£15.00

R. G. BARLOW'S KANGAROO

R. G. BARLOW,

LANCASHIRE COUNTY

Football & Athletic Depot,

7, VICTORIA STATION APPROACH,

MANCHESTER.

FOOTBALLS.

The " KANGAROO " - - 8/6

The " RED ROSE " - - 7/6

The " DURABLE " - - 7/-

The " WONDER " - - 5/6

GUARANTEED BEST VALUE IN TRADE.

R. G. B. supplies Goods of the First Quality only, and at exceptionally Low Prices. See Price List, sent Free on application to

R. G. BARLOW,

7, Victoria Station Approach,

MANCHESTER.

=== PRICE ONE PENNY. ===

THE OLDEST AND BEST PAPER OF ITS KIND.

— THE —

ATHLETIC ❦ NEWS

PUBLISHED EVERY MONDAY MORNING,

IS SIMPLY THE

BEST PAPER IN THE WORLD

FOR NEWS AND COMMENTS ABOUT

FOOTBALL & LACROSSE.

OFFICES: 2, MARK LANE, WITHY GROVE, MANCHESTER.

MANCHESTER UNITED
Pictorial History
& Club Record

THE PICTORIAL HISTORY
AND CLUB RECORD OF
MANCHESTER UNITED

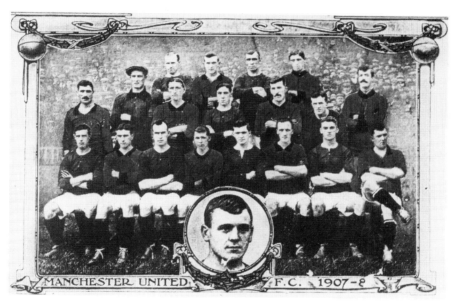

Football League Champions 1908

'United We Stand'

*Above: Billy Meredith (Left), Newton Heath LYR player of c1880 (Centre) &
Jesper Olsen (Right). Below: 'The Last Line-up.' The Busby Babes prior to the
match with Red Star Belgrade in February 1958.*

MANCHESTER UNITED

Pictorial History and Club Record

by

CHARLES ZAHRA
Statistics and Records

JOSEPH MUSCAT
Club History

IAIN McCARTNEY
Players' Biographies

KEITH MELLOR
Origins and Pictorial History

 TEMPLE  NOSTALGIA

Nottingham
England

MCMLXXXVI

PUBLISHED & PRINTED BY
TEMPLE NOSTALGIA PRESS
TEMPLE PRINTING LIMITED
NOTTINGHAM ENGLAND

PHOTOLITHOGRAPHY & ARTWORK BY
SPECTRUM GRAPHICS LIMITED
AND ROGER HEATON

COVER JACKET PRODUCED BY
ELECTRONIC COLOUR SYSTEMS LIMITED

COVER JACKET & BOOK DESIGN BY
KEITH MELLOR
AOY ASSOCIATES

© Temple Nostalgia Press

All rights reserved. No part of this publication may be reproduced, stored in a
retrieval system, or transmitted, in any form or by any means, electronic,
mechanical, photocopying, recording or otherwise, without the prior permission of
Temple Printing Ltd.

ISBN 1 870010 01 9

02732554

AUTHORS NOTE

This volume is the result of a decade and a half of painstaking research into the historical record of Manchester
United. We believe that it contains an unequalled combination of unique pictorials, club memorabilia and
records. The statistical content is as accurate as can be established by the authors at the time of going to press.
Fresh evidence of early records is continually being discovered and it would be unrealistic to guarantee
absolute accuracy. Very early information on teams, scorers and attendances is notoriously uncertain, and
even club's own records are known to conflict with newspapers and journals of the period, the football
authorities themselves are aware that some early teams included illegal players using anagrams of real names.
There are instances of players being included in team line-ups of press match reports and even having scored!
but who according to official archives did not play in the fixture. The statistical authors take full responsibility
for the authenticity of the club records in the book and would welcome any further information to add to it, or
to revise current records.

FOOTBALL MEMORABILIA

*Historically valuable memorabilia and photographs concerning Manchester United and other football clubs is continually being
discovered. With other publications in preparation, the publishers are always grateful to receive news of any old football material,
particularly newscuttings, photos and ephemora, either for purchase or on loan for copying. Any supporter wishing to advise of items of
this nature should contact Temple Printing Ltd., Wilford Crescent East, Nottingham. NG2 2EF.*

Contents

European Cup Winners, 1968.

A TRIBUTE TO SIR MATT BUSBY, C.B.E.

Above: *SIR MATT THE PLAYER. As a proud member of the F.A. Cup winning Manchester City team of 1934. (KM)*

Below: *THIS IS YOUR LIFE. With relatives and friends on the BBC TV programme transmitted on 6 January 1958, exactly one month before the Munich Air Disaster. (JM)*

SIR MATT BUSBY C.B.E. WITH SWORD OF HONOUR. (JM)

THE PICTORIAL HISTORY & CLUB RECORD OF MANCHESTER UNITED

FOREWORD
by
SIR MATT BUSBY, C.B.E.
President - Manchester United
Football Club

Over the years there have been many books written about Manchester United but I doubt if we have ever seen one that contains such a wealth of detail as this work, more appropriately for being the labour of love of some of the club's most dedicated followers.

Charles Zahra and Joseph Muscat are members of Manchester United's large supporters club in Malta, and I know first hand of the enthusiasm for our club that has run so high there for so long. Their efforts to produce this document of United's glorious history deserves the highest praise.

Joseph is President of the Malta Club, and also their historian and keeper of records, whilst Charles has, for over fifteen years been collating the teams statistics, ably assisted by Iain McCartney.

They have all now put it to excellent use with this historical and statistical account of matches played along with the many fascinating illustrations compiled by the editor, Keith Mellor. There are now a great many more facts and figures which I am glad to see recorded for posterity.

Finally, this book is all the more gratifying as Manchester United have always tried to foster our friendship with Malta. I personally have many happy memories of visits to the George Cross island so it gives me tremendous pleasure to see their book coming as an important contribution to the history of Manchester United.

All good wishes

Matt Busby

Sir Matt Busby, C.B.E.

THE STORY OF NEWTON HEATH
LYR AND MANCHESTER UNITED

ORIGINS

THE FIRST DECADE 1878–1888

"It is necessary to go back to far off days for the contrasting scene, and to imagine a little roped enclosure in which a thin ring of spectators stood watching a troupe of players in nondescript jerseys. Both players and watchers were humble railway workers whose hearts were in the game, and whose only thoughts were of victory."
Scene at North Road ground of Newton Heath L & YR 1878 (from *Association Football* published 1905 Caxtons).

The scribe who penned that graphic description of the North Road ground adjacent to the Carriage and Wagon Works and Shunting Yards of the Lancashire and Yorkshire Railway at Newton Heath presents a rare insight into the humble beginnings of Manchester United Football Club. The original Newton Heath team was spawned at a time when rugby football was the vogue in the Manchester region, but many other areas of the British Isles had long since adopted the association code, and some of the earliest surviving clubs from the Midlands like Notts County, Stoke City and Nottingham Forest had already enjoyed the recreation for a decade and a half. We have to go back to very early Victorian times to identify the genesis of football in its first recognisable form. In an elementary fashion, it had been pioneered by public schoolboys and military men, and the first rules devised at Cambridge University in 1846. This early attempt at conformity was largely ignored outside the immediate area, each school or regiment adopting a code peculiar to its own convenient interpretation, though uniform in combining both handling and kicking. By the later 1850's, young sporting gentlemen who had learned the game at college were forming teams to challenge the University and Army teams, predominantly in Sheffield and the Home Counties. Games were still generally a combination of what we know as soccer and rugby, but the increasing interest and rapid spread of the pastime initiated the formation of the London Football Association in 1863 and the adoption, for the South at least, of a set of uniform rules. These laws did introduce some element of conformity, but they still differed from other areas, mainly in the use of 'hacking', which was still a feature of the Northern game, and the South's move to outlaw it was considered effeminate. As conformity continued to spread, albeit slowly, throughout the remainder of the 1860's, there was little evidence of enthusiasm for the game in the North-West, although a form of rugby code was practised. Soccer continued to contain features of the rugby game and in 1870 was still generally confined to the professional class and white-collar workers. But it was to be the age of reform throughout Victorian Britain that would enable the lower working classes to benefit from a shorter working week, and coinciding with the increasingly widespread adoption of the Saturday half-holiday soccer's popularity began to traverse social, and geographical boundaries. The cradle of Association Football in Lancashire was a small village near Bolton, where in 1872, a Mr. J.J. Bentley (you would do well to remember the name) formed the Turton Football Club, to Harrow rules. The sport was soon identified as ideal recreation for cotton workers who found themselves with some leisure time that did not conflict with Sunday Worship. More teams were formed in the neighbourhood of Turton by local churches and millworkers, and soccer quickly spread throughout the region, spawning the emergence of teams in Bolton, Blackburn, Darwen and across the Pennines. Whilst the North-Eastern Lancastrians preferred the 'dribbling-game', Association was slow to gain influence in a Manchester region that had remained staunchly 'rugger', with clubs scattered abundantly throughout the City environs. But in this year of 1878 there was at least one small Mancunian suburb where soccer was gaining a foothold.

Manchester 1878

Towards the North East aspect of the city was situated those Carriage and Wagon Works of the Lancashire and Yorkshire Railway at Newton Heath. It occupied an area where only scant evidence of the original heathland remained, but there was nevertheless still areas where the employees of the Railway Company could find recreation by kicking at a ball of chrome-leather in a manner after their counterparts in the North of the county. As the pastime gained in popularity the workers obtained permission to play more organised sport on a disused piece of grassless chalkland owned by the local church. it lay adjacent to the works in North Road, and enthusiasm was such that players eagerly turned up for evening games with blackened faces and carrying dinner-baskets straight from the workshops and Yards. The L & Y Railway Football Club was thus formed. Though difficulties in working rosta's hampered the arrangement of suitable fixtures, as fervour persisted matches against neighbouring church and village sides became a feature of the 'free' Saturday afternoons.

The motley attire of the players was discarded on the purchase of a set of Cashmerette jerseys in the adopted club colours of Green and Gold halves, and by 1879 the club had become more widely known as Newton Heath (L & YR) F.C. The same year the Lancashire F.A. Cup was instituted for the County's leading sides, and won by Darwen. Newton Heath were not entered, but that year evidence of Mancunian progress under Association rules was emphasised when the Manchester Wanderers held the famous Blackburn Rovers to a 2–2 draw.

With no changing facilities and a pitch described at the time as 'in places hard as flint with ashes underneath that had become like iron, and in others thick mud', it is perhaps not surprising that the Newton Heath players sometimes favoured excursions to opponents grounds, and a grass playing surface. But it was evidently not always to advantage of 'The Coachbuilders', as the team was affectionately called, the *Bolton Evening News* reported what appears to have been a most colourful occasion on 24 November 1880. At the Pikes Lane ground, the second eleven of the Wanderers club of Bolton entertained the Newton Heath side. The green and gold of the Newtonians clashed with the scarlet and white quarters of the hosts, who proved far too strong on the day, despatching the visitors back to Manchester on the end of a 0–6 reverse. The Bolton team of that period also sported the borough coat of arms embroidered onto their vivid jerseys. A fortnight after the Pikes Lane encounter, on 4 December, the team fought out a goalless draw on the ground of Manchester Arcadians, but an inability to find the net was proving costly that season, opportunists in the 'Heathens' front ranks conspicuous by absence. In a return match with Wanderers Seconds on 22 January 1881, the Bolton men repeated their 6–0 winning margin, and although goals did come, from Cramphorne and Minchley, to secure a 2–0 home success over Bootle Seconds on 5 February, the familiar failings were evident again ten days later at North Road. Hurst were allowed to snatch a single goal victory.

The President of the club was the Carriage and Wagon Superintendent, Mr. Attock, and the running of the team was the responsibility of the Dining Room Committee of the Railway Company. Their untiring work was rewarded by equal effort on the field. The early players were of hardy stock, toiling long hours at the works during the week and showing admiral zeal for sporting combat on Saturday afternoons. The club coveted one advantage over local rivals, able to secretly operate a camouflaged form of professionalism, long before its legal adoption.

The team was gradually strengthened, with skill increasingly an arbitrary requisite allied to the players undoubted enthusiasm. In the campaign of 1881/2 goals were somewhat more in evidence than previously. Rigby, Cramphorne and Hopwood steered winning efforts past the Manchester Arcadians custodian, without reply, on October 15 at the Heath and although they suffered on a 0–4 reverse at Blackburn Olympic the following week they were back on the goal standard on 12 November, beating West Gorton St. Marks 3–0. St. Marks did manage revenge on their own ground later that season, winning 2–1.

In the early 1880's the emergent interest in the Association game was increasingly reflected by the rugby orientated local press. The *Manchester Guardian,* in November 1882, reported that Newton Heath (L & YR) had entertained Bentfield — 'the home team scoring three goals to their opponents one goal and two disputed goals. The Newtonians scored all their goals in the last half, when some good play was shown'. The 'Heathens' team that day can be recorded for posterity: C. Fulton (Goal): S. Black, J. Rigby (Backs): J. Edmonson, C. Charlton (Half Backs): E. Latham, J. Thompson (Right Wing): J. Jarrett, J. Jones (Left Wing): E. Thomas (Capt) and H. Kenyon (Centres). A week later Middleton were vanquished 4–3 and early in January Astley Bridge succumbed 4–1 to the Heath men.

Evocative names enriched the fixtures list — Pendleton Olympic, Haughton Dale, Dalton Hall, Eaglestorm, Oughtrington Park, and teams from Levenshulme, Heywood, Eccles, Gorton and Greenhays returned from North Road unrewarded.

THE 'SPIRITED' EDGE OF COMPETITION

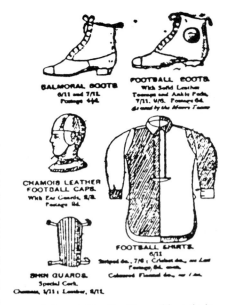

A new era, one of competitive soccer, began for Newton Heath at the start of the 1883/4 campaign, with entry for the Lancashire Senior Cup. As it was, the initial foray was short-lived, but it did provide the club with an appetite for the more spirited edge of competition hitherto not experienced. The advent of this new enterprise could not have attracted more illustrious visitors to the Heath. Fresh from having broken the mould of Association Football for all time, just six months after defeating the Old Etonians 2−1 at Kennington Oval to release the stranglehold of the Academic and Military to bring the F.A. Cup to the North of England, Blackburn Olympic paraded before an excited Manchester public. On the 27 October 1883 the 'Heathens' fought a first round reargard action but were powerless to prevent the Olympians, with a late rush, run up a score of 7 goals to 2. It is amusing to imagine the English Cup holders' thoughts as they wended their way on foot in full 'riguer' past the curious throng who lined their route to the playing pitch from the changing facilities, at the Three Crowns Inn on the Oldham Road. Another milestone marked that same season when in March 1884, full-back Sam Black became the first ever Newton Heath player to gain representative honours, selected for Manchester and District against Liverpool at Bootle. His second appearance, against Hallamshire, brought another honour to the Heath, club official Mr. B. Ainsworth refereed the match. Sam Black had also impressed the mighty Blackburn Olympic in the famous cup-tie and actually turned down an opportunity to move to the 'Hole-I'-th'-Wall', the Olympic home ground and quarters in Blackburn.

The Manchester F.A. Senior Cup was introduced in 1884/5, and Newton Heath so nearly were inaugural winners. Old rivals Hurst beat them 3−0 in the Final at Whalley Range on 25 April 1885, but the cup run had provided much excitement to reflect upon, none more so than the first round when the opponents had to be defeated twice. The 'Coachbuilders' won 3−2 at Eccles, but the home team so vehemently protested at the validity of the winning goal that their appeal to the Manchester F.A. was upheld. The replay was held at the neutral ground of Manchester Arcadians, where this time the Newtonians confirmed their superiority by winning 3−0.

The disappointment of losing that first Final was redeemed in the most satisfying way in the following campaign of 1885/6, at their second attempt the 'Heathens' won the Manchester Senior Cup for the first time, but again attracted fierce controversy.

Repeating the previous year's first round success against Eccles, this time by 2−0 with goals from Watkin and Gotheridge, the team again reached the Final, by vanquishing Gorton Villa 5−0 in round two, and Hurst 3−1 in the Semi-Final at Salford. The Cup Final opponents at Whalley Range on 3 April was Manchester, and the scene was set for such controversy that the dispute was recalled for many years in the locale. Newton Heath went ahead with a goal so blatantly illegal on two counts. Davies was clearly offside when he shot goalwards. The hand of Watkins was seen by most to divert the ball between the posts, and to the consternation of the Manchester players the referee allowed the point to stand, dismissing the offside calls and claiming afterwards not to have heard the appeal for 'hands'. In the ensuing disarray, Sam Black emerged to fire home a second, and winning, goal. Manchester replied just once, and the Newton Heath players were engulfed by jubilant supporters who surrounded the grandstand for the presentation of the Cup, to the strains of Handel performed by the Newton Heath Brass Band.

↱ L. & Y. Rʸ. ↰
EXCURSIONS
FROM
MANCHESTER & LIVERPOOL.

To LONDON from MANCHESTER on February 20, 22, 24, 27, etc., and from LIVERPOOL on February 21, 24, etc.

The Saturday to Monday Tickets to London issued by any train every Saturday.

FOOTBALL MATCHES
MIDDLESBROUGH, NEWCASTLE
OLDHAM, BRADFORD,
HUDDERSFIELD, WAKEFIELD,
and NORMANTON.

It was the start of an impressive record in the Manchester competition. The name of Newton Heath was to figure prominently for nearly a decade, winning the trophy again in 1888, 1889, 1890 and 1893, as well as Runners-Up in 1885, 1887 and 1891. So, allowing for an unaccountable lapse in 1892 when Bolton beat them in the Semi-Final, the 'Heathens' were to reach the final eight times in the first nine years of the tournament.

The Lancashire clubs had for long been at odds with the sport's London administrators on the thorny subject of professionalism. With players drawn from the working classes, the Northern game was fashioned around the 'Professors', imported from Scotland and other areas to hawk their skills to the highest bidder on the pretext of work in the cottonmills and factories of North-Western England. This cut sharply across the Corinthian ideals of the South, but the irresistible tide of professionalism finally breached amateur resistance in July 1885, and Newton Heath were among those first to exploit the legalised system, with an influx of Welshmen lured by the prospect of work in the railway workshops. Jack Powell was one of the first to arrive at North Road, following dispute over residential qualification whilst with Preston he was offered a job as a fitter with the L & Y Railway with the proviso that he played for the football team. Powell went on to captain the side into league soccer, and was one of several players from the Druids team of Ruabon to sport the green and gold jersey. Roger Doughty, and his brother Jack (he was described as a 'Crasher of the first order'), Jack Owen, J.E. Davies and Tom Burke were illustrious names that were to become synonymous with the 'Heathens' in those early days of professionalism. Progress on the field proved to the detriment of the financial status of the club. The absence of adequate resources always seemed chronic at North Road, and the Spectre of Bankruptcy often loomed. It was said that "those forerunners of dissolution — the bailiffs — had many experiences of the Newton Heath club", and it was reputed that one director had his home sold over his head, after putting every penny he had into the club to stave off the threat of the official receiver.

It was as well that the club could offer civilian jobs, players wages were only around £1 per week. There were times when money was so tight that the directors could only count up the 'gate' money, and, after deducting an amount for ground upkeep, divide it up amongst the players. Harry Renshaw, probably the first-known sports journalist to regularly report the fortunes of the club, could recall the occasion when one player was handed the princely sum of 7s. 6d. "I shall have to spend Sunday at home, my best suit is at the pawnbrokers for 15 shillings", the player observed ruefully, upon which officials and other players held a collection to redeem the suit, as it was considered that "a professional footballer should not be the subject to such indignity".

Despite its financial embarrassments, the club was at least able to gain some prestige by enlisting some very eminent local personalities as Vice-Presidents. These included three city Members of Parliament — Mr. A.J. Balfour, Mr. C.E. Schwann and Sir James Ferguson Bart., all of whom occasionally braved the spartan conditions of North Road, to see the team play.

Since the success of Blackburn Olympic in bringing the F.A. Cup to the North in 1883, the trophy remained in the town for four years, the Rovers having won it on three successive occasions. This Lancastrian domination encouraged increased participation in the County Palatine. Season 1886/7 saw Newton Heath's initial challenge for the 'English' cup, but this historic venture was prematurely truncated in ignominious circumstances. On 30 October 1886 the 'Heathens' visited Fleetwood Rangers in the Qualifying Round, and the score was level at two goals each at the end of normal time. The Newtonians refused to play the extra-time as instructed by the Referee, who then abandoned the tie and awarded it to Fleetwood. It was to be another three years before Newton Heath again participated in the competition.

Realising the necessity of regular competitive fixtures, the leading clubs of the North and Midlands instituted the formation of the Football League in 1888. Membership was to be restricted to twelve clubs to fit in the available dates that did not conflict with English Cup and County F.A. competitions. Understandably there was great anxieties amongst clubs to gain admittance, and Newton Heath's cautious hopes had some element of justification. They had regained the Manchester Senior Cup, defeating Denton in the 1888 Final by a record score of 7−1. Their record against the 'elite' sides during 1887/8 included victories over Aston Villa and Accrington and drawn games with Preston, Bolton and Burnley. Some very high scores had been registered against lesser opposition, Nottingham Jardines (8−0), Ten Acres (9−0), Earlestown (7−0), West Manchester (6−0), Gorton Assoc. (8−1), Rawtenstall (7−0) and Derby Midland (6−1) had all fell victim to the dead-eye 'Heathen' forwards. Newtonian hopes however, were not to be realised, the club obtained just one vote in favour, and the application failed. The Heath men's chagrin was hightened when in friendly encounters early in 1888/9, successful league aspirants Bolton and Blackburn Rovers were defeated at North Road. To compensate, along with other disappointed clubs Newton Heath attended a meeting chaired by Mr. R.M. Sloane of Bootle F.C. in the April of 1888, at the Royal Hotel in Crewe, where a series of home and home fixtures were agreed to on a league basis, and to be called the Football Combination. The fourteen club secretaries present pledged their clubs "to support each other in the arranging of matches between themselves, and that no fixture must be cancelled on account of any cup competition or other match". A further six clubs were admitted to the original members and a fixtures committee formed to administer the Football Combination programme.

A new chapter in the story of Newton Heath LYR was about to begin.

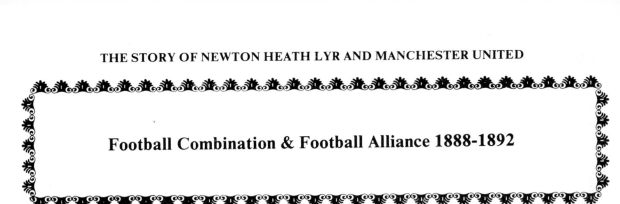

Football Combination & Football Alliance 1888-1892

The year 1880 was historic for Association Football. In the autumn of that year the Football League programme opened for the first time, and though less significantly it then seemed, on September 1st the commencing fixtures in the Football combination were played. For Newton Heath, and ultimately its lusty offspring Manchester United, the latter would prove as important as the League was to it's privileged dozen founder-members. Though not then realised, the combination was the embryo of the Football Alliance, which, in just three short years, would be adopted by McGregor's League for it's Second Division.

Newton Heath's committments to the Combination did not begin until 22 September, when they received and defeated Darwen 4-3 before a 'gate' of 4,000, the goals coming from Gale and a Jack Doughty hat-trick. Before this the Newtonians had beaten Bolton, Blackburn Rovers and Walsall Town Swifts at North Road, and the following week they travelled to Gainsborough and won 5-1.

On 6 October International Soccer came to the Heath with the visit of the Canadian Touring XI, who won 2-0 in front of 5,000 curious spectators. A week later the 'Heathens' journeyed to Derby Midland for the second Combination fixture, and this was the team that secured a 1-1 draw; T. Hay; J. Powell, J. Mitchell; T. Burke, R. Doughty, J. Owen; Walton, Kirkham, J. Doughty, J. Gale and J. Gotheridge. The system worked well at first but by early in 1889, the Football Combination looked to be in trouble, with some clubs not honouring their fixtures. Newton Heath were not among them, they had already played eight matches, losing only once, away to Darwen. The team had been rearranged somewhat, and when they defeated Bootle 4-0 on 26 January the line-up was: Hay; Powell, Mitchell; Burke, J. Davies, J. Owen; W. Tait, J. Doughty, R. Doughty, Gale, G. Owen. By the end of March they had played 11, won 7, drawn twice and lost twice. It was a record second-to-none amongst contesting teams and Newton Heath could consider themselves unofficial winners of the competition.

Whilst not a complete success, only one team failed to fulfil its commitments, the Combination fueled interest in a regular league contest. Newton Heath were among those instrumental in the formation of the Football Alliance, organised on the same principles of the hugely successful Football League. It was yet another momentous step for the Club, and the 'Heathens' commenced their fixtures under Alliance Rules against Sunderland Albion on 21 September 1889. Despite a 4-1 success against the Wearsiders, the team soon found it tough going in a highly competitive environment, and were satisfied to finish eighth in the league. In that season the Heath men gained entry to the F.A. Cup once again, three years after the Fleetwood controversy. The draw dealt them a cruel hand, an away excursion to the 'Invincibles' of Preston, and the great 'Double' champions of that year dashed Newtonian hopes by winning 6-1. Season 1890/1 saw another struggle and a slip to ninth place, but in the following campaign of 1891/2 the team emerged to mount a serious challenge for the Alliance title. It was unfortunate that the opening game, at Burton Swifts, was lost 2-3, but the goals were scored by new signing Donaldson and established favourite Farman. Though the loss of those two points were to prove critical at the seasons end, it was the goalscoring exploits of that pair which inspired the challenge. Together they hit 36 goals, and it was not until the end of February when the team next lost, at Small Heath. On 19 March the 'Heathens' clashed head-on with their closest rivals Nottingham Forest at the Town ground. A 0-3 reverse virtually handed the championship to the Foresters, but only two points separated the teams at the close of fixtures.

It was to prove the final season for the Football Alliance. With increasing pressure from outside clubs to gain membership, the Football League was extended to two sections, the majority of Alliance clubs forming the Second Division. As Champions and Runners-up of the Alliance the Forest and Newton Heath were admitted to Division One, along with Sheffield Wednesday, who replaced Darwen. So, fourteen years after it's formation in the railway yards and workshops, Newton Heath LYR had joined the elite clubs in the Football League.

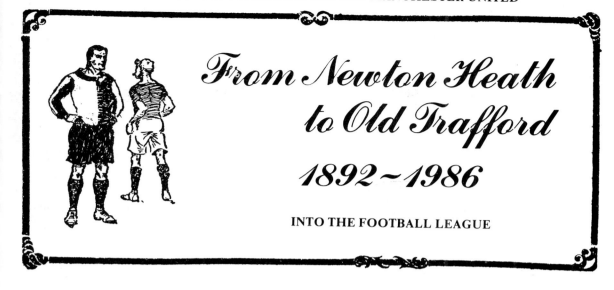

From Newton Heath to Old Trafford

1892~1986

INTO THE FOOTBALL LEAGUE

As fully-fledged members of the First Division the club had to adopt a more professional approach and image. First, a new company was floated and at the same time L & YR dropped, the team simply known as Newton Heath F.C. Also, the company affairs would require a full-time administrator, and Mr. A.H. Albut previously with Aston Villa, was appointed Secretary, and the club's first paid official. The registered office was a tiny cottage at 33 Oldham Road but later, improved facilities were secured, a disused schoolroom at the Institute in Silver Street at Miles Platting.

Season 1892/3 heralded the Football League career of the club, but it was to prove a hard baptism and many troubled times would be encounted in those early years of League life. Newton Heath commenced their fixtures against one of of the great teams of the age, away to the Rovers at Blackburn. The 'Heathens' appeared to look worthy of their new status and only lost an exciting match by the odd goal of seven. In fact, the team soon realised life in this new environment was always going to be less than easy, and they collected only two points from the first six matches. An exception to the rule occured on 15 October. Still without a single victory, the Heath men unaccountably went on the rampage and scored ten times against Wolverhampton Wanderers, that first-ever League win 10-1, still stands as the team's highest score in the competition. Never the less, the struggle continued and apart from that record win, there was little to cheer during that initial season. The team occupied the bottom position for most of the campaign and by April they were firmly rooted at the foot of the table.

But in those days relegation was not automatic, it was determined by a series of test matches between the bottom clubs of Division One and the leading clubs in Division Two. Everything depended on their clash with Small Heath, a sort of final played at Stoke. If they won, the 'Heathens' would remain in the First Division.

The match, played in front of 4,000 spectators, ended in a 1-1 draw, but in the replay the following Thursday at Sheffield, Newton Heath defeated Small Heath 5-2 after twice going behind—thus survival, and another season amongst the elite in the First Division. The crushing of Small Heath could perhaps have been foreseen for only a few days previous fifth-placed Bolton had been beaten in the Final of the Manchester Senior Cup, the team's fifth success in eight years. They had come good at the finale of the season in time to save their status.

To further enhance the club's standing, a new ground was acquired for the start of 1893/4. The new venue at Bank Street in Clayton was three miles from North Road, but was more spacious and could accommodate larger crowds. The new enclosure lay adjacent to Chemical works and was to become notorious to visiting sides. It's skyline, a forest of chimney stacks shrouded in pernicious smoke, cast a bizarre setting and the noxious fumes polluted the air. But the move enabled the club to build a fine stadium over years at Clayton, which one day, a decade hence, would be described as 'palatial'.

The Bank Street ground was used for the first time against Burnley on 2 September 1893, and although the new campaign started well with a 3-2 win in front of 10,000 spectators, the 'Heathens' struggled again. At the end of the season they were again to be found at the bottom of the First Division with an even worse record than the year before, losing twenty-two matches and winning only six. Yet again the team had to endure the extra matches of the test series. This time it was a different story from the previous year. Liverpool beat Newton Heath in the crucial final match of the test series and after just two seasons they were relegated to the Second Division.

The relegation season did have it's moments of sensation — notably the match against West Bromwich Albion at Bank Street where Newton Heath emerged winners by 4 − 1. 'Observer', reporting the match in the *Birmingham Daily Gazette* on 16 October, 1893, said that Newton Heath's play was "rough, brutal and cowardly" and characterised by "dirty tricks".

The Newton Heath club sued the proprietors of the *Birmingham Daily Gazette* for damages for libel, they were found guilty and fined just ONE FARTHING!

Life in the Second Division was a little rosier than in the First and the Newtonians managed third place behind Bury and Notts County. It seemed that each season Newton Heath had one outstanding match to stand out above all others. This time their opponents were another Midlands team — Walsall Town Swifts.

The match was played in terrible weather at Bank Street, Newton Heath leading 3 − 0 at half-time. The 'Heathens' put added pressure on Walsall and in an amazing second half scored another eleven times! After the match Walsall protested claiming the pitch was unplayable. The protest was upheld, and the match was replayed three weeks later. The result? — Newton Heath 9, Walsall 0! This time the result stood.

Finishing a meritorious third behind Bury and Notts County, the team was again involved in the test matches, but in the deciding final game they lost to Stoke by three clear goals — thus missing promotion at the first time of asking.

Newton Heath's financial situation was brightened when at the end of the season it was revealed that the total debts, which were accumulated over the years, had been reduced considerably.

Still, Newton Heath had to be content with Second Division football. In the following seasons the 'Heathens' had some notable successes in F.A. Cup games and managed to achieve good placings in the League. Sixth in 1895/6, runners-up in 1896/7 but failing in the test matches, and fourth in three consecutive seasons 1897/8, 1898/9 and 1899/1900.

During this period they also had some considerable success in the local competitions. In 1898 they reached the semi-final of the Manchester Senior Cup and won the Lancashire Cup for the first time by defeating Blackburn Rovers 2 − 1.

This honour was somewhat blemished because the 'Heathens' had a congestion of fixtures that led them to cancel a League match against Luton in order to play in a Manchester Cup tie — they were fined £63. 4s. 0d.

During this time the nature of the team was changing with new faces coming in and players who had performed in the First Division departing.

In came Caesar Augustus Llewellyn Jenkyns, a Welshman; new goalkeeper Frank Barrett, a Scottish international who played with Newton Heath for five years. Another Scotsman to join the ranks was Joe Cassidy from Motherwell, a striker of immense power. But perhaps the most important signing of that period was that of Harry Stafford who in the not too distant future was to play a very important part in the club's fate. Stafford was a typical right-back of the era.

On the other side of Manchester, rivals City gained promotion to the First Division and, with a certain William Meredith in their ranks, had assembled a very useful side.

The 'Heathens', who had in 1896/7 discarded their traditional colours of green and gold in favour of white shirts and blue knickers were operating more ambitiously. Several quality players were added to the squad, but success in the shape of promotion eluded them.

By the turn of the century Newton Heath were still to be found usually between the promotion pack and mid-table. Tenth place in season 1900/01 was followed by worsening League fortunes the following year, finishing fourth from bottom in the 1901/2 Second Division. That season was somewhat redeemed when they won the Manchester Cup for the first time in nine years, defeating Manchester City in the Final.

Generally though, the outlook for the Newton Heath club at this period was bleak, with financial troubles forcing the club into it's biggest crisis since formation.

During a fateful season, at the beginning of 1902, the creditors foreclosed and steps towards bankrupting the company were initiated. However, the club did manage to stay afloat — with the players in doubt whether they were going to be paid their wages.

On the 18th March, 1902, a meeting of the shareholders was called at the New Islington Hall with Mr. F. Palmer as President. It was revealed that the Football Association agreed to the re-formation of the club.

Club captain Harry Stafford was one of the main speakers and after Mr. Palmer reported that it would cost £2,000 to save the club, the amiable full-back sensationally revealed that four gentlemen were prepared to raise that sum between them. The four gentlemen were Mr. J.H. Davies, Mr. Taylor, Mr. Bown and Mr. Jones. The meeting was adjourned for further talks between the Football Association and the consortium.

On April 28th, 1902, the Athletic News reported that Mr. Bown, a member of the consortium had suggested that the name of Newton Heath be changed . . . and it was — to MANCHESTER UNITED. A month later the Lancashire F.A. gave the formal permission for the change of title.

The most powerful man behind the consortium was, in fact, Mr. John H. Davies. He was the financial power behind the group and is generally known to be the saviour of Newton Heath.

Davies was born in 1864 and he began on the road to fortune by becoming a commission agent's clerk, then on to innkeeper, a brewer, and for many years chairman of the Manchester brewery of Walker and Pomfray.

However, it is interesting to note how John H. Davies came to be involved in the takeover and saving of Newton Heath from extinction. This is the story, in brief, as recalled Harry Renshaw:-

A dog, belonging to Harry Stafford the club captain, was let loose to collect subscriptions in the bazaar of 1901 in aid of the football club. The dog wandered, and was found by a Mr. Thomas, licensee of one of Mr. Davies's pubs. Thomas showed the dog to Davies, who bought it. Then, presumably, after having transacted canine business with the lawful owner, Davies installed Stafford in another licensed house, and proceeded to the matter of reviving the moribund Newton Heath FC.

Davies recognised that the club had potential and could be made profitable. Even in those early days he began thinking of making the new Manchester United into an international concern.

The first board of directors was formed with Davies as President and Chairman, along with Messrs. Taylor, Bown, Jones, Andrew and Mr. J.J. Bentley — at that time President of the Football League, but more notably, the same who formed the Turton club way back in 1872.

A sum of £3,000, a huge amount then, was put down to buy any players needed to strengthen the team. Harry Stafford was the man mainly responsible to scout for and buy players and by the beginning of season 1902/03 the team was a class above their Second Division status. They even changed their colours again, donning for the first time the famous red jersey and white shorts.

United started the campaign with a 1−0 away win at Gainsborough Trinity and followed that with a similar score against Burton United in front of 20,000 supporters. United finished the season in fifth position, but the season was to be largely remembered for activity in the transfer market.

In came T. Arkesden from Derby County for £150; W. Griffiths from a local junior side; Moger, a goalkeeper from Southampton; Irish international T.H. Morrison from Burnley; T.H. Read from Manchester City; Albert Schofield from Everton; J.H. Peddie from Newcastle; and another goalkeeper, the former rugby international, J.W. Sutcliffe.

James West, who had been appointed as Secretary/Manager in 1900, surprisingly resigned on the 29 September 1903 saying in his letter ''my name may be associated with the failure of the newer members of the club to sustain the high reputation they had previously gained in first-class football''.

West was succeeded by Mr. J.E. Mangnall from Burnley. Mangnall clearly was not satisfied with the players already there and wanted to further strengthen the team. In came Bonthron, Bell and a player by the name of Charlie Roberts from Grimsby. His transfer was the master stroke by Mangnall. Roberts cost United the sum of £400 after being trailed by many clubs including Manchester City, Derby County and Nottingham Forest — but he opted for United.

At the end of the 1903/04 season United were to be found in third position and apart from good performances in the League, United also enjoyed good results in the F.A. Cup. It took six hours for United to dispose of Small Heath in the Intermediate Round and then account for Notts County in the First Round. The good run came to an abrupt end with a 0−6 thrashing at the hands of Sheffield Wednesday.

In that same season neighbours City upstaged United and had one of their most successful seasons. City won the F.A. Cup led by Welsh international wizard Billy Meredith and finished runners-up in the First Division.

Two months into season 1904-05 scandal broke out in the rival camp of Manchester City. The F.A. investigated the club's dealings in respect of transfer negotiations with Glossop North End. It was proved that negotiations relating to certain players had been concluded without a too nice appreciation of legal formalities. Further, it was suggested that City's directors had attempted to pull the wool over the eyes of the legislators.

City suffered heavy penalties. The team was banned from playing from 11 October to 8th November except for three away matches; five directors were suspended for three years and the club was also fined £250.

City's troubles triggered a chain reaction and among other clubs to be investigated were Uniteds, who in that season just failed again to gain promotion, finishing third.

But Manchester City's troubles were not over yet. Billy Meredith was suspended from the 4th August, 1905 to the 30th April, 1908 for allegedly having offered a sum of money to an Aston Villa player to allow Manchester City win the match, which was vital to the outcome of the League Championship.

The following March, another F.A. Commission, instigated by directors of Manchester City, enquired into the charge that Meredith, while under suspension, demanded his wages and visited the dressing rooms. It was revealed that Meredith was indeed promised guarantees of compensation and that he was carrying other people's guilt.

Later Meredith was allowed to negotiate his own transfer and Mangnall acted quickly to secure the signature of the Welsh wizard for a fee of £500 despite knowing that he still had to serve eighteen months of his suspension.

At the end of May the F.A. gave their final verdict on City's affairs and seventeen players who had received improper payments and bonuses were fined and suspended until New Year's Day 1907. More damaging for City, all players concerned were barred from ever playing for the club again.

Mangnall knew that City possessed many talented players and duly signed another four to join Meredith in the red colours of United. They were Sandy Turnbull, George Livingstone, Jimmie Bannister and Herbert Burgess.

United could not yet make use of their new signings, but Mangnall's side was one of the favourites for promotion in season 1905/06 and they disappointed neither punters or the supporters, finishing second behind Bristol City to gain promotion after twelve years in the Second Division.

Promotion was ensured with a 6−0 thrashing of Burton United at Clayton and celebrated with fireworks and brass bands. The team on that fateful April day was:- Moger, Holden. Blackstock, Downie, Roberts, Duckworth, Wombwell, Peddie, Sagar, Picken, Wall.

For the first time ever, in 1906/07 the First Division included among its members both the Manchester teams. Although newly promoted, United were considered to be among the best teams in the League, and when, on New Year's Day 1907, the recruits from City were finally available for selection, Manchester United appeared a formidable force.

However, the F.A. Cup was still proving an unlucky competition for the team, losing to Portsmouth in the First round, although in the previous year 1905/06 they had reached the Fourth round for the first time.

1906/07 saw Roberts, Meredith and Co. help United to a respectable eighth place. During that season Bonthron left for Sunderland and another player was added to the Clayton ranks — James Turnbull, a centre-forward from Leyton Orient.

Another close season passed and United went into 1907/08 with high hopes of success. By Christmas the Reds were leading the First Division with a record worthy of Champions. From eighteen matches played, they had won fifteen, drawn two and lost only one, and had scored fifty-four (54) goals for an impressive average of three goals per match.

With Manchester City also back in form and putting in a brave challenge, United had an indifferent spell in the second half of the season and struggled to keep up the pace.

Fortunately, their form returned and they won the League Championship for the first time, pulling nine points clear ahead of Aston Villa, with neighbours Manchester City in third place.

In recognition, for the second time in three years, Mangnall was given a £1 raise by the club and a further bonus of £100. The first successful era of Manchester United had begun.

During that successul season, the President and Chairman of the club, John H. Davies, announced eventual plans for a new ground at Old Trafford that would accommodate 100,000 people.

During the summer of 1908 the club embarked upon another new venture, touring the continent and playing several friendly matches. They travelled to Austria and Hungary and one of the matches, against Ferenczvaros of Hungary, was won 7−0 and it was reported that there was some trouble on the terraces.

The tag of 'Champions of England' seemed alien to United the following season, 1908/09, as their League fortunes declined to the point of finishing the season in 13th position. However, the F.A. Cup was altogether a different story.

With the news that the Stretford District Council had approved the plans for the new stadium, United embarked on their F.A. Cup trail. In the previous twenty-seasons of participation United had only progressed as far as round four twice, in 1906 and 1908.

United eliminated both Brighton and Everton at Clayton with similar 1−0 scorelines. Another Lancashire side, Blackburn Rovers were hammered by United in the third round 6−1, also at Clayton.

Mangnall's team were understandably apprehensive about the next match at Burnley. They had never gone further than the fourth round and, for the first time in the 1909 competition, they had been drawn to play away from home.

With the pitch covered by ice and Burnley leading 1−0, the referee decided to call off the match after 72 minutes play. United took fullest advantage, by winning the replay a few days later 3−2. At last they were within sight of their first English Cup Final, but the formidable Newcastle United stood between them and an appearance at the Crystal Palace.

The semi-final was played at Bramall Lane, home of Sheffield United, and to the joy of the travelling United fans, Mangnall's men emerged the winners by the only goal of the match.

Bristol City, their opponents in the Final, were considered an ordinary side and had only one player of real stature — defender William Wedlock, the England international. United were considered hot favourites to lift the trophy and they entered onto the Crystal Palace pitch on Saturday, 24 April, 1909, with this team: Moger, Hayes, Stacey, Duckworth, Roberts, Bell, Meredith, Halse, J. Turnbull, A. Turnbull, Wall.

In front of 71,000 fans United gave a persistent performance of attacking football in which is generally recorded as a disappointing Final. Meredith displayed the wing wizardry that was his trademark. He tormented the City defenders time and again in a generally one-sided match.

Unaccountably, United could score just once, without reply, the winning goal coming from Sandy Turnbull who was doubtful before the match, but played on the insistence of captain Charlie Roberts. Three days later the team paraded the Cup through the streets of Manchester and were welcomed by thousands of jubilant Mancunians.

The two major trophies in successive years had proved a good investment for Chairman John H. Davies and also gave him and the other United directors courage to press on with the building plans for the new ground.

United were now established among the top sides in England. They possessed perhaps the best manager of that era in J.E. Mangnall and some of the outstanding players. Who could boast a better half-back line than Duckworth, Roberts, and Bell. These three, along with Billy Meredith, were legends in those early days of the nineteenth century.

The following season United considerably improved their League position, finishing 5th, but the outstanding event of 1909/10 was their move from Clayton to the new ground Old Trafford.

The final match at Clayton was played on 22nd January, 1910 against Tottenham Hotspur, with United bidding farewell to their home of many years with a 5−0 win in front of 5,000 spectators.

By contrast, 50,000 were present at Old Trafford for the inaugural match on 19th February, 1910, against Liverpool. Spectators came from everywhere, but although the match provided seven goals, United lost 4−3 after leading 2−0 at one period. The modern stadium had been launched and United now possessed the best ground in the Football League.

New players were recruited for the 1910/11 campaign. Most notable of these new players were Hofton, a full-back who came from Glossop North End, James Hodge who came from Scottish League club Stenhousemuir and Enoch 'Knocker' West, a centre-forward of repute from Nottingham Forest.

United possessed a strong squad of players and fancied their chances for honours on the two fronts. They started the season well enough and when they beat Newcastle by two clear goals on 15th October, 1910, United went top of the League, a point ahead of Sunderland.

The men from Old Trafford kept up their good form during the long winter months, but unlike the last Championship season of 1907/08, there were many teams in contention for the League Championship. The 'Reds' remained to the fore and when it came to the last weeks of the season the race developed into a straight fight between United and their arch-rivals from the Midlands, Aston Villa.

Before the very last match of the season, Villa were leading United by one point. To win the Championship, United had to win at home to Sunderland, while Villa must lose at Liverpool.

United went about their business with style and demolished the Wearsiders, lying third in the table, 5−1. Amid mounting excitement, news was coming in from Liverpool that the home side were two goals up. At the end of ninety minutes that scoreline was confirmed, and United were once again League Champions, with the same points — 52 — as in their previous success, in 1908.

United had attracted an average 30,000 fans at home and to crown the League success Old Trafford was chosen as the venue for the F.A. Cup Final replay between Bradford City and Newcastle United on 26 April, 1911.

The side that won the Championship contained seven members of the previous championship team and the new additions were Stacey and Donnelly at full-back, 'Knocker' West replacing J. Turnbull and Harold Halse for Bannister at inside-right. Halse had joined the club from Southend in season 1906/07.

United were at their peak and seemingly destined to become an even greater force. But this promise failed to materialise, and between that second Championship success and the outbreak of World War I the team's fortunes declined.

Some of the players were admittedly getting on in age, but the main blow came in September, 1912 when J.E. Mangnall left United to join neighbours City. Assistant Secretary Thomas Wallworth took over for a period until Mr. J.J. Bentley stepped in.

A disappointing 13th position in 1911/12 was followed by a much improved, albeit false, fourth place in 1912/13.

Mangnall's departure at the beginning of 1912/13 signalled the end of an era and many of the established names disappeared from Old Trafford. Moger, the goalkeeper, was replaced by Beale of Norwich City. The famous half-back line of Duckworth, Roberts and Bell was dismantled. Roberts went to Oldham, and Bell to Blackburn. Only Duckworth remained.

In the immediate years before the outbreak of The Great War the struggle continued and the team could only manage 14th in 1913/14 and 18th in 1914/15.

The only headlines coming out of Old Trafford were of a notorious nature. For in the last season before hostilities, a scandal to revive memories in Manchester of 1905, broke in the newspapers.

A match on Good Friday, 1915 at Old Trafford in which United defeated Liverpool 2−0, appeared merely to have provided a surprise result. United were battling against relegation whilst Liverpool had been in good form of late. A few days after the game a letter appeared in the press, signed by 'Football King', claiming to have evidence that the match was 'fixed'.

Uproar followed. The Football Association and the Football League, each of which had received copies of the letter, set up an inquiry. Seven months later ''Football King's'' claim proved to be right, the match was ''fixed''. Four players of Liverpool and three of United were found guilty and banned for life. United's players were Turnbull, Whalley and the mercurial Enoch ''Knocker'' West. (Ultimately, all were to be forgiven by the F.A., their life bans rescinded — ''In appreciation of their services to the country in wartime'').

But the shocking and scandalous episode had other far reaching effects. United had staved off relegation by one point, leaving Spurs and Chelsea in the bottom places.

At the end of that season many opinions were voiced as to whether United's survival was legitimate. Many football officials argued that United should be relegated instead of Chelsea.

In an effort to deflate controversy, the Football League enlarged the First Division so that United and Chelsea should both stay up. But "Football King" had had his way, and he was never identified.

War broke out in 1915 and with it the end of the regular League football. But United, like all other teams, played in War-time organised football with several guest players from other club sides.

United were hit very harshly by the war and suffered more than most, losing three of their players in action — P. McGuire, O. Linkson and the legendary 'Sandy' Turnbull, a member of United's Championship sides and the player who scored the goal which gave United the F.A. Cup in 1909.

When peace was restored in 1919 United were a shadow of the team that had dominated the early 1900's. Jack Mew, a goalkeeper signed before the war was the star along with Jack Silcock, an England international, and 'Cal' Hilditch, the captain.

United only managed 12th place in that first post-war campaign of 1919/20, but that season United made an important signing, Jack Spence came from amateur team Scotswood. Charlie Moore also joined United, but some of the old stars departed. Herbert Burgess and Dick Duckworth were given free transfers and George Wall moved to Oldham for a fee of £200.

United's dark days continued and after achieving 13th position in season 1920/21, the fateful drop to Division Two came in 1921/22, after winning only eight matches and finishing bottom of the division.

Mr. J.R. Robson (appointed manager in 1914) resigned his post to be replaced by John A. Chapman, although the former stayed on as Assistant Manager.

During that period, Mr. W.R. Deakin, who was appointed club Chairman in 1909 (John H. Davies was President) died and was replaced by G.H. Lawton.

Back in the Second Division, the club wanted a quick return to the higher division and went about solving their problems with the cheque book.

John H. Davies was still a powerful man at United and only wanted the best for them. He asked Aston Villa to release their England centre-half Frank Barson, around whom he could rebuild the team, and in August, 1922, the legendary Barson moved to Old Trafford for a fee of £5,000, a huge sum at that time.

United pinned their hopes on the experienced Barson, and Jack Spence, to help them get promoted at the first time of asking. In fact they very nearly did it and came a whisker away from promotion. United had a slight chance of finishing before Notts County or Leicester City on goal average if they won their last match at Barnsley. United could only draw 2−2 but as events turned out even a win would not have been enough as Notts County won their two matches in hand to win promotion outright. The following season, 1923/24, proved a struggle, United finished 14th and again disappointing in the F.A. Cup, going out to Huddersfield in the Second Round.

A dramatic improvement achieved their objective in 1924/5, a strong defence, built around Barson and an adequate forward line with Spence as the star gave United a good start to the season. They faltered a bit in mid-season, but a late rally saw them fight out the second promotion spot with Derby County.

Before the last match of the season, the position was that United would NOT have gained promotion had they lost their last match at Barnsley 0−1, 0−2, 0−3, 0−4, or 0−5 and if Derby were to win their match by 12−0, 9−0, 6−0, 3−0 or 1−0 respectively. In the event, both drew their matches and United, after three years in the doldrums, were up.

Back in the First Division United gained a respectable 9th place in 1925/26, but the highlight of the season was United's F.A. Cup semi-final clash with neighbours and rivals Manchester City. During their run up to the semi-final United had eliminated the likes of Port Vale, Tottenham Hotspur, Sunderland and Fulham, and the clash with City on the 27th March at Bramall Lane caught the imagination of the city.

Although engaged in a constant battle against relegation, City were the better team on the day, and won comfortably 3−0. City went on to lose the Final to Bolton Wanderers and were also relegated, so, once again, Manchester was left with only one team in the First Division.

During that season an International was played at Old Trafford — between England and Scotland on April 17, 1926. Scotland won 1−0.

In October, 1926, the club's Secretary-Manager John Chapman was suspended from management by the F.A. for the rest of the season. Clarence G. Hilditch, a centre-half of some fame with the club, replaced him and acted as player-manager. When Chapman's suspension was over he did not resume his duties with United and Herbert Bamlett was appointed in April 1927, by which time United had completed an average season finishing 15th in Division One.

The days of the Secretary-Manager were also finished. While Bamlett was now the Manager of the club, a new Secretary was appointed — Walter Crickmer was to serve the club for many years to come.

The third season among the elite started on a sad note. On the 24 October, 1927 John H. Davies the President and saviour of the club, died. His death was announced at a board meeting the following day.

This was crisis time once again at Old Trafford. Season 1927/28 ended with United just escaping relegation and occupying 18th position. The great Frank Barson had left for Watford during the season.

Matters improved somewhat in 1928/29 with a good final run-up that saw United collect 24 points from the last fifteen matches to finish 12th.

Season 1929/30 was not much better, they finished 17th and although seasoned campaigners like Silcock, Spence, Steward and Moore were still in the team, United's future looked uncertain.

But worse was still to come. United started season 1930−31 with twelve successive defeats,leaving them rock-bottom of the First Division.

The efforts of new striker James Bullock from Chesterfield proved fruitless and by the end of the season United, apart from finishing bottom of the Division and being relegated, had the shame of their worst-ever statistics to live with:- Played 42, won 7, drew 8, lost 27, goals for 53, against 115, points 22!

During the season various protests were made against the board and there were fruitless calls for their resignations. The only resignation that did come was that of Manager Herbert Bamlett, leaving Walter Crickmer with the added duties of management apart from those of Secretary.

Apart from difficulties on the field, the club had many problems off it. United were in deep financial trouble. The brewery company which owned Old Trafford was requested to allow payment of the mortgage interest to stand over and there were also back arrears with Income Tax. Then, in December, the Bank refused more credit and the management were unable to pay the players wages.

History sometimes repeats itself, and as in 1902 when John H. Davies rescued the club, another benefactor stepped in. His name — J.W. Gibson.

Gibson was one of the founders of the clothing firm Biggs, Jones and Gibson Ltd. He placed £2,000 at the club's disposal and also arranged for the players to be paid their wages. He also announced that if he received sufficient backing from the public, he would provide further help. He agreed with the directors to be responsible for the liabilities of the club until 9th January, 1932, and, furthermore, that the directors resign their office if Mr. Gibson saw fit, in order to re-organise the company.

In season 1931/32, with United back in Division Two, the financial picture looked brighter, although results on the field did not improve and United finished in mid-table.

On 5th January, 1932, just four days before the agreement with Mr. Gibson was to end, a board meeting had taken place.

With Mr. Gibson also present at the meeting he was elected as a director of the club with the terms that were agreed upon.

A further meeting was held six days later under the chairmanship, for the last time, of G.H. Lawton, and Gibson clearly pointed out that financial support from the supporters had not been encouraging, but, nevertheless, announced that four gentlemen were prepared to come in and help the club out of it's financial difficulties.

The gentlemen were Colonel George Westcott, Hugh Shaw, Matthew Newton and A.E. Thomson. On January 20 Gibson was elected as Chairman and President of the company and Messrs. Westcott, Shaw, Newton and Thomson as the directors.

During that very important season the club started a junior team, run by 'Cal' Hilditch and called the 'A' team.

The new directors injected a new confidence into the club and went about their business in efficient manner. Scott Duncan, a good manager with Hamilton Academicals and Cowdenbeath, was appointed manager to relieve Walter Crickmer of his extra duties.

New players were also brought in, but the new season of 1932/33 started with a 0−2 home defeat at the hands of Championship contenders Stoke City. That defeat alarmed Scott Duncan and his directors, and United went shopping yet again to solve their problems.

Many new players were recruited, especially from Scotland where Duncan was familiar with the scene. Old players were sold, including Uniteds great servant and goalscorer Joe Spence. 'Cal' Hilditch retired. At the end of it all United finished 6th, which was an improvement on the previous campaign.

It was back to familiar problems in season 1933/34. By mid-season, the club was fighting against the threat of relegation to Division Three! The threat was serious and the implications had a far reaching effect with the resignations of directors Westcott and Thomson. They were replaced by Dr. W. McLean and former director Mr. H.P. Hardman.

During the latter half of the season the colours of the club were changed to white shirts with cherry hoops and white shorts, but this move only brought further bad luck. Other players were signed but no improvement was shown, and as the season went on the situation worsened and came to a dramatic crisis point at the very last match of the season.

The situation was that United, bottom but one in the table, faced Millwall, one place above them and with one point more. To save themselves, United had to win at Millwall. United did just that, conquering the London team 2−0 on the 5th day of May, 1934, and the two sides of Manchester celebrated different occasions — United staving off relegation and City their F.A. Cup triumph.

The summer activity was focussed on the appointment of Tom Curry as trainer and Bill Inglis as his assistant to aide manager Scott Duncan for the forthcoming season. The appointments were effective as United had a fairly successful season in 1934/35, finishing 5th behind Brentford, Bolton, West Ham and Blackpool.

The usual activity in the transfer market meant that United bought Bryant and Bamford from Wrexham while Hall replaced Hacking in goal. On the financial side the club made a profit of £4,490, the best since 1928.

The improvement carried on to the next season, 1935/36, and the formation of the team was largely the same as for the previous year. J. Brown came from Burnley to fill the right wing-half berth and Tommy Breedon was installed as goalkeeper from Sheffield Wednesday. Although Scott Duncan tried to persuade clubs to part with several top players, nothing further materialised and he had to be content with the young players coming through from the club's junior team.

The season saw United play with distinction from the outset. The team ended the campaign with a run of nineteen unbeaten matches that enabled the Manchester 'Reds' to win the Second Division Championship. Promotion was ensured on 28 April, 1936, when United, needing only a point to secure themselves a First Division place, won 3−2. The club celebrated with a ceremonial dinner at the Midland Hotel and the opinion of most was that the 'Reds' were back to stay.

Celebrations were to turn into utter disappointment for whilst United were very good in the Second Division they were not quite good enough for the First. Scott Duncan's team paid a short, one-year visit to the First Division .

What a contrast on the other side of Manchester! City won the League Championship to confirm their golden age of success.

The blame for that disastrous season was put down to the long list of injuries. United went long stretches without winning and injuries alone were a lame excuse.

On one occasion during the season, Tommy Breen, newly arrived goalkeeper from Belfast Celtic, touched the ball for the first time in his United career after sixty-seconds — he picked the ball from the back of the net after conceding a goal!

United prepared for another season in Division Two. John Smith, a £6,500 buy from Newcastle, was one of the new faces, along with a lad named Stan Pearson, who made his debut against Chesterfield in mid-October and performed well in a resounding 7−1 victory. Pearson went on to have an excellent season and one particular game stood out — his four goals in a 5−1 win over Swansea.

On November 9, 1937, manager Scott Duncan shocked United when he resigned, and finding a successor proved a real headache. In the end the board of directors decided not to engage a new manager and, with the help of Walter Crickmer, did not appoint a new boss until the end of the second world war.

Crickmer had a job on his hands, but the seemingly hopeless situation in the first half of the season turned to genuine promotion prospects by April. With only one match left United were lying joint third with Coventry, behind Aston Villa and Sheffield United.

While Villa had 55 points and one match to play, Sheffield had 53 with their programme completed. So, although Villa were assured of top spot whatever their result, both United and Coventry had a chance of equalling Sheffield's points tally if they won their respective matches. Then the second promotion spot would be decided on goal average.

Sheffield had a goal average of 1.30, United at 1.60 and Coventry at 1.47. In the final match against Bury, United won 2−0 and with the superior goal average jumped straight back to Division One.

At this time Chairman Gibson launched the Manchester United Junior Athletic Club, more widely known as the MUJACS. The team served as a nursery for United and was perhaps the first of it's kind in those days before the War.

The MUJACS competed in the Chorlton Amateur League and in winning the trophy they scored 223 goals in the process. Among the stars of that junior side was John Aston, who played at inside-right, and who was to prove a stalwart in the post-war golden era.

Season 1938-39 arrived with United possessing a good squad of young players, with no pretentions but to hold their own in the First Division.

Craven at inside-right and Jack Smith, a centre-forward, arrived from Grimsby and Newcastle respectively, but the biggest impact was made by Johnny Carey, who had a great season. Carey was already a Republic of Ireland international and his genius attracted many clubs to ask United about his availability — Gibson always firmly rejected such approaches.

Although United could only manage 14th place in the last full pre-war season it was clear that the team had potential, possessing style and class in contrast to the rugged approach of United teams of the past.

Johnny Carey, Stan Pearson and Jack Rowley, all relative youngsters, made a big impact. Breedon, Redwood, Roughton, Vose, McKay and Welsh international Warner in defence were as strong as they come, and but for a lack of goals from the front men, a better position would have been achieved.

To confirm the air of optimism, United won the Central League Championship for the first time for 18 years; the Manchester League was won by the 'A' team, the MUJAC's won the Chorlton League; and the Manchester Senior Cup was again on United's shelves.

Even the financial position of the club looked healthier with the balance sheet showing a profit for five successive seasons. Indeed, there was grounds for optimism in the Manchester United camp.

Then in 1939 War was declared and the dreams of many, not only those of Manchester United, were shattered, and League soccer was again abandoned until the ending of hostilities.

Part of the premises at Old Trafford as well as the Cliff training ground at Lower Broughton were taken over by the military and R.A.F. respectively. On the suspension of the League programme regional leagues were introduced.

The coaching staff could no longer call on the regular players as most of them had joined the armed forces and were posted around England and Europe. Tommy Breen went to Ireland and played for Belfast Celtic, while Jack Rowley turned out for Shrewsbury and Wolves, his first club.

In turn, United had several players guest for them including Butt of Blackburn Rovers and Woodward of Bolton Wanderers. Young players made their breakthrough in the first team at this period including Charlie Mitten, John Aston and Henry Cockburn.

The nucleus of the team that was destined for great things after the War was taking shape now and war competition honours came United's way in the process. They won the War League Championship Trophy (2nd competition) in 1942 and reached the final of the North Cup in 1945 where they lost 3−2 on aggregate over two games against Bolton Wanderers.

The Second World War, like the 1915-1919 war, claimed victims in the Manchester United camp. B. Carpenter was killed in active service, while Redwood died of tuberculosis in the Spring of 1944. Gladwin was so badly wounded that he had to give up playing, and Allenby Chilton, another of the up-and-coming stars, was wounded, although not seriously.

The biggest setback during the War came on the night between the 11th and 12th March, 1941, when Old Trafford was blitzed by enemy bombs. The grandstand and buildings had been so extensively damaged, that competitive football could not be played. The club was in debt to the tune of £74,000, without a manager, and players scattered all over Europe. The picture was a bleak one.

The directors wrote to the War Damage Commission for the demolition of the grandstand and rebuilding of a new one. But the Commission, in a letter to the directors in November, 1944, stated that 'the property at Old Trafford is not considered as a total loss'.

United sought the help of Ellis Smith, a United supporter since a boy and an MP representing Stoke-on-Trent in Parliament. United were granted the sum of £17,478 for repairs, the highest allowance given to any club, but, without a new stand, League football could not be staged.

In the meantime, Manchester City came to the rescue. They offered Maine Road to be used by United for their League and Cup matches, which offer was duly and happily accepted by the directors. In return, United gave City the chance to play reserve matches at the Cliff Training Ground, which was released by the military in 1944.

For the next eight years, United were to play their matches at Maine Road.

When V.E. Day finally signalled peace in 1945, the British public, after five years of hostilities were very much thirsty for the excitement and drama of competitive football.

United, with Old Trafford still out of commission, went about their business to get the playing affairs organised, but the top priority was the appointment of a new manager. The directors had several men in mind, but, at a board meeting held on the 15th February, 1945, a name was mentioned that would figure forever in United's fairytale road to success.

The chairman told his fellow directors that a certain Mr. Matthew Busby had contacted him about the post of manager of the club. Although Busby had several offers from other clubs, he preferred the United job because of family reasons and wanted to stay in the Manchester area.

The chairman stated that he was impressed with Busby's ideas and after persuading his fellow directors to his way of thinking, the former Liverpool, Manchester City and Scottish international wing-half was offered a five-year contract to come into effect after his demobilisation.

Some of the old players did not play again for United. Eric Roughton became manager of Exeter City, while Bryant was transferred to Bradford City.

A chance meeting in Italy with former West Bromwich Albion and Wales wing-half, Jimmy Murphy, gave Matt Busby the opportunity to lure him to Old Trafford as his assistant — certainly Busby's most important signing.

Matt Busby began instilling confidence in the players. He was a player's manager, capable of getting the very best out of his players. He was a born leader and always got respect from his players.

He experimented positionally until he came up with a fine combination. Busby's first venture into the transfer market was the signing of Jimmy Delaney from Celtic for £40,000. Here was a small man, who was already advancing in years for a winger. But, as he was to prove many times during his days as manager, Matt Busby had bought wisely. At the end of his first season at the helm Busby piloted the team to fourth place in the 1945/46 war-time Northern League and the typical first Busby team read:- Crompton, Hamlett, Chilton, Aston, Whalley, Cockburn, Delaney, Pearson, Rowley, Buckle, Wrigglesworth.

It was evident that Busby was welding together a very useful team and upon demob from the services of Johnny Carey, Johnny Morris, Charlie Mitten, Jack Rowley and others, United had, at last, something to look forward with hope.

League football was back and when season 1946/47 got under way United immediately made their mark. Results in the League were very impressive, and although the Reds made an early exit from the F.A. Cup — losing 0−2 to Nottingham Forest in the fourth round — United finished the season as runners-up to Liverpool.

Busby had worked wonders with the team. The potential was there to see and the football public was now taking notice of the Red revolution at United.

Johnny Carey, at that time operating at half-back, was majestic throughout the season; at the back Chilton and Cockburn were considered the most stylish defenders in the country; and up front, Morris, Pearson, Rowley, Delaney and Mitten interchanged bewilderingly and weaved their wizardry.

United scored 95 goals that season, the highest they had ever achieved in their history. They even lost the fewest matches in the First Division with eight.

Busby had moulded together a strong side but above all they were exciting to watch and season 1947-48 proved an even greater success. Yet again, United finished runners-up in the League seven points behind Champions Arsenal.

But the real excitement was reserved for the F.A. Cup. In the third round United were drawn to meet Aston Villa at Villa Park. The match proved one of the most exciting ever as Villa went ahead immediately from the kick-off. Jack Rowley equalised, and from then on United overran Villa and by half-time Busby's boys were 5−1 up.

It looked as all was lost for Villa, but, amazingly, they fought back to 5−4 before Stan Pearson killed off their hopes to make it 6−4 in United's favour — a classic!

United then disposed of champions Liverpool (3−0), Cup holders Charlton Athletic (2−0), and Preston North End (4−1). Busby had steered United to the semi-final for the first time since 1909. There they met Derby County. In a highly charged match at Hillsborough, United won 3−1 with the in-form Stan Pearson notching a magnificent hat-trick.

United were at Wembley and there they were to meet Blackpool, a team that had finished in ninth place in the First Division, but possessed two players of individual brilliance in England internationals Stan Mortensen and Stanley Matthews.

The Final was played on the 24 April, 1948, and United were everybody's favourites to win the trophy. They did win — in style — 4−2 with goals from Rowley (2), Pearson and Anderson after Blackpool had taken an early lead and that Final is still regarded by many as the best of all-time for skill and sheer entertainment.

The F.A. Cup win made the season of 1947/48 a very successful campaign. The team was splendidly blended with highly skilful players. Johnny Carey has moved successfully to left-back position, while his manager, Matt Busby, also had time to lead the British Olympic team with the assistance of trainer Tom Curry.

Season 1948/49 saw United finish runners-up in the League for the third successive season, this time behind Portsmouth. The League Championship was Busby's prime aim, but somehow the honour was eluding the team.

The team had another good run in the F.A. Cup beating Bournemouth, Bradford and Hull before going out to eventual winners Wolves in the semi-final. The match was played in front of 74,000 fans at Goodison Park and was decided by a Sammy Smyth goal.

In the meantime Busby added Johnny Downie to his squad by paying Bradford Park Avenue £18,000.

Old Trafford was by now nearing it's restoration and in August, 1949, the club returned to it's proper headquarters. A practice game took place on the 13th August and eleven days later the homecoming was celebrated with a 3−0 League victory over Bolton Wanderers.

With the team finally back at Old Trafford, United had high hopes for the new season, 1949/50, and went about their business in a grand manner — unbeaten in their first eight games. In December Busby paid Darlington £5,000 for Ray Wood, a young goalkeeper of immense promise who was to be reared as Jack Crompton's successor.

But as the season progressed, United's form declined, Warner was sick for most of the period and Carey was out with injury for long spells. Fourth place behind Portsmouth, Wolves and Sunderland was a respectable performance although United had been seriously hampered by a run of nine games without a win. In the end only three points separated them from Portsmouth who won the League Championship.

For Matt Busby and Jimmy Murphy things were taking shape. Youngsters were coming through the junior teams. Jeff Whitefoot made his league debut at Portsmouth, and Mark Jones, Jackie Blanchflower, Denis Viollet, Tom McNulty, Bill Redman and Roger Byrne, were also blooded in the first team.

At the end of the season United travelled on the *Queen Mary* for a tour in the United States where they played two friendly matches defeating Turkish champions Besiktas 2−1 and an American Soccer League XI, 9−2.

The tour was a highly pleasing experience for United, although winger Charlie Mitten then left United to play in the F.I.F.A.− banned Bogota.

On return to England, Busby's boys were again among the favourites for the League's top honour. More young players were knocking on the first-team door. Some of the senior players nearing the end of their careers and Bill Redman and Mark Jones were given their chance in the first-team as early as October.

Jimmy Delaney moved to Aberdeen, and Reg Allen, one of the League's top goalkeepers, arrived from QPR for £11,000. Allen took over from Jack Crompton, and with Ray Wood still learning his trade in the reserves, United had adequate cover in the goalkeeper position.

Some positional changes reaped rewards. John Aston was tried at centre-forward in place of the injured Jack Rowley. Roger Byrne came in at left-back while Aston, in his stint up front scored a remarkable 16 goals, before Rowley returned. Then Aston moved back to full-back and Byrne was moved to the left-wing.

United, for an agonising fourth time in five years, finished runners-up in season 1950/51. Harry McShane joined United from Bolton in exchange for Ball, as Spurs pipped them to the League Championship. The F.A. Cup saw United eclipsed by Birmingham in the sixth round.

In August, 1951, Busby added yet another player to his already strong squad. He paid £25,000 for the services of Johnny Berry from Birmingham City and the nippy little winger was to prove a lucky omen to the team's fortunes.

The League campaign of 1951/52 was one of the most closely contested for a very long time. At least six clubs, including United, led the table at some stage of the season. Then Arsenal, led by Joe Mercer, established a stronghold and seemed favourites to take the crown.

But United had other ideas and gave them a run for their money. In the last weeks of the season United overtook the Gunners, but as fate had planned it, Arsenal and United were to meet at Old Trafford in the last match of the season. By then the London club retained only a remote chance of the Championship, United held a two-point lead at the top, and Arsenal had to win by a margin of 7−0 to take the title on goal average.

Unfortunately for them, United were in no mood for upsets and before 53,000 spectators defeated Arsenal to the tune of 6−1, with Jack Rowley notching a hat-trick. The other goals were scored by Stan Pearson (2) and Roger Byrne.

United were the Champions after a lapse of over 40 years. Matt Busby's first great side had won the ultimate honour with a team that oozed class and was the toast of England.

Reg Allen was perhaps the best uncapped player in England. The defence in which Carey, Chilton and Cockburn dominated, was a rock, and the partnership of Rowley and Pearson produced 52 League goals.

The general look of the Championship winning side was:- Allen, McNulty, Aston (or Byrne), Carey, Chilton, Cockburn, Berry, Downie, Rowley (or Aston), Pearson, Bond (or Byrne).

Right through that team, nearly every name was a star in his own right, but some of them were at the veteran stage. Matt Busby knew this but decided to stay loyal to the players who had served him so well for the defence of the title in season 1952/53.

By mid-October the alarm bells were ringing — United were paired with neighbours Manchester City at the foot of the table. It was clear that for the first time since Matt Busby took over, United were in trouble. The shareholders were also concerned about the situation and they aired their views in no uncertain terms.

Busby refused to panic. He knew that there were youngsters in the reserve and junior sides ready to come in. It was at this time that Busby and Murphy decided to experiment and arranged a friendly match against Kilmarnock. Busby introduced many young players like Jackie Blanchflower and Jeff Whitefoot, both of whom had already been blooded in the first team. Relative newcomers in the team were Eddie Colman, Wilf McGuinness, Duncan Edwards and David Pegg. The gamble paid off as the NEW United won 3−0.

It was the birth of . . . . , . .

The Busby Babes

SUMMER SCHOOL 1952. United were the first club to run a close-season coaching course for promising schoolboys. Jimmy Murphy and Bert Whalley (coach), along with Scout Joe Armstrong, (far left) and trainer Bill Ingris watch club stewardess Mrs Ann Evans pour Duncan Edwards a cup of tea. (BNPC)

The significance of the match at Kilmarnock was soon apparent. The manner in which it was won encouraged Busby to keep most of the youngsters together for the next two League fixtures, against Huddersfield and Arsenal, both of which were drawn.

Then came another Busby masterstroke. He invested a record fee of £29,999 in Barnsley's talented centre-forward Tommy Taylor, whose Hotspur-style leadership proved an instant success. Ray Wood established himself in goal and Roger Byrne moved to left-back and paired with Bill Foulkes. Allenby Chilton was the only player from the Championship team still able to hold a first-team place.

Johnny Carey retired and joined Blackburn Rovers as their manager, and Chilton replaced him as the club skipper. Stan Pearson, Jack Rowley and Henry Cockburn also parted company with United in the next two years.

The arrival of Tommy Taylor had made a big difference to United's fortunes and helped by the injection of the young players, the team managed to climb to eighth place by the end of the season.

During the season the F.A. introduced a new trophy — the F.A. Youth Cup. United, captained by young Duncan Edwards won the inaugural competition beating Wolves in the final, 8 – 4 on aggregate, with this team:- Clayton, Fulton, Kennedy, Colman, Cope, Edwards, McFarlane, Doherty, Lewis, Pegg, Scanlon.

The young United side went on to win the trophy for the next four seasons, making it five times in a row between 1953 and 1957. That success showed that United possessed the best group of young talent in England and sometimes crowds exceeding 20,000 watched their matches in the Youth Cup.

In the two seasons that followed Matt Busby kept faith with the young players, gradually blooding them one by one.

In season 1953/54 United were placed 4th, and then 5th the following year 1954/55. The average age of the team was only 21, and they had done extremely well to finish as high as they did in the league. However, their inexperience was evident, especially in the F.A. Cup, when they made quick exits. However, Matt Busby was patient in the knowledge that it was only a matter of time before the club started reaping the rich rewards of the successful youth policy.

Season 1955/56 started with a positive run of results, and victory over Cardiff City on the last Saturday of October saw United go top of the First Division. A lean spell during the next six weeks meant a temporary shift from top spot, which was regained on December 3 after victory over Sunderland. United were now one point ahead of Blackpool.

The second half of the season saw United's youngsters reassert themselves again and they retained their lead until

Left: *BUSBY BABES Wilf McGuinness, Eddie Colman, Mark Jones and Denis Viollet pictured as the team leaves Manchester's Ringway Airport for Madrid and the 1956/7 European Cup Semi-final. (BNPC)*

Right: *BOBBY CHARLTON. Schoolboy International (JG).*

Left: *IN MEMORIUM.   A sad page from a Supporter's autograph book, all these players died at Munich. David Pegg, Eddie Colman, Mark Jones, Duncan Edwards, Roger Byrne and Tommy Taylor. (KB)*

the end of the campaign to win the League Championship, eleven points ahead of runners-up Blackpool. No team had managed quite such a feat in the twentieth century. United were also unbeaten at home and the striking partnership of Tommy Taylor and Denis Viollet produced 45 goals in the League.

Although the average age of the team was only 22, nearly all the squad had played at international level for their countries. The general formation of the team for that great season was:-

Wood, Foulkes, Byrne, Colman, Jones, Edwards, (from) Berry, Whelan, Doherty, Taylor, Viollet, Blanchflower, Pegg, though Ian Greaves replaced the injured Foulkes towards the end of the season.

The emergence of that team clearly illustrated the success of United's persistence on priming their own players. Only Wood, Berry and Taylor cost transfer fees.

Matt Busby was aware that he had assembled a potentially great team and football personalities showered universal praise upon his collection of young gems. Bernard Joy, a former Arsenal stalwart believed that United needed another three or four years to be . . . "strong claimants for the unofficial title of the greatest English club side of all time."

Winning a major trophy made the young lions of Manchester United hungry for further success. By now they were familiarly, and affectionately known as the 'Busby Babes'.

The team took season 1956/57 by storm and brushed aside all opposition as they repeated the success of the season before — League Champions for the second successive year. Not only that, United also reached the Final of the F.A. Cup, which they lost in controversial fashion, and became the first English club side to take part in European competition.

Making his mark in the first-team was a young lad by the name of Bobby Charlton who made thirteen appearances at inside left.

United's main rivals were Tottenham Hotspur, but even with such a strong side in pursuit, Busby's babes won the title with a margin of eight points.

The team also came close to becoming the first side this century to win the League and Cup double. United disposed of Hartlepool, Wrexham, Everton, Bournemouth and Birmingham City in the semi-final at Hillsborough, to reach the F.A. Cup Final.

Only Aston Villa stood between them and the historic 'double'.

Left: *Detail from a cartoon by Bill Tidy from the Everton v Man. Utd. programme on 4 Sept. 1957. (KM)*

Right: *DUNCAN EDWARDS. Signed by Matt Busby after a tip-off from Joe Mercer that he would be "a world beater." (JG)*

United were without the services of the injured pair Mark Jones and Denis Viollet, who were replaced by Jackie Blanchflower and Bobby Charlton respectively. With only eight minutes played, disaster struck United.

Ray Wood fractured a cheek-bone in a clash with Villa's Peter McParland. Wood went off for treatment and Jackie Blanchflower replaced him between the posts. When Wood returned, he was just a spectator on the flank with United effectively playing with ten men.

Blanchflower performed heroics, but could not prevent Peter McParland scoring two goals for Villa in the first half.

United rallied after reorganising for the second period and with seven minutes left Tommy Taylor scored from a Duncan Edwards corner. At this point Busby responded with a do-or-die decision. He sent instructions for Wood to return to goal and Blanchflower returned to his outfield duties.

The Busby Babes pressed on and a Liam Whelan goal was disallowed for infringement. In the end United's gallant efforts proved fruitless and the 'double' dream was shattered.

Busby's team had ventured into Europe for the first time, despite the strong opposition from the Football League, who claimed that additional commitments would result in a congestion of fixtures.

United fared well in the circumstances and in the first round of the competition disposed of the Belgian Champions Anderlecht on a 12 − 0 aggregate — United created a club record win of 10 − 0 under the Maine Road floodlights in the second leg. In the second round Borussia Dortmund of West Germany were accounted for 3 − 2 on aggregate.

It was in the next round that United really made the headlines. Their opponents were Atletico Bilbao of Spain. United lost the first leg in Spain 5 − 3 and naturally enough, hopes were not high for the second leg. On 6th February, 1957, United produced yet another magnificent performance and beat Bilbao 3 − 0 with goals by Denis Viollet, Tommy Taylor and Johnny Berry.

In the semi-final United met the best side in Europe at that time — Spain's other giants Real Madrid. A team with an array of great players including Puskas, Di Stefano, Kopa and Gento.

The Spanish Maestros were too strong in Madrid and built up a 3 − 1 advantage to take to Manchester. United made a strong challenge in the second leg at Old Trafford (by now suitable floodlights had been installed) and held Real to a 2 − 2 draw, but losing the tie 5 − 3 on aggregate. United's first season in Europe had established the club as an international force and Busby's reputation as manager further enhanced. In retaining their Football League Championship the team had ensured a second challenge on Europe, and with Real Madrid there again to defend their supremacy, all Britain and the Continent anticipated with relish another Battle of the European Giants in 1957/58.

THE BUSBY BABES 1957/8. Back Row: Edwards, Foulkes, Jones, Wood, Colman, Pegg. Front Row: Berry, Whelan, Byrne, Taylor, Viollet. (MMUSC)

THE SEASON OF 1957−8
COUNTDOWN TO MUNICH

Manchester United's exceptional young side, with European experience behind them, started the campaign of 1957/8 as everybody's favourites for the League Championship. Who could stop them?

The Busby Babes started the season with six successive League wins and averaged three goals per match. But like any other sides they had their bad days — Blackpool were the first visitors to win at Old Trafford that season, and Bolton inflicted a sobering 4−0 defeat at Burnden Park.

At this early stage of the season United were lying fourth in the table, two points behind leaders Nottingham Forest and well under way in another European campaign — Shamrock Rovers of Ireland were eliminated without difficulty.

The Reds kept up the momentum, beating Aston Villa twice by four goals on each occasion — once in the League and then to lift the F.A. Charity Shield. Life in the League was not as smooth as Busby would have liked and Wolves and West Bromwich Albion had opened up a gap, with the Babes well adrift by December.

Dukla Prague were disposed of over two legs at the next European Cup hurdle and early in 1958 Matt Busby bought his first player in five years. In doing so he paid a world record fee for a goalkeeper — the talented Doncaster and Northern Ireland star Harry Gregg.

Workington were United's first opponents in the new year and were beaten 3−1 on their own ground a few days before the first leg of the European Cup, quarter final tie against Red Star Belgrade of Yugoslavia at Old Trafford. Bobby Charlton and Eddie Colman both scored to establish a slender 2−1 victory.

Ipswich were comfortably beaten 2−0 in another F.A. Cup tie before two remarkable League matches which together produced 18 goals! Bolton were crushed 7−2 at Old Trafford and on 1 February 1958, just four days before their second leg match in the European Cup against Red Star in Belgrade, United visited Arsenal for an important League game.

This match will always be remembered as an epitaph to the Busby Babes. A crowd of over 50,000 packed into Highbury to see the famous Babes in action against the 'Gunners'. United responded in magnificent fashion.

Duncan Edwards powered United into the lead in typical fashion after just ten minutes, Bobby Charlton scored a second on the half-hour and Tommy Taylor slotted in a third to send United ahead by three clear goals at half-time.

The second-half seemed a formality, but Arsenal had other ideas and within the space of two minutes they scored on three occasions to level the scores — 3−3. Any other team might have been demoralised, but not this United side. They stepped up a gear and Denis Viollet headed United in front once again. Tommy Taylor made it 5−3 and Tapscott scored a late one for Arsenal for the final score to read, Arsenal 4, Manchester United 5.

This was to be the last match that the Busby Babes would play on British soil . It was a happy bunch of players that flew off to Belgrade for the next of their European hurdles, and on 5 February they met Red Star Belgrade in Yugoslavia and secured their place in the semi-final with a 3−3 draw after leading 3−0 at half-time.

The Manchester party left Belgrade for home in cheerful mood, content in the knowledge of a semi-final place guaranteed. Their opponents would be Italy's A.C. Milan.

The Elizabethan airliner refuelled at Munich airport. The weather was fearful, with ice and snow blanketing the runway. Despite the atrocious conditions the pilot, Captain James Thain, and his crew decided to go ahead. After all — they had many experiences of similarly hazardous take-offs.

The pilot made two attempts but on each occasion the plane would not respond. Then a third take-off attempt was made and the plane appeared to lift slightly, but not enough to avoid a house on the fringe of the airfield. The rest is history — THE PLANE CRASHED AND BURST INTO FLAMES.

Disaster had struck United at their zenith. The death toll was shattering. Manchester United players that died instantly were Geoffrey Bent, captain Roger Byrne, Eddie Colman, Mark Jones, David Pegg, Tommy Taylor and Liam Whelan. Trainer Tom Curry, Coach Herbert Whalley, Secretary Walter Crickmer, eight journalists and another three passengers also died in the crash.

Eight other United players and Matt Busby were injured, while Duncan Edwards, the supreme player of British soccer, lost his own fight for life two weeks later.

Of the surviving players, Harry Gregg risked his life in heroic fashion, trying to save some of the passengers by going in amongst the wreckage. He managed to save a young mother and her baby from the smouldering, tangled mass of metal that had minutes before been an aircraft.

Across the world newspapers reported the tragedy. Flags were flown at half-mast.

The injured were being treated at the Rechts der Isaar Hospital under the expert care of Professor George Maurer, the chief surgeon. The surviving players fought bravely for their lives. The wounds received by Johnny Berry and Jackie Blanchflower were so bad that neither were to kick a football again. Others, including Bobby Charlton and Denis Viollet recovered sufficiently to continue in that same season.

On 8th February, 1958, the British sporting public paid homage to the dead of Manchester United by observing a two-minute silence at every sports ground.

Association Football

AN OCCASION TO REMEMBER

Skill the only arbiter at Nottingham

BY AN OLD INTERNATIONAL

Nottingham F. 1, Manchester U. 2

All that was needed to make Saturday's league match between Nottingham Forest and Manchester United at Nottingham the perfect sporting occasion for 98 per cent of the record crowd of 47,675 enthusiasts who saw it (the other 2 per cent were camp followers from Manchester) was a reversal of the score—United 2, Nottingham Forest 1. .

And few would gainsay that but for a masterful—nay, a unique—exhibition of roving, inexhaustible, intuitive wing half-back play by Edwards, and two breath-taking saves by Wood, Forest might easily have drawn the match if not, indeed, come out on top.

For one traveller at least this WAS the perfect occasion; a case where the flawless manners of players, officials, and spectators alike gave to a routine league match the flavour almost of an idyll There was the glorious sunshine for a start, so comforting to those who had queued from 8 a.m.; the impeccable turf; the cosy intimate atmosphere of a ground where spectators are not held back by concrete walls or wooden palings but are allowed—nay welcomed—to advance and sit on the fringe of the turf itself.

Air of ballet

There was the tingling sense of a great occasion, the excited chatter, the ringing of bells, the occasional demented howl as of a lunatic at large, swelling to a great roar as the gladiators appeared. Since the club colours clashed, United danced out on to the pitch in their Tennysonian strip—"clothed in white samite, mystic, wonderful "—white stockings and all. It lent an air of ballet to the scene. One almost expected Robert Helpmann to emerge dribbling a ball. Instead Forest poured out in blood-red shirts and with that high-stepping action so beloved of modern footballers, as of lusty gamecocks spoiling for a fight. If one were to say that 47,000 mouths simultaneously watered, the expression might seem crude, but it would nevertheless be true. Rarely, if ever, has expectation of a football treat been more thoroughly roused: rarely, if ever, has it been so quickly and completely satisfied

Consider United's opening goal, drafted by Pegg, and signed, sealed, and delivered by Whelan. Pegg dashed seventy yards along the touchline, sent across a swift, low centre, and though Whelan, after the match, was inclined to scale down his success and attribute it to luck, his shot was a model of timing. Coming so soon as it did, within four minutes of the kick off, it might have

Above: *TOMMY TAYLOR Scores the last goal on British soil for the Babes, at Highbury against Arsenal just five days before Munich. (MMUSC)*

Left: *THE PERFECT OCCASION. This classic report by Don Davies, who also died at Munich, for the "Manchester Guardian" on 14 October 1956, perfectly sums up the pleasures of watching the babes. (MG)*

OPPOSITE PAGE:

Top: *MUNICH, 6 FEBRUARY 1958–The burned-out aircraft. (BNPC)*

Centre Left: *HARRY GREGG Inspects the wreckage after heroically saving several lives. (MMUSC)*

Bottom Left: *FUNERAL CORTEGE carries the victims past mourners on 12 February 1958. (BNPC)*

Right:*AIR CRASH VICTIMS are carried aboard an aircraft at Munich, bound for home. (BNPC)*

Naturally enough, the club had to go on. Jimmy Murphy, who only missed the trip because he was on duty as Manager of the Wales International side, travelled to Munich to visit the critically-injured Matt Busby at his bedside. The United Manager's immortal words to Murphy were — *"Keep the flag flying Jimmy"*

Murphy did just that. The match scheduled for 8 February against Wolves at Old Trafford was postponed to allow the club to organise something from its remaining resources. Even the F.A. postponed the Cup-tie with Sheffield Wednesday for some ten days and gave special consent for the purchase of players within the normally prohibited period prior to a cup-tie. Murphy immediately went out and bought two experienced players. These were 'wee' Ernie Taylor from Blackpool, and defender Stan Crowther from Aston Villa. Together with Gregg and Foulkes, the only players to come away unscathed from the crash, and a blend of reserve and junior players, Murphy named his side to meet Sheffield Wednesday at Old Trafford on February 19, 1958. The match programme for that day showed only blank spaces on the United team's page, as it was they lined up on that momentous occasion like this — Gregg, Foulkes, Greaves, Goodwin, Cope, Crowther, Webster, Taylor, Dawson, Pearson, Brennan.

On an emotional night in Manchester, the patchwork United side beat Sheffield Wednesday 3−0, with Seamus Brennan, then a left-winger and making his first-team debut, scoring two of the goals. Supporters celebrated through the night, the people of Manchester were caught in the euphoria and even people who had never seen a football match asked how the gallant United had fared.

The remainder of the season was a fairytale to behold. The team managed to finish in ninth place in the League and gave a fine account for themselves in the European Cup semi-final against A.C. Milan, even winning the first leg, 2−1.

But their epic performances were reserved for the F.A. Cup, for, after beating Sheffield Wednesday, they amazingly went on to reach the Final. To get there, they had to dispose of the persistent attentions of both West Bromwich Albion and Fulham, each tie decided in replays.

The Final was played on 3 May, 1958, just three months after the Munich disaster. United's opponents were Bolton Wanderers who had finished below United in the League. They were no more than a competent side but possessed one of the game's legends — England centre-forward Nat Lofthouse.

Matt Busby had made a remarkable recovery from his injuries and was allowed to travel to Wembley and watch the match from the United bench alongside Jimmy Murphy.

The match was only two minutes old when Lofthouse was put clear by a sharply executed Bolton counter attack, and he slammed the ball past Gregg to put his team one goal up. From that point Wanderers dominated the play.

Any hopes that United retained of a comeback were shattered when a Stevens shot was parried by Gregg. As the ball rose high above the goalkeeper's head and with Gregg poised to catch the ball, Lofthouse charged in and barged the unprepared custodian and ball into the net. It was a cruel moment, Lofthouse had connected in Gregg's back but the referee ruled that it was a valid goal.

Play was stopped for several minutes while Gregg received treatment. United never recovered and Bolton's 2−0 win secured them the F.A. Cup.

So the curtain fell on 1957/8. A season which will always be remembered as the year when arguably the best club team in the history of English football perished in the snow and ice of Munich.

THE GRAVE OF MARK JONES. (MMUSC)

 # THE PHOENIX RISES

Although it took some time for Busby to regain his appetite for the game, at one time he was on the point of quitting, he knew the club could not live on memories. So he set out to build another great team.

Manchester United's patchwork team consisted of players who had performed out of their skins in the aftermath of Munich, and they were not expected to figure in any of the honours for season 1958/59.

To the surprise of all they were in the thick of the battle for the League title and gave Wolves, the favourites, a remarkable challenge.

Matt Busby, sensing that his United side might just go all the way strengthened the squad by paying a record £45,000 to Sheffield Wednesday for their 'Golden Boy', England international Albert Quixall.

Warren Bradley, an England amateur international, also made his debut during that season.

Quixall failed to impress initially but his class emerged in the final few weeks of the season, adding neat skills to the brilliant form shown by Bobby Charlton, and the continuous goals of Denis Viollet.

But Stan Cullis's Wolves produced a great finish to the season and pipped United for the title. Runners-up in the First Division, United also managed to score 103 league goals. Amazing, coming just one season after Munich.

Many football experts doubted whether the teams effort and enthusiasm was sufficient to carry them to another League challenge. Indeed, season 1959/60 saw United struggle to repeat the performance. Busby had seen his team suffer a bad run of injuries as well as players like Bobby Charlton and Warren Bradley lose their form.

United bought Maurice Setters, a strong and tireless West Bromwich Albion wing-half for £30,000 and gave young Dave Gaskell his chance between the posts in place of Harry Gregg. Another new arrival was Tony Dunne, a £5,000 buy from Shelbourne of Ireland.

Of the few memorable matches of the season, most notable were the two prestigious encounters with Real Madrid, in England and Spain. Both matches ended in defeat and were seen by a total of 150,000 people.

The other positive note was Denis Viollet's 32 League goals which established a United club record, beating Jack Rowley's 30 in season 1951/52.

The following season saw a repeat of the story. United obtained seventh position in the League, went out to Sheffield Wednesday in the Fourth Round of the Cup, and bought another defender — Noel Cantwell from West Ham for £22,000.

These were lean times for the team and Busby faced the most critical period in his managerial career. In fact, the next two seasons were to prove United's worst in the League since 1937.

Season 1961 – 62 saw United finish in 15th place in the First Division, although they reached the semi-finals of the F.A. Cup losing to the great Spurs side 3 – 1.

That season David Herd joined United from Arsenal for £35,000 and two familiar faces left the Old Trafford scene — Alex Dawson joined Preston, and Denis Viollet, one of the original 'Busby Babes' and prolific goalscorer, left for the Midlands to join Stoke City for £25,000.

During the summer of 1962 United caused a sensation by signing Scottish international Denis Law from Italian Club Torino for a then record British fee of £115,000. Law, once of Huddersfield and Manchester City was disillusioned with Italy and Matt Busby wanted him to help revive the fortunes of United.

Denis Law certainly produced the goods in 1962/63, scoring 23 league goals and forming a lethal partnership with David Herd, but the pair were unable to restore immediately the club fortunes as they fought against relegation all season. United finished the season fourth from the bottom, just three points above Manchester City, who went down to Division Two with Leyton Orient.

Even the signing of Pat Crerand from Celtic for £56,000 early in 1963 had failed to revive fortunes in the League. However, the Scotsman's arrival brought better reward in the F.A. Cup.

A Denis Law hat-trick in a 5 – 0 win against Huddersfield put United on the Wembley trail. Aston Villa, Chelsea and Coventry were United's next victims before Busby's men met Second Division Southampton in the semi-final at Villa Park. United won the match with a solitary goal by the mercurial Law. The Reds were back at Wembley.

Leicester City were no match to United as the team shed the problems of the League struggle and at last produced a performance worthy of the star names that formed the side. The irrepressible Denis Law put United ahead in the 29th minute and David Herd added a second before half time.

United controlled the match for most of the second half, but received a set-back when Keyworth halved United's lead. David Herd dispelled any fears for United with his second goal and United's third, in the last five minutes. The Cup was back at Old Trafford and after six years another major honour.

The success at Wembley served as a big boost for the preparations of season 1963/64 in which they were once again to take part in Europe.

The season however, was to be remembered for the emergence of youngsters like in the early days of the Busby Babes. The youth team won the FA Youth Cup side with players like David Sadler, John Fitzpatrick, John Aston, Willie Anderson — and a young Irishman by the name of George Best.

United had a tremendous season, finishing runners-up to Liverpool in the League and of the ninety goals scored in the League, fifty came from the smash and grab partnership of Denis Law (30) and David Herd (20).

In the Cup competitions United also fared well. They made a satisfying return to European competition with a run to the Quarter Finals of the Cup Winners' Cup, before losing to Sporting Lisbon 6 − 4 on aggregate.

West Ham United defeated the 'Reds' 3 − 1 in the semi-final of the F.A. Cup to end their hopes of retaining it.

Denis Law confirmed United's return among the best when he was voted European Footballer of the Year in 1964, the first such honour won by a United player, and later emulated by Best and Charlton. So ended a very successful season and one in which Matt Busby had finally put together another outstanding team. In fact United started the following season of 1964/65 as one of the favourites for the League Championship.

The first weeks of the season did not give much indication as United managed only one win in six matches. Then a win over Nottingham Forest signalled an unbeaten run of 15 matches.

As the season progressed, United, Chelsea and Leeds fought out a battle for supremacy. United produced a run of seven wins in a row which included a vital 1 − 0 win over Leeds. By the end of the season the championship battle had developed into a direct tussle between United and Leeds.

A 3 − 1 win over Arsenal clinched the League title for the 'Reds' but a curious situation emerged.

With one game still to play, United were level on points with Leeds United who had completed their programme with a draw at Birmingham. However United had a superior goal average, and although they lost their matches against Aston Villa, the Championship still ended up at Old Trafford, by 0.686 of a goal.

The team did very well in Europe, reaching the semi-finals of the Inter Cities Fairs' Cup, as well as the same stage in the F.A. Cup, where Leeds beat them with a last minute goal in the replay at the City Ground, Nottingham.

The great incentive in season 1965/66 was of course United's first participation in the European Cup since 1958.

United's defence of the League Championship ended in a respectable 4th place and for the fourth successive season United reached the semi-final of the F.A. Cup, where they lost 1 − 0 to Everton at Burnden Park.

But the real excitement for that season was left for the European Cup. In the early rounds United disposed of HJK Helsinki of Finland 9 − 2 on aggregate, and then ASK Vorwarts of East Germany 5 − 1 on aggregate, the Reds winning all matches home and away.

They drew strong Portuguese opposition in the quarter-final. Benfica, twice winners of the competition and on another two occasions beaten finalists, threatened to put an end to any chances United had of winning the trophy for the first time. They were one of the outstanding teams of the era and their star player in the team, Eusebio, nicknamed the 'Black Panther', was challenging Pele's claim as the world's greatest footballer.

United's prospects were not improved in the first leg at Old Trafford. Despite winning 3 − 2, Busby knew that Benfica had never lost on their Stadium of Light in Lisbon, and the odds were stacked against the 'Reds'.

75,000 partisan fans filled the stadium with noise, but the players stayed calm and to everyone's surprise they attacked the home team. The Portuguese did not expect this kind of tactics, and were not used to having to defend on their home territory.

The United team clicked right from the start and in the first quarter of an hour scored three goals. George Best was having the game of his life, and scored twice. John Connelly scored the other to take United's 3 − 2 advantage of Old Trafford to an unbelievable 6 − 2 aggregate.

Benfica pressed hard in the second half, and when they scored through a Brennan own goal, they put further pressure on Gregg's goal but to no avail. United pressed again and with only minutes left scored another two goals — Pat Crerand and Bobby Charlton scoring for a memorable 5 − 1 victory that many consider as the club's finest-ever performance.

But the night belonged to young George Best who was nicknamed 'El Beatle' by the Portuguese fans after he destroyed them in one of the most exciting, individual virtuoso performances anywhere in Europe.

It was a pity that United did not continue their good work to the semi-final, where, to everyone's surprise they were eliminated by Patizan Belgrade of Yugoslavia. The 'Reds' had lost the first leg in Belgrade 0 − 2, but after their exploits in Lisbon, they were favourites to overturn the score and reach the Final. But United could only manage a 1 − 0 win and another European Cup dream was over.

In the summer of 1966 Old Trafford was used as one of the venues for the World Cup tournament held in England. England went on to win the Cup, defeating West Germany 4 − 2 after extra-time in the Final at Wembley. Bobby Charlton and Nobby Stiles formed part of the England team and for them 1966 was a year to remember.

England's World Cup win, achieved with a team without the traditional 'English' winger, generated a big increase on the terraces. Some of the teams adopted the patient approach employed so successfully by Ramsey, but mercifully not United who continued to excite crowds with a bold and adventurous attacking style — naturally so, being blessed with three of the world's top forwards in Law, Charlton and Best.

United embarked upon 1966/67 with participation again in the League Cup, but lasted only one round, suffering a heavy 1 − 5 defeat at the hands of Blackpool.

Matt Busby paid Chelsea a fee of £50,000 for goalkeeper Alex Stepney early in the season and winger John Connelly moved on to Blackburn Rovers.

Bobby Noble, a very promising young full-back, came into the team, but after 29 League appearances he was involved in a horrific car crash that put him out of action, from which he never really recovered. David Sadler came in at centre-forward and David Herd moved to inside left. Another new name was that of John Aston who played at outside-left with Best filling Connelly's berth on the right.

Liverpool made all the early running and it looked likely that they would win the title for the second season in succession.

They were still leading the table in January, but United put together an unbeaten run of twenty games in the last half of the season to close the gap. United went top on March 11th after a goalless draw at Newcastle and stayed there, holding off the close attentions of Forest who were runners-up. The team was unbeaten at home that season, and clinched the League title with an impressive 6 − 1 win at West Ham. The League title was Busby's fifth in his long career with Manchester United, but during that season, he had to see his team fail in the Cups — the defeat at Blackpool in the League Cup, and the fourth round surprise exit at home to Norwich in the F.A. Cup. The League Championship success gave yet another opportunity to challenge for the European Cup.

So the 1967/68 campaign kicked off as one of the most important to Matt Busby since he took over in 1945. He knew that the team would be among the favourites to lift the European Cup, and there was also the League Championship to retain.

The League contest took a dramatic route as both United and neighbours Manchester City fought out a fierce battle throughout the season. They arrived at the final Saturday level on points with 56 each, but with City on better goal difference.

United's final game was at Old Trafford against Sunderland, while Mercer and Allison took their team to Newcastle. The odds were in favour of United but as events turned out, the opposite happened.

While United lost 1 − 2 at home City figured in a dramatic match at St. James Park which they won 4 − 3. City took the League Championship by two points to cheer the blue half of Manchester.

But United had other targets and the European Cup was the big one. The European journey started against the amateurs from Malta, Hibernians. United won the first leg 4 − 0 at Old Trafford but were held to a 0 − 0 draw in Malta, where it was an occasion to remember, United have a large following on the George Cross Island.

United then drew F.K. Sarajevo of Yugoslavia and another 0 − 0 away draw, the Reds won the return at Old Trafford 2 − 1. Gornik Zabrze of Poland proved an even more difficult encounter and the 'Reds' had to fight hard to create a 2 − 0 home advantage, and lost the second leg 0 − 1. But the Reds were through to the semi-final and another clash with European legends Real Madrid who were no longer the strong team they were in the fifties and early sixties, but any Real team is a force to be reckoned with over two legs.

A solitary George Best goal was the only advantage United carried over to Madrid for the second leg. Hopes were not high on May 15, 1968 as United stepped out into the cauldron of the Bernabeu Stadium.

United held out Real's offensive and were succeeding in keeping their forwards at bay. Then, all hell broke loose. On the half hour Pirri headed Madrid into the lead and 1 − 1 on aggregate; Gento made it 2 − 0 with a burst of speed, and then a long ball from Tony Dunne caused such confusion in the Real defence that they conceded an own goal — 2 − 1 and at this stage United would be through. But wait — Amancio made it 3 − 1 and that's how they went in at half-time.

If hopes were not high at the beginning of the match, at the beginning of the second half they were even lower. It all looked over, Sadler was moved up front in a last desperate measure, United attacked and were now proving a headache to the Real defence. Sadler dramatically headed in a free-kick by Crerand to make the score 3 − 2 on the night but 3 − 3 on aggregate. Then with twelve minutes left Best started on a run that left Sanchis and Zoco for dead, pulled the ball back from the goal-line to the heart of the Real defence and veteran Bill Foulkes, survivor of Munich and the longest serving player at the club, scored to make the score 3 − 3.

United managed to hold on and won the tie 4 − 3 on aggregate. At last, Manchester United had reached the European Cup Final. It was a joyous night for Manchester, but especially for Bobby Charlton, Bill Foulkes and manager Matt Busby who had all survived Munich and now, ten years on, were on they way to the European pinnacle. The final was scheduled for Wembley Stadium and United's opponents were Benfica, who had a score to settle from two seasons before.

The first half produced little of significance, with United always the better side, and the Portuguese champions dishing up some rough treatment. No goals were scored.

The second half was an improvement over the first and at last United began putting their game together. Only a few minutes had gone when Bobby Charlton, whose heading abilities were perhaps his only weakness, headed in a cross to put United 1 − 0 up. Wembley erupted, United were in front and from then on United built in confidence. United had chances to increase on their lead, but chances were missed.

Then, with ten minutes left, Wembley was stunned to silence. Torres rose high above the United defence and headed down for Graca to stab the ball into the net. 1 − 1 and the game went into extra time.

United had not played well in those first ninety minutes, but on the opening exchanges of extra time they began playing the football they were renowned for. Seven minutes into the first half of extra time, George Best picked up a ball from Kidd, ran at the defence and finished by dribbling past Benfica goalkeeper Henrique to put the ball into the net. Almost immediately, Brian Kidd, who was celebrating his nineteenth birthday, headed United into a 3 − 1 lead, and Bobby Charlton hammered in the fourth.

The night belonged to one man — Matt Busby. His dream of leading United to the European Cup had finally come true. He was the happiest man on earth that May evening in London and to this day, 29 May 1968 will always be remembered as the finest day in his career.

Matt Busby was made a Knight of the British Empire in June 1968 and United went into season 1968/69 with high hopes for another good campaign.

But, as had happened with the 1951/52 League Championship team, the side failed to live up to the European Champions tag. Some of the players lost form and United started the season with several heavy defeats.

Willie Morgan was signed from Burnley for £100,000 and although the League position did not improve dramatically, United were going stronger in their defence of the European Cup. Waterford of Ireland and Anderlecht of Belgium, albeit narrowly, were eliminated by December.

In January Sir Matt Busby announced that he would retire as manager of Manchester United to make way for a new man at the helm.

United ended the season in mid-table but managed to reach the semi-final of the European Cup. They took care of Rapid Vienna in the quarter-finals and for the second time in their history, United had to meet A.C. Milan of Italy in the semi-final.

United lost the first leg in Milan 0 − 2 in a match that was dominated by the Italians. In the second leg United put the Italian side under heavy pressure and Bobby Charlton scored the only goal of the match, which meant United were again eliminated.

During that season the 'Reds' also played two matches against Argentina's Estudiantes De Plata to determine the World Club Championship. In two fiery and controversial matches United went down to a 2 − 1 aggregate, losing 0 − 1 in Argentina and drawing 1 − 1 at home.

This was a transitional period for the club, Wilf McGuiness, one of the original 'Busby Babes' and a member of the coaching staff at Old Trafford, took over as manager.

The season of 1969/70 started very badly for McGuiness with the team failing to win any of the first six matches. Then he made his first move into the transfer market and paid £80,000 for Arsenal's Scottish centre-half Ian Ure. Ure's arrival meant an improvement in United's fortunes and they picked themselves up to finish in a very good eighth position by the end of the season.

McGuiness also steered them to two semi-finals, in both the League and F.A. Cup. The team beat Middlesbrough, Wrexham, Burnley and Derby County in the League Cup without conceding a single goal on their way to a semi-final clash with neighbours City.

Both legs were titanic clashes with lots of excitement, but City took the honours beating United 2 − 1 at Old Trafford after the first leg at Maine Road had ended in a 2 − 2 draw.

The F.A. Cup trail was as exciting, but with an equally disappointing outcome. Ipswich were the first victims, before a 3 − 0 win over Manchester City. Then came the George Best Show, with United beating Northampton Town 8 − 2 and the Gaelic genius scoring six of them.

Middlesbrough, who like City had met United in the League Cup, were beaten after a replay and, the team was drawn to meet mighty Leeds United in the semi-finals.

United refused to be intimidated by Leeds and it was only after three epic matches that the 'Reds' surrendered.

The following season 1970/71, was also disappointing as far as the League was concerned, United continued to struggle and it was evident that McGuiness was not making progress with the team. They started badly and were dangerously close to the relegation zone when at a board meeting held on 28 December, 1970. McGuiness was relieved of his post. The ideal clubman, Wilf gracefully accepted his old job back, that of trainer-coach to the Central League side.

Sir Matt Busby was pursuaded to resume the managerial duties again until a suitable replacement was found. United ended the season in eighth place and again reached the semi-finals of the League Cup, to be beaten 3 − 2 on aggregate by Aston Villa.

United advertised the post of manager and among the favourites were Jock Stein of Celtic, Don Revie of Leeds, and Jimmy Adamson of Burnley. But the choice fell on Frank O'Farrell, the quiet boss of Leicester City who had built quite a reputation at Filbert Street. He was his own man and was one of the academy of former West Ham footballers that graduated as top class managers.

O'Farrell was installed at Old Trafford in July and his first move was to appoint another ex-Hammer, Malcolm Musgrove, as his chief coach.

United's opening to season 1971/72 appeared to prove that the board had made an excellent choice. They were playing some entertaining stuff, taking seven points from their first four matches and by December were leading the First Division with only two defeats.

George Best, whose form had declined in the last two years, was at last again providing the magic. Bobby Charlton and Denis Law also hit form and young players like Alan Gowling, Tommy O'Neil and Paul Edwards had found their niche in the team. All seemed well and the fans and the directors were happy with the situation.

Then, suddenly the team lost an amazing seven games in a row! In consequence, United lost the leadership of the First Division to Manchester City and never fully recovered from the crisis.

O'Farrell attempted to get back among the leaders by strengthening the team with two new signings — Martin Buchan came from Aberdeen for £130,000, and Ian Storey-Moore joined the then select band of players to exceed the £200,000 threshold when he arrived from Nottingham Forest in controversial circumstances.

Storey-Moore's transfer caused a sensation at that time. United agreed a fee with his club Forest and the England international seemed set for Old Trafford when Brian Clough persuaded him to join Derby County. Clough even paraded the player as his new signing prior to a match at the Baseball Ground, much to the disapproval of both United and Forest. In the end, Forest stood by their agreement with United, of course knowing that a move of their best player to high-riding Derby County just a few miles away would lose them support at the turnstiles.

Storey-Moore joined United's fight to regain their form of early season, but could only help the team to finish 8th The following season, 1972/73, was a continuation of the last. United were looking a poor side and failed to win any of their first nine League matches. The team sank to bottom of the First Division with the threat of relegation a firm reality. George Best resumed his disappearing acts and United were a doomed side.

O'Farrell signed Wyn Davies, the Welsh International, from Manchester City and then paid a record £220,000 for Ted MacDougall from third division Bournemouth. MacDougall was one of the most prolific scorers in the lower divisions and his move created much publicity and helped deviate the attention from the real troubles.

The critical situation came to a head in December when United were thrashed 0 – 5 in a league match at Crystal Palace. That was the last straw for the board. They knew they had to do something to stop the rot and they acted drastically. Frank O'Farrell received his Christmas present — the sack. The atmosphere at Old Trafford was one of depression, and confusion, and morale at it's lowest ebb.

They searched for a successor to O'Farrell and came up with a choice that seemed the most popular at the time — Tommy Docherty, the controversial manager of the Scottish national side.

At that time Scotland were in the middle of their World Cup qualifying programme, but Docherty was unable to resist the unique challenge at Old Trafford. To quote the 'Doc', he was . . . "Born to be Manager of Manchester United". Nevertheless, he arrived at a club in disarray, and a poor team. He immediately raided the transfer market and by the end of the season he signed SIX new players. Alex Forsyth a full back from Partick Thistle; George Graham, a £120,000 signing from Arsenal; Lou Macari from Celtic, beating Liverpool for his signature; Jim Holton, a young powerfully-built centre half from Shrewsbury; Stewart Houston from Brentford; and Jim McCalliog, a player of great experience from Wolves. A curious feature about these six players was that all the players were Scotsmen! No wonder United were nicknamed "MacUnited"!

Anyway, Docherty managed to save United from relegation, the team finished in 18th place. However, the season contained many sad memories, not least George Best's troubles.

But perhaps the saddest moment came at the very last match of the season at Chelsea. Bobby Charlton had already announced that he would hang up his boots and the match at Chelsea was his last for the club. It was the end of an era, and Denis Law's free transfer signified a time of change at Old Trafford.

The wholesale changes continued into the next season 1973/74, when the programme opened with some bad results. Docherty sold MacDougall to West Ham United and George Best came out of retirement briefly, but then finally to leave Old Trafford for good.

United struggled all season and this time the threat of relegation was real. The team staged a late run of six games without defeat at the very end of the season, but things worsened again. Their fate was sealed in the last match of the season, ironically, against Manchester City at Old Trafford – United lost 0 – 1. The goal came from Denis Law who scored with a back-heel only minutes from time. There was an invasion of the pitch and the referee had to abandon the match. The Football League later ruled that the result of the match would stand and United, after 36 years in the First Division, were relegated to the Second Division.

The club was in a state of shock, but the directors refused to panic and kept faith in Tommy Docherty to lead the team back to the big time. A prolonged spell of Second Division soccer was unthinkable at Old Trafford and the 'Doc' knew that failure to get promotion at the first attempt would have meant his departure from the club. During the summer he paid £180,000 for centre-forward Stuart Pearson from Hull City and United embarked on season 1974/75 with one target only — Promotion.

The 'Reds' attracted big crowds not only at Old Trafford, but also at away matches where attendance records were broken at several grounds. Apart from their good perfomances in the League, United had an impressive run in the Football League Cup and reached the semi-finals only to lose 2 – 3 on aggregate to Norwich City.

The biggest cheer was reserved for United's away match at Southampton when the team won 1 – 0 and clinched promotion to the First Division. They went on to win the Second Division Championship trophy with a 2 – 2 draw at Notts County. The good times were back at Old Trafford and Tommy Docherty had proved that United were heading on the right trail again.

United won the first three matches of 1975/76 and topped the League table. Tommy Docherty paid £80,000 for Gordon Hill, a young winger from Millwall, and United turned the clock back many years when they played with two wingers — Coppell and Hill.

Tommy Doc's side made a brave fight for the League Championship and along with Liverpool and Q.P.R. dominated the season. The situation at the very end of the season was that United were four points behind Liverpool with two games in hand. The 'Reds' failed to capitalize and a home defeat against Stoke and another loss at Leicester saw the Championship going to Liverpool, with United finishing in third position.

That was not the end of United's season. They had also made a big impact in the F.A. Cup and after eliminating Oxford, Peterborough, Leicester, Wolves, and Derby County in the Semi-Final, they were to meet Second Division Southampton in the Final at Wembley Stadium.

United were overwhelming favourites and looked set for their first major honour since the 1968 European Cup win. United started the match with their now familiar marauding style, but as the game progressed they failed to penetrate the solid Southampton defence.

Then Jim McCalliog, who had helped in United's fight for survival in the wake of Tommy Docherty's arrival at Old Trafford, stunned his old colleagues, setting up the winning goal. With just seven minutes to go, a beautiful through pass from the Scotsman sent Bobby Stokes away to place his shot past Alex Stepney into the net.

The United end of Wembley Stadium stood in silence, not quite believing that their team was one down to the Second Division club. Southampton survived the last frantic minutes and United were surprisingly beaten in one of the biggest ever F.A. Cup Final upsets in history.

Gerry Daly left for Derby County soon after the beginning of season 1976/77 when United, after a slow start to the campaign, improved their position in the League by finishing sixth. Jimmy Greenhoff arrived from Stoke to join his brother Brian and his partnership with Stuart Pearson in attack proved vital in the fine Cup exploits.

The team reached the fifth round of the Football League Cup, where they lost 0 – 3 to Everton. It also made a reappearance in European competition and took part in the U.E.F.A Cup, they were eliminated by Juventus after, in an earlier round, they had proved the better of crack Dutch side Ajax Amsterdam.

The team was suited for Cup football and for the second successive season they reached the F.A Cup Final.

Their route to the Twin Towers took them past Walsall, Queen's Park Rangers, Southampton, Aston Villa and finally Leeds United in the semi-finals. Their opponents at Wembley Stadium were the mighty Liverpool, at their very peak. Liverpool were already League Champions and on course for a unique treble with the European Cup Final only four days after the Wembley showpiece. Needless to say, the Merseysiders were favourites, but United were determined to erase the disappointment of the previous year.

Liverpool played in the familiar style that saw them dominating that season and in the first half were by far the better side, though United defended well.

Five minutes into the second half, Jimmy Greenhoff managed to get a back header past Hughes and Smith to Pearson, who shot immediately, and Clemence was beaten.

Joy was short-lived as within three minutes Liverpool drew level, but two minutes later another goal arrived. Jimmy Greenhoff and Lou Macari worked past Smith, and the Scot shot through, the ball hitting Greenhoff on the way past Clemence and into the net.

The final whistle signalled the club's first F.A. Cup triumph since 1963, and that famous victory should have assured Tommy Docherty's future, but events during the summer took a sensational turn.

In a Sunday newspaper a story broke out that Tommy's marriage had broken down because of his affair with Mary Brown, the wife of United's physiotherapist.

The sensational stories continued for some days with more expose's and after an emergency board meeting United decided that they had no option but to terminate Tommy's contract.

Just two months after United's finest hour since their 1968 European Cup win Docherty was sacked and in came Dave Sexton, manager of Queen's Park Rangers. Sexton's beliefs on how football should be played proved completely different from the Doc's. Whilst Docherty's style was based on quick attacking football, Sexton based his football on a more cautious approach, based on the continental system.

United under Sexton had an uninspired 1977/78, and it was clear that the supporters missed the excitements of the Docherty era.

Sexton paid a record £500,000 for Leeds United's Scottish defender Gordon McQueen and then a further £350,000 for his Leeds and international team-mate Joe Jordan. United ended the season in tenth place and were knocked out by West Brom in the Fourth Round of the F.A. Cup.

On the European scene United made the headlines for the wrong reasons. The 'Reds' were drawn with St. Etienne of France in the first round of the Cup Winners' cup, with the first match to be played away from home. An impressive performance succeeded in holding the French to a 1 − 1 draw, but some of the fans were involved in fighting with St. Etienne followers and the brutal Gendarmerie. The violence resulted in United being ordered to play their return leg on a neutral ground, and behind closed doors.

The match was played at Plymouth and United beat St. Etienne 2 − 0 to go through to the next round where they were eliminated by FC Porto of Portugal, 5 − 6 on aggregate.

During 1978/79 Sexton paid another £300,00 for Wrexham's Welsh international Mike Thomas and introduced a new goalkeeper in Gary Bailey. In this centenary season, again United came good in the F.A. Cup, reaching the Final for the third time in four years.

Though the Cup Final was to be the highlight of the club's celebrations it was achieved only after two epic encounters with Liverpool in the Semi-Finals.

After drawing the first match at Maine Road 2 − 2, United went to Goodison Park, home of Liverpool's neighbours Everton, and in an emotional night, the Manchester Reds, this time playing in white, won 1 − 0.

100,000 fans gathered at Wembley Stadium on a sunny Saturday in May to see United take on the 'Gunners' of Arsenal. This was predicted as one of the most balanced finals ever.

United, with only five mintues to go, were 0 − 2 down to Arsenal, the goals coming from Brian Talbot and Frank Stapleton. It seemed a hopeless situation and some United supporters were already leaving the stadium. Then, United got a goal back through Gordon McQueen — a consolation goal, it seemed.

The goal inspired the Red Devils. Two minutes later Sammy McIlroy went on a jinking run that took him through a cluster of players in the penalty area, a move which seemed to go on, and on, and on. But the Irishman kept calm and placed a shot past Pat Jennings into the net. United were level at 2 − 2, drama was not yet over. With the Arsenal team stunned and the match seemingly heading for extra-time, the London team launched a last desperate attack . . . Graham Rix crossed, Bailey missed the ball and it landed at the feet of Alan Sunderland, who shot into an empty net and made the score 3 − 2 to Arsenal.

In the close season Dave Sexton paid £750,000 for Chelsea's talented England midfield player Ray Wilkins in the hope of strengthening the team for the beginning of next season.

In fact, United's fortunes in the League improved considerably in season 1979/80. The team started with several good results and even led the table early in the season, United persisted with their challenge, but Liverpool always seemed a step ahead and in the end, United finished runners-up, just two points behind the men from Anfield.

United were getting results, but it was evident that their brand of football was not pleasing the fans and some of the board. The club boasted a tradition for attacking football, but under Sexton, the pattern of play had changed. The team possessed a very good midfield but were in desperate need for new ideas up front. This was emphasised in their moderate start the the 1980/81 campaign. United suffered a quick exit in the U.E.F.A. Cup at the hands of Poland's Widzew Lodz on the away goals rule.

Dave Sexton's answer was to pay £1.2 million to Nottingham Forest for their England striker Garry Birtles.

He had been a consistent scorer for Forest, and with him came the hope that United's problems would be solved, especially with Joe Jordan playing alongside him up front.

Disappointingly, Birtles found it hard to settle and it was several frustrating months before he opened his account for United. The team continued to drift between the top six and mid-table throughout the season and made quick exits in both the F.A. and League Cups.

The general outlook at Old Trafford looked bleak until a late rally at the end of the season which saw United win all of their last seven League matches.

It failed to impress the board, however, and, with a new chairman in Martin Edwards, they decided that it was time for a change in management and their choice fell on one of the most colourful characters in management — Ron Atkinson, who had done a magnificent job with West Bromwich Albion.

Life under Atkinson was certainly to be eventful and he immediately set about returning Manchester United to their attacking traditions. He wasted no time in implementing his own regime. Out went all the coaching staff, to be replaced by his own men from the Hawthorns. He paid Arsenal £900,000 for Eire International striker Frank Stapleton to replace crowd favourite Joe Jordan, who moved to Italy.

United had a very good season in the League, finishing third to improve on the previous season. They won a place in the U.E.F.A Cup but the headlines highlighted Ron Atkinson's moves in the transfer market.

He went back to West Bromwich again, and paid £650,00 for Remi Moses and a British record fee of £1.8 million for England international Bryan Robson.

During the summer prior to 1982/83, United moved quickly to sign Dutch international Arnold Muhren on a free transfer after the termination of his contract with Ipswich Town. As in the previous season, United and Liver pool were the main challengers but the Merseysiders finished on top yet again, with United in third place .

The Manchester 'Reds' managed to reach the Milk Cup Final for the first time in their history, only to lose to Liverpool 2 − 1 after extra time. They were compensated in May, returning to Wembley to win the F.A. Cup after two exciting matches with relegated Brighton. Having drawn the first match 2 – 2, United went on to register a Wembley record 4 – 0 win in the replay. It was the first honour for United under Ron Atkinson.

The F.A. Cup win was just reward for United's admiral attacking ambitions that season, and made up for the tragic loss of Steve Coppell who had to retire at the age of 28 because of an injury. Arthur Graham was signed from Leeds as a replacement, and once again the main target for season 1983/84 was the League Championship. United started the season well and went 16 games without defeat as well as heading the table for several weeks. Elimination from the Milk Cup by Third Division Oxford served as an impetus to do even better in the League. Further disappointment in the F.A. Cup — another Third Division side, Bournemouth beat the 'Reds' 2 – 0 was followed by another good run in the League and after a 4 – 0 victory over Arsenal, United went top. That was March, when United also eliminated Spain's Barcelona from the Cup Winners Cup 3 – 2 on aggregate.

In the semi-final they faced the might of Juventus of Italy and after drawing the first leg at Old Trafford 1 – 1 with several regular players missing, United lost the second leg in Turin 2 – 1 to a last minute goal by Poalo Rossi. Their challenge to Liverpool in the League faded and a poor run at the end saw United finish fourth.

More new players arrived at Old Trafford — Jesper Olsen from Ajax, Gordon Strachan from Aberdeen and Alan Brazil from Spurs.

In 1984/85 it was the other Merseyside outfit Everton who dominated and United had to be content with another 4th place, 14 points behind the 'Toffeemen' from Goodison.

Everton had not only beaten United to the Championship, but also won 2 – 1 at Old Trafford in the Milk Cup. However, United had another chance to restore the balance when the two teams met in the F.A. Cup Final.

United had eliminated Liverpool after a replay in the semi-finals, but Everton were favourites for the 'double'. The Blues looked an even better bet when in the second half of the Final, Kevin Moran was sent off. United's ten men fought gallantly and survived to play an extra 30 minutes of extra time.

Against the odds, and the run of play Norman Whiteside scored one of the best individual goals ever seen at Wembley to give United a memorable victory and the F.A. Cup for the second time in three years.

Two F.A. Cups, and in the top four in each of Ron Atkinson's first four seasons was success by anyone's standards. Although it was now eighteen years since United had won the Championship, no manager since Sir Matt Busby had enjoyed more success.

United started 1985/86 with a sound 4 – 0 win over Aston Villa at Old Trafford.

In fact, United kept on winning, and playing brilliant football they went into their eleventh match away at Luton with an amazing ten straight wins behind them. Had they beaten Luton, they should have equalled Spurs's record of 11 straight opening wins. They drew 1 – 1, but they continued their good form and at one stage were ten points ahead of second placed Liverpool.

Such was United's supremacy that it seemed that nobody could live with United — they looked unbeatable, and were being compared with the great 'double' Spurs side of 1961.

But defeat had to come, and Sheffield Wednesday were the team to do it on November 9. That result had dramatic consequences, United failed to win any of their next four matches and were eliminated by Liverpool in the Milk Cup. By December, what had seemed a certain League Championship had turned into a five horse race. United still headed the table but their lead was diminishing weekly.

The team was cruelly disrupted by injury. Bryan Robson, Gordon Strachan, Graeme Hogg and Peter Barnes all suffered long-term injuries. That brilliant early season form deserted them and at the beginning of February, they lost their lead to Everton.

In a bid to revive the challenge, Ron Atkinson plunged into the transfer market yet again. In November he paid £275,000 for Aston Villa defender Colin Gibson. He was joined by Danish international Johnn Sivebaek from Velje of Denmark, Terry Gibson in exchange for Alan Brazil and £300,000 from Coventry, and Peter Davenport for £600,000 from Nottingham Forest.

Despite these new signings, United's brave challenge fizzled out and at the end of the season Ron Atkinson was left to ponder on that magnificent start to the campaign, and more poignantly, on what might have been.

MANCHESTER UNITED

FORMED 1878 AS NEWTON HEATH LYR

CLUB HONOURS 1878-1986

European Champions Cup
Winners: 1968
Semi-Finals: 1957 1958 1966 1969

World Club Championship
Finalists: 1968

Football League Division One
Champions: 1908 1911 1952 1956
1957 1965 1967
Runners-up: 1947 1948 1949 1951
1959 1964 1968 1980

Football League Division Two
Champions: 1936 1975
Runners-up: 1897 1906 1925 1938

FA Challenge Cup
Winners: 1909 1948 1963 1977
1983 1985
Finalists: 1957 1958 1976 1979
Semi-Finals: 1926 1949 1962 1964
1965 1966 1970

Football League (Milk) Cup
Finalists: 1983
Semi-Finals: 1970 1971 1975

European Cup-Winners' Cup
Semi-Finals: 1984

Inter Cities Fairs Cup
Semi-Finals: 1965

FA Charity Shield
Winners: 1908 1911 1952 1956
1957 1983
Joint Holders: 1965 1967 1977
Runners-up: 1948 1963 1985

FA Youth Cup
Winners: 1953 1954 1955 1956
1957 1964
Finalists: 1982 1986

Lancashire FA Youth Cup
Winners: 1972 1975 1976
Runners-up: 1973 1978
Semi-Finals: 1971

Football Alliance
Runners-up: 1891

Central League
Champions: 1913 1921 1939 1947
1956 1960

Lancashire FA Senior Cup
Winners: 1898 1913 1914 1920
1938 1943 1946 1951
1969
Joint Winners: 1929

Manchester FA Senior Cup
Winners: 1886* 1888 1889 1890
1893 1908 1910 1912
1913 1920 1924 1926
1931 1934 1936 1937
1939 1948 1955 1957
1959 1964

*The first cup won by United

Watney Cup
Finalists: 1971

Coronation Soccer Cup
Semi-Final: 1953

Daily Mail Fair Play League
Winners: 1976 1977 1979
Runners-up 1978

THE PICTORIAL HISTORY

AND CLUB RECORD 1878-1986

Newton Heath LYR

FACT FILE ON NEWTON HEATH & MANCHESTER UNITED

PRESIDENTS & CHAIRMEN
c1882-1891 F. Attock.
1891-1902 T. Connelly, Cllr. James Bowes,
James Taylor, W. Crompton, W. Healey, James Taylor
1902-1927 J. H. Davies
1909-1919 President — J. H. Davies
                Chairman — W. R. Deakin.
1927-1932 G. H. Lawton
1932-1951 J. W. Gibson
1951-1965 H. P. Hardman
1965-1980 L. C. Edwards
1980-present: President — Sir Matt Busby
                  Chairman — Martin Edwards

MANAGERS AND SECRETARIES
Secretary 1892-1900 A. H. Albot
Secretary 1900-1903 James West
Secretary 1903-1912 J. E. Magnall
Temporary Secretary 1912 T. J. Wallworth
Secretary 1912-1916 J. J. Bentley
Manager 1914-1921 J. R. Robson
Sec/Manager 1921-1926 John A. Chapman
Player-Manager 1926-1927 Clarence Hilditch
Manager 1927-1931 Herbert S. Bamlett
Secretary 1928-1958 Walter Crickmer
Manager 1932-1937 A. Scott Duncan
Manager 1945-1969 Matt Busby
Secretary 1958 to present Les Olive
Manager 1970-1970 Wilf McGuiness
Manager 1970-1971 Sir Matt Busby
Manager 1971-1972 Frank O'Farrell
Manager 1972-1977 Tommy Docherty
Manager 1977-1981 Dave Sexton
Manager 1981 to present Ron Atkinson

CLUB GROUNDS
c1880-1893 North Road, Newton Heath
1893-1910 Bank Street, Clayton
1910 to present Old Trafford
*Between 1941 and 1949 senior home matches played at
Maine Road

TEAM COLOURS
c1878-1896 Green & Gold Jerseys
1896-1902 White Jerseys, Blue Shorts
1902-1923 Red Jerseys, White Shorts
1923-1927 White Jerseys with Red "V", White Shorts
1927-1934 Red Jerseys, White Shorts
1934 (Part) Cherry and White hooped Jerseys, White
Shorts
1934 to present Red Jerseys, White Shorts

RECORD ATTENDANCES PRE-WAR
F.A. CUP at Old Trafford
76,962 25 March 1939 Semi-Final tie
Wolves v Grimsby Town
73,000 24 March 1923 Semi-Final tie
Bolton Wanderers v Sheffield United
65,101 4 February 1911 4th Round tie
Manchester United v Aston Villa

F.A. CUP at Old Trafford (cont.)
59,300 9 March 1912 4th Round tie
Manchester United v Blackburn Rovers
56,607 26 April 1911 F.A. Cup Final Replay
Bradford City v Newcastle United

at Clayton
c35,500 24 February 1906 3rd Round tie
Manchester United v Aston Villa

FOOTBALL LEAGUE at Old Trafford
70,504 26 December 1920
Manchester United v Aston Villa

at Clayton
c40,000 5 September 1903
Manchester United v Bristol City

RECORD ATTENDANCES POST-WAR
FOOTBALL LEAGUE at Old Trafford
66,123 22 February 1958
Manchester United v Nottingham Forest

at Maine Road
82,950 1 January 1949
Manchester United v Arsenal

RECORD SCORES PRE-WAR
FOOTBALL LEAGUE
15 October 1892 Newton Heath 10 Wolves 1
9 March 1895 Newton Heath 14 Walsall 0
(declared void due to state of pitch)
3 April 1895 Newton Heath 9 Walsall 0 (Replay)

F.A. CUP
1896/7 Qual Rd 4 Newton Heath 7 West Manchester 0
1 November 1902 Qual Rd 3 Manchester United 7
Accrington Stanley 0
13 January 1906 Rd 1 Manchester United 7 Staple Hill 0
14 January 1928 Rd 3 Manchester United 7 Brentford 1

RECORD SCORES POST-WAR
FOOTBALL LEAGUE
19 March 1969 Manchester United 8 QPR 1

F.A. CUP
12 Feb 1949 Rd 5 Manchester United 8 Yeovil Town 0
7 Feb 1970 Rd 5 Northampton Town 2 Manchester Utd 8

EUROPEAN CUP
26 Sept 1956 Manchester United 10 R.S.C Anderlecht 0

RECORD APPEARANCES (F.L./F.A.C./F.L.C.)
706 Bobby Charlton (606 League)
627 Bill Foulkes (563 League)

RECORD GOALSCORERS (F.L./F.A.C./F.L.C.)
223 Bobby Charlton (198 League)
209 Jack Rowley (182 League)
207 Denis Law (171 League)

RECORD LEAGUE GOALS — ONE SEASON
32 Denis Viollet Season 1959-60

Newton   Heath LYR

NEWTON HEATH
1878

The Newton Heath LYR F.C. was
formed by railway company
workers at the carriage and wagon
works of the Lancashire and
Yorkshire Railway.

*Top Right: Badge of the Lancashire & Yorkshire
Railway. (IM)*

*Top Left: THE THREE CROWNS INN on Oldham
Road, Newton Heath. The early players used the
changing facilities there before walking to the pitch on
North Road. (KM)*

*Middle Right: SAM BLACK. The first club player to
be selected for representative honours. (MMUSC)*

Results of Challenge, Friendly, Charity, Benefit & Testimonial Matches

1880-1

Nov 20	A	Bolton Wanderers XI	0-6
Dec 4	A	Manchester Arcadians	0-0
Jan 22	H	Bolton Wanderers XI	0-6
Feb 5	H	Bootle Reserves	2-0
Feb 15	H	Hurst	0-1

1881-2

Oct 15	H	Manchester Arcadians	3-0
Oct 22	A	Blackburn Olympic XI	0-4
Nov 12	H	West Gorton St. Marks	3-0
Mar 4	A	West Gorton St. Marks	1-2

1882-3

Nov 25	H	Bentfield	3-1
Dec 2	H	Middleton	4-3
Jan 13	A	Astley Bridge 'A'	4-1
Jan 20	A	Bentfield	2-4
Feb 10	A	Manchester Arcadians	0-0

1883-4

Oct 6	A	Pendleton Olympic Res	1-4
Oct 13	H	Haughton Dale	2-2
Dec 1	H	Manchester Arcadians	4-0
Dec 8	A	Earlstown	0-8
Jan 5	H	Bootle Wanderers	6-0
Jan 12	A	Bentfield	1-1
Jan 19	H	St. Helen's	3-1
Feb 2	H	Greenhays	1-0
Feb 9	A	Bootle Wanderers	1-1
Feb 23	H	Blackburn Olympic XI	0-0
Mar 8	A	Manchester Arcadians	4-0
Mar 15	A	Astley Bridge Reserves	0-0
Mar 29	A	Greenhays	1-5

1884-5

Oct 4	H	Earlstown Reserves	2-1
Oct 11	A	Haughton Dale Reserves	7-0
Nov 8	H	Greenhays	3-1
Nov 22	A	Oughtrington Park	4-2
Nov 29	H	Heywood	5-1
Dec 13	H	Dalton Hall	4-1
Dec 20	A	Levenshume	4-0
Dec 27	A	Heywood	1-1
Jan 3	H	Eccles	0-0
Jan 10	H	Oughtrington Park	3-2
Jan 17	A	Gorton Association	3-1
Jan 24	H	Stretford	1-2
Feb 7	A	Doncaster Rovers	3-1
Mar 14	A	Greenhays	3-1
Mar 21	H	West Manchester	5-3
Mar 22	A	Earlstown	0-2
Apr 4	H	Blackburn Olympic XI	0-1
Apr 11	A	Stretford	0-0

1885-6

Aug 29	H	Crewe Alexandra	1-3
Sept 12	A	Kearsley	11-2
Sept 19	H	Blackburn Olympic XI	3-4
Sept 26	H	Bolton Wanderers Swifts	0-3
Oct 10	A	Macclesfield	4-3
Oct 17	A	Baxenden	2-2
Oct 24	A	Blackpool St. John	2-0
Oct 31	H	Crewe Alexandra	3-1
Nov 7	H	Darwen and District	1-1
Nov 14	H	Crewe Britannia	3-0
Nov 21	A	Darwen Hibernian	2-1

1885-6 (cont.)

Nov 28	H	Furness Vale Rovers	2-0
Dec 5	H	Greenhays	4-1
Dec 12	H	West Manchester	1-0
Jan 2	H	Pendleton Plympic	5-0
Jan 16	H	Macclesfield	3-3
Jan 30	H	Southport Central	4-0
Feb 6	H	Lower Hurst	2-3
Feb 13	H	Thornhall	10-0
Feb 20	H	Blackburn Olympic XI	3-1
Feb 27	H	Irwell Springs	2-0
Mar 20	H	Baxenden	4-3
Mar 27	A	Pendleton Olympic	2-2
Mar 29	A	Blackburn Olympic	0-3
Apr 10	A	Furness Vale Rovers	2-1
Apr 17	H	Accrington Reserves	2-1
Apr 23	H	Bell's Temperance	1-1
Apr 24	H	Darwen and District	2-1
Apr 26	H	West Bromwich Alb Res	1-0
May 8	H	Manchester	2-3
May 15	A	Salford and District	2-0
May 22	H	South Shore	1-1

1886-7

Sept 4	A	Northwich Victoria	0-5
Sept 11	H	Oswaldtwistle Rovers	2-4
Sept 18	A	Stanley	2-0
Sept 25	A	Hurst	1-3
Oct 2	H	Manchester	8-0
Oct 9	A	Oswaldtwistle Rovers	2-1
Oct 16	A	Rawtenstall	3-3
Oct 23	H	Burslem Port Vale	4-0
Nov 6	H	Blackburn Olympic	4-2
Nov 13	H	Irwell Springs	0-3
Nov 20	H	Rawtenstall	0-0
Nov 27	H	Macclesfield	1-0
Dec 4	A	Manchester	3-2
Dec 11	H	Hurst	5-0
Dec 18	A	Bury	0-0
Dec 25	H	Burton Wanderers	0-0
Dec 27	H	Nottingham Rovers	0-1
Jan 1	A	Crewe Alexandra	0-2
Jan 15	H	Irwell Springs	1-0
Jan 22	H	Witton	0-0
Jan 29	H	Stanley	2-0
Feb 5	A	Macclesfield	4-1
Feb 26	A	Hurst	3-1
Mar 5	H	Derby Midland	3-1
Mar 12	H	Nottingham Jardines	2-2
Mar 19	H	Gorton Association	8-0
Apr 8	H	Halliwell	0-0
Apr 9	H	Gainsborough Trinity	1-0
Apr 11	H	Accrington	0-3
Apr 16	H	Crewe Alexandra	2-3
Apr 30	H	Bolton Wanderers	0-5
May 14	H	Blackburn Rovers	1-0

1887-8

Sept 3	H	Accrington	2-1
Sept 10	A	Bell's Temperance	1-2
Sept 17	H	Earlstown	7-0
Sept 24	H	West Manchester	6-0
Oct 1	A	Derby Midland	3-0
Oct 8	H	Hurst	3-1
Oct 15	H	Padiham	3-0
Oct 22	A	Accrington	1-2
Oct 29	H	Burnley	0-0

1887-8 (cont.)

Nov 5	H	Ten Acres	9-0
Nov 12	A	Hurst	2-1
Nov 19	H	Nottingham Jardines	8-0
Nov 26	A	Crewe Alexandra	1-0
Dec 3	A	Ten Acres	1-0
Dec 10	A	West Manchester	2-2
Dec 17	A	Astley Bridge	0-1
Dec 24	H	Leek	3-0
Dec 26	H	Burslem Port Vale	0-0
Dec 31	H	Casuals	2-1
Jan 2	H	Burton Wanderers	1-1
Jan 7	H	Bolton Wanderers	0-1
Jan 14	H	Astley Bridge	3-0
Jan 21	H	Gorton Association	8-1
Jan 28	H	Oswaldtwistle Rovers	1-0
Feb 4	H	Bell's Temperance	4-2
Feb 11	A	Crewe Alexandra	0-0
Feb 18	A	Oswaldtwistle Rovers	0-6
Feb 25	A	Bootle	0-1
Mar 3	H	Blackburn Olympic	1-2
Mar 24	H	Rawtenstall	7-0
Mar 31	H	Mitchell St. George's	2-2
Apr 7	A	Burnley	1-7
Apr 21	H	Derby Midland	6-1
Apr 23	H	Bolton Wanderers	3-3
Apr 30	A	Hyde	1-1
May 5	H	Preston North End	1-1
May 12	A	Denton	4-1
May 21	H	Aston Villa XI	1-0

1888-9

Sept 1	H	Bolton Wanderers	1-0
Sept 8	H	Blackburn Rovers	2-1
Sept 15	H	Walsall Town Swifts	2-1
Sept 29	A	Gainsborough Trinity	5-1
Oct 6	H	Canadian Team XI	0-2
Oct 27	H	Witton	2-2
Nov 17	H	West Manchester	5-0
Nov 24	H	Halliwell	2-0
Dec 8	A	West Manchester	1-2
Dec 22	H	Darwen Old Wanderers	4-0
Dec 25	H	West Manchester	4-0
Dec 26	A	Wolves	1-6
Dec 29	H	Corinthians	0-4
Dec 31	H	3rd Lanark Rifle Volun.	1-0
Jan 1	A	Heart of Midlothian	1-2
Jan 2	H	Casuals	1-0
Jan 12	A	The Wednesday	1-2
Feb 2	A	Bolton Wanderers	1-3
Feb 16	H	Rotherham Town	7-2
Feb 23	H	Preston North End	1-0
Mar 9	A	Nottingham Forest	2-2
Mar 23	H	Nottingham Forest	3-1
Apr 13	A	South Shore	2-2
Apr 20	H	The Wednesday	1-2
Apr 22	H	West Bromwich Albion	1-3
May 4	A	Grimsby Town	0-3
May 11	H	Preston North End	1-1
May 18	H	Derby St. Duke's	2-1
May 20	A	Ardwick	1-2
May 25	H	Darwen	3-2

(continued on page 46)

MANCHESTER CUP WINNERS 1887-8

SATURDAY'S PASTIMES.

FOOTBALL.

ASSOCIATION.

MANCHESTER CUP.

FINAL TIE.

NEWTON HEATH (L. & Y.) v. DENTON.—The competition for the above cup was brought to a close yesterday (Saturday) afternoon, on the ground of the Manchester Rugby Club, at Whalley Range, this having been the venue of three previous final ties. The games have been closely fought, the biggest score being scored by Hurst, when they beat Newton Heath by 8 goals to nil, this being in the 1884-5 season. One of the contestants in this match have always been in the final—viz., Newton Heath, this being the fourth time they have got so far in the competition, whilst their opponents have been beaten in the first stage on two occasions. Both clubs are rapidly rising to the front rank, and have had fairly successful seasons. Newton Heath have played 39 games, of which 23 have been won, 6 drawn, and 10 lost—103 goals scored to 43 goals against them. Denton have played 34 games, out of which 22 were won, 5 drawn, and 7 lost, whilst the goals scored have been 79 for and 42 against. Neither team is able to play its full strength, Denton being the worst sufferers, as there are four second team men playing, whilst Newton Heath are without Tom Hay, their goalkeeper, a host in himself.

The ball was kicked off at 3-30, by Denton, against the wind, and their opponents at once began to press, and shots were poured in one after the other, but Lowe was in grand form, and he was ably assisted by Seddon and Arrandale. J and R Doughty, with Gotheredge, played a rattling game, and plagued the defence a lot. The play was only relieved by one or two runs by the Denton forwards. It was quite forty minutes from the start when the first goal was scored for Newton Heath by Burke, and this was followed by another by R Doughty, which brought half-time. The second half was also all in favour of the Newton Heath men, as they were constantly pressing, and goals were scored by J Davies, J Doughty (3), R Doughty, and another. Newton Heath winning a very one-sided game. Score:—

NEWTON HEATH .... 7 goals.
DENTON .... 1 goal.

The cup was presented to Powell by Mrs Colbeck.

Teams—NEWTON HEATH: Pedley, goal; Mitchell and Powell, backs; Burke, Davies, and Owen, half-backs; Earp, Wright, J Doughty, R Doughty, and Gotheridge, forwards. DENTON: Lowe, goal; Seddon and Arrandale, backs; Moss, Cooke, and O Arrandale, half-backs; Bromley, Howard, Seddon, Arrowsmith, and Jenkins, forwards.

ROGER DOUGHTY

JACK OWEN

A RECORD CUP WIN. Newton Heath (L&Y) Scored a record seven goals to win the Manchester Cup, as reported in the UMPIRE, *Sunday 29 April 1888. (KM)*

1880   NEWTON HEATH   1902
Results of Challenge, Friendly, Charity, Benefit & Testimonial Matches

(Continued from page 44)

1889-90

Sept 2	A	Stoke-on-Trent	1-2
Sept 3	A	Gorton Villa	2-0
Sept 7	H	Bolton Wanderers	1-1
Sept 14	H	Witton	2-1
Sept 16	A	Burslem Port Vale	1-0
Nov 16	H	Sheffield United	7-1
Jan 1	H	Heart of Midlothian	4-2
Jan 2	A	Cambuslang	2-1
Feb 1	A	Ardwick	3-0
Mar 3	A	Sheffield United	1-2

1890-1

Sept 1	H	Burslem Port Vale	5-1
Sept	A	Hyde	2-1
Sept 8	A	Burslem Port Vale	4-4
Sept 22	A	Burnley	4-3
Oct 25	H	Darwen	1-6
Nov 15	H	Ardwick	4-1
Dec 6	H	South Shore	3-1
Dec 25	H	Belfast Distillery	8-4
Jan 1	H	Cambridge Trinity	6-1
Jan 2	A	Ardwick	1-1
Jan 3	H	Walsall Town Swifts	5-2
Jan 31	H	Preston North End	3-1
Feb 28	A	Ardwick	3-1
Mar 9	A	Burslem Port Vale	1-2
Mar 27	H	Clapton Orient	3-1
Mar 30	H	Accrington	2-5
Apr 4	A	South Shore	2-1
April 8	H	Bury	2-1
Apr 13	H	Burnley	1-2
Apr 20	A	West Manchester	0-4
Apr 25	H	Bootle	1-1
Apr 27	H	Preston North End	1-1

1891-2

Nov 23	A	Sheffield United	2-3
Jan 2	H	Canadian Team XI	5-1
Jan 23	H	Small Heath	7-2
Apr 4	H	Sheffield United	2-1

1892-3

Jan 2	A	Ardwick	5-3
Feb 18	H	Burnley	2-1
Mar 11	A	Burnley	0-3
Mar 27	H	Ardwick	3-2
Apr 10	A	Ardwick	2-1
Apr 29	A	Ardwick	0-3

1893-4

Sept 6	A	Liverpool	0-1
Sept 20	H	Liverpool	0-3
Dec 25	H	Ardwick	2-1
Mar 1	A	Liverpool	0-3
Apr 9	A	Ardwick	2-1

1894-5

Sept 1	H	Edinburgh St. Bernards	2-5
Sept 24	A	Stockport County	3-0
Sept 27	H	Queen's Park	3-3
Sept 29	H	Edinburgh Hibernians	2-1
Dec 25	H	Sunderland	1-3
Jan 26	A	Liverpool	3-0
Feb 9	A	Bury	0-1
Feb 16	A	West Manchester	2-0
Feb 23	H	Derby County	1-1
Feb 27	A	Bury	2-3
Mar 16	A	Liverpool	1-1
Apr 29	A	Blackburn Rovers	2-2

1895-6

Nov 11	A	Luton Town	1-4
Dec 25	A	Manchester City	1-3

1896-7

Oct 31	A	Fairfield	2-2
Nov 14	A	Luton Town	1-0
Nov 21	A	Fairfield	5-0
Apr 30	A	Manchester City	5-2

1897-8

Sept 1	H	Blackpool	0-0
Sept 7	A	Bury	2-2
Oct 6	H	Bury	1-3
Oct 20	A	Grimsby Town	1-3
Jan 16	H	Grimsby Town	3-0
Apr 12	A	Sheffield United	4-1
Apr 27	H	Manchester City	2-4
Apr 30	H	Gainsborough Trinity	2-1

1898-9

Oct 29	A	Manchester City	1-2
Jan 7	H	Manchester City	2-0
Apr 24	H	Manchester City	1-2

1899-1900

Oct 2	H	Renton	2-1
Nov 18	H	Blackpool	0-0
Nov 29	H	Manchester City	0-1
Jan 1	A	Manchester City	1-2
Feb 27	H	Manchester City	1-0

1900-1

Sept 26	H	Manchester City	0-0

1902   MANCHESTER UNITED   1935
Results of Friendlies, Charity, Benefit, and Testimonial Matches

1902-3

Sept 1	A	Preston North End	1-5

1904-5

Sept 26	A	Kettering Town	2-0
Nov 26	A	Corinthians	3-11

1907-8

May 24	A	Ferenezvaros	7-0

1909-10

Sept 13	A	Southend United	2-2
Apr 27		Football League XI Played at Burnley	1-4

1913-4

Nov 12		Bradford City Played at Belfast	1-2

1914-5

Oct 12	A	Hull City	2-3

1915-6

May 6	A	Manchester City	2-2

1916-7

Dec 26	H	Manchester City	1-0
Jan 1	A	Manchester City	0-0

1917-8

Dec 25	A	Manchester City	2-0
Jan 1	H	Manchester City	3-0

1918-19

Dec 25	A	Manchester City	1-2
Jan 1	H	Manchester City	2-0
May 17	H	Liverpool	3-1

1922-3

Mar 10	A	MAnchester City	0-5
Feb 24	A	Birmingham	1-1
May 5	H	Airdrieonians	0-2

1923-4

Sept 12	H	Heart of Midlothian	2-2
Apr 14	H	Heart of Midlothian	3-0
Apr 16	H	Glasgow Celtic	1-0
Apr 23	H	Glasgow Rangers	1-1

Switzerland Tour 1926

	F.C. Basle	3-1
	F.C. Lausanne	9-1
	Geneva	5-1
	F.C. Zurich	3-2
	Berne	5-1

1926-7

Dec 21	A	South Shields	1-1
Apr 27	H	Motherwell	5-1

1927-8

Dec 28	H	Corinthians	2-0

1932-33

Feb 18	H	Cowdenbeath	10-1

1933-4

Feb 17	H	Newcastle United	3-4

1934-5

Feb 16	H	Third Lanark	1-1

GRAND FOOTBALL MATCH.

NEWTON HEATH v. THE CANADIANS,

NEWTON HEATH TEAM.

Referee: Mr. J. J. BENTLEY (Bolton).

Umpire: Mr. H. McINTYRE.

Goal:
o
T. Hay.

Right Back:
o
J. Powell.

Left Back:
o
A. N. Other

Half Backs:
o
J. Davies.

T. Bourke.

J. Owen.

Right Wing:

Left Wing:

A. B. Other   R. Doughty.

J. Gotheridge   J. Gale.

RESERVES: Walton and Bridgewater

Centre:
o
J. Doughty

Centre:
o
T. Gibson

Left Wing:

Right Wing:

A. Webster.   W. P. Thompson

A. Gibson.   W. Bowman

H. Pirie

Half Backs:
o
C. Kranz.

E. P. Gordon.

Left Back:
o
S. Brubacher.

Right Back:
o
F. Killer.

Goal:
o
A. N. Garrett.

RESERVES: H. Bingham and W. P. Mustad.

Umpire: Mr. D. FORSYTH.

CANADIAN TEAM.

On Saturday, October 6th, 1888.

TO BE PLAYED AT NEWTON HEATH.

NEWTON HEATH 0 CANADIAN XI 2. 6 October 1888. This historic occasion, the 'Heathens' first match against International opposition, was marked by the presence of one of the club's distinguished Vice-Presidents. Sir Jamnes Ferguson, BART, MP saw the tourists spoil that seasons unbeaten record of Newton Heath. (BNPC)

MANCHESTER F.A SENIOR CUP RESULTS 1884-1964

1884-5

Rd 1	A	Eccles (Void)	3-2
Rd 1 R	N	Eccles	3-0
Rd 2	A	Manchester	3-0
S/F	N	Dalton Hall	4-3
Final		Hurst	0-3

1885-6

Rd 1	A	Eccles	2-0
Rd 2		Gorton Villa	5-0
S/F		Hurst	3-1
Final	N	Manchester	2-1

1886-7

Rd 1	A	Hooley Hill	7-0
Rd 2	A	Gorton Association	11-1
S/F	N	Ten Acres	1-0
Final	N	West Manchester	1-2

1887-8

Rd 2	H	Hooley Hill	3-0
S/F		Hurst	2-0
Final	N	Denton	7-1

1888-9

Rd 1	A	West Manchester	2-1
Rd 2	H	Ardwick	4-1
S/F	H	Manchester Welsh XI	2-1
Final	N	Hooley Hill	7-0

1889-90

| S/F | | Denton | 4-1 |
| Final | | Royton | 5-2 |

1890-1

| S/F | N | Stockport County | 3-1 |
| Final | N | Ardwick | 0-1 |

1891-2

| Rd 3 | H | West Manchester | 3-1 |
| S/F | N | Bolton Wanderers | 1-3 |

1892-3

Rd 3	A	West Manchester	2-1
S/F	N	Bury	3-1
Final	N	Bolton Wanderers	2-1

1893-4

| Rd 1 | A | Bolton Wanderers | 2-3 |

1895-6

| Rd 3 | H | Fairfield | 2-5 |

1896-7

| Rd 3 | A | Manchester City | 1-0 |
| S/F | N | Bury | 0-2 |

1897-8

Rd 3	H	Bury	2-2
Rd 3 R	A	Bury	3-2
S/F	H	Manchester City	1-1
S/F R	H	Manchester City	1-2

1898-9

| Rd 3 | H | Bury | 1-4 |

1899-1900

| Rd 3 | A | Bury | 0-5 |

1900-1

Rd 3	H	Rochdale	4-0
S/F	N	Glossop North End	0-0
S/F R	N	Glossop North End	1-0
Final	A	Manchester City	0-4

1901-2

Rd 3	A	Rochdale	3-2
S/F	N	Bolton Wanderers	1-1
S/F R	N	Bolton Wanderers	1-0
Final	A	Manchester City	2-1

1902-3

| Rd 3 | H | Bury | 0-4 |

1903-4

Rd 3	H	Stockport County	3-1
S/F	A	Manchester City	1-1
S/F R	H	Manchester City	1-2

1904-5

Rd 3	A	Stockport County	2-2
Rd 3 R	N	Stockport County	4-2
S/F	N	Glossop North End	5-1
Final	N	Bury	1-3

1906-7

| Rd 3 | H | Glossop North End | 5-0 |
| S/F | A | Manchester City | 1-2 |

1907-8

Rd 3	H	Manchester City	1-0
S/F	N	Stockport Coutny	3-1
Final	N	Bury	1-0

1908-9

| Rd 3 | H | Stockport County | 2-4 |

1909-10

Rd 3	A	Manchester City	6-2
S/F	N	Northern Nomads	2-0
Final	N	Stockport County	4-1

1910-11

Rd 3	H	Northern Nomads	3-0
S/F	N	Glossop North End	2-1
Final	A	Manchester City	1-3

1911-12

Rd 3	A	Bury	2-2
Rd 3 R	H	Bury	0-0
Rd 3 R2	H	Bury	4-0
S/F	A	Bolton Wanderers	4-0
Final		Rochdale	0-0
Final R		Rochdale	1-1
Fin R2	A	Rochdale	5-0

1912-3

Rd 3	H	Oldham Athletic	3-0
S/F	A	Glossop North End	4-1
Final		Bolton Wanderers	4-1

1913-4

| Rd 3 | H | Rochdale | 5-0 |
| S/F | N | Oldham Athletic | 1-2 |

1914-5

| Rd 3 | H | Manchester City | 3-1 |
| S/F | N | Stockport County | 1-2 |

1919-20

Rd 3	H	Bolton Wanderers	5-2
S/F	A	Bury	2-1
Final	A	Oldham Athletic	1-0

1920-1

Rd 1	H	Bury	1-0
S/F	H	Rochdale	2-0
Final	A	Bolton Wanderers	0-2

1921-2

| Rd 3 | H | Hurst | 1-1 |
| Rd 3 R | A | Hurst | 3-4 |

1922-3

| Rd 1 | H | Stalybridge Celtic | 1-2 |

1923-4

Rd 1	H	Manchester University	4-0
Rd 2	A	Stockport County	1-1
Rd 2 R	H	Stockport County	0-0
Rd 2 R2	A	Stockport County	1-1
Rd 2 R3	H	Stockport County	3-0
S/F	H	Bolton	4-0
Final	H	Manchester City	3-0

1924-25

Rd 1	A	Hurst	1-1
Rd 1 R	H	Hurst	6-2
Rd 2	H	Manchester City	2-2
Rd 2 R2	A	Manchester City	4-7

1925-26

Rd 3	H	Bury	1-0
S/F	H	Stockport County	4-0
Final	H	Manchester City	2-0

1926-7

Rd 3	H	Bury	4-0
S/F	A	Wigan Borough	0-0
S/F R	H	Wigan Borough	1-0
Final	N	Crewe Alexandra	1-2

1927-8

Rd 3	H	Crewe Alexandra	2-2
Rd 3 R	A	Crewe Alexandra	3-1
S/F	H	Bury	3-0
Final	A	Manchester City	2-4

1928-9

| Rd 3 | A | Bolton Wanderers | 1-4 |

1929-30

| Rd 3 | H | Oldham Athletic | 1-3 |

1930-1

Rd 3	A	Wigan Borough	3-1
S/F	H	Rochdale	2-0
Final	N	Bury	5-1

1931-2

| Rd 3 | | Manch'ter North End | 5-1 |
| S/F | H | Oldham Athletic | 0-1 |

1932-33

| S/F | H | Bury | 2-1 |
| Final | A | Manchester City | 0-2 |

1933-4

| S/F | H | Bury | 5-0 |
| Final | H | Manchester City | 1-0 |

1934-5

| S/F | H | Manchester City | 3-1 |
| Finla | H | Bury | 1-2 |

1935-6

| Final | H | Oldham Athletic | 5-1 |

1936-7

| S/F | H | Bolton Wanderers | 1-0 |
| Final | A | Bury | 1-0 |

1937-8

| S/F | H | Bury | 2-1 |
| Final | H | Bolton Wanderers | 1-2 |

1938-9

| S/F | A | Manchester City | 1-0 |
| Final | H | Oldham Athletic | 4-1 |

1958-9

| Final | H | Manchester City | 4-0 |

1961-2

| Final | H | Bolton Wanderers | 0-1 |

1963-4

| Final | H | Manchester City | 5-3 |

LANCASHIRE F.A SENIOR CUP RESULTS 1884-1947

1883-4

| Rd 1 | H | Blackburn Olympic XI | 2-7 |

1884-5

| Rd 1 | H | Haydock Temperance | 4-0 |
| Rd 2 | A | Baxenden | 1-4 |

1885-6

| Rd 1 | A | Lytham | 0-1 |

1889-90

| Rd 1 | A | Halliwell | 1-2 |

1890-1

| Rd 1 | A | Witton | 4-3 |
| Rd 2 | A | Preston North End | 1-3 |

1891-2

| Rd 1 | H | Bury | 2-3 |

1892-3

| Rd 1 | A | Bury | 0-4 |

1893-4

| Rd 1 | A | Everton | 1-7 |

1894-5

| Rd 1 | A | Bolton Wanderers | 1-2 |

1895-6

| Rd 1 | H | Bury | 1-2 |

1896-7

| Rd 1 | H | West Manchester | 4-1 |
| Rd 2 | A | Burnley | 1-2 |

1897-8

Rd 1	H	Wigan Borough	6-0
Rd 2	H	Manchester City	1-0
S/F	H	Bolton Wanderers	4-1
Final	N	Blackburn Rovers	2-1

1898-9

| Rd 1 | A | Darwen | 5-0 |
| Rd 2 | A | Blackburn Rovers | 1-6 |

1899-1900

| Rd 1 | H | Bolton Wanderers | 3-2 |
| Rd 2 | A | Southport Central | 0-1 |

1900-1

| Rd 1 | A | Manchester City | 0-2 |

1901-2

Rd 1	A	Nelson	0-0
Rd 1 R	H	Nelson	4-1
Rd 2	A	Southport Central	0-5

1902-3

| Rd 1 | A | Preston North End | 1-3 |

1903-4

Rd 1	A	Accrington	2-2
Rd 1 R	H	Accrington	2-1
Rd 2	H	Blackpool	2-1
S/F	N	Blackburn Rovers	1-1
S/F R	N	Blackburn Rovers	0-1

1904-5

| Rd 1 | A | Bolton Wanderers | 2-4 |

1905-6

| Rd 1 | H | Blackburn Rovers | 1-2 |

1906-7

| Rd 1 | A | Liverpool | 1-4 |

1907-8

Rd 1	A	Manchester City	3-0
Rd 2	H	Bolton Wanderers	2-0
S/F	N	Oldham Athletic	1-3

1908-9

| Rd 2 | H | Bolton Wanderers | 3-0 |
| Rd 3 | A | Blackburn Rovers | 1-2 |

1909-10

| Rd 1 | A | Blackburn Rovers | 0-3 |

1910-1

Rd 1	H	Nelson	8-0
Rd 2	H	Oldham Athletic	0-0
Rd 2 R	A	Oldham Athletic	3-1
S/F	N	Burnley	0-0
S/F R	N	Burnley	1-2

1911-2

Rd 1	A	Bacup	5-1
Rd 2	H	Everton	2-1
S/F	A	Bolton Wanderers	1-2

1912-3

Rd 1	A	Oldham Athletic	3-3
Rd 1 R	H	Oldham Athletic	4-1
Rd 2	A	Bolton Wanderers	3-0
S/F		Blackpool	0-0
S/F R		Blackpool	5-0
Final	N	Blackburn Rovers	3-2

1913-4

Rd 1	A	Bury	1-1
Rd 1 R	H	Bury	2-1
Rd 2	A	Liverpool	3-1
S/F	A	Manchester City	1-1
S/F R	H	Manchester City	2-0
Final	N	Blackpool	1-0

1914-5

| Rd 1 | A | Burnley | 0-5 |

1915-19

SEE WARTIME RECORDS

1919-22

REGIONAL LEAGUES COMPETITION

1919-20

	H	Manchester City	1-0
	H	Manchester City	3-3
	H	Oldham Athletic	1-1
	A	Oldham Athletic	3-0
		Group Winners	
S/F	H	Burnley	2-0
Final	H	Liverpool	1-1
		Cup shared	

1920-1

	H	Manchester City	1-1
	H	Manchester City	0-3
	H	Oldham Athletic	4-1
	A	Oldham Athletic	2-2

1921-2

	H	Manchester City	3-1
	H	Manchester City	0-3
	H	Oldham Athletic	0-3
	A	Oldham Athletic	1-1

1922-3

| Rd 2 | A | Rochdale | 0-1 |

1923-4

| Rd 2 | H | Stockport County | 2-2 |
| Rd 2 R | A | Stockport County | 0-4 |

1924-5

| Rd 1 | H | Liverpool | 0-0 |
| Rd 1 R | A | Liverpool | 2-4 |

1925-6

| Rd 2 | H | Southport | 9-0 |
| Rd 3 | A | Manchester City | 2-3 |

1927-8

| Rd 2 | H | Rochdale | 4-2 |
| Rd 3 | H | Bury | 0-4 |

1928-9

Rd 2	A	New Brighton	4-0
Rd 3	H	Wigan	4-4
Rd 3 R	A	Wigan	2-1
S/F	A	Bolton Wanderers	2-2
S/F R	A	Bolton Wanderers	1-0
Final	H	Blackburn Rovers	2-1

1929-30

Rd 2	H	Rochdale	5-0
Rd 3	H	Bolton Wanderers	6-1
S/F	A	Manchester City	1-3

1930-1

Rd 2	H	Oldham Athletic	2-0
Rd 3	A	Rochdale	1-0
S/F	H	Blackburn Rovers	4-2
Final	A	Liverpool	0-4

1931-2

| Rd 2 | H | Manchester City | 2-3 |

1933-4

| Rd 1 | H | Barrow | 1-2 |

1934-5

| Rd 1 | A | Lancaster City | 3-2 |
| Rd 2 | H | Rossendale | 1-2 |

1935-6

| S/F | H | Wigan | 0-2 |

1936-7

| Rd 2 | H | Everton | 2-0 |
| S/F | A | Blackpool | 1-4 |

1937-8

| S/F | H | Blackburn Rovers | 4-1 |
| Final | A | Southport | 1-0 |

1938-9

| Rd 1 | | Preston North End | |

1939-46

WARTIME
L.S.C. matches counted also as Football League North Second Competition

1940-1

Rd 1-1	A	Blackburn Rovers	2-0
Rd 1-2	H	Blackburn Rovers	0-0
Rd 2-1	A	Bolton Wanderers	2-3
Rd 2-2	H	Bolton Wanderers	4-1
S/F	A	Chester	6-4
Final	H	Burnley	1-0

1941-2

Rd 1-1	A	Oldham Athletic	5-1
Rd 1-2	H	Oldham Athletic	2-1
Rd 2-1	A	Blackburn Rovers	1-1
Rd 2-2	H	Blackburn Rovers	0-1

1942-3

Rd 1-1	H	Bury	4-1
Rd 1-2	A	Bury	5-3
Rd 2-1	H	Crewe Alexandra	4-1
Rd 2-2	A	Crewe Alexandra	6-0
S/F-1	H	Oldham Athletic	3-0
S/F-2	A	Oldham Athletic	1-3
Final-1	H	Liverpool	3-1
Final-2	H	Liverpool	3-3

1945-6

Rd 1-1	H	Rochdale	5-1
Rd 1-2	H	Rochdale	0-2
Rd 2-1	H	Bury	4-1
Rd 2-2	A	Bury	1-0
S/F	H	Manchester City	3-0
Final	H	Burnley	1-0

1946-7

Rd 1-1	A	Preston North End	1-0
Rd 1-2	H	Preston North End	2-1
Rd 2-1	H	Burnley	4-3
Rd 2-2	A	Burnley	0-2

Top: NEWTON HEATH LYR FIXTURES CARD for 1888-9. After failing in their application for membership of the Football League in 1888, the 'Heathers' joined forced with other disapointed clubs to form the Football Combination. (MMUSC).

Top Right: J. SNEDDON. Top Centre: F. SLATER. Middle Centre: R. MCFARLANE. Middle Right: MR SMITH Club Umpire.

BOTTOM: FOOTBALL ALLIANCE. The first fixtures for the Alliance league in its inaugural season. (MMUSC)

NEWTON HEATH L.Y.R.
Cricket and Football Club

FIXTURES for Season 1888-89

President:
F. ATTOCK, Esq.

Vice=Presidents:
The Hon. A. J. BALFOUR, M.P.
The Hon. C. E. SCHWANN, M.P.
Sir JAMES FERGUSSON, Bart., M.P.
C. R. CRESWELL, Esq.   W. H. ROTHWELL, Esq.
J. GRIMSHAW, Esq.   H. G. SADLER, Esq.
J. TAYLOR Esq., J.P.   I. HILTON, Esq.
C. P. SCOTT, Esq., J.P.   W. TORKINGTON, Esq.
G. TURTON, Esq.   Alderman W. BROWN.
W. S. LAYCOCK, Esq.   Councillor PAYNE, &c.

Treasurer: Mr. J. HANDLEY.

Financial Secretary:
Mr. GEORGE FARROW, 637, Oldham Road,
Newton Heath.

Corresponding Secretary:
Mr. T. SADLER, 7, Marsden Street,
Newton Heath.

Committee:
Mr. J. PANTER.   Mr. T. RIGBY.
Mr. T JACKSON.   Mr. J. WHITEHEAD.
Mr. J. B. DODD.

Captain (1st Team): Mr. JOHN POWELL.
Captain "Swifts": Mr. JOHN EARP.
Club House: SHEARS HOTEL.

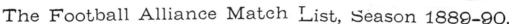

The Football Alliance Match List, Season 1889-90.

Date. 1889.	BIRMINGHAM ST. GEORGE'S.		W	L	BOOTLE.		W	L	CREWE ALEXANDRA		W	L	DARWEN.		W	L	GRIMSBY TOWN.		W	L	LONG E RANGERS		W	L
Sept. 7	Small Heath	h..			Sheffield Wed	a..							Sunderld Albion	h..							Grimsby Town	a..		
" 14	Sheffield Wednesday	h..			Small Heath	a..			Walsall T Swifts	h..							Long E Rangers	h..			Crewe Alexandra	h..		
" 21	Darwen	a..							Long E Rangers	h..			B St George's	h..			Notts Forest	h..						
" 28					Newton Heath	h..			Newton Heath	h..							Walsall T Swifts	a..			Sheffield Wed	h..		
Oct. 5	Bootle	h..			Notts Forest	a..											Notts Forest	a..			Walsall T Swifts	h..		
" 12	Notts Forest	a..			Bir St George's	a..			Sheffield Wed	a..														
" 19	Grimsby Town	a..							Notts Forest	a..			Long E Rangers	a..			B St George's	h..			Darwen	a..		
" 26	Newton Heath	a..			Sunderld Albion	h..							Sheffield Wed	a..										
Nov. 2	Long Eaton Rangers	h..			Walsall T Swifts	a..			Walsall T Swifts	a..							Sunderld Albion	h..			Bir St George's	a..		
" 9									Grimsby Town	h..			Bootle	a..			Crewe Alexandra	a..			Newton Heath	a..		
" 16	Walsall Town Swifts	a..			Darwen	a..							Walsall T Swifts	h..			Small Heath	h..			Notts Forest	h..		
" 23									Sunderld Albion	a..			Sunderld Albion	h..			Walsall T Swifts	h..			Bootle	a..		
" 30					Long E Rangers	h..											Sheffield Wed	h..			Walsall T Swifts	a..		
Dec. 7					Newton Heath	a..																		
" 14									Notts Forest	a..							Darwen	h..						
" 21	Long Eaton Rangers	a..											Grimsby Town	a..										
" 25	Small Heath	h..											B St George's	h..			Small Heath	h..						
" 26	Darwen	h..			Walsall T Swifts	h..			Sunderld Albion	a..			Newton Heath	a..							Small Heath	h..		
Jan. 4	Sunderland Albion	h..			Darwen	a..			Small Heath	a..			Bootle	h..			Newton Heath	h..						
" 11					Sunderld Albiona	a..			Long E Rangers	h..			Sheffield Wed	h..							Crewe Alexandra	a..		
" 18									Darwen	h..			Crewe Alexandra	a..										
" 25	Notts Forest	a..			Crewe Alexandra	a..			Bootle	h..			Grimsby Town	h..			Darwen	a..			Sheffield Wed	h..		
Feb. 1													Notts Forest	h..							Sunderld Albion	h..		
" 8									Sheffield Wed	h..							Newton Heath	h..			Bootle	a..		
" 15	Crewe Alexandra	h..			Long E Rangers	a..			B St George's	a..			Small Heath	a..							Bootle	h..		
" 22	Walsall Town Swifts	a..			Grimsby Town	a..			Small Heath	h..							Bootle	h..			Notts Forest	a..		
Mar. 8	Bootle	a..			B St George's	h..			Newton Heath	a..			Walsall T Swifts	a..			Sunderld Albion	a..						
" 15					Sheffield Wed	h..			Darwen	a..			Crewe Alexandra	a..							Darwen	h..		
" 22					Crewe Alexandra	h..							Long E Rangers	h..			Sheffield Wed	h..			Newton Heath	h..		
" 29	Crewe Alexandra	a..							Bootle	a..			Notts Forest	a..										
Apr. 4	Grimsby Town	a..			Small Heath	h..			B St George's	h..			Newton Heath	a..			B St George's	h..			Crewe Alexandra	h..		
" 5	Sheffield Wednesday	a..																						
" 8	Sunderland Albion	a..			Notts Forest	h..			Grimsby Town	a..			Small Heath	h..			Bootle	h..			Sunderld Albion	a..		
" 12	Newton Heath	a..			Grimsby Town	h..											Long E Rangers	h..			Grimsby Town	h..		

Date. 1889.	NEWTON HEATH.		W	L	NOTTS FOREST.		W	L	SHEFFIELD WED.		W	L	SMALL HEATH.		W	L	SUNDERLND ALBION.		W	L	WALSALL T SWIFTS.		W	L
Sept. 7					Walsall T Swifts	a..			Bootle	h..			Bir St George's	a..			Darwen	a..			Notts Forest	h..		
" 14					Grimsby Town	a..			Bir St George's	a..			Bootle	h..							Crewe Alexandra	a..		
" 21	Sunderland Albion	h..											Walsall T Swifts	h..			Newton Heath	a..			Small Heath	a..		
" 23	Bootle	a..																						
" 28	Crewe Alexandra	a..			Bootle	h..			Long E Rangers	a..											Grimsby Town	h..		
Oct. 5					Bir St George's	h..											Small Heath	h..			Long E Rangers	a..		
" 12					Crewe Alexandra	h..			Crewe Alexandra	h..			Sunderld Albion	a..			Bootle	a..						
" 19	Walsall Town Swifts	a..							Small Heath	h..			Sheffield Wed	a..							Newton Heath	h..		
" 26	Birmingham St George's	a..			Small Heath	h..			Darwen	h..							Grimsby Town	h..			Bootle			
Nov. 2					Sunderld Albion	h..							Notts Forest	a..							Crewe Alexandra	h..		
" 9	Long Eaton Rangers	h..											Walsall T Swifts	h..			Crewe Alexandra	a..			Small Heath	a..		
" 16					Long E Rangers	a..			Small Heath	a..			Sheffield Wed	h..			Darwen	a..			Bir St George's	h..		
" 23													Grimsby Town	a..			Notts Forest	h..			Darwen	h..		
" 30	Sheffield Wednesday	h..			Sunderld Albion	a..			Newton Heath	a..											Grimsby Town	a..		
Dec. 7	Bootle	h..			Crewe Alexandra	h..			Grimsby Town	a..							Sheffield Wed	h..			Long E Rangers	h..		
" 14									Sunderld Albion	a..														
" 21	Walsall Town Swifts	h..											Bir St George's	a..							Newton Heath	a..		
" 25									Sunderld Albion	a..			Grimsby Town	a..			Sheffield Wed	h..						
" 28	Darwen	a..			Sheffield Wed	a..			Notts Forest	h..			Long E Rangers	a..			Crewe Alexandra	h..			Bootle	a..		
Jan. 4	Grimsby Town	h..			Sheffield Wed	h..			Notts Forest	a..			Crewe Alexandra	h..			Bir St George's	h..						
" 11					Bir St George's	h..			Darwen	h..							Bootle	a..						
" 18					Darwen	h..			Long E Rangers	h..							Newton Heath	h..			Sunderland Albion	a..		
" 25	Sunderland Albion	h..											Long E Rangers	a..			Long E Rangers	h..			Bir St George's	a..		
Feb. 1	Grimsby Town	a..			Newton Heath	h..			Crewe Alexandra	h..			Darwen	a..			Walsall T Swifts	h..			Darwen	a..		
" 15	Notts Forest	a..			Long E Rangers	h..							Crewe Alexandra	h..							Sunderld Albion	a..		
" 22																	Grimsby Town	h..						
Mar. 8	Crewe Alexandra	h..			Small Heath	h..			Newton Heath	a..			Notts Forest	a..			Walsall T Swifts	a..			Grimsby Town	h..		
" 15	Sheffield Wednesday	h..							Bootle	h..			Newton Heath	h..			Small Heath	a..			Walsall T Swifts	h..		
" 22	Small Heath	a..			Darwen	h..															Sunderld Albion	h..		
" 29	Long Eaton Rangers	a..			Walsall T Swifts	h..			Grimsby Town	h..											Bir St George's	a..		
Apr. 4	Darwen	h..															Sunderld Albion	h..			Darwen			
" 5	Notts Forest	h..			Newton Heath	a..							Bir St George's	h..			Bootle				Sunderld Albion			
" 8	Small Heath	h..			Bootle				Bir St George's	h..			Darwen				Bir St George's	h..						
" 12													Newton Heath				Long E Rangers	a..			Sheffield Wed	a..		
" 19	Birmingham St George's	h..							Walsall T Swifts	a..														

1888-9
The Football Combination
Unofficial Winners

1889-90
The Football Alliance
Position: 8th

Newton Heath L. & Y.R.

1889-90 — The Football Alliance

Match No.	Date	Venue	Opponents	Result	Goalscorers	Attendance
1	Sept 21	H	Sunderland Albion	W 4-1	Wilson 2, Stewart, J. Doughty	3,000
2	23	A	Bootle	L 1-4	1.o.g.	
3	28	A	Crewe Alexandra	D 2-2	Stewart, 1.o.g.	
4	Oct 19	A	Walsall Town Swifts	L 0-4		2,000
5	26	A	Birmingham St. George's	L 1-5	J. Doughty	
6	Nov 9	A	Long Eaton Rangers	W 3-0	J. Doughty 2, Farman	
7	30	A	The Wednesday	L 1-3	J. Doughty	
8	Dec 7	H	Bootle	W 3-0	Farman, J. Doughty, Stewart	4,000
9	28	A	Darwen	L 1-4	G. Owen	
10	Jan 25	H	Sunderland Albion	L 0-2		2,400
11	Feb 8	H	Grimsby Town	L 0-7		
12	15	H	Nottingham Forest	W 3-1	Wilson, Stewart 2	
13	Mar 1	H	Crewe Alexandra	L 1-2	G. Owen	
14	15	A	Small Heath	D 1-1	Wilson	
15	22	A	Long Eaton Rangers	W 3-1	Wilson 2, Farman	
16	29	A	Darwen	W 3-1	Wilson, Stewart	
17	Apr 5	H	Nottingham Forest	L 0-1		
18	14	H	Small Heath	W 9-1	Craig, Stewart 3, Wilson, Farman, J. Doughty 2, R. Doughty	
19	14	H	Grimsby Town	L 0-1		
20	19	H	Birmingham St. George's	W 2-1	J. Doughty, Craig	
21	21	A	Walsall Town Swifts	W 2-1	J. Doughty, Farman	
22	26	H	The Wednesday	L 1-2	Craig	4,000

F.A. CUP

	Date	Venue	Opponents	Result	Goalscorers	Attendance
Rd 1	Jan 18	A	Preston North End	L 1-6	Craig	7,000

Alliance League Appearances
Alliance League Scorers

Players:
Hay, T.
Mitchell, J.
Powell, J.
Doughty, R.
Davies, Jos.
Owen, J.
Tait, W.
Stewart, W.
Doughty, J.
Wilson, E.
Gotheridge, J.
Burke, T.
Pedley, J.
Owen, G.
Felton, C.
Farman, A. H.
Craig, T.
Harrison, C.

1888-9 — The Football Combination

Match No.	Date	Venue	Opponents	Result	Goalscorers (where known)	Attendance
1	Sept 22	H	Darwen	W 4-3	J. Doughty 3, Gale	4,000
2	Oct 13	A	Derby Midland	D 1-1		4,000
3	20	H	Leek	W 4-1	J. Doughty, R. Doughty, Gotheridge, 1 scrimmage	3,000
4	Nov 3	H	Leek	W 5-0	J. Doughty 3, R. Doughty, Tait	3,000
5	10	A	Burslem Port Vale	D 1-1	J. Davies	
6	Dec 1	A	Bootle	W 1-0		
7	Jan 5	A	Darwen	L 0-6		
8	19	H	Burslem Port Vale	W 3-0		2,500
9	26	H	Bootle	W 4-0	R. Doughty, J. Doughty, J. Davies, Gale	
10	Mar 2	H	Derby Midland	W 2-0	W. Tait, J. Gotheridge	3,000
11	30	H	South Shore	L 0-1		

THE F.A. CUP

Newton Heath L. & Y.R. first entered the 'English Cup' in 1886/7, their opponents were Fleetwood Rangers on 30 October. With the full-time score at 2-2 the 'Heathers' refused to play extra-time and the match was abandoned and awarded to Fleetwood. Newton Heath did not enter again until 1889-90, when they were drawn at Preston North End.

DID YOU KNOW? The Football Combination was formed in 1888 by clubs failing to gain admittance to the Football League, Newton Heath's own application having received just one vote. The Combination was only loosely based on league rules, the twenty participating clubs agreed to play a minimum 8 matches against other member teams. It worked well initially, and despite a period of strife with some clubs not honouring fixtures, only Blackburn Olympic failed to fulfill their commitment. Whilst difficult to establish who fared best, considering all the results Newton Heath had the best record, just ahead of Notts Rangers, though these teams had not met. When the Combination ceased on 5 April 1889, the balance of its funds was donated to an orphanage in Derby, and most of the teams became founder members of the Football Alliance.

THE FOOTBALL ALLIANCE 1889/90

Above: MANCHESTER CUP WINNERS 1889/90. This was the Newton Heath team that won the Manchester Cup during the clubs first season in the Football Alliance. Back Row: Mitchell, Slater, McMillan. Middle Row: R. Doughty, Ramsey, Owen. Bottom: Smith (Umpire), Farman, J. Doughty, Evans, Malarvie, Sharp, Preddy (Trainer). (JG)

THE FOOTBALL ALLIANCE: NEWTON HEATH LYR 4 SUNDERLAND ALBION 1.

About 3,000 spectators witnessed the first of the Newton Heath games under the Alliance rules. The Albion were understood to have organised a strong team to represent the club, and great interest was felt in the result of this match by the Newton Heath supporters.

Smith kicked off for Sunderland, and the visitors with excellent passing at first pressed. Mitchell and Davies relieved, and the other end was the scene of operations. Repeated attempts to score by the home players were defeated with Angus and McDermid getting the ball away. Hard and fast play was the order of the day for a time, during which each side was called on to defend its goal. At length the home team players fairly gained the upper hand, after Angus had knocked out several shots, Wilson, from a pass by J. Doughty, scored for Newton Heath. The visitors roused up, and with good combined play they brought the ball to the front of the home goal, where, after Hay had kept out one or two good shots, they, out of a scrimmage, equalised the score.

The ball was taken to the Albion end after the kick off, and Wilson shot into the hands of Angus. A goal was claimed, but disallowed. Stewart, however regained the lead for Newton Heath, after neat passing by the home side, and a few minutes before half-time Tait passed to J. Doughty, and the third goal was scored.

In the second half the game was again in favour of the home team, but the Albion defence was strong, and attempt after attempt was made to lower the visitors colours. Hay, the Newton Heath goalkeeper was also at times much pressed, but he also repelled all attacks on his goal. Just before time, the home forwards again got away, and Wilson sent in a shot which Angus allowed to pass him, giving Newton Heath a 4-1 victory.

The above report appeared in THE MANCHESTER GUARDIAN, 23 September 1889.

Newton Heath L. & Y. R.

1891-2

No.	Date	Venue	Opponents	Result	Goalscorers	Attendance
1	Sept 12	A	Burton Swifts	L 2-3	Donaldson, Farman	
2	19	H	Bootle	W 4-0	Farman, Edge 3	5,000
3	26	A	Birmingham St. George's	W 3-1	Donaldson 2, Stewart	300
4	Oct 10	A	Ardwick	W 3-1	Donaldson, Farman 2	4,000
5	17	A	Grimsby Town	D 2-2	Donaldson 2	3,000
6	31	H	Burton Swifts	W 3-1	J. Doughty, Edge, Farman	3,000
7	Nov 7	A	Crewe Alexandra	W 2-0	Donaldson, 1 o.g.	3,000
8	21	H	Lincoln City	W 10-1	Donaldson 3, Hood 2, Stewart 2, Sneddon, Farman, 1 o.g.	6,000
9	28	A	Walsall Town Swifts	W 4-1	Farman, Donaldson 3	
10	Dec 12	A	Ardwick	W 4-2	Farman 2, Edge, Sneddon	13,000
11	26	A	Small Heath	D 2-2	Farman 2	4,000
12	Jan 2	H	Nottingham Forest	D 3-3	Edge 2, Farman	4,000
13	9	A	Bootle	D 1-1	Edge	12,000
14	30	H	Crewe Alexandra	W 5-3	Donaldson 3, Sneddon, R. Doughty	2,000
15	Feb 20	H	The Wednesday	D 1-1	Hood	6,000
16	27	A	Small Heath	L 2-3	Farman, Sneddon	300
17	Mar 5	H	Walsall Town Swifts	W 5-0	Farman, Sneddon, McFarlane, Donaldson	4,000
18	19	A	Nottingham Forest	L 0-3		9,000
19	26	H	Grimsby Town	W 6-1	Sneddon, unknown 5	2,000
20	Apr 2	A	Lincoln City	W 4-0	Donaldson 2, Farman	4,000
21	9	H	Birmingham St. George's	W 3-0	Donaldson 2, Hood	

Alliance League Appearances

Alliance League Scorers — 3 o.g.s

F.A. CUP

	Date	Venue	Opponents	Result	Goalscorers	Attendance
Qual 1	Oct 3	H	Ardwick	W 5-1	Farman 2, Edge, Sneddon, R. Doughty	10,000
Qual 2			BYE			
Qual 3	Nov 14	A	South Shore	W 2-0		4,000
Qual 4	Dec 5	A	Blackpool	L 3-4		

1890-1

No.	Date	Venue	Opponents	Result	Goalscorers	Attendance
1	Sept 6	H	Darwen	W 4-2	Farman, Evans, J. Doughty, Owen	
2	13	H	Grimsby Town	L 1-3	Stewart	
3	20	H	Nottingham Forest	D 1-1	J. Doughty	
4	27	A	Stoke	L 1-2	Milarvie	
5	Oct 11	A	Bootle	L 0-5		
6	18	H	Grimsby Town	W 3-1	Ramsey, Evans, Sharpe	4,000
7	Nov 1	H	Crewe Alexandra	W 6-3	Farman, Stewart 2, Craig, Evans, Ramsey	
8	8	A	Walsall Town Swifts	L 1-2	Sharpe	
9	22	A	Nottingham Forest	L 2-8	Ramsey, Farman	
10	29	H	Sunderland Albion	L 1-5	Ramsey	
11	Dec 13	A	Small Heath	W 4-1	Sharpe, Milarvie, 1 o.g.	2,000
12	27	H	Bootle	W 2-1	Stewart, Milarvie	2,000
13	Jan 5	H	Stoke City	L 0-1		
14	10	A	Birmingham St. Georges	L 1-6	Farman	2,000
15	17	H	Walsall Town Swifts	D 3-3	Owen, Milarvie, Ramsey	3,000
16	24	A	The Wednesday	L 2-1	Sharpe, Stewart	4,000
17	Feb 14	A	Crewe Alexandra	D 1-1	Craig	
18	21	A	The Wednesday	L 1-2	Sharpe	
19	Mar 7	H	Small Heath	L 1-3	Sharpe	2,000
20	14	H	Birmingham St. George's	L 1-3	Sharpe, Milarvie, 1 o.g.	2,000
21	28	A	Darwen	L 1-2	Ramsey	3,500
22	Apr 11	H	Bootle	L 1-2	Ramsey	

Alliance League Appearances

Alliance League Scorers — 2 o.g.s

F.A. CUP

	Date	Venue	Opponents	Result	Goalscorers	Attendance
Qual 1	Oct 4	A	Higher Walton	W 2-0	Farman, Evans	3,000
Qual 2	Oct 25	A	Bootle	L 0-1 *		

* This match was played by Newton Heath reserve team.

Players

- Slater, J.
- Mitchell, J.
- McMillan, J.
- Doughty, R.
- Ramsey, R.
- Owen, J.
- Farman, A. H.
- Doughty, J.
- Evans, G.
- Sharpe, W. H.
- Milarvie, R.
- Stewart, W.
- Powell, J.
- Sadler, E.
- Clements, J. E.
- Craig, T.
- Phasey, I.
- Felton, C.
- Denman, J.
- McFarlane, A.
- Henrys, A.
- Donaldson, A.
- Sneddon, A.
- Edge, A.
- Cash
- Hood, W.
- Davies, J.
- Mathieson, W.

ALLIANCE RUNNERS-UP 1891-2

ALLIANCE LEAGUE TABLES 1889-1892

SEASON 1889-90

	P	W	D	L	F	A	Pts
Sheffield Wednesday	22	15	2	5	70	38	32
Bootle	22	13	2	7	69	38	28
Sunderland Albion	22	13	2	7	65	39	28
Grimsby	22	12	2	8	58	47	24
Crewe Alexandra	22	11	2	9	68	59	24
Darwen	22	10	2	10	70	72	22
Birmingham St. George's	22	9	3	10	58	47	21
Newton Heath	22	9	2	11	38	43	20
Walsall Town Swifts	22	8	3	11	40	54	19
Small Heath	22	6	5	11	41	67	17
Nottingham Forest	22	6	5	11	31	62	17
Long Eaton Rangers	22	4	2	16	34	76	10

SEASON 1890-1

	P	W	D	L	F	A	Pts
Stoke	22	12	7	2	57	39	33
Sunderland Albion	22	12	6	4	69	28	30
Grimsby	22	11	5	6	43	27	27
Birmingham St. George's	22	12	2	8	64	62	26
*Nottingham Forest	22	9	7	6	66	39	23
Darwen	22	10	3	9	64	59	23
Walsall Town Swifts	22	9	3	10	34	61	21
Crewe Alexandra	22	8	4	10	59	62	20
Newton Heath	22	7	3	12	37	55	17
Small Heath	22	7	2	13	58	66	16
Bootle	22	3	7	12	40	61	13
Sheffield Wednesday	22	4	5	13	39	66	13

*Two points deducted for including ineligible players.

SEASON 1891-2

	P	W	D	L	F	A	Pts
Nottingham Forest	22	14	5	3	59	22	33
Newton Heath	22	12	7	3	69	33	31
Small Heath	22	12	5	5	53	36	29
Sheffield Wednesday	22	12	4	6	65	35	28
Burton Swifts	22	12	2	2	54	53	26
Crewe Alexandra	22	7	4	11	44	49	18
Ardwick	22	6	6	10	39	51	18
Bootle	22	8	2	12	42	64	18
Lincoln City	22	6	5	11	37	65	17
*Grimsby	22	6	6	10	40	39	16
Walsall Town Swifts	22	6	3	13	39	59	15
Birmingham St. George's	22	5	3	14	34	64	11

*Two points deducted

Top: FOOTBALL ALLIANCE RUNNERS-UP 1891-2. Newton Heath made a valiant effort to win the Alliance, finishing a close second to Champions Forest in the third, and final season of the competition. This is the team that took the field against Walsall Town Swifts on 5 March 1892. Back Row (Standing): Mr. Preddy (Trainer), H. Jones, Mr. Bird, R. McFarlane, J. F. Slater, J. E. Clements; Middle Row (Seated): R. Doughty, W. Stewart, J. Owen; Front (Kneeling): A. H. Farman, W. Hood, R. Donaldson, J. Sneddon, A. Edge. (KM)

Middle Right: Back: Massey (Trainer); Front: T. Fairbrother (Director), A. Mitchell, G. Perrins. (MMUSC)

Bottom Right: Back: J. Davies; Front: W. Stewart, W. Brown, F. C. Errentz, J. E. Clements. (MMUSC)

Newton Heath

Match No.	Date	Venue	Opponents	Result	Goalscorers	Attendance
1	Sept 3	A	Blackburn Rovers	L	3-4	Donaldson, Coupar, Farman	3,000
2	10	H	Burnley	D	1-1	Donaldson	10,000
3	17	A	Burnley	L	1-4	Donaldson	7,000
4	24	A	Everton	L	0-6		
5	Oct 1	A	West Bromwich Albion	D	0-0		4,000
6	8	H	West Bromwich Albion	L	2-4	Donaldson, Hood	8,000
7	15	H	Wolverhampton Wanderers	W	10-1	Hendry, Stewart 3, Farman, Donaldson 4, Hood	4,000
8	19	H	Everton	L	3-4	Donaldson, Hood, Farman	
9	22	A	The Wednesday	L	0-1		6,000
10	29	A	Nottingham Forest	D	1-1	Farman	8,000
11	Nov 5	H	Blackburn Rovers	D	4-4	Hood, Farman 2, Carson	12,000
12	12	H	Notts County	L	1-3	Carson	8,000
13	19	H	Aston Villa	W	2-0	Fitzsimmons, Coupar	6,000
14	26	A	Accrington	D	2-2	Fitzsimmons, Colville	1,500
15	Dec 3	H	Bolton Wanderers	L	1-4	Coupar	5,000
16	10	H	Bolton Wanderers	W	1-0	Donaldson	4,000
17	17	A	Wolverhampton Wanderers	L	0-2		5,000
18	24	H	The Wednesday	L	1-5	Hood	4,000
19	26	A	Preston North End	L	1-2	Hood	4,000
20	31	H	Derby County	W	7-1	Donaldson 4, Farman 2, Fitzsimmons	3,000
21	Jan 7	A	Stoke City	L	1-7	Coupar *Newton Heath fielded only 10 players	1,000
22	14	H	Nottingham Forest	L	1-3	Donaldson	8,000
23	26	A	Notts County	L	0-4		1,000
24	Feb 11	A	Derby County	L	1-5	Fitzsimmons	5,000
25	25	H	Sunderland	L	0-5		15,000
26	Mar 4	H	Aston Villa	L	0-2		4,000
27	31	H	Stoke City	W	1-0	Farman	10,000
28	Apr 1	H	Preston North End	W	2-1	Donaldson 2	9,000
29	4	A	Sunderland	L	0-6		3,500
30	8	H	Accrington	D	3-3	Fitzsimmons, Donaldson, Stewart	3,000

Football League Appearances
Football League Scorers

TEST MATCHES TO DECIDE RELEGATION

Rd	Date	Venue	Opponents	Result	Goalscorers	Attendance
Rd 1	Apr 22	N	Small Heath	D	1-1	Farman (played at Stoke)	4,000
Play-off	Apr 27	N	Small Heath	W	5-2	Cassidy, Coupar, Farman 3 (played at Sheffield)	

F.A. CUP

Rd	Date	Venue	Opponents	Result	Attendance
Rd 1	Jan 21	A	Blackburn Rovers	L	0-4	7,000

Players: Warner, J.; Clements, J. E.; Brown, W.; Perrins, G.; Stewart, W.; Errentz, F. C.; Farman, A. H.; Coupar, J.; Donaldson, R.; Carson, A.; Mathieson, W.; Mitchell, A.; Hood, W.; Hendry, J.; Kinloch, J.; Fitzsimmons, T.; Colville, J.; Hendry, A.; Davies, J.; Brady, W.; Cassidy, J.

DID YOU KNOW? In Newton Heath's first season in the Football League, they finished bottom of Division One, and had to contest 'Test Matches' with Stoke City to decide the relegation issue, surviving to compete for another season in the senior section. The first ever league victory was remarkably a 10-1 success over Wolves, but the 6 league wins, equalled only in 1893/4, is the lowest registered in the clubs history. The club's North Road ground was the property of the Cathedral Authorities in Manchester, and during 1892/3 these well-meaning people decided that they could no longer allow an admission charge at the gate. The club could not agree to this but the Dean and Canons were adamant, and the notice to quit was issued. A piece of muddy wasteland at Bank Street, Clayton was secured, and a spacious enclosure was built in time for the 1893/4 season. The club dropped L & YR from its name in 1892/3 becoming known simply as Newton Heath F.C.

INTO THE LEAGUE 1892−3
Newton Heath Officials

MR. PREDDY
Committee & Trainer

MR. H. JONES
Vice President

MR. A. H. ALBUT
Secretary

No. 16.—Vol. 1. [Entered at Stationers' Hall.] JANUARY 28, 1893. [Registered at G.P.O. as a Newspaper.] ONE PENNY.

No. 15.—THE NEWTON HEATH TEAM.

Bottom: THE FOOTBALL LEAGUE 1892/3. Newton Heath's first season in the league started badly, matters came to a head on 7 January 1893 when the team took the field against Stoke City with only ten players, and without a recognised goalkeeper. W. Stewart went between the posts at Stoke and this team group photo must be unique amongst first-class clubs, not a custodian in sight! (BNPC)

Newton Heath

Match No.	Date	Venue	Opponents	Result		Goalscorers	Attendance
1	Sept 2	H	Burnley	W	3-2	Farman 3 (First Match at Clayton)	10,000
2	9	A	West Bromwich Albion	L	1-3	Donaldson	4,500
3	16	H	The Wednesday	W	1-0	Farman	7,000
4	23	A	Nottingham Forest	D	1-1		10,000
5	30	H	Darwen	L	0-1		4,000
6	Oct 7	A	Derby County	L	0-2		7,000
7	14	H	West Bromwich Albion	W	4-1	Donaldson, Errentz, Peden, 2	8,000
8	21	A	Burnley	L	1-4	Hood	7,000
9	28	H	Wolverhampton Wanderers	L	0-2		4,000
10	Nov 4	H	Darwen	L	0-1		8,000
11	11	H	Wolverhampton Wanderers	W	1-0	Davidson	5,000
12	25	A	Sheffield United	L	1-3	Fitzsimmons	2,000
13	Dec 2	H	Everton	L	0-3		6,000
14	9	A	Sunderland	L	1-4	Campbell	8,000
15	16	A	Bolton Wanderers	L	1-3		5,000
16	23	H	Aston Villa	L	1-3	Peden	8,000
17	23	A	Preston North End	L	0-2		5,000
18	Jan 6	H	Everton	L	0-2		9,000
19	13	A	The Wednesday	L	1-2	Peden	9,000
20	Feb 3	A	Aston Villa	L	1-5	Mathieson	5,000
21	Mar 3	H	Sunderland	L	2-4	Peden, McNaught	10,000
22	10	A	Sheffield United	L	0-2		5,000
23	12	H	Blackburn Rovers	W	5-1	Clarkin, Donaldson 3, Farman	5,000
24	17	H	Derby County	L	2-6	Clarkin 2	7,000
25	23	A	Stoke	W	6-2	Peden 2, Errentz, Clarkin, Farman 2	8,000
26	24	H	Bolton Wanderers	D	2-2	Farman, Donaldson	10,000
27	26	A	Blackburn Rovers	L	0-4		5,000
28	31	A	Stoke City	L	1-3	Clarkin	4,000
29	Apr 7	A	Nottingham Forest	L	0-2		4,000
30	14	H	Preston North End	L	1-3	Mathieson	4,000

TEST MATCH TO DECIDE RELEGATION

	Apr 28	N	Liverpool	L	0-2	(played at Blackburn) Newton Heath relegated	3,000

F.A. CUP

Rd 1	Jan 27	H	Middlesbrough	W	4-0	Donaldson 2, Peden, Farman	5,000
Rd 2	Feb 10	H	Blackburn Rovers	D	0-0	(after extra time)	18,000
Replay	Feb 17	A	Blackburn Rovers	L	1-5	Donaldson	5,000

Players:
Fall, J. W.; Mitchell, A.; Clements, J. E.; Perrins, G.; Stewart, W.; Davisdons, J.; Farman, A. H.; McNaught, J.; Fitzsimmons, T.; Peden, J.; Donaldson, R.; Errentz, F. C.; Hood, W.; Thompson, W.; Prince, D.; Graham, J.; Campbell, W. C.; Rothwell, C.; Clarkin, J.; Parker, B.; Douglas, W.; Mathieson, W.; Woods, M. J.; Stones, H.

League Appearances / League Scorers

DID YOU KNOW? Newton Heath finished their second season in the First Division at the bottom of the table again. This time they suffered relegation to the Second Division after losing their Test Match. During the 1893/4 Season the club caused a sensation by suing a newspaper for libel! Following a match against West Bromwich Albion at Bank Street the Birmingham Daily Gazette reported that the home players used excessive roughness and brutality in achieving their 4-1 victory. The clubs demand for "an apology, suitable compensation and legal charges" was refused. With testimonials from both the referee and the match reporter form the Manchester Guardian, they brought their action for libel before the Manchester Civil Court on 2 March 1894. The presiding Judge, Mr. Justice Day found in favour of Newton Heath, but because the defence had successfully argued that the article had not injured the business operations of the plaintiffs, he awarded damages of just ONE FARTHING!!!

THE 'HEATHENS' ENTER THE FOOTBALL LEAGUE

BLACKBURN ROVERS 4 NEWTON HEATH 3

played at Blackburn on 3 September 1892

A rainstorm made the ground heavy. NEWTON HEATH kicked off, but the Rovers first became dangerous. Clements relieved, and clever play by Stewart carried the ball into the Rovers half, but Forest sent the ball back, and Southworth worked through the Newton defence and scored a splendid goal for the home side.

The game continued in favour of the Rovers, and immediately afterwards Hall scored number two. Newton Heath were being kept back in defence, and after fifteen minutes play, Rovers went three goals in front, after Chippendale secured the ball on the line and made a tricky pass to Hall to score his second goal of the game.

Slowly Newton Heath came more into the game and after one attack, Donaldson finished a nice piece of work by scoring. The game became much more even, and at length the visitors made several efforts to score, and shortly before the half time break, Coupar managed to pull back a second goal.

In the second half, the game continued to be evenly fought and the Rovers were unlucky not to go further in front as Mathieson shot close, and Southworth was brought to the ground several times when he was about to shoot.

Newton Heath kept pressing for the equaliser, but it failed to come, and after withstanding more Blackburn pressure, they evenually conceded a fourth goal, scored by outside right Chippendale. Ten minutes later, Farman brought the visitors back into the game again, but it was now too late in the game to get a result, and the final score stood at 4-3 in Blackburn's favour.

Above: Match Report from the MANCHESTER GUARDIAN, 5 September 1892, covering Newton Heath's first Football League fixture.

Right: R. DONALDSON, scored Newton Heath's first-ever goal in the Football League.

Newton Heath

Match No.	Date	Venue	Opponents	Result		Goalscorers	Attendance
1	Sept 8	A	Burton Wanderers	L	0-1		3,000
2	15	H	Crewe Alexandra	W	6-1	Smith 2, Dow 2, Clarkin, McCartney	6,000
3	22	A	Leicester Fosse	W	3-2	Dow 2, Peters	4,000
4	Oct 6	A	Darwen	D	1-1	Donaldson	4,000
5	13	H	Woolwich Arsenal	D	3-3	Clarkin, Donaldson 2	40,000
6	20	A	Burton Swifts	W	2-1	Donaldson 2	5,000
7	27	H	Leicester Fosse	D	2-2	McNaught, Smith	5,000
8	Nov 3	A	Manchester City	W	5-2	Smith 4, Clarkin	14,400
9	10	H	Rotherham Town	W	3-2	Davidson, Peters, Donaldson	4,000
10	17	A	Grimsby Town	L	1-2	Clarkin	5,000
11	24	A	Darwen	D	1-1	McCartney	5,000
12	Dec 1	A	Crewe Alexandra	W	2-0	Smith, Clarkin	3,000
13	8	H	Burton Swifts	W	5-1	Peters 2, Smith 2, Dow	3,500
14	15	A	Notts County	D	0-0		3,000
15	22	H	Lincoln City	W	3-0	Millar, Donaldson, Smith	2,000
16	24	A	Burslem Port Vale	W	5-2	Millar, Smith, Clarkin, Donaldson, McNaught	1,000
17	26	H	Walsall Town Swifts	W	2-1	Stewart, Millar	1,000
18	29	A	Lincoln City	L	0-3		1,500
19	Jan 1	H	Burslem Port Vale	W	3-0	Millar 2, Rothwell	5,000
20	5	H	Manchester City	W	4-1	Clarkin 2, Donaldson, Smith	12,000
21	12	A	Rotherham Town	L	1-2	Errentz	6,000
22	Mar 2	H	Burton Wanderers	D	1-1	Peters	6,000
23	23	H	Grimsby Town	W	2-0	Cassidy 2	9,000
24	30	A	Woolwich Arsenal	L	2-3	Clarkin, Donaldson	6,000
25	Apr 3	H	Walsall Town Swifts	W	9-0	Donaldson 2, Peters 2, Smith 2, Cassidy 2, Clarkin	6,000
26	6	H	Newcastle United	W	5-1	Cassidy 2, Smith 2, 1 o.g.	5,000
27	12	H	Bury	D	2-2	Donaldson, Cassidy	4,000
28	13	A	Newcastle United	L	0-3		10,000
29	15	A	Bury	L	1-2	Peters	
30	20	H	Notts County	D	3-3	Smith, Cassidy, Clarkin	

League Appearances
League Scorers

F.A. CUP

Rd 1	Feb 2	H	Stoke City	L	2-3	Peters, Smith	7,000

TEST MATCH TO DECIDE PROMOTION

	Apr 27	N	Stoke City	L	0-3	Not Promoted (played at Cobridge, Port Vale)	8,000

Players: Douglas, W.; McCartney, J.; Errentz, F. C.; Stewart, W.; McNaught, J.; Davidson, W. R.; Clarkin, J.; Farman, A. H.; Dow, J. M.; Smith, R.; Peters, J.; Perrins, J.; Donaldson, R.; Millar, G.; Stones, H.; Rothwell, J.; Cassidy, J.; McFettridge, D.; Cairns, J.; Longair, W.

DID YOU KNOW? The move to Clayton in 1893 had mixed fortunes for Newton Heath. The ground lay adjacent to chemical works, and noxious smells polluted the atmosphere of the neighbourhood. The 'Heathens' were able on occasions to turn this to advantage, when losing at half-time they would send instructions to the boilerman at the works to belch more fumes from the chimneys. This added to the discomfort of the visitors, but the home players were so accustomed that they were not affected. This home advantage may have contributed to a successful first season in the Second Division. The team finished third, but missed out on promotion, losing their 'Test Match' 0-3 to Stoke City. On 9 March 1895, the 'Heathens' defeated Walsall Town Swifts 14-0, but the visitors appealed against the state of the ground and the inclement weather. It was upheld, but Newton Heath still won the replay 9-0.

A RECORD SCORE 1895

NEWTON HEATH 1894/5

A RECORD SCORE. Newton Heath 14 Walsall Town Swifts 0. 9 March 1895. This is the 'Heathens' side (in their Green shirts with Gold collars and cuffs) that scored a club record fourteen goals. Then, after Walsall had successfully appealed against the result because of the state of the pitch, these players beat the 'Swifts' again, by 9-0.
Back Row: Albut (Sec), Paley (Trainer), Dow, Douglas, Palmer (Director), Errentz, Davidson, Faulkner (Director). Middle Row: Crompton (President), Perrins, McNaught, Stewart, Jones, (Vice-President). Front: Clarkin, Donaldson, Cassidy, Smith, Peters. (JG)

W. HOOD   J. E. CLEMENTS   A. EDGE

Newton Heath

Match No.	Date		Venue	Opponents	Result	Goalscorers	Attendance
1	Sept	7	H	Crewe Alexandra	W 5-0	Kennedy, Cassidy 2, Aitken, Smith	6,000
2		14	A	Loughborough Town	D 3-3	McNaught, Cassidy 2	
3		21	H	Burton Swifts	W 5-0	Donaldson 2, Cassidy 2, Kennedy	9,000
4		28	A	Crewe Alexandra	W 2-0	Smith 2	
5	Oct	5	H	Manchester City	D 1-1	Clarkin	12,000
6		12	A	Liverpool	L 1-7	Cassidy	7,000
7		19	H	Newcastle United	W 2-1	Peters, Cassidy	8,000
8		26	A	Newcastle United	L 1-2	Kennedy	8,000
9	Nov	2	H	Liverpool	W 5-2	Peters 3, Smith, Clarkin	8,000
10		9	A	Arsenal	L 1-2	Cassidy	9,000
11		16	H	Lincoln City	W 5-5	Clarkin 2, Peters, Cassidy, Collinson	8,000
12		23	A	Notts County	W 2-0	Cassidy, Kennedy	6,000
13		30	H	Arsenal	W 5-1	Kennedy, Cartwright 2, Clarkin, Peters	8,000
14	Dec	14	H	Manchester City	L 1-2	Cassidy	18,000
15		21	H	Notts County	W 3-0	Donaldson, Cassidy, Clarkin	3,000
16		21	A	Darwen	L 0-3		
17	Jan	1	H	Grimsby Town	W 3-2	Cassidy 3 (1 pen)	8,000
18		4	H	Leicester Fosse	L 0-3		7,000
19		11	H	Rotherham Town	W 3-0	Donaldson 2, Stephenson	
20	Feb	3	H	Leicester Fosse	W 2-0	Kennedy, Smith	1,000
21		8	H	Burton Swifts	L 1-4	Dow	2,000
22		29	H	Burton Wanderers	L 1-2	McNaught	1,000
23	Mar	7	A	Rotherham Town	W 3-2	Smith, Donaldson, Kennedy	
24		14	A	Grimsby Town	L 2-4	Kennedy, Smith	1,000
25		18	A	Burton Wanderers	L 1-5	Dow	
26		23	A	Burslem Port Vale	L 0-3		
27	Apr	3	H	Darwen	W 4-0	Kennedy 3, McNaught	4,000
28		4	H	Loughborough Town	W 2-0	Smith, Donaldson	
29		6	H	Burslem Port Vale	W 2-1	Smith, Clarkin	5,000
30		11	A	Lincoln City	L 0-2		

F.A. CUP

	Date		Venue	Opponents	Result	Goalscorers	Attendance
Rd 1	Feb	1	H	Kettering	W 2-1	Donaldson, Smith	6,000
Rd 2		15	H	Derby County	D 1-1	Kennedy	20,000
Replay		19	A	Derby County	L 1-5	Smith	6,000

Players: Douglas, W.; Dow, J. M.; Errentz, F. C.; Fitzsimmons, D.; McNaught, J.; Cartwright, W. G.; Clarkin, J.; Kennedy, W.; Cassidy, J.; Smith, R.; Aitken, J.; Peters, J.; Perrins, G.; Donaldson, R.; Collinson, J.; Ridgway, J. A.; Stephenson, R.; Vance, J.; Whitney, J.; Whittaker, W.; Stafford, H.

(Bottom summary rows: *League Appearances* and *League Scorers*.)

DID YOU KNOW? The Newton Heath club had some generous benefactors and enthusiastic followers in the early days. 'Father' Bird was a local chimney-sweep who had a great interest in the team, his hospitality regularly included entertaining the players and officials at his home with a supper of potato-pie or Lancashire Hot-Pot, followed by refreshments and a 'sing-song'.

As befits a club which sprang from the railways, it was appropriate that it was rendered great service by Mr. Sedgwick, who was then the Station Master at Manchester's Victoria Station. He ensured that the players journeyed to away fixtures in the luxury of reserved apartments, and was a familiar figure at home matches, where his voice was heard by all, and he was always dressed in silk hat and frock coat.

CLAYTON 1893-1910

THE UNIQUE ROOF PAVILION ON THE STAND AT CLAYTON

THE BANK STREET GROUND

The ground at Clayton was acquired following a dispute over admission charges to the North Road ground with the owners, the Cathedral authorities. An agreement was reached with the Bradford & Clayton Recreative Committee for use of the new ground for eight months of the year, with some evenings for practice and training. The ground lay adjacent to chemical works for which Clayton was famous, the neighbourhood being well-known for the noxious smells thus:

> "As Satan was flying over Clayton for Hell,
> He was chained in the breeze, likewise the smell.
> Quoth he "I'm not sure in what country I roam,
> But I'm sure by the smell I'm not far from home."

Newton Heath's first match at Bank Street was against Burnley on 2 September 1893, a hat-trick by Farman clinched a 3-2 win for the "Heathens".

Right: A. H. FARMAN scored the first goal for Newton Heath at Bank Street.

61

Newton Heath

Match No.	Date	Venue	Opponents	Result		Goalscorers	Attendance	Ridgway, J. A.	Stafford, H.	Errentz, F. C.	Draycott, W. L.	Jenkyns, C. A. L.	Cartwright, W. G.	Bryant, W.	Donaldson, R.	Brown, W.	McNaught, J.	Cassidy, J.	Smith, R.	Wetherell, J.	Brisly	Barrett, F.	Kennedy, W. J.	Vance, J.	Gillespie, M.	Griffiths, W.	Boyd, H.	Morgan, W.	Doughty	Match No.
1	Sept 1	H	Gainsborough Trinity	W	2-0	McNaught 2		1	2	3	4	5	6	7	8	9	10	11												1
2	5	A	Burton Swifts	W	5-3	Brown, Bryant, Cassidy, Draycott, McNaught		1	2	3	4	5	6	7	8	9	10	11												2
3	7	H	Walsall	W	2-0	Cassidy, Donaldson	7,000	1	2	3	4	5	6	7	8	9	10	11												3
4	12	H	Lincoln City	W	3-1	Donaldson, Cassidy 2 (1 pen)	6,000	1	2	3		5	6	7	8	9	10	11	4											4
5	19	A	Grimsby Town	L	0-2			2			4	5	6	7	8	9	10	11		1	3									5
6	21	A	Walsall	W	3-2	Brown, McNaught, Draycott	7,000	2	3	4	5			7	8	9	10	11	6	1										6
7	26	H	Newcastle United	W	4-0	Cassidy 3 Donaldson		2	3	4	5	6	7	8			10	11	9			1								7
8	Oct 3	A	Manchester City	D	0-0		20,000	2	3	4	5	6	7	8			10	9	11			1								8
9	10	H	Small Heath	D	1-1	1 scrimmage	6,000	2	3	4	5	6	7	8			10	9	11	1										9
10	17	A	Blackpool	L	2-4	Bryant, Draycott	5,000	2	3	4	5	6	7	8	9		10		11			1								10
11	21	A	Gainsborough Trinity	L	0-2		4,000	2	3	4	5	6	7	9			10	11				1	8							11
12	24	H	Burton Wanderers	W	3-0	Cassidy 3	4,000	2	3	4	5	6	7				8	9	11			1		10						12
13	Nov 7	H	Grimsby Town	W	4-2	Donaldson, Jenkyns, Cassidy 2	5,000	2	3	4	5	6	7	11			8	9	10			1								13
14	28	A	Small Heath	L	0-1		5,000	2	3	4	5	6	7	11			8	9				1		10						14
15	Dec 19	A	Notts County	L	0-3		5,000	2	3	4	5	6	7	11			8	9				1			10					15
16	25	H	Manchester City	W	2-1	Smith, Donaldson	18,000	2	3	4	5		7	11		6	9	8				1		10						16
17	26	H	Blackpool	W	2-0	Cassidy 2	9,000	2	3	4	5		7	11		6	9	8				1			10					17
18	28	A	Leicester Fosse	L	0-1		8,000	2		4	5	3	7	11		6	9	8				1		10						18
19	Jan 1	A	Newcastle United	L	0-2			2	3	4	5		7	9		6	10	11				1	8							19
20	9	H	Burton Swifts	D	1-1	Donaldson		2	3	4	5	6	7	11			8	9				1		10						20
21	Feb 6	H	Loughborough Town	W	6-0	Smith 2, Donaldson, Draycott, Boyd, Jenkyns	5,000	2	3	4	5			8			6	11	7			1		10		9				21
22	20	H	Leicester Fosse	W	2-1	Boyd, Donaldson	8,000	2		4	5	3	7	8			6	11				1		10		9				22
23	Mar 2	H	Darwen	W	3-1	Cassidy 2, Boyd	3,000	2		4		3	7	8			6	11				1		10		9	5			23
24	13	A	Darwen	W	2-0	Gillespie, Cassidy	3,000		3	4	5	2	7	8			6	11				1		10		9				24
25	20	A	Burton Wanderers	W	2-1	Gillespie, 1 o.g.			3	4		2	7	8			6	11				1		10		9	5			25
26	22	H	Woolwich Arsenal	D	1-1	Boyd	3,000		3	4	5	2	7	8			6		11			1		10		9				26
27	27	H	Notts County	D	1-1	Bryant	10,000		3	4	5	2	7	8			6	11				1		10		9				27
28	Apr 1	A	Lincoln City	W	3-1	Jenkyns 3	1,000		3	4	5	2	7	8			6	11				1		10		9				28
29	3	A	Woolwich Arsenal	W	2-0	Boyd, Donaldson	6,000		3	4	5	2	7	8			6	11				1		10		9				29
30	10	A	Loughborough Town	L	0-2			2	3	4			6	7	8		5	11				1		10		9				30
						League Appearances		4	24	26	29	27	25	29	29	7	30	28	14	3	1	23	2	15	1	10	2	0	
						League Scorers						4	5				9	2	4	17	3		3		2	5		1 o.g.	

TEST MATCHES TO DECIDE PROMOTION

	Date	Venue	Opponents	Result		Goalscorers	Attendance					Jenkyns		Bryant	Donaldson		McNaught	Cassidy				Barrett			Gillespie		Boyd	Morgan		
	Apr 19	A	Burnley	L	0-2		10,000		3	4	5	2	7	8			6	11			1		10		9				
	21	H	Burnley	W	2-0	Jenkyns, Boyd	6,000		3	4	5		7	8			6	11			1		10		9	2			
	24	H	Sunderland	D	1-1	Boyd	18,000		3	4	5		7	8			6	11			1		10		9	2			
	26	A	Sunderland	L	0-2	(Newton Heath not promoted)	6,000		3	4	5		7	8			6	11			1		10		9	2			

F.A. CUP

	Date	Venue	Opponents	Result		Goalscorers	Attendance					Jenkyns		Bryant	Donaldson			Cassidy				Barrett			Gillespie		Boyd	Morgan		
Qual 3	Dec 12	H	West Manchester	W	7-0	Gillespie 2, Cassidy 2, Rothwell, Bryant, 1 o.g																						
Qual 4	Jan 2	H	Nelson	W	3-0	Cassidy, Donaldson, Gillespie																						
Qual 5	15	A	Blackpool	D	2-2	Gillespie, Donaldson	1,000		2	3		5	6	7	9			4	10	8		1		11					
Replay	20	H	Blackpool	W	2-1	Bryant, 1 o.g.	2,000																					
Rd 1	30	H	Kettering	W	5-1	Cassidy 2, Donaldson 2, Bryant	5,000		2	3	4	5	6	7	9			8	11			1		10					
Rd 2	Feb 13	H	Southampton St. Marys	D	1-1	Donaldson	8,000		2	3		5	6	7	8			4	11			1		10		9			
Replay	17	A	Southampton St. Marys	W	3-1	Bryant 2, Cassidy			2			5	3	7	8			4	11	6		1		10		9			
Rd 3	27	A	Derby County	L	0-2		11,244		2		4	5	3	7	8			6	11			1		10		9			

DID YOU KNOW? The 1896/7 season marked the end of an era for Newton Heath, when they abandoned their traditional green and gold shirts for a new strip of white shirts and blue shorts. The change heralded some success, the team was runners-up in Division Two, but were again unable to secure promotion, failing in the series of Test matches.

TEST MATCHES LEAGUE TABLE 1896-7
To decide Promotion and Relegation

	Pl.	W	D	L	F	A	Pts
NOTTS COUNTY	4	2	2	0	3	1	6
SUNDERLAND	4	1	2	1	3	2	4
BURNLEY	4	1	1	2	3	4	3
NEWTON HEATH	4	1	1	2	3	5	3

Note: Notts County Promoted/Burnley Relegated

Newton Heath 1896-7

The first photograph of the 'Heathens' in their new colours of White Shirts and Blue Shorts. (BNPC)

Standing: A. Norris (Trainer), Mr. J. Taylor (President), H. Stafford, F. Barrett, F. C. Errentz, Mr. A. H. Albut (Secretary), Mr. W. Healey (Director).
Middle Row: W. L. Draycott, J.R. McNaught, C. A. L. Jenkyns, W. Cartwright.
Front Row: W. Bryant, R. Donaldson, H. Boyd, M. Gillespie, J. Cassidy.

Newton Heath

Match No.	Date		Venue	Opponents	Result		Goalscorers	Attendance
1	Sept	4	H	Lincoln City	W	5-0	Boyd 3, Cassidy, Bryant	5,000
2		11	A	Burton Swifts	W	4-0	Boyd 3, Cassidy	
3		18	H	Luton Town	L	1-2	Cassidy	8,000
4		25	A	Blackpool	W	1-0	Smith	
5	Oct	2	H	Leicester Fosse	W	2-0	Boyd 2	6,000
6		9	A	Newcastle United	L	0-2		12,000
7		16	A	Manchester City	D	1-1	Gillespie	20,000
8		23	H	Small Heath	L	1-2	Bryant	6,000
9		30	H	Walsall	W	6-0	Cassidy 2, Donaldson 2, Bryant, Gillespie	
10	Nov	6	H	Lincoln City	L	0-1		7,000
11		13	A	Newcastle United	L	0-1		
12		20	A	Leicester Fosse	D	1-1	Wedge	5,000
13		27	H	Grimsby Town	W	2-1	Wedge, Bryant	
14	Dec	11	A	Walsall	D	1-1	Boyd	
15		25	H	Manchester City	W	1-0	Cassidy	16,000
16		27	A	Gainsborough Trinity	L	1-2	Boyd	3,000
17	Jan	1	H	Burton Swifts	W	4-0	Bryant, Carman, McNaught, Boyd	8,000
18		8	A	Woolwich Arsenal	L	1-5	Boyd	7,000
19		12	A	Burnley	D	0-0		
20		15	H	Blackpool	W	4-0	Cassidy, Boyd 2, Cartwright	4,000
21	Feb	26	H	Woolwich Arsenal	W	5-1	Boyd, Cassidy, Bryant 2, Collinson	6,000
22	Mar	7	A	Burnley	L	3-6	Bryant 2, Collinson	3,000
23		19	A	Darwen	W	3-2	Boyd 2, McNaught	2,000
24		21	A	Luton Town	D	2-2	Cassidy, Boyd	
25		29	H	Loughborough Town	W	5-1	Cassidy 2, Boyd 3	3,000
26	Apr	2	A	Grimsby Town	W	3-1	Cassidy 2 (1 pen), Boyd	5,000
27		8	H	Gainsborough Trinity	W	1-0	Cassidy	4,000
28		9	H	Small Heath	W	3-1	Morgan, Boyd, Gillespie	4,000
29		16	A	Loughborough Town	D	0-0		1,200
30		23	H	Darwen	W	3-2	Bryant, Collinson 2	4,000

F.A. CUP

			Venue	Opponents	Result		Goalscorers	Attendance
Rd 1	Jan	29	H	Walsall	W	1-0	1 o.g.	10,000
Rd 2	Feb	12	H	Liverpool	D	0-0		10,000
Replay		16	A	Liverpool	L	1-2	Collinson	10,000

Players:
Barrett, F.; Stafford, H.; Errentz, F. C.; Morgan, W.; McNaught, J.; Cartwright, W. G.; Bryant, W.; Dunn, W.; Boyd, H.; Gillespie, M.; Cassidy, J.; Jenkyns, C. A. L.; Donaldson, R.; Smith, R.; Ridgway, J. A.; Draycott, W.; Wedge, F. E.; Carman, J.; Errentz, H.; Collinson, J.

League Appearances and League Scorers totals are given at the foot of each player column.

DID YOU KNOW? Among the novel schemes to attract crowds to Clayton involved a Goose, and a Goat! It was once announced that spectators would be able to hear the 'Bank Street Canary' in "full-song". But the bird referred to was in fact a goose which was housed in a pen in the corner of the ground and being fattened for the club's Christmas dinner! The goat belonged to one of the players, who would entertain onlookers by taking the animal to the adjacent public house, and encourage it to drink ale until it fell down.

Newton Heath won the Lancashire Senior Cup in 1897/8, beating the favourites Blackburn Rovers 2-1 at Goodison Park. The team that day was: Barrett, Errentz (H.), Errentz (F.C.), Draycott, McNaught, Cartwright, Bryant, Collinson, Boyd, Cassidy and Gillespie.

LANCASHIRE CUP WINNERS 1897-8

Above: LANCASHIRE SENIOR CUP WINNERS 1898. Back Row: A. Norris (Trainer), H. Errentz, F. C. Errentz, F. Barrett, H. Stafford, W. L. Draycott, J. R. McNaught, W. Morgan.
Front Row: W. Cartwrigth, J. Collinson, H. Boyd, M. Gillespie, W. Bryant, J. Cassidy. (JG)

Below: LANCASHIRE CUP FINAL. Newton Heath 2 Blackburn Rovers 1. Match Report from The Umpire *27 March 1989. The 'Heathens goals were scored by Boyd and Collinson. (KM)*

LANCASHIRE SENIOR CUP.—Final

Blackburn Rovers v. Newton Heath. By the Everton Ground, Goodison Park, Liverpool, before 8000 spectators. Teams :—

BLACKBURN ROVERS.—Carter, goal; Brandon and Killean, backs; Ball, Booth, and Chambers, half backs; Briercliffe, Blackburn, Proudfoot, Wilkie, and Campbell, forwards.

NEWTON HEATH.—Barrett, goal; F Errentz, and F Errentz, backs; Cartwright, Draycott, and Bryant, half-backs; Collinson, Boyd, Cassidy, and Gillespie forwards.

Referee : Mr R Lythgoe, Liverpool.

Newton won the toss, and had a strong wind in their favour. Newton charged down the first minute but were quickly repulsed. Proudfoot and Briercliffe being prominent, particularly the former, whose shot from the left was spoilt by the wind. Then Boyd and Gillespie got away, the latter landing the ball in Carter's hands. Newton were decidedly dangerous in the next few minutes. Bryant sending in a splendid shot which just tipped the corner of the goal. The pressure continued, and the play was exciting. Blackburn defending magnificently. Eventually, in clearing Killean placed the ball for Boyd, who seized the opportunity and scored the first goal for Newton. When play was resumed it was confidently expected that Blackburn would have all the play, but the opening stages hardly justified expectations, although the wind was as strong as ever. However, Blackburn were soon busy attacking, and Barrett was called again and again. Briercliffe and Proudfoot shooting well. A clever run between Bryant and Collinson took play away up the field, but the Rovers' backs were ready, and forced the ball behind. Newton came on again, and play was very fast. Gillespie shot from the left

and just after Carter cleared Collinson charged him, an incident which aroused hooting from the spectators. Blackburn again advanced, but Barrett and his backs repelled manfully. Newton maintained the aggressive for some time, but at last clever forward play took Blackburn up, and Campbell carried the ball before the Newton goal. Barrett ran out and fell on it, but Proudfoot dashing up kicked the ball through, so equalising the score. The ensuing play was practically all in the Blackburn quarters. Newton placing the ball all round the goal, but nothing was added to the score which was at the interval one goal each. Newton were playing strongly, despite the wind, and had quite as much of the game as Blackburn. Campbell once just skimmed the Newton crossbar, but the Newton players showed the best form, and the left wing attacked several times, and Boyd shot an offside goal. Newton's energy was rewarded by Collinson scoring grandly from a pass by Gillespie. The Rovers pressed wildly, but the Newton defence was impenetrable. Final :—

| NEWTON HEATH | 2 GOALS |
| BLACKBURN ROVERS | 1 GOAL |

REMARKS ON THE GAME.

Taken altogether, the game was very disappointing, nothing like first-class football being exhibited by either team. Barrett and the brothers Errentz formed the Heathens' defence, and played a hard game, the goalkeeper successfully negotiating several difficult shots. The half-backs tackled well, while the forwards took advantage of every opportunity, and made ground rapidly. Brandon and Proudfoot were the only men of the Rovers who displayed anything like form. Campbell and Wilkie were extremely disappointing. The Heathens certainly were the better team, and deserved victory.

Newton Heath

Match No.	Date		Venue	Opponents	Result		Goalscorers	Attendance
1	Sept	3	A	Gainsborough Trinity	W	2-0	Jones 2	2,000
2		10	H	Manchester City	W	3-0	Boyd, Cassidy 2	20,000
3		17	A	Glossop North End	W	2-1	Bryant, Cassidy	6,000
4		24	H	Walsall	W	1-0	Gillespie	8,000
5	Oct	1	A	Burton Swifts	L	1-5	Boyd	2,000
6		8	H	Burslem Port Vale	W	2-1	Bryant, Cassidy	10,000
7		15	A	Small Heath	L	1-4	Cassidy	5,000
8		22	H	Loughborough Town	W	6-1	Cassidy 2, Collinson 2, Brooks 2	5,000
9	Nov	5	A	Grimsby Town	W	3-2	Cassidy 2 (1 pen), Gillespie	
10		12	H	Barnsley	D	0-0		5,000
11		19	A	New Brighton Tower	W	3-0	Cassidy, Cunningham Collinson	6000
12		26	H	Lincoln City	W	1-0	Bryant	4,000
13	Dec	3	A	Woolwich Arsenal	L	1-5	Collinson	7,000
14		10	H	Blackpool	W	3-1	Cunningham, Collinson, Cassidy	8,000
15		17	A	Leicester Fosse	L	0-1		8,000
16		24	H	Darwen	W	9-0	Gillespie 2, Bryant 3, Cassidy 3, 1 o.g.	20,000
17		26	H	Manchester City	L	0-4		20,000
18		31	H	Gainsborough Trinity	W	6-1	Collinson 3, Bryant, Cartwright, Draycott	6,000
19	Jan	2	H	Burton Swifts	D	2-2	Boyd, Cassidy	6,000
20		14	A	Glossop North End	W	3-0	Cunningham, Errentz, Gillespie	12,000
21		21	A	Walsall	L	0-2		12,000
22	Feb	4	A	Burnham Port Vale	L	0-1		6,000
23		18	A	Loughborough Town	W	1-0	Bryant	
24		25	H	Small Heath	W	2-0	Roberts, Boyd	12,000
25	Mar	4	A	Grimsby Town	L	0-3		
26		18	H	New Brighton Tower	L	1-2	Gillespie	
27		25	A	Lincoln City	L	0-2		3,000
28	Apr	1	H	Woolwich Arsenal	D	2-2	Cassidy, Bryant	5,000
29		3	A	Blackpool	W	1-0	Bryant	3,000
30		4	A	Barnsley	W	2-0	Lee 2	4,000
31		8	A	Luton Town	W	1-0	Lee	3,000
32		12	H	Luton Town	W	5-0	Gillespie, Lee, Cassidy, Morgan, Cartwright	6,000
33		15	H	Leicester Fosse	D	2-2	Cassidy, Gillespie	6,000
34		22	A	Darwen	D	1-1	Morgan	1,000

F.A. CUP

	Date		Venue	Opponents	Result		Goalscorers	Attendance
Rd 1	Jan	28	A	Tottenham Hotspur	D	1-1	Cassidy	15,000
Replay	Feb	1	H	Tottenham Hotspur	L	3-5	Bryant 3	6,000

Players:

Barrett, F.; Stafford, H.; Errentz, F. C.; Draycott, W. L.; Morgan, W.; Cartwright, W.G.; Bryant, W.; Collinson, J.; Jones, O. J.; Cassidy, J.; Gillespie, M.; Boyd, H.; Turner, J.; Cairns, J.; Owen, W.; Brooks, W. H.; Connachan, J.; Cunningham J.; Turner, R.; Pepper, F.; Walker, R.; Gourlay, J.; Roberts; Hopkins, J; Lee, E.; Griffiths, W.; Ratcliffe, G.

League Appearances

League Scorers

DID YOU KNOW? Newton Heath contested the William Healey Cup Final in 1898/9, but as in the previous season, they lost to local rivals Manchester City. 1898 marked the departure of one of the club's great characters, the redoubtable Caesar Jenkyns. He was described as a big, burly fellow, and very vigorous in his play, with ways of expressing his exultation or disgust. It was said that one "Heathen' goalkeeper returned home to Scotland, after hearing of Caesar's opinion of his attempt to prevent a goal being scored. Also in 1898, the first of the Players Union movements was formed. The early meeting to organise the Union of Professional Football Players were held at the Spread Eagle Hotel in Manchester, at which players representing Newton Heath were prominent speakers. Better pay and conditions were indeed needed, the 'Heathens' players did not received win bonuses, they were rewarded in victory by a visit to the local fish and chip shop for supper paid for by the directors!

LEAGUE LINES AND TABLES.

THE LEAGUE CHAMPIONSHIP.

FIRST DIVISION.

Record up to date:

	P.	Won	Lost	Dr'n	Goals For	Agst	Pts
Sheffield United	30	17	5	8	56	31	42
Sunderland	29	15	9	5	39	30	35
Wolverhampton Wan.	30	14	9	7	57	41	35
Everton	30	13	8	9	48	39	35
Sheffield Wednesday	30	15	12	3	51	42	33
West Bromwich Albion	30	11	9	10	44	45	32
Notts. Forest	28	11	8	9	47	43	31
Aston Villa	29	13	11	5	59	51	31
Liverpool	30	11	13	6	43	43	28
Derby County	30	11	13	6	57	61	28
Bolton Wanderers	30	11	15	4	28	41	26
Preston North End	30	8	14	8	35	43	24
Notts. County	30	8	14	8	35	46	24
Bury	30	8	14	8	39	51	24
Blackburn Rovers	30	7	13	10	39	54	24
Stoke	30	8	14	8	33	55	24

TO-DAY'S RESULTS.

Bury	1	Blackburn Rovers	0
Wolverhampton Wan.	5	Sheffield Wednesday	0
Liverpool	4	Aston Villa	0

SECOND DIVISION.

Record up to date:

	P.	Won	Lost	Dr'n	Goals For	Agst	Pts
Burnley	30	20	2	8	80	24	48
Newcastle United	30	21	6	3	64	32	45
Manchester City	30	15	6	9	63	36	39
Woolwich Arsenal	30	16	8	5	68	47	37
Newton Heath	29	15	8	6	61	33	36
Small Heath	29	15	10	4	56	49	34
Leicester Fosse	30	13	10	7	46	35	33
Luton	29	13	9	7	68	49	33
Gainsborough Trinity	29	12	12	5	49	53	29
Walsall	30	12	13	5	58	58	29
Grimsby Town	30	10	16	4	52	62	24
Blackpool	28	8	15	5	44	61	21
Burton Swifts	29	8	17	4	37	68	20
Lincoln City	30	6	19	5	43	82	17
Darwen	29	6	21	2	29	73	14
Loughborough	29	6	21	2	24	84	14

TO-DAY'S RESULTS.

Manchester City	9	Burton Swifts	0
Leicester Fosse	3	Gainsborough Trinity	1
Small Heath	4	Lincoln City	0
Blackpool	1	Grimsby Town	1
Loughborough	0	Newton Heath	0

MIDLAND LEAGUE.

Record up to date:

	P.	Won	Lost	Dr'n	Goals For	Agst	Pts
Mexborough	21	15	3	3	53	24	33
Barnsley St. Peter's	22	14	5	3	47	32	31
Chesterfield	22	11	4	7	63	23	29
Ilkeston	22	9	7	6	37	39	24
Rushden	21	9	7	5	34	42	23
Burslem Port Vale	22	10	9	3	45	35	23
Long Eaton Rangers	22	7	10	5	26	45	19
Kettering	22	7	10	5	19	28	19
Burton Wanderers	22	6	10	6	31	44	18
Glossop North End	21	7	12	2	59	45	16
Doncaster Rovers	21	4	11	6	31	35	14
Wellingborough Town	22	5	14	3	22	46	13

TO-DAY'S RESULTS.

Wellingborough	2	Burslem Port Vale	0
Rushden	4	Barnsley St. Peter's	1
Burton Wanderers	1	Mexborough	1
Glossop North End	2	Long Eaton Rangers	1

LEAGUE—DIVISION II

LOUGHBOROUGH v. NEWTON HEATH.

Loughborough: Beardsley, goal; Ward and Hardy, backs; Smith, Hodgkin, and White, half-backs; Hall, Roulston, Pegg, Tuthill, and Wright, forwards.

Newton Heath: Barrett, goal; Stafford and F. Errentz, backs; Draycott, McNaught, and H. Errentz, half-backs; Bryant, Morgan, Boyd, Cassidy, and Gillespie, forwards.

This was the last home match in Division II. at Loughborough, and the supporters hoped for victory so as to give them the chance of handing on the wooden spoon to Darwen's careful custody. The same eleven represented Loughborough which defeated Grimsby a week ago, and Newton Heath were also strongly represented. The weather was beautifully fine, but the "gate" was hardly in keeping with the weather. Loughborough started punctually before 1,000 spectators, and Gillespie soon got a centre in which Hardy headed. Tuthill and Wright went away, but were deprived, and Gillespie again secured on the left wing and placed into the centre for Boyd to shoot, Beardsley saving. Hall received a good pass from Pegg, but shot wide. Hardy took a free kick, and after a spell of futile kicking in the "Heathens'" goal Hall charged foully and was penalised. Then the visitors sent behind several times, Ward playing a good back game. Tuthill and Pegg tried to get through, and then Roulston was tripped, the result of the free kick being a header past the post by Tuthill. The referee then gave a free kick to the "Heathens"—an error—and a couple of shots from Draycott were nicely put out of the way by Beardsley. At the other end Stafford cleared in time from Tuthill, and a backheeler by Pegg made the goalkeeper kick away. The "Heathens" returned, and Bryant sent the ball whizzing over the bar, and McNaught narrowly missed. Then Loughborough were away again, and from Hall's centre Tuthill forced a corner. This was fruitless, but soon after Loughborough were again in evidence, and when Wright shot in Pegg went for the goalkeeper, stafford clearing the goal mouth. A minute later Hall received a pass from the centre, and sent right across the goal mouth, with Tuthill and Wright losing a glorious opportunity. The "Heathens" had a corner without result, and there was another siege of the visitors' goal in vain, White finally sending wide. Beardsley handled once more to the right wing, and another centre by Hall, though dangerous, produced nothing. The home left wing again put in some good work, and after Stafford had deprived, White sent in a long dropper which Barrett was rather lucky to successfully dispose of. The "Heathens" pressed from a free, and Cassidy was given off-side. Pegg was also given off-side close to the centre line, and this was followed by a free kick close to goal, a return header being played on to the bar by Beardsley and then cleared at the expense of a corner. Just before half-time Gillespie rattled one in, and Beardsley fell on the ball and prevented any score before half-time.

After the interval Loughborough visited first, but Hall ran the ball out of bounds. Then Wright was yards off-side, and immediately after Loughborough had a free kick, Stafford interposing between Tuthill and the goal. White gave Wright a capital pass, but the left winger missed his kick. Cassidy got past Hardy, but Ward beat him smartly. The "Heathens" came again, and McNaught kicked wide. Result:—

Loughborough **0**
Newton Heath **0**

Newton Heath

Match No.	Date		Venue	Opponents	Result		Goalscorers	Attendance
1	Sept	2	H	Gainsborough Trinity	D	2-2	Cassidy, Lee	8,000
2		9	A	Bolton Wanderers	L	1-2	Ambler	5,000
3		16	A	Loughborough Town	W	4-0	Bain, Cassidy, Griffiths, 1 o.g.	6,000
4		23	H	Burton Swifts	D	0-0		6,000
5		30	A	The Wednesday	L	1-2	Bryant	8,000
6	Oct	7	H	Lincoln City	W	1-0	Cassidy	6,000
7		14	A	Small Heath	L	0-1		10,000
8		21	H	New Brighton Tower	W	2-1	Cassidy 2	10,000
9	Nov	4	H	Woolwich Arsenal	W	2-0	Roberts, Morgan	5,000
10		11	A	Barnsley	D	0-0		
11		25	A	Luton Town	W	1-0	Jackson	3,000
12	Dec	2	H	Burslem Port Vale	W	3-0	Jackson 2, Cassidy	
13		16	H	Middlesbrough	W	2-1	Parkinson 2	4,000
14		23	A	Chesterfield	L	1-2	Griffiths	
15		26	H	Grimsby Town	W	7-0	Parkinson, Cassidy 2, Bryant 2, Jackson, 1 o.g.	4,000
16		30	H	Gainsborough Trinity	W	1-0	Parkinson	2,000
17	Jan	6	A	Bolton Wanderers	L	1-2	Parkinson	5,000
18		13	A	Loughborough Town	W	2-0	Jackson, Parkinson	1,000
19		20	H	Burton Swifts	W	4-0	Gillespie 3, Parkinson	5,000
20	Feb	3	H	The Wednesday	W	1-0	Bryant	10,000
21		10	A	Lincoln City	L	0-1		3,000
22		17	H	Small Heath	W	3-2	Godsmark, Cassidy, Parkinson	10,000
23		24	A	New Brighton Tower	W	4-1	Godsmark, Collinson 2, R. Smith	8,000
24	Mar	3	H	Grimsby Town	W	1-0	Smith	
25		10	A	Woolwich Arsenal	L	1-2	Cassidy	4,000
26		17	H	Barnsley	W	3-0	Cassidy 2, Leigh	3,000
27		24	A	Leicester Fosse	L	0-2		6,000
28		31	H	Leicester Fosse	W	5-0	Godsmark 2, Cassidy 3	
29	Apr	7	H	Burslem Port Vale	L	0-1		
30		13	A	Luton Town	W	3-2	Griffiths, Gillespie, Jackson	10,000
31		14	H	Walsall	W	5-0	Errentz, Jackson 2, Gillespie, Foley	4,000
32		17	A	Walsall	D	0-0		3,000
33		21	A	Middlesbrough	L	0-2		8,000
34		28	H	Chesterfield	W	2-1	Holt, Grundy	

F.A. CUP

			Venue	Opponents	Result		Goalscorers
Qual 1	Oct	28	H	South Shore	L	1-3	Jackson

Players:
Barrett, F.; Stafford, H.; Errentz, F. C.; Morgan, W.; Fitzsimmons, D.; Cartwright, W.G.; Bryant, W.; Jackson, W.; Lee, E.; Cassidy, J.; Ambler, G.; Griffiths, W.; Bain, J.; Roberts; Collinson, J.; Gillespie, M.; Sawyer, F.; Blackmore, P.; Clark, J.; Parkinson, R.; Heathcote, J.; Godsmark, G.; Smith, R.; Foley, G.; Leigh, T.; Holt, J.; Grundy, J.

League Appearances / League Scorers

DID YOU KNOW? The first floodlit match played at Clayton was a benefit match for players Harry Stafford and Walter Cartwright, in recognition of their sterling service to the Newton Heath club. The opponents were Manchester City, the ball was gilded and the pitch illuminated by a system called 'Welles Lights'. Unfortunately the match was played in a strong gale, and there was great difficulty in keeping the lights working. As one was re-lit, another would blow-out, and when only one lamp remained alight, the referee abandoned the game. On reaching the dressing rooms the officials discovered that half the 22 players were already dressed, having left the field unnoticed in the darkness. In their anxiety to find the exit gates the spectators were falling over each other.

NEWTON HEATH v. SHEFFIELD WEDNESDAY.

Taking into consideration the importance of this fixture, the attendance of 10,000 people at Clayton, Manchester, on Saturday, was by no means gratifying. The bitterly cold weather, of course, had a deterrent effect, but all the same a much better gathering was expected. The game was of a rather rough character, and during the initial half Sheffield had somewhat the best of it, Barrett's charge being dangerously threatened on several occasions. Cassidy, Godsmark, and Parkinson put in good shots for the Heathens, but at the interval there was no score. On resuming, a disgraceful exhibition was witnessed, the referee having frequently to blow his whistle, fouls being numerous. Much ill-feeling was shown between the two teams, and Bryant, from a corner, eventually scored the only goal of the match for Newton Heath. Result: Newton Heath, one goal; Sheffield Wednesday, love. Teams:

Newton Heath: Barrett (goal), Stafford and Erentz (backs), Morgan, Griffiths, and Cartwright (half-backs), Bryant, Godsmark, Parkinson, Jackson, and Cassidy (forwards).

Sheffield Wednesday: Massey (goal), Layton and Langley (backs), Ferrier, Crawshaw, and Ruddlesdin (half-backs), Davis, Brash, Pryce, Wright, and Spiksley (forwards).

Right:
WILLIAM OWEN
Newton Heath
& Wales

Left:
WILLIAM
HEALEY
Director

SMALL HEATH v. NEWTON HEATH.

These teams were engaged at Small Heath on Saturday, 10,000 people watching the match. The home team had their captain, Alec Leake, back in his old position at centre-half, Wigmore going on the wing. Newton Heath were short of their noted outside right, Bryant. In the first half the advantage rested with Small Heath, but such a splendid defence did Barrett, in goal, and Stafford and Erentz, at back, offer, that the local team could not score, and at the interval no single point had been obtained. Five minutes after the restart Main shot past Barrett, and this proved to be the only point of the match. Both goalkeepers had plenty of work, but were equal to the demands made upon them, and Small Heath won by a goal to nothing. Teams:

Small Heath: Robinson (goal), Archer and Pratt (backs), Wigmore, Leake, and Farnall (half-backs), Wilcox, Scriven, McRoberts, Main, and Wharton (forwards).

Newton Heath: Barrett (goal), Stafford and Erentz (backs), Morgan, Griffiths, and Cartwright (half-backs), Sawyer, Jackson, Collinson, Cassidy, and Gillespie (forwards).

Referee: Mr H. Shelton (Nottingham).

Above: THE WILLIAM HEALEY CUP. Presented by Mr. Healey, the Cup was contested by Newton Heath and Manchester City in 1898 and 1899. City won on both occasions at Bank Street, by 4-2 in 1898 and 2-1 in 1899. (KM)

Top Left and Bottom Right: Match Reports from 1899/1900 season against Sheffield Wednesday, and Small Heath, later Birmingham City. (CZ)

Mr. James West appointed Secretary/Manager   *Position: 10th*

Newton Heath

Match No.	Date		Venue	Opponents	Result		Goalscorers	Attendance
1	Sept	1	A	Glossop North End	L	0-1		8,000
2		8	H	Middlesbrough	W	4-0	Jackson, Grundy, Griffiths 2	
3		15	A	Burnley	L	0-1		
4		22	H	Burslem Port Vale	W	4-0	Leigh, Schofield 2, Grundy	4,000
5		29	A	Leicester Fosse	L	0-1		
6	Oct	6	H	New Brighton Tower	W	1-0	Jackson	6,000
7		13	A	Gainsborough Trinity	W	1-0	Leigh	
8		20	H	Walsall	D	1-1	Schofield	8,000
9		27	A	Burton Swifts	L	1-3	Leigh	
10	Nov	10	A	Woolwich Arsenal	L	1-2	Jackson	8,000
11		24	A	Stockport County	L	0-1		5,000
12	Dec	1	H	Small Heath	L	0-1		
13		8	A	Grimsby Town	L	0-2		
14		15	H	Lincoln City	W	4-1	W. Morgan, Leigh 3	
15		22	A	Chesterfield	L	1-2	1 scrimmage	
16		26	H	Blackpool	W	4-0	Griffiths, Leigh, Schofield, H. Morgan	10,000
17		29	A	Glossop North End	W	3-0	Leigh 2, H. Morgan	
18	Jan	1	H	Middlesbrough	W	2-1	Schofield 2	12,000
19		12	H	Burnley	L	0-1		
20		19	A	Burslem Port Vale	L	0-2		
21	Feb	16	H	Gainsborough Trinity	D	0-0		
22		19	A	New Brighton Tower	L	0-2		
23		25	A	Walsall	D	1-1	W. Morgan	
24	Mar	2	H	Burton Swifts	W	1-0	Leigh	
25		13	H	Barnsley	W	1-0	Leigh	
26		16	H	Woolwich Arsenal	W	1-0	Leigh	
27		20	A	Leicester Fosse	L	2-3	Fisher 2	2,000
28		23	A	Blackpool	W	2-1	Griffiths 2	
29		30	H	Stockport County	W	3-1	Leigh, H. Morgan, Schofield	
30	Apr	5	A	Lincoln City	L	0-2		
31		6	H	Small Heath	L	0-1		
32		9	A	Barnsley	L	2-6	H. Morgan, Jackson	
33		13	H	Grimsby Town	W	1-0	H. Morgan (pen)	
34		27	H	Chesterfield	W	1-0	Leigh	

F.A. CUP

*Int 1	Jan	5	H	Portsmouth	W	3-0	Griffiths, Jackson, 1 o.g.	3,000
Rd 1	Feb	9	H	Burnley	D	0-0		8,000
Replay	Feb	13	A	Burnley	L	1-7	Schofield	3,000

*Int denotes Intermediate Round

Players (League): Garvey, J.; Stafford, H.; Errentz, F. C.; Morgan, W.; Griffiths, W.; Cartwright, W. G.; Schofield, J. A.; Lawson, R. R.; Leigh, T.; Jackson, J.; Grundy, J.; Whitehouse, J.; Smith, W.; Ambler, G.; Fisher, J.; Greenwood, W.; Collinson, J.; Morgan, H.; Booth, W.; Heathcote, J.; Hayes, J. V.; Whitney, J.; Johnson, S.; Sawyer; Lappin, H. H.

DID YOU KNOW? So financially destitute did the Newton Heath club become that to raise sufficient funds for the rail fares to away matches, a 'whip-round' among supporters was often necessary, and frequently the menu for the players dinner en route consisted of bottled beer and cheese. In those days of strife, the arrival of a new player at the club would cause great excitement in the environs of Clayton. Large crowds would gather at the local railway station, anxious to greet the newest capture. The crowds at Bank street however did not match the proportion, and support became so weak that the players were paid according to the gate receipts. When the attendance was particularly sparse, one player is reported to have excused himself from playing thus: "I don't think I can play today; my foot isn't right", and changed back into his civilian clothes.

Top: *NEWTON HEATH F.C. GRAND BAZAAR. February 1902. Held at the St. James Hall, Oxford Street, to aid the club's fight against bankruptcy, and from which Harry Stafford's dog's escape and capture led to Staffords meeting with Mr. J. H. Davies, and ultimately the club's reformation as Manchester United in 1902/3. (MMUSC)*

Botom: *MANCHESTER CUP WINNERS 1901/2. Newton Heath 2 Manchester City 1. 26 April 1902. This match report on the very last match played as Newton Heath is from* The Umpire *dated 27 April 1902. (KM)*

MANCHESTER CUP WINNERS 1901/2

"Good to begin well, better to end well"

NEWTON HEATH FOOTBALL CLUB.

GRAND · BAZAAR,

REPRESENTING

"SUNNY LANDS,"

IN THE

St. James's Hall,
Manchester,

WEDNESDAY, FEBRUARY 27TH.
THURSDAY, FEBRUARY 28TH.
FRIDAY, MARCH 1ST.
SATURDAY, MARCH 2ND.

Season Tickets, 3s. 6d.

PRICES OF ADMISSION
FIRST DAY 2s. 6d., after 6 p.m. 1s.
SECOND DAY 1s. all day.
THIRD DAY 1s., after 6 p.m. 6d.
FOURTH DAY, 6d. all day.

CHILDREN, HALF-PRICE.

MANCHESTER CUP.—Final.

Manchester City v. Newton Heath.— This tie was decided at Hyde-road in splendid weather, in the presence of upwards of 12,000 spectators. City played their full team, while Newton Heath were represented by Saunders in goal. It was soon apparent in which direction the sympathies of the crowd lay, for right from the initial appearance on the field of the respective teams the cheering which greeted the Heathens stood in distinct contrast to that meted out to the Manchester City players. The operations for the first fifteen minutes were almost totally in favour of Newton Heath, who, aided by the wind, kept the City defence continually on the alert. During this pressure Morgan was injured as a result of a charge by Di Jones, while on perhaps half-a-dozen occasions Hillman was called upon to display his abilities in order to keep out the Newton Heath forwards, who were striving with might and main to get the ball into the net. Presently McOustra broke away, and on nearing goal Meredith tried his hand with a shot which came in contact with a Newton Heath player, and the ball travelling to Threlfall that player dashed in and opened the score for the home side. The resumption saw the visitors on the attack, and Lappin, with a surprise shot which came in contact with a City player, forced a corner, which, however, was neutralised in consequence of a smart clearance by Hosie. The play for some time afterwards was fairly even, though the Heathens had a big advantage in the wind, but as regards actually getting the ball into goal the advantage lay with the visitors, who eventually forced a corner which was grabbed away by Hillman. In doing so, however, the City custodian sent the ball over the post line, and from the succeeding flag-kick, well placed by Threlfold, Lappin equalised the scores, a performance which was greeted by a wild outburst of enthusiasm. On resuming, Meredith and McOustra were prominent, and the former was brought down inside the penalty line, but the referee, Mr. Lewis, awarded an ordinary free kick. From this, however, Saunder's charge had a miraculous existence, the ball hovering about the goal, the Heathens' custodian once saving from Drummond from close quarters, the danger not being cleared until Threlfall had shot the ball over the line. A free kick to Manchester City, in consequence of supposed illegitimate tactics by Stafford against Threlfall, was followed by a similar concession to Newton Heath as a result of Drummond fouling an opponent, a piece of work which caused the referee to lecture the latter player, but neither kick availed the sides anything. Towards the interval, however, a splendid save by Hillman was succeeded by McOustra being presented by a practically open goal, but he shot over the bar, and half-time arrived with the score 1 goal each.

The second half opened with an attack by Newton Heath, and Hillman had the utmost difficulty in keeping his charge intact to a clever shot by Griffiths. Threlfall responded on behalf of the City, but his pass to the right failed to be reached by McOustra ere the ball crossed the goal-line. Meredith was then well fed by McOustra, but the Welshman's centre was fully accounted for by Saunders, who dashed out of goal and punched away. Soon afterwards Schofield made his way along the wing, and Jones being in a tight corner, Hunter came to his aid. The latter, however, fouled the Newton Heath forward just as he had crossed the twelve yards' line, and from the penalty kick awarded Fred Brettz gave his side the winning goal. The end came shortly afterwards with Newton Heath winners of a game in which they played with more spirit and cohesion than their opponents. Final:—

NEWTON HEATH .... 2 GOALS
MANCHESTER CITY .... 1 GOAL

Manchester F.A. Senior Cup Winners   *Position: 15th*

Newton Heath

Match No.	Date	Venue	Opponents	Result	Goalscorers	Attendance
1	Sept 7	H	Gainsborough Trinity	W 3-0	Preston 2, Lappin	3,000
2	14	A	Middlesbrough	L 0-5		12,000
3	21	H	Bristol City	W 1-0	Griffiths	7,000
4	28	A	Blackpool	W 4-2	Preston, Schofield, Griffiths, Smith	3,000
5	Oct 5	A	Stockport County	W 3-3	Schofield, Preston, Smith	5,000
6	12	A	Burton United	D 0-0		3,000
7	19	H	Glossop North End	D 0-0		3,000
8	26	H	Doncaster Rovers	W 6-0	Schofield, Coupar 2, Griffiths, Preston 2	7,000
9	Nov 9	A	West Bromwich Albion	L 1-2	Fisher	13,029
10	16	A	Woolwich Arsenal	L 0-2		3,000
11	23	H	Barnsley	W 1-0	Griffiths	4,000
12	30	A	Leicester Fosse	L 2-3	Cartwright 2	4,000
13	Dec 7	A	Preston North End	L 1-5	Preston	3,000
14	21	H	Burslem Port Vale	W 1-0	Richards	3,000
15	26	A	Lincoln City	L 0-2		4,000
16	Jan 1	H	Preston North End	L 0-1		10,000
17	4	A	Gainsborough Trinity	D 1-1	Schofield	2,000
18	18	A	Bristol City	L 0-4		6,000
19	25	H	Blackpool	L 0-1		2,500
20	Feb 1	A	Stockport County	L 0-1		1,000
21	11	H	Burnley	W 2-0	Lappin, Preston	1,000
22	15	A	Glossop North End	W 1-0	Errentz	5,000
23	22	A	Doncaster Rovers	L 0-4		3,000
24	Mar 1	H	Lincoln City	D 0-0		6,000
25	8	A	West Bromwich Albion	L 0-4		10,206
26	15	H	Woolwich Arsenal	L 0-1		4,000
27	17	A	Chesterfield	L 0-3		2,000
28	22	A	Barnsley	L 2-3	Higson, Cartwright	2,500
29	28	H	Burnley	L 0-1		1,000
30	29	H	Leicester Fosse	W 2-0	Morgna, Cartwright	2,000
31	Apr 7	H	Middlesbrough	L 1-2	Errentz	2,000
32	19	A	Burslem Port Vale	D 1-1	Coupar	
33	21	A	Burton United	W 3-1	Cartwright, Griffiths, Preston	
34	23	H	Chesterfield	W 2-0	Coupar, Preston	

F.A. CUP

Match No.	Date	Venue	Opponents	Result	Goalscorers
Int 1	Dec 14	H	Lincoln City	L 1-2	Fisher

League Appearances / League Scorers

Player	League Appearances	League Scorers
Whitehouse, J.	23	
Stafford, H.	27	
Errentz, F. C.	25	2
Morgan, W.	33	1
Banks, J.	30	
Cartwright, W. G.	29	5
Schofield, J. A.	4	4
Williams, W.	29	
Preston, S.	20	10
Lappin, H. H.	17	2
Fisher, J.	14	1
Smith, W.	8	2
Griffiths, W.	5	5
Higgins	5	
Coupar, J.	10	4
Heathcote, J.	10	
Richards, W.	3	1
Saunders, J.	8	
Hayes, J. V.	11	
Higson, J.	16	1
O'Brien, W.	7	

DID YOU KNOW? A St. Bernard dog is credited with playing a major part in saving the Newton Heath club from extinction in 1901/2, and ultimately in the formation of Manchester United. With impending fate of bankruptcy again looming, Harry Stafford organised a Bazaar in St. James Hall to raise funds. The event proved an expensive failure, but worse still for Stafford, his pet St. Bernard, acting as overnight guard-dog and still wearing a collecting box, escaped the attentions of his keeper Louis Rocca, and went out of a door into Oxford Street. Stafford advertised the loss in the press, receiving a reply from a Mr. J. H. Davies, a local Brewery owner. On collecting his pet he fell into conversation with Davies on the plight of the club. The Newton Heath club crumbled into bankruptcy and the Bailiffs took possession of the club office and contents, triumphantly seizing and carrying away a clock! An emergency meeting was called at the Islington Public Hall, Ancoats — and out of darkness cometh light! Harry Stafford announced to the assembly that he and the said Mr. Davies had devised a plan to raise sufficient capital to save the club.

Farewell to
Newton Heath

Newton Heath

HARRY STAFFORD

Mr. J. W. DAVIES

Above Top: HARRY STAFFORD, Captain of Newton Heath.

Above Bottom: MR. J. H. DAVIES, local brewery owner, who between them proposed the financial rescue plan that was to save the club from extinction and lead to the formation of Manchester United F.C.

THE FOUNDERS OF MANCHESTER UNITED

MANCHESTER UNITED

Match No.	Date	Venue	Opponents	Result	Goalscorers	Attendance
1	Sept 6	H	Gainsborough Trinity	W 1-0	Richards	20,000
2	13	H	Burton United	W 1-0	Hurst	
3	20	A	Bristol City	L 1-3	Hurst	8,000
4	27	H	Glossop North End	D 1-1	Hurst	12,000
5	Oct 4	H	Chesterfield	L 1-2	Preston, Peddie	14,000
6	11	A	Stockport County	W 1-0	Pegg	6,000
7	25	H	Woolwich Arsenal	W 1-0	Beadsworth	
8	Nov 8	A	Lincoln City	W 3-1	Peddie 2, Hurst	6,000
9	15	H	Small Heath	W 1-0	Downie	9,000
10	22	A	Leicester Fosse	D 1-1	Downie	5,000
11	Dec 6	A	Burnley	W 2-0	Pegg, 1 o.g.	2,000
12	20	H	Burslem Port Vale	D 1-1	Peddie	2,000
13	25	A	Manchester City	D 1-1	Peddie	35,000
14	26	H	Blackpool	D 2-2	Downie, Morrison	12,000
15	27	H	Barnsley	W 2-1	Peddie, Lappin	9,000
16	Jan 3	H	Gainsborough Trinity	W 3-1	Peddie, Downie, Pegg	8,000
17	10	A	Burton United	L 1-3	Peddie	5,000
18	24	H	Bristol City	L 1-2	Peddie	10,000
19	31	A	Glossop North End	W 3-1	Downie, Morrison, Griffiths	
20	Feb 14	A	Chesterfield	L 1-2	Preston	
21	21	H	Blackpool	L 0-2		
22	28	A	Doncaster Rovers	D 2-2	Morrison 2	2,000
23	Mar 7	H	Lincoln City	L 1-2	Downie	
24	9	A	Woolwich Arsenal	W 3-0	Arkesden, Pegg 2	8,000
25	21	H	Leicester Fosse	W 5-1	Griffiths, Morrison, Smith, Pegg, Peddie	
26	23	H	Stockport County	D 0-0		
27	30	A	Preston North End	L 0-1		
28	Apr 4	H	Burnley	W 4-0	Griffiths, Morrison, Peddie 2	6,000
29	10	A	Manchester City	W 2-0	Schofield 2	30,000
30	11	H	Preston North End	L 1-3	Pegg	4,000
31	13	A	Doncaster Rovers	W 4-0	Arkesden, Bell 2, Griffiths	4,000
32	18	H	Burslem Port Vale	W 2-1	Schofield 2	8,000
33	20	A	Small Heath	L 1-2	Peddie	8,000
34	25	A	Barnsley	D 0-0		2,000

F.A. CUP

Round	Date	Venue	Opponents	Result	Goalscorers	Attendance
Qual 3	Nov 1	H	Accrington	W 7-0	Williams 2 (1 pen), Morgan, Pegg, Richards, Peddie	6,000
Qual 4	Nov 13	H	Oswaldtwistle Rovers	W 3-2	Pegg, Williams (pen), unknown	8,000
Qual 5	29	H	Southport Central	W 4-1	Pegg 3, Banks	8,000
Int 1	Dec 13	H	Burton United	D 1-1	Griffiths	6,000
Replay	17	H	Burton United	W 3-1	Pegg, Peddie, Schofield	7,000
Rd 1	Feb 7	H	Liverpool	W 2-1	Peddie 2	12,000
Rd 2	21	A	Everton	L 1-3	Griffiths	15,000

League Appearances

League Scorers

Players:
Whitehouse, J.; Stafford, H.; Read, T. H.; Morgan, W.; Griffiths, W.; Cartwright, W. G.; Richards, C. H.; Schofield, J. A.; Peddie, J. H.; Williams, F.; Hurst, D. J.; Pegg, E.; Bruce, W.; Hayes, J. V.; Banks, J.; Preston, S.; Birchenough, H.; Rothwell, H.; Ball, W. H.; Beadsworth, A.; Downie, A. L. B.; Morrison, T.; Lappin, H. H.; Saunders, J.; Bell, A.; Arkesden, T. A.; Smith, L.; Street, E.; Marshall, A. G.; Fitchett, J.; Christie, J.; Cleaves, H.; Turner

DID YOU KNOW? The historic meeting that transformed the club from Newton Heath to Manchester United took place on 18 March 1902. Harry Stafford's proposal was for himself and Mr. Davies, along with three other gentlemen to each invest £500 to ensure the continuation of the club. The platform announced that a new name should be adopted, along with a new playing strip. Louis Rocca was at the meeting and related that when those present were asked for suggestions, both Manchester Celtic and Manchester Central were put forward. When neither found favour, Rocca himself shouted, "What about United?", to which there was general agreement, and the club became MANCHESTER UNITED F.C. A change of colours, to Red Shirts and White Shorts was also decided upon. The first-ever match under the new banner was actually a friendly five days later. Chas Richards was the player to score the first ever league goal for Manchester United.

A NEW GOLDEN AGE 1902-3

MANCHESTER
UNITED F.C.

Left
**ERNEST
MAGNELL**

*Appointed Secretary/Manager
in September 1903. (MMUSC)*

*CHAS E. RICHARDS
He scored the first-ever
League goal for Manchester
United, against Gainsborough
Trinity on 6 September 1902. (KM)*

MANCHESTER UNITED

Match No.	Date	Venue	Opponents	Result	Goalscorers	Attendance
1	Sept 5	A	Bristol City	D 2-2	Griffiths 2	40,000
2	12	A	Burnley	L 0-2		40,000
3	19	H	Burslem Port Vale	L* 0-1		
4	26	A	Glossop North End	W 5-0	Griffiths 2, Schofield, Downie, S. Robertson	30,000
5	Oct 3	H	Bradford City	W 3-1	Pegg 3	20,000
6	10	A	Woolwich Arsenal	L 0-4		20,000
7	17	H	Barnsley	W 4-0	Griffiths, S. Robertson, Pegg 2	20,000
8	24	A	Lincoln City	D 0-0		
9	Nov 7	H	Stockport County	W 3-1	Pegg, Arkesden, J. A. Schofield	25,000
10	14	A	Bolton Wanderers	D 0-0		
11	21	H	Preston North End	L 0-2		22,000
12	Dec 19	H	Gainsborough Trinity	W 4-2	Pegg, Arkesden, S. Robertson, Duckworth	8,000
13	25	H	Chesterfield	W 3-1	Arkesden 2, A. Robertson	8,000
14	26	A	Burton United	D 2-2	Arkesden 2	8,000
15	Jan 2	A	Bristol City	D 1-1	Griffiths	8,000
16	9	H	Burslem Port Vale	W 2-0	Arkesden, Grassam	10,000
17	16	H	Glossop North End	W 3-1	Arkesden 2, Downie	10,000
18	23	A	Bradford City	D 3-3	Griffiths, Downie, Wilkinson	15,000
19	30	H	Woolwich Arsenal	W 1-0	S. Robertson	40,000
20	Feb 13	A	Lincoln City	W 2-0	Downie, Griffiths	8,000
21	Mar 9	A	Blackpool	L 1-2	Grassam	8,000
22	12	H	Burnley	W 3-1	Grassam 2, Griffiths	
23	19	H	Preston North End	D 1-1	Arkesden	8,000
24	26	H	Grimsby Town	W 2-0	A. Robertson 2	40,000
25	28	A	Stockport County	W 3-0	Hall, Pegg, A. Robertson	6,000
26	Apr 1	A	Chesterfield	W 2-0	Bell, Hall	5,000
27	2	A	Leicester Fosse	W 1-0	McCartney	5,000
28	5	H	Barnsley	W 2-0	J. A. Schofield, Grassam	10,000
29	9	H	Grimsby Town	W 3-1	Grassam 2, J. A. Schofield	5,000
30	12	A	Blackpool	L 1-3	Grassam	10,000
31	16	H	Gainsborough Trinity	W 1-0	A. Robertson	8,000
32	23	A	Burton United	W 2-0	Arkesden, Grassam	8,000
33	25	A	Bolton Wanderers	D 0-0		5,000
34	Apr 30	H	Leicester Fosse	W 5-2	Bonthron, Griffiths, S. Robertson 2, J. A. Schofield	5,000

F.A. CUP

Int 1	Dec 12	H	Small Heath	D 1-1	J. A. Schofield	10,000
Replay	16	A	Small Heath	D 1-1	Arkesden (after extra time)	4,000
2 Replay	21	A	Small Heath	W 1-1	S. Robertson (a.e.t.) (at Bramall Lane, Sheffield)	
3 Replay	Jan 11	N	Small Heath	W 3-1	Arkesden 2, Grassam (at Hyde Road, Manchester)	12,000
Rd 1	Feb 6	H	Notts County	D 3-3	Downie, A. Robertson, Arkesden	15,000
Replay	10	A	Notts County	W 2-1	Morrison, Pegg	23,000
Rd 2	20	H	The Wednesday	L 0-6		

League Appearances
League Scorers

Players:
Sutcliffe, J. W.; Bonthron, R. P.; Read, T. H.; Downie, A. L. B.; Griffiths, W.; Robertson, A.; McCartney, J.; Gaudie, R; Robertson, T.; Arkesden, T. A.; Robertson, S.; Cartwright, W. G.; Schofield, J. A.; Hayes, J. V.; Bell, A.; Pegg, E.; Blackstock, T.; Grassam, W.; Morrison, T.; Moger, H. H.; Duckworth, R.; Wilkinson, H.; Kerr, H.; Hall, P.; Schofield, J.; Roberts, C.; Lyons, G.; Hartwell, W.

DID YOU KNOW? On the formation of the Manchester United club, Harry Stafford was appointed to take charge of team affairs, whilst James West continued as Secretary/Manager. On 29 September 1903, Mr. West resigned and was succeeded by Mr. Ernest Magnell.

During the F.A. Cup 2nd round tie against Everton at Clayton, United wore two completely different playing kits. The club's red shirts were worn as usual in the first half but due to the atrocious weather conditions, United had a change of kit at half time, and re-appeared after the break in blue and white stripes.

MANCHESTER UNITED 3 GLOSSOP NORTH END 1. 16th January 1904. The match programme for this local 'derby' at Bank Street, Clayton. Arkesden 2 and Downie scored the United goals. (JG)

THE UMPIRE. The Best Weekly Paper

Read the Special Article each week by

J. J. BENTLEY,

President of The League, and Chairman of the
Manchester United F.C.

Piccadilly Restaurant,

3 LEVER STREET, Opposite Infirmary.

All cars from the ground finish journey at the door.	Everything of the best quality and every satisfaction given.

Manchester United v. Glossop.

Saturday, January 16th.

Manchester United.

Goal
Sutcliffe
1
Full backs
Bonthron   Read
2   3
Half backs
Downie   Griffiths   Cartwright
4   5   6
Forwards
Schofield   Wilkinson
7   11
Morrison   Grassam   Arkesden
8   9   10

O

Murphy   Bainbridge
12   16
Coates   Morton   Thornley
13   14   15
Forwards
Galley   Coodall   Boden
17   18   19
Half backs
Norgrove   Hancock
20   21
Full backs
Clarke
22
Goal

Left   Right

GLOSSOP.

Referee   -   -   -   -   Mr. J. COOPER

NOTE—In case of any alteration in the teams a
notice will be sent round the ground giving the name
of the substituted player and the number of the position
in which he will play.

Manchester Evening News

FOOTBALL EDITION—

SATURDAY EVENING

Special Lengthy Reports of
MANCHESTER UNITED MATCHES.

THE MANCHESTER UNITED F.C.

OFFICIAL PROGRAMME

SEASON 1903-4

PRICE ONE PENNY

PUBLISHED UNDER THE PATRONAGE
OF THE OFFICIALS OF THE CLUB.

DYSON,

Pioneer of the Tripe Trade.

TEN SHOPS—FIND ONE.

OFFICIAL PROGRAMME 1904

MANCHESTER UNITED

Match No.	Date		Venue	Opponents	Result	Goalscorers	Attendance
1	Sept	3	A	Burslem Port Vale	D 2-2	Allan 2	10,000
2		10	H	Bristol City	W 4-1	Williams, Peddie, Robertson, Schofield	
3		17	H	Bolton Wanderers	L 1-2	Mackie	3,000
4		24	A	Glossop North End	W 2-1	Roberts, Allan	
5	Oct	8	A	Bradford City	D 1-1	Arkesden	12,000
6		15	H	Lincoln City	W 2-0	Schofield, Arkesden	
7		22	A	Leicester Fosse	W 3-0	Schofield, Peddie, Arkesden	8,000
8		29	H	Barnsley	W 4-0	Downie, Schofield, Allan, Peddie	
9	Nov	5	A	West Bromwich Albion	W 2-0	Arkesden, Williams	5,578
10		12	H	Burnley	W 1-0	Arkesden	6,500
11		19	A	Grimsby Town	W 1-0	Bell	
12	Dec	3	H	Doncaster Rovers	W 1-0	Peddie	2,500
13		10	A	Gainsborough Trinity	W 3-1	Arkesden 2, Allan	
14		17	A	Burton United	W 3-2	Peddie 3	
15		24	H	Liverpool	W 3-1	Williams, Roberts, Arkesden	30,000
16		26	H	Chesterfield	W 3-0	Allan 2, Williams	
17		31	H	Burslem Port Vale	W 6-1	Allan 3, Hayes, Arkesden, Roberts	30,000
18	Jan	2	H	Bradford City	W 7-0	Roberts 2, Peddie, Arkesden 2, Allan, 1 o.g.	30,000
19		3	A	Bolton Wanderers	W 4-2	Allan 2, Peddie, Williams	20,000
20		7	A	Bristol City	D 1-1	Arkesden	20,000
21		21	H	Glossop North End	W 4-1	Mackie 2, Arkesden, Grassam	
22	Feb	11	A	Lincoln City	L 0-3		
23		18	H	Leicester Fosse	W 4-1	Allan, Peddie 3	7,000
24		25	A	Barnsley	D 0-0		
25	Mar	4	H	West Bromwich Albion	W 2-0	Peddie, Williams	9,960
26		11	A	Burnley	L 0-2		7,500
27		18	H	Grimsby Town	W 2-1	Allan, Duckworth	
28		25	H	Blackpool	W 1-0	Grassam	
29	Apr	1	A	Doncaster Rovers	W 6-0	Duckworth 3, Beddowes, Peddie, Wombwell	8,000
30		8	A	Gainsborough Trinity	D 0-0		
31		15	H	Burton United	W 5-0	Duckworth 2, Peddie 2, Arkesden	
32		21	A	Chesterfield	L 0-2		
33		22	A	Liverpool	L 0-4		
34		24	H	Blackpool	W 3-1	Allan 2, Peddie	

League Appearances
League Scorers

F.A. CUP

Int 1	Jan	14	H	Fulham	D 2-2	Mackie, Arkesden	15,000
Replay		18	A	Fulham	D 0-0		
2 Replay		23	N	Fulham	L 0-1	(at Villa Park, Birmingham)	8,000

Players:
Moger, H. H.; Bonthron, R. P.; Hayes, J. V.; Downie, A. L. B.; Roberts, C.; Robertson, A.; Schofield, J. A.; Allan, J. T.; Mackie, C.; Peddie, J. H.; Arkesden, T. A.; Williams, H.; Bell, A.; Robertson, A.; Duckworth, R.; Hartwell, W.; Grassam, W.; Blackstock, T.; Fitchett, J.; Beddowes, J. H.; Griffiths, W.; Wombwell, R.; Valentine, R.; Holden, R. H.; Lyons, G.

DID YOU KNOW? Charlie Roberts was the first United player to be selected to represent England in 1904/5. In the same season United won 14 consecutive league matches in Division Two and enjoyed their longest run without conceding a goal. This was for 7 matches played between 15 October 1905 and 3 December 1904, and only equalled in 1924/5.

OPPOSITE PAGE:

Top Right: CHARLIE ROBERTS was the first United player to win England caps, when in 1905 he appeared in all the Home Internationals. (MMUSC).

Top Left: ENGLAND 1 SCOTLAND 0. 1 April 1905. Roberts (right) watches Herbert Smith cut out a Scottish attack. (KM)

Bottom: OFFICIAL PROGRAMME for the England v Scotland match. (KM).

UNITED'S FIRST ENGLAND CAP 1905

ENGLAND v SCOTLAND

CHARLIE ROBERTS

CRYSTAL PALACE.

OFFICIAL PROGRAMME.

INTERNATIONAL FOOTBALL MATCH.
SATURDAY, APRIL 1st, 1905.

/ England v. Scotland. O

TEAMS.

ENGLAND.	SCOTLAND.
1. Linacre (Notts Forest) *Goal.*	12. G. Wilson (Heart of Midlothian).
2. Spencer (*Capt.*) (Aston Villa).	13. P. Somers (Celtic).
3. H. Smith (Reading).	14. A. Young (Everton).
4. Ruddlesdin (Sheffield Wednesday).	15. Howie (Newcastle United).
5. Roberts (Manchester United).	16. R. Walker (Heart of Midlothian).
6. Leake (Aston Villa).	17. McWilliam (Newcastle United).
7. Sharp (Everton).	18. E. Thomson (Heart of Midlothian).
8. Bloomer (Derby County).	19. A. Aitken (Newcastle United).
9. V. J. Woodward (Tottenham Hotspur).	20. J. Watson (Sunderland).
10. Bache (Aston Villa).	21. McCombie (Newcastle United).
11. Bridgett (Sunderland).	22. Lyall (Sheffield Wednesday) *Goal.*

Colours—**White Shirts and Blue Knickers.**   *Colours*—**Primrose and Pink.**

Referee	...	...	...	...	W. NUNNERLEY (Wales).
Linesman	...	...	...	...	G. W. SIMMONS (Herts).

KICK OFF AT 3.30.   [P.T.O.

FOR CONTINUATION OF PROGRAMME SEE OTHER SIDE.

MANCHESTER UNITED

Match No.	Date	Venue	Opponents	Result	Goalscorers	Attendance
1	Sept 2	H	Bristol City	W 5-1	Sagar 3, Picken, Beddowes	20,000
2	4	H	Blackpool	W 2-1	Peddie 2	
3	9	A	Grimsby Town	W 1-0	Sagar	6,000
4	16	H	Glossop North End	W 2-1	Beddowes, Bell	10,000
5	23	A	Stockport County	W 3-1	Sagar, Peddie 2	18,000
6	30	H	Blackpool	W 1-0	Roberts	6,000
7	Oct 7	H	Bradford City	D 0-0		15,000
8	14	A	West Bromwich Albion	L 0-1		7,024
9	21	H	Leicester Fosse	W 3-2	Sagar, Peddie 2	10,000
10	28	A	Gainsborough Trinity	D 2-2	Bonthron 2	
11	Nov 4	A	Hull City	W 1-0	Picken	12,000
12		H	Lincoln City	W 2-1	Picken, Roberts	
13		A	Chesterfield	L 0-1		8,000
14	18	H	Burslem Port Vale	W 3-0	Peddie, Beddowes, 1 o.g.	
15	25	A	Barnsley	W 3-0	Beddowes, Picken, 1 o.g.	
16	Dec 2	H	Clapton Orient	W 4-0	Peddie 2, Picken 2	16,000
17	9	A	Burnley	W 3-1	Beddowes, Picken, Peddie	12,000
18	23	A	Burton United	W 2-0	Schofield 2	
19	25	H	Chelsea	D 0-0		36,000
20	30	A	Bristol City	D 1-1	Roberts	18,800
21	Jan 6	H	Grimsby Town	W 5-0	Beddowes, Picken 2	15,000
22		A	Leeds City	L 0-3		
23	20	H	Glossop North End	W 8-2	Picken 2, Peddie, Beddowes, Roberts	12,000
24	27	A	Stockport County	W 1-0	Roberts	14,000
25		H	Bradford City	W 5-1	Bell, Beddowes, Roberts, Schofield, Wombwell	10,000
26	Feb 17	H	West Bromwich Albion	D 0-0		8,000
27	Mar 3	A	Hull City	W 5-0	Picken 2, Sagar, Peddie, Peddie	16,000
28		H	Chesterfield	W 4-1	Picken 3, Sagar	
29	24	A	Burslem Port Vale	L 0-1		5,000
30	29	A	Leicester Fosse	W 5-2	Sagar 3, Peddie, Picken	
31	31	H	Barnsley	W 5-1	Sagar 2, Bell, Picken	
32	Apr 7	A	Clapton Orient	W 1-0	Wall	67,000
33	13	H	Chelsea	D 1-1	Peddie	
34	14	H	Burnley	W 2-0	Sagar	20,000
35	16	A	Gainsborough Trinity	W 1-0	Allan 2	
36	21	A	Leeds City	W 3-1	Wombwell, Peddie, Allan	10,000
37	28	H	Lincoln City	W 3-2	Allan 2, Wall	
38		H	Burton United	W 6-0	Sagar 2, Picken 2, Wall, Peddie	10,000

League Appearances / League Scorers

F.A. CUP

Round	Date	Venue	Opponents	Result	Goalscorers	Attendance
Rd 1	Jan 13	H	Staple Hill	W 7-2	Beddowes 3, Picken 2, Williams, Allan	7,500
Rd 2	Feb 3	H	Norwich City	W 3-0	Downie, Peddie, Dyer	10,000
Rd 3	24	H	Aston Villa	W 5-1	Picken 3, Peddie 2	36,500
Rd 4	Mar 10	H	Woolwich Arsenal	L 2-3	Sagar, Peddie	26,500

Players: Moger, H. H.; Bonthron, R. P.; Blackstock, T.; Downie, A. L. B.; Roberts, C.; Bell, A.; Beddowes, J. H.; Picken, J. B.; Sagar, C.; Peddie, J. H.; Arkesden, T. A.; Wombwell, R.; Montgomery, A.; Valentine, R.; Lyons, G.; Dyer, J. A.; Schofield, J. A.; Holden, R. H.; Donaghy, B.; Duckworth, J.; Williams, H.; Blew, H.; Allan, J. T.; Robertson, A.; Wall, G.

DID YOU KNOW? During the Season of 1905/6 when United clinched promotion by finishing second to Bristol City, and reached the FA Cup Quarter-Finals, they set up two club records. The 28 league wins is a record from their 38 games, not equalled until 1956/7, and the 4 defeats in 1905/6 is the fewest number incurred by a United team in a single season. The match on 31 March 1906 against Barnsley at Clayton was awarded as a Benefit for players J. A. Schofield and J. V. Hayes.

Top: MANCHESTER UNITED — DIVISION TWO RUNNERS-UP 1905/6. Back Row: Downie, Moger, Bonthron. Middle Row: J. E. Magnell (Secretary), Picken, Sagar, Blackstock, Peddie, Bacon (Trainer). Front Row: Beddowes, Roberts, Bell, Arkesden. (JG).

Bottom: WOOLWICH ARSENAL'S WIN. Cartoon from Athletic News, *12 March 1906, on United's 4th Round F.A. Cup defeat by Arsenal at Clayton. (JG).*

PROMOTION TO FIRST DIVISION 1905-6

Freeman equalizes.

Peddie gives United the lead

Bailbron puts in some vigourous kicking.

Fine tackling by Roberts.

Ritchie and Templeton provide plenty of work for Downie

Club formed into Limited Company   *Position: 8th*

MANCHESTER UNITED

Match No.	Date	Venue	Opponents	Result		Goalscorers	Attendance
1	Sept 1	A	Bristol City	W	2-1	Roberts, Picken	21,000
2	3	A	Derby County	D	2-2	Schofield 2	5,000
3	8	H	Notts County	D	0-0		20,000
4	15	A	Sheffield United	W	2-0	Downie, Bell	10,000
5	22	H	Bolton Wanderers	L	1-2	Peddie	45,000
6	29	H	Derby County	D	1-1	Bell	5,000
7	Oct 6	A	Stoke City	W	2-1	Duckworth 2	10,000
8	13	H	Blackburn Rovers	D	1-1	Wall	20,000
9	20	A	Sunderland	L	1-4	Peddie	20,000
10	27	H	Birmingham	D	1-1	Peddie 2	30,000
11	Nov 3	A	Everton	L	0-3		20,000
12	10	H	Woolwich Arsenal	W	1-0	Downie	20,000
13	17	H	The Wednesday	L	2-5	Menzies, Peddie	9,000
14	24	H	Bury	L	2-4	Peddie, Wall	30,000
15	Dec 1	A	Manchester City	L	0-3		40,000
16	15	H	Middlesbrough	W	3-1	Wall 2, Sagar	15,000
17	22	A	Preston North End	L	0-3	Turnbull	7,000
18	25	H	Newcastle United	L	1-3	Menzies	
19	26	H	Liverpool	D	0-0		
20	29	A	Aston Villa	L	0-2		
21	Jan 1	A	Bristol City	D	0-0		16,000
22	5	H	Aston Villa	W	1-0	Turnbull	4,000
23	19	H	Notts County	L	0-3		10,000
24	26	H	Sheffield United	W	2-0	Wall, Sagar	20,000
25	Feb 2	A	Bolton Wanderers	W	1-0	Turnbull	25,000
26	9	A	Newcastle United	L	0-5		35,000
27	16	H	Stoke	W	4-1	Picken 2, Meredith, 1 o.g.	16,000
28	16	H	Blackburn Rovers	W	4-2	Meredith 2, Wall, Sagar	5,000
29	23	H	Preston North End	W	3-0	Wall 2, Sagar	20,000
30	Mar 2	A	Birmingham	D	1-1	Menzies	16,000
31	16	H	Woolwich Arsenal	L	0-4		
32	25	H	Sunderland	W	2-0	Turnbull, Williams	10,000
33	30	A	Bury	W	2-1	Meredith, Menzies	20,000
34	Apr 1	H	Liverpool	W	1-0	Turnbull	40,000
35	6	H	Manchester City	D	1-1	Roberts	40,000
36	10	H	The Wednesday	W	5-0	Wall 3, Picken, Sagar	9,000
37	13	A	Middlesbrough	L	0-2		
38	22	H	Everton	W	3-0	Bannister, Turnbull, Meredith	

F.A. CUP

Rd 1	Jan 12	A	Portsmouth	D	2-2	Picken, Wall	24,329
Replay	16	H	Portsmouth	L	1-2	Wall	15,000

Player columns (with Match No. repeated at foot):

Moger, H. H.; Bonthron, R. P.; Holden, R. H.; Downie, A. L. B.; Roberts, C.; Bell, A.; Schofield, J. A.; Peddie, J. H.; Sagar, C.; Picken, J. B.; Wall, G.; Beddowes, J. H.; Yates, W.; Wombwell, R.; Buckley, F. C.; Allan, J. T.; Blackstock, T.; Duckworth, R.; Young, J.; Berry, W.; Menzies, A.; Burgess, H.; Meredith, W. H.; Bannister, J.; Turnbell, A.; Williams, S. H.

League Appearances

League Scorers

DID YOU KNOW? It was during the 1906/7 season that Billy Meredith was introduced to the United team, along with his former Manchester City team-mates Sandy Turnbull, George Livingstone, Jimmie Bannister and Herbert Burgess. All had been suspended by the F.A. and banned from playing for City again, after allegations against that club during 1904/5. Turnbull scored a winning goal on his debut against Aston Villa on New Year's Day 1907. Meredith, Burgess and Bannister also appeared in United's colours for the first time in the same match.

Top: 'A CLAYTON RECEPTION'. Manchester United 3 Manchester City 1. 21 December 1907. The noxious cloud of fumes belching from the Chemical works adjacent to Bank Street is illustrated in this cartoon from the Athletic News. *(MMUSC).*

Middle: RETURN TO FIRST DIVISION. The United playing squad for 1906/7, before the introduction following suspension of former City Stars Billy Meredith, Herbert Burgess, Sandy Turnbull, Jimmie Bannister and George Livingstone. (JG)

A Clayton reception.

A fine shot by Conlin saved by Mogrer.

HERBERT BURGESS

C. SAGAR

'MERRY' MEREDITH

MANCHESTER UNITED

Match No.	Date	Venue	Opponents	Result		Goalscorers	Attendance	Moger, H. H.	Holden, R. H.	Burgess, H.	Duckworth, R.	Roberts, C.	Bell, A.	Meredith, W. H.	Bannister, J.	Menzies, A.	Turnbull, A.	Wall, G.	Thomson, E.	Turnbull, J.	Stacey, G.	Picken, J. B.	Williamson, H.	Whiteside, K. D.	McGillivray, J.	Downie, A. L. B.	Wilson, T.	Berry, W.	Broomfield, H. C.	Halse, H. J.	Dalton, E.	Hulme, A.	Match No.
1	Sept 2	A	Aston Villa	W	4-1	Meredith 2, Bannister, Wall	20,000	1	2	3	4	5	6	7	8	9	10	11															1
2	7	H	Liverpool	W	4-0	A. Turnbull 3, Wall	20,000	1	2	3	4	5	6	7	8	9	10	11															2
3	9	H	Middlesbrough	W	2-1	A. Turnbull 2	20,000	1	2	3	4	5		7	8	9	10	11	6														3
4	14	A	Middlesbrough	L	1-2	Bannister	20,000	1	2	3	4	5	6	7	8	9	10	11															4
5	21	A	Sheffield United	W	2-1	A. Turnbull 2	25,000	1	2	3	4	5	6	7	8	9	10	11															5
6	28	A	Chelsea	W	4-1	Meredith 2, Bannister, A. Turnbull	40,000	1	2	3	4	5	6	7	8		10	11		9													6
7	Oct 5	H	Nottingham Forest	W	4-0	Bannister, Wall, J. Turnbull, 1 o.g.	30,000	1	2	3	4	5	6	7	8		10	11		9													7
8	12	A	Newcastle United	W	6-1	Wall 2, A. Turnbull, Roberts, J. Turnbull, Meredith	30,000	1	2		4	5	6	7	8		10	11		9	3												8
9	19	A	Blackburn Rovers	W	5-1	A. Turnbull 3, J. Turnbull 2	30,000	1	2	3	4	5	6	7	8		10	11		9													9
10	26	H	Bolton Wanderers	W	2-1	A. Turnbull, J. Turnbull	30,000		1	2	3	4	5	6	7	8		10	11	9													10
11	Nov 2	A	Birmingham	W	4-3	Meredith 2, J. Turnbull, Wall	25,000	1	2	3	4	5	6	7	8			11		9		10											11
12	9	H	Everton	W	4-3	Wall 2, Meredith, Roberts	35,000	1	2	3	4	5	6	7	8		10	11		9													12
13	16	A	Sunderland	W	2-1	A. Turnbull 2	32,000	1	2	3	4	5	6	7	8		10	11		9													13
14	23	H	Woolwich Arsenal	W	4-2	A. Turnbull 4	8,000	1	2	3	4	5	6	7	8		10			9		11											14
15	30	A	The Wednesday	L	0-2		43,143	1	2	3	4	5	6	7	8		10	11		9													15
16	Dec 7	H	Bristol City	W	2-1	Wall 2	30,000	1	2		4	5	6	7	8		10	11		9	3												16
17	14	H	Notts County	D	1-1	Meredith	8,000	1	2	3	4	5	6	7	8		10	11		9													17
18	21	H	Manchester City	W	3-1	A. Turnbull 2, Wall	40,000	1	2	3	4	5	6	7	8		10	11		9													18
19	25	H	Bury	W	2-1	Meredith, J. Turnbull	45,000	1	2		4	5	6	7	8		10	11		9	3												19
20	28	A	Preston North End	D	0-0		18,000	1	2		4	5	6	7	8		10	11		9	3												20
21	Jan 1	A	Bury	W	1-0	Wall	29,500	1	2		4	5	6	7	8		10	11		9	3												21
22	18	A	Sheffield United	L	0-2		20,000	1	2	3			6	7	8			11		9		10	4	5									22
23	25	H	Chelsea	W	1-0	J. Turnbull	30,000	1	2	3		5	6	7		10		11		9		8			4								23
24	Feb 8	A	Newcastle United	D	1-1	J. Turnbull	50,000	1	2	3	4		6	7	8		10	11		9			5										24
25	15	H	Blackburn Rovers	L	1-2	A. Turnbull	10,000	1	2	3	4	5	6	7	8		10			9				11									25
26	29	H	Birmingham	W	1-0	A. Turnbull	14,000	1	2		4	5	6	7	8		10	11		9	3												26
27	Mar 14	H	Sunderland	W	3-0	Bell, Wall, Berry	12,000	1		3	4	5	6	7	8		10	11										9					27
28	21	A	Woolwich Arsenal	L	0-1					3	4	5	6	7	8			11				2	10					9	1				28
29	25	A	Liverpool	L	4-7	Wall 2, J. Turnbull, Bannister	15,000			3	4	5	6	7	8			11		9		2	10						1				29
30	28	H	The Wednesday	W	4-1	Wall 2, A. Turnbull, Halse	12,000			3	4		6	7	8		10	11				2					5		1	9			30
31	Apr 4	A	Bristol City	D	1-1	Wall	15,000			3	4	5	6	7	8		10	11				2							1	9			31
32	8	A	Everton	W	3-1	Halse, A. Turnbull, Wall	17,000			3	4	5		7	8		10	11				2					6		1	9			32
33	11	H	Notts County	L	0-1		20,000			3	4		6	7	8		10	11		9	2						5	7	1				33
34	17	A	Nottingham Forest	L	0-2		20,000			3	4	5	6	7		10	11			9	2								1	8			34
35	18	A	Manchester City	D	0-0		40,000			2		5	6	7	8		10	11		9	3						4		1				35
36	20	H	Aston Villa	L	1-2	Picken	25,000			2		5	6	7	8			11		10	3	9					4		1				36
37	22	A	Bolton Wanderers	D	2-2	Halse, Stacey	16,000			2				7	8		11	5			3	10					4		1	9	6		37
38	25	H	Preston North End	W	2-1	Halse, 1 o.g.	20,000	1				6	7	8		11	5		2	10						4			9	3			38

| | | League Appearances | | 28 | 26 | 28 | 35 | 32 | 35 | 37 | 36 | 6 | 26 | 36 | 3 | 26 | 18 | 18 | 1 | 1 | 1 | 9 | 1 | 3 | 10 | 6 | 1 | 1 |
| | | League Scorers | | | | | | | 2 | 1 | 10 | 5 | | 25 | 19 | | 10 | 1 | 1 | | | | | | 1 | 4 | | 2 o.g.s |

F.A. CUP

	Date	Venue	Opponents	Result		Goalscorers	Attendance	Moger	Holden	Burgess	Duckworth	Roberts	Bell	Meredith	Bannister	Menzies	A.Turnbull	Wall	Thomson	J.Turnbull	Stacey	Picken												
Rd 1	Jan 11	H	Blackpool	W	3-1	Wall 2, Meredith	11,747	1	2			5	7	8			10	11		6	9	3												
Rd 2	Feb 1	H	Chelsea	W	1-0	A. Turnbull	25,184	1	2	3	4	5	6	7	8		10	11		9														
Rd 3	Feb 22	A	Aston Villa	W	2-0	A. Turnbull, Wall	45,000	1		3	4		5	6	7	8		10	11		2							9						
Rd 4	Mar 7	A	Fulham	L	1-2	J. Turnbull	41,000	1		3	4	5	6	7	8			10	11		9	2												

DID YOU KNOW? At the end of Season 1907/8 which had seen United become League Champions for the first time, many of the teams players found themselves ostracised by the authorities because of their influence in the reformation of the Players Union. A strike was threatened in 1909, the United Union contingent called themselves 'The Outcasts' and had to do their pre-season training at Fallowfield. The F.A. and the Football League averted a strike by the players by recognising the Union just prior to the following season. United were the first-ever winners of the F.A. Charity Shield, defeating QPR 4-0 on 29 August 1908 at Stamford Bridge, after a 1-1 draw at Park Royal.

FOOTBALL LEAGUE CHAMPIONS 1907-8

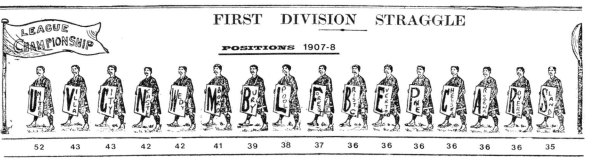

FIRST DIVISION STRAGGLE

POSITIONS 1907-8

LEAGUE CHAMPIONSHIP

UNITED	V'LLA	CITY	N'ASTL	WED'Y	M'DRO	BURY	L'POOL	P'REST	BRISTOL C	EVERTON	P'NE	C'ELSEA	ARSENAL	R'OVERS	S'LAND
52	43	43	42	42	41	39	38	37	36	36	36	36	36	36	35

Top: LEAGUE CHAMPIONS & CHARITY SHIELD WINNERS 1908. The team also won the Manchester Cup, which is on the right. (JG)

Middle: SANDY TAKES A TUMBLE. Fulham 2 Manchester United 1. F.A. Cup 4th Round. 9 March 1908. Sandy Turnbull in typical aggressive style at Craven Cottage. (KM)

Bottom Right: 'THE OUTCASTS'. Some of the United players who helped form the Players' Union. (KM)

MANCHESTER UNITED

Match No.	Date	Venue	Opponents	Result	Goalscorers	Attendance
1	Sept 5	A	Preston North End	W 3-0	J. Turnbull 2, Halse	16,000
2	7	H	Bury	W 2-1	J. Turnbull 2	28,000
3	12	H	Middlesbrough	W 6-3	J. Turnbull 4, Wall, Halse	40,080
4	19	A	Manchester City	W 2-1	J. Turnbull, Halse	28,000
5	26	A	Liverpool	W 3-2	Halse 2, J. Turnbull	25,000
6	Oct 3	A	Bury	D 2-2	Halse, Wall	14,000
7	10	H	Sheffield United	D 2-2	Bell 2	50,000
8	17	A	Aston Villa	L 1-3	Halse	15,000
9	24	H	Sunderland	W 2-2	A. Turnbull 2	30,000
10	31	A	Nottingham Forest	L 1-6	A. Turnbull	15,000
11	Nov 7	H	Chelsea	L 0-1		16,000
12	14	A	Blackburn Rovers	W 3-1	Wall, J. Turnbull, Halse	28,000
13	21	H	Bradford City	W 2-0	Picken, Wall	15,000
14	28	A	The Wednesday	W 3-1	Halse, J. Turnbull, Picken	20,000
15	Dec 5	H	Everton	L 2-3	Halse, Bannister	38,000
16	12	H	Leicester Fosse	W 4-2	Wall 3, Picken	14,000
17	19	A	Woolwich Arsenal	W 1-0	Wall	12,000
18	25	H	Newcastle United	L 1-2	Wall	45,000
19	26	A	Newcastle United	L 1-2		40,000
20	Jan 1	H	Notts County	W 4-3	Halse 2, A. Turnbull, Roberts	18,000
21	2	H	Preston North End	L 0-2		18,000
22	9	A	Middlesbrough	L 0-5		12,000
23	23	A	Manchester City	W 3-1	Livingstone 2, Wall	30,000
24	30	A	Liverpool	L 1-3	A. Turnbull	40,000
25	Feb 13	A	Sheffield United	D 0-0		12,000
26	27	A	Nottingham Forest	L 0-2		
27	Mar 13	A	Chelsea	D 1-1	Wall	28,000
28	15	H	Sunderland	D 2-2	J. Turnbull, Payne	
29	20	H	Blackburn Rovers	L 0-3		
30	31	H	Aston Villa	L 0-2		
31	Apr 3	A	The Wednesday	L 0-1		10,000
32	10	H	Bristol City	L 0-1		20,000
33	12	H	Everton	D 2-2	J. Turnbull 2	10,000
34	12	A	Bristol City	L 0-1		20,000
35	13	A	Notts County	W 1-0	Picken	15,471
36	17	A	Leicester Fosse	W 2-3	Wall, J. Turnbull	25,000
37	27	H	Woolwich Arsenal	L 1-4	J. Turnbull	10,000
38	29	A	Bradford City	L 0-1		

F.A. CUP

Rd 1	Jan 16	H	Brighton	W 1-0	Halse	8,074
Rd 2	Feb 6	H	Everton	W 1-0	Halse	38,217
Rd 3	20	H	Blackburn Rovers	W 6-1	A. Turnbull 3, J. Turnbull 2, Livingstone	40,000
Rd 4	Mar 6	A	Burnley	L 0-1	Abandoned after 72 minutes — inclement weather	15,471
Rd 4	10	A	Burnley	W 3-2	Halse, J. Turnbull 2	(Replayed Tie) 25,000
S/F	27	N	Newcastle United	W 1-0	Wall, J. Turnbull	(at Bramall Lane, Sheffield) 40,118
FINAL	Apr 24	N	Bristol City	W 1-0	A. Turnbull	(at Crystal Palace) 71,401

Players: Moger, H. H.; Stacey, G.; Burgess, H.; Duckworth, R.; Roberts, C.; Bell, A.; Meredith, W. H.; Halse, H. J.; Turnbull, J.; Picken, J. B.; Wall, G.; Christie, D.; Bannister, J.; Downie, A. L. B.; Hardman, H. P.; Turnbull, A.; Hulme, A.; Wilcox, T. W. J.; Linkson, O. H. S.; Thomson, E.; Hayes, J. V.; Curry, J.; Berry, W.; Livingstone, G. T.; Payne, E.; Donnelly, A.; Holden, R. H.; McGillivray, J.; Ford, J. B.; Quinn, J. J.

DID YOU KNOW? When United won the F.A. Cup in 1908/9, it is recorded that a proud Mancunian businessman had a replica of the Cup made for himself. This was against F.A. Cup rules, the F.A. ordered a new trophy to be made — the present cup — and copyrighted.

OPPOSITE PAGE:

Top: F.A. CUP WINNERS 1909. A Civic Reception was held in honour of the United players who beat Bristol City in the Cup Final. Captain Charlie Roberts shows off the trophy on the steps of the Manchester Town Hall. (BNPC)

Middle: MANCHESTER UNITED 1908/9 Playing Squad. (JG)

Bottom Right: CUP WINNERS RETURN: A horse-drawn carriage embarks from Central Station carrying the United party on a triumphant return to Manchester. (MMUSC)

Bottom Left: MEREDITH'S SUSPENSION. This cartoon comments on the suspension of Billy Meredith, after being sent-off in the 1st Round match against Brighton. He missed the cup-ties against Everton and Blackburn. (MMUSC)

F.A. CUP WINNERS 1908/9

THE ENGLISH CUP

MAROONED.

NO CUP TIES PLAYED HERE

SUSPENSION ISLAND

MANCHESTER UNITED

Match No.	Date	Venue	Opponents	Result	Goalscorers	Attendance
1	Sept 1	H	Bradford City	W 1-0	Wall	13,000
2	4	H	Bury	W 2-0	J. Turnbull 2	15,000
3	6	A	Notts County	W 2-1	J. Turnbull, Wall	15,000
4	11	A	Tottenham Hotspur	D 2-2	J. Turnbull, Wall	32,375
5	18	H	Preston North End	D 1-1	Roberts	15,000
6	25	A	Notts County	W 2-3	A. Turnbull 2	12,000
7	Oct 2	H	Newcastle United	D 1-1	Wall	27,000
8	9	A	Liverpool	L 2-3	A. Turnbull 2	30,000
9	16	H	Aston Villa	W 2-0	Halse, A. Turnbull	
10	23	A	Sheffield United	W 1-0	Wall	
11	30	H	Woolwich Arsenal	W 1-0	Wall	10,000
12	Nov 6	A	Bolton Wanderers	W 3-2	Homer 2, Halse	
13	13	H	Chelsea	W 2-0	A. Turnbull, Wall	14,000
14	20	A	Blackburn Rovers	L 2-3	Homer 2	35,000
15	27	H	Nottingham Forest	L 2-6	Halse, Wall	10,000
16	Dec 4	A	Sunderland	L 0-3		14,000
17	18	H	Middlesbrough	W 2-1	A. Turnbull, Homer	12,000
18	25	H	The Wednesday	L 0-3		30,000
19	27	A	The Wednesday	L 1-4	Homer	25,000
20	Jan 1	H	Bradford City	W 2-0	Wall (pen), A. Turnbull	30,000
21	8	A	Bury	D 1-1	Homer	30,000
22	22	H	Tottenham Hotspur	W 5-0	Roberts 2, Hooper, Connor, Meredith	8,000
23	Feb 5	H	Preston North End	L 0-1		
24	12	A	Newcastle United	W 4-3	A. Turnbull 2, Roberts, Blott	30,000
25	19	A	Liverpool	L 3-4	A. Turnbull, Homer, Wall (at Old Trafford)	50,000
26	26	A	Aston Villa	L 1-7	Meredith	40,000
27	Mar 5	H	Sheffield United	W 1-0	Picken	40,000
28	12	A	Woolwich Arsenal	D 0-0		40,000
29	19	H	Bolton Wanderers	W 5-0	Picken, Meredith, Wall, J. Turnbull, Halse	45,000
30	25	H	Bristol City	W 2-1	J. Turnbull, Picken	30,000
31	26	A	Chelsea	D 1-1	J. Turnbull	
32	28	A	Bristol City	L 1-2	Meredith	18,000
33	Apr 2	H	Blackburn Rovers	W 2-0	Halse 2	
34	6	H	Everton	W 3-2	J. Turnbull 2, Meredith	
35	9	A	Nottingham Forest	L 0-2		8,000
36	16	H	Sunderland	W 2-0	A. Turnbull, Wall	
37	23	A	Everton	D 3-3	Homer, Wall, A. Turnbull	
38	30	H	Middlesbrough	W 4-1	Picken 4	

League Appearances / League Scorers

Players: Moger, H. H.; Stacey, G.; Hayes, J. V.; Duckworth, R.; Roberts, C.; Bell, A.; Halse, H. J.; Bannister, J.; Turnbull, J.; Turnbull, A.; Wall, G.; Livingstone, E. T.; Picken, J. B.; Downie, A. L. B.; Blott, S. P.; Meredith, W. H.; Round, E.; Ford, J. B.; Homer, T. P.; Holden, R. H.; Burgess, H.; Donnelly, A.; Whalley, A.; Connor, E.; Quinn, J. J.; Hooper, A.; Curry, J.

F.A. CUP						
Rd 1	Jan 15	A	Burnley	L 0-2		

DID YOU KNOW? United moved grounds again in 1909/10 after nearly eighteen years at Clayton. The whole club was moved "lock, stock and barrel" to Old Trafford, on a site chosen and purchased personally by the Chairman Mr. J. H. Davies, for a sum of £60,000. The final match at the Bank Street ground was against Tottenham Hotspur before 8,000 spectators on 22 January 1910, the players signed off winning 5-0 and Billy Meredith is credited with scoring the last goal on that ground. Old Trafford was opened on 19 February 1910, with Liverpool the visitors and a crowd of 50,000. Sandy Turnbull scored United's first goal on the new ground, but Liverpool won 4-3.

OPPOSITE PAGE:

Top Right: OLD TRAFFORD 1910. An aerial view of the new ground, opened in February 1910. (MMUSC)

Top Left: THE CUP TEAM OF 1909. From 'The Complete Collection of English Cup Winners 1884-1933. (KM)

Middle: FA CUP FINAL 1909. Manchester United 1 Bristol City 0. Crystal Palace. 24 April 1909. The Official Match Programme. (BH)

Bottom Right: CUP WINNING GOAL. Billy Meredith (left) watches Sandy Turnbull's shot deceive the City keeper to enter the net in the Final. (MMUSC)

Bottom Left: CAPTAIN CHARLIE ROBERTS leads out the team for the final at the Palace. (MMUSC)

Bottom Centre: THE NEW F.A. CUP. The present Cup was introduced in 1910, the old trophy was withdrawn (after being illegally reproduced in Manchester) and presented to Lord Kinnaird.

FA CUP HOLDERS MOVE TO OLD TRAFFORD 1910

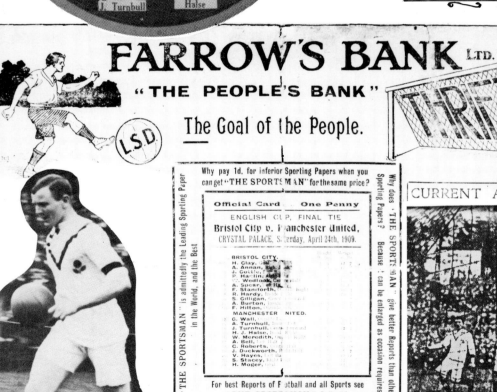

MANCHESTER UNITED

Match No.	Date		Venue	Opponents	Result		Goalscorers	Attendance	Moger, H. H.	Holden, R. H.	Stacey, G.	Duckworth, R.	Roberts, C.	Bell, A.	Meredith, W. H.	Halse, H. J.	West, E. J.	Turnbull, A.	Wall, G.	Hayes, J. V.	Linkson, O. H. S.	Livingstone, G. T.	Picken, J. B.	Connor, E.	Curry, J.	Hooper, A.	Homer, T. P.	Whalley, A.	Donnelly, A.	Sheldon, J.	Edmonds, H.	Hofton, L.	Hodge, J.	Blott, S. P.	Match No.
1	Sept	1	A	Woolwich Arsenal	W	2-1	West, Halse		1	2	3	4	5	6	7	8	9	10	11																1
2		3	H	Blackburn Rovers	W	3-2	West, Meredith, Turnbull		1	2	3	4	5	6	7	8	9	10	11																2
3		10	A	Nottingham Forest	L	1-2	Turnbull	20,000	1		2	4	5	6	7	8	9	10	11	3															3
4		17	H	Manchester City	W	2-1	West, Turnbull	50,000	1		3	4	5	6	7	8	9	10	11		2														4
5		24	A	Everton	W	1-0	Turnbull	30,000	1	2	3	4	5	6	7	8	9	10	11																5
6	Oct	1	H	The Wednesday	W	3-2	Wall 2, West	22,000	1	2	3	4	5	6	7	8	9	10	11																6
7		8	A	Bristol City	W	1-0	Halse	20,000	1	2	3		5	6	7	8	9		11		4	10													7
8		15	H	Newcastle United	W	2-0	Halse, Turnbull	50,000	1	2	3	4	5	6	7	8	9	10	11		6														8
9		22	A	Tottenham Hotspur	D	2-2	West 2	28,000	1	2	3	4	5		7	8	9	10			6		11												9
10		29	H	Middlesbrough	L	1-2	Turnbull		1		3	4	5		7	8	9	10		2	6		11												10
11	Nov	5	A	Preston North End	W	2-0	West, Turnbull		1		3	4	5		7	8	9	10		2		11	6												11
12		12	H	Notts County	D	0-0		16,000	1		3	4	5		7	8	9	10	11	2			6												12
13		19	A	Oldham Athletic	W	3-1	Turnbull 2, Wall	20,000	1		3		5		7	8	9	10	11	2	4		6												13
14		26	A	Liverpool	L	2-3	Roberts, Turnbull		1		3		5		7	8		10	11	2	4			6	9										14
15	Dec	3	H	Bury	W	3-2	Homer 2, Turnbull		1		3		5					10	11	2	4	8		6	9										15
16		10	A	Sheffield United	L	0-2		9,500	1	2	3		5		7			10	11		4	8			9	6									16
17		17	H	Aston Villa	W	2-0	West, Turnbull		1		3		5		7		9	10	11		8					4	2								17
18		24	A	Sunderland	W	2-1	Meredith, Turnbull	24,000	1		3		5	6	7		9	10	11		8					4	2								18
19		26	H	Woolwich Arsenal	W	5-0	West 2, Picken 2, Meredith		1		3		5	6	7		9	10	11		8					4	2								19
20		27	A	Bradford City	L	0-1		38,000	1		3		5				9	10	11	6	8					4	2	7							20
21		31	A	Blackburn Rovers	L	0-1			1		3		5	6			9	10	11		8					4	2	7							21
22	Jan	2	H	Bradford City	W	1-0	Meredith	35,000	1		3			6	7		9	10	11	4	8					5	2								22
23		7	A	Nottingham Forest	W	4-2	Wall, Picken, Homer, 1 o.g.	18,000	1		3			6	7		9		11		10					8	4	2							23
24		21	A	Manchester City	D	1-1	Turnbull		1		3	4	5	6	7	8	9	10	11								2								24
25		28	H	Everton	D	2-2	Duckworth, Wall		1		3	4	5	6			8	9	10	11							2	7							25
26	Feb	11	H	Bristol City	W	3-1	Picken, West, Homer	17,000			3	4	5	6	7		9		11							8			2	1				26
27		18	A	Newcastle United	W	1-0	Halse				4	5	6	7	8	9		11							3		1	2					27
28	Mar	4	A	Middlesbrough	D	2-2	West, Turnbull				3	4		6	7		9	10	11							8	5	2		1				28
29		11	H	Preston North End	W	5-0	West, Duckworth, Turnbull, Connor				3	4	5	6	7		9	10				8	11					1	2				29
30		15	H	Tottenham Hotspur	W	3-2	Meredith, West, Turnbull	13,000			3	4	5	6	7		9	10				8	11					1	2				30
31		18	A	Notts County	L	0-1		14,000			3	4	5	6	7		9	10				8	11			2		1					31
32		25	H	Oldham Athletic	D	0-0		35,000			3	4	5	6	7		9	10								8	1	2				32
33	Apr	1	H	Liverpool	W	2-0	West 2	25,000			3		5	6	7	8	9	10					4			11	1	2				33
34		8	A	Bury	W	3-0	Homer 2, Halse				3		5	6	7	8		11	10						9	4		1	2				34
35		15	A	Sheffield United	D	1-1	West	25,000			3		5	6	7	8		11	10						9	4		1	2				35
36		17	A	The Wednesday	D	0-0		25,000					5	7	8	11	10					9			4	3		1	2	6			36
37		22	A	Aston Villa	L	2-4	Halse 2	50,000			3	4		6	7	8	9	10				11				5			1	2			37
38		29	H	Sunderland	W	5-1	Halse 2, West, Turnbull, 1 o.g.	12,000			3	4		6	7	8	9	10								5	2		1		6	11	38
				League Appearances					25	8	36	22	33	27	35	23	35	35	26	1	7	10	14	7	5	2	7	15	15	5	13	9	2	1	
				League Scorers								2	1		5	9	19	18	5				4	1									2 o.g.s		

		F.A. CUP																																		
Rd 1	Jan	14	A	Blackpool	W	2-1	Picken, West	20,000	1		3	4	5	6	7		9	10	11							8			2					
Rd 2	Feb	4	H	Aston Villa	W	2-1	Halse, Wall	65,101	1		3	4	5	6	7	8	9	10	11										2					
Rd 3		25	A	West Ham United	L	1-2	A. Turnbull	26,000			3	4	5	6	7	8	9	10	11										2	1				

DID YOU KNOW? United won their second League Championship in 1910/11. During the League match at Oldham on 19 November 1910, Sandy Turnbull was cautioned for remarks he made to the referee Mr. Lewis, who warned him that if he repeated the offence he would be sent-off. Sandy remained quiet until the end of the game, when he approached the referee, who was expecting an apology. "Well Turnbull, what do you want?" he queried. "I only want to tell you that I have said it again — but you didn't hear me", replied Sandy. Mr. Lewis returned to his dressing room with a smile on his face. The League match against Newcastle on 15 October 1910 was awarded a Benefit for Richard Holden and John Picken.

OPPOSITE PAGE:

Top: MANCHESTER UNITED CHAMPIONS. The news headlines tell the story in The Umpire 30 April 1911. (KM)

Middle: LEAGUE CHAMPIONS 1910/11. Back Row: Green, Halse, A. Nuttall, J. Nuttall, J. Broad. Middle Row: Bacon (Trainer), Meredith, Hodge, Stacey, Whalley, Holden, Moger, Stanford, Turnbull, Mr. Magnall (Secretary). Front Row: Homer, Conner, C. Roberts, West, Bell, Linkson. Squatting: Aspinall, Sheldon, Donnelly. (JG)

Bottom: FIRST DIVISION STRAGGLE. Final positions in United's Second Championship season. (KM)

FOOTBALL LEAGUE CHAMPIONS 1910/11

MANCHESTER UNITED CHAMPIONS.

VILLA DISAPPOINTED.

Bristol City Drop Out.

EVERTON SAVE BURY.

ROVERS WIN ON TEESSIDE.

(By "RARA AVIS.")

After much moaning and groaning, intermixed with ventilation, the football season has come to a close. Rarely, indeed, have the vital issues been delayed until the very last, as they have been on this occasion, which in a way is just as it should be—at any rate the treasurers of the League clubs will tell you so.

To win the Championship the Villa had to draw at Liverpool, though in the event of Manchester United beating Sunderland at Old Trafford by a fairly substantial margin. As

second goal of the afternoon with a fast shot. Stewart put the ball into the net close on the interval, but was ruled offside, to the indignation of the crowd.

The teams dispensed with the customary rest, and on re-starting the home eleven tried desperately to get on level terms. Duncan once giving Smith a rare handful to save, but taking Newcastle's shooting all round it was generally too wild to be effective, although thrice in succession Smith saved well-meant attempts at scoring. Manchester, with a goal ahead, were playing a cool game, and dealt with Newcastle's rushes in a business-like manner, and it did not appear as if the Tynesiders would manage to equalise affairs until hands just outside the penalty area against Kelso enabled Willis to score the United's second goal, thus placing the teams on a level footing, this being after 17 minutes work. Then a penalty was given against Holford for handling, and M'Cracken made no mistake with his kick, sending the ball swiftly past Smith; but Manchester should have got on level terms again on resuming, Wynn putting the ball over the bar with no one to beat—a glorious chance wasted. Allan followed this up with an offside goal for Newcastle, and then we had a sensational rush away, and the United defence being drawn out of goal, Roe had an easy task to place

BRAVO, UNITED !

Sunderland Well Beaten.

GOOD WIND-UP.

(By "THE GENERAL")

MANCHESTER UNITED 5 SUNDERLAND 1

When Manchester United won the League Championship at the close of the season 1907-8 they put up a new record in scoring fifty-two points. Yesterday they equalled that performance and the same number of points proved enough to again carry off the championship, Liverpool helping the Manchester team to this end by beating Aston Villa.

It has been a strenuous season, and I feel sure the Manchester players would have created another record in points had it not been for rank bad luck in the shape of injuries, as well as other misfortunes on the field of play. But as these accidents come to all teams and have to be counted in the game, the Manchester United players and directors will rest content that matters have ended so well, and that they can go away until next September with the knowledge that they have done their best and have pleased their many thousands of faithful followers. I hope and trust they will be as keen next season, when the club will have been formed into a limited

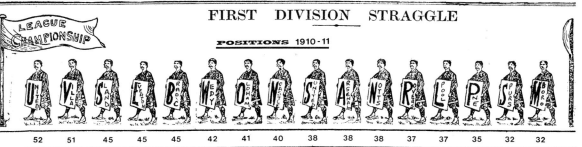

FIRST DIVISION STRAGGLE

POSITIONS 1910-11

UNITED	VILLA	S'LAND	EVER	B.RC'D	W'DY	L'HAM	C'ASTLE	U'NITED	A'RS'L	N'OTTS	R'OV'RS	L'POOL	P'NE	S'PURS	M'BORO
52	51	45	45	45	42	41	40	38	38	38	37	37	35	32	32

MANCHESTER UNITED

Match No.	Date		Venue	Opponents	Result	Goalscorers	Atten-dance	Edmonds, H.	Holton, L.	Stacey, G.	Duckworth, R.	Roberts, C.	Bell, A.	Meredith, W. H.	Halse, H.	Homer, T. P.	Turnbull, A.	Wall, G.	Anderson, G.	Hamill, M.	Sheldon, J.	West, E. J.	Holden, R. H.	Donnelly, A.	Whalley, A.	Blott, S. P.	Moger, H. H.	Linkson, O. H. S.	McCartney, P.	Livingstone, G. T.	Hodge, J.	Royals, E. J.	Nuttall, T. A.	Capper, A.	Knowles, F.	Match No.
1	Sept	2	A	Manchester City	D	0-0	40,000	1	2	3	4	5	6	7	8	9	10	11																		1
2		9	H	Everton	W	2-1	Halse, Turnbull	30,000	1	2	3	4	5	6	7	8		10	11	9																		2
3		16	A	West Bromwich Albion	L	0-1		34,921	1	2	3	4	5	6	7	9		10	11	8																		3
4		23	H	Sunderland	D	2-2	Stacey 2	15,000	1	2	3	4	5	6	7	9		10	11	8																		4
5		30	A	Blackburn Rovers	D	2-2	West 2	30,000	1	2	3	4	5	6		8		10	11			7	9															5
6	Oct	7	H	The Wednesday	W	3-1	Halse 2, West	30,000	1	2	3	4	5	6	7	8		10	11			9																6
7		14	A	Bury	W	1-0	Turnbull	14,000	1	2	3	4	5	6	7	8		10	11			9																7
8		21	H	Middlesbrough	L	3-4	Halse, Turnbull, West	18,000	1		3	4	5	6	7	8		10	11			9	2															8
9		28	A	Notts County	W	1-0	Turnbull		1		3		5	6	7	8		10				9		2	4	11												9
10	Nov	4	H	Tottenham Hotspur	L	1-2	Halse	25,000	1		3		5	6	7	8		10	11			9		2	4													10
11		11	H	Preston North End	D	0-0		15,000	1		3	4	5	6	7	8		10				9		2		11												11
12		18	A	Liverpool	L	2-3	West, Roberts		1		3	4	5	6	7	8		10				9		2		11												12
13		25	H	Aston Villa	W	3-1	West 2, Roberts	25,101			3	4	5	6	7	8		10	11			9					1	2									13
14	Dec	2	A	Newcastle United	W	3-2	West 2, Halse	40,000			3	4	5	6	7	8		10	11			9						2									14
15		9	H	Sheffield United	W	1-0	Halse		1		3	4	5	6	7	8		10	11			9						2									15
16		16	A	Oldham Athletic	D	2-2	West, Turnbull		1		3	4	5	6	7	8		10	11			9						2									16
17		23	H	Bolton Wanderers	W	2-0	Halse, Turnbull	35,000	1		3	4	5	6	7	8		10	11			9						2									17
18		25	H	Bradford City	L	0-1		50,000			3	4	5		7	8		10	11			9		6			1	2									18
19		26	A	Bradford City	W	1-0	West	38,000			3	4	5		7			10	11	8		9		6				2									19
20		30	H	Manchester City	D	0-0		41,743			3	4	5		7			10	11	8		9						2									20
21	Jan	1	H	Woolwich Arsenal	W	2-0	Meredith, West				3	4	5	6	7			10	11	8		9						2									21
22		6	A	Everton	L	0-4						4	5	6	7				11		8	9	2	3		10											22
23		20	H	West Bromwich Albion	L	1-2	Wall	12,000			3	4	5	6	7	8		10	11					2					9								23
24		27	A	Sunderland	L	0-5					3	4	5	6	7			10	11	8				2		9											24
25	Feb	10	A	The Wednesday	L	0-3		19,000	1					6	7			10	11		8	9	2		5	4											25
26		17	H	Bury	D	0-0			1				5	7	8			10	11		9	2										4	6				26
27	Mar	2	H	Notts County	W	2-0	West 2		1		3	4	5			8		10	11			7	9					2					6				27
28		16	A	Preston North End	D	0-0			1			4	5		7	8			11		10	9	3					2					6				28
29		23	H	Liverpool	D	1-1	Nuttall					4	5		7					8		9	3					2			6	1	10	11			29
30		30	A	Aston Villa	L	0-6		15,000				4			7	8		10				9	3		11			2			6	1				5	30
31	Apr	5	A	Woolwich Arsenal	L	1-2	Turnbull		1					7	4		10	11		8		9	3					2			6					5	31
32		6	A	Newcastle United	L	0-2								6	7			10	11		8	9	3				1	2			4				5	32
33		9	A	Tottenham Hotspur	D	1-1	Wall	14,600	1					6	7			10	11		8	9	3					2			4					5	33
34		13	A	Sheffield United	L	1-6	Nuttall	8,000	1			5	6						11		8	7	9	3				2			4		10				34
35		17	A	Middlesbrough	L	0-3													11		7	9	3		1	2			4		10				35
36		20	H	Oldham Athletic	W	3-1	West 2, Wall	14,000			3		5	6	7				11		8	9						1	2				10	4			36
37		27	A	Bolton Wanderers	D	1-1	Meredith				3		5	6	7				11		8	9						1	2				10	4			37
38		29	H	Blackburn Rovers	W	3-1	Meredith, Hamill, West	59,300			3		5	6	7				11		8	9						1	2				10	4			38

| | | League Appearances | | | 29 | 7 | 29 | 26 | 32 | 31 | 35 | 24 | 1 | 30 | 33 | 11 | 16 | 5 | 32 | 6 | 13 | 6 | 8 | 7 | 21 | 1 | 1 | 10 | 2 | 6 | 1 | 7 |
| | | League Scorers | | | | | | | | | 1 | | 2 | | 3 | 8 | | 8 | 3 | | 1 | | 17 | | | | | 2 | | |

				F.A. CUP																														
Rd 1	Jan	13	H	Huddersfield Town	W	3-1	West 2, Halse	19,759	1		3	4	5	6	7	8		10	11			9	2													
Rd 2	Feb	3	H	Coventry City	W	5-1	Halse 2, Wall, West, Turnbull	17,131	1		3	4		6	7	8		10	11			9	2	5													
Rd 3		24	A	Reading	D	1-1	West		1		3	4	5	6	7	8		10	11			9						2									
Replay		29	H	Reading	W	3-0	Turnbull 2, Halse		1		3	4	5	6	7	8		10	11			9						2									
Rd 4	Mar	9	H	Blackburn Rovers	D	1-1	l o.g.	59,300	1		3	4	5	6	7	8		10	11			9	2														
Replay		14	A	Blackburn Rovers	L	2-4	West 2	39,286	1		3	4	5	6	7	8		10	11			9		2													

DID YOU KNOW? The Central League was formed in 1911/12, the United reserve team was entered in the new League as founder members. Harold Halse scored 6 goals in United's 8-4 FA Charity Shield victory over Swindon Town at Stamford Bridge in 1911.

OPPOSITE PAGE:

United were the first winners of the Charity Shield, beating QPR at Stamford Bridge on 29 August 1908. The Daily Graphic carried this photographic feature on the cover. The match in fact was a replay, the first game being drawn 1-1 at the Park Royal. In 1911, United defeated Swindon Town 8-4, again at Stamford Bridge, on 25 September. (BL).

F.A. CHARITY SHIELD WINNERS 1908 & 1911

THE DAILY GRAPHIC

One Penny

No. 5840.—Vol. LXXV.   LONDON: MONDAY, AUGUST 31, 1908   Registered as a Newspaper.

FOR THE FOOTBALL ASSOCIATION CHARITY CUP.

EXCITING MOMENTS AT THE MOUTH OF THE GOAL: PUNCHING THE BALL ON THE NET.   RECEIVING A THROW.

SIR WILLIAM TRELOAR PRESENTING THE CHARITY SHIELD AND MEDALS TO THE WINNERS.

MANCHESTER UNITED BEAT THE QUEEN'S PARK RANGERS AT STAMFORD BRIDGE. ("Daily Graphic" Photograph.)   93

MANCHESTER UNITED

Match No.	Date	Venue	Opponents	Result	Goalscorers	Attendance
1	Sept 2	A	Woolwich Arsenal	D 0-0		40,000
2	7	H	Manchester City	L 0-1	*BILL MEREDITH'S BENEFIT MATCH*	38,911
3	14	A	West Bromwich Albion	W 2-1	Livingstone, Turnbull	26,000
4	21	H	Everton	W 2-0	West 2	38,000
5	28	A	The Wednesday	D 3-3	West 2, Turnbull	27,000
6	Oct 5	H	Derby County	D 1-1	West	40,000
7	12	A	Blackburn Rovers	L 1-2	Turnbull	16,000
8	19	H	Tottenham Hotspur	W 2-0	West, Turnbull	12,000
9	26	A	Middlesbrough	L 2-3	Nuttall 2	
10	Nov 2	H	Notts County	W 2-1	Meredith, Anderson	
11	9	A	Aston Villa	L 2-4	West, Wall	
12	16	H	Sunderland	L 1-3	Wall	
13	23	A	Liverpool	W 3-1	Anderson 2, Wall	14,000
14	30	H	Bolton Wanderers	L 1-2	Wall	
15	Dec 7	A	Sheffield United	W 4-0	West, Wall, Turnbull, Anderson	
16	14	H	Newcastle United	W 3-1	West 3	
17	21	A	Oldham Athletic	D 0-0		36,000
18	25	H	Chelsea	W 4-1	West 2, Whalley, Anderson	30,000
19	26	A	Chelsea	W 4-2	Turnbull 2, Wall, Anderson	28,000
20	28	H	Manchester City	W 2-0	West 2	40,000
21	Jan 1	H	Bradford City	W 2-0	Anderson 2	28,000
22	4	A	West Bromwich Albion	D 1-1	Roberts	15,000
23	18	H	Everton	L 1-4	Hamill	38,000
24	25	A	The Wednesday	W 2-0	West, Whalley	38,000
25	Feb 8	H	Blackburn Rovers	D 0-0		
26	15	A	Derby County	W 4-0	West 2, Turnbull, Anderson	30,000
27	Mar 1	A	Middlesbrough	W 2-1	Meredith, Whalley	
28	8	H	Notts County	W 2-1	Turnbull, Anderson	
29	15	A	Woolwich Arsenal	L 1-3	Sheldon	
30	21	H	Sunderland	W 4-0	Whalley, Anderson	
31	22	H	Aston Villa	W 4-0	Stacey, Wall, West, Turnbull	23,000
32	28	A	Bradford City	L 0-1		
33	29	H	Liverpool	W 2-0	West, Wall	
34	31	A	Tottenham Hotspur	D 1-1	Blott	12,762
35	Apr 5	H	Bolton Wanderers	W 2-1	Anderson, Wall	20,000
36	19	H	Sheffield United	L 1-2	Wall	21,700
37	19	H	Newcastle United	W 3-0	Hunter 2, West	17,000
38	26	A	Oldham Athletic	D 0-0		5,000

F.A. CUP

	Date	Venue	Opponents	Result	Goalscorers	Attendance
Rd 1	Jan 11	H	Coventry City	D 1-1	Wall	11,500
Replay	16	A	Coventry City	W 2-1	Roberts, Anderson	20,042
Rd 2	Feb 1	A	Plymouth Argyle	W 2-0	Anderson, Wall	21,000
Rd 3	22	A	Oldham Athletic	D 0-0		26,932
Replay	26	H	Oldham Athletic	L 1-2	West	31,180

League Appearances
League Scorers

Players:
Beale, R. H.; Linkson, O. H.; Stacey, G.; Duckworth, R.; Roberts, C.; Bell, A.; Meredith, W. H.; Hamill, M.; West, E. J.; Turnbull, A.; Wall, G.; Holden, R. H.; Whalley, A.; Livingstone, G.; Nuttall, T. A.; Donnelly, A.; Hodge, J.; Anderson, G.; Sheldon, J.; Knowles, F.; Gripps, T.; Blott, S. P.; Mew, J. W.; Hunter, W.

DID YOU KNOW? After United's Manchester Senior Cup Final 4-1 victory over Bolton Wanderers on 21 April 1913, one of the Wanderers players congratulated United's brilliant Irishman Micky Hamill. "Well done Micky, what a side you have!" he said. "Oh, you should watch us when we are really trying" answered Hamill cheekily. United defeated Blackburn Rovers 3-2 at Blackpool on 9 December 1912 to win the Lancashire Senior Cup.

MANCHESTER UNITED 1912-13

Back Row: W. Chamberlain, R. Beale, W. Meredith, J. Mew, A. Whalley, J. T. Haywood. Middle Row: H. Taylor (Trainer), C. Shreeve, T. Briddon, R. Roberts, J. Hodge, F. Knowles, G. Anderson, T. Gipps, G. Bracegirdle (Ass. Trainer). Front Row: A. Potts, J. Lee, A. Hopper, M. Hamill, G. T. Livingstone, G. Stacey, J. Sheldon, E. J. West, J. Thomson. (JG)

Bottom Left: G. STACEY. He had a fine career with United. Between 1907 and 1915 he made 267 League and F.A. Cup appearances. (MMUSC)

Bottom Right: PLUMSTEAD PRESSURE: Woolwich Arsenal 0 Manchester United 0. 2 September 1912. United custodian Beale clears a Gunners attack, with Stacey in support. (MMUSC)

G. STACEY

Lancashire Senior Cup Winners

MANCHESTER UNITED

Match No.	Date		Venue	Opponents	Result		Goalscorers	Attendance
1	Sept	6	A	The Wednesday	W	3-1	West, Turnbull, 1 o.g.	25,000
2		8	H	Sunderland	W	3-1	Anderson, Whalley, Turnbull	
3		13	H	Bolton Wanderers	L	0-1		
4		20	A	Chelsea	W	2-0	Anderson, Wall	40,000
5		27	H	Oldham Athletic	W	4-1	West 2, Anderson, Wall	
6	Oct	4	A	Tottenham Hotspur	W	3-1	Stacey, Whalley, Wall	39,000
7		11	A	Burnley	W	2-1	Anderson 2	30,000
8		18	H	Preston North End	W	3-0	Anderson 3	38,000
9		25	A	Newcastle United	W	1-0	West	35,000
10	Nov	1	H	Liverpool	W	3-0	Wall 2, West	35,000
11		8	A	Aston Villa	L	1-3	Woodcock	28,000
12		15	H	Middlesbrough	L	0-1		
13		22	A	Sheffield United	L	0-2		
14		29	H	Derby County	D	3-3	Turnbull 2, Meredith	27,249
15	Dec	6	A	Manchester City	W	2-0	Anderson 2	20,000
16		13	H	Bradford City	D	1-1	Knowles	36,000
17		20	A	Blackburn Rovers	W	1-0	1 o.g.	20,000
18		25	H	Everton	L	0-1		30,000
19		26	A	Everton	L	0-5		
20		27	H	The Wednesday	W	2-1	Meredith, Wall	17,000
21	Jan	1	H	West Bromwich Albion	W	1-0	Wall	16,400
22		3	A	Bolton Wanderers	L	1-6	West	20,000
23		17	H	Chelsea	L	0-1		
24		24	A	Oldham Athletic	D	2-2	Wall, Woodcock	28,000
25	Feb	7	A	Tottenham Hotspur	L	1-2	Wall	30,000
26		14	H	Burnley	L	0-1		
27		21	A	Middlesbrough	D	2-2	Anderson	
28		28	H	Newcastle United	D	2-2	Anderson, Potts	
29	Mar	5	A	Preston North End	L	2-4	Travers, Wall	
30		14	H	Aston Villa	L	0-6		
31	Apr	4	A	Derby County	L	2-4	Anderson, Travers	5,000
32		10	H	Sunderland	L	0-2		
33		11	A	Manchester City	L	0-1		36,440
34		13	H	West Bromwich Albion	L	1-2	Travers	17,907
35		15	A	Liverpool	W	2-1	Travers, Wall	6,000
36		18	A	Bradford City	L	0-1		10,000
37		22	H	Sheffield United	W	2-1	Thompson	5,000
38		25	H	Blackburn Rovers	D	0-0		

F.A. CUP

Rd	Date		Venue	Opponents	Result		Goalscorers	Attendance
Rd 1	Jan	10	A	Swindon Town	L	0-1		18,187

Player columns (League Appearances / League Scorers):
Beale, R. H.; Hodge, James; Stacey, G.; Duckworth, R.; Whalley, A.; Hamill, M.; Meredith, W.; Turnbull, A.; Anderson, G.; West, E. J.; Wall, G.; Knowles, F.; Cashmore, A.; Hooper, A.; Chorlton, T.; Gipps, T.; Woodcock, W.; Mew, J. W.; Haywood, J.; Thompson, J.; Potts, A.; Roberts, R. H.; Hodge, John; Livingstone, C.; Hudson, E.; Norton, J.; Travers, G. E.; Rowe, J.; Hunter, G. C.; Royals, E. J.

DID YOU KNOW? United won the Lancashire Senior Cup for the second successive season in 1913/4. They defeated Blackpool 1-0 with a goal from Cashmore at Bolton on 8 December 1913. Keeper Jack Mew began his long career in the United senior side in 1913. He made his debut at Old Trafford at home to Middlesbrough on 1 March 1913 having signed for the club in 1910 from Marley Hill Colliery in Co. Durham, much to the chagrin of Sunderland officials and supporters who had anticipated him joining the Roker Club.

Top: MANCHESTER UNITED 1913-14. Back Row: Hodge, Gipps, Knowles, Beale, Stacey, Hamill, Whalley. Front Row: Meredith, Woodcock, Anderson, West, Wall. (JG)

Bottom Right: MANCHESTER UNITED 2 NOTTS COUNTY 1. 2 November 1912. Meredith walks away after Sandy Turnbull (at near post) scores for United, in this Weekly News picture.

Bottom Left: Postcard celebrating Swindon Town's FA Cup victory over United in 1914

ENOCH WEST   T. MEEHAN

Swindon 1
Manchester 0
United

In Memory of
MANCHESTER
UNITED
WHO FELL, FIGHTING FOR THE
ENGLISH CUP,
(First Round)
At County Ground, Swindon.
JANUARY 10TH, 1914.

Manchester United
  Didn't want to die,
They didn't want to do it
  There was a reason why,
But Swindon had to kill them
  (It may have been a sin),
They really didn't want to,
  But they did want to win.

A.A.

MANCHESTER UNITED

Match No.	Date	Venue	Opponents	Result	Goalscorers	Attendance	Beale, R. H.	Hodge, John	Stacey, G.	Hunter, G. C.	O'Connell, P.	Knowles, F.	Meredith, W.	Travers, G. E.	West, E. J.	Woodcock, W.	Wall, G.	Norton, J.	Gipps, T.	Turnbull, A.	Anderson, G.	Potts, A.	Hudson, A.	Whaley, A.	Mew, J. W.	Hodge, James	Cookson, S. P.	Spratt, W.	Haywood, J.	Allman, A.	Prince, H.	Montgomery,	Fox	Match No.
1	Sept 2	H	Oldham Athletic	L	1-3	O'Connell		1	2	3	4	5	6	7	8	9	10	11																	1
2	5	H	Manchester City	D	0-0		20,000	1	2	3	4	5	6	7	8	9	10	11																	2
3	12	A	Bolton Wanderers	L	0-3			1	2	3	4	5	6		8	9	10	11	7																3
4	19	H	Blackburn Rovers	W	2-0	West 2	12,000	1	2	3	5			6	7		10		11			4	8	9											4
5	26	A	Notts County	L	2-4	Turnbull, Wall		1	2	3	5			6	7		10		11			4	8	9											5
6	Oct 3	H	Sunderland	W	3-0	Anderson, Stacey, West	20,000	1	2	3	5	4	6	7		10			11				8	9											6
7	10	A	The Wednesday	L	0-1		12,000	1	2	3	5	4	6	7	8	10			11					9											7
8	17	H	West Bromwich Albion	D	0-0		13,200	1	2	3		5	6			10	7		11	4			9	8											8
9	24	A	Everton	L	2-4	Anderson, Wall		1	2			4	6		8	10			7		3		9	5											9
10	31	H	Chelsea	D	2-2	Anderson, Hunter	16,000	1	2	3	5		6		8			7	11	4		10	9												10
11	Nov 7	A	Bradford City	L	2-4	Hunter, West	12,000	1	2	3	5		6			10			7	11	4		8	9											11
12	14	H	Burnley	L	0-2		15,000		2	3	5	4	6	7	9		10	11			8				1										12
13	21	A	Tottenham Hotspur	L	0-2		11,000		1		2	6	4			10			7	11		8	9		3		5								13
14	28	H	Newcastle United	W	1-0	West	5,000	1	2	3	5	4	6			10			7	11		8	9												14
15	Dec 5	A	Middlesbrough	D	1-1	Anderson	7,000	1	2	3	5	4	6			10			7	11		8	9												15
16	12	H	Sheffield United	L	1-2	Anderson	8,000	1	2	3	5	4	6			10			7	11		8	9												16
17	19	A	Aston Villa	D	3-3	Norton 2, Anderson	10,000	1	2	3	5	4			7	10				11	6		9	8											17
18	26	A	Liverpool	D	1-1	Stacey	20,000	1	2	3		5			7	10				11	6		9	8			4								18
19	Jan 1	H	Bradford Park Avenue	L	1-2	Anderson		1	2	3		5			7	10				11	4		9	8			6								19
20	2	A	Manchester City	D	1-1	West	31,000	1	2	3		5			7	10				11	4		9	8			6								20
21	16	H	Bolton Wanderers	W	4-1	Potts 2, Woodcock, Stacey (pen)	12,000	1	2	3		5	4	7		10	9			11			8				6								21
22	23	A	Blackburn Rovers	D	3-3	Woodcock 2, 1 o.g.	7,000	1	2	3		5	4	7		10	9			11			8				6								22
23	30	H	Notts County	D	2-2	Stacey, Potts		1	2	3		5	4	7		10	9			11			8				6								23
24	Feb 6	A	Sunderland	L	0-1			1		3		5		7		10	9			11			8					6	2	4					24
25	13	H	The Wednesday	W	2-0	West, Woodcock		1				5		7		10	9			11			8					6	3	4	2				25
26	20	A	West Bromwich Albion	D	0-0		10,169	1				5			10		9	7	11				8					6	3	4	2				26
27	27	H	Everton	L	1-2	Woodcock		1				5		7		9			11	6			8						3	4	2	10			27
28	Mar 13	H	Bradford City	W	1-0	Potts	14,000	1				5				10	9	11	7				8					6	3		2		4		28
29	20	A	Burnley	L	0-3			1				5				10	9	11	7				8					6	3		2		4		29
30	27	H	Tottenham Hotspur	D	1-1	Woodcock	7,000	1				5		7		10	9	11					8						3	6	2		4		30
31	Apr 2	H	Liverpool	W	2-0	Anderson 2	18,000	1	2			5		7		10				11			9	8					3	6			4		31
32	3	H	Newcastle United	L	0-2			1	2			5		7		10				11			9	8					3	6			4		32
33	5	A	Bradford Park Avenue	L	0-5		15,000	1				5		7		10	9			11					8	9			8	3	6	2		4		33
34	6	A	Oldham Athletic	L	0-1			1				5	6	7		10									8	9				11	3	4	2		4	34
35	10	A	Middlesbrough	D	2-2	O'Connell, Turnbull	15,000	1				5		7			8					10	9						11	3	6	2		4	35
36	17	A	Sheffield United	L	1-3	West		1				5		7		8	9					10							11	3	6	2		4	36
37	19	A	Chelsea	W	3-1	West, Woodcock, Norton	30,000	1	3			5		7		10	8			11			9								6	2		4	37
38	26	H	Aston Villa	W	1-0	Anderson	8,000	1	3			5		7		10	8			11			9								6	2		4	38
			League Appearances					37	26	23	15	34	19	26	8	33	20	17	29	10	13	22	17	2	1	1	4	12	13	12	12	1	11	
			League Scorers							4	2	2				9	7	2	3			2	10	4									1 o.g.	

F.A. CUP

Rd 1	Jan 9	A	The Wednesday	L	0-1		23,248	1	2	3	4	5		7		10		11				9						6			8			

DID YOU KNOW? *Season 1914/15 was the last season of the Football League programme prior to the competition being suspended, due to The Great War. During the period of hostilities, and until 1919, Wartime Regional Leagues were introduced. Following a league match between United and Liverpool on 2 April 1915 allegations were made against players on both teams for match 'fixing'. As a result of an F.A. enquiry several players from each club were suspended for life, but after the war their suspensions were rescinded for the contributions to the War effort.*

98

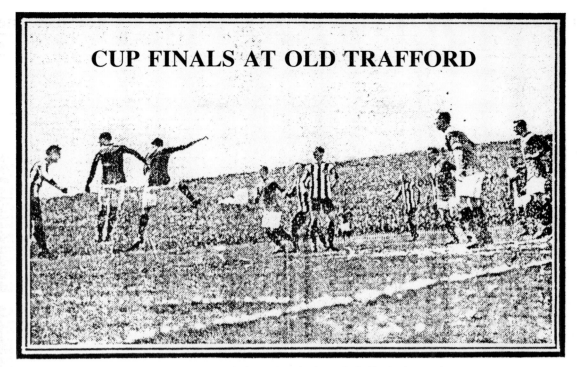

CUP FINALS AT OLD TRAFFORD

Bradford's robust play which gave them the Cup — Daily Sketch *photograph.*

F.A. CUP FINALS 1911 & 1915

Top:
BRADFORD CITY 1
NEWCASTLE UNITED 0.
After a 0-0 draw at the Crystal Palace Bradford were appropriate winners in the replay. the new trophy, the present one, was made in Bradford and 1911 was the first year it was competed for. (K.M.)

Bottom Right:
SHEFFIELD UNITED 3
CHELSEA 0
The 1915 Final was the first staged, other than replays, outside London since 1894. It was called the "Khaki Cup Final", because of the large presence of servicemen in the crowd, who watched the game in typical Manchester weather. (MMUSC)

OLD TRAFFORD

When John Davies, United's saviour and chairman at the turn of the century, decided to build a new stadium he was determined that it would be the best in the country. Davies paid out £60,000 for the land to build the new stadium and originally the ground was planned to hold 100,000 spectators, by later develepments. The contractors were Humprey's Ltd of London and even in those early days Old Trafford was acknowledged as the best in the country.

The new stadium was ready for it's inaugural match on February 19th, 1910 when United met Lancashire rivals Liverpool. A large crowd of around 50,000 — using forty turnstiles — packed into the ground in a festive mood. But Liverpool ignored any sense of occasion and spoiled United's party with a 4-3 win after being 2-0 behind at one stage.

Old Trafford was soon selected to stage important matches. The first was an F.A. Cup semi-final between Barnsley and Everton in 1910, but a year later it was the venue of the F.A. Cup Final replay between Bradford City and Newcastle United.

The biggest honour was staging the 1915 'Khaki' Cup Final (so called because of the many soldiers in the crowd), the only time in the twentieth century that a Final had been initially played for outside London.

Sheffield United beat Chelsea 3-0 that year and it is a strange quirk of history that Old Trafford was not to stage another F.A. Cup Final until Chelsea won a replay there in 1970. Since World War Two United have been Britain's major attraciton, pulling in enormous crowds. The Reds hold the record for the biggest Football League crowd — 82,950 against Arsenal in 1949, but the match was played at Maine Road due to the bombing of Old Trafford during the War.

The biggest gate at Old Trafford involving United in a League match was on Boxing Day, 1920, when they played Aston Villa before a crowd of 70,504. By coincidence, that same season also saw the lowest ever attendance at Old Trafford — 13! The unlucky thirteen paid to see a Second Division match between Stockport County and Leicester City on 7 May, 1921, Stockport's ground was closed due to suspension at the time.

It was during the nineteen-twenties that Old Trafford increased further in stature, and on 17 April, 1926, the ground was used for the first time as an international arena — staging the England v Scotland match. Then, a decade later, in 1938 it was chosen for England's fixture with Northern Ireland.

Three F.A. Cup Semi-Finals were staged between the wars and in the last one, that between Wolverhampton Wanderers and Grimsby Town on 25th March, 1939 — a crowd of 76,962 crammed the terraces to register the highest ever attendance for the enclosure. It is a record that still holds as the present capacity is reduced to 52,000 for safety regulations. So, ironically, the highest-ever crowd at Old Trafford didn't involve United.

Europe was on the verge of World War II and among the Football League teams, United suffered the most as a consequence of the hostilities, League Football was postponed during the war, but Old Trafford as ever, was in the news, albeit this time, not good.

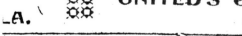

Above: MANCHESTER UNITED 3 LIVERPOOL 4. The opening match at Old Trafford, as reported in The Umpire, *20 February 1910. (K.M.).*

Two German air raids over Manchester — one just before Christmas 1940 and the other on 11 March, 1941 — left the ground blitzed. The main stand, dressing rooms and offices were all extensively damaged, later declared a complete loss.

After the war Matt Busby was appointed manager and the amiable Scotsman began rebuilding a side that was to be a force for years to come. With Old Trafford out of action, United played their immediate post-war seasons at Maine Road, home of Manchester neighbours, City.

Under the chairmanship of James Gibson, the board worked hard to restore the stadium to it's former grandeur, and their efforts were rewarded on 24 August, 1949. Ten years after United's last League game on their home pitch, Bolton Wanderers were the first visitors to the rebuilt enclosure.

The advent of European competition emphasised the importance of emulating the other top grounds and to install floodlights. They were erected in 1956 and the first match was against Bolton, which resulted in a 2-0 defeat for United. A month later they met Real Madrid in the European Cup, a game televised direct which ended in a 2-2 draw and United's elimination.

The stadium underwent many structural changes during the late fifties and early sixties. The Stretford End was covered in 1959 and the seats at the back installed in 1962.

Further developments coincided with the 1966 World Cup which was hosted by England. In preparation for the big event, a new Cantelever Stand was built at a cost of £350,000 — this stand incorporating private boxes which were then a novelty at British stadiums.

Three World Cup matches were staged featuring, Hungary, Bulgaria and Portugal.

With United the outstanding team of that decade, Old Trafford was the venue for many memorable matches. For the first and only time on English soil, a World Club Championship match was played there — United drawing 1-1 with Estudiates de La Plata of Argentina in a very physical match.

1969 also saw two away matches — against Arsenal in the League and AC Milan in the European Cup — transmitted live on to a big screen on the Old Trafford pitch, Again United were one of the pioneers of this new system of watching matches, and large crowds paid at the turnstiles.

In 1970, Old Trafford was again chosen to stage an FA Cup Final — the replay between Chelsea and Leeds. But unfortunate times were imminent and the ground fell victim to the growing problems aflicting society. A year later during a match against Newcastle, a knife was thrown from the Stratford End on to the pitch, narrowly missing it's intended target, a Newcastle player. The referee reported the incident and a tribunal found United guilty and closed their ground for the first two League matches of the following 1971/2 season.

That was one of the incidents that heralded a new era of violence at British grounds. But thankfully for the Manchester public the club responded positively to combat this trend by improving still further the amenities, generating a family atmosphere — and a fierce pride in the club. Old Trafford, now the most modern and comfortable stadium in Britain, has reaped the benefits of providing the best of facilities for its supporters, and today stands as a Mecca for world soccer.

Above: OLD TRAFFORD. An aerial view prior to completion of fully covered stands in 1966. (BNPC)

Our Football Portrait Gallery.

WM. MEREDITH (Manchester United.)

"Without doubt, the finest outside right ever seen in this or any other country," is the considered opinion of an expert judge of the "Soccer" game in regard to "Billy" Meredith.

Meredith was born at Chirk, North Wales, and joined the Manchester City in its first year. He scored the goal which won City the English Cup in 1904, and sent the supporters of that famous combination delirious with joy. In 1906 Meredith put his wonderful powers of dribbling at the service of Manchester United, and it is a poor day when "Billy's" mathematically precise "centres" and "sandy" Turnbull's miraculous head do not furnish at least one good goal for the skilful "Reds." Not so fast, probably, by a yard or so in a hundred, as of yore, Meredith's sprint is still equal to shaking off the attention of the average back, and he is constantly "acquiring merit" in the matter of subtlety in tactics. "Billy" Meredith holds the record for Welsh International Caps.

He will continue to add to his collection of fancy head-gear for some years yet, one may venture to prophesy, for he is a model athlete as to physical fitness and powers of retaining it.

Photos reproduced by courtesy of Messrs. E. HULTON & Co. LTD.

BILLY MEREDITH. Feature from The Manchester Programme, *a Theatre and entertainments magazine, dated 4 September 1911. (KM)*

THE GREAT WAR

The Footballers Battalion—17th Batt. (Football) Middlesex Regt.

Above:
SOCCER AT WAR. The Footballers Battalion, 17th Middlesex Regiment included Manchester United's Sheldon, back row, extreme right. (KM)

IN MEMORIUM
'SANDY' TURNBULL

Left: United favourite Sandy Turnbull, scorer of the 1909 FA Cup winning goal, and seen here in training, was killed in action during the First World War. (BNPC)

Matches No. 1 to 26 Lancashire Section Principal Tournament — Position: 11th

Matches No. 27 to 36 Lancashire Section Southern Division Subsidiary Tournament — Position: 6th

Match No.	Date	Venue	Opponents	Result		Goalscorers	Attendance
1	Sept 4	A	Oldham Athletic	L	2-3	Wilson, Halligan	5,000
2	11	H	Everton	L	2-4	Wilson 2	12,000
3	18	A	Bolton Wanderers	W	5-3	West 2, Woodcock 2, A. Davies	
4	25	H	Manchester City	D	1-1	Halligan	20,000
5	Oct 2	A	Stoke city	D	0-0		6,000
6	9	H	Burnley	L	3-7	D. Davies, Wilson, Woodcock	12,000
7	16	A	Preston North End	D	0-0		2,500
8	23	H	Stockport County	W	3-0	Halligan, Hughes, Woodcock	7,000
9	30	A	Liverpool	W	2-0	West, Wilson	15,000
10	Nov 6	H	Bury	D	1-1	Woodcock	7,000
11	13	H	Rochdale	W	2-0	Gipps, A. Davies	4,000
12	20	A	Blackpool	L	1-5	Woodcock	
13	27	H	Southport Central	D	0-0		5,000
14	Dec 4	H	Oldham Athletic	W	2-0	Anderson, Halligan	
15	11	A	Everton	L	0-2		7,000
16	18	H	Bolton Wanderers	W	1-0	Bracegirdle	6,000
17	25	A	Manchester City	L	1-2	Halligan	20,000
18	Jan 1	H	Stoke City	L	1-2	Woodcock	8,000
19	8	A	Burnley	L	4-7	Travis 4	7,000
20	15	H	Preston North End	W	4-0	Woodcock 2, Hughes, Halligan	7,000
21	22	A	Stockport County	L	1-3	Woodcock	5,000
22	29	H	Liverpool	D	1-1	Cookson	10,000
23	Feb 5	A	Bury	L	1-2	Travis	
24	12	A	Rochdale	D	2-2	Woodcock, Halligan	3,000
25	19	H	Blackpool	D	1-1	Woodcock	
26	26	A	Southport Central	L	0-5		
27	Mar 4	H	Everton	L	0-2		
28	11	A	Oldham Athletic	L	0-1		
29	18	H	Liverpool	D	0-0		
30	25	H	Manchester City	L	0-2		
31	Apr 1	A	Stockport County	L	3-5	Campney 2, Winterburn	5,000
32	8	A	Everton	L	1-3	Forster	
33	15	H	Oldham Athletic	W	3-0	Crossley, Knowles, Halligan	5,000
34	21	H	Stockport County	W	3-2	Crossley, Woodcock, Halligan	9,000
35	22	A	Liverpool	L	1-7	Woodcock	
36	29	A	Manchester City	L	1-2	Crossley	

NOTE: Matches 27 to 36 were also counted as Lancashire F.A. Senior Cup Ties.

LEAGUE APPEARANCES (Matches 1 to 26 only)

Allman, A. 5; Anderson G. 5; Armstrong, 2; Barlow, C. 21; Bracegirdle, 7; Brown, 1; Chorley, 1; Cookson, S. P. 1; Cubberly, 3; Davies, A. 21; Davies D. 4; Davies, J. 1; Forster, T. 5; Gipps, T. 21; Gipps, W. 3; Halligan, W. 23; Hallworth, 1; Harmwzit, 1; Hayes, 1; Haywood, J. 9; Hilditch, C. G. 3; Hodge, J. 1; Holt, 1; Hudson, E. 20; Hughes, 2; Ireland, 1; Knighton, 1; Knowles, F. 5; Lofthouse, 2; Mew, J. W. 26; O'Connell, P. 18; Pennington, 2; Robinson, J. W. 1; Spratt, W. 1; Travis, A. 9; Wall, G. 7; West, E. J. 11; Wilson, D. 11; Winterburn, A. 2; Woodcock, W. 26.

GOALSCORERS (Matches 1 to 36)

Woodcock, W. 14; Halligan, W. 9; Trains, A. 5; Wilson, D. 5; West, E. J. 3; Crossley, Private 3; Campney, 2; Davies, A. 2; Hughes, 2; Anderson, G. 1; Bracegirdle, 1; Cookson, S. P. 1; Davies, D. 1; Forster, T. 1; Gipps, T. 1; Knowles, F.; Winterburn, A. 1.

Matches No. 1 to 30 Lancashire Section Principal Tournament   *Position: 7th*

Matches No. 31 to 36 Lancashire Section Subsidiary Tournament   *Position: 4th*

Match No.	Date	Venue	Opponents	Result		Goalscorers	Attendance
1	Sept 2	H	Port Vale	D	2-2	Woodcock 2	
2	9	A	Oldham Athletic	W	2-0	Armstrong, O'Connell	
3	16	H	Preston North End	W	2-1	Woodcock 2	
4	23	A	Burnley	L	1-7	Armstrong	
5	30	A	Blackpool	D	2-2	Woockcock 2	
6	Oct 7	H	Liverpool	D	0-0		
7	14	A	Stockport County	L	0-1		
8	21	H	Bury	W	3-1	Armstrong 2, Crossley	
9	28	A	Stoke City	L	0-3		
10	Nov 4	H	Soutport Central	W	1-0	Woodcock	
11	11	A	Blackburn Rovers	W	2-1	Woodcock, Anderson	
12	18	H	Manchester City	W	2-1	Woodcock, Anderson	
13	25	A	Everton	L	2-3	Anderson, Woodcock	
14	Dec 2	H	Rochdale	D	1-1	Anderson	3,000
15	9	A	Bolton Wanderers	L	1-5	Anderson	
16	23	H	Oldham Athletic	W	3-2	Anderson 2, Lees	
17	30	A	Preston North End	L	2-3	Anderson, Woodcock	
18	Jan 6	H	Burnley	W	3-1	Anderson 2, Woodcock	
19	13	H	Blackpool	W	3-2	Woodcock 2, Crossley	
20	20	A	Liverpool	D	3-3	Anderson 3	
21	27	H	Stockport County	L	0-1		
22	Feb 3	A	Bury	D	1-1	Woodcock	
23	10	H	Stoke City	W	4-2	Woodcock 2, Robinson, Ellis	
24	17	A	Southport Central	W	1-0	Ellis	
25	24	H	Blackburn Rovers	W	1-0	Anderson	
26	Mar 3	A	Manchester City	L	0-1		
27	10	H	Everton	L	0-2		
28	17	A	Rochdale	L	0-2		2,000
29	24	H	Bolton Wanderers	W	6-3	Woodcock 3, Anderson 2, Hilditch	
30	Apr 6	A	Port Vale	L	0-3		
31	Mar 31	A	Stoke City	L	1-2	Ellis	
32	Apr 7	H	Manchester City	W	5-1	Anderson 3, Woodcock 2	
33	9	H	Port Vale	W	5-1	Anderson 3, Travis 2	
34	14	H	Stoke City	W	1-0	Woodcock	
35	21	A	Manchester City	W	1-0	Anderson	
36	28	A	Port Vale	L	2-5	Woodcock, McMenemy	

NOTE: Matches 31 to 36 were also counted as Lancashire F.A. Senior Cup Ties.

LEAGUE APPEARANCES (Matches 1 to 30 only)

Anderson G. 18; Armstrong, 8; Bailey, 1; Barlow, C. 26; Barnett, 11; Bennett, 1; Brennan, 1; Brooks, 4; Buckley,, 13; Bunting, W. 1; Capper, 1; Connor, 4; Cookson, S. P. 1; Crossley, Private 11; Cubberley, 1; Davies, W. 2; Ellis, 12; Forster, T. 29; Frith, 1; Goddard, 1; Hamill, 1; Heath, 1; Hilditch, C. G. 24; Hudson, E. 2; Hughes, 2; Kite, 1; Lees, 2; Leigh, 10; Lomas, 5; Martin, 1; McMenemy, 2; Mew, J. W. 21; Molyneaux, 14; Montgomery, J. 1; O'Connell, P. 8; Ogden, 1; Pennington, 1; Preece, 1; Robinson, J. W. 16; Siddall, 1; Silcock, J. 27; Spooner, 1; Swann, 6; Tattum, 1; Travis, A. 2; Tremlow, 1; Wall, G. 1; Wilson, D. 2; Wilson, P. 1; Winterburn, A. 2; Woodcock, W. 25; Wright, W. 1; Wroe, 1.

GOALSCORERS (Matches 1 to 36)

Woodcock, W. 24; Anderson, G. 23; Armstrong, 4; Ellis, 3; Crossley, Private 2; Trains, A. 2; Hilditch, C. G. 1; Lees, 1; McMenemy, 1; O'Connell, P. 1; Robinson, J. W. 1.

Match No.	Date	Venue	Opponents	Result		Goalscorers	Attendance
1	Sept 1	A	Blackburn Rovers	W	5-0	Anderson 3, Woodcock, Meehan	
2	8	H	Blackburn Rovers	W	6-1	Anderson 4, Woodcock 2	
3	15	A	Rochdale	L	0-3		3,000
4	22	H	Rochdale	D	1-1	Woodcock	3,000
5	29	A	Manchester City	L	1-3	Anderson	
6	Oct 6	H	Manchester City	D	1-1	Woodcock	
7	13	A	Everton	L	0-3		
8	20	H	Everton	D	0-0		
9	27	H	Port Vale	D	3-3	Anderson, Ellis, Connor	
10	Nov 3	A	Port Vale	D	2-2	Ellis, Anderson	
11	10	H	Bolton Wanderers	L	1-3	Ellis	
12	17	A	Bolton Wanderers	L	2-4	Anderson, Ellis	
13	24	H	Preston North End	W	2-1	Anderson 2	
14	Dec 1	A	Preston North End	D	0-0		
15	8	H	Blackpool	W	1-0	Elliott	
16	15	A	Blackpool	W	3-2	Woodcock 2, Meehan	
17	22	A	Burnley	W	5-0	Meehan, Connor, Anderson 3	
18	29	H	Burnley	W	1-0	Connor	
19	Jan 5	A	Southport Central	L	0-3		
20	12	H	Southport Central	D	0-0		
21	19	A	Liverpool	L	1-5	Woodcock	
22	26	H	Liverpool	L	0-2		
23	Feb 2	A	Stoke City	L	1-5	Woodcock	
24	9	H	Stoke City	W	2-1	Woodcock (pen), Ellis	10,000
25	16	H	Bury	D	0-0		
26	23	A	Bury	W	2-1	Massey, Woodcock	
27	Mar 2	H	Oldham Athletic	W	2-1	Ellis, Woodcock	
28	9	A	Oldham Athletic	L	0-2		
29	16	H	Stockport County	W	2-0	Buckley 2	
30	23	A	Stockport County	L	1-2	Buckley	
31	Mar 29	A	Manchester City	L	0-3		
32	30	H	Stoke City	W	2-1	Stafford, Woodcock	
33	Apr 1	H	Manchester City	W	2-0	Woodcock, Buckley	
34	6	A	Stoke City	D	0-0		
35	13	H	Port Vale	W	2-0	Bourne 2	
36	20	A	Port Vale	L	0-3		

NOTE: Matches 31 to 36 were also counted as Lancashire F.A. Senior Cup Ties.

LEAGUE APPEARANCES (Matches 1 to 30 only)

Allsop, 2; Anderson, G. 15; Bell, 2; Best, 1; Birks, 3; Buckley, 7; Bunting, W. 6; Chamberlain, W. T. 4; Connor, 23; Cookson, S. P. 1; Coyne, 1; Daniels, 4; Davies, 1; Ellis, 27; Harrison, 1; Hilditch, C. G. 28; Hilton, 1; Holt, 4; Hopkin, F. 1; Hopkinson, 10; Johnstone, 6; Johnston, 1; Kinsella, 17; Knowles, F. 1; Leah, 2; Lloyds, 1; Mann, 1; Massey, 1; Marsden, 8; McLachlan , 1; McLaughlin, 1; McMenamy, 2; Meehan, T. 26; Mew, J. W. 30; Montgomery, J. 1; Moores, 1; Muskett, 2; Peplow, 1; Rainford, 3; Roberts, 2; Robinson, J. W. 4; Scarley, 1; Silcock, J. 29; Southern, 4; Stafford, 1; Thomas, 1; Walker, A. 2; Wallworth, 1; Whitehead, 1; Williams, 10; Woodcock, W. 26.

GOALSCORERS (Matches 1 to 36)

Anderson, G. 16; Woodcock, W. 14; Ellis, 6; Buckley, 4; Connor, 3; Meehan, T. 3; Bourne, 2; Elliott, 1; Massey, 1; Stafford, 1.

Matches No. 1 to 30 Lancashire Section Principal Competition

Position: 9th

Matches No. 31 to 36 Lancashire Section C Subsidiary Tournament

Position: 3rd

Match No.	Date	Venue	Opponents	Result		Goalscorers	Attendance
1	Sept 7	H	Oldham Athletic	L	1-4	Meehan	
2	14	A	Oldham Athletic	W	2-0	Myers 2	
3	21	H	Blackburn Rovers	W	1-0	Ellis	
4	28	A	Blackburn Rovers	D	1-1	Ellis	
5	Oct 5	H	Manchester City	L	0-2		
6	12	A	Manchester City	D	0-0		
7	19	H	Everton	D	1-1	Woodcock	
8	26	A	Everton	L	2-6	Howarth, Woodcock	
9	Nov 2	A	Rochdale	W	3-1	Coombes, Tickle	3,000
10	9	H	Rochdale	L	0-1		6,000
11	16	A	Preston North End	L	2-4	Green 2	
12	23	H	Preston North End	L	1-2	1 o.g.	
13	30	A	Bolton Wanderers	L	1-3	Hilditch	
14	Dec 7	H	Bolton Wanderers	W	1-0	Woodcock	
15	14	A	Port Vale	L	1-3	Woodcock	
16	21	H	Port Vale	W	5-1	Woodcock 4, W. Jones	
17	28	A	Blackpool	D	2-2	Woodcock, Ellis	
18	Jan 11	A	Stockport County	L	1-2	Cookson	
19	18	H	Stockport County	L	0-2		
20	25	A	Liverpool	D	1-1	Langford	
21	Feb 1	H	Liverpool	L	0-1		
22	8	A	Southport Vulcan	L	1-2	J. T. Jones	
23	15	H	Southport Vulcan	L	1-3	Meehan	
24	22	A	Burnley	L	2-4	Hodge 2	
25	Mar 1	H	Burnley	W	4-0	Makin, Hodge 2, Woodcock	
26	8	A	Stoke City	W	2-1	J. T. Jones, Albinson	
27	15	H	Stoke City	W	3-1	Woodcock 2, Hodge	
28	22	A	Bury	W	2-0	Woodcock, Lomas	
29	29	H	Bury	W	5-1	Spence 4, Woodcock	
30	30	H	Blackpool	W	5-1		
31	Apr 5	A	Port Vale	W	3-1	Hopkins, Woodcock, J. T. Jones	
32	12	H	Port Vale	W	2-1	Woodcock 2	
33	18	A	Manchester City	L	0-3		35,000
34	19	H	Stoke City	L	0-1		
35	21	H	Manchester City	L	2-4	Potts, Spence	
36	27	A	Stoke City	L	2-4	Smith, Spence	

NOTE: Matches 31 to 36 were also counted as Lancashire F.A. Senior Cup Ties.

LEAGUE APPEARANCES (Matches 1 to 30 only)

Albinson, 2; Barlow, C. 1; Bowne, 1; Bradwick, 1; Buckley, 1; Carr, 2; Clayton, 4; Connor, 2; Cookson, S. P. 6; Coombes, 9; Cope, 1; Davies, 2; Dunn, 6; Ellis, 19; Forster, T. 2; Green, 1; Hall, 1; Haywood, 10; Hilditch, C. G. 26; Hilton, 1; Hodge, J. 11; Hopkin, F. 5; Howarth, 5; Hudson, E. 3; Jones, J. T. 13; Jones, W. 2; Kinsella, 5; Langford, 10; Lomas, 3; Lumberg, 3; Makin, N. 14; Manual, 1; Masserof, 1; Meehan, T. 29; Mew, J. W. 29; Molyneaux, 1; Murray, 2; Muskett, 1; Myers, 6; Nightingale, 2; Nuttall, 1; Peplow, 3; Reid, 1; Scott-Duncan, 1; Silcock, J. 29; Smith, 1; Spence, J. W. 1; Tickle, 2; Wall, G. 3; Williams, 4; Woodcock, W. 27; Worrall, 1; Worsencroft, 1.

GOALSCORERS (Matches 1 to 36)

Woodcock, W. 17; Spence, J. W. 6; Hodge, J. 5; Ellis, 3; Jones, J. T. 3; Green, 2; Meehan, T. 2; Myers, 2; Albinson, 1; Cookson, S. P. 1; Coombes, 1; Hilditch, C. G. 1; Hopkins, F. 1; Howarth, 1; Jones, W. 1; Langford, 1; Lomas, 1; Makin, N. 1; Potts, A. 1; Smith, 1; Tickle, 1; 1 o.g.

MANCHESTER UNITED

Match No.	Date	Venue	Opponents	Result	Goalscorers	Attendance
1	Aug 30	A	Derby County	D	1-1	Woodcock	12,000
2	Sept 1	H	The Wednesday	D	0-0		6,000
3	6	H	Derby County	L	0-2		15,000
4	8	A	The Wednesday	W	3-1	Meehan, Spence, Woodcock	12,000
5	13	A	Preston North End	W	3-2	Spence 2, Meehan	20,000
6	20	H	Preston North End	W	5-1	Woodcock 2, Spence 2, Meehan	20,000
7	27	A	Middlesbrough	W	5-1	Woodcock 2, Spence 2, Montgomery	20,000
8	Oct 4	H	Middlesbrough	D	1-1	Woodcock	30,000
9	11	A	Manchester City	D	3-3	Hodge, Spence, Hopkin	30,000
10	18	H	Manchester City	W	1-0	Spence	49,360
11	25	H	Sheffield United	D	2-2	Woodcock, Hopkin	20,000
12	Nov 1	A	Sheffield United	W	3-0	Hodges, Spence, Woodcock	20,000
13	8	H	Burnley	L	0-1	Hodge	18,000
14	15	A	Burnley	L	1-2	Hodge	25,000
15	22	H	Oldham Athletic	W	3-0	Hodges, Spence, Hopkin	18,000
16	Dec 6	A	Aston Villa	L	1-2	Hilditch	30,000
17	13	H	Aston Villa	L	1-2	Bissett	30,000
18	20	H	Newcastle United	W	2-1	Hodges, Spence	20,000
19	26	A	Liverpool	D	0-0		
20	27	H	Newcastle United	L	1-2	Hilditch	45,000
21	Jan 1	A	Liverpool	D	0-0		
22	3	H	Chelsea	L	0-2		25,000
23	17	A	Chelsea	L	0-1		40,000
24	24	A	West Bromwich Albion	L	1-2	Woodcock	30,192
25	Feb 7	A	Sunderland	L	0-3		30,000
26	11	H	Oldham Athletic	D	1-1	Bissett	
27	14	H	Sunderland	W	2-0	Harris, Hodges	58,661
28	21	A	Arsenal	W	3-0	Spence 2, Hopkin	
29	25	H	West Bromwich Albion	L	1-2	Spence	21,000
30	28	H	Arsenal	L	0-1		
31	Mar 6	A	Everton	W	1-0	Bissett	30,000
32	13	H	Everton	D	0-0		30,000
33	20	H	Bradford City	D	0-0		
34	27	A	Bradford City	L	1-2	Bissett	18,000
35	Apr 2	H	Bradford Park Avenue	L	0-1		28,000
36	3	H	Bolton Wanderers	D	1-1	Toms	
37	6	A	Bradford Park Avenue	W	4-1	Woodcock, Toms, Bissett, Grimwood	11,000
38	10	A	Bolton Wanderers	W	5-3	Bissett 2, Meredith, Toms, Woodcock	
39	17	H	Blackburn Rovers	D	1-1	Hopkin	
40	24	H	Blackburn Rovers	L	0-5		20,000
41	26	H	Notts County	D	0-0		20,000
42	May 1	A	Notts County	W	2-0	Spence, Meredith	20,000

F.A. CUP

Rd 1	Jan 10	A	Port Vale	W	1-0	Toms	14,549
Rd 2	31	H	Aston Villa	L	1-2	Woodcock	48,600

League Appearances   League Scorers

Players:
Mew, J. W.
Moore, C.
Silcock, J.
Montgomery, J.
Hilditch, C. G.
Whalley, A.
Hodge, J.
Woodcock, W.
Spence, J. W.
Potts, A.
Hopkin, F.
Meehan, T.
Toms, W.
Grimwood, J. B.
Hodges, F. C.
Forster, T.
Bissett, G.
Meredith, W. H.
Robinson, J. W.
Barlow, C.
Harris, C.
Spratt, W.
Prentice, J. H.
Williamson, J.
Sapsford, G.

DID YOU KNOW? The peacetime Football League programme resumed on 30 August 1919, United opened their peacetime fixtures at the Baseball Ground where Woodcock scored in a 1-1 draw.

OPPOSITE PAGE

Top: RETURN TO PEACETIME 1919/20. United resumed their Football League programme with these players:
Back Row: W. Makin, J. S. Wood, C. Hilditch, C. Moore, J. Mew, J. Silcock, T. Meehan. Front: G. Bissett, F. Goodwin, W. Meredith, G. Sapsford, F. Hopkins.
Insets: (above): E. Partridge & (below) J. Spence. (BNPC)

Bottom Middle: 'THE REAL THING'. Manchester United 1 Middlesbrough 1. 4 October 1919. Match report after United had embarked on their 'Real' League fixtures. (CZ)

Bottom Left: FRED HOPKIN. Joined United in 1919. (KM)

Bottom Right: C. RADFORD on 'Pinnace' Cigarettes Card. (BH)

RETURN TO PEACETIME

F. HOPKIN

THE REAL THING.

Middlesbrough's Draw After Thrilling Struggle.

Manchester United..1 Middlesbrough.....1

[BY IMPRESSIONIST.]

WHEN Manchester United equalised the score with Middlesbrough, at Old Trafford, in the last fleeting moments it was a fitting and dramatic conclusion to a game that breathed the essence of the real football, with all the concomitants of exciting incident to please the appetite of the most insatiable.

The scheming of both teams was carried to an appropriate finish, with the result that a rare battle of skill and wits ensued between attack and defence.

The visitors were the purveyors of the football artistic, but United took their share of the honours by virtue of their speed and their cleverness, by keeping the ball open, and by prompt distribution. Still, they did not shoot nearly so accurately as the Middlesbrough attacks, else it is conceivable that the one weak spot in the latter's armour —the backs—would have succumbed to more than one goal. However, it was a result thoroughly justified, and infinitely creditable to both sides.

The exuberant Manchester men began with every appearance of overpowering a wavering defence, but once the Middlesbrough machine became attuned the balance was restored.

C. RADFORD

MANCHESTER UNITED

March No.	Date	Venue	Opponents	Result		Goalscorers	Attendance
1	Aug 28	H	Bolton Wanderers	L	2-3	Hopkin, Meehan	
2	30	H	Arsenal	L	0-2		
3	Sept 4	A	Bolton Wanderers	D	1-1	Sapsford	
4	6	A	Arsenal	D	1-1	Spence	
5	11	A	Chelsea	W	3-1	Meehan 2, Leonard	40,000
6	18	H	Chelsea	W	2-1	Leonard 2	30,000
7	25	A	Tottenham Hotspur	L	0-1		52,000
8	Oct 2	H	Tottenham Hotspur	L	1-4	Spence	34,600
9	9	H	Oldham Athletic	W	4-1	Sapsford 2, Meehan, Miller	
10	16	A	Oldham Athletic	D	2-2	Spence, 1 o.g.	20,000
11	23	H	Preston North End	W	1-0	Miller	
12	30	A	Preston North End	L	0-1		
13	Nov 6	A	Sheffield United	W	2-1	Leonard 2	
14	13	H	Sheffield United	D	0-0		20,000
15	20	A	Manchester City	D	1-1	Miller	60,000
16	27	H	Manchester City	L	0-3		40,000
17	Dec 4	H	Bradford Park Avenue	W	5-1	Miller 2, Myerscough 2, Partridge	35,000
18	11	A	Bradford Park Avenue	W	4-2	Myerscough 2, Miller, Partridge	12,000
19	18	A	Newcastle United	W	2-0	Miller, Hopkin	35,000
20	25	A	Aston Villa	W	4-3	Harrison, Grimwood 2, Partridge	40,000
21	26	H	Aston Villa	L	1-3	Harrison	70,504
22	Jan 1	H	Newcastle United	L	3-6	Silcock, Hopkin, Partridge	5,000
23	15	H	West Bromwich Albion	L	1-4	Partridge	40,104
24	22	A	West Bromwich Albion	W	2-0	Partridge, Myerscough	26,826
25	Feb 5	H	Liverpool	D	1-1	Grimwood	35,000
26	9	A	Liverpool	L	0-2		25,000
27	12	A	Everton	L	1-2	Meredith	40,000
28	26	H	Sunderland	W	3-0	Robinson, Hilditch, Harrison	
29	Mar 5	A	Sunderland	L	1-4	Sapsford 2, Goodwin	
30	9	A	Everton	L	0-2		
31	12	H	Bradford City	D	1-1	Robinson	22,000
32	19	A	Bradford City	L	0-1		
33	25	H	Burnley	D	1-1	Sapsford	40,000
34	26	A	Huddersfield Town	L	2-5	Harris, Partridge	30,000
35	28	A	Burnley	L	0-3		30,000
36	Apr 2	H	Huddersfield Town	W	2-0	Bissett 2	30,000
37	9	A	Middlesbrough	W	4-2	Spence 2, Grimwood, Bissett	15,000
38	16	H	Middlesbrough	L	0-1		
39	23	A	Blackburn Rovers	L	0-2		20,000
40	30	H	Blackburn Rovers	L	0-1		33,000
41	May 2	A	Derby County	D	1-1	Bissett	8,000
42	7	H	Derby County	W	3-0	Spence 2, Sapsford	10,000

F.A. CUP

	Date	Venue	Opponents	Result		Goalscorers	Attendance
Rd 1	Jan 8	A	Liverpool	D	1-1	Miller	40,000
Replay	12	H	Liverpool	L	1-2	Partridge	30,000

Players (League Appearances / League Scorers):

Player	League Appearances	League Scorers
Mew, J.	40	
Moore, C.	26	
Silcock, J.	37	1
Meehan, T.	15	4
Grimwood, J. B.	25	4
Hilditch, C. G.	34	1
Meredith, W. H.	14	1
Bissett, G.	12	3
Goodwin, W.	5	1
Sapsford, G. D.	21	7
Hopkin, F.	31	3
Hofton, L.	1	
Harris, F. E.	26	1
Spence, J. W.	19	7
Barlow, C.	13	
Myerscough, J.	1	5
Schofield, G. W.	1	
Toms, W.	1	
Hodges, F. C.	2	
Leonard, H.	10	5
Miller, T.	25	7
Montgomery, J.	1	
Forster, T.	2	
Partridge, E.	28	7
Steward, A.	23	
Harrison, W. E.	7	3
Robinson, J. W.	1	2
Radford, C.		

1 o.g.

DID YOU KNOW? A record league attendance for Old Trafford was established on 26 December 1920, when a crowd of 70,504 saw United lose 1-3 to Aston Villa. Billy Meredith was given a free transfer at the end of 1920/1 after fifteen years with the club, and rejoined Manchester City in August 1921.

END OF 'THE MEREDITH ERA'

─── ·o· ───

HOME RECORD LOST.

UNITED "BAG A BRACE" AT VILLA PARK

BY "TOUCHSTONE."

Aston Villa 3, Manchester United 4.

Manchester United celebrated Christmas Day by overcoming Aston Villa at Villa Park, and thus being the first club to take away both points from the ground. The score was far more generous than the margin—four goals to three—and a crowd of some 40,000 thoroughly enjoyed the remarkable sequence of goals which featured the last half-hour.

FIRST HALF PROMISE.

The match was played under almost ideal conditions, and it was a genuine Christmassy setting in which the rivals disported themselves to fine purpose.

From the personal standpoint chief interest centred in the debut of Spiers, from Halesowen, who was entrusted with the charge of goal in place of Lee. It was of course a severe ordeal for a young player to face a vanguard of the capacity of Manchester, and it must be confessed that his success was only partial.

With his first half display no fault can be found, but he was sadly at fault with the second and third goals, and was out of position with the fourth. He fields the ground balls with much greater acumen than he displays when gathering high shots, and it was the latter that proved

COPE'S "CLIPS" CIGARETTES

No. 125—MEREDITH
Manchester United

Noted Footballers

2175   **J. MYERSCOUGH**

Top Right: BILLY MEREDITH. 'Clips' Cigarettes 'Noted Footballers' series No. 125, by Cope Bros of Liverpool. Meredith left United at the end of 1920/1. (KM)

Top Middle: ASTON VILLA 3 MANCHESTER UNITED 4. Xmas Day 1920. Match report of the stirring win at Villa Park. The following days return match drew Old Trafford's record league attendance of 70,504. (CZ).

Top Left: J. MYERSCOUGH on 'Pinnace' Cigarettes Card. (BH)

Bottom: UNITED 1920/1. Back Row: J. Spence, T. Forster, J. Greenwood, C. Moore, J. Mew, J. Silcock, T. Meehan, E. Partridge. Front Row: W. Harrison, T. Miller, A. Leonard, G. Sapsford, F. Hopkin. (BNPC)

Relegated to Division Two

M.U.F.C.

MANCHESTER UNITED

Match No.	Date	Venue	Opponents	Result		Goalscorers	Attendance
1	Aug 27	A	Everton	L	0-5		30,000
2	Aug 29	H	West Bromwich Albion	L	2-3	Partridge, Robinson	20,000
3	Sept 3	A	West Bromwich Albion	W	2-1	Harrison, Spence	25,000
4	Sept 7	H	Everton	D	0-0		20,500
5	Sept 10	A	Chelsea	D	0-0		30,000
6	Sept 17	H	Chelsea	D	0-0		28,000
7	Sept 24	A	Preston North End	L	2-3	Partridge, Lochhead	
8	Oct 1	H	Preston North End	D	1-1	Spence	
9	Oct 8	A	Tottenham Hotspur	D	2-2	Sapsford, Spence	36,113
10	Oct 15	H	Tottenham Hotspur	W	2-1	Sapsford, Spence	40,000
11	Oct 22	A	Manchester City	L	1-4	Spence	60,000
12	Oct 29	H	Manchester City	W	3-1	Spence 3	56,000
13	Nov 5	A	Middlesbrough	L	3-5	Lochhead, Sapsford, Spence	
14	Nov 12	H	Middlesbrough	W	3-1	Spence 3	
15	Nov 19	A	Aston Villa	L	1-3	Spence	23,000
16	Nov 26	H	Aston Villa	W	1-0	Henderson	
17	Dec 3	A	Bradford City	L	1-2	Spence	15,000
18	Dec 10	H	Bradford City	D	1-1	Henderson	20,000
19	Dec 17	A	Liverpool	L	1-2	Sapsford	
20	Dec 24	H	Liverpool	L	0-1		50,000
21	Dec 26	A	Burnley	L	0-1		
22	Dec 27	H	Burnley	L	2-4	Sapsford, Lochhead	25,000
23	Dec 31	A	Newcastle United	L	0-3		
24	Jan 2	H	Newcastle United	L	0-1		25,000
25	Jan 14	A	Sheffield United	L	0-1		
26	Jan 21	H	Sunderland	L	1-2	Sapsford	
27	Jan 28	A	Sunderland	W	3-1	Spence, Lochhead, Sapsford	30,000
28	Feb 11	H	Huddersfield Town	D	1-1	Spence	20,000
29	Feb 18	A	Birmingham	W	1-0	Spence	
30	Feb 25	H	Birmingham	D	1-1	Sapsford	20,000
31	Feb 27	A	Huddersfield Town	D	1-1	Sapsford	26,000
32	Mar 11	H	Arsenal	W	1-0	Spence	
33	Mar 18	A	Arsenal	L	0-1		
34	Mar 25	A	Blackburn Rovers	L	0-3		15,000
35	Mar 25	H	Blackburn Rovers	L	0-1		
36	Apr 1	H	Bolton Wanderers	L	1-3	Lochhead	28,000
37	Apr 5	A	Bolton Wanderers	L	0-1		
38	Apr 8	A	Oldham Athletic	L	0-3		
39	Apr 15	H	Sheffield United	W	3-2	Harrison, Lochhead, P.Partridge	45,000
40	Apr 22	A	Oldham Athletic	D	1-1	Lochhead	20,000
41	Apr 29	H	Cardiff City	D	1-1	P.Partridge	19,000
42	May 6	A	Cardiff City	L	1-3	Lochhead	

F.A. CUP

	Date	Venue	Opponents	Result		Goalscorers	Attendance
Rd 3	Jan 7	H	Cardiff City	L	1-4	Sapsford	28,726

Players:

Mew, J. W.; Brett, F. B.; Silcock, J.; Bennion, S. R.; Grimwood, J. B.; Scott, J.; Gibson, R.; Myerscough, J.; Lochhead, A. W.; Sapsford, G. D.; Partridge, E.; Harris, F. E.; Harrison, W. E.; Spence, J. W.; Goodwin, W.; Robinson, J. W.; Bissett, G.; Hilditch, C. G.; Radford, C.; Schofield, C. W.; Forster, T.; Barlow, C.; McBain, N.; Henderson, W.; Steward, A.; Howarth, J. T.; Taylor; Haslam, G.; Thomas, H.; Pugh, J.

(Columns record League Appearances and League Scorers for each player.)

DID YOU KNOW? United were relegated to Division Two at the end of the 1921-22 Season, finishing bottom of the table with 28 points from 42 matches. On 31 October 1921, Mr. John A. Chapman was appointed Secretary/Manager on the resignation of Mr. J. R. Robson, who later accepted the position of Assistant Manager.

M.U.F.C.

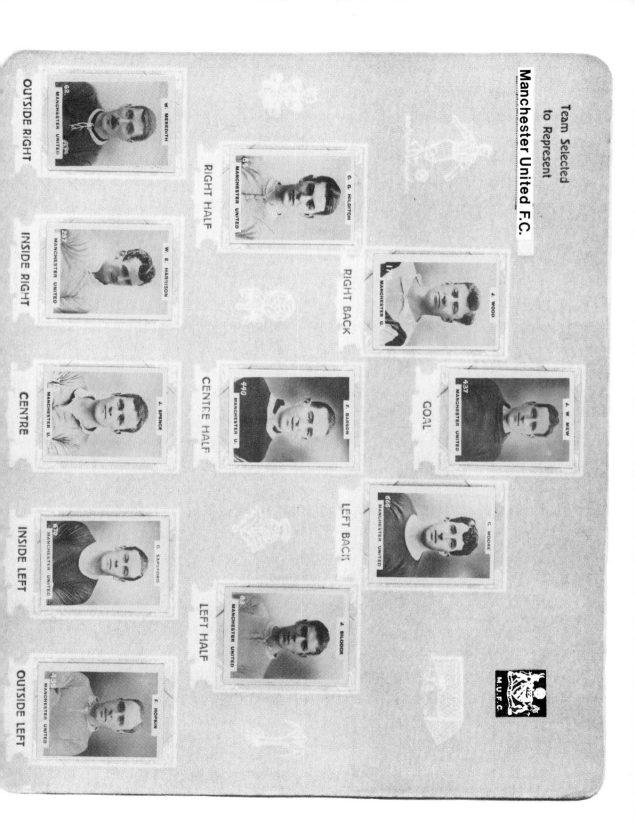

Team Selected to Represent

Manchester United F.C.

OUTSIDE RIGHT — W. MEREDITH — MANCHESTER UNITED

RIGHT HALF — C. G. HILDITCH — MANCHESTER UNITED

RIGHT BACK — J. WOOD — MANCHESTER U.

INSIDE RIGHT — W. E. HARRISON — MANCHESTER UNITED

CENTRE — J. SPENCE — MANCHESTER U.

CENTRE HALF — F. BARSON — MANCHESTER U.

GOAL — J. W. MEW — MANCHESTER UNITED

INSIDE LEFT — C. SAPSFORD — MANCHESTER UNITED

LEFT BACK — C. MOORE — MANCHESTER UNITED

LEFT HALF — J. SILCOCK — MANCHESTER UNITED

OUTSIDE LEFT — F. HOPKIN — MANCHESTER UNITED

M.U.F.C.

Above: Pinnace *series of soccer photos, produced by 'Pinnace' Cigarettes. (BH)*

113

MANCHESTER UNITED

M.U.F.C.

Match No.	Date		Venue	Opponents	Result	Goalscorers	Attendance
1	Aug	26	H	Crystal Palace	W 2-1	Wood, Spence	30,000
2		28	A	The Wednesday	L 0-1		20,000
3	Sept.	2	A	Crystal Palace	W 3-2	Spence 2, Williams	12,000
4		4	H	The Wednesday	W 1-0	Spence	35,000
5		9	A	Wolverhampton Wanderers	W 1-0	Williams	
6		16	H	Wolverhampton Wanderers	W 1-0	Spence	
7		23	A	Coventry City	L 0-2		17,000
8		30	H	Coventry City	W 2-1	Henderson, Spence	20,000
9	Oct	7	A	Port Vale	L 1-2	Spence	
10		14	H	Port Vale	L 0-1		20,000
11		21	A	Fulham	D 1-1	Myerscough	20,000
12		28	A	Fulham	D 0-0		22,000
13	Nov	4	H	Clapton Orient	D 0-0		25,000
14		11	A	Clapton Orient	D 1-1	Goldthorpe	15,000
15		18	H	Bury	D 2-2	Goldthorpe 2	20,000
16		25	A	Bury	L 0-1		10,000
17	Dec	2	H	Rotherham County	W 3-0	Lochhead, Spence, McBain	
18		9	A	Rotherham County	D 1-1	Goldthorpe	
19		16	H	Stockport County	D 0-0		15,000
20		23	A	Stockport County	W 1-0	McBain	30,000
21		25	A	Leeds United	W 6-1	Goldthorpe 4, Myerscough 2	24,745
22		26	H	Leeds United	W 2-0	Goldthorpe 2	30,000
23		30	A	Hull City	L 1-2	Lochhead	
24	Jan	1	H	Hull City	W 1-0	Lochhead	20,000
25		6	H	Barnsley	W 3-2	Goldthorpe, Lochhead, 1 o.g.	15,000
26		20	H	Rotherham County	D 0-0		30,000
27		27	A	Leeds United	W 1-0	Lochhead	23,000
28	Feb	10	A	Notts County	D 0-0		
29		17	H	Notts County	D 1-1	Spence	20,000
30		21	H	Derby County	D 1-1	Lochhead	30,000
31	Mar	3	A	Southampton	L 1-2	Lochhead	
32		14	H	Southampton	D 1-1	McDonald	12,000
33		17	A	Derby County	D 1-1	Goldthorpe	23,000
34		21	H	Bradford City	W 3-0	Lochhead, Goldthorpe 2	
35		30	H	South Shields	W 3-0	Lochhead, Spence	
36		31	A	South Shields	L 0-1		
37	Apr	2	A	Blackpool	W 3-0	Hilditch, Goldthorpe, Spence	
38		7	H	Blackpool	W 2-1	Lochhead, Radford	
39		11	A	Southampton	W 1-0	Bain	
40		14	A	Leicester City	W 1-0		24,000
41		21	H	Leicester City	L 0-2		28,000
42		28	A	Barnsley	D 2-2	Spence, Lochhead	

F.A. CUP

	Date		Venue	Opponents	Result	Goalscorers	Attendance
Rd 1	Jan	13	A	Bradford City	D 1-1	Partridge	27,000
Replay		17	H	Bradford city	W 2-0	Goldthorpe, Barker	27,791
Rd 2	Feb	3	A	Tottenham Hotspur	L 0-4		38,333

Players: Mew, J. W.; Radford, C.; Silcock, J.; Hilditch, C. G.; McBain, N.; Grimwood, J. B.; Wood, J.; Lochhead, A. W.; Spence, J. W.; Partridge, E.; Thomas, H.; Williams, H.; Moore, C.; Barson, F.; Lyner; Sarvis; Henderson, W.; Bain, D.; Pugh, J.; Myerscough, J.; Goldthorpe, E. H.; Cartman, H. R.; Bennion, S. R.; Barber, J.; Lievesley; McDonald, K.; Mann, F. D.; Steward, A.; Broome, A. H.

DID YOU KNOW? When Frank Barson signed for United in August 1922 he was promised a public-house if the club secured promotion. When they did, 3 years later, Frank lasted for just 15 minutes as a licensee! On the day he opened his hotel, he was besieged by United well-wishers. Within minutes his patience had become exhausted with the flattery – he told the Head Waiter to take over – and walked out for good.

MANCHESTER'S FATE SEALED.

Leicester Steadiness Reaps Its Reward at Old Trafford.

Manchester United 0 Leicester City 2

Manchester United gave one of their worst exhibitions of the season in their home game with Leicester City and suffered a defeat by two goals to nothing that permanently seals their fate. They have sacrificed no fewer than 16 points to teams at Old Trafford to date.

Whereas the United, who had Mew back in goal, were at full strength, Leicester had to play John Duncan, their inside-right, at left-half.

As usual, it was, as far as the home side were concerned, a tale of missed chances brought on by nerves. The importance of the occasion upset the equilibrium of the attack, and with the exception of Spence, there was not a forward in the line who could execute anything worthy of the name of a shot. The first half was void of scoring, but with the wind behind them Leicester opened their account through John Duncan. This set-back caused the United captain to rearrange his attack, Spence going to the centre and Bain outside-right. The alterations had an effect for a time, and Spence actually got the ball into the net on one occasion—with the aid of his hands.

Fifteen minutes from the end, Smith increased the visitors' lead.

Leicester deserved their success. They were steadier and on the day a much better balanced side.

H. WILLIAMS

Top Left: JOHN A. CHAPMAN. Appointed Secretary/Manager in October 1921. (MMUSC)

Top Right: MANCHESTER UNITED 3 ROTHERHAM COUNTY 0. 2 December 1922. United's right-back Radford tackles the Rotherham winger, in this photo from 'Quality Cigarettes' card by J. A. Pattreiouex. (KM).

Bottom Left: MANCHESTER UNITED 0 LEICESTER CITY 2. 21 April 1923. Report of the match in which United lost their chance of promotion. (CZ)

Middle Bottom: E. H. GOLDTHORPE on 'Casket' Cigarette Card. (KM)

Bottom Right: H. WILLIAMS on 'Pinnace' Cigarette Card. (BH)

MANCHESTER UNITED

Match No.	Date	Venue	Opponents	Result	Goalscorers	Attendance
1	Aug 25	H	Bristol City	W 2-1	McDonald, Lochhead	30,000
2	27	A	Southampton	W 1-0	Goldthorpe	35,000
3	Sept 1	A	Bristol City	W 2-1	Lochhead, Spence	25,000
4	3	H	Southampton	D 0-0		20,000
5	8	H	Bury	L 0-2		
6	15	A	Bury	L 0-1		
7	22	A	South Shields	L 0-1		
8	29	H	South Shields	D 1-1	Lochhead	
9	Oct 6	A	Oldham Athletic	L 2-3	2 o.g.s	
10	13	H	Oldham Athletic	W 2-0	Bain 2	
11	20	A	Stockport County	W 3-0	Mann 2, Bain	
12	27	H	Stockport County	L 2-3	Barber, Lochhead	
13	Nov 3	A	Leicester City	D 2-2	Lochhead 2	17,000
14	10	H	Leicester City	W 3-0	Spence, Mann, Lochhead	20,000
15	17	A	Coventry City	D 1-1	1 o.g.	16,100
16	Dec 1	H	Coventry City	D 0-0		19,475
17	8	A	Leeds United	D 0-0		30,000
18	15	H	Leeds United	W 3-1	Lochhead 2, Spence	14,000
19	22	H	Port Vale	W 5-0	Bain 3, Lochhead, McPherson	14,000
20	25	H	Barnsley	L 1-2	Grimwood	40,000
21	26	A	Barnsley	L 0-1		
22	29	A	Bradford City	D 0-0		
23	Jan 2	H	Coventry City	D 1-2	Bain	14,000
24	5	H	Bradford City	W 3-0	Bain, Lochhead, McPherson	18,000
25	19	A	Fulham	L 1-3	Lochhead	12,000
26	26	H	Fulham	D 0-0		
27	Feb 6	A	Blackpool	L 0-1		
28	9	H	Blackpool	D 0-0		
29	16	A	Derby County	L 0-3		12,000
30	23	H	Derby County	D 0-0		25,000
31	Mar 1	A	Nelson	W 2-0	Spence, Kennedy	
32	8	H	Nelson	L 0-1		25,000
33	15	H	Hull City	D 1-1	Lochhead	
34	22	A	Hull City	D 0-0		8,000
35	29	H	Stoke City	D 2-2	Smith 2	
36	Apr 5	A	Stoke City	L 0-3		
37	12	H	Crystal Palace	W 5-1	Spence 4, Smith	
38	18	A	Clapton Orient	L 0-1		
39	19	A	Crystal Palace	D 1-1	Spence	
40	21	H	Clapton Orient	D 2-2	Evans 2	
41	26	H	The Wednesday	W 2-0	Smith, Lochhead	20,000
42	May 3	A	The Wednesday	L 0-2		10,000

F.A. CUP

	Date	Venue	Opponents	Result	Goalscorers	Attendance
Rd 1	Jan 12	H	Plymouth Argyle	W 1-0	McPherson	35,700
Rd 2	Feb 2	H	Huddersfield Town	L 0-3		66,678

Players (with shirt-number appearances recorded across the season):

Mew, J. • Moore, C. • Silcock, J. • Meehan, T. • Grimwood, J. B. • Hilditch, C. G. • Meredith, W. H. • Bissett, G. • Goodwin, W. • Sapsford, G. D. • Hopkin, F. • Hofton, L. • Harris, F. E. • Spence, J. W. • Barlow, C. • Myerscough, J. • Schofield, G. W. • Toms, W. • Hodges, F. C. • Leonard, H. • Miller, T. • Montgomery, J. • Forster, T. • Partridge, E. • Steward, A. • Harrison, W. E. • Robinson, J. W. • Radford, C.

League Appearances and League Scorers are recorded in the totals rows at the foot of the grid (3 o.g.s).

DID YOU KNOW? United's record attendance for an F.A. Cup match at Old Trafford was established in 1923/4, when 66,678 spectators saw the 'Reds' lose 0-3 to Huddersfield Town. United changed their colours in 1923 to white shirts with a red 'V' and white shorts, which they continued to wear until 1927.

Bottom Left: UNITED SUPREME: Manchester United 5 Port Vale 0. 22 December 1923. Match report of the Old Trafford destruction of Port Vale. (CZ)

Centre: H. THOMAS on 'Pinnace' Cigarette Card. (BH)

Middle Right: JACK SPENCE 'Footballers Series' No. 50. From 'Trawler' Cigarettes by J. A. Pattreioex of Manchester. (KM)

THE MANCHESTER UNITED

League Champions 1908 1911

Winners English Cup 1909

OFFICIAL — SEASON 1923-24 — PROGRAMME

VOL. XI. No. 37.   SATURDAY, APRIL 26, 1924.   2d.

NOTABLE COLLAPSES.

Christmas Cheer For Manchester United and The Wednesday.

UNITED SUPREME.

Vale Meet Day of Dire Disaster.

Manchester U....5 Port Vale........0

[BY JACQUES.]

FOURTEEN thousand people at Old Trafford on Saturday saw Manchester United move on a heavy ground with such pace and combination that Port Vale, though struggling pluckily, were completely outclassed. At the interval the home team led by two goals, and three were added in the second half. The Vale had wind and rain at their backs in the opening forty-five minutes, but they were never able to hold their own.

DAVID BAIN headed the first goal, and the same player forced the second in a scrimmage. Lowe and Prince, the Vale outside wing men, made new centres at times, and Bridgett made bold efforts to break down the home defence, but generally the visiting half-backs were kept on the run by a virile forward line, who were not only good in midfield, but finished strongly.

The first goal of the second half was the result of a fine effort by M'Pherson, who, going away on the United left wing with great speed, turned the ball sharply back from near the flag instead of driving it across.

This left LOCHHEAD so placed that he was able to meet the ball on the run, and his shot gave Lonsdale no chance. Another Manchester onslaught saw BAIN rush in as the ball fell between Birks and Pursell and drive it home, and SPENCE scored the last goal of the game.

The Vale had made changes, Page moving from inside left to inside right, and Prince coming in to partner Bridgett on the left flank of the vanguard, while Hampson figured at left half-back. The home side had M'Pherson in the forward line again, Thomas standing down. Page had an early opportunity, but his hurried volley passed wide of the right hand post, and it was just after this that Spence's run and centre led to the opening goal.

H. THOMAS

J. W. SPENCE
MANCHESTER UNITED.

A Barson Story.—Frank Barson, the former Manchester United centre-half, was a wit as well as a great player. Once he was badly fouled by an opposing centre-forward, and the referee went to caution the player. Before he could speak, Barson had limped over and said with a grin : " Don't send him off, ref. —I'll kick him off in the second half ! "

MANCHESTER UNITED

Match No.	Date	Venue	Opponents	Result	Goalscorers	Attendance
1	Aug 30	H	Leicester City	W 1-0	Goldthorpe	
2	Sept 1	A	Stockport County	L 1-2	Lochhead	
3	6	A	Stoke City	D 0-0		
4	8	H	Barnsley	W 1-0	Henderson	20,000
5	13	H	Coventry City	W 5-1	Henderson 2, Lochhead, Spence, McPherson	17,000
6	20	A	Oldham Athletic	W 3-0	Henderson 3	
7	27	H	The Wednesday	W 2-0	Smith, McPherson	
8	Oct 4	A	Clapton Orient	W 1-0	Lochhead	
9	11	H	Crystal Palace	W 1-0	Lochhead	40,000
10	18	A	Southampton	W 2-0	Lochhead 2	14,000
11	25	A	Wolverhampton Wanderers	D 0-0		
12	Nov 1	H	Fulham	W 2-0	Henderson, Lochhead	
13	8	A	Portsmouth	D 1-1	Smith	25,000
14	15	H	Hull City	W 2-0	Hanson, McPherson	30,000
15	22	H	Blackpool	D 1-1	Hanson	
16	29	A	Derby County	D 1-1	Hanson	59,448
17	Dec 6	A	South Shields	W 2-1	Henderson, McPherson	
18	13	H	Bradford City	W 3-0	Henderson 2, McPherson	25,000
19	20	A	Port Vale	L 1-2	Lochhead	
20	25	H	Middlesbrough	D 1-1	Henderson	
21	26	H	Middlesbrough	W 2-0	Smith, Henderson	
22	27	A	Leicester City	L 0-3		
23	Jan 1	H	Chelsea	W 1-0	Grimwood	28,000
24	3	H	Stoke City	W 2-0	Henderson 2	
25	17	A	Coventry City	L 0-1		12,000
26	24	H	Oldham Athletic	L 0-1		
27	Feb 7	H	Clapton Orient	W 4-2	Kennedy 2, Pape, McPherson	
28	14	A	Crystal Palace	L 1-2	Lochhead	
29	23	A	The Wednesday	D 1-1	Pape	8,000
30	28	H	Wolverhampton Wanderers	W 3-0	Spence 2, Kennedy	
31	Mar 7	A	Fulham	L 0-1		
32	14	H	Portsmouth	W 2-0	Spence, Lochhead	27,525
33	21	A	Hull City	W 1-0	Lochhead	8,000
34	28	H	Blackpool	D 0-0		
35	Apr 4	A	Derby County	L 0-1		24,438
36	10	H	Stockport County	W 2-0	Pape 2	
37	11	A	South Shields	W 1-0	Lochhead	34,000
38	13	A	Chelsea	W 1-0	Smith	40,000
39	18	H	Bradford City	D 1-1	Pape	17,000
40	22	H	Southampton	W 1-0	Smith	40,000
41	25	H	Port Vale	W 4-0	Spence, Smith, McPherson, Lochhead	40,000
42	May 2	A	Barnsley	D 0-0		

F.A. CUP

Rd 1	Jan 10	A	The Wednesday	L 0-2		35,079

Players:
Steward, A.; Moore, C.; Silcock, J.; Bennion, S. R.; Barson, F.; Hilditch, C. G.; Spence, J. W.; Smith, T. G.; Goldthorpe, F. H.; Lochhead, A. W.; McPherson, F.; Henderson, W.; Mann, F. D.; Grimwood, J. B.; Jones, T.; Thomas, H.; Hanson, J.; Kennedy, F.; Haslam, G.; Taylor, J.; Bain, J.; Pape, A.; Partridge, E.; Rennox, C.

League Appearances

League Scorers

DID YOU KNOW? In securing promotion back to Division One in 1924-5, United conceded only 23 goals in 42 matches – a record for Division Two. Albert Pape arrived with his club Clapton Orient for the match at Old Trafford on 7 February 1925, but was signed by United just before the kick-off and made his debut against his former team mates.

PROMOTION YEAR 1924/5

Top: PROMOTION 1925. Manchester United 1 Leicester City 0. 30 August 1924. Goldthorpe gives United a good start to the season with this penalty goal winner at Old Trafford. (MMUSC)

Bottom: TOTTENHAM HOTSPUR 2 MANCHESTER UNITED 2. FA Cup 4th Round, 30 January 1926. 'Cal' Hilditch leads out the United team at White Hart Lane. United won the replay 2-0. (MMUSC)

MANCHESTER UNITED

League

Match No.	Date		Venue	Opponents	Result		Goalscorers	Attendance
1	Aug	29	A	West Ham United	L	0-1		40,000
2	Sept	2	H	Aston Villa	W	3-0	Spence, Barson, Lochhead	
3		5	H	Arsenal	L	0-1		
4		7	A	Aston Villa	D	2-2	Hanson, Rennox	
5		12	A	Manchester City	D	1-1	Rennox	70,000
6		16	H	Leicester City	W	3-2	Rennox 2, Lochhead	
7		19	H	Liverpool	L	0-5		
8		26	A	Burnley	W	6-1	Rennox 3, Hilditch, Hanson, Smith	26,000
9	Oct	3	A	Leeds United	L	0-2		26,500
10		10	H	Newcastle United	W	2-1	Thomas, Rennox	
11		17	A	Tottenham Hotspur	W	1-0	Thomas	30,000
12		24	H	Cardiff City	D	0-0		15,000
13		31	A	Huddersfield Town	D	1-1	McPherson	27,000
14	Nov	7	A	Everton	W	3-1	Spence, McPherson, Rennox	
15		14	H	Birmingham	W	3-1	Spence, Barson, Thomas	16,654
16		21	A	Bury	W	3-1	McPherson 2, Spence	
17		28	H	Blackburn Rovers	W	2-0	McPherson, Thomas	
18	Dec	5	A	Sunderland	L	1-2	Rennox	
19		12	H	Sheffield United	L	1-2	McPherson	
20		19	A	West Bromwich Albion	L	1-5	McPherson	30,000
21		25	H	Bolton Wanderers	W	2-1	Spence, Hanson	30,000
22		26	A	Leicester City	W	3-1	McPherson 3	26,996
23		28	H	Liverpool	D	3-3	Hanson, Rennox, Spence	
24	Jan	2	H	West Ham United	W	2-1	Rennox 2	28,000
25		16	A	Arsenal	L	2-3	Spence, McPherson	
26		23	H	Manchester City	L	1-6	Rennox	50,000
27	Feb	6	H	Burnley	W	1-0	McPherson	30,000
28		13	A	Leeds United	W	2-1	McPherson, Sweeney	
29		27	H	Tottenham Hotspur	W	1-0	Smith	
30	Mar	10	H	Huddersfield Town	D	0-0		30,000
31		17	A	Bolton Wanderers	L	1-3	McPherson	
32		20	H	Everton	D	0-0		28,000
33		2	A	Notts County	W	3-0	McPherson, Rennox 2	25,000
34	Apr	2	H	Notts County	L	0-1		
35		3	H	Bury	L	0-1		
36		5	A	Blackburn Rovers	L	0-7		15,000
37		10	A	Newcastle United	L	1-4	Hanson	10,000
38		14	H	Birmingham	L	1-2	Rennox	20,000
39		19	A	Sunderland	W	5-1	Taylor 3, Thomas, Smith	
40		21	H	Sheffield United	L	0-2		18,000
41		24	A	Cardiff City	W	1-0	Inglis	
42	May	1	H	West Bromwich Albion	W	3-2	Taylor 3	11,198

F.A. CUP

Round	Date		Venue	Opponents	Result		Goalscorers	Attendance
Rd 3	Jan	9	A	Port Vale	W	3-2	Spence 2, McPherson	14,841
Rd 4		30	H	Tottenham Hotspur	D	2-2	Spence, Thomas	40,000
Replay	Feb	3	A	Tottenham Hotspur	W	2-0	Rennox, Spence	45,000
Rd 5		20	H	Sunderland	W	2-0	McPherson, Smith 2	50,500
Replay		24	A	Sunderland	D	3-3	McPherson, Smith	58,661
Rd 6	Mar	6	H	Fulham	W	2-1	Smith, Spence	28,699
S/F		27	N	Manchester City	L	0-3		46,450

Players

Steward, A.
Moore, C.
Silcock, J.
Bennion, S. R.
Barson, F.
Bain, J.
Spence, J. W.
Smith, T. G.
Iddon, R.
Lochhead, A. W.
McPherson, F.
Mann, F. D.
Hilditch, C. G.
Pape, A.
Hanson, J.
Rennox, C.
Grimwood, J. B.
Thomas, H.
Haslam, G.
Taylor, J.
Hannaford, C.
Jones, T.
McCrae, J. J.
Mew, J.
Hall, J.
Sweeney, E.
Partridge, E.
Astley, J.
Inglis, W.
Richardson, L.

League Appearances

League Scorers

MANCHESTER UNITED FOOTBALL CLUB

CUP SEMI-FINAL TEAM—1925-6.

Top: F.A. CUP SEMI-FINAL TEAM 1925/6. Back Row: C. Hilditch, C. Moore, A. Steward, J. Silcock, F. Barson, F. D. Mann.
Front Row: J. Spence, R. Iddon, F. McPherson, C. Rennox, H. Thomas. Inset: J. McCrae. (BNPC)

Bottom: SEMI-FINAL AT BRAMALL LANE. Manchester United 0 Manchester City 3. 27 March 1926. Alf Steward saves in this City attack,
with Barson (left) and Moore (right) in attendance. (MMUSC)

M.U.F.C.

MANCHESTER UNITED

Match No.	Date		Venue	Opponents	Result		Goalscorers	Attendance
1	Aug	28	A	Liverpool	L	2-4	McPherson 2	45,000
2		30	A	Sheffield United	D	2-2	McPherson 2	
3	Sept	4	H	Leeds United	D	2-2	McPherson 2	28,000
4		11	A	Newcastle United	L	2-4	McPherson, Spence	
5		15	H	Arsenal	D	2-2	McPherson, Hanson	33,000
6		18	H	Burnley	W	2-1	Spence 2	10,000
7		25	A	Cardiff City	D	1-1	Spence, Rennox	
8	Oct	2	H	Aston Villa	W	2-1	Barson, Rennox	30,000
9		9	A	Bolton Wanderers	L	0-4		12,000
10		16	H	Bury	W	3-0	Spence 2, McPherson	30,000
11		23	A	Birmingham	L	0-1		35,000
12		30	H	West Ham United	L	0-4		20,000
13	Nov	6	A	The Wednesday	L			
14		13	A	Leicester City	W	3-2	McPherson 2, Rennox	15,000
15		20	H	Everton	W	2-1	Rennox 2	
16		27	A	Blackburn Rovers	L	1-2	Spence	
17	Dec	4	H	Huddersfield Town	D	0-0		16,000
18		11	A	Sunderland	L	0-6		
19		18	H	West Bromwich Albion	W	2-0	Sweeney 2	
20		25	A	Tottenham Hotspur	D	1-1	Spence	37,762
21		27	H	Tottenham Hotspur	W	2-1	McPherson 2	50,000
22		28	A	Arsenal	L	0-2		35,000
23	Jan	1	H	Sheffield United	W	5-0	McPherson 2, Barson, Rennox, Sweeney	30,000
24		15	A	Leeds United	L	0-1		
25		22	H	West Bromwich Albion	W	3-2	Spence, Rennox, McPherson	
26	Feb	5	A	Burnley	L	0-1		
27		9	H	Newcastle United	W	3-1	Spence, Hanson, Harris	28,000
28		12	A	Cardiff City	D	1-1	Hanson	
29		19	H	Aston Villa	L	0-2		36,000
30		26	H	Bolton Wanderers	D	0-0		15,000
31	Mar	5	H	Bury	L	1-2	A. Smith	15,000
32		12	H	Birmingham	D	1-1	Spence	12,000
33		19	H	West Ham United	L	0-3		20,000
34		26	A	The Wednesday	W	1-0	Spence	12,000
35	Apr	2	H	Leicester City	W	1-0	Spence	18,000
36		9	A	Everton	D	0-0		35,000
37		15	H	Derby County	D	0-0		
38		16	H	Blackburn Rovers	W	2-0	Hanson, Spence	17,676
39		18	A	Derby County	D	2-2	Spence 2	13,582
40		23	A	Huddersfield Town	D	0-0		
41		30	H	Sunderland	D	0-0		11,022
42	May	7	A	West Bromwich Albion	D	2-2	Spence, Hanson	

League Appearances

League Scorers

Players:
Steward, A.; Inglis, W. W.; Silcock, J.; Hilditch, C. G.; Barson, F.; Mann, F. D.; Spence, J. W.; Smith, T. G.; McPherson, F.; Howarth, H.; Thomas, H.; Bennion, S. R.; Haslam, G.; Hanson, J.; Wilson, J. T.; Partridge, E.; Rennox, C.; Jones, T.; Grimwood, J. B.; Chapman, W.; Hannaford, J.; Sweeney, .E; Moore, C.; Harris, T.; Smith, A.; Iddon, R.; Astley, J.

F.A. CUP

	Date		Venue	Opponents	Result		Goalscorers	Attendance
Rd 3	Jan	8	A	Reading	D	1-1	McPherson	28,961
Replay		12	H	Reading	D	2-2	Spence, Sweeney (after extra time)	29,122
2nd Replay		17	N	Reading	L	1-2	McPherson (at Villa Park, Birmingham)	16,500

DID YOU KNOW? United's Secretary/Manager Mr. John A. Chapman was suspended by the F.A. for alleged management irregularities on 8 October 1926. He was replaced by Walter Crickmer as Secretary, and Clarence Hilditch as caretaker Player-Manager. On 13 April 1927, Mr. Herbert Bamlett was appointed Team Manager, along with Louis Rocca in capacity of Assistant Manager.

M.U.F.C.

SEMI-FINAL ACTION 1926

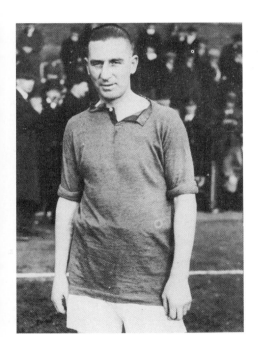

Top: SEMI-FINAL ACTION March 1926. United full-back Moore tries to cut out this shot from a City forward, with Mann (right) and Silcock behind him. (BNPC)

Bottom Right: SEMI-FINAL CROWD at Bramall Lane. The placard advises United to 'Give it to Joe' Spence. (MMUSC)

Bottom Left: FRANK BARSON. (MMUSC)

MANCHESTER UNITED

Match No.	Date		Venue	Opponents	Result	Goalscorers
1	Aug 27		H	Middlesbrough	W 3-0	Spence 2, Hanson
2	" 29		H	The Wednesday	W 2-0	Partridge, Hanson
3	Sept 3		A	Birmingham	D 0-0	
4	" 7		H	The Wednesday	D 1-1	McPherson
5	" 10		A	Newcastle United	L 1-7	Spence
6	" 17		H	Huddersfield Town	L 2-4	Spence 2
7	" 19		A	Blackburn Rovers	L 0-3	
8	" 24		H	Tottenham Hotspur	W 3-0	Hanson 2, Spence
9	Oct 1		A	Leicester City	L 0-1	
10	" 8		A	Everton	L 2-5	Bennion, Spence
11	" 15		H	Cardiff City	D 2-2	Spence, Sweeney
12	" 22		H	Derby County	W 5-0	Spence 3, Johnston, McPherson
13	" 29		A	West Ham United	W 2-1	McPherson, 1 o.g.
14	Nov 5		H	Portsmouth	W 2-0	Hanson, McPherson
15	" 12		A	Sunderland	L 1-4	Spence
16	" 19		H	Aston Villa	W 5-1	Partridge 2, Johnston, McPherson, Spence
17	" 26		A	Burnley	L 0-4	
18	Dec 3		H	Bury	L 0-1	
19	" 10		A	Sheffield United	L 1-2	Spence
20	" 17		H	Arsenal	W 4-1	Spence, Partridge, Hanson, McPherson
21	" 24		A	Liverpool	L 0-2	
22	" 26		H	Blackburn Rovers	W 2-1	Spence (pen)
23	" 31		H	Middlesbrough	W 2-1	Hanson, Johnston
24	Jan 7		H	Birmingham	D 1-1	Hanson
25	" 21		A	Newcastle United	L 1-4	Partridge
26	Feb 4		H	Tottenham Hotspur	L 1-3	Johnston
27	" 11		A	Leicester City	W 5-2	Spence 2, Nicol 2, Hanson
28	" 25		A	Cardiff City	L 0-2	Johnston
29	Mar 7		H	Huddersfield Town	D 0-0	
30	" 10		H	Everton	W 1-0	Johnston
31	" 14		H	West Ham United	W 1-0	Rawlings
32	" 17		A	Portsmouth	L 0-1	
33	" 28		A	Derby County	L 0-5	
34	" 31		A	Aston Villa	L 1-3	Rawlings
35	Apr 6		A	Bolton Wanderers	L 2-3	Spence, Thomas
36	" 7		H	Burnley	W 4-3	Rawlings 3, Hanson
37	" 9		H	Bolton Wanderers	W 2-1	Johnston, Rawlings
38	" 14		H	Bury	L 3-4	McLenahan, Williams, Johnston
39	" 21		A	Sheffield United	L 2-3	Rawlings, Thomas
40	" 25		H	Sunderland	W 2-1	Hanson, Johnston
41	" 28		A	Arsenal	W 1-0	Rawlings
42	May 5		H	Liverpool	W 6-1	Spence 3, Rawlings 2, Hanson

League Appearances

League Scorers

F.A. CUP

	Date		Venue	Opponents	Result	Goalscorers	Attendance
Rd 3	Jan 14		H	Brentford	W 7-1	Hanson 4, Spence, McPherson, Johnston	18,558
Rd 4	" 28		A	Bury	D 1-1	Johnston	22,439
Rd 4 Replay	Feb 1		H	Bury	W 1-0	Spence	48,001
Rd 5	" 18		H	Birmingham City	W 1-0	Johnston	52,568
Rd 6	Mar 3		A	Blackburn Rovers	L 0-2		42,312

Players: Steward, A.; Moore, C.; Silcock, J.; Bennion, S. R.; Barson, F.; Wilson, J. T.; Chapman, W.; Hanson, J.; Spence, J. W.; Partridge, E.; McPherson, F.; Jones, T.; Hilditch, C. G.; Thomas, H.; Haslam, G.; Bain, J.; Richardson, L.; Mann, F. D.; Ramsden, C. W.; Sweeney, E.; Williams, D. R.; Johnston, W. G.; Taylor, C.; McLenahan, H.; Nicol, G.; Rawlings, W. E.; Ferguson, D.

DID YOU KNOW? 'Dixie' Dean hammered all Everton's five goals against United at Goodison Park on 8 October 1927.

Top: UNITED 1927/8. Back Row: T. Jones, G. Hilditch, J. Silcock, A. Steward, J. Pullar, R. Bennion, C. Moore, H. Bamlett (Manager), J. Wilson. Front Row: W. Chapman, J. Hanson, J. Spence, E. Partridge, F. McPherson, F. Barson. (JG)

Bottom: WHITE CHRISTMAS: Arsenal 1 Manchester United 0. 28 December 1926 at Highbury. Alf Steward saves from this Gunners attack with (L to R) Bennion, Jones and Mann in attendance for United. (NW)

MANCHESTER UNITED

Match No.	Date	Venue	Opponents	Result	Goalscorers	Attendance
1	Aug 25	H	Leicester City	D 1-1	Rawlings	18,000
2	27	A	Aston Villa	D 0-0		
3	Sept 1	A	Manchester City	D 2-2	Wilson, Johnston	62,000
4	8	H	Leeds United	L 2-3	Spence, Johnston	30,000
5	15	H	Liverpool	D 2-2	Silcock, Hanson	
6	22	A	West Ham United	L 1-3	Rawlings	30,000
7	29	H	Newcastle United	W 5-0	Rawlings 2, Spence, Hanson, Johnston	
8	Oct 6	A	Burnley	W 4-3	Spence 2, Hanson 2	
9	13	H	Cardiff City	D 1-1	Johnston	
10	20	H	Birmingham	W 1-0	Johnston	15,000
11	27	A	Huddersfield Town	W 2-1	Spence, Hanson	13,600
12	Nov 3	H	Bolton Wanderers	D 1-1	Hanson	
13	10	A	The Wednesday	L 1-2	Hanson	18,800
14	17	H	Derby County	L 0-1		30,000
15	24	A	Sunderland	L 1-5	Rowley	16,000
16	Dec 1	H	Blackburn Rovers	L 1-4	Ramsden	
17	8	A	Arsenal	L 1-3	Hanson	
18	15	H	Everton	D 1-1	Hanson	
19	22	A	Portsmouth	L 0-3		10,000
20	25	H	Leeds United	W 2-1	Ramsden	
21	26	A	Sheffield United	L 1-6	Rawlings	
22	29	A	Leicester City	L 1-2	Hanson	20,000
23	Jan 1	H	Aston Villa	D 2-2	Hilditch, Rowley	
24	5	H	Manchester City	L 1-2	Rawlings	50,000
25	19	H	Leeds United	L 1-2	1 o.g.	20,000
26	Feb 2	H	West Ham United	L 2-3	Reid, Rowley	15,000
27	9	A	Newcastle United	L 0-5		40,000
28	13	A	Liverpool	W 3-2	Thomas 2, Reid	
29	16	H	Burnley	W 1-0	Rowley	
30	23	A	Cardiff City	D 2-2	Hanson, Reid	
31	Mar 2	A	Birmingham	D 1-1	Hanson	12,000
32	9	H	Huddersfield Town	W 1-0	Hanson	30,000
33	16	A	Bolton Wanderers	D 1-1	Hanson	
34	23	H	The Wednesday	W 2-1	Reid, Rowley	20,000
35	29	H	Bury	W 3-1	Reid 3	
36	30	A	Derby County	L 1-6	Hanson	14,397
37	Apr 1	H	Bury	W 1-0	Thomas	
38	6	H	Sunderland	W 3-0	Mann, Hanson, Reid	30,000
39	13	A	Blackburn Rovers	W 3-0	Reid 2, Ramsden	
40	20	H	Arsenal	W 4-1	Reid 2, Hanson, Thomas	
41	27	A	Everton	W 4-2	Hanson 2, Reid 2	
42	May 4	H	Portsmouth	D 0-0		18,000

League Appearances
League Scorers

F.A. CUP

Rd	Date	Venue	Opponents	Result	Goalscorers	Attendance
Rd 3	Jan 12	A	Port Vale	W 3-0	Spence, Hanson, Taylor	17,519
Rd 4	26	H	Bury	L 0-1		40,558

Player names:

Steward, A.
Dale, W.
Silcock, J.
Bennion, S. R.
Mann, F. D.
Wilson, J. T.
Spence, J. W.
Hanson, J.
Rawlings, W. E.
Johnston, W. G.
Williams, D. R.
Moore, C.
McLenahan, H.
Spencer, C. W.
Taylor, C.
Rowley, H. B.
Thomas, H.
Hilditch, C. G.
Ramsden, C. W.
Richardson, L.
Nicol, G.
Sweeney, E.
Partridge, E.
Inglis, W. W.
Reid, T.
Boyle, T.
Thomson, A.

DID YOU KNOW? Hughie McLenahan cost United three freezers of ice cream when he arrived at Old Trafford in 1928. Louis Rocca was a well-known ice cream manufacturer, and he heard that Hughie's team, Stockport County had organised a Bazaar to aid club funds. He offered County the ice cream free in return for McLenahan being released from his amateur contract to sign for United.

Top Right: FRANK MANN. A fine action study on Players *Cigarettes card 'Footballers 1928' Series No. 25. Frank stepped in as emergency centre-half when Barson was injured, and helped United successfully avoid relegation in 1927/8. He made 197 League and Cup appearances. (KM)*

Top Left: BLEAK CHRISTMAS. Alf Steward is beaten to the cross as Jimmy Bain scores Arsenals winner at Highbury on 28 December 1926.

Bottom: MANCHESTER UNITED 4 BURNLEY 3. 7 April 1928 at Old Trafford. In this enlargement of Gallahers *Cigarette Card 'Footballers' series No. 49, Richardson (on ground) and Jones fail to stop Beel scoring for Burnley. (KM)*

MANCHESTER UNITED

M.U.F.C.

Match No.	Date		Venue	Opponents	Result	Goalscorers	Attendance
1	Aug 31		A	Newcastle United	L 1-4	Spence	40,000
2	Sept 2		H	Leicester City	L 1-4	Rowley	14,000
3		7	A	Blackburn Rovers	W 1-0	Mann	28,000
4		14	H	Leicester City	W 2-1	Spence, Ball	18,000
5		21	H	Middlesbrough	W 3-2	Rawlings 3	
6		28	A	Liverpool	L 1-2	Spence	
7	Oct 5		H	West Ham United	L 1-2	Hanson	20,000
8		7	A	Manchester City	L 1-3	Hanson	50,000
9		12	H	Sheffield United	L 1-3	Thomas	
10		19	A	Grimsby Town	L 2-5	Ball, Rowley	
11		26	H	Portsmouth	L 0-3		20,000
12	Nov 2		A	Aston Villa	W 1-0	Ball	
13		9	H	Arsenal	W 1-0	Ball	
14		16	A	Derby County	W 3-2	Hanson, Rowley, Ball	15,000
15		23	H	Sheffield Wednesday	L 2-7	Hanson, Ball	
16		30	A	Burnley	W 1-0	Rowley	
17	Dec 7		H	Sunderland	W 4-2	Spence 2, Hanson, Ball	19,000
18		14	A	Bolton Wanderers	D 1-1	Ball	20,000
19		21	H	Everton	D 0-0		
20		25	A	Birmingham	W 3-0	Ball 2, Hanson	20,000
21		26	H	Birmingham	D 0-0		
22		28	H	Leeds United	W 1-0	Rowley	
23	Jan 4		A	Newcastle United	W 5-0	Boyle 2, McLachlan, Rowley, Spence	
24		18	A	Blackburn Rovers	L 4-5	Boyle 2, Ball, Rowley	
25		25	H	Middlesbrough	L 0-3		
26	Feb 1		A	Liverpool	L 0-1		
27		8	H	West Ham United	W 4-2	Spence 4	20,000
28		15	A	Manchester City	W 1-0	Reid	63,018
29		22	H	Grimsby Town	D 2-2	Reid, Rowley	
30	Mar 1		A	Portsmouth	W 3-0	Boyle, Reid 2	18,000
31		8	H	Aston Villa	L 1-4	Reid	18,000
32		12	A	Arsenal	L 2-4	Warburton, McLachlan	
33		15	H	Derby County	D 1-1	Wilson, Ball	19,179
34		29	A	Burnley	L 0-4		11,778
35	Apr 5		H	Sunderland	W 2-1	McLenahan 2	15,000
36		14	H	Sheffield Wednesday	D 2-2	Rowley, McLenahan	15,000
37		18	A	Huddersfield Town	W 1-0	McLenahan	15,000
38		19	H	Everton	D 3-3	Spence, McLenahan, Rowley	25,000
39		22	A	Huddersfield Town	D 2-2	Hilditch, McLenahan	13,000
40		26	A	Leeds United	L 1-3	Spence	10,000
42	May 3		H	Sheffield United	L 1-5	Rowley	16,000

F.A. CUP

		Venue	Opponents	Result	Goalscorers	Attendance
Rd 3	Jan 11	H	Swindon Town	L 0-2		33,226

Players (appearances / goals)

Steward, A.		Spence, J. W.	12
Moore, C.		Hanson, J.	6
Dale, W.		Reid, T.	5
Bennion, S. R		Rowley, H. B.	11
Spencer, C. W.		Thomas, H.	1
Mann, F. D.	1	Silcock, J.	
Ball, J.	12	Rawlings, W. E.	3
Wilson, J. T.	1	Boyle, T.	5
Sweeney, E.		Hilditch, C. G.	1
Taylor, C.		McLenahan, H.	6
Jones, T.		McLachlan, G.	2
Chesters, S.		Warburton, A.	1
Thomson, A.			

League Appearances — League Scorers

M.U.F.C.

DID YOU KNOW? Matt Busby nearly became a United player early in his career. Then with Manchester City, he was the subject of a telephone enquiry from Louis Rocca at a time United had several injury problems. "I want one player for Saturday", Louis told Peter Hodge, the City Manager. "And who is that?" he replied, to which Rocca admitted he wanted Matt Busby. "Give us £150, and he's yours" replied Hodge. "But Peter, we haven't 150 cents, never mind £150" lamented Rocca, and Matt stayed at Maine Road.

PARK YOUR CAR at the
COUNTY CRICKET GROUND GARAGE,
OLD TRAFFORD.

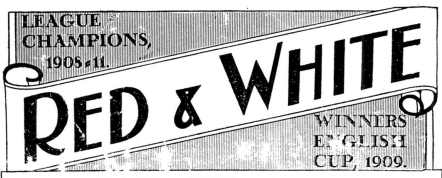

LEAGUE CHAMPIONS, 1908-11.

RED & WHITE

WINNERS ENGLISH CUP, 1909.

MANCHESTER UNITED
OFFICIAL PROGRAMME

SEASON 1929-30.

VOL. XVII. No. 33.   SATURDAY, MARCH 22nd, 1930.   **2D.**

F.A. CUP—Semi-Final.

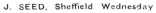

J. SEED, Sheffield Wednesday.   T. WILSON, Huddersfield Town.

THE RIVAL CAPTAINS.

ALLIED NEWSPAPERS LIMITED, Printers, Withy Grove, Manchester.

Above: FA CUP SEMI-FINAL AT OLD TRAFFORD 1929/30.
Huddersfield Town 2 Sheffield Wednesday 1. 22 March 1930.
Official Match Programme. (PC)

Relegated to Division Two and Manchester Senior Cup Winners

Position: 22nd

MANCHESTER UNITED

Match No.	Date	Venue	Opponents	Result		Goalscorers	Attendance
1	Aug 30	H	Aston Villa	L	3-4	Warburton, Reid, Rowley	
2	Sept 3	A	Middlesbrough	L	1-3	Rowley	
3	6	A	Chelsea	L	2-6	Spence, Reid	48,000
4	10	A	Huddersfield Town	L	0-6		
5	13	H	Newcastle United	L	4-7	Reid 3, Rowley	14,067
6	15	A	Huddersfield Town	L	0-3		
7	20	A	Sheffield Wednesday	L	0-3		
8	27	H	Grimsby Town	L	0-2		20,000
9	Oct 4	A	Manchester City	L	1-4	Spence	45,000
10	11	H	West Ham United	L	1-5	Reid	26,000
11	18	H	Arsenal	L	1-2	McLachlan	28,000
12	25	A	Portsmouth	L	1-4	Rowley	20,000
13	Nov 1	H	Birmingham	W	2-0	Rowley, Gallimore	12,000
14	8	A	Leicester City	L	4-5	Bullock, McLachlan	20,000
15	15	H	Blackpool	D	0-0		
16	22	A	Sheffield United	L	0-7		
17	29	H	Sunderland	D	1-1	Gallimore	7,000
18	Dec 6	A	Blackburn Rovers	L	1-4	Rowley	8,000
19	13	H	Derby County	W	2-1	Spence, Reid	
20	20	A	Leeds United	L	0-5		12,000
21	25	H	Bolton Wanderers	L	1-3	Reid	
22	26	A	Bolton Wanderers	D	1-1	Reid	
23	27	A	Aston Villa	L	0-7		
24	Jan 1	H	Leeds United	D	0-0		7,000
25	3	A	Chelsea	W	1-0	Warburton	
26	17	H	Newcastle United	L	3-4	Warburton 2, Reid	7,000
27	28	H	Sheffield Wednesday	W	4-1	Spence, Warburton, Reid, Hopkinson	
28	31	A	Grimsby Town	L	1-2	Reid	
29	Feb 7	H	Manchester City	L	1-3	Spence	50,000
30	14	A	West Ham United	W	1-0	Gallimore	10,000
31	21	A	Arsenal	L	1-4	Thomson	
32	Mar 7	A	Birmingham	D	0-0		18,000
33	16	H	Portsmouth	D	0-0		5,000
34	21	H	Blackpool	L	1-5	Hopkinson	
35	28	A	Sunderland	D	0-0		12,000
36	28	H	Leicester City	L	1-2	Hopkinson	
37	Apr 3	A	Liverpool	D	1-1	Wilson	
38	4	A	Sunderland	W	2-1	Reid, Hopkinson	
39	6	H	Liverpool	W	4-1	Reid 2, Rowley, McLenahan	
40	11	H	Blackburn Rovers	L	0-1		6,722
41	18	A	Derby County	L	1-6	Spence	20,000
42	May 2	H	Middlesbrough	D	4-4	Reid 2, Bennion, Gallimore	10,000

F.A. CUP

	Date	Venue	Opponents	Result		Goalscorers	Attendance	
Rd 3	Jan 10	A	Stoke City	D	3-3	Reid 3	23,415	
Replay	14	H	Stoke City	D	0-0		22,013	(after extra time)
2nd Replay	19	N	Stoke City	W	4-2	Hopkinson 2, Spence, Gallimore	10,000	(at Anfield)
Rd 4	24	A	Grimsby Town	L	0-1		20,000	

Players: Steward, A.; Jones, T.; Silcock, J.; Bennion, S. R.; McLenahan, H.; Wilson, J. T.; Spence, J. W.; Warburton, A.; Reid, T.; Rowley, H. B.; McLachlan, G.; Chesters, A.; Dale, W.; Ramsden, C. W.; Hilditch, C. G.; Williams, F.; Mellor, J.; Bullock, J.; Parker, T. A.; Gallimore, S.; Lydon, G.; Hopkinson, S.; Thomson, A.

League Appearances / League Scorers

DID YOU KNOW? United set unwanted records in 1930/1. They conceded a club record 115 goals, the most club defeats, 27, in a season, along with the fewest wins, 7, in a 42 match programme. The 12 opening consecutive League defeats is a First Division record.

A BOYCOTT ATTEMPT — AND RELEGATION 1930-1

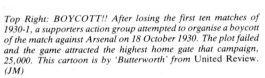

Top Right: BOYCOTT!! After losing the first ten matches of 1930-1, a supporters action group attempted to organise a boycott of the match against Arsenal on 18 October 1930. The plot failed and the game attracted the highest home gate that campaign, 25,000. This cartoon is by 'Butterworth' from United Review. *(JM)*

Bottom: OLD TRAFFORD, Photographed in the nineteen-thirties. (JG)

MANCHESTER UNITED

Match No.	Date	Venue	Opponents	Result	Goalscorers	Attendance
1	Aug 29	A	Bradford Park Avenue	L 1-3	Reid	16,466
2	Sept 2	A	Southampton	L 2-3	Johnston, Ferguson	30,000
3	5	A	Swansea Town	W 2-1	Reid, Hopkinson	
4	7	H	Stoke City	L 0-3		
5	12	H	Tottenham Hotspur	D 1-1	Johnston	8,000
6	16	H	Stoke City	D 1-1	Spence	5,000
7	19	A	Nottingham Forest	L 1-2	Gallimore	10,000
8	26	H	Chesterfield	W 3-1	Warburton 2, Johnston	
9	Oct 3	A	Burnley	L 0-2		5,383
10	17	H	Barnsley	D 0-0		
11	10	H	Preston North End	W 3-2	Johnston, Spence, Gallimore	
12	24	A	Notts County	D 3-3	Mann, Gallimore, Spence	
13	31	A	Plymouth Argyle	L 1-3	Johnston	24,000
14	Nov 7	H	Leeds United	L 2-5	Spence 2	10,000
15	14	A	Oldham Athletic	W 5-1	Johnston 2, Spence, 1 o.g.	
16	21	H	Bury	L 1-2	Spence	
17	28	A	Port Vale	W 2-1	Spence 2	6,000
18	Dec 5	H	Millwall	W 2-0	Spence, Gallimore	6,000
19	12	A	Bradford City	L 3-4	Spence 2, Johnston	13,279
20	19	H	Bristol City	L 0-1		4,000
21	25	H	Wolverhampton Wanderers	W 3-2	Spence, Reid, Hopkinson	10,000
22	26	A	Wolverhampton Wanderers	L 0-7		
23	Jan 2	A	Bradford Park Avenue	L 0-2		8,000
24	16	A	Swansea Town	L 1-3	Warburton	
25	23	H	Tottenham Hotspur	L 1-4	Reid	20,743
26	30	H	Nottingham Forest	W 3-2	Reid 3	12,000
27	Feb 6	A	Chesterfield	W 3-1	Reid 2, Spence	11,000
28	17	A	Burnley	W 5-1	Johnston 2, Gallimore, Ridding 2	
29	20	A	Preston North End	D 0-0		
30	27	H	Barnsley	W 3-0	Hopkinson 2, Gallimore	20,000
31	Mar 5	A	Notts County	W 2-1	Hopkinson, Reid	24,000
32	12	H	Plymouth Argyle	W 2-1	Spence 2	
33	19	A	Leeds United	W 4-1	Reid 2, Ridding, Johnston	14,000
34	25	H	Charlton Athletic	L 0-2		40,000
35	26	H	Oldham Athletic	W 5-1	Spence, Reid 3, Fitton	
36	28	A	Charlton Athletic	L 0-1		
37	Apr 2	A	Bury	D 0-0		
38	9	H	Port Vale	W 2-0	Reid, Spence	
39	16	H	Millwall	D 1-1	Reid	10,000
40	23	H	Bradford City	W 1-0	Black	20,000
41	30	A	Bristol City	L 1-2	Black	
42	May 7	A	Southampton	D 1-1	Black	6,128

F.A. CUP

	Date	Venue	Opponents	Result	Goalscorers	Attendance
Rd 3	Jan 9	A	Plymouth Argyle	L 1-4	Reid	28,000

Players: Steward, A.; Mellor, J.; Silcock, J.; Bennion, S. R.; Parker, T. A.; McLachlan, G.; Ferguson, J.; Warburton, A.; Reid, T.; Johnston, W. G.; Mann, H.; McLenahan, H.; Spence, J.; Hopkinson, S.; Rowley, H. B.; Hilditch, C. G.; Wilson, J. T.; Gallimore, S.; Jones, T.; Dean, H.; Robinson, M.; Dale, W.; Lydon, G.; Manley, T.; Chesters, A.; Ridding, W.; Whittle, J.; Vincent, E.; Lievesley, L.; Page, L. A.; Moody, J.; Fitton, G. A.; McDonald, W.; Black, R.

League Scorers: Ferguson 1, Warburton 3, Reid 17, Johnston 11, Mann 1, Spence 19, Hopkinson 5, Gallimore 6, Ridding 3, Fitton 1, Black 3, 1 o.g.

DID YOU KNOW? United had to be rescued from financial crisis again in 1931. Walter Crickmer was unable to obtain enough money from the bank to purchase the player's Xmas turkey's — never mind the wages! Mr. James Gibson saved the club from extinction by guaranteeing payment of the wage bill until the end of the season, when he was elected Chairman.

ANOTHER FINANCIAL CRISIS 1931/2

J. GRIFFITHS

WILL'S CIGARETTES

G. VOSE (MANCHESTER UNITED)

Top Right: MR. JAMES GIBSON. Saved the club from bankruptcy in 1931/2, and was elected Chairman at the end of the season. (MMUSC)

Bottom: TOMMY JONES, JACK MELLOR, JACK SILCOCK. (KM)

Mr. Scott Duncan appointed Manager

MANCHESTER UNITED

Match No.	Date		Venue	Opponents	Result		Goalscorers	Attendance
1	Aug	27	H	Stoke City	L	0-2		28,000
2		29	A	Charlton Athletic	W	1-0	Spence	
3	Sept	3	A	Southampton	L	2-4	Reid, 1 o.g.	7,987
4		7	H	Charlton Athletic	D	1-1	McLenahan	12,000
5		10	A	Tottenham Hotspur	L	1-6	Ridding	24,177
6		17	H	Grimsby Town	D	1-1	Brown	
7		24	A	Oldham Athletic	D	1-1	Spence	
8	Oct	1	H	Preston North End	D	0-0		20,000
9		8	A	Bury	W	3-2	Brown, Gallimore, Spence	5,393
10		15	H	Bradford Park Avenue	W	2-1	Reid 2	15,000
11		22	A	Millwall	W	7-1	Reid 3, Brown 2, Gallimore, Spence	35,000
12		29	H	Port Vale	D	3-3	Ridding 2, Brown	
13	Nov	5	A	Notts County	W	2-0	Gallimore, Ridding	28,000
14		12	H	Bury	D	2-2	Ridding, Brown	
15		19	A	Fulham	W	4-3	Gallimore 2, Brown, Ridding	28,000
16		26	H	Chesterfield	D	1-1	Ridding	
17	Dec	3	A	Bradford City	L	0-1		28,000
18		10	H	West Ham United	L	1-3	Ridding	15,000
19		17	A	Lincoln City	W	4-1	Reid 3, 1 o.g.	15,000
20		24	A	Swansea Town	L	1-2	Brown	
21		26	H	Plymouth Argyle	W	3-2	Spence 2, Reid	34,000
22		31	A	Stoke City	D	0-0		
23	Jan	2	H	Plymouth Argyle	W	4-0	Ridding 2, Spence, Chalmers	31,000
24		7	A	Southampton	L	1-2	McDonald	31,000
25		21	H	Tottenham Hotspur	W	2-1	Frame (pen), McDonald	28,000
26		31	A	Grimsby Town	D	1-1	Stewart	
27	Feb	4	H	Oldham Athletic	W	2-0	Ridding, Stewart	
28		11	A	Preston North End	D	3-3	Dewar, Stewart, Hopkinson	15,000
29		22	H	Burnley	W	2-1	Warburton, McDonald	
30	Mar	4	A	Millwall	L	0-2		20,000
31		11	H	Port Vale	D	1-1	Hine	
32		18	A	Notts County	L	0-1		
33		25	H	Bury	L	1-3	McLenahan	
34	Apr	1	A	Fulham	L	1-3	Dewar	6,238
35		5	A	Bradford Park Avenue	D	1-1	Vincent	
36		8	H	Chesterfield	W	2-1	Frame, Dewar	
37		14	A	Nottingham Forest	W	2-3	Dewar, Brown	13,257
38		15	A	Bradford City	W	2-1	Brown, Hine	11,196
39		17	H	Nottingham Forest	W	2-1	Hine, McDonald	20,000
40		22	A	West Ham United	L	1-2	Dewar	18,000
41		29	A	Lincoln City	L	2-3	Dewar, Hine	
42	May	6	H	Swansea Town	D	1-1	Hine	

League Appearances

League Scorers

F.A. CUP

Rd 3	Jan 14	H	Middlesbrough	L	1-4	Spence	36,991

Players: Moody, J.; Mellor, J.; Silcock, J.; McLenahan, H.; Vincent, E.; McLachlan, G.; Spence, J. W.; Ridding, W.; Black, R.; McDonald, W.; Page, L.; Warburton, A.; Reid, T.; Fitton, G. A.; Hopkinson, S.; Gallimore, S.; Manley, T.; Brown, H.; Frame, T.; Chalmers, W. S.; Jones, T.; Stewart, W.; Hine, E.; Dewar, N.; Mitchell, A.; Topping, H.; Heywood, H.

DID YOU KNOW? The MUJACS (Manchester United Junior Athletic Club) was the idea of Walter Crickmer, for the development of young players. The scheme soon payed dividends, supplying the first team with several players in the 'thirties, and providing the nucleus of the great post-war team. Aston, Morris, Pearson, Mitten and Walton were to all graduate from the MUJAC ranks.

134

Top: TARTAN ARMY. This cartoon appeared in the United match programme in December 1932, with observations on the number of Scottish players recruited by new manager Scott Duncan. (BH)

Bottom: ON PARADE: Players lining up for the camera are (L to R): Bryant, McKay, Smith, Bellis, McDonald. (BNPC)

M.U.F.C.

MANCHESTER UNITED

Match No.	Date		Venue	Opponents	Result		Goalscorers	Attendance
1	Aug	26	A	Plymouth Argyle	L	0-4		27,000
2		30	A	Nottingham Forest	L	0-1		20,000
3	Sept	2	H	Lincoln City	D	1-1	Green	10,399
4		7	A	Nottingham Forest	W	1-0	Stewart	20,000
5		9	A	Bolton Wanderers	L	1-5	Stewart	10,389
6		16	H	Brentford	W	4-3	Hine, Frame, Brown 2	18,000
7		23	H	Burnley	W	5-2	Dewar 4, Brown	
8		30	A	Oldham Athletic	L	0-2		
9	Oct	7	H	Preston North End	W	1-0	Hine	11,419
10		14	A	Bradford Park Avenue	L	1-6	Hine	
11		21	H	Bury	L	1-2	Byrne	10,000
12		28	H	Hull City	W	4-1	Heywood 2, Hine, Green	
13	Nov	4	A	Fulham	W	2-0	Stewart, 1 o.g.	
14		11	H	Southampton	W	1-0	Manley	15,000
15		18	A	Blackpool	L	1-3	Brown	
16		25	H	Bradford City	W	2-1	1 o.g., Dewar	
17	Dec	2	A	Port Vale	W	3-2	Brown, Black, Dewar	
18		9	H	Notts County	L	1-2	Dewar	
19		16	A	Swansea Town	L	1-2	Hine	
20		25	H	Millwall	L	1-2	Dewar	15,000
21		25	H	Grimsby Town	L	1-3	Vose	20,000
22		26	A	Grimsby Town	L	3-7	Byrne, Frame (pen), McGillivray	12,800
23		30	H	Plymouth Argyle	L	0-3		
24	Jan	6	A	Lincoln City	L	1-5	Brown	
25		20	H	Bolton Wanderers	L	1-3	Ball	
26		27	A	Brentford	L	1-3	Ball	15,000
27	Feb	3	H	Burnley	W	4-1	Cape 2, Green, Stewart	9,026
28		10	A	Oldham Athletic	L	2-3	Cape, Green	6,000
29		21	A	Preston North End	L	2-3	Gallimore 2	6,000
30		24	A	Bradford Park Avenue	L	0-4		15,000
31	March	3	H	Bury	W	2-1	Ball, Gallimore	
32		10	A	Hull City	L	1-4	Ball	6,000
33		17	H	Fulham	W	1-0	Ball	20,000
34		24	A	Southampton	L	0-1		4,900
35		30	H	West Ham United	L	0-1		32,000
36		31	A	Blackpool	W	2-0	Cape, Hine	
37	April	2	H	West Ham United	L	1-2	Cape	18,000
38		7	A	Bradford City	W	2-0	Cape	9,349
39		14	H	Port Vale	W	2-0	McMillen, Brown	18,000
40		21	A	Notts County	D	0-0		
41		28	H	Swansea Town	D	1-1	Topping	18,000
42	May	5	A	Millwall	W	2-0	Manley, Cape	35,000

F.A. CUP

Rd 3	Jan	14	H	Portsmouth	D	1-1	McLenahan	23,283
Replay		17	A	Portsmouth	L	1-4	Ball	18,748

Player columns: Hillam, Mellor, Jones, McLenahan, Vose, Manley, McGillivray, Hine, Dewar, Green, Stewart, Vincent, Frame, Chalmers, Silcock, McMillan, Brown, Warburton, Hall, Hopkinson, Ridding, Byrne, Heywood, Black, Topping, McDonald, Ball, Nevin, Cape, Manns, Newton, Gallimore, Behan, Ainsworth, Hacking, Griffiths, Robertson, McKay

League Appearances / League Scorers (with 2 o.g.s)

DID YOU KNOW? United managed to avoid relegation to Division Three in 1933/4, by winning their final game at Millwall 2-0 with goals by Manley and Cape. Millwall themselves were relegated instead. During their desperate fight to avoid the drop, United changed their colours, adopting white shirts with cherry hoops, hoping for a change of luck. They used a club record number of players during the season, 38 in all.

M.U.F.C.

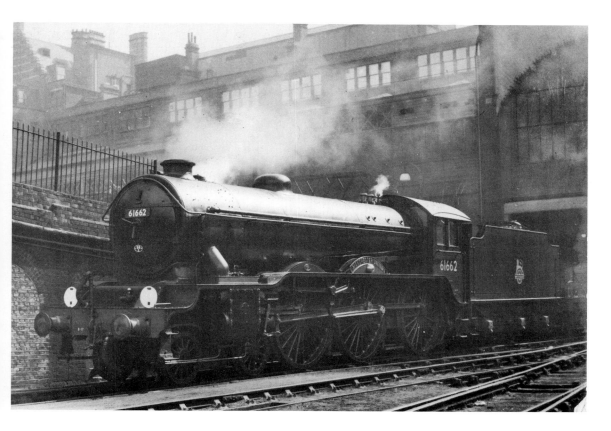

G. MUTCH (PRESTON NORTH END)

FOOTBALL - W. PORTER, MANCHESTER UNITED

W. M'KAY (MANCHESTER UNITED)

Top: UP STEAM! This London & North Eastern Railway *Locomotive was named* Manchester United *and one of twenty four Class B17's given the names of famous football teams. It was built during the nineteen-thirties at Darlington, but the photograph was taken after nationalization of British Railways. The name-plate was presented to the club when the loco was scrapped in 1960. (CZ)*

Bottom: UNITED PLAYERS ON CIGARETTE CARDS: (Left): GEORGE MUTCH, on Churchmans 'Association Footballers' *No. 31, seen whilst playing for Scotland during his Preston days. (Centre): W. PORTER on* Senior Service 'Sporting Events and Stars' *No. 54, and W. McKAY on* Churchmans 'Association Footballers' *No. 26. (KM)*

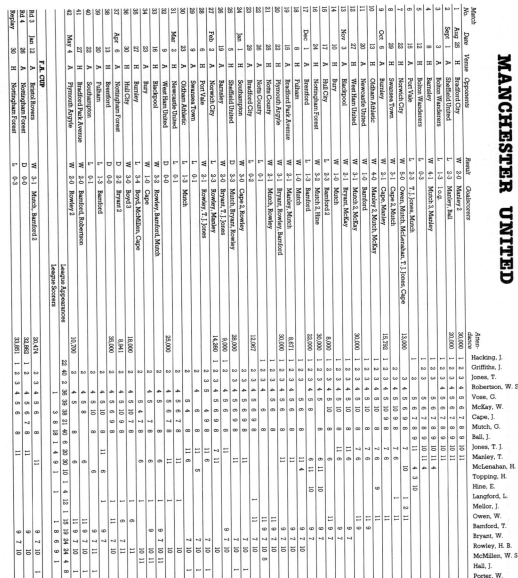

MANCHESTER UNITED

Match No.	Date	Venue	Opponents	Result	Goalscorers	Attendance
1	Aug 25	H	Bradford City	W 2-0	Manley 2	30,000
2	Sept 1	A	Sheffield United	L 1-3	l.o.g.	20,000
3	3	A	Bolton Wanderers	L 2-3	Manley, Ball	20,000
4	8	H	Barnsley	W 4-1	Mutch 3, Manley	
5	12	A	Bolton Wanderers	L 0-3		
6	15	H	Port Vale	W 2-1	T.J.Jones, Mutch	
7	22	H	Norwich City	W 5-0	Owen, Mutch, McLenahan, T.J.Jones, Cape	13,000
8	29	A	Swansea Town	W 3-1	Cape 2, Mutch	
9	Oct 6	H	Burnley	W 2-1	Cape, Manley	
10	13	A	Oldham Athletic	W 4-0	Manley 2, Mutch, McKay	15,792
11	20	H	Newcastle United	W 1-0	Bamford	
12	27	A	West Ham United	W 3-1	Mutch 2, McKay	30,000
13	Nov 3	H	Blackpool	W 2-1	Bryant, McKay	
14	10	A	Bury	W 1-0	Mutch	
15	17	H	Hull City	L 2-3	Bamford 2	8,000
16	24	A	Nottingham Forest	W 3-2	Mutch 2, Hine	
17	Dec 1	A	Brentford	L 1-3	Bamford	22,000
18	8	H	Fulham	W 1-0	Mutch	
19	15	A	Bradford Park Avenue	W 2-1	Manley, Mutch	8,671
20	22	H	Plymouth Argyle	W 3-1	Bryant, Rowley, Bamford	30,000
21	25	H	Notts County	W 2-1	Mutch, Manley	
22	26	A	Notts County	L 0-1		
23	29	A	Bradford City	L 0-2		12,067
24	Jan 1	H	Southampton	W 3-0	Cape 2, Rowley	
25	5	H	Sheffield United	D 3-3	Mutch, Bryant, Rowley	28,000
26	19	A	Barnsley	W 2-0	Bryant, T.J.Jones	9,000
27	Feb 2	H	Port Vale	L 2-3	Rowley, Manley	14,260
28	6	H	Norwich City	W 2-1	Rowley, T.J.Jones	
29	9	A	Swansea Town	L 0-1		
30	23	A	Oldham Athletic	D 0-0		25,000
31	Mar 2	A	Newcastle United	L 0-1		
32	9	H	West Ham United	L 1-3	Mutch	
33	16	A	Blackpool	D 0-0		
34	23	H	Bury	W 3-2	Rowley, Bamford, Mutch	
35	27	H	Burnley	W 1-0	Cape	
36	30	H	Hull City	L 3-4	Boyd, McMillen, Cape	18,000
37	Apr 6	A	Nottingham Forest	W 3-0	Boyd 3	
38	13	H	Brentford	D 2-2	Bryant 2	38,000
39	20	A	Fulham	L 1-3	Bamford	
40	22	A	Southampton	L 0-1		
41	27	H	Bradford Park Avenue	W 2-0	Bamford, Robertson	
42	May 4	A	Plymouth Argyle	W 2-0	Rowley 2	10,700

F.A. CUP

	Date	Venue	Opponents	Result	Goalscorers	Attendance
Rd 3	Jan 12	A	Bristol Rovers	W 3-1	Mutch, Bamford 2	20,474
Rd 4	26	A	Nottingham Forest	D 0-0		32,862
Replay	30	H	Nottingham Forest	L 0-3		33,851

Players: Hacking, J.; Griffiths, J.; Jones, T.; Robertson, W. S; Vose, G.; McKay, W.; Cape, J.; Mutch, G.; Ball, J.; Jones, T. J.; Manley, T.; McLenahan, H.; Topping, H.; Hine, E.; Langford, L.; Mellor, J.; Owen, W.; Bamford, T.; Bryant, W.; Rowley, H. B.; McMillen, W. S.; Hall, J.; Porter, W.; Boyd, W.

League Appearances: 22, 40, 2, 36, 38, 21, 40, 2, 6, 20, 30, 10, 1, 4, 12, 1, 8, 19, 24, 24, 4, 8, 15, 6

League Scorers: 3, 18, 1, 4, 9, 1, 8, 6, 9, 1, 4, 1 l.o.g.

DID YOU KNOW? The least number of drawn games by United in a 42-match League programme is 4, in 1934/5. Billy Bryant and Tommy Bamford both arrived at Old Trafford from Wrexham, and both scored on their debuts.

OPPOSITE PAGE:

Top: UNITED 1934/5. Back Row: Mellor, Robertson, Bryant, Manley, Langford, Hacking, McMillen, Griffiths. Middle Row: Jones, T., Hine Jones, T. J., Mutch, Bamford, Owen, Vose. Front Row: Cape, McLenahan, McKay. (KM,)

Bottom Left: MANCHESTER UNITED 1 THIRD LANARK 1. 16 February 1935. Official programme of the friendly match at Old Trafford Boyd scored United's goal. (BH)

Bottom Right: TOM BAMFORD & BILL BRYANT appeared on these Topical Times photocards after arriving from Wrexham in 1935. (KM)

MANCHESTER UNITED

Back Row (*left to right*): MELLOR, ROBERTSON, BRYANT, MANLEY, LANGFORD, HACKING, McMILLEN GRIFFITHS.
Middle Row: JONES (T.), HINE, JONES (T. J.), MUTCH, BAMFORD, OWEN, VOSE.
Front Row: CAPE, McLENAHAN, McKAY.

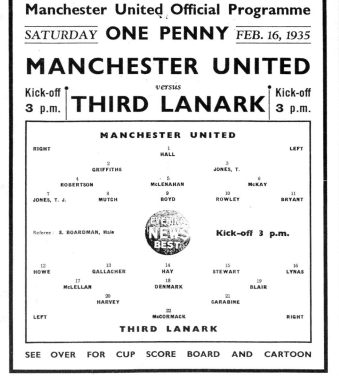

Manchester United Official Programme

SATURDAY **ONE PENNY** FEB. 16, 1935

MANCHESTER UNITED

Kick-off
3 p.m.
versus
THIRD LANARK
Kick-off
3 p.m.

MANCHESTER UNITED

RIGHT				LEFT
		1 HALL		
	2 GRIFFITHS		3 JONES, T.	
	4 ROBERTSON	5 McLENAHAN	6 McKAY	
7 JONES, T. J.	8 MUTCH	9 BOYD	10 ROWLEY	11 BRYANT

Referee: S. BOARDMAN, Hale

EVENING NEWS BEST

Kick-off 3 p.m.

12 HOWE	13 GALLACHER	14 HAY	15 STEWART	16 LYNAS
	17 McLELLAN	18 DENMARK	19 BLAIR	
	20 HARVEY		21 CARABINE	
LEFT		22 McCORMACK		RIGHT

THIRD LANARK

SEE OVER FOR CUP SCORE BOARD AND CARTOON

TOM BAMFORD,   Topical
Manchester United F.C.   Times

WILLIAM BRYANT,   Topical
Manchester Utd. F.C.   Times

MANCHESTER UNITED

Match No.	Date	Venue	Opponents	Result	Goalscorers	Attendance
1	Aug 31	A	Plymouth Argyle	L 1-3	Bamford	22,544
2	Sept 4	H	Charlton Athletic	W 3-0	Chester, Cape, Bamford	
3	7	H	Charlton Athletic	W 3-1	Bamford 2, Mutch	
4	9	A	Bradford City	W 3-1	Bamford 2, Mutch	30,731
5	14	A	Charlton Athletic	D 0-0		
6	18	H	Newcastle United	W 2-0	Rowley, Bamford	18,000
7	21	H	Hull City	W 2-0	Bamford 2	30,000
8	28	A	Tottenham Hotspur	D 0-0		17,678
9	Oct 5	A	Southampton	L 1-2	Rowley	23,000
10	12	H	Port Vale	W 3-0	Mutch 2, Bamford	
11	19	H	Fulham	W 1-0	Rowley	
12	26	A	Sheffield United	W 3-1	Cape, Mutch, Rowley	12,316
13	Nov 2	H	Bradford Park Avenue	L 0-1		10,000
14	9	A	Leicester City	L 1-4	Mutch	
15	16	A	Swansea Town	L 1-2	Bamford	25,000
16	23	H	West Ham United	L 2-3	Rowley 2	17,254
17	30	H	Norwich City	W 5-3	Rowley 3 (1 pen), Manley 2	24,007
18	Dec 7	A	Doncaster Rovers	D 0-0		
19	14	H	Nottingham Forest	W 5-0	Rowley, Mutch, Bamford 2, Manley	15,000
20	26	H	Barnsley	D 1-1	Bamford	21,000
21	28	H	Plymouth Argyle	W 3-2	Mutch 2, Manley	21,000
22	Jan 1	H	Barnsley	W 7-2	Manley 4 (1 pen), Rowley 2, Mutch	21,000
23	4	A	Bradford City	L 0-1		11,278
24	18	H	Newcastle United	W 3-1	Mutch, Gardner, Manley	
25	Feb 1	H	Southampton	W 4-0	Bryant, Mutch 2, lo.g.	20,000
26	5	A	Tottenham Hotspur	D 0-0		20,456
27	8	A	Port Vale	W 2-0	Rowley 2, Mutch	23,000
28	22	H	Sheffield United	D 1-1	Manley	26,322
29	29	H	Blackpool	W 3-2	Manley, Bryant, Mutch	
30	Mar 7	A	West Ham United	W 2-1	Mutch, Bryant	31,000
31	14	H	Swansea Town	W 3-0	Rowley, Mutch, Manley	
32	21	A	Leicester City	D 1-1	Bryant	15,000
33	28	H	Norwich City	W 2-1	Rowley 2	38,000
34	Apr 1	A	Fulham	D 2-2	Bryant, Griffiths	
35	4	A	Doncaster Rovers	D 0-0		13,574
36	10	H	Burnley	D 2-2	Bamford 2	26,166
37	11	H	Bradford Park Avenue	W 4-0	Mutch 2, Bryant, Bamford	
38	13	H	Burnley	W 4-0	Bryant 2, Rowley 2	39,661
39	18	A	Nottingham Forest	D 1-1	Bamford	32,286
40	25	H	Bury	W 2-1	Lang, Rowley	11,271
41	29	A	Bury	W 3-2	Manley 2, Mutch	
42	May 2	A	Hull City	D 1-1	Bamford	34,440

League Appearances — 5,000

Player columns: Breedon, J.; Griffiths, J.; Porter, W.; Brown, J.; Vose, G.; McKay, W.; Bryant, W.; Mutch, G.; Bamford, T.; Rowley, H. B.; Chester, R.; Hall, J.; Cape, J.; Ferrier, R.; Manley, T.; Redwood, H.; Robbie, D.; Owen, W.; Wassall, J.; Morton, B.; Langford, L.; Whalley, H.; Robertson, W.; Gardner, R.; Lang, T.

League Scorers

F.A. CUP

	Date	Venue	Opponents	Result	Goalscorers	Attendance
Rd 3	Jan 11	H	Reading	W 3-1	Manley, Mutch 2	28,844
Rd 4	25	A	Stoke City	D 0-0		33,286
Replay	29	H	Stoke City	L 0-2		34,440

DID YOU KNOW? United looked anything but a promotion outfit half way through season 1935/6, but then went 19 consecutive matches without defeat to secure a place in Division One.

THE
Premier Football Team of Manchester
◄◄◄◄
MANCHESTER UNITED

English Cup winners 1908-09;
First Division Champions 1907-1908, 1910-1911
Second Division Champions 1935-36.

◄◄◄◄

Have accomplished what the following Clubs have not ——

ARSENAL Couldn't do it.
BOLTON W. Couldn't do it.
DERBY COUNTY Couldn't do it.
MANCHESTER CITY Couldn't do it!
HUDDERSFIELD T. Couldn't do it.
NEWCASTLE U. Couldn't do it.
SHEFFIELD U. Couldn't do it.
Billy Meredith couldn't do it against P.C. Walter Cartwright

The elite of the Football World—
Burnley, Everton, West Brom, Preston, Sheffield Wednesday
Who have won the English Cup and First and Second Div. Championships

AND MANCHESTER UNITED
has now joined the select band of
TRIPLE CROWN HEROES

MANCHESTER IS PROUD OF—
Mr. J. W. GIBSON, the Gamest Sportsman in the Kingdom ;
Mr. SCOTT DUNCAN, Football's Greatest Manager ; also
The gallant band of United Supporters not forgetting the Ladies!

And the bravest man was Captain Brown,
Who played his Ukelele when they won the Triple Crown !

SECOND DIVISION CHAMPIONS 1935-6

Below: The United players on their triumphant tour of Manchester as the open-top bus wends its way down Warwick Street to Old Trafford on 2 May 1936. The Trafford Hotel is in the background. (BNPC)

Top Left: This postcard was issued to celebrate the team's successful campaign. (MMUSC)

MANCHESTER UNITED

M.U.F.C.

Match No.	Date	Venue	Opponents	Result	Goalscorers	Attendance
1	Aug 29	H	Wolverhampton Wanderers	D 1-1	Bamford	
2	Sept 2	A	Huddersfield Town	L 1-3	Manley	
3	5	A	Huddersfield Town	L 4-5	Wassall, Bamford 3	22,000
4	9	H	Derby County	W 3-1	Mutch, Bryant, Bamford	30,000
5	12	H	Manchester City	W 3-2	Bamford, Manley, Bryant	69,000
6	19	A	Sheffield Wednesday	D 1-1	Bamford	40,000
7	26	H	Preston North End	L 1-3	Bamford	
8	Oct 3	A	Arsenal	W 2-0	Rowley, Bryant	
9	10	H	Brentford	L 0-4		25,000
10	17	A	Portsmouth	L 1-2	Manley	21,000
11	24	H	Chelsea	D 0-0		30,000
12	31	A	Stoke City	L 0-3		
13	Nov 7	H	Charlton Athletic	D 0-0		20,000
14	14	A	Grimsby Town	L 2-6	Bamford, Mutch	
15	21	H	Liverpool	L 2-5	Thompson, Manley	17,600
16	28	A	Leeds United	L 1-2	Bryant	15,000
17	Dec 5	H	Birmingham	L 1-2	Mutch	15,000
18	12	A	Middlesbrough	L 2-3	Halton, Manley	15,000
19	19	H	West Bromwich Albion	D 2-2	McKay, Mutch	25,107
20	25	A	Bolton Wanderers	W 1-0	Bamford	
21	26	H	Wolverhampton Wanderers	L 1-3	McKay	
22	28	H	Bolton Wanderers	W 4-0	Bryant 2, McKay 2	48,000
23	Jan 1	A	Sunderland	W 2-1	Mutch, Bryant	47,000
24	2	H	Derby County	D 2-2	Rowley 2	32,000
25	9	A	Manchester City	L 0-1		62,895
26	23	H	Sheffield Wednesday	D 0-1		9,021
27	Feb 3	A	Preston North End	D 1-1	Wrigglesworth	
28	6	A	Arsenal	D 1-1	Rowley	30,000
29	13	H	Brentford	L 1-3	Baird	
30	20	A	Portsmouth	L 0-1		15,000
31	27	H	Chelsea	L 2-4	Gladwin, Bamford	
32	Mar 6	A	Stoke City	W 2-1	McClelland, Baird	28,000
33	13	H	Charlton Athletic	L 0-3		
34	20	H	Grimsby Town	D 1-1	Cape	28,000
35	27	A	Liverpool	W 2-1	Baird, Mutch	
36	27	H	Everton	L 0-2		
37	29	A	Everton	W 3-2	Mutch, Bryant (pen), Ferrier	28,395
38	Apr 3	H	Leeds United	D 0-0		
39	10	H	Birmingham	D 2-2	Bamford 2	18,000
40	17	H	Middlesbrough	W 2-1	Bamford, Bryant	
41	21	A	Sunderland	D 1-1	Bamford	
42	24	A	West Bromwich Albion	L 0-1		16,245

F.A. CUP

Match No.	Date	Venue	Opponents	Result	Goalscorers	Attendance
Rd 3	Jan 16	H	Reading	W 1-0	Bamford	36,668
Rd 4	30	A	Arsenal	L 0-5		45,637

League Appearances
League Scorers

Players:
John, W. R. · Redwood, H. · Porter, W. · Brown, J. · Vose, G. · McKay, W. · Bryant, W. · Mutch, G. · Bamford, T. · Rowley, H. B. · Manley, T. · McLenahan, H. · McClelland, J. · Wassall, J. · Ferrier, R. · Mellor, J. · Roughton, G. W. · Griffiths, J. · Whalley, J. · Thompson, J. E. · Breen, W. · Winterbottom, W. · Halton · Lang, T. · Cape, J. · Baird, H. · Wrigglesworth, W. · Gladwin, G. · Jones, T. · Gardner, R.

M.U.F.C.

DID YOU KNOW? United made a quick return to Division Two, when they were relegated in 1936/7. Tommy Breen, the Irish 'keeper, made his United debut against Leeds on 28 November 1936, and conceded a goal inside the first minute without having touched the ball.

OPPOSITE PAGE:
SECOND DIVISION CHAMPIONS 1935/6. The successful playing squad. (JG)
Bottom Right: STAN PEARSON made rapid progress in the United side after his debut in 1937. (MMUSC)
Bottom Centre: JACK ROWLEY. (KM)
Middle Right: UNITED'S 1936/7 First Division prospects reviewed in Littlewoods Football Annual. *(KM)*
Bottom Left: WALTER WINTERBOTTOM TOPICAL TIMES photocard. (KM)

Presented with Topical Times.

MANCHESTER UNITED.

I am delighted that once again I can include the United in my First Division prospects. They have been too long away. I am wondering whether they will be able to " carry corn." Oh, the defence is all right, and I cannot fault the side so far as half-backs are concerned ; but even the most biased United supporter would not, and could not, describe the attack as being quite up to First Division requirements. Such as Mutch, Rowley and Manley have definite ability, but the Old Trafford men will have to introduce more cohesive skill if they are to cut much ice against the many Gibraltar-like defences to be located in the First Division. I expect that Manager Scott-Duncan will sign a couple more forwards before the ball is set rolling. If he does I shall be pleased, for it would make the side into a really good one. As it is, the United following should be content with a mid-table position as the reward for this " come-back " to grace. Newcomers are Roy John, the Welsh International goalkeeper, to take the place of Hall ; McMahon, an inside-left from St. Rochs ; and Montgomery, centre-forward, from Coltness.

16

WALTER WINTERBOTTOM,
Manchester United F.C.

Promoted to Division One & Lancashire Senior Cup Winners — Position: Runners-Up

MANCHESTER UNITED

Match No.	Date	Venue	Opponents	Result	Goalscorers	Attendance
1	Aug 28	H	Newcastle United	W 3-0	Bryant, Manley 2	30,566
2	30	A	Coventry City	L 0-1		
3	Sept 4	A	Luton Town	L 0-1		
4	8	H	Coventry City	D 2-2	Bryant, Bamford	18,000
5	11	H	Barnsley	W 4-1	Manley, Bamford 3	
6	13	A	Bury	W 2-1	Ferrier 2	
7	18	A	Stockport County	L 0-1		
8	25	H	Southampton	L 1-2	Manley	20,000
9	Oct 2	H	Sheffield United	L 0-1		
10	9	A	Tottenham Hotspur	W 1-0	Manley	31,905
11	16	A	Blackburn Rovers	D 1-1	Bamford	20,000
12	23	H	Sheffield Wednesday	W 1-0	McKay	20,000
13	30	A	Fulham	L 0-1		
14	Nov 6	H	Plymouth Argyle	D 0-0		18,000
15	13	A	Chesterfield	W 7-1	Manley, Bamford 4, Baird, Bryant	
16	20	H	Aston Villa	W 3-1	Manley, Bamford, Pearson	
17	27	A	Norwich City	W 3-2	Baird, Bryant, Pearson	17,397
18	Dec 4	H	Swansea Town	W 5-1	Rowley 4, Bryant	
19	11	A	Bradford Park Avenue	L 0-4		12,004
20	27	H	Nottingham Forest	W 4-3	Baird 2, McKay, Wrigglesworth	30,000
21	Jan 1	H	Nottingham Forest	W 3-2	Carey, Bryant, Bamford	16,894
22	15	A	Newcastle United	D 2-2	Rowley, Bamford	40,000
23	29	A	Luton Town	W 4-2	Bamford, Bryant, McKay, Carey	
24	Feb 2	H	Stockport County	W 3-1	Bryant, Baird, Bamford	
25	5	A	Barnsley	D 2-2	Smith, Rowley	7,889
26	19	H	Southampton	D 3-3	Redwood 2, Baird	20,654
27	17	H	Sheffield United	W 2-1	Smith, Bryant	40,000
28	19	A	Tottenham Hotspur	L 0-1		38,000
29	23	H	West Ham United	W 4-0	Wassall, Smith, Baird 2	15,000
30	26	A	Blackburn Rovers	W 2-1	Baird, Bryant	
31	Mar 5	H	Sheffield Wednesday	W 3-1	Brown, Baird Rowley	37,000
32	12	H	Fulham	W 1-0	Baird	
33	19	H	Plymouth Argyle	D 1-1	Rowley	
34	26	A	Chesterfield	W 4-1	Carey, Smith 2, Bryant	20,762
35	Apr 2	A	Aston Villa	L 0-3		
36	9	H	Norwich City	L 0-1		30,000
37	15	A	Burnley	L 0-1		26,864
38	16	H	Swansea Town	D 2-2	Smith, Rowley	13,811
39	18	A	Burnley	W 4-0	Bryant, Baird, McKay 2	33,000
40	23	H	Bradford Park Avenue	W 3-1	McKay, Smith, Baird	15,000
41	30	A	West Ham United	L 0-1		17,000
42	May 7	H	Bury	W 2-0	Smith, McKay	55,000

F.A. Cup

Match No.	Date	Venue	Opponents	Result	Goalscorers	Attendance
Rd 3	Jan 8	A	Yeovil and Petters United	W 3-0	Pearson, Baird, Bamford	49,004
Rd 4	22	A	Barnsley	D 2-2	Carey, Baird	38,549
Replay	26	H	Barnsley	D 2-2		33,601
Rd 4	12	H	Barnsley	W 1-0	Baird	24,147
Rd 5	Feb 12	A	Brentford	L 0-2		

League Appearances & Goals

Player	League Apps	League Goals
Breen, W.	33	
Griffiths, J.	18	
Roughton, W. G.	39	
Gladwin, G.	6	
Vose, G.	33	
McKay, W.	37	7
Bryant, W.	39	12
Murrey, R. D.	23	
Bamford, T.	36	14
Baird, H.	21	13
Manley, T.	9	6
Mutch, G.	4	
Wassall, J.	5	1
Brown, J.	16	1
Winterbottom, W.	4	
Ferrier, R.	2	2
Thompson, J. E.	3	
Carey, J. J.	16	3
Wrigglesworth, W.	25	1
Breedon, J.	9	
Rowley, J. F.	11	9
Whalley, H.	2	
Redwood, H.	10	2
Pearson, S. C.	2	2
Jones, D.		
Savage, R.		
Porter, W.	2	
Smith, J.	17	8

DID YOU KNOW? Stan Pearson and Jack Rowley were both introduced into the Second Division Championship team in 1937/8, when United made an immediate return to the First Division.

PROMOTION YEAR 1937-8

Top Right: PROMOTION 1937/8. Official Programme cover for the promotion year. (KM)

Bottom: THE M.U.J.A.C.'s 1937/8. The players and officials of the Manchester United Junior Athletic Club, United's first-ever Youth team. (JG)

Top Left: GRAND SLAM. 5 November 1938. All United's five teams won their matches on that day. This Butterworth cartoon appeared a week later in the programme for the Wolves game. (KM)

Manchester Senior Cup Winners

MANCHESTER UNITED

Match No.	Date		Venue	Opponents	Result		Goalscorers	Attendance
1	Aug	27	A	Middlesbrough	L	1-3	Smith	28,000
2		31	H	Bolton Wanderers	D	2-2	Craven, 1 o.g.	
3	Sept	3	H	Birmingham	W	4-1	Smith 2, Craven, Bryant	30,000
4		7	A	Liverpool	L	0-1		
5		10	A	Grimsby Town	L	0-1		
6		17	H	Stoke City	D	1-1	Smith	25,000
7		24	A	Chelsea	W	5-1	Manley, Redwood, Carey, Rowley, Smith	30,000
8	Oct	1	A	Preston North End	D	1-1	Bryant	23,000
9		8	H	Charlton Athletic	L	0-2		30,000
10		15	H	Blackpool	D	0-0		
11		22	A	Blackpool	L	1-5	Smith	26,638
12		29	H	Derby County	L	0-1		30,000
13	Nov	5	A	Sunderland	W	1-0	Rowley	30,000
14		12	H	Aston Villa	W	2-0	Rowley, Wrigglesworth	35,000
15		19	A	Wolverhampton Wanderers	L	1-3	Rowley	31,809
16		26	H	Everton	L	0-3		18,000
17	Dec	3	A	Huddersfield Town	D	1-1	Hanlon	10,000
18		10	H	Portsmouth	W	1-0	Bryant	10,000
19		17	A	Arsenal	D	0-0		15,000
20		24	H	Brentford	W	5-2	Manley, Rowley, Bryant, Hanlon 2	15,000
21		26	A	Middlesbrough	D	1-1	Wassall	26,000
22		31	H	Leicester City	W	3-0	Wrigglesworth 2, Carey	23,000
23	Jan	14	A	Leicester City	D	1-1	Hanlon	20,000
24		21	H	Birmingham	D	3-3	Pearson, McKay, Hanlon	25,000
25	Feb	4	A	Grimsby Town	L	0-1		25,000
26		11	H	Stoke City	W	3-0	Rowley 2, Wassall	35,000
27		28	H	Chelsea	W	1-0	Bradbury	40,000
28		11	H	Preston North End	L	1-7	Hanlon	28,000
29		18	A	Charlton Athletic	L	0-3		15,000
30		25	A	Blackpool	W	5-3	Hanlon 3, Bryant, Carey	35,000
31	Mar	4	A	Derby County	D	1-1	Carey	10,000
32		11	A	Sunderland	D	1-1	Wassall	25,000
33		18	H	Aston Villa	W	3-1	Rowley 2, Wassall	10,000
34		21	A	Wolverhampton Wanderers	L	0-1		25,000
35		29	H	Everton	L	0-2		18,000
36	Apr	1	A	Huddersfield Town	D	1-1	Rowley	14,007
37		7	H	Leeds United	D	0-0		38,000
38		8	H	Portsmouth	W	1-0	Rowley	28,000
39		10	A	Leeds United	L	1-3	Carey	25,000
40		15	A	Arsenal	L	1-2	Hanlon	13,700
41		22	H	Brentford	W	3-0	Bryant, Carey, Wassall	25,000
42		29	A	Bolton Wanderers				
42	May	6	H	Liverpool	W	2-0	Hanlon 2	

League Appearances / League Scorers

Player	Appearances	Goals
Breen, W.	7	
Redwood, H.	36	1
Roughton, W. G.	14	
Gladwin, G.	12	
Vose, G.	39	
McKay, W.	20	1
Bryant, W.	27	6
Wassall, J.	19	4
Smith, J.	11	6
Craven, C.	38	2
Rowley, J. F.	21	10
Breedon, J.	9	
Pearson, S. C.	35	1
Griffiths, J.	32	
Manley, T.	12	2
Carey, J. J.	32	7
Wrigglesworth, W.	13	3
Brown, J.	3	
Warner, J.	29	
Whalley, H.	2	
Hanlon, J.	27	9
Tapken, N.	14	
Bradbury, L.	2	1
Dougan, T.	4	
1 o.g.		

F.A. CUP

			Venue	Opponents	Result		Goalscorers	Attendance
Rd 3	Jan	7	A	West Bromwich Albion	D	0-0		23,900
Replay		11	H	West Bromwich Albion	L	1-5	Redwood	17,641

DID YOU KNOW? Old Trafford's record attendance was established in March 1939, when a crowd of 76,692 watched the F.A. Cup Semi-Final tie between Wolves and Grimsby Town. United's reserve side won the Central League Championship in 1938/9.

146

A RETURN TO THE FIRST DIVISION

Top: UNITED RETURNED TO DIVISION ONE in 1938/9 with this squad of players: (L to R) Back Row: Brown, Roughton, Breedon, Manley, Breen, McKay, Baird. Middle Row: B. Inglis (Asst. Trainer), Bryant, Craven, Smith, J. Griffiths, G. Vose, T. Curry (Trainer). Front: Redwood, Gladwin, Pearson. (MMUSC)

Bottom Right: INTERNATIONAL SOCCER AT OLD TRAFFORD. England 7 Ireland 0. 16 November 1938. Cover of Match Programme. (KM)

Bottom Left: JOHN WASSALL from Topical Times Annual 1939/40. (KM)
W. ROUGHTON on Churchmans Cigarette Card 'Association Footballers' Series No. 37. (KM)

Matches No. 1 to 3 Football League Division One. Suspended for duration of War

Matches No. 4 to 25 Regional League (Western) Division

Matches No. 26 to 29 The League Cup

Match No.	Date	Venue	Opponents	Result		Goalscorers	Attendance
1	Aug 26	H	Grimsby Town	W	4-0	Carey, Wrigglesworth, Bryant, Pearson	20,000
2	30	A	Chelsea	D	1-1	Bryant	15,000
3	Sept 2	A	Charlton Athletic	L	0-2		6,000
4	Oct 21	H	Manchester City	L	0-4		7,000
5	28	A	Chester	W	4-0	Pearson 2, Smith 2	5,500
6	Nov 11	H	Crewe Alexandra	W	5-1	Smith, Pearson, Carey, Vose, Hanlon	3,000
7	18	A	Liverpool	L	0-1		5,000
8	25	H	Port Vale	W	8-1	Wrigglesworth 5, Pearson, Asquith, Smith	2,000
9	Dec 2	A	Tranmere Rovers	W	4-2	Smith 2, Warner, Hanlon	2,500
10	9	A	Stockport County	W	7-4	McKay (pen), Smith 2 Pearson 2, Hanlon, 1 o.g.	3,392
11	23	H	Wrexham	W	5-1	Pearson 2, Roughton, Butt, Hanlon	2,000
12	Jan 6	A	Everton	L	2-3	Smith, McKay	2,500
13	20	H	Stoke City	W	4-3	Pearson, Jones 2, Butt	3,000
14	Feb 10	A	Manchester City	L	0-1		5,000
15	24	H	Chester	W	5-1	Manley, Pearson, Carey, 2 o.g.s	6,000
16	Mar 9	A	Crewe Alexandra	W	4-1	Smith 2, Pearson, Butt	3,000
17	16	H	Liverpool	W	1-0	Pearson	6,000
18	23	A	Port Vale	W	3-1	McKay 2, Pearson	5,000
19	30	H	Tranmere Rovers	W	6-1	Smith 3, Roberts, McKay, Roughton (pen)	6,000
20	Apr 6	H	Stockport County	W	6-1	Roughton, Pearson 2, Butt 2, Wrigglesworth	8,000
21	May 6	H	New Brighton	W	6-0	Smith 2, Asquith, Whalley, Butt, Wrigglesworth	
22	13	A	Wrexham	L	2-3	Butt 2	
23	18	A	New Brighton	L	0-6		
24	25	A	Stoke City	L	2-3	Burdett 2	
25	Jun 1	H	Everton	L	0-3		
26	Apr 20	H	Manchester City	L	0-1		21,874
27	27	A	Manchester City	W	2-0	Wrigglesworth, Pearson	21,569
28	May 4	A	Blackburn Rovers	W	2-1	Smith, Carey	8,800
29	11	H	Blackburn Rovers	L	1-3	Carey	12,551

NOTES:

1) On the 3rd September War was declared against Germany and the Football League was abandoned after only three matches were played by each club.

2) On 16th September Manchester United played for the first time in a Friendly against Bolton Wanderers after War was declared.

3) On 21st October Manchester United began playing in the Regional League Western Division with a game against Manchester City.

APPEARANCES

Anderson, J. 1; Asquith, B. 9; Breedon, J. 25; *Briggs, C. (Accrington Stanley) 2; Bryant, W. 4; *Burdett, T. (Bury) 2;
*Butt, L. (Blackburn Rovers) 11; Carey, J. J. 25; *Carter, D. F. (Bury) 1; Chilton, A. C. 1; *Doherty, P. D. (Manchester City) 1; *Dougal, P. 1;
*Fairhurst, W. G. 2; *Gemmell, J. (Bury) 2; *Goodall, E. I. (Bolton Wanderers) 2; Griffiths, J. 4; Hanlon, J. 11; *Herd, A. (Manchester City) 1;
*Kilshaw, E. (Bury) 7; *Jones, D. (Bury) 2; *Jones, (Bolton Wanderers) 1; *Manley, T. (Brentford) 8; *Matthews, S. (Stoke City) 1; McKay, W. 25;
Mitten, C. 3; *Nicholson, W. E. (Aberdeen) 4; Pearson, S. C. 22; Porter, W. 6; Redwood, H. 28; *Roberts, F. (Bury) 5; Roughton, W. G. 23;
Smith J. 23; *Toseland, E. 1; Vose, G. 7; Warner, J. 23; Wassall, J. V. 1; Whalley, H. 3; *Woodward, T. (Bolton Wanderers) 1; Wrigglesworth, W. 20.

* denotes guest player

GOALSCORERS

Pearson, S. C. 17; Smith, J. 17; Wrigglesworth, W. 9; Butt, L. 8; Carey, J. J. 5; McKay, W. 5 (1 pen); Hanlon, J. 4; Roughton, W. G. 3 (1 pen);
Asquith, B. 2; Bryant, W. 2; Burdett, T. 2; Jones, D. 2; Manley, T. 1; Roberts, F. 1; Vose, G. 1; Warner, J. 1; Whalley, H. 1; 3 own goals.

Above: DESTRUCTION OF OLD TRAFFORD 1941. (JG)

Below: FOOTBALL IN GASMASKS. Cartoon from the cover of Post Football Guide *1958/9. (KM)*

MANCHESTER
UNITED AT WAR
1939-46

Matches No. 1 to 19 Football League (North) 1st Competition

Matches No. 20 to 21 League War Cup

Matches No. 22 to 31 North Regional League 2nd Competition

Match No.	Date	Venue	Opponents	Result		Goalscorers	Attendance
1	Aug 31	A	Rochdale	W	3-1	Smith, Aston, Carey	3,000
2	Sept 7	H	Bury	D	0-0		2,000
3	14	A	Oldham Athletic	L	1-2	Farrow	5,096
4	21	H	Oldham Athletic	L	2-3	Smith 2	3,000
5	28	A	Manchester City	L	1-4	Smith	10,000
6	Oct 5	H	Manchester City	L	0-2		10,000
7	12	A	Burnley	W	1-0	Warner	2,500
8	19	H	Preston North End	W	4-1	Buchan, Dodds 2, Carey	3,500
9	26	A	Preston North End	L	1-3	Bryant	2,200
10	Nov 2	H	Burnley	W	4-1	Carey, Butt 2, Smith	1,000
11	9	A	Everton	L	2-5	Smith, Dodds	1,000
12	16	H	Everton	D	0-0		2,000
13	23	A	Liverpool	D	2-2	Warner, Smith	4,000
14	30	H	Liverpool	W	2-0	Butt, Smith	700
15	Dec 7	A	Blackburn Rovers	D	5-5	Mitten, Bryant, Dodds 2, Aston	2,000
16	14	H	Rochdale	L	3-4	Carey, Smith 2	1,000
17	21	A	Bury	L	1-4	McKay	2,000
18	25	A	Stockport County	W	3-1	Smith 2, Burrows	1,500
19	28	N	Blackburn Rovers	W	9-0	Smith 5, Carey 2, Aston, Mitten (at Stockport)	1,500
20	Feb 15	H	Everton	D	2-2	Rowley, 1 o.g.	5,000
21	22	A	Everton	L	1-2	Rowley	3,000
22	Mar 1	A	Chesterfield	D	1-1	Smith	2,000
23	8	H	Bury	W	7-3	Rowley 3, Carey 3, Smith	3,000
24	22	A	Oldham Athletic	W	1-0	Smith	1,500
25	29	A	Blackpool	L	0-2		4,000
26	Apr 5	H	Blackpool	L	2-3	Mears, Smith	2,000
27	12	A	Everton	W	2-1	Rowley 2	4,000
28	14	A	Manchester City	W	7-1	Rowley 4, Pearson 2, Smith	7,000
29	26	A	Liverpool	L	1-2	Rowley	2,000
30	May 3	H	Liverpool	D	1-1	Rowley	1,500
31	10	A	Bury	L	1-5	Rowley	2,000

NOTES:

1) On 11th March 1941 part of the ground and Main Stand were destroyed by a German bombing raid.

2) On 14th April 1941 United beat City at Maine Road 7-1, this was City's heaviest defeat on the ground since the opening in 1923.

3) Following heavy air raids on Manchester, United played their home game on the 28th December 1940 at the Stockport, County Ground.

APPEARANCES

*Ainsley, G. E. (Leeds United) 1; Asquith, B. 4; Aston, J. 10; *Bagley, T. H. (Bury) 1; *Bartholomew, R. (Grimsby Town) 2;
*Bellis, A. (Port Vale) 4; Breedon, J. 30; *Briggs, C. (Accrington Stanley) 1; *Brown, A. (Huddersfield Town) 13; Bryant, W. 19;
*Buchan, W. R. M. (Blackpool) 2; *Burbanks, W. E. (Sunderland) 2; *Burrows, A. (Stockport County) 5; *Butt, L. (Blackburn Rovers) 2;
Carey, J. J. 28; Carey, W. J. 1; Couser, H. M. (Bangor) 2; *Dodds, E. (Blackpool) 4; *Emptage, A. (Manchester City) 1; *Farrow, G. (Blackpool) 3;
*Gemmell, J. (Bury) 1; *Gorman, W. C. (Bury) 2; Griffiths, J. 1; *Johnson, R. 1; *Jones, B. (Bolton Wanderers) 1; *Jones, S. (Blackpool) 1;
McKay, W. 18; *McPhillips, L. (Cardiff City) 1; Mears, S. 2; Mitten, C. 15; *O'Donnell, H. (Blackpool) 5; *Olsen, T. B. (Bury) 1; Pearson, S. C. 2;
Porter, W. 15; Redwood, H. 23; Roughton, W. G. 23; Rowley, G. A. 1; Rowley, J. F. 11; Smith, J. 28; *Stork, H. (Stockport County) 1;
*Topping, H. W. (Stockport County) 1; Vose, G. 3; Warner, J. 30; *Watkins, T. (Home Guard) 1; Whalley, H. 16; Wrigglesworth, W. 1;
Wyles, T. C. (Everton) 1. (denotes guest player)

GOALSCORERS

Smith, J. 24; Rowley, J. F. 14; Carey, J. J. 9; Dodds, E. 5; Aston, J. 3; Butt, L. 3; Bryant, W. 2; Mears, S. 2; Mitten, C. 2; Pearson, S. C. 2;
Warner, J. 2; Buchan, W. R. M. 1; Burrows, A. 1; Farrow, G. 1; McKay, W. 1; 1 own goal.

Matches No. 1 to 18 Football League (North) Section 1st Competition

Matches No. 19 to 32 League War Cup

Match No. 33 League Championship 2nd Competition

Match No.	Date	Venue	Opponents	Result		Goalscorers	Attendance
1	Aug 30	H	New Brighton	W	13-1	Rowley, 7, Mitten, Bryant, 2, Smith 3	2,000
2	Sept 6	A	New Brighton	D	3-3	Carey, Whalley, Morris	1,500
3	13	A	Stockport County	W	5-1	Rowley 4, Mitten	3,000
4	20	H	Stockport County	W	7-1	Warner, Rowley 4, Carey, Mitten	2,000
5	27	H	Everton	L	2-3	Smith, Rowley	4,000
6	Oct 4	A	Everton	W	3-1	Rowley, Smith, Carey	6,000
7	11	A	Chester	W	7-0	Smith 2, Mitten 2, Morris, Whalley, Warner	3,500
8	18	H	Chester	W	8-1	Smith 2, Carey, Rowley 4, Bryant	2,000
9	25	A	Stoke City	D	1-1	Carey	5,000
10	Nov 1	H	Stoke City	W	3-0	Whalley, Carey, Rowley	4,000
11	8	H	Tranmere Rovers	W	6-1	Rowley 5, Smith	2,000
12	15	A	Tranmere Rovers	D	1-1	Rowley	2,000
13	22	A	Liverpool	D	1-1	Smith	10,000
14	29	H	Liverpool	D	2-2	Rowley, J. 2	3,000
15	Dec 6	H	Wrexham	W	10-3	Smith 2, Carey 4, Rowley 3, Bryant	2,000
16	13	A	Wrexham	W	4-3	Morris 4	2,500
17	20	A	Manchester City	L	1-2	Morris	10,000
18	25	H	Manchester City	D	2-2	Smith, Rowley	20,000
19	27	H	Bolton Wanderers	W	3-1	Morris, Rowley 2	5,000
20	Jan 3	A	Bolton Wanderers	D	2-2	Pearson, Rowley	2,500
21	10	H	Oldham Athletic	D	1-1	Morris	5,000
22	17	A	Oldham Athletic	W	3-1	Carey 2, Rowley	6,000
23	31	A	Southport	W	3-1	Rowley, Smith, Carey	2,000
24	Feb 14	A	Sheffield United	W	2-0	Carey, Rowley	12,000
25	21	H	Preston North End	L	0-2		4,000
26	28	A	Preston North End	W	3-1	Rowley 2, Carey	6,000
27	Mar 21	H	Sheffield United	D	2-2	Catterick, Smith	6,000
28	28	H	Southport	W	4-2	Carey 2, Catterick 2	3,000
29	Apr 4	A	Blackburn Rovers	W	2-1	Warner, Catterick	5,000
30	6	H	Blackburn Rovers	W	3-1	Bryant, Carey 2	9,000
31	11	H	Wolverhampton Wanderers	W	5-4	Morris, Catterick 2, Smith, Carey	9,000
32	18	A	Wolverhampton Wanderers	L	0-2		12,000
33	May 23	A	Manchester City	W	3-1	Worrall 2, Whalley	6,000

NOTES:

4) Manchester United played their last game of the Wartime period at Old Trafford against Bury on 8th March 1941. Next official League match played at Old Trafford was against Bolton Wanderers on 24th August 1949.

5) On 5th April 1941 Manchester United commenced their series of home games at Maine Road.

APPEARANCES

*Breedon, J. 32; Bryant, W. 30; Carey, J. J. 31; *Catterick, H. (Everton) 6; Chilton, A. C. 1; *Dougal, J. (Preston North End) 1; Dougal, T. 1; *Emptage, A. T. (Manchester City) 1; Griffiths, J. 6; *Holdcroft, G. (Preston North End) 1; *Hornby, R. (Burnley) 1; Lee, J. 3; Mitten, C. 13; Morris, J. 20; Pearson, S. C. 6; Porter, W. 32; Redwood, H. 18; *Roach, J. E. (Accrington Stanley) 3; *Robinson, A. (Burnley) 1; Roughton, W. G. 27; Rowley, A. G. 1; Rowley, J. F. 23; Shore, H. 6; Smith, J. 30; *Taylor, E. W. (Manchester University) 1; Waddington, A. 2; Warner, J. 29; Whalley, H. 33; *Worrall, H. (Portsmouth) 1; Wrigglesworth, W. 3.
* denotes guest player

GOALSCORERS

Rowley, J. F. 42; Carey, J. J. 20; Smith, J. 17; Morris, J. 10; Catterick, H. 6; Bryant, W. 5; Mitten, C. 5; Whalley, H. 4; Warner, J. 3; Worrall, H. 2; Pearson, S. C. 1.

Matches No. 1 to 18 Football League (North) 1st Competition

Matches No. 19 to 30 Football League War Cup (North)

Match No. 31 Football League (North) 2nd Competition

Match No.	Date	Venue	Opponents	Result		Goalscorers	Attendance
1	Aug 29	A	Everton	D	2-2	Pearson, Catterick	8,000
2	Sept 5	H	Everton	W	2-1	Carey, Mitten	4,000
3	12	H	Chester	L	0-2		
4	19	A	Chester	D	2-2	Catterick, Roughton	3,000
5	26	A	Blackburn Rovers	L	2-4	Bryant, Catterick	2,000
6	Oct 3	H	Blackburn Rovers	W	5-2	Smith 3, Morris, Mitten	4,000
7	10	H	Liverpool	L	3-4	Smith 2, Mitten	4,000
8	17	A	Liverpool	L	1-2	Carey	12,786
9	24	A	Stockport County	W	4-1	Bellis 2, Carey, 1 o.g.	2,000
10	31	H	Stockport County	W	3-1	Bellis, Smith 2	3,000
11	Nov 7	H	Manchester City	W	2-1	Pearson, 1 o.g.	9,301
12	14	A	Manchester City	W	5-0	Bryant 2, Smith 3	7,000
13	21	A	Tranmere Rovers	W	5-0	Morris 2, Smith 2, 1 o.g.	4,000
14	28	H	Tranmere Rovers	W	5-1	Rowley 2, Smith, Pearson 2	3,000
15	Dec 5	H	Wrexham	W	6-1	Smith 3, Bellis 2, Bryant	2,000
16	12	A	Wrexham	W	5-2	Bryant, Carey, Smith 3	3,500
17	19	A	Bolton Wanderers	W	2-0	Mitten, Carey	2,000
18	25	H	Bolton Wanderers	W	4-0	Roughton, Carey 2, Bryant	
19	26	H	Chester	W	3-0	Bellis 2, Mitten	10,449
20	Jan 2	A	Chester	L	1-4	Smith	1,500
21	9	A	Blackpool	D	1-1	Pearson	5,000
22	16	H	Blackpool	W	5-3	Smith, Bryant, Buchan 3	17,381
23	23	H	Everton	L	1-4	Smith	7,764
24	30	A	Everton	W	5-0	Pearson, Smith 3, Buchan	14,000
25	Feb 6	A	Manchester City	D	0-0		17,577
26	13	H	Manchester City	D	1-1	Smith	16,326
27	20	H	Crewe Alexandra	W	7-0	Smith 3, Pearson 2, Morris, Bryant	5,000
28	27	A	Crewe Alexandra	W	3-2	Bryant 2, Broadis	4,000
29	Mar 6	H	Manchester City	L	0-1		26,962
30	13	A	Manchester City	L	0-2		36,453
31	May 1	H	Sheffield United	W	2-0	Carey, Smith	5,000

APPEARANCES

Anderson, W. 1; *Asquith, B. (Barnsley) 1; *Barkas, S. (Manchester City) 1; *Bellis, A. (Port Vale) 19; Breedon, J. 27;
*Broadis, I. A. (Tottenham Hotspur) 1; *Brocklebank, R. (Burnley) 1; Bryant, W. 28; *Buchan, W. R. M. (Blackpool) 7; *Burnett, G. G. (Everton) 1;
Carey, J. J. 22; *Catterick, H. (Everton) 5; *Chadwick, C. (Middlesbrough) 1; *Dainty, A. (Preston North End) 1; Dimond, S. 2;
*Eastwood, E. (Manchester City) 1; Griffiths, J. 22; Hall, J. L. 1; *Harrison, H. (Burnley) 1; *King, F. O. 1; *Kippax, F. (Burnley) 1; *Kirkman, N. 1;
Lee, J. S. 4; McKay, W. 8; Mitten, C. 8; Morris, J. 9; Pearson, S. C. 11; Porter, W. 26; ,*Roach, J. E. (Accrington Stanley) 4;
*Robinson, J. J. (Manchester City) 1; Roughton, W. G. 25; Rowley, A. G. 3; Rowley, J. F. 2; *Scales, G. (Manchester City) 1; Shore, J. 2;
Smith, J. 25; *Smith, T. M. (Preston North End) 1; Vose, G. 8; Walton, J. W. 1; Warner, J. 27; *Westwood, E. (Manchester City) 1; Whalley, H. 26;
*Williams, W. J. H. (Manchester City) 1; *Worrall, H. (Portsmouth) 1.
* denotes guest player

GOALSCORERS

Smith, J. 30; Bryant, W. 10; Carey, J. J. 8; Pearson, S. C. 8; Bellis, A. 7; Mitten, C. 5; Buchan, W. R. M. 4; Morris, J. 4; Catterick, H. 3;
Roughton, W. G. 2; Rowley, J. F. 2; Broadis, I. A. 1; 3 own goals.

Matches No. 1 to 18 Football League (North) 1st Championship

Matches No. 19 to 32 Football League War Cup (North)

Matches No. 33 to 39 Football League (North) 2nd Championship

Match No.	Date	Venue	Opponents	Result		Goalscorers	Attendance
1	Aug 28	H	Stockport County	W	6-0	Bellis 2, Smith 2, McKay, McDonald	3,000
2	Sept 4	A	Stockport County	D	3-3	McDonald 2, Bryant	2,000
3	11	H	Everton	W	4-1	Broadis, McDonald 2, Smith	10,000
4	18	A	Everton	L	1-6	Bellis	
5	25	H	Blackburn Rovers	W	2-1	Bryant 2	5,000
6	Oct 2	A	Blackburn Rovers	L	1-2	Roughton	3,000
7	9	H	Chester	W	3-1	Bellis 3	5,000
8	16	A	Chester	L	4-5	Smith 2, McKay, 1 o.g.	4,000
9	23	A	Liverpool	W	4-3	Smith, McDonald, Pearson 2	15,000
10	30	H	Liverpool	W	1-0	McKay	13,647
11	Nov 6	A	Manchester City	D	2-2	Smith, Pearson	15,157
12	13	H	Manchester City	W	3-0	Morris, Bryant, Smith	8,958
13	20	H	Tranmere Rovers	W	6-3	Mitten 4, Smith 2 (Abandoned 85 minutes)	2,000
14	27	A	Tranmere Rovers	W	1-0	McKay	2,500
15	Dec 4	A	Wrexham	W	4-1	Smith, Morris 2, Bryant	3,500
16	11	H	Wrexham	W	5-0	Smith 2, Pearson 3	2,500
17	18	H	Bolton Wanderers	W	3-1	Warner, Morris, Smith	4,800
18	25	A	Bolton Wanderers	W	3-1	Smith 2, Bryant	8,000
19	26	H	Halifax Town	W	6-2	Pearson 3, Smith 2, Rowley	
20	Jan 1	A	Halifax Town	D	1-1	Smith	4,000
21	8	A	Stockport County	W	3-2	Brook 2, Bryant	4,500
22	15	H	Stockport County	W	4-2	Smith 3, Brook	5,000
23	22	H	Manchester City	L	1-3	Smith	12,372
24	29	A	Manchester City	W	3-2	Rowley 2, Smith	18,569
25	Feb 5	A	Bury	W	3-0	Pearson 2, Smith	5,159
26	12	H	Bury	D	3-3	Bryant, McKay, Brook	6,896
27	19	H	Oldham Athletic	W	3-2	Smith 3	7,028
28	26	A	Oldham Athletic	D	1-1	Bryant	6,768
29	Mar 4	A	Wrexham	W	4-1	Bryant, Rowley, Smith, Morris	12,000
30	11	H	Wrexham	D	2-2	Pearson, Smith	12,248
31	18	A	Birmingham	L	1-3	Smith	16,000
32	25	H	Birmingham	D	1-1	Rowley	32,992
33	Apr 1	A	Bolton Wanderers	L	0-3		2,500
34	8	H	Bolton Wanderers	W	3-2	Bryant 2, Morris	13,044
35	10	A	Manchester City	L	1-4	Bryant	19,000
36	15	H	Burnley	W	9-0	Smith 3, Bryant 2, Rowley 2, Brook 2	4,000
37	22	A	Burnley	D	3-3	Smith, Brook 2	2,500
38	29	H	Oldham Athletic	D	0-0		2,000
39	May 6	A	Oldham Athletic	W	3-1	Morris, Sloan, 1 o.g.	1,658

APPEARANCES

*Bailey, A. 1; *Barker, L. 1; *Bellis, A. (Port Vale) 16; *Black, W. 1; *Bootle, W. (Manchester City) 1; Breedon,. J. 32; *Brierley, G. N. (R.A.F.) 1; *Broadis, I. A. (Tottenham Hotspur) 2; *Brook, H. (Sheffield United) 13; Bryant, W. 36; 1; Carey, J. J. 1; Cochrane, A. M. 1; Cockburn, H. 1; Davies, 1; Dimond, S. 1; *Ferrer, D. 6; *Gallon, J. W. 3; *Gardner, T. 1; Gibson, R. 1; Griffiths, J. 20; Grundy, T. 2; Hacking, J. 1; *Hyde, E. W. (Stockport County) 1; *Liddell, J. (Stockport County) 3; *McDonald, J. C. (R.A.F.) 8; McKay, W. 33; Mitten, C. 4; Morris, J. 18; Murray, 1; Norris, F. 3; Pearson, L. 1; Pearson, S. C. 16; Porter, W. 36; *Rudman, H. 1; Roughton, W. G. 30; Rowley, J. F. 5; *Sloan, J. W. (Tranmere Rovers) 1; Smith, J. 33; *Tilling, H. K. 1; Tomlinson, F. 1; Tynell, L. 1; Vose, G. 1; *Walmsley, J. 1; Walton, J. A. 24; Warner, J. 36; *Watton, G. D. (Birmingham) 1; *Watson, W. T. 1; Whalley, H. 21; Williams, W. J. H. 1; Wilson, J. H. 1; *Wood, D. (Hearts) 1; *Woodruff, H. 1. (denotes guest player)

GOALSCORERS

Smith, J. 35; Bryant, W. 15; Pearson, S. C. 12; Brook, H. 8; Morris, J. 7; Bellis, A. 6; McDonald, J. C. 6; Rowley, J. F. 6; McKay, W. 5; Mitten, C. 4; Broadis, I. A. 1; Roughton, W. G. 1; Sloan, J. W. 1; Warner, J. 1; 2 own goals.

Matches No. 1 to 19 Football League (North) 1st Championship

Matches No. 20 to 31 and 33 to 40 Football League (North) Cup

Match No. 32 Football League (North) 2nd Championship

Match No.	Date	Venue	Opponents	Result		Goalscorers	Attendance
1	Aug 26	A	Everton	W	2-1	Mycock, Currier	15,000
2	Sept 2	H	Everton	L	1-3	Bryant	10,000
3	9	H	Stockport County	L	3-4	Mycock 2, Bryant	8,000
4	16	A	Stockport County	D	4-4	Smith, Mycock 2, Bryant	6,000
5	23	H	Bury	D	2-2	Mycock, Walton	6,000
6	30	A	Bury	L	2-4	Woodcock, Mycock	4,636
7	Oct 7	A	Chester	L	0-2		5,000
8	14	H	Chester	W	1-0	Freer	3,000
9	21	H	Tranmere Rovers	W	6-1	Dougan, Bryant, Mycock 2, Mitten, Chadwick	8,000
10	28	A	Tranmere Rovers	W	4-2	Mycock, Bryant 2, 1 o.g.	1,500
11	Nov 4	A	Liverpool	L	2-3	Woodcock, Mycock	17,610
12	11	H	Liverpool	L	2-5	Mitten, Mycock	5,000
13	18	H	Manchester City	W	3-2	Morris 2, Mycock	20,764
14	25	A	Manchester City	L	0-4		18,657
15	Dec 2	A	Crewe Alexandra	W	4-1	Bryant 2, Mycock, Chadwick	7,000
16	9	H	Crewe Alexandra	W	2-0	Bowden, Morris	5,000
17	16	H	Wrexham	W	1-0	Ireland	6,000
18	23	A	Wrexham	L	1-2	Morris	7,200
19	26	A	Sheffield United	W	4-3	Chadwick, Bainbridge, Morris 2	12,000
20	30	A	Oldham Athletic	W	4-3	Chadwick, Smith, Mycock 2	6,617
21	Jan 6	H	Huddersfield Town	W	1-0	Smith	8,000
22	13	A	Huddersfield Town	D	2-2	Smith, Cockburn	6,146
23	Feb 3	H	Manchester City	L	1-3	Mitten	30,000
24	10	A	Manchester City	L	0-2		22,923
25	17	H	Bury	W	2-0	Whalley, Mitten	5,000
26	24	A	Bury	L	1-3	Bainbridge	6,000
27	Mar 3	H	Oldham Athletic	W	3-2	Chadwick, Whalley, Rowley	10,000
28	10	A	Halifax Town	L	0-1		6,000
29	17	H	Halifax Town	W	2-0	Chadwick, Roach	8,000
30	24	A	Burnley	W	3-2	Chadwick, Rowley 2	15,000
31	31	H	Burnley	W	4-0	Bryant, Smith 3	25,523
32	Apr 2	A	Blackpool	L	1-4	Wrigglesworth	14,000
33	7	H	Stoke City	W	6-1	Bryant, Wrigglesworth 2, Smith, Rowley 2	45,616
34	14	A	Stoke City	W	4-1	McCulloch, Bryant 2, 1 o.g.	5,000
35	21	A	Doncaster Rovers	W	2-1	Smith, Bellis	29,177
36	28	H	Doncaster Rovers	W	3-1	Wrigglesworth	31,728
37	May 5	H	Chesterfield	D	1-1	Bellis	32,013
38	12	A	Chesterfield	W	1-0	McDowell	32,000
39	19	A	Bolton Wanderers	L	0-1		40,000
40	26	H	Bolton Wanderers	D	2-2	Wrigglesworth, Bryant	57,395

APPEARANCES

*Astbury, T. A. (Chester) 1; Bainbridge, W. 4; *Bartholomew, R. (Grimsby Town) 3; *Bellis, A. (Port Vale) 6; *Bowden, N. H. 2; *Boyes, W. (Everton) 1; Breedon, J. 14; *Briggs, C. J. (Accrington Stanley) 8; Bryant, W. 35; Capper, G. 3; *Chadwick, C. (Middlesbrough) 25; Chilton, A. C. 6; Cockburn, H. 9; Crompton, J. 26; *Currier, J. (Bolton Wanderers) 3; Dougan, T. 3; Freer, C. 1; *Gallon, J. W. 1; Glaister, G. (Blackburn Rovers) 1; Glidden, G. S. (Tranmere Rovers) 1; Heffion, T. 1; *Ireland, H. W. (Reading) 1; *Johnson, A. A. (R.A.F.) 1; Jones, A. 1; *Keeley, W. (Accrington Stanley) 2; *Makin, G. 1; *McCulloch, W. D. (Stockport County) 3; McDonald, H. 1; *McDowell, J. 1; *McInnes, J. S. (Liverpool) 2; McKay, W. 21; *Mercer, S. (Leicester City) 1; Mitten, C. 6; Morris, J. 11; Mycock, A. 25; Porter, W. 6; *Roach, J. E. (Accrington Stanley) 18; *Robinson, P. (Manchester City) 2; Roughton, W. G. 29; Rowley, J. F. 3; *Sloan, J. W. (Tranmere Rovers) 2; Smith, J. 26; Walton, J. W. 36; Warner, J. 31; Whalley, H. 35; *White, R. (Tottenham Hotspur) 3; *Woodcock, A. 7; Wrigglesworth, W. 11. (* denotes guest player).

GOALSCORERS

Mycock, A. 16; Bryant, W. 13; Smith, J. 9; Chadwick, C. 7; Wrigglesworth, W. 7; Morris, J. 6; Rowley, J. F. 5; Mitten, C. 4; Bainbridge, W. 2; Bellis, A. 2; Whalley, H. 2; Woodcock, A. 2; Bowden, N. H. 1; Cockburn, H. 1; Currier, J. 1; Dougan, T. 1; Freer, C. 1; Ireland, H. W. 1; McCulloch, W. D. 1; McDowell, J. 1; Roach, J. E. 1; Walton, J. W. 1; 2 own goals.

Football League (North)   *Position: 4th*

Home Matches played at Maine Road

Match No.	Date	Venue	Opponents	Result		Goalscorers	Attendance
1	Aug 25	A	Huddersfield Town	L	2-3	Smith 2	7,672
2	Sept 1	H	Huddersfield Town	L	2-3	Rowley, Koffman	28,000
3	8	H	Chesterfield	L	0-2		15,000
4	12	A	Middlesbrough	L	1-2	Daine	10,000
5	15	A	Chesterfield	D	1-1	Bryant	10,000
6	20	A	Stoke City	W	2-1	Reid, Hullett	18,000
7	22	A	Barnsley	D	2-2	Hullett, Cockburn	11,000
8	29	H	Barnsley	D	1-1	Smith	20,000
9	Oct 6	H	Everton	D	0-0		30,697
10	13	A	Everton	L	0-3		35,000
11	20	A	Bolton Wanderers	D	1-1	Wrigglesworth	20,000
12	27	H	Bolton Wanderers	W	2-1	Carey, Worrall	27,272
13	Nov 3	H	Preston North End	W	6-1	Rowley 2, Smith 2, Worrall, Warner	22,072
14	10	A	Preston North End	D	2-2	Bainbridge, Smith	13,000
15	17	A	Leeds United	D	3-3	Hanlon 2, Buckle	10,000
16	24	H	Leeds United	W	6-1	Wrigglesworth 2, Buckle 2, Rowley, Hanlon	21,312
17	Dec 1	H	Burnley	D	3-3	Hullett 3	17,429
18	8	A	Burnley	D	2-2	Smith, Hanlon	8,000
19	15	H	Sunderland	W	2-1	Smith 2	19,500
20	22	A	Sunderland	L	2-4	Wrigglesworth, Smith	18,000
21	25	A	Sheffield United	L	0-1		13,000
22	26	H	Sheffield United	L	2-3	Hullett, Carey	35,000
23	29	H	Middlesbrough	W	4-1	Smith 2, Rowley 2	18,937
24	Jan 12	H	Grimsby Town	W	5-0	Rowley 3, Smith, Bainbridge	20,789
25	19	A	Grimsby Town	L	0-1		9,000
26	Feb 2	H	Blackpool	W	4-2	Rowley 2, Wrigglesworth, Bainbridge	18,033
27	9	H	Liverpool	W	2-1	Smith 2	33,000
28	16	A	Liverpool	W	5-0	Rowley 2, Hanlon 2, Wrigglesworth	37,197
29	23	A	Bury	D	1-1	Hanlon	16,391
30	Mar 2	H	Bury	D	1-1	Hanlon	30,912
31	9	H	Blackburn Rovers	W	6-2	Rowley 3, Hanlon 2, Delaney	31,422
32	16	A	Blackburn Rovers	W	3-1	Smith 2, Pearson	8,000
33	23	A	Bradford Park Avenue	L	1-2	Carey	13,498
34	27	A	Blackpool	W	5-1	Pearson 3, Carey, Wrigglesworth	10,000
35	30	H	Bradford Park Avenue	W	4-0	Wrigglesworth, Aston, Rowley, Delaney	36,791
36	Apr 6	H	Manchester City	L	1-4	Aston	62,144
37	13	A	Manchester City	W	3-1	Pearson, Hanlon, Rowley	50,440
38	19	A	Newcastle United	W	1-0	Pearson	50,000
39	20	H	Sheffield Wednesday	W	4-0	Pearson 2, Delaney, Rowley	34,000
40	22	H	Newcastle United	W	4-1	Wrigglesworth, Delaney, Rowley, Mitten (pen)	39,173
41	27	A	Sheffield Wednesday	L	0-1		12,000
42	May 4	H	Stoke City	W	2-1	Pearson, Buckle	37,773

APPEARANCES

Aston, J. 5; Bainbridge, W. 7; Bryant, W. 8; Buckle, E. W. 6; Carey, J. J. 27; Chilton, A. C. 32; Cockburn, H. 37; Comer, D. 1; Crompton, J. 30; *Davie, J. (Chesterfield) 1; Delaney, J. 15; Dimond, S. 1; *Gallacher, J. 1; *Hamlett, T. L. (Bolton Wanderers) 1; Hanlon, J. 24; Hullett, W. 5; Koffman, J. 2; Landers, T. 1; Langford, L. 1; McKay, W. 1; Mitten, C. 4; Mycock, A. 3; Pearson, S. C. 12; *Reid, D. J. (Stockport County) 1; Rhodes, D. 1; *Roach, J. E. (Accrington Stanley) 13; Roughton, W. G. 5; Rowley, J. F. 29; Smith, J. 22; Tapkin, N. 12; Vose, G. 1; Walton, J. W. 37; Warner, J. 33; Whalley, H. 37; Wilson, J. H. 3; *Worrall, F. 7; Wrigglesworth, W. 36. (* denotes guest player)

GOALSCORERS

Rowley, J. F. 20; Smith, J. 17; Hanlon, J. 11; Pearson, S. C. 9; Wrigglesworth, W. 9; Hullett, W. 6; Buckle, E. W. 4; Carey, J. J. 4; Delaney, J. 4; Bainbridge, W. 3; Aston, J. 2; Worrall, H. 2; Bryant, W. 1; Cockburn, H. 1; Daine, J. 1; Koffman, J. 1; Mitten, C. 1 (pen); Reid, D. J. 1; Warner, J. 1.

THEY'VE LOST THEIR HOME BUT NOT THEIR SPIRIT

United, like all other clubs, reduced their ranks and went onto a war time austerity basis when Hitler declared war. They had a first-class ground at Old Trafford; it was only a shell when war ended.

One night, during a March blitz on Manchester, in 1941, the Luftwaffe spread its carpet of bombs around that part of the Manchester area. Some hit the ground, and left it a pile of rubble.

When officials went there a few hours after the raid the scene almost brought tears. The club's offices, its dressing rooms, its stands, and all the expensive apparatus bought for treating injuries formed merely a big mound of rubbish.

It has been variously estimated that the repair bill may total as much as £100,000. That will have to more seriously considered when building of football grounds is allowed once again.

Meanwhile, the club is without a proper home. Fortunately Manchester City's ground at Maine Road escaped bombing, and so the first team is playing there, while the reserves manage to turn out at Old Trafford, where the police allow only crowds of small dimension to assemble.

If there had been no neighbouring soccer ground, it is difficult to imagine what United could have done. As it is, they do a certain amount of training on the Manchester University ground at Fallowfield.

CITY TO THE RESCUE

CHARLIE MITTEN   JACK ROWLEY

When Old Trafford was blitzed out of use in 1941, neighbours Manchester City were quick to offer the use of the Maine Road ground.

Top: "THEY'VE LOST THEIR HOME, BUT NOT THEIR SPIRIT', reprinted from Manchester United Over The Years, *a booklet published in 1947. (JG)*

Middle Left: UNITED REVIEW. When United resumed their Football League fixtures, they were still at Maine Road, and this famous programme cover was used for the first time for the opening match of 1946/7. (JG)

JOHNNY HANLON   SAMMY LYNN   HENRY COCKBURN

1941 OLD TRAFFORD BLITZED

-Manchester United F.C.

W. G. ROUGHTON views the tree that grew in MANCHESTER UNITED'S blitzed grandstand.

DESTRUCTION OF OLD TRAFFORD

Of all the Football League club grounds, it was Old Trafford that received the most devastating damage from the Luftwaffe bombers. Though both Sheffield United and West Ham also "copped it", Manchester United suffered the most, they were unable to use their home ground until 1949. Two German air raids over Manchester, one just prior to Christmas 1940, and the other on 11 March 1941 left the Stadium blitzed. The Main Stand, dressing rooms and offices were destroyed. Photographs from Athletic News Football Annual 1945-6. (KM)

CASUAL COMMENTS

By ALF CLARKE
OF THE "MANCHESTER EVENING CHRONICLE"

Photo : *Manchester Evening Chronicle*

Seven years ago . . . I remember the occasion. Vivid recollections—United in London, and the venue of their game, the following day, was Charlton. The soccer season had just begun. We reached Euston around 9 p.m. on the Friday night. All street lighting was extinguished. Searchlights played around in the sky.

Came the dawn. We went to Charlton. Barrage balloons were flying round the ground. The atmosphere was electric. But football was not the public fancy at that moment. If I remember rightly only about 5,000 spectators watched the match.

Next day came the dreaded news. WAR !

Seven years have passed. United's grand ground at Old Trafford was blitzed in March, 1941, and has not since been used for a league game, though Central League matches of United and City will take place this season. But the loss of ground did not mean loss of prestige. United carried on, like most other clubs, entertaining the public. Players joined up, fighting for right and liberty all round the world.

We lost three of our young players. George Curless used to answer the 'phone in the United offices. He was a young full back, of rich promise. Soon, he had grown up and became a pilot in the R.A.F. with commissioned rank. Then, one day, he went to bomb Germany . . . He never came back.

Ben Carpenter had been signed on by United from Burton early in 1939. An inside forward, and United the envy of many clubs because they had him signed on the dotted line. Ben was in the retreat to Dunkirk, and he did not come back.

Bert Redwood died as a civilian. He had been invalided from the Army.

Remember Redwood ? I rated him high. He was already established as United's first team right full back before the war broke out. Recall how he

deposed Jack Griffiths from the side ? He had to be good to keep a player like Griffiths from the team. Then one day, I saw him in the dressing room at Maine Road. He was ill and a dying man. I never saw him alive after that.

And George Gladwin, the diminutive inside right from Doncaster whose nimble feet had defenders guessing. Well, George came back, but he will never play football again. The Japs slashed his legs to ribbons.

But United carried on, remembering, and watching the career of their players scattered around and about. When they were home on leave, they gave us of their best. The United had periods of ascendancy. They got to the Cup Final (the North section) one season, losing narrowly to Bolton Wanderers. They won the Lancashire Cup. But, more than that, they carried on. And they contrived to unearth new talent, Crompton, Walton, Cockburn. Walton now an England player. Cockburn knocking at the door. Mitten, too, now matured and a recent England choice. Remember my telling you of his 13-goals record scoring in a match in the Azores, where he was stationed. Now England honours him.

Rowley, too, an England player in wartime football. Pearson, who showed wonder form in Denis Compton's touring side in India. Hanlon, back from a German prisoner-of-war camp. The signing of Jimmy Delaney, from Glasgow Celtic, and Scotland fame. Johnny Carey, now installed as captain of the side. Johnny Morris (back later in the year from India) as another potential star in a team of stars.

Yes, that's Manchester United. This is my twenty-second year with them as sports reporter. I have never known them with greater possibilities. They'll go places, will this United team.

ALF CLARKE.

Top: BRITISH ARMY XI 1940. This photograph shows Matt Busby and Reg Allen, both later to come to Old Trafford, with the Army team at the Army, Navy and Air Force Leave Club in Paris. Busby was appointed United Manager at the end of the war, and Allen was one of his early major signings, at a record fee for a goalkeeper. (Left to right): Back Row: A. Geldard, Stevenson, D. Compton, A. Beattie, Army XI secretary, Col. Green, J. Mercer, Reg Allen, B. Sproston, S. Cullis, Team Trainer, T. Lawton. Front Row: W. Copping B. Cook, Matt Busby, D. Welch, M. Eddleston. (JM)

Inset: LES OLIVE. The present United Secretary, he served in the R.A.F. in Egypt, after joining the Old Trafford office staff in 1942. (MMUSC)

Bottom Left: JIMMY MURPHY. Joined United as Assistant Manager at the end of the war. (MMUSC)

Bottom Right: MATT BUSBY takes a training session. (MMUSC)

MATT BUSBY
watches the field

Photo.: Manchester Evening News

To all United Fans I say " How do you do ? " This is my first opportunity of having a word with you since my arrival here last year, and what better means than by the Club programme ? This represents the written words and thoughts of the Manchester United F.C., and I am certain you and I have an equal interest in it. As it is intended that I have a regular article to discuss football from many view-points I hope it will bring us even closer together. You and I look forward to the opening of the 1946-47 season and what it has in store for us. How often have I felt that tingle run through me, known to all players on the first match of a new season, wondering in what form it would find me and how kindly the ball would run. I am finding all the same reactions as a manager.

A great number of people have asked me about our prospects for the coming season. To this I have replied that our boys are in good heart and excellent physical condition, and will hold their own. Others have remarked that the team should do very well if they start off as they finished last season. Yes, I would be a very happy man if they start off as they finished, but I realise from experience the number of things that can crop up to influence this. After all, each player is human and not a mechanical engine which, when you press a button, goes through its work every minute of the day. I do wish all followers of football would remember this very important point when a player has an " off day."

However, we must get on to the battle which starts this afternoon. We will all find the pace of the game stepping up, the tackling keener and the teamwork improved with a view to getting back to 1939 standards—which is all to the good of the game. Whether we start off on the right foot this afternoon or not, I do feel our

boys will provide many happy afternoons for us all.

When I came here, I set out to have a team play methodical and progressive football. Without method a team gets nowhere. Without making progress after creating an opening or a position, the opportunity is lost and the team is back where it started. This will always be my policy, so I leave it to the players to supply the answer, and I hope you will have something good to shout about !

M Busby

Manager.

Walter Crickmer Still Smiling

It is indeed like old times to see Walter Crickmer, our genial secretary, in his usual office. The war years have not left the marks upon him which we might have expected He was on police duty during the blitz and the station received a direct hit by a high explosive bomb. Walter was a lucky one who escaped alive. Also he has been doing tremendously strenuous and important work during the war—of which storage of Government supplies was not the least. In spite of these troubles and trials he is bubbling over with enthusiasm for the old team. His great grudge against the universe is that it has proved impossible to rebuild the stands—thus the games at Maine Road.

MATT BUSBY'S FIRST PROGRAMME ARTICLE. Reproduced from United Review Vol 1 No 1 1946. (JG)

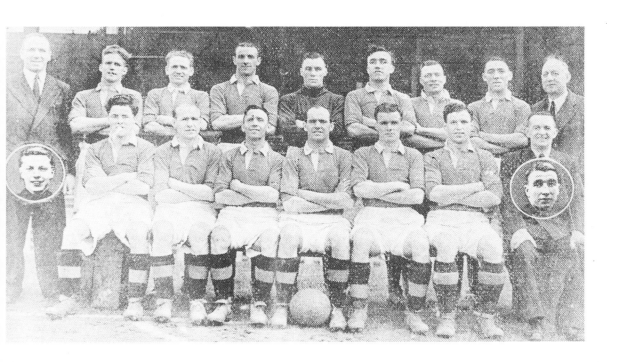

BRICKS AND BOKAYS
By BUTTERWORTH

"3 MORE FLUTTERS AND WE'RE AT WEMBLEY!"

WATCH US MIGRATE TO THE SOUTH!

WE'VE GOT THE WINGS!

I'M PUTTING ALL MY EGGS IN ONE BASKET—!

UNITED

WALTER

FOR CUP CASH

KNOTS FOREST

"A TREE THAT MAY IN WINTER, WEAR...... A NEST OF ROBINS IN HER HAIR!"

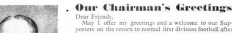

Photo : Lafayette

Our Chairman's Greetings

Dear Friends,

May I offer my greetings and a welcome to our Supporters on the return to normal first division football after the interlude of watching teams comprised of strange personnel, weary war-workers and travel stained servicemen, who, despite numerous difficulties, gallantly succeeded in keeping our grand game alive through the darkest days of a world war. Yes, I think you will agree, everybody did their best to keep the "United" flag flying. all anxiously waiting and looking forward to this day when we embark on the first post-war season of serious competitive football. It is indeed gratifying to know practically all our service players are with us once more, fully trained and fit to do battle with the best. I was with them on an occasion during training and was really impressed with their activities. Mr. Busby, our manager, tells me he is satisfied the team will do well, so we open up full of confidence. A number of the 1939 older players are no longer with us—six years is a long time and changes were imminent, but as you will see, our policy in fostering junior talent is now proving its worth.

A lump rises in my throat when I think of our premises at Old Trafford damaged beyond repair by fire and blast in March 1941, and still looking a sorry spectacle owing to the Government policy of issuing only limited licences for building materials whilst the housing problem is so manifest. As against this, we are fortunate that our neighbours, Manchester City, to whom we are greatly indebted, came to the rescue and offered us a temporary home, which we still enjoy.

In conclusion I must say how much I appreciate your loyalty during the past war-years and sincerely trust you will be rewarded with real, enterprising football.

Yours faithfully,

Jw Gibson

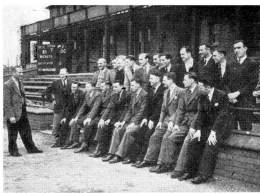

MANCHESTER UNITED

Match No.	Date	Venue	Opponents	Result	Goalscorers	Attendance
1	Aug 31	H	Grimsby Town	W 2-1	Rowley, Mitten	40,000
2	Sept 4	H	Chelsea	W 3-0	Pearson, Rowley, Mitten	28,000
3	7	A	Charlton Athletic	W 3-1	Hanlon, Rowley, 1 o.g.	43,000
4	11	A	Liverpool	W 5-0	Pearson 3, Rowley, Mitten	41,657
5	14	H	Middlesbrough	W 1-0	Rowley	65,112
6	18	H	Chelsea	D 1-1	Chilton	29,000
7	21	A	Stoke City	L 2-3	Delaney, Hanlon	41,699
8	28	H	Arsenal	W 5-2	Hanlon 2, Rowley 2, Wrigglesworth (pen)	62,718
9	Oct 5	H	Preston North End	D 1-1	Wrigglesworth	55,395
10	12	A	Sheffield United	D 2-2	Rowley 2	35,543
11	19	A	Blackpool	L 1-3	Delaney	30,000
12	26	H	Sunderland	L 0-3		48,385
13	Nov 2	A	Aston Villa	D 0-0		54,000
14	9	H	Derby County	W 4-1	Pearson 2, Mitten, Rowley	57,540
15	16	A	Everton	D 2-2	Pearson, Rowley	45,832
16	23	H	Huddersfield Town	W 5-2	Mitten 2, Rowley, Morris 2	39,216
17	30	A	Wolverhampton Wanderers	L 2-3	Delaney, Hanlon	40,704
18	Dec 7	H	Brentford	W 4-1	Rowley 3, Mitten	31,962
19	14	A	Blackburn Rovers	L 1-2	Morris	21,400
20	25	H	Bolton Wanderers	D 2-2	Rowley 2	28,505
21	26	H	Bolton Wanderers	W 1-0	Pearson	57,186
22	28	H	Grimsby Town	D 0-0		17,000
23	Jan 4	A	Charlton Athletic	W 4-1	Burke 2, Pearson, Buckle (pen)	43,406
24	18	A	Middlesbrough	W 4-2	Pearson 2, Morris, Buckle	37,435
25	Feb 1	A	Arsenal	L 2-6	Pearson, Morris	35,000
26	5	H	Stoke City	D 1-1	Buckle (pen)	7,000
27	22	H	Blackpool	W 3-0	Rowley 2 (pen), Hanlon	29,993
28	Mar 1	A	Sunderland	D 1-1	Delaney	20,000
29	8	A	Aston Villa	W 2-1	Pearson, Burke	36,965
30	15	A	Derby County	L 3-4	Burke 2, Pearson	19,579
31	22	H	Everton	W 3-0	Burke, Delaney, Warner	43,441
32	29	H	Huddersfield Town	D 2-2	Delaney, Pearson	18,509
33	Apr 5	A	Wolverhampton Wanderers	W 3-1	Rowley 2, Hanlon	66,967
34	7	H	Blackpool	W 3-1	Buckle 2, Delaney	36,965
35	8	A	Leeds United	W 2-0	McGlen, Burke	15,000
36	12	H	Brentford	D 0-0		21,714
37	19	H	Blackburn Rovers	W 4-0	Pearson 2, Rowley, 1 o.g.	46,196
38	26	H	Portsmouth	W 1-0	Delaney	32,000
39	May 3	A	Liverpool	L 0-1		48,800
40	10	A	Preston North End	D 1-1	Pearson	22,000
41	17	H	Portsmouth	W 3-0	Morris, Mitten, Rowley	37,614
42	26	H	Sheffield United	W 6-2	Rowley 3, Morris 2, Pearson	34,059

Players:
Crompton, J. · Carey, J. · McGlen, W. · Warner, J. · Chilton, A. C. · Cockburn, H. · Delaney, J. · Pearson, S. C. · Hanlon, J. · Rowley, J. F. · Mitten, C. · Whalley, H. · Aston, J. · Walton, J. W. · Wrigglesworth, W. · Morris, J. · Burke, R. S. · Collinson, C. · Worrall, H. · Buckle, E. W. · Fielding, W. J.

(League Appearances and League Scorers totals given per player.)

F.A. Cup

Round	Date	Venue	Opponents	Result	Goalscorers	Attendance
Rd 3	Jan 11	A	Bradford Park Avenue	W 3-0	Rowley 2, Buckle	26,990
Rd 4	25	H	Nottingham Forest	L 0-2		58,641

DID YOU KNOW! When the Football League programme resumed in 1946/7, Allenby Chilton made his second league appearance — seven years after his debut!! The two games were separated by the War. His debut was on 2 September 1939 against Charlton Athletic, and his second match was on 31 August 1946 against Grimsby Town.

OPPOSITE PAGE

F.A. Cup Winners

1948

HERE YOU SEE THE MANCHESTER UNITED F.A. CUP WINNERS 1947/48 IN THEIR "NEW LOOK" OUTFITS, SUPPLIED BY DEMMARK CLOTHING CO.

Front Row: left to right sitting, C. Mitten, Mr. B. Demmy, H. Cockburn, J. Carey (Capt.), Mr. A. Demmy, J. Anderson, J. Morris, and Mr. Matt Busby (Manager).

Back Row: standing, Mr. T. Curry (trainer), J. Rowley, J. Delaney, J. Aston, A. Chilton, J. Crompton, J. Warner (reserve), S. Pearson, and Alf Clarke (author of this History).

UNITED WANTED THE BEST: WE HAVE IT.

MANCHESTER UNITED

Match No.	Date	Venue	Opponents	Result	Goalscorers	Attendance
1	Aug 23	A	Middlesbrough	D 2-2	Rowley 2	36,600
2	27	H	Liverpool	W 2-0	Pearson, Morris	52,385
3	30	A	Charlton Athletic	W 6-2	Rowley 4, Morris, Pearson	52,659
4	Sept 3	A	Liverpool	D 2-2	Pearson, Mitten	48,081
5	6	A	Arsenal	L 1-2	Morris	62,000
6	8	H	Burnley	D 0-0		37,517
7	13	A	Sheffield United	L 0-1		49,808
8	20	H	Manchester City	D 0-0		72,000
9	27	A	Preston North End	L 1-2	Hanlon	33,600
10	Oct 4	H	Stoke City	D 1-1	Morris	45,745
11	11	H	Grimsby Town	W 3-1	Morris, Rowley, Mitten	40,035
12	18	A	Sunderland	W 4-1	Morris 3, Rowley	34,748
13	25	H	Aston Villa	W 1-0	Carey	47,078
14	Nov 1	A	Wolverhampton Wanderers	W 4-2	Morris 2, Pearson, Delaney	44,309
15	8	A	Huddersfield Town	D 4-4	Rowley 4	59,772
16	15	H	Derby County	W 3-1	Morris, Rowley, Mitten	32,990
17	22	A	Everton	D 2-2	Morris, Cockburn	36,509
18	29	H	Chelsea	L 0-2		43,617
19	Dec 6	H	Blackpool	D 1-1	Pearson	63,683
20	13	A	Blackburn Rovers	D 1-1	Morris	22,600
21	20	H	Middlesbrough	L 2-3	Pearson 2	46,666
22	25	H	Portsmouth	W 3-1	Morris 2, Rowley	42,776
23	27	A	Portsmouth	W 3-1	Morris 2, Delaney	28,000
24	Jan 1	H	Burnley	W 5-0	Rowley 3, Mitten 2	59,838
25	3	H	Charlton Athletic	W 2-1	Pearson, Morris	39,000
26	17	H	Arsenal	D 1-1	Rowley	81,962
27	31	H	Sheffield United	L 1-2	Rowley	45,189
28	Feb 14	A	Preston North End	D 1-1	Delaney	61,765
29	21	A	Stoke City	W 2-0	Pearson, Buckle (pen)	36,794
30	Mar 6	H	Sunderland	W 3-1	Delaney, Rowley, Mitten (pen)	55,160
31	17	A	Grimsby Town	W 1-0	Rowley	13,000
32	20	H	Wolverhampton Wanderers	W 3-2	Delaney, Morris, Mitten	50,667
33	22	A	Aston Villa	D 1-1	Pearson	50,000
34	26	H	Bolton Wanderers	W 1-0	Pearson	71,623
35	27	A	Huddersfield Town	W 2-0	Pearson, Burke	38,266
36	29	H	Bolton Wanderers	W 1-0	Anderson	44,205
37	Apr 7	A	Derby County	L 0-2		49,609
38	10	A	Manchester City	D 1-1	Rowley	71,690
39	17	H	Everton	D 0-0		44,198
40	28	A	Chelsea	W 5-0	Pearson 2, Mitten (pen), Rowley, Delaney	43,225
41	May 1	A	Blackpool	L 0-1		30,000
42		H	Blackburn Rovers	W 4-1	Pearson 3, Delaney	44,439

F.A. CUP

Round	Date	Venue	Opponents	Result	Goalscorers	Attendance
Rd 3	Jan 10	A	Aston Villa	W 6-4	Morris 2, Pearson 2, Rowley 2, Delaney	58,683
Rd 4	24	N	Liverpool	W 3-0	Rowley, Morris, Mitten (at Goodison Park)	74,721
Rd 5	Feb 7	N	Charlton Athletic	W 2-0	Warner, Mitten (at Huddersfield)	33,312
Rd 6	28	H	Preston North End	W 4-1	Mitten, Pearson 2, Rowley	74,213
S/F	Mar 13	N	Derby County	W 3-1	Pearson 3 (at Hillsborough, Sheffield)	62,250
FINAL	Apr 24	N	Blackpool	W 4-2	Rowley 2, Pearson, Anderson (at Wembley)	100,000

Players (shirt-number appearance columns 1–11):
Crompton, J.; Carey, J.; Aston, J.; Warner, J.; Chilton, A. C.; McGlen, W.; Delaney, J.; Morris, J.; Rowley, J.; Pearson, S. C.; Mitten, C.; Burke, R. S.; Cockburn, H.; Dale, J.; Hanlon, J.; Walton, J. W.; Worrall, H.; Pegg, J. K.; Anderson, J.; Lynn, S.; Brown, R. B.; Buckle, E. W.; Lowrie, T.; Ball, J.; Cassidy, L.

League Appearances / League Scorers (season totals shown at foot of appearance grid).

DID YOU KNOW! United played in Blue Shirts in the 1948 F.A. Cup Final against Blackpool, they had created history again by beating First Division opposition in every round.

Top: THE TEAM THAT WON THE CUP. (Left to Right): Standing: J. Carey (captain), J. Anderson, J. Crompton, A. Chilton, H. Cockburn, J. Aston. Seated: J. Delaney, J. Morris, J. Rowley, S. Pearson, C. Mitten. (CPS)

Bottom Right: FA CUP WINNERS 1948. Players souvenir with autographs. (BNPC)

Middle Left: FA CUP FINAL Manchester United 4 Blackpool 2. Wembley 24 April 1948. Captain Johnny Carey introduces King George VI to Allenby Chilton. (MMUSC)

Bottom Left: ALBERT SQUARE: The team arrives with the FA Cup aboard the open-top bus for a civic reception.

THE TEAM THAT WON THE CUP

MANCHESTER UNITED

J. CROMPTON
J. CAREY (Capt.)
J. ASTON
J. ANDERSON
A. CHILTON
H. COCKBURN
J. MORRIS
J. ROWLEY
S. PEARSON
C. MITTEN

Home Fixtures played at Maine Road

MANCHESTER UNITED

Match No.	Date	Venue	Opponents	Result		Goalscorers	Attendance
1	Aug 21	H	Derby County	L	1-2	Pearson	52,620
2	23	A	Blackpool	W	3-0	Mitten 2, Pearson	30,000
3	28	A	Arsenal	W	1-0	Mitten	62,000
4	Sept 1	H	Blackpool	L	3-4	Mitten (pen), Morris, Delaney	51,187
5	4	H	Huddersfield Town	W	4-1	Pearson 2, Mitten (pen), Delaney	57,714
6	8	A	Wolverhampton Wanderers	W	1-0	Morris, Rowley	42,000
7	11	A	Manchester City	L	2-3	Morris, Rowley	64,502
8	15	H	Wolverhampton Wanderers	W	2-0	Pearson, Buckle	33,871
9	18	H	Sheffield United	D	2-2	Buckle, Pearson	76,880
10	25	A	Aston Villa	W	3-1	Rowley 2, Mitten (pen)	36,880
11	Oct 2	A	Sunderland	L	1-2	Rowley	54,419
12	9	H	Charlton Athletic	L	1-2	Burke	66,964
13	16	A	Stoke City	L	1-2	Morris	45,830
14	23	H	Burnley	D	1-1	Mitten	47,093
15	30	A	Preston North End	W	6-1	Pearson 2, Mitten 2, Rowley, Morris	37,574
16	Nov 6	H	Everton	W	2-0	Morris, Delaney	42,789
17	13	A	Chelsea	D	1-1	Rowley	62,542
18	20	H	Birmingham City	W	3-0	Morris, Rowley, Pearson	45,482
19	27	A	Middlesbrough	W	4-1	Rowley 3, Delaney	31,331
20	Dec 4	H	Newcastle United	D	1-1	Mitten	70,787
21	11	A	Portsmouth	D	2-2	Mitten (pen), McGlen	30,000
22	18	H	Derby County	W	3-1	Burke 2, Pearson	31,498
23	25	H	Liverpool	D	0-0		47,788
24	27	A	Liverpool	W	2-0	Pearson, Burke	53,325
25	Jan 1	H	Arsenal	W	2-0	Mitten, Burke	82,950
26	22	H	Manchester City	D	0-0		66,485
27	Feb 19	A	Aston Villa	L	1-2	Rowley	70,000
28	Mar 12	A	Charlton Athletic	W	2-0	Pearson 2, Downie	56,000
29	19	A	Stoke City	W	3-0	Rowley, Mitten, Downie	55,949
30	Apr 6	H	Birmingham City	W	1-0	Rowley	47,000
31	9	H	Huddersfield Town	D	1-1	Rowley	17,256
32	15	H	Chelsea	D	1-1	Mitten (pen)	27,304
33	16	A	Bolton Wanderers	W	1-0	Carey	44,999
34	18	A	Burnley	W	2-0	Rowley 2	37,722
35	21	H	Bolton Wanderers	W	3-0	Rowley 2, Mitten	47,663
36	23	H	Sunderland	W	5-0	Rowley 4, Mitten	30,640
37	27	A	Preston North End	L	1-2	Downie	43,214
38	30	A	Everton	L	0-2	Downie 2	39,106
39	May 2	H	Newcastle United	W	1-0	Burke	48,000
40	4	A	Middlesbrough	W	1-0	Rowley	20,158
41	4	H	Sheffield United	W	3-2	Downie, Mitten, Pearson	20,880
42	7	H	Portsmouth	W	3-2	Rowley 2, Mitten (pen)	49,808

F.A. CUP

Round	Date	Venue	Opponents	Result		Goalscorers	Attendance
Rd 3	Jan 8	H	Bournemouth	W	6-0	Burke 2, Pearson, Rowley 2, Mitten	55,012
Rd 4	29	H	Bradford Park Avenue	D	1-1	Mitten	82,771
Replay	Feb 5	A	Bradford Park Avenue	D	1-1	Mitten (after extra time)	29,092
2nd Replay	7		Bradford Park Avenue	W	5-0	Burke, Rowley 2, Pearson	70,434 (after extra time)
Rd 5	12	H	Yeovil Town	W	8-0	Rowley 5, Burke 2, Mitten	81,565
Rd 6	26	A	Hull City	W	1-0	Pearson	55,019
S/F	Mar 26	N	Wolverhampton Wanderers	D	1-1	Mitten (at Hillsborough)	62,250
Replay	Apr 2	N	Wolverhampton Wanderers	L	0-1	(at Goodison Park, Liverpool)	73,000

Players:

Crompton, J. · Carey, J. · Aston J. · Anderson, J. · Chilton, A. C. · Cockburn, H. · Delaney, J. · Morris, J. · Rowley, J. · Pearson, S. C. · Mitten, C. · McGlen, W. · Hanlon, J. · Brown, R. B. · Buckle, E. W. · Ball, J. · Warner, J. · Burke, R. S. · Downie, J. D. · Lowrie, T. · Cassidy, L.

OPPOSITE PAGE

Top: MANCHESTER UNITED 3 PORTSMOUTH 3. FA Cup 5th Round 11 February 1950 at Old Trafford. Pearson is at the near post to head the second goal, from a Mitten corner. (BNPC)

Middle Right: BACK TO OLD TRAFFORD. This petition was signed by thousands of United supporters in an effort to obtain planning permission to rebuild Old Trafford. The ground was re-opened in August 1949. (BNPC)

Middle Left: CHELSEA 1 MANCHESTER UNITED 1. 13 November 1948. United defenders in aerial action with Roy Bentley in this Chelsea attack. (MMUSC)

UNITED TEAM GROUP 1949-50. Back Row: M. Busby (Manager), Carey, Feenan, Chilton, Crompton, Aston, Lynn T. Curry (Trainer). Front Row: Cockburn, Delaney, Warner, Rowley, Pearson, Mitten. (JG)

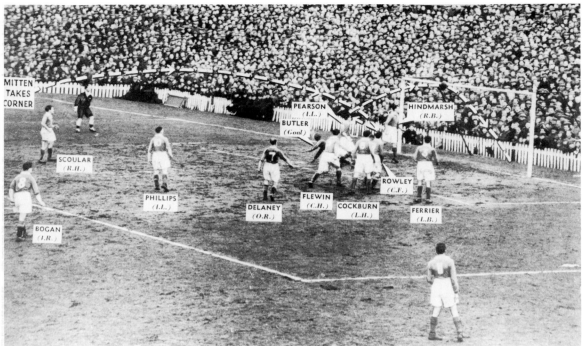

MITTEN TAKES CORNER

SCOULAR (R.H.)

PHILLIPS (I.L.)

BOGAN (I.R.)

DELANEY (O.R.)

FLEWIN (C.H.)

COCKBURN (L.H.)

PEARSON (I.L.)

BUTLER (Goal)

ROWLEY (C.F.)

HINDMARSH (R.B.)

FERRIER (L.B.)

PETITION

TO THE MINISTRY OF WORKS

Appealing for the necessary permits and licences to restore the accommodation at

MANCHESTER UNITED FOOTBALL CLUB GROUND

Old Trafford, which was destroyed by enemy action during the last war. This is our only form of recreation to which we look forward after a week's hard work & we, the undersigned spectators, hereby appeal to you for your consideration

ORGANISER To whom all forms should be returned H. S. THOMPSON, 58 WELLINGTON ROAD SOUTH, STOCKPORT.

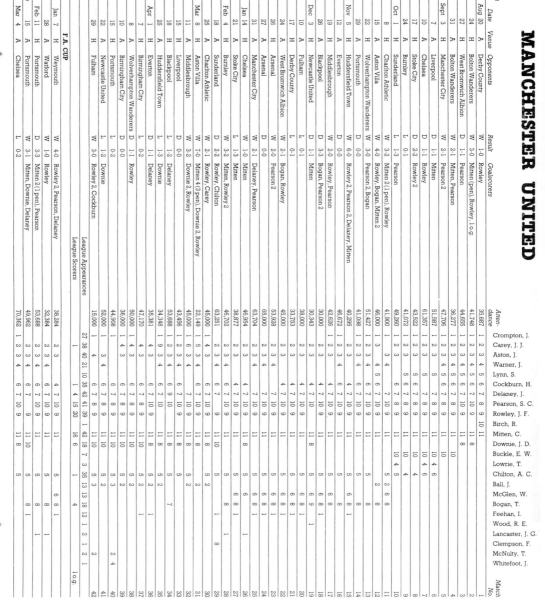

MANCHESTER UNITED

Match No.	Date		Venue	Opponents	Result	Goalscorers	Attendance
1	Aug	20	H	Derby County	W 1-0	Rowley	35,687
2		24	A	Bolton Wanderers	W 3-0	Mitten (pen), Rowley, 1 o.g.	41,748
3		27	A	West Bromwich Albion	D 1-1	Pearson	44,655
4		31	H	Bolton Wanderers	W 2-1	Mitten, Pearson	36,277
5	Sept	3	H	Manchester City	W 2-1	Pearson 2	47,706
6		7	A	Liverpool	D 1-1	Mitten	51,587
7		10	A	Chelsea	D 1-1	Rowley	61,357
8		17	H	Stoke City	D 2-2	Rowley 2	43,522
9		24	A	Burnley	L 0-1		41,072
10	Oct	1	H	Sunderland	L 1-3	Pearson	49,260
11		8	A	Charlton Athletic	W 3-2	Mitten 2(1 pen), Rowley	41,900
12		15	H	Aston Villa	W 4-0	Rowley, Bogan, Mitten 2	46,000
13		22	A	Wolverhampton Wanderers	W 3-0	Pearson 2, Bogan	51,427
14		29	H	Portsmouth	D 0-0		41,098
15	Nov	5	H	Huddersfield Town	W 6-0	Rowley 2, Pearson 2, Delaney, Mitten	40,295
16		12	A	Everton	W 2-0	Rowley, Pearson	46,672
17		19	H	Middlesbrough	W 2-0	Rowley, Pearson	42,626
18		26	A	Blackpool	D 3-3	Bogan, Pearson 2	30,000
19	Dec	3	H	Newcastle United	D 1-1	Mitten	30,343
20		10	A	Fulham	D 0-1		38,000
21		17	H	Derby County	L 0-1		33,753
22		24	A	West Bromwich Albion	W 2-0	Pearson 2	45,000
23		26	H	Wolverhampton Wanderers	W 2-0	Pearson 2	53,928
24		27	A	Arsenal	D 0-0		65,000
25		31	H	Manchester City	W 2-1	Delaney, Pearson	63,704
26	Jan	14	A	Chelsea	W 1-0	Mitten	46,954
27		21	H	Stoke City	L 1-3	Mitten	38,877
28	Feb	4	A	Burnley	W 3-2	Mitten, Rowley 2	46,702
29		18	A	Sunderland	D 2-2	Rowley, Chilton	63,251
30		25	H	Charlton Athletic	W 2-1	Rowley, Carey	45,000
31	Mar	8	A	Aston Villa	W 7-0	Mitten 4(3 pen), Downie 2, Rowley	22,149
32		11	H	Middlesbrough	W 3-2	Downie 2, Rowley	45,000
33		18	A	Liverpool	D 0-0		43,456
34		25	H	Blackpool	L 1-2	Delaney	53,688
35		29	A	Huddersfield Town	L 1-3	Downie	34,348
36	Apr	1	A	Everton	D 1-1	Delaney	35,381
37		7	H	Birmingham City	L 0-2		47,170
38		8	A	Wolverhampton Wanderers	D 1-1	Rowley	50,000
39		10	H	Birmingham City	D 0-0		36,000
40		15	A	Portsmouth	L 0-2		44,908
41		22	A	Newcastle United	L 1-2	Downie	52,000
42		29	H	Fulham	W 3-0	Rowley 2, Cockburn	15,000

F.A. CUP

Rd 3	Jan	7	H	Weymouth	W 4-0	Rowley 2, Pearson, Delaney	38,284
Rd 4		28	A	Watford	W 1-0	Rowley	32,384
Rd 5	Feb	11	H	Portsmouth	D 3-3	Mitten 2(1 pen), Pearson	53,688
Replay		15	A	Portsmouth	W 3-1	Mitten, Downie, Delaney	49,962
Rd 6	Mar	4	A	Chelsea	L 0-2		70,362

Players appearances and League Scorers columns:
Crompton, J.; Carey, J. J.; Aston, J.; Warner, J.; Lynn, S.; Cockburn, H.; Delaney, J.; Pearson, S. C.; Rowley, J. F.; Birch, R.; Mitten, C.; Downie, J. D.; Buckle, E. W.; Lowrie, T.; Chilton, A. C.; Ball, J.; McGlen, W.; Bogan, T.; Feehan, I.; Wood, R. E.; Lancaster, J. G.; Clempson, F.; McNulty, T.; Whitefoot, J.

League Appearances 27; *League Scorers* (various)

DID YOU KNOW! Charlie Mitten scored a hat-trick of penalties against Aston Villa on 8 March 1950.

OPPOSITE PAGE

Top: ATLAS CLUB MEXICO 6 MANCHESTER UNITED 6. 4 June 1950 Los Angeles. Atlas captain Juan Gomez disputes a decision with referee A. Thompson. (BNPC)

Bottom Right: US TOUR POSTER announcing two matches between United and Atlas Club in Los Angeles. (BNPC)

Bottom Left: AMERICAN LEAGUE ALL STARS 2 MANCHESTER UNITED 9. 14 May 1950. United's John Ball beats Al Carro in the exhibition game in New York. (BNPC)

AMERICAN TOUR 1950

INTERNATIONAL SOCCER

MANCHESTER UNITED
MILLION DOLLAR ENGLISH TEAM

AND

ATLAS CLUB
Of GUADALAJARA · CHAMPIONS of MEXICO

See these Two Dream Teams in Action!

TWO DOUBLE - HEADERS

Wednesday Night » MAY 31 « 6:45 and 8:15 p. m.
Sunday Afternoon » JUNE 4 « 1:00 and 3:00 p. m.

GILMORE STADIUM
BEVERLY BOULEVARD at FAIRFAX · LOS ANGELES

POPULAR PRICES: RESERVED SEATS - $2.20, Including Tax
GENERAL ADMISSION - $1.80, Including Tax

TICKETS AVAILABLE FOREIGN TOURS 6151 W. 98th St. L.A. 45 - Oregon 8-2591
6920 S. Central Ave., L. A. 2 - Kimball 1189

MANCHESTER UNITED

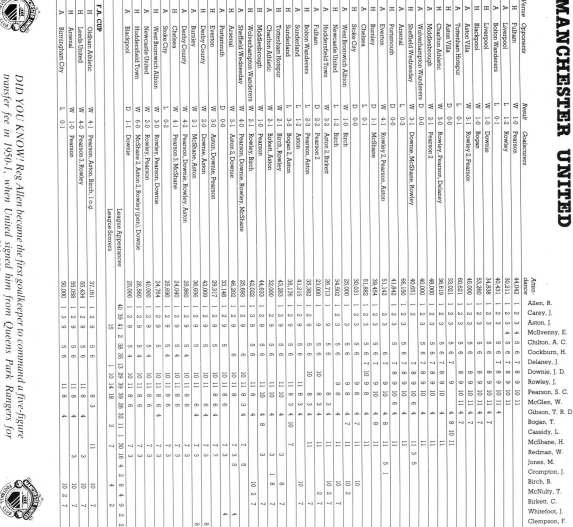

Match No	Date	Venue	Opponents	Result		Goalscorers	Attendance
1	Aug 19	H	Fulham	W	1-0	Pearson	44,042
2	23	A	Liverpool	L	1-2	Rowley	30,211
3	26	A	Bolton Wanderers	L	0-1		40,431
4	30	H	Liverpool	W	1-0	Downie	34,838
5	Sept 2	H	Blackpool	W	1-0	Bogan	53,260
6	4	A	Aston Villa	W	3-1	Rowley 2, Pearson	45,000
7	9	A	Tottenham Hotspur	L	0-1		60,621
8	13	H	Aston Villa	D	0-0		33,021
9	16	H	Charlton Athletic	W	3-0	Rowley, Pearson, Delaney	36,619
10	23	A	Middlesbrough	W	2-1	Pearson 2	48,000
11	30	A	Wolverhampton Wanderers	D	0-0		40,000
12	Oct 7	H	Sheffield Wednesday	W	3-1	Downie, McShane, Rowley	40,651
13	14	A	Arsenal	L	0-3		66,150
14	21	H	Portsmouth	D	0-0		41,842
15	28	A	Everton	W	4-1	Rowley 2, Pearson, Aston	51,142
16	Nov 4	H	Burnley	D	1-1	McShane	39,454
17	11	A	Chelsea	L	0-1		51,882
18	18	H	Stoke City	D	0-0		30,031
19	25	A	West Bromwich Albion	L	1-2	Birch	25,000
20	Dec 2	H	Newcastle United	W	3-2	Aston 2, Birkett	34,502
21	9	A	Huddersfield Town	L	2-3	Pearson 2	26,713
22	16	A	Fulham	D	2-2	Pearson 2	23,000
23	23	H	Bolton Wanderers	L	2-3	Pearson, Aston	35,382
24	25	A	Sunderland	L	1-2	Aston	41,215
25	26	H	Sunderland	L	3-5	Bogan 2, Aston	35,176
26	Jan 13	A	Tottenham Hotspur	W	2-1	Birch, Rowley	43,283
27	20	H	Charlton Athletic	W	2-1	Birkett, Aston	32,000
28	Feb 3	H	Middlesbrough	W	1-0	Pearson	44,633
29	17	H	Wolverhampton Wanderers	W	2-1	Rowley, Birch	42,022
30	26	A	Sheffield Wednesday	W	4-0	Pearson, Downie, Rowley, McShane	25,693
31	Mar 3	A	Arsenal	W	3-1	Aston 2, Downie	46,202
32	17	A	Portsmouth	D	0-0		33,148
33	23	H	Everton	W	3-0	Downie, Aston, Pearson	29,317
34	24	H	Derby County	W	2-0	Downie, Aston	42,009
35	26	A	Burnley	W	2-1	McShane, Aston	36,656
36	31	A	Derby County	W	4-2	Pearson, Downie, Rowley, Aston	25,860
37	Apr 7	H	Chelsea	W	4-1	Pearson 3, McShane	24,040
38	14	H	Stoke City	L	0-2		25,690
39	21	A	West Bromwich Albion	W	3-0	Rowley, Pearson, Downie	24,764
40	28	A	Newcastle United	W	2-0	Rowley, Pearson	40,000
41		H	Huddersfield Town	W	6-0	McShane 2, Aston 2, Rowley (pen), Downie	26,560
42	May 5	A	Blackpool	D	1-1	Downie	25,000

League Appearances
League Scorers

F.A. CUP

Rd No	Date	Venue	Opponents	Result		Goalscorers	Attendance
Rd 3	Jan 6	H	Oldham Athletic	W	4-1	Pearson, Aston, Birch, 1 o.g.	37,161
Rd 4	27	H	Leeds United	W	4-0	Pearson 3, Rowley	55,434
Rd 5	Feb 10	H	Arsenal	W	1-0	Pearson	55,058
Rd 6	24	A	Birmingham City	L	0-1		50,000

Players:
Allen, R. · Carey, J. · Aston, J. · McIlvenny, E. · Chilton, A. C. · Cockburn, H. · Delaney, J. · Downie, J. D. · Rowley, J. · Pearson, S. C. · McGlen, W. · Gibson, T. R. D. · Bogan, T. · Cassidy, L. · McShane, H. · Redman, W. · Jones, M. · Crompton, J. · Birch, B. · McNulty, I. · Birkett, C. · Whitefoot, J. · Clempson, F. · Lowrie, T.

DID YOU KNOW! Reg Allen became the first goalkeeper to command a five-figure transfer fee in 1950-1, when United signed him from Queens Park Rangers for £11,000.

OPPOSITE PAGE

Top: UNITED V ARSENAL CUP-TIE. Queues for tickets stretched for over a mile. United won the 5th Round tie with a Stan Pearson goal. (BNPC)

Middle Left: CARTOON from the match programme. (JM)

Middle Right: OLD TRAFFORD June 1951. New stand building in progress, to replace the blitzed Main Stand, which had been without cove[r] since the war. (BNPC)

MANCHESTER UNITED 4 LEEDS UNITED 0. F.A. Cup 4th Round 27 January 1951. Thousands of supporters were locked out of Old Trafford with over 55,000 packed inside. (BNPC)

1951

MANCHESTER UNITED

Match No.	Date	Venue	Opponents	Result	Goalscorers	Attendance
1	Aug 18	A	West Bromwich Albion	D 3-3	Rowley 3	27,486
2	22	A	Middlesbrough	W 4-2	Rowley 3, Pearson	37,331
3	25	H	Newcastle United	W 2-1	Rowley, Downie	51,880
4	29	H	Middlesbrough	W 4-1	Pearson 2, Rowley 2	44,212
5	Sept 1	H	Bolton Wanderers	L 0-1		52,239
6	5	A	Charlton Athletic	W 3-2	Rowley 2, Downie	26,773
7	8	A	Stoke City	W 4-0	Rowley 3, Pearson	43,660
8	12	A	Charlton Athletic	D 2-2	Downie 2	28,806
9	15	A	Manchester City	W 2-1	Berry, McShane	52,571
10	22	H	Tottenham Hotspur	L 0-2		70,822
11	29	H	Preston North End	L 1-2	Aston	53,494
12	Oct 6	H	Derby County	W 2-1	Pearson, Berry	39,767
13	13	A	Aston Villa	W 5-2	Pearson 2, Rowley 2, Bond	46,000
14	20	H	Sunderland	L 0-1		40,915
15	27	A	Wolverhampton Wanderers	W 2-0	Pearson, Rowley	46,167
16	Nov 3	A	Huddersfield Town	D 1-1	Pearson	25,616
17	10	H	Chelsea	L 2-4	Pearson Rowley	48,960
18	17	H	Portsmouth	L 1-3	Downie	42,378
19	24	A	Liverpool	D 0-0		36,915
20	Dec 1	H	Blackpool	W 3-1	Downie 2, Rowley	34,154
21	8	A	Arsenal	W 3-1	Rowley, Pearson, 1 o.g.	55,451
22	15	A	West Bromwich Albion	W 5-1	Pearson 2, Downie 2, Berry	27,684
23	22	H	Newcastle United	D 2-2	Cockburn, Bond	45,414
24	25	A	Fulham	W 3-2	Bond, Rowley, Berry	33,802
25	26	H	Fulham	D 3-3	Rowley, Pearson, Bond	35,000
26	29	H	Bolton Wanderers	W 1-0	Pearson	53,205
27	Jan 5	A	Stoke City	D 0-0		33,000
28	19	H	Manchester City	D 1-1	Carey	54,284
29	26	A	Tottenham Hotspur	W 2-0	Pearson, 1 o.g.	40,845
30	Feb 9	A	Preston North End	W 2-1	Aston, Berry	38,000
31	16	H	Derby County	W 3-0	Pearson, Rowley, Aston	27,693
32	Mar 1	H	Aston Villa	D 1-1	Berry	39,910
33	8	A	Sunderland	W 2-1	Rowley, Cockburn	48,078
34	15	H	Wolverhampton Wanderers	W 2-0	Clempson, Aston	45,109
35	22	A	Huddersfield Town	L 2-3	Clempson, Pearson	30,316
36	Apr 5	A	Portsmouth	L 0-1		28,522
37	11	H	Burnley	D 1-1	Byrne	28,907
38	12	H	Liverpool	W 4-0	Byrne 2 (1 pen), Downie, Rowley	42,970
39	14	A	Burnley	W 6-1	Byrne 2, Rowley, Pearson, Downie, Carey	44,508
40	19	A	Blackpool	D 2-2	Byrne, Rowley	39,118
41	21	A	Chelsea	W 3-0	Pearson, Carey, 1 o.g.	37,434
42	26	H	Arsenal	W 6-1	Rowley 3 (1 pen), Pearson 2, Byrne	53,661

F.A. CUP

Rd	Date	Venue	Opponents	Result	Goalscorers	Attendance
Rd 3	Jan 12	H	Hull City	L 0-2		43,517

Player summary (League Appearances / League Scorers):

Player	Appearances	Goals
Allen, R.	33	
Carey, J.	38	3
Redman, W.	18	
Cockburn, H.	38	2
Chilton, A. C.	42	
McGlen, W.	2	
McShane, H.	12	1
Pearson, S. C.	41	22
Rowley, J. F.	40	30
Downie, J. D.	31	11
Bond, J. E.	17	4
Gibson, T. R. D.	36	
Berry, J. J.		6
Cassidy, L.		
Walton, J. A.		
Aston, J.		4
McNulty, T.		
Birch, B.		
Crompton, J.		
Byrne, R.	24	7
Blanchflower, J.		
Jones, M.		
Clempson, F.		2
Whitefoot, J.		
o.g.s		3

DID YOU KNOW! After finishing Runners-Up 4 times in the previous 5 years, United were League Champions in 1951/2 for the third time in the club's history. Paradoxically, winning the Championship was to mark the end of one illustrious era at Old Trafford, with several of the team nearing the ends of their careers, and lead ultimately to another golden age. The necessary influx of its home-reared young talent was to herald the birth of the legendary 'Busby Babes'.

Top: LEAGUE CHAMPIONS & CHARITY SHIELD WINNERS 1951/2. Back Row: Downie, Rowley, Aston, Allen, Chilton, Byrne, Pearson. Front Row: Berry, Carey, Cockburn, McNulty. (JG)

Bottom: MANCHESTER UNITED 6 ARSENAL 1. 26 April 1952. Johnny Carey leads the United players from the field to receive the Championship trophy after they had demolished Runners-up Arsenal to clinch the title. (BNPC)

FOOTBALL LEAGUE CHAMPIONS 1951-2

MANCHESTER UNITED

Match No.	Date		Venue	Opponents	Result		Goalscorers	Attendance	Wood, R. E.	McNulty, T.	Aston, J.	Carey, J.	Chilton, A. C.	Gibson, T. R. D.	Berry, J. J.	Downie, J. D.	Rowley, J.	Pearson, S. C.	Byrne, R.	Crompton, J.	Cockburn, H.	Clempson, E.	Bond, J. E.	Allen, R.	Jones, M.	Scott, J.	Whitefoot, J.	McShane, H.	Lewis, E.	Doherty, J.	Pegg, D.	Foulkes, W.	Redman, W.	Taylor, T.	Blanchflower, J.	Edwards, D.	Olive, R. L.	Viollet, D. S.	Match No.
1	Aug 23	H		Chelsea	W	2-0	Downie, Berry	41,805	1	2	3	4	5	6	7	8	9	10	11																				1
2	27	A		Arsenal	L	1-2	Rowley	58,831	1	2	3	4	5	6	7	8	9	10	11																				2
3	30	A		Manchester City	L	1-2	Downie	56,140	1	2	3	4	5	6	7	8	9	10	11																				3
4	Sept 3	H		Arsenal	D	0-0		37,636	1	2	3	4	5	6	7	8	9	10	11																				4
5	6	H		Portsmouth	L	0-2		37,278	1	2	3	4	5	6	7	8	9	10	11																				5
6	10	A		Derby County	W	3-2	Pearson 3	20,226	1	2	3	4	5	6	7	8	9	10	11																				6
7	13	A		Bolton Wanderers	W	1-0	Berry	40,531	1	2	3	4	5	6	7	8	9	10	11																				7
8	20	H		Aston Villa	D	3-3	Downie, Rowley (2 pens)	40,000	1	2	3	4	5	6	7	8	9	10	11				1																8
9	27	A		Sunderland	L	0-1		28,967	1	2	3	4	5	6	7	8	9	10	11																				9
10	Oct 4	H		Wolverhampton Wanderers	L	2-6	Rowley 2	40,132	1	2	3	4	5	6	7	8	9	10	11																		1		10
11	11	A		Stoke City	L	0-2		29,968	1	2	3	4	5	6	7	8	9	10	11			8														11			11
12	18	A		Preston North End	W	5-0	Pearson 2, Aston 2, Rowley	40,600	1	2	3	4	5	6	7	8	9	10	11															4					12
13	25	H		Burnley	L	1-3	Aston	36,913	1	2	3	4	5	6	7	8	9	10	11															4					13
14	Nov 1	A		Tottenham Hotspur	W	2-1	Berry 2	44,300	1	2	3	4	5	6	7	8	9	10																4	11				14
15	8	H		Sheffield Wednesday	D	1-1	Pearson	48,571	1	2	3	4	5	6	7	8	9	10																4	11				15
16	15	A		Cardiff City	W	2-1	Aston, Pearson	40,000	1	2	3	4	5	6	7	8	9	10																4	11				16
17	22	H		Newcastle United	D	2-2	Pearson, Aston	33,528	1	2	3	4	5	6	7	8	9	10																4	11				17
18	29	A		West Bromwich Albion	L	1-3	Lewis	24,000	1	2	3	4	5	6		8	9	10											11					4					18
19	Dec 6	H		Middlesbrough	W	3-2	Pearson 2, Aston	27,617	1	2	3	4	5	6	7	8	9	10											11					4					19
20	13	A		Liverpool	W	2-1	Aston, Pearson	34,450	1	2	3	4	5	6	7	8	9	10											11					4					20
21	20	A		Chelsea	W	3-2	Doherty 2, Aston	23,261	1	2	3	4	5	6	7		9	10											11	8				4					21
22	25	A		Blackpool	D	0-0		27,778	1	2	3	4	5	6	7		9	10											11	8				4					22
23	26	H		Blackpool	W	2-1	Carey, Lewis	48,077	1	2	3	4	5	6	7		9	10											11	8				4					23
24	Jan 1	H		Derby County	W	1-0	Lewis	34,813	1	2	3	4	5	6	7		9	10											11	8				4					24
25	3	H		Manchester City	D	1-1	Pearson	47,883	1	2	3	4	5	6	7		9	10									6		11	8				4					25
26	17	A		Portsmouth	W	1-0	Lewis	32,341	1	2	3	4	5	6	7		9	10											11	8				4					26
27	24	A		Aston Villa	L	1-2	Lewis	43,638	1	2	3	4	5	6	7		9	10											11	8				4					27
28	Feb 7	H		Bolton Wanderers	W	3-1	Rowley 2, Lewis	34,339	1	2	3	4	5	6	7		9	10											11	8				4					28
29	18	A		Sunderland	W	2-2	Pegg Lewis	24,263	1	2	3	4	5	6			9	10											11	8		7		4					29
30	21	H		Wolverhampton Wanderers	L	0-3		38,269	1	2	3	4	5	6			9	10											11	8		7		4					30
31	28	A		Stoke City	L	1-3	Berry	30,219	1	2	3	4	5	6	7		9	10											11	8				4					31
32	Mar 7	H		Preston North End	W	5-2	Taylor 2, Pegg 2, Rowley	52,590	1	2	3	4	5	6	7		9												11			10		4	8				32
33	14	A		Burnley	L	1-2	Byrne (pen)	45,682	1	2		4	5	6	7		9		3										11			10		4	8				33
34	25	H		Tottenham Hotspur	W	3-2	Pegg, Pearson 2	18,384	1	2		4	5	6	7		9	10	3										11			8		4					34
35	28	A		Sheffield Wednesday	D	0-0		37,101	1	2		4	5	6	7		9	10	3										11			8		4		6			35
36	Apr 3	A		Charlton Athletic	D	2-2	Taylor, Berry	42,000	1	2		4	5		7		9		3										11			10		4	8	6			36
37	4	H		Cardiff City	L	1-4	Byrne (pen)	37,163	1	2		4	5		7		9		3										11			10		4	8	6			37
38	6	H		Charlton Athletic	W	3-2	Taylor 2, Rowley	30,105	1	2		4	5		7		9		3										11			10		4	8	6			38
39	11	A		Newcastle United	W	2-1	Taylor 2	38,970	1	2		4	5		7		9		3										11			10		4	8	6			39
40	18	H		West Bromwich Albion	W	2-2	Pearson, Viollet	31,380	1	2		4	5		7			10	3										11					4	8	6		9	40
41	20	H		Liverpool	W	3-1	Pearson, Rowley, Berry	20,869	1	2		4	5		7		9	10	3										11					4	8	6			41
42	25	A		Middlesbrough	L	0-5		38,000	1	2		4	5		7		9	10	3										11					4	8	6			42

League Appearances — Wood 42, McNulty 41, Aston 23, Carey 20, Chilton 42, Gibson 26, Berry 39, Downie 20, Rowley 40, Pearson 27, Byrne 11, Crompton, Cockburn, Clempson, Bond, Allen, Jones, Scott, Whitefoot 10, McShane, Lewis 11, Doherty, Pegg, Foulkes 6, Redman, Taylor 11, Blanchflower 6, Edwards, Olive, Viollet

League Scorers — Pearson 12, Lewis 23, Rowley 2, Byrne (pen) (Highbury) 49,119

F.A. CUP

Rd 3	Jan 10	A	Millwall	W	1-0	Pearson	35,682
Rd 4	31	A	Walthamstow Avenue	D	1-1	Lewis	34,748
Replay	Feb 5	N	Walthamstow Avenue	W	5-2	Pearson, Lewis, Rowley 2, Byrne (pen) (Highbury)	49,119
Rd 5	14	A	Everton	L	1-2	Rowley	77,920

DID YOU KNOW? United used five different goalkeepers in 1952/3, a club record (equalled only in 1895/6). One of these was Les Olive, then working in the Old Trafford ticket office and registered on amateur forms. Mr. Olive is the present Club Secretary.

OPPOSITE PAGE

Top: PRESTON 0 MANCHESTER UNITED 5. 18 October 1952 at Deepdale. Jack Rowley heads home with keeper Newlands grounded. (BNPC)

Middle Left: EUROPEAN YOUTH CUP WINNERS 1954. United's Youth team show the Lord Mayor of Manchester the trophy at a civic reception in their honour. (BNPC)

Middle Right: WALTHAMSTOW AVENUE 2 MANCHESTER UNITED 5. 5 February 1953 at Highbury. Allenby Chilton tackles Jim Lewis in the F.A. Cup 4th Round Replay.

Bottom: MANCHESTER UNITED 'A' v WARD ST. OLD BOYS at The Cliff Ground, Salford. Played under floodlights on 15 November 1952. (BNPC)

MANCHESTER UNITED

Match No.	Date		Venue	Opponents	Result	Goalscorers	Attendance
1	Aug	19	H	Chelsea	D 1-1	Pearson	29,936
2		22	A	Liverpool	D 4-4	Byrne (pen), Rowley, Taylor, Lewis	48,422
3		26	A	West Bromwich Albion	L 1-3	Taylor	31,806
4		29	H	Newcastle United	D 1-1	Chilton	27,837
5	Sept	5	A	West Bromwich Albion	L 0-2		32,000
6		9	H	Manchester City	L 0-2		53,097
7		12	H	Middlesbrough	D 2-2	Rowley 2	18,161
8		16	A	Bolton Wanderers	D 0-0		43,544
9		19	A	Middlesbrough	W 4-1	Taylor 2, Rowley, Byrne (pen)	22,037
10		26	H	Preston North End	W 1-0	Byrne (pen)	41,171
11	Oct	3	H	Tottenham Hotspur	D 1-1	Rowley	52,837
12		10	A	Burnley	L 1-2	Pearson	37,696
13		17	H	Sunderland	W 1-0	Rowley	34,617
14		24	H	Wolverhampton Wanderers	L 1-3	Taylor	38,000
15		31	A	Aston Villa	W 1-0	Berry	30,266
16	Nov	7	H	Huddersfield Town	D 0-0		34,175
17		14	A	Arsenal	D 2-2	Rowley, Blanchflower	28,141
18		21	A	Cardiff City	W 6-1	Viollet 2, Blanchflower, Taylor, Rowley, Berry	24,000
19		28	H	Blackpool	W 4-1	Taylor 3, Viollet	49,853
20	Dec	5	A	Portsmouth	D 1-1	Taylor	29,233
21			H	Sheffield United	D 2-2	Blanchflower 2	31,693
22		12	A	Chelsea	L 1-3	Berry	37,153
23		19	H	Liverpool	W 5-1	Taylor 2, Blanchflower 2, Viollet	26,074
24		25	H	Sheffield Wednesday	W 5-2	Taylor 3, Viollet, Blanchflower	27,123
25		26	A	Sheffield Wednesday	W 1-0	Viollet	44,196
26	Jan	2	A	Newcastle United	W 2-1	Foulkes, Blanchflower	55,780
27		16	H	Manchester City	D 1-1	Berry	46,379
28		23	H	Bolton Wanderers	L 1-5	Taylor	46,663
29	Feb	6	A	Preston North End	W 3-1	Blanchflower, Rowley, Taylor	34,000
30		13	A	Tottenham Hotspur	W 2-0	Rowley, Taylor	38,485
31		20	A	Burnley	L 0-2		31,402
32		27	H	Sunderland	W 2-0	Taylor, Blanchflower	58,440
33	Mar	6	A	Wolverhampton Wanderers	W 1-0	Berry	38,939
34		13	H	Aston Villa	D 2-2	Taylor 2	27,000
35		20	H	Huddersfield Town	W 3-1	Rowley, Viollet, Blanchflower	40,181
36		27	A	Arsenal	L 1-3	Taylor	42,753
37	Apr	3	H	Cardiff City	L 2-3	Viollet, Rowley	22,832
38		10	A	Blackpool	L 0-2		28,996
39		16	H	Charlton Athletic	W 2-0	Aston, Viollet	31,876
40		17	H	Portsmouth	W 2-0	Blanchflower, Viollet	29,663
41		19	A	Charlton Athletic	L 0-1		19,111
42		24	A	Sheffield United	W 3-1	Aston, Blanchflower, Viollet	32,000

F.A. CUP

Rd 3	Jan	9	A	Burnley	L 3-5	Viollet, Taylor, 1 o.g.	52,847

League Appearances

League Scorers

Players: Crompton, J.; Aston, J.; Byrne, R. W.; Gibson, T. R. D.; Chilton, A. C.; Cockburn, H.; Berry, J. J.; Rowley, J. F.; Taylor, T.; Pearson, S. C.; Pegg, D.; Lewis, E.; Wood, R. E.; McNulty, T.; Whitefoot, J.; Viollet, D. S.; McShane, H.; Foulkes, W. A.; Edwards, D.; Blanchflower, J.; Webster, C.; McFarlane, N. W.; Redman, W.

DID YOU KNOW? Duncan Edwards was United's youngest player when he made his debut at Old Trafford on Easter Monday 4 April 1953, against Cardiff City, aged 15 years and 285 days. Duncan also made International history when, aged 18 years and 183 days, he became England's youngest-ever player, making his debut against Scotland at Wembley on 2 April 1955. England won 7-2.

Top: PLAYING SQUAD at the start of the 1953/4 season. Back Row: Pearson, Berry, Clayton, Lewis, Whitefoot, Pegg, Blanchflower, McNulty. Centre Row: J. Murphy (Chief Coach), W. Inglis (2nd Team Trainer), Aston, Crompton, Jones, Gannon, Hamilton, Fulton, Downie, Kennedy, T. Dalton (Physiotherapist), T. Curry (1st Team Trainer). Front Row: Rowley, Taylor, Chilton, Webster, McFarlane, Mooney, Scanlon, Whelan, Cockburn, Gibson, B. Whalley (Coach). (JG)

Middle Left: CORONATION CUP 1953. Semi-Final tie. Celtic 2 Manchester United 1 at Hampden Park with an attendance of 73,436. United beat Rangers 2-1 in the first round of this Tournament between top teams of England and Scotland, to commemorate the Coronation of Queen Elizabeth II. (KM)

Middle Right: F.A. YOUTH CUP PLAQUE. Awarded in 1955 to the club, to commemorate winning the competition for three successive seasons. (BNPC)

Bottom: FIVE IN A ROW: United's Youth team dominated the FA Youth Cup, winning the trophy in each of the first five seasons, here Alex Dawson is in action against Blackburn Rovers Youth in March 1956. (BNPC)

official souvenir programme

CORONATION CUP

SEMI-FINAL TIES

CELTIC v.
MANCHESTER UNITED
AT HAMPDEN PARK

NEWCASTLE UNITED
v. HIBERNIAN
AT IBROX STADIUM

Saturday, 16th May, 1953—Kick-Off 3 p.m.

6ᴰ

THE FOOTBALL ASSOCIATION

YOUTH CHALLENGE CUP COMPETITION

PRESENTED TO MANCHESTER UNITED F.C.
TO COMMEMORATE THEIR ACHIEVEMENT
IN WINNING THE COMPETITION
IN THREE CONSECUTIVE SEASONS
1952-1953   1953-1954
1954-1955

MANCHESTER UNITED

Match No.	Date		Venue	Opponents	Result		Goalscorers	Attendance
1	Aug	21	H	Portsmouth	L	1-3	Rowley	38,203
2		23	A	Sheffield Wednesday	W	4-2	Viollet, Blanchflower 2	38,118
3		28	A	Blackpool	W	4-2	Webster 2, Viollet, Blanchflower	31,885
4	Sept	1	H	Sheffield Wednesday	W	2-0	Viollet 2	29,556
5		4	H	Charlton Athletic	W	3-1	Rowley 2, Taylor	38,105
6		8	A	Tottenham Hotspur	W	2-0	Berry, Webster	44,661
7		11	H	Bolton Wanderers	D	1-1	Webster	35,161
8		15	A	Tottenham Hotspur	W	2-1	Viollet, Rowley	29,212
9		18	H	Huddersfield Town	D	1-1	Viollet	45,648
10		25	A	Manchester City	L	2-3	Taylor, Blanchflower	54,105
11	Oct	2	A	Wolverhampton Wanderers	L	2-4	Viollet, Rowley	39,617
12		9	H	Cardiff City	W	5-2	Taylor 4, Viollet	39,328
13		16	A	Chelsea	W	6-5	Viollet 3, Taylor 2, Blanchflower	55,966
14		23	H	Newcastle United	W	5-2	Taylor 4, Viollet	29,217
15		30	A	Everton	D	2-2	Rowley, Taylor	63,021
16	Nov	6	H	Preston North End	L	2-4	Taylor 1 o.g.	30,063
17		13	A	Sheffield United	L	0-3		26,857
18		20	H	Arsenal	W	2-1	Viollet 2	33,373
19		27	A	West Bromwich Albion	L	0-2		33,931
20	Dec	4	H	Leicester City	W	3-1	Taylor, Blanchflower	19,369
21		11	A	Leicester City	W	4-2	Webster, Rowley, Viollet	24,967
22		18	H	Portsmouth	D	0-0		26,019
23		27	A	Burnley	L	0-1		49,136
24		28	A	Aston Villa	L	1-2	Taylor	51,000
25	Jan	1	H	Blackpool	W	4-1	Blanchflower 2, Edwards, Viollet	51,918
26		22	H	Bolton Wanderers	D	1-1	Taylor	39,873
27	Feb	5	A	Huddersfield Town	W	3-1	Pegg, Edwards, Berry	31,408
28		12	H	Manchester City	L	0-5		47,914
29		23	A	Wolverhampton Wanderers	L	2-4	Taylor, Edwards	15,679
30		26	A	Cardiff City	L	0-3		15,500
31	Mar	5	H	Burnley	W	1-0	Edwards	31,729
32		19	H	Everton	L	1-2	Scanlon	32,295
33		26	A	Preston North End	W	2-0	Scanlon, Byrne (pen)	13,327
34	Apr	2	H	Sheffield United	W	5-0	Taylor 2, Whelan, Viollet, Berry	21,158
35		8	A	Sunderland	L	3-4	Edwards 2, Scanlon	43,882
36		9	A	Leicester City	W	0-1	Edwards	34,362
37		11	H	Sunderland	D	2-2	Byrne (pen), Taylor	36,013
38		16	H	West Bromwich Albion	D	2-2	Taylor 2, Viollet	24,165
39		18	A	Newcastle United	L	0-2		35,540
40		23	A	Arsenal	W	3-2	Blanchflower 2, 1 o.g.	42,754
41		26	H	Charlton Athletic	D	1-1	Viollet	13,149
42		30	H	Chelsea	W	2-1	Scanlon, Taylor	33,602

F.A. CUP

			Venue	Opponents	Result		Goalscorers	Attendance
Rd 3	Jan	8	A	Reading	D	1-1	Webster	26,000
Replay		12	H	Reading	W	4-1	Webster 2, Rowley, Viollet	24,578
Rd 4		29	A	Manchester City	L	0-2		75,000

Players (columns): Wood, R. E.; Foulkes, W. A.; Byrne, R. W.; Whitefoot, J.; Chilton, A. C.; Edwards, D.; Berry, J. J.; Blanchflower, J.; Webster, C.; Viollet, D. S.; Rowley, J. F.; Taylor, T.; Gibson, T. R. D.; Crompton, J.; Greaves, I. D.; Kennedy, P. A.; Cockburn, H.; Goodwin, F. J.; Scanlon, A.; Bent, G.; Pegg, D.; Jones, M.; Whelan, W. A.

League Appearances / League Scorers totals per player.

DID YOU KNOW? United's Youth team completed a hat-trick of F.A. Youth Cup victories in 1954/5. They were presented with a commemorative plaque from the F.A. to mark the occasion, then went on to retain the trophy in 1956 and 1957 to register a record 5 successive triumphs.

Top: F.A. YOUTH CUP WINNERS 1955. This is the team that completed a hat-trick of wins in this tournament.
(Left to right): Back Row: D. Edwards, T. Becket, S. Brennan, T. Hawksworth, A. Rhodes, J. Queenan. Front Row: R. Jones, L. Fidler, E. Colman, W. McGuinness, R. Charlton. (BNPC)

Bottom: MANCHESTER UNITED 1954/5. Back Row: J. Whitefoot, B. Foulkes, J. Blanchflower, R. Wood, J. Rowley, D. Edwards. Front Row: E. Lewis, J. Berry, A. Chilton, D. Viollet, R. Byrne. Insets: T. Taylor, M. Jones. (JG)

MANCHESTER UNITED

Match No.	Date	Venue	Opponents	Result	Goalscorers	Attendance
1	Aug 20	A	Birmingham City	D 2-2	Viollet 2	37,994
2	24	A	Tottenham Hotspur	D 2-2	Webster, Berry	25,406
3	27	H	West Bromwich Albion	W 3-1	Lewis, Viollet, Scanlon	31,996
4	31	H	Tottenham Hotspur	W 2-1	Edwards 2	27,453
5	Sept 3	A	Manchester City	L 0-1		59,162
6	7	H	Everton	W 2-1	Edwards, Blanchflower	27,843
7	10	A	Sheffield United	L 0-1		28,241
8	14	A	Everton	L 2-4	Webster, Blanchflower	34,897
9	17	H	Preston North End	W 3-2	Pegg, Taylor, Viollet	33,078
10	24	A	Burnley	D 0-0		26,873
11	Oct 1	H	Luton Town	W 3-1	Webster, Taylor 2	34,409
12	8	A	Wolverhampton Wanderers	W 4-3	Taylor 2, Doherty, Pegg	48,638
13	15	H	Aston Villa	D 4-4	Webster, Blanchflower, Pegg 2	30,000
14	22	H	Huddersfield Town	W 3-0	Berry, Taylor, Pegg	34,150
15	29	A	Cardiff City	W 1-0	Taylor	27,500
16	Nov 5	H	Arsenal	D 1-1	Taylor	41,586
17	12	A	Bolton Wanderers	L 1-3	Taylor	38,109
18	19	H	Chelsea	W 3-0	Byrne (pen), Taylor 2	22,192
19	26	A	Blackpool	D 0-0		26,240
20	Dec 3	H	Sunderland	W 2-1	Doherty, Viollet	39,901
21	10	A	Portsmouth	L 2-3	Taylor, Pegg	24,594
22	17	H	Birmingham City	W 2-1	Viollet, Jones	27,704
23	24	A	West Bromwich Albion	W 4-1	Taylor, Viollet 3	31,500
24	26	H	Charlton Athletic	W 5-1	Viollet 2, Taylor, Byrne (pen), Doherty	44,611
25	27	A	Charlton Athletic	L 0-3		42,040
26	31	H	Manchester City	W 2-1	Berry (pen), Taylor	60,956
27	Jan 14	H	Sheffield United	W 3-1	Taylor, Berry, Pegg	30,162
28	21	A	Preston North End	L 1-3	Whelan	28,047
29	Feb 4	H	Burnley	W 2-0	Taylor, Viollet	27,342
30	11	A	Luton Town	W 2-0	Viollet, Whelan	16,354
31	18	H	Wolverhampton Wanderers	W 2-0	Taylor 2	40,014
32	25	A	Aston Villa	W 1-0	Whelan	36,277
33	Mar 3	H	Chelsea	W 4-2	Viollet 2, Pegg, Taylor	32,050
34	10	A	Arsenal	W 1-0	Byrne (pen)	44,693
35	17	H	Arsenal	D 1-1	Viollet	50,758
36	24	H	Bolton Wanderers	W 1-0	Taylor	46,114
37	30	H	Newcastle United	W 5-2	Viollet 2, Taylor, Pegg, Doherty	58,748
38	31	A	Huddersfield Town	W 2-0	Taylor 2	37,780
39	Apr 2	A	Newcastle United	D 0-0		37,395
40	7	H	Blackpool	W 2-1	Berry (pen), Taylor	62,277
41	14	A	Sunderland	D 2-2	Whelan, McGuinness	19,865
42	21	H	Portsmouth	W 1-0	Viollet	38,417

F.A. CUP

Match	Date	Venue	Opponents	Result
Rd 3	Jan 7	A	Bristol Rovers	L 0-4

League Appearances / League Scorers

Player	Appearances	Scorers
Wood, R. E.	41	
Foulkes, W. A.	26	
Byrne, R. W.	39	3
Whitefoot, J.	15	
Jones, M.	42	1
Edwards, D.	33	3
Webster, C.	31	4
Blanchflower, J.	18	3
Taylor, T.	33	25
Viollet, D. S.	34	20
Scanlon, A.	5	1
Berry, J. J.	34	4
Lewis, E.	1	1
Goodwin, F. J.	8	
Whelan, W. A.	13	4
Doherty, J.	16	4
Whitehurst, W.	1	
Pegg, D.	35	9
Bent, G.	6	
McGuinness, W.	3	1
Crompton, J.	1	
Colman, E.	25	
Greaves, I. D.	15	
Scott, J.	1	

DID YOU KNOW? When United won the League Championship in 1955/6 they finished 11 points ahead of Runners-up Blackpool, to equal the same record of Preston (1888/9), Sunderland (1892/3) and Aston Villa (1896/7). Two club records were established in 1956. United's longest unbeaten run in all Senior competitions is 29 matches played between 4 February 1956 and 17 October 1956. During the same period the team enjoyed its longest unbeaten run of 26 Football League games.

OPPOSITE PAGE

Top: CHAMPIONS! Roger Byrne holds the Championship trophy aloft after the presentation ceremony following the match against Portsmouth on 21 April. (BNPC)

Bottom: MANCHESTER UNITED 2 BLACKPOOL 1. 7 April 1956. Jubilant supporters and officials greet the United players at the end of the match in which they clinched the league title. (BNPC)

MANCHESTER UNITED

Match No.	Date	Venue	Opponents	Result	Goalscorers	Attendance
1	Aug 18	H	Birmingham City	D 2-2	Viollet 2	32,752
2	20	A	Preston North End	W 3-1	Taylor 2, Whelan	32,569
3	25	A	West Bromwich Albion	W 3-2	Taylor, Viollet, Whelan	26,850
4	29	H	Preston North End	W 3-2	Viollet 3	32,240
5	Sept 1	H	Portsmouth	W 3-0	Berry, Viollet, Pegg	40,369
6	5	A	Chelsea	W 2-1	Taylor, Whelan	29,082
7	8	A	Newcastle United	D 1-1	Whelan	50,130
8	15	H	Sheffield Wednesday	W 4-1	Viollet, Whelan, Berry, Taylor	48,078
9	22	H	Manchester City	W 2-0	Viollet, Whelan	53,515
10	29	A	Arsenal	W 2-1	Whelan, Berry (pen)	62,479
11	Oct 6	H	Charlton Athletic	W 4-2	Charlton 2, Berry, Whelan	42,439
12	13	A	Sunderland	W 3-1	Viollet, Whelan, Taylor	49,487
13	20	H	Everton	L 2-5	Viollet, Whelan, 1 o.g.	43,451
14	27	A	Blackpool	D 2-2	Taylor 2	32,632
15	Nov 3	H	Wolverhampton Wanderers	W 3-0	Whelan, Pegg, Taylor	54,835
16	10	A	Bolton Wanderers	L 0-2		39,922
17	17	H	Leeds United	W 3-2	Berry, Colman	51,131
18	24	A	Tottenham Hotspur	D 2-2	Edwards, Taylor, Pegg	57,724
19	Dec 1	H	Luton Town	W 3-1	Edwards, Taylor, Pegg	34,736
20	8	A	Aston Villa	W 3-1	Taylor 2, Viollet	44,000
21	15	H	Birmingham City	L 1-3	Whelan	38,600
22	26	H	Cardiff City	W 3-1	Whelan, Taylor, Viollet	28,607
23	29	A	Portsmouth	W 3-1	Edwards, Pegg, Viollet	32,147
24	Jan 1	H	Chelsea	W 3-0	Taylor 2, Whelan	42,116
25	12	H	Newcastle United	W 6-1	Whelan 2, Viollet 2, Pegg 2	44,911
26	19	A	Sheffield Wednesday	L 1-2	Taylor	51,068
27	Feb 2	A	Manchester City	W 4-2	Whelan, Taylor, Viollet Edwards	63,872
28	9	H	Arsenal	W 6-2	Whelan 2, Berry 2 (1 pen), Edwards, Taylor	60,384
29	23	H	Charlton Athletic	W 5-1	Charlton 3, Taylor 2	16,308
30	Mar 2	A	Blackpool	L 0-2		42,602
31	6	H	Everton	W 2-1	Webster 2	34,029
32	9	A	Aston Villa	D 1-1	Charlton	55,484
33	16	H	Wolverhampton Wanderers	D 1-1	Charlton	53,228
34	25	H	Bolton Wanderers	L 0-2		60,862
35	30	A	Leeds United	W 2-1	Berry, Charlton	47,000
36	Apr 6	H	Tottenham Hotspur	D 0-0		60,349
37	13	A	Luton Town	W 2-0	Taylor 2	21,227
38	19	A	Burnley	W 2-0	Whelan 2	41,321
39	20	H	Sunderland	W 4-0	Whelan 2, Taylor, Edwards	58,489
40	22	H	Burnley	W 2-1	Whelan 2, Taylor	41,321
41	27	A	Cardiff City	W 3-2	Scanlon 2 (1 pen), Dawson	18,000
42	29	H	West Bromwich Albion	D 1-1	Dawson	20,357

League Appearances

League Scorers

F.A. CUP

Round	Date	Venue	Opponents	Result	Goalscorers	Attendance	
Rd 3	Jan 5	A	Hartlepool United	W 4-3	Whelan 2, Taylor, Berry	17,264	
Rd 4	26	H	Wrexham	W 5-0	Whelan 2, Taylor 2, Byrne (pen)	34,445	
Rd 5	Feb 16	H	Everton	W 1-0	Edwards	61,803	
Rd 6	Mar 2	A	Bournemouth	W 2-1	Berry 2 (1 pen)	28,799	
S/F	23	N	Birmingham City	W 2-0	Berry, Charlton	65,107	(at Hillsborough, Sheffield)
FINAL	May 4	N	Aston Villa	L 1-2	Taylor	100,000	(at Wembley)

Players: Wood, R. E.; Foulkes, W. A.; Byrne, R. W.; Colman, E.; Jones, M.; Edwards, D.; Berry, J. J.; Whelan, W. A.; Taylor, T.; Viollet, D. S.; Pegg, D.; Cope, R.; Bent, G.; McGuinness, W.; Charlton, R.; Hawksworth, A.; Blanchflower, J.; Goodwin, F. J.; Webster, C.; Doherty, J.; Clayton, G.; Scanlon, A.; Greaves, I. D.; Dawson, A. D.

DID YOU KNOW! United's floodlights were first used for a league match on 25 March 1957 against Bolton Wanderers.

OPPOSITE PAGE

Top: LEAGUE CHAMPIONS 1956/7: Back Row: Dr. W. Maclean (Director), Mr. H. P. Hardman (Chairman), Mr. G. E. Whittaker (Director), Mr. W. Crickmer (Secretary), Mr. J. Gibson (Director). Middle Row: T. Curry (Trainer), Blanchflower, Foulkes, Taylor, Jones, Wood, Greaves, Edwards, Whelan, Doherty, M. Busby (Manager). Front Row: Webster, Pegg, Coleman, Byrne, Berry, Whitefoot, Viollet. (JG)

Middle Right: EUROPEAN CUP SEMI-FINALISTS. United were Englands first representatives in Europe, and reached the semi-finals before losing 3-5 on aggregate to eventual winners Real Madrid. Here Roger Byrne shakes hands with Munoz before the 1st leg in Madrid.

Middle Left: SOUVENIR FROM MADRID. Roger Byrne and Matt Busby with the trophy presented by Real to commemorate the game. The trophy is still at Old Trafford. (BNPC).

Bottom: F.A. CUP FINAL 1957. Aston Villa 2 Manchester United 1 at Wembley. (Right): The teams take the field and (Left): Ray Wood with Peter McParland of Villa, whose challenge after 6 minutes left Wood an injured passenger on the wing. (MMUSC)

MANCHESTER UNITED

Match No.	Date	Venue	Opponents	Result	Goalscorers	Attendance
1	Aug 24	A	Leicester City	W 3–0	Whelan 3	40,214
2	28	H	Everton	W 3–0	T. Taylor, Viollet, 1 o.g.	59,103
3	31	H	Manchester City	'W' 4–1	Edwards, Berry, Viollet, T. Taylor	63,103
4	Sept 4	A	Everton	D 3–3	Berry, Whelan, Viollet	72,077
5	7	H	Leeds United	W 5–0	T. Taylor, Berry 2, Viollet	50,400
6	14	A	Blackpool	W 4–1	Viollet 2, Whelan 2	34,181
7	18	A	Bolton Wanderers	L 0–4		48,003
8	21	H	Blackpool	L 1–2	Viollet	40,763
9	28	A	Arsenal	W 4–2	Whelan 2, T. Taylor, Pegg	47,142
10	Oct 5	H	Wolverhampton Wanderers	L 1–3	Doherty	48,825
11	19	A	Aston Villa	W 4–1	Whelan, Viollet	47,654
12	26	H	Nottingham Forest	L 0–3		38,283
13	Nov 2	A	Portsmouth	L 3–4	T. Taylor 2, Whelan	52,839
14	9	H	West Bromwich Albion	D 1–1	T. Taylor	49,449
15	16	A	Burnley	L 1–2	Whelan	39,063
16	23	H	Preston North End	W 2–1	Webster 2	40,866
17	30	A	Sheffield Wednesday	D 1–1	Edwards, T. Taylor	53,890
18	Dec 7	H	Newcastle United	L 3–4	Pegg 2, Whelan	43,077
19	14	A	Tottenham Hotspur	L 3–4	T. Taylor, Viollet 2	36,791
20	21	H	Birmingham City	D 3–3	Viollet	36,883
21	25	A	Chelsea	L 0–1	Viollet, Charlton	41,631
22	26	H	Chelsea		Viollet, Charlton	39,444
23	28	A	Leicester City			26,488
24	Jan 11	H	Leeds United			70,483
25	18	H	Bolton Wanderers	W 7–2	Charlton 3, Viollet 2, Scanlon, Edwards (pen)	39,400
26	Feb 1	A	Arsenal	W 5–4	T. Taylor 2, Edwards, Charlton, Viollet	51,302
27	22	H	Nottingham Forest	D 1–1	Dawson	47,186
28	Mar 1	A	West Bromwich Albion		Dawson	47,187
29	8	H	Chelsea		Viollet 2, Scanlon, Charlton	37,247
30	15	A	Sheffield Wednesday		Edwards (pen), T. Taylor, Charlton	63,278
31	29	H	Burnley		T. Taylor, Scanlon	66,123
32	31	A	Aston Villa		Dawson, Webster	63,578
33	Apr 4	H	Sunderland		Dawson, Charlton	63,578
34	5	H	Preston North End		Dawson, Webster, E. Taylor	41,141
35	7	A	Sunderland		Dawson 3	53,890
36	12	H	Sunderland		Dawson	28,393
37	16	A	Tottenham Hotspur		Webster	33,267
38	19	H	Portsmouth		E. Taylor, Dawson	38,991
39	21	H	Birmingham City		Charlton 2	39,975
40	23	H	Wolverhampton Wanderers		Charlton 2	59,836
41	26	A	Newcastle United		Viollet 3	51,302
42	26	A	Chelsea	L 1–2	E. Taylor	45,011

F.A. CUP

	Date	Venue	Opponents	Result	Goalscorers	Attendance
Rd 3	Jan 4	A	Workington Town	W 3–1	Viollet 3	21,000
Rd 4	25	H	Ipswich Town	W 2–0	Charlton 2	53,550
Rd 5	Feb 19	H	Sheffield Wednesday	W 3–0	Brennan 2, Dawson	59,848
Rd 6	Mar 1	A	West Bromwich Albion	D 2–2	Dawson, E. Taylor	58,250
Replay	5	H	West Bromwich Albion	W 1–0	Webster	60,560
S/F	22	N	Fulham	D 2–2	Charlton 2 (at Villa Park, Birmingham)	69,745
Replay	26	N	Fulham	W 5–3	Dawson (3), Brennan, Charlton (at Highbury)	38,258
FINAL	May 3	N	Bolton Wanderers	L 0–2	(at Wembley)	100,000

League Appearances
League Scorers

Players:
Wood, R. E.; Foulkes, W. A.; Byrne, R. W.; Colman, E.; Blanchflower, J.; Edwards, D.; Berry, J. J.; Whelan, W. A.; Taylor, T.; Viollet, D. S.; Pegg, D.; McGuinness, W.; Goodwin, F. J.; Doherty, J.; Charlton, R.; Jones, M.; Jones, E. P.; Dawson, A. D.; Webster, C.; Scanlon, A.; Gaskell, J. D.; Gregg, H.; Morgans, K. G.; Greaves, I. D.; Cope, R.; Crowther, S.; Taylor, E.; Pearson, M.; Brennan, S. A.; Harrop, R.; Heron, T. R. F.

Top Right: PRE-SEASON TOUR 1957. The United party leaves Ringway Airport in optimistic mood for the club tour of Berlin and Hanover.

Top Left: 'UNITED WILL GO ON' Manchester United 1 Nottingham Forest 1. 22 February 1958. From United's first league match after the Munich disaster, the programme carried this defiant message from chairman Harold Hardman. (KM)

Middle: MUNICH DISASTER: Right: The Daily Mirror headline on 7 February (BNPC) and Left: the burning wreckage of the aircraft. (MMUSC)

Bottom Right: F.A. CUP FINALISTS 1958. The United Cup team is interviewed for BBC Sportsview by commentator Ken Wolstenholme.

UNITED WILL GO ON . . .

On 6th February 1958 an aircraft returning from Belgrade crashed at Munich Airport. Of the twenty-one passengers who died twelve were players and officials of the Manchester United Football Club. Many others still lie injured.

It is the sad duty of we who serve United to offer the bereaved our heart-felt sympathy and condolences. Here is a tragedy which will sadden us for years to come, but in this we are not alone. An unprecedented blow to British football has touched the hearts of millions and we express our deep gratitude to the many who have sent messages of sympathy and floral tributes. Wherever football is played United is mourned, but we rejoice that many of our party have been spared and wish them a speedy and complete recovery. Words are inadequate to describe our thanks and appreciation of the truly magnificent work of the surgeons and nurses of the Rechts der Isar Hospital at Munich. But for their superb skill and deep compassion our casualties must have been greater. To Professor Georg Maurer, Chief Surgeon, we offer our eternal gratitude.

Although we mourn our dead and grieve for our wounded we believe that great days are not done for us. The sympathy and encouragement of the football world and parti-cularly of our supporters will fortify and inspire us. The road back may be long and hard but with the memory of those who died at Munich, of their stirring achieve-ments and wonderful sportsmanship ever with us, Manchester United will rise again.

H. P. HARDMAN, CHAIRMAN

MANCHESTER UNITED

Match No.	Date		Venue	Opponents	Result		Goalscorers	Attendance
1	Aug	23	H	Chelsea	W	5-2	Charlton 3, Dawson 2	52,122
2		27	A	Nottingham Forest	W	3-0	Charlton 2, Scanlon	44,721
3		30	A	Blackpool	L	1-2	Viollet	36,719
4	Sept	3	H	Nottingham Forest	D	1-1	Charlton	51,670
5		6	H	Blackburn Rovers	W	6-1	Viollet 2, Charlton 2 (1 pen), Scanlon, Webster	64,962
6		8	A	West Ham United	L	2-3	Webster, McGuinness	36,000
7		13	A	Newcastle United	D	1-1	Charlton	60,490
8		17	H	West Ham United	W	4-1	Webster, Scanlon 3	53,057
9		20	H	Tottenham Hotspur	D	2-2	Webster 2	62,036
10		27	A	Manchester City	D	1-1	Charlton (pen)	62,812
11	Oct	4	A	Wolverhampton Wanderers	L	0-4		36,840
12		8	H	Preston North End	L	0-2		49,555
13		11	H	Arsenal	D	1-1	Viollet	55,909
14		18	A	Everton	L	2-3	Cope 2	64,079
15		25	H	Leicester City	W	4-1	Scanlon, Viollet, Bradley, Charlton	51,948
16	Nov	1	A	Leeds United	W	2-1	Scanlon, Goodwin	48,500
17		8	H	Burnley	L	1-3	Quixall	48,628
18		15	A	Bolton Wanderers	L	3-6	Dawson 2, Charlton	33,358
19		22	A	Luton Town	D	2-2	Viollet, Charlton	41,196
20		29	H	Birmingham City	W	4-0	Charlton 2, Scanlon, Bradley	28,618
21	Dec	6	H	Leicester City	W	3-1	Viollet, Charlton, Bradley	38,251
22		13	A	Preston North End	W	4-0	Viollet, Charlton, Scanlon, Bradley	26,288
23		20	H	Chelsea	W	3-2	Goodwin, Charlton, Scanlon, Bradley	48,550
24		26	A	Aston Villa	W	2-1	Goodwin, Charlton, 1 o.g.	62,761
25		27	H	Aston Villa	W	2-0	Quixall, Viollet	56,000
26	Jan	3	A	Blackpool	W	2-1	Viollet, Pearson	61,720
27		31	H	Newcastle United	D	4-4	Charlton (pen), Quixall, Scanlon, Viollet	48,777
28	Feb	7	A	Tottenham Hotspur	W	3-1	Scanlon, Charlton 2 (1 pen)	48,401
29		14	H	Manchester City	W	4-1	Goodwin, Bradley 2, Scanlon	59,604
30		21	A	Wolverhampton Wanderers	W	2-1	Viollet, Charlton	62,547
31		28	H	Arsenal	L	2-3	Viollet, Bradley	67,386
32	Mar	2	A	Blackburn Rovers	W	3-1	Bradley 2, Scanlon	40,300
33		7	H	Everton	W	2-1	Goodwin, Scanlon	51,044
34		14	A	West Bromwich Albion	W	3-1	Goodwin, Scanlon	38,608
35		21	H	Leeds United	W	4-0	Viollet, Scanlon, Bradley	45,289
36		27	H	Portsmouth	W	6-1	Bradley, Charlton 2 (1 pen), Viollet 2, 1 o.g.	51,783
37		28	A	Burnley	L	2-4	Goodwin, Ciollet	44,086
38		30	A	Portsmouth	W	3-0	Charlton 2, Bradley	29,359
39	Apr	4	H	Bolton Wanderers	W	3-0	Charlton, Scanlon, Violet	61,283
40		11	A	Luton Town	D	0-0	Quixall (pen)	27,025
41		18	H	Birmingham City	W	1-0	Bradley	42,827
42		25	A	Leicester City	L	1-2	Bradley	38,466

F.A. CUP

			Venue	Opponents	Result			Attendance
Rd 3	Jan	10	A	Norwich City	L	0-3		38,000

Players (League appearances / goals summarised at foot of grid):

Gregg, H. · Foulkes, W. A. · Greaves, I. D. · Goodwin, F. J. · Cope, R. · McGuiness · Dawson, A. D. · Taylor, E. · Viollet, D. S. · Charlton, R. · Scanlon, A. · Webster, C. · Crowther, S. · Quixall, A. · Wood, R. E. · Harrop, W. · Pearson, M. · Morgans, K. G. · Bradley, W. · Carolan, J. · Hunter, R. · Brennan, S. A.

League Scorers: Charlton, Viollet, Scanlon, Bradley, Dawson, Goodwin, Webster, Quixall, Cope, McGuinness, Pearson, 2 o.g.s

DID YOU KNOW? Manchester United were the first British club to record a profit of six-figures when they declared a surplus of £100,000 in 1958. In season 1958/9 the team equalled the club record of 103 goals scored in a season of 42 games, previously set in 1956/7.

THE PHEONIX RISES

Top: FOOTBALL LEAGUE RUNNERS-UP 1958/9. Just a year after Munich, United were second in Division One.
(Left to Right): Back Row: Charlton, Scanlon, Carolan, Gregg, Goodwin, Cope. Front Row: McGuinness, Viollet, Foulkes, Quixall, Morgans.

Bottom: MUNICH THANKSGIVING. August 1958. United returned to Munich for a friendly match and Thanksgiving Service.
Left: Wilf McGuinness signs the visitors book at the City Hall, watched by some of his team-mates.
Right: Matt Busby is greeted by Herr A. W. Wetzel, the President of Munich F.C. (BNPC)

MANCHESTER UNITED

Match No.	Date	Venue	Opponents	Result	Goalscorers	Attendance
1	Aug 22	A	West Bromwich Albion	L 2-3	Viollet 2	40,733
2	26	H	Chelsea	L 0-1		57,674
3	29	H	Newcastle United	W 3-2	Viollet 2, Charlton	53,257
4	Sept 2	A	Chelsea	W 6-3	Bradley 2, Viollet 2, Quixall, Charlton	66,579
5	5	A	Birmingham City	D 1-1	Quixall	38,220
6	9	H	Birmingham City	D 1-1	Quixall	48,407
7	12	H	Leeds United	W 6-0	Bradley 2, Charlton 2, Viollet, Scanlon	55,402
8	16	A	Tottenham Hotspur	L 1-5	Viollet	55,000
9	19	A	Leeds United	D 2-2	2 o.g.s	34,000
10	26	H	Manchester City	L 0-3		58,300
11	Oct 3	A	Preston North End	L 0-4		41,403
12	10	H	Leicester City	W 4-1	Viollet 2, Charlton, Quixall	35,026
13	17	A	Arsenal	W 4-2	Quixall, Charlton, Viollet, 1 o.g.	51,626
14	24	H	Sheffield Wednesday	L 2-3	Viollet, 1 o.g.	39,289
15	31	A	Blackburn Rovers	W 3-1	Viollet, Dawson, Scanlon	39,600
16	Nov 7	H	Fulham	W 4-1	Viollet, Bradley	44,063
17	14	A	Bolton Wanderers	D 3-3	Viollet, Scanlon, Charlton	37,882
18	21	H	Luton Town	D 1-1	Quixall	40,572
19	28	A	Everton	W 4-1	Viollet 2, Quixall, Goodwin	46,086
20	Dec 5	H	Blackpool	D 1-1	Pearson, Viollet 2	45,558
21	12	A	Nottingham Forest	L 1-2	Dawson	31,666
22	19	H	West Bromwich Albion	W 4-1	Quixall	33,677
23	26	A	Wolverhampton Wanderers	L 2-3	Viollet, Dawson, Scanlon	45,000
24	28	H	Burnley	W 4-1	Viollet, Bradley	62,376
25	Jan 2	A	Newcastle United	L 3-7	Dawson, Quixall 2 (1 pen)	57,200
26	16	A	Birmingham City	W 2-1	Viollet 2, Scanlon 2	47,361
27	23	H	Tottenham Hotspur	W 2-1	Quixall (pen), Viollet	62,602
28	Feb 6	H	Manchester City	D 0-0		59,450
29	13	A	Preston North End	D 1-1	Viollet	44,014
30	24	H	Leicester City	L 1-3	Scanlon	33,191
31	27	A	Blackpool	W 6-0	Charlton 3, Viollet 2, Scanlon	23,996
32	Mar 5	H	Wolverhampton Wanderers	L 0-2		60,860
33	19	H	Nottingham Forest	W 3-1	Charlton 2, Dawson	45,269
34	26	A	Fulham	W 5-0	Viollet 3, Dawson, Scanlon	38,250
35	30	H	Sheffield Wednesday	W 2-4	Viollet 2, Dawson, Giles, Pearson	26,821
36	Apr 2	H	Bolton Wanderers	W 2-0	Charlton, Dawson	45,298
37	9	A	Luton Town	W 3-2	Bradley, Dawson 2	21,242
38	15	H	West Ham United	L 1-2	Dawson	38,000
39	16	H	Blackburn Rovers	W 1-0	Dawson	45,945
40	18	A	West Ham United	W 5-3	Dawson 2, Charlton 2, Quixall	34,676
41	23	A	Arsenal	L 2-5	Pearson, Giles	41,067
42	30	H	Everton	W 5-0	Dawson 3, Quixall, Bradley	43,823

F.A. CUP

	Date	Venue	Opponents	Result	Goalscorers	Attendance
Rd 3	Jan 9	H	Derby County	W 4-2	Scanlon, Charlton, Goodwin, 1 o.g.	33,897
Rd 4	30	A	Liverpool	W 3-1	Charlton 2, Bradley	56,736
Rd 5	Feb 20	H	Sheffield Wednesday	L 0-1		66,350

Players (League Appearances / League Scorers):
Gregg, H.; Greaves, I. D.; Carolan, J.; Goodwin, F. J.; Foulkes, W. A.; McGuinness, W.; Bradley, W.; Quixall, A.; Viollet, D. S.; Charlton, R.; Scanlon, A.; Dawson, A. D.; Cope, R.; Brennan, S. A.; Giles, J. M.; Gaskell, J. D.; Pearson, M. M.; Setters, M. E.; Heron, T. R. F.; Lawton, N.

DID YOU KNOW? Denis Viollet set a club record of 32 goals in 1959/60, and was the Football League's top scorer for that season. Alex Dawson scored a unique 'Hat-trick of Hat-tricks', in three consecutive games for the reserves.

OPPOSITE PAGE

Top: UNITED PLAYING SQUAD FOR 1958/9. Back Row: English, Brennan, Clayton, Dawson, Hawksworth, Goodwin, Wood, Harrop, Carolan. Middle Row: T. Dalton (Physiotherapist), J. Murphy (Ass. Manager), Smith, Gregg, Elms, Bratt, Holland, Pearson, Crowther, Cope, Greaves, W. Bradley, Heron, McGuinness, Shiels, Giles, W. Inglis (Trainer), J. Crompton (Trainer). Front Row: Taylor, Webster, Foulkes, M. Busby C.B.E. (Manager), Morgans, Scanlon, Viollet, Charlton. (JG)

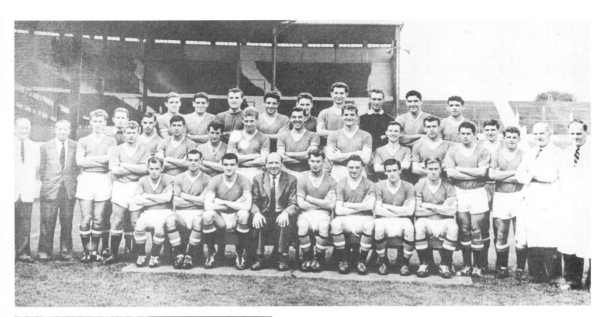

Middle Left: BOBBY CHARLTON — 21 TODAY! Matt Busby has a word with birthday boy Charlton and an otherwise occupied Wilf McGuinness over lunch at the Davyhulme Golf Clubhouse prior to the Arsenal match on 10 Oct 1958. (BPNC)

Bottom: REAL MADRID 6 MANCHESTER UNITED 5. 11 November 1959. An attendance of 83,000 saw this 11-goal thriller. Gregg is seen saving from Di Stefano. (BPNC).

MANCHESTER UNITED

No.	Date	Venue	Opponents	Result	Goalscorers	Attendance
1	Aug 20	H	Blackburn Rovers	L 1-3	Charlton	47,778
2	24	A	Everton	L 0-4		51,602
3	31	H	Everton	W 4-0	Viollet	51,818
4	Sept 3	A	Tottenham Hotspur	L 1-4	Viollet	55,445
5	5	H	West Ham United	L 1-2	Viollet	30,506
6	10	H	Leicester City	D 1-1	Giles	35,493
7	14	A	West Ham United	W 6-1	Charlton 2, Viollet 2, Quixall (pen), Scanlon	33,696
8	17	A	Aston Villa	L 1-3	Viollet	44,000
9	24	H	Wolverhampton Wanderers	L 1-3	Charlton	44,458
10	Oct 1	A	Bolton Wanderers	D 1-1	Giles	39,197
11	15	H	Burnley	L 3-5	Viollet 3	32,011
12	22	A	West Bromwich Albion	W 3-2	Dawson, Viollet, Quixall (pen)	32,756
13	24	H	Newcastle United	W 3-2	Dawson, Stiles, Setters	37,516
14	29	A	Nottingham Forest	W 2-1	Viollet 2	23,628
15	Nov 5	H	Arsenal	L 1-2	Quixall	45,715
16	12	A	Sheffield Wednesday	D 0-0		36,685
17	19	H	Birmingham City	L 1-3	Charlton	31,549
18	26	A	Cardiff City	W 1-0	Dawson	32,756
19	Dec 3	H	Preston North End	W 1-0	Dawson	24,904
20	10	A	Fulham	D 4-4	Charlton, Quixall 2 (1 pen), Dawson	26,700
21	17	H	Blackburn Rovers	W 2-1	Pearson 2	17,200
22	24	A	Chelsea	W 2-1	Charlton, Dawson	37,601
23	26	H	Chelsea	W 2-1	Charlton, Dawson	50,213
24	31	A	Manchester City	W 6-0	Dawson 3, Nicholson 2, Charlton	50,479
25	Jan 16	H	Tottenham Hotspur	W 5-1	Charlton 2, Dawson 3	65,295
26	21	A	Aston Villa	W 2-0	Stiles, Pearson	31,308
27	Feb 4	H	Leicester City	L 0-3		33,525
28	11	A	Wolverhampton Wanderers	L 1-2	Nicholson	38,526
29	18	H	Bolton Wanderers	L 1-2	Nicholson	38,870
30	25	A	Nottingham Forest	W 3-1	Quixall (pen), Dawson 2	26,700
31	Mar 4	A	Manchester City	W 3-1	Dawson, Charlton, Pearson	50,479
32	11	H	Newcastle United	W 1-0	Charlton	37,508
33	18	A	Arsenal	D 1-1	Moir	29,732
34	25	H	Sheffield Wednesday	D 1-1	Charlton	35,901
35	31	A	Blackpool	L 1-5	Charlton	30,835
36	Apr 1	H	Fulham	L 0-2		24,664
37	3	H	Blackpool	W 3-1	Charlton, Viollet, Quixall	27,750
38	8	A	West Bromwich Albion	W 2-0	Nicholson, 1 o.g.	21,750
39	12	H	Burnley	W 6-0	Viollet 3, Quixall 3	25,019
40	15	H	Birmingham City	W 4-1	Pearson 2, Quixall (pen), Viollet	28,376
41	22	A	Preston North End	W 4-2	Charlton 2, Setters 2	21,262
42	29	H	Cardiff City	D 3-3	Charlton 2, Setters	30,320

F.A. CUP

	Date	Venue	Opponents	Result	Goalscorers	Attendance
Rd 3	Jan 7	H	Middlesbrough	W 3-0	Cantwell, Dawson 2	49,184
Rd 4	28	A	Sheffield Wednesday	D 1-1	Cantwell (pen)	58,000
Replay	Feb 1	H	Sheffield Wednesday	L 2-7	Dawson, Pearson	65,243

League Appearances — *League Scorers*

Players: Gregg, H.; Cope, R.; Carolan, J.; Setters, M. E.; Haydock, F.; Brennan, S. A.; Giles, J. M.; Quixall, A.; Viollet, D. S.; Charlton, R.; Scanlon, A.; Nicholson, J. J.; Foulkes, W. A.; Dawson, A. D.; Stiles, N. P.; Moir, I.; Dunne, A. P.; Pearson, M.; Heron, T. R. F.; Bradley, W.; Cantwell, N.; Briggs, W. R.; Pinner, M. J.; Morgans, K. G.; Lawton, N.; Gaskell, D.

DID YOU KNOW: United embarked on a Tour of North America in the summer of 1960, playing a total 9 matches in Canada and the United States, against opposition from Germany, Scotland (Hearts), Ukraine as well as New York, St. Louis, San Francisco and New England.

OPPOSITE PAGE

MANCHESTER UNITED 1959/60: (Left to Right) Back Row: Brennan, Cope, Greaves, Goodwin, Gregg, Dawson, Sheils, Foulkes, Carolan. Front Row: Bradley, McGuinness, Viollet, Quixall, Charlton, Scanlon. (JG)

Centre: U.S TOUR 1960. Catholic Youth All-Stars 0 Manchester United 4. St. Louis USA. Menu Brochure from the pre-match Banquet. (KM)

Bottom Left: F.A YOUTH CUP 1959/60. Ian Moir cracks home his second goal against Middlesbrough Youth at Old Trafford. (BNPC)

INTERNATIONAL SOCCER
KICK OFF BANQUET

M A N C H E S T E R   U N I T E D

C Y C   A L L   S T A R S

CF
HARDMAN

OL
FR. POELKER

OR
FR. MEYER

IL
MSGR. SULLIVAN

IR
GUELKER

LHB
STEWART

RHB
GOCKEL
FLAVIN

CHB
SOLARI

LFB
FR. GALLAGHER

RFB
BURNES

ENGLAND

ST LOUIS

GOAL
BISHOP FLAVIN

EPIPHANY GYM
MAY 24, 1960
6:30 p.m.

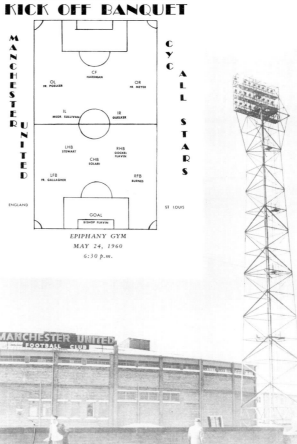

MANCHESTER UNITED

Match No.	Date	Venue	Opponents	Result	Goalscorers	Attendance
1	Aug 19	A	West Ham United	D 1-1	Stiles	32,606
2	23	H	Chelsea	W 3-2	Herd, Viollet, Pearson	45,589
3	26	H	Blackburn Rovers	W 6-1	Charlton, Quixall 2 (1 pen), Herd 2, Setters	44,872
4	30	A	Chelsea	L 0-2		42,248
5	Sept 2	A	Blackpool	W 3-2	Viollet 2, Charlton	28,156
6	9	H	Tottenham Hotspur	W 1-0	Quixall	56,745
7	16	A	Cardiff City	W 2-1	Quixall (pen), Dawson	28,000
8	18	H	Aston Villa	D 1-1	Stiles	39,000
9	23	A	Manchester City	W 3-2	Stiles, Viollet, 1 o.g.	56,933
10	30	H	Wolverhampton Wanderers	L 0-2		39,300
11	Oct 7	A	West Bromwich Albion	D 1-1	Dawson	25,645
12	14	H	Birmingham City	L 0-2		30,086
13	21	A	Arsenal	L 1-5	Viollet	54,099
14	28	H	Bolton Wanderers	L 0-3		31,359
15	Nov 4	A	Sheffield Wednesday	L 1-3	Viollet	36,808
16	11	H	Leicester City	D 2-2	Giles, Viollet	21,306
17	18	A	Ipswich Town	L 1-4	McMillan	25,755
18	25	H	Burnley	L 1-4	Herd	40,858
19	Dec 2	A	Everton	L 1-5	Herd	48,199
20	9	H	Fulham	W 3-0	Herd 2, Lawton	22,479
21	16	A	West Ham United	L 1-2	Herd	29,472
22	26	H	Nottingham Forest	W 6-3	Lawton 3, Herd, Charlton, Brennan	31,366
23	Jan 13	H	Blackpool	L 0-1		27,061
24	15	H	Aston Villa	W 2-0	Quixall, Charlton	21,683
25	20	A	Tottenham Hotspur	D 2-2	Charlton, Stiles	55,225
26	Feb 3	H	Cardiff City	W 3-0	Stiles, Giles, Lawton	28,211
27	10	A	Manchester City	W 2-0	Chisnall, Herd	49,959
28	24	H	West Bromwich Albion	W 4-1	Charlton 2, Setters, Quixall	26,000
29	28	A	Wolverhampton Wanderers	D 2-2	Lawton, Herd	25,777
30	March 3	A	Birmingham City	D 1-1	Herd	34,366
31	17	A	Bolton Wanderers	L 0-1		25,777
32	20	A	Nottingham Forest	L 0-1		27,833
33	24	H	Sheffield Wednesday	D 1-1	Charlton	31,322
34	April 4	H	Leicester City	L 3-4	McMillan 2, Quixall (pen)	15,318
35	7	A	Ipswich Town	W 5-0	Quixall 3, Stiles, Setters	25,194
36	10	H	Blackburn Rovers	L 0-3		14,600
37	14	A	Burnley	W 3-1	Cantwell, Brennan (pen), Herd	36,817
38	16	H	Arsenal	L 2-3	McMillan, Cantwell	24,788
39	21	H	Everton	D 1-1	Herd	31,950
40	23	A	Sheffield United	L 0-1		29,536
41	24	H	Sheffield United	W 3-2	McMillan 2, Stiles	29,234
42	28	A	Fulham	L 0-2		40,113

F.A. CUP

Round	Date	Venue	Opponents	Result	Goalscorers	Attendance
Rd 3	Jan 6	H	Bolton Wanderers	W 2-1	Herd, Nicholson	42,202
Rd 4	31	H	Arsenal	W 1-0	Setters	54,082
Rd 5	Feb 17	H	Sheffield Wednesday	D 0-0		65,623
Replay	21	A	Sheffield Wednesday	W 2-0	Giles, Charlton	65,009
Rd 6	Mar 10	A	Preston North End	D 0-0		37,521
Replay	14	H	Preston North End	W 2-1	Charlton, Herd	63,382
SF	31	N	Tottenham Hotspur	L 1-3	Herd	65,000 (at Hillsbrough, Sheffield)

Players

Gregg, H.; Brennan, S. A.; Cantwell, N.; Stiles, N. P.; Foulkes, W. A.; Setters, M. E.; Quixall, A.; Viollet, D. S.; Herd, D. G.; Pearson, M.; Charlton, R.; Bradley, W.; Dawson, A. D.; Gaskell, J. D.; Dunne, A. P.; Lawton, N.; Giles, J. M.; Moir, I.; Haydock, F.; Nicholson, J. J.; McMillan, S. T.; Chisnall, J. P.; Briggs, W. R.

League Scorers: Herd 14, Quixall 10, Stiles 7, Viollet 7, Charlton 7, Lawton 6, McMillan 6, Setters 4, Brennan 2, Cantwell 2, Dawson 2, Giles 2, Pearson 1, Chisnall 1, 1 o.g.

OPPOSITE PAGE

Top: WOLVERHAMPTON WANDERERS 2 MANCHESTER UNITED 2   28th February 1962   This Wolves attack at Molyneux is foiled by United 'keeper Briggs and Shay Brennan, watched anxiously by Bill Foulkes, with Maurice Setters in the background. (JG).

Bottom: SUITED FOR SUCCESS: After United's FA Cup 4th Round 1-0 success over Arsenal on 13th January 1962, winning goal scorer Maurice Setters chooses suit material at the menswear department of the C.W.S in Balloon Street the following Thursday. Salesman Mr. Dover gets the approval of Albert Quixall, David Herd, "Nobby" Lawton and Matt Busby. (BNPC).

MANCHESTER UNITED

Match No.	Date	Venue	Opponents	Result	Goalscorers	Attendance
1	Aug 18	H	West Bromwich Albion	2-2	Herd, Law	51,685
2	22	A	Everton	1-3	Moir	69,501
3	25	A	Arsenal	3-1	Herd 2, Chisnall	62,308
4	29	H	Everton	0-1		63,431
5	Sept 1	H	Birmingham City	2-0	Giles, Herd	39,847
6	5	A	Bolton Wanderers	0-3		44,859
7	8	A	Leyton Orient	0-1		24,901
8	12	H	Bolton Wanderers	3-0	Cantwell, Herd 2	37,721
9	15	H	Manchester City	2-3	Law 2	49,193
10	22	A	Burnley	2-5	Stiles, Law	45,954
11	29	H	Sheffield Wednesday	0-1		40,520
12	Oct 6	A	Blackpool	2-2	Herd 2	33,242
13	13	H	Blackburn Rovers	0-3		42,252
14	20	A	Tottenham Hotspur	2-6	Herd, Quixall, Law	51,314
15	27	H	West Ham United	3-1	Quixall 2 (1 pen), Law	29,204
16	Nov 3	A	Ipswich Town	5-3	Law 4, Herd	18,475
17	10	H	Liverpool	3-3	Herd, Quixall (pen), Giles	43,810
18	17	A	Wolverhampton Wanderers	3-2	Herd, Law 2	27,305
19	24	H	Aston Villa	2-2	Quixall 2 (1 pen)	36,882
20	Dec 1	A	Sheffield United	1-1	Charlton	25,173
21	8	H	Nottingham Forest	5-1	Herd 2, Charlton, Law, Giles	27,392
22	15	A	West Bromwich Albion	0-3		17,596
23	26	H	Fulham	1-0	Charlton	23,298
24	Feb 23	H	Blackpool	1-1	Herd	43,121
25	26	A	Blackburn Rovers	2-2	Law, Charlton	27,800
26	March 2	A	Tottenham Hotspur	0-2		53,416
27	9	H	West Ham United	1-3	Herd	28,950
28	18	A	Ipswich Town	1-0	Quixall (pen)	32,792
29	April 1	H	Fulham	0-2		28,124
30	9	A	Aston Villa	2-1	Stiles, Charlton	26,867
31	13	H	Liverpool	0-1		51,529
32	15	A	Leicester City	2-2	Herd, Charlton	50,005
33	16	H	Leicester City	3-4	Law 3	37,002
34	20	A	Sheffield United	1-1	Law 3	31,179
35	22	H	Wolverhampton Wanderers	2-1	Herd, Law	36,197
36	May 1	H	Sheffield United	1-3	Setters	31,878
37	4	H	Burnley	1-0	Law	30,266
38	6	H	Arsenal	2-3	Law 2	36,000
39	10	A	Birmingham City	1-2	Law	21,814
40	15	A	Manchester City	1-1	Quixall	52,424
41	18	H	Leyton Orient	3-1	Law, Charlton, 1 o.g.	32,759
42	20	A	Nottingham Forest	2-3	Giles, Herd	16,130

F.A. CUP

Round	Date	Venue	Opponents	Result	Goalscorers	Attendance
Rd 3	Mar 4	H	Huddersfield Town	5-0	Law (3), Quixall, Giles	47,703
Rd 4	Mar 11	H	Aston Villa	1-0	Quixall	52,265
Rd 5	16	H	Chelsea	2-1	Law, Quixall	48,298
Rd 6	30	H	Coventry City	3-1	Charlton (2), Quixall	44,200
S/F	Apr 27	N	Southampton	1-0	Law *(at Villa Park, Birmingham)*	68,312
FINAL	May 25	N	Leicester City	3-1	Law, Herd (2) *(at Wembley)*	100,000

Players: Gaskell, J. D.; Brennan, S. A.; Dunne, A. P; Stiles, N. P.; Foulkes, W. A.; Setters, M. E.; Giles, J. M.; Quixall, A.; Herd, D. G.; Law, D.; Moir, I.; Pearson, M.; Nicholson, J. J.; Lawton, N.; Chisnall, J. P.; McMillan, S. T.; Cantwell, N.; Gregg, H.; Charlton, R.; Crerand, P. T.; Haydock, F.; Walker, D.

League Appearances / League Scorers (totals shown by column)

DID YOU KNOW? United were the first British club to pay a six-figure transfer fee when they signed Denis Law for £115,000 from Torino in July 1962.

OPPOSITE PAGE

Top: F.A. CUP SEMI-FINAL: MANCHESTER UNITED 1 SOUTHAMPTON 0   27 April 1963. John Giles eludes Tony Knapp to get in a shot at Villa Park. (BNPC).

Top Inset: Scorer of the winning goal, Denis Law is congratulated by Nobby Stiles.

Middle Left: TEAM GROUP 1962/3: Back Row: Cantwell, Charlton, Gaskell, Foulkes, Quixall. 3rd Row: Matt Busby, Nicholson, Brennan, McMillan, Crompton (coach). 2nd Row: Giles, Herd, Setters, Dunne. Front: Stiles, Lawton. (MMUSC).

Middle Right: FA CUP WINNERS: MANCHESTER UNITED 3 LEICESTER CITY 1   25th May 1963. United players celebrate winning the FA Cup at Wembley. (Left to right): Charlton, Crerand, Cantwell, Quixall, and Herd. (MMUSC).

Bottom: United come home with the F.A. Cup and Albert Square is the scene of celebrations. (MMUSC).

F.A. CUP WINNERS 1962-3

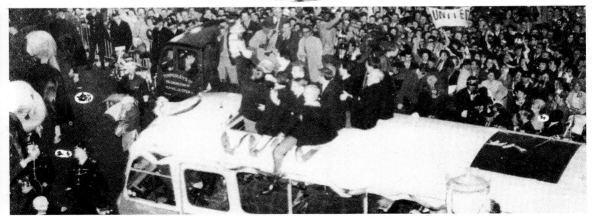

MANCHESTER UNITED

Match No.	Date	Venue	Opponents	Result	Goalscorers	Attendance
1	Aug 24	A	Sheffield Wednesday	D 3-3	Moir, Charlton 2	32,177
2	28	H	Ipswich Town	W 2-0	Law 2	39,921
3	31	H	Ipswich Town	W 7-2	Law 3(1 pen), Sadler, Setters, Moir, Chisnall	62,965
4	Sept 3	A	Everton	W 5-1	Chisnall 2, Law 2, Sadler	28,113
5	7	A	Birmingham City	D 1-1	Chisnall	36,874
6	11	H	Blackpool	W 3-0	Law, Charlton 2	47,400
7	14	H	West Bromwich Albion	W 1-0	Sadler	50,453
8	16	A	Blackpool	L 0-1		29,806
9	21	A	Arsenal	L 1-2	Moir	56,776
10	28	H	Leicester City	W 3-1	Setters, Herd 2	41,374
11	Oct 2	A	Chelsea	D 1-1	Setters	45,381
12	5	A	Bolton Wanderers	D 1-1	Herd	35,872
13	19	H	Nottingham Forest	W 2-1	Chisnall, Quixall	41,169
14	26	A	West Ham United	W 1-0	Herd	45,120
15	Nov 2	A	Blackburn Rovers	L 2-2	Herd, Law 4	41,426
16	9	H	Wolverhampton Wanderers	W 4-1	Law 3, Herd	34,189
17	16	A	Tottenham Hotspur	W 4-1	Law, Moore, Charlton	57,415
18	23	H	Aston Villa	W 4-1	Law 3, Herd	30,000
19	30	A	Liverpool	L 0-1		54,684
20	Dec 7	H	Sheffield United	W 2-1	Law 2	30,613
21	14	A	Stoke City	W 5-2	Herd, Law 4	52,232
22	21	H	Sheffield Wednesday	W 3-1	Herd 3	35,139
23	26	H	Everton	L 0-4		48,027
24	28	A	Burnley	L 1-6	Herd	35,764
25	Jan 11	H	Burnley	W 5-1	Herd 2, Moore 2, Best	25,624
26	18	A	Birmingham City	W 2-1	Sadler	44,686
27	Feb 1	H	West Bromwich Albion	W 4-1	Charlton, Best, Law 2	47,834
28	8	A	Arsenal	W 3-1	Herd, Law, Setters	25,624
29	11	H	Leicester City	L 2-3	Law, Herd	48,340
30	19	A	Bolton Wanderers	W 5-0	Best 2, Herd 2, Charlton	36,538
31	22	H	Blackburn Rovers	W 3-1	Chisnall, Law 2	33,926
32	March 7	A	West Ham United	W 2-0	Sadler, Herd	36,726
33	21	H	Tottenham Hotspur	W 3-2	Law, Moore, Charlton	27,027
34	23	A	Chelsea	L 1-1	Law	56,392
35	28	H	Fulham	D 2-2	Herd, Law	42,931
36	28	A	Wolverhampton Wanderers	D 2-2	Herd, Charlton	41,769
37	30	H	Fulham	W 3-0	Crerand, Foulkes, Herd	44,470
38	April 4	H	Liverpool	L 0-3		44,279
39	6	A	Aston Villa	W 1-0	Law	52,589
40	11	H	Sheffield United	L 1-3	Law, Moir	28,848
41	18	A	Stoke City	L 1-3	Charlton	27,587
42	25	H	Nottingham Forest	W 3-1	Law 2, Moore	45,670

F.A. CUP

Round	Date	Venue	Opponents	Result	Goalscorers	Attendance
Rd 3	Jan 4	H	Southampton	W 3-2	Moore, Herd, Crerand	29,164
Rd 4	25	A	Bristol Rovers	W 4-1	Law (3), Herd	35,772
Rd 5	Feb 15	A	Barnsley	W 4-0	Best (2), Law, Herd	38,076
Rd 6	29	H	Sunderland	D 3-3	Charlton, Best, 1 o.g.	63,700
Replay	Mar 4	A	Sunderland	D 2-2	Law, Charlton (after extra time)	68,000
2nd Replay	9	N	Sunderland	W 5-1	Law (3)(1 pen), Chisnall, Herd (at Huddersfield)	54,952
SF	14	N	West Ham United	L 1-3	Law (at Hillsborough, Sheffield)	65,000

League Appearances: 25, 40, 28, 41, 41, 33, 18, 20, 19, 30, 40, 17, 17, 30, 9, 18, 17, 17, 2, 1

Players: Gregg, H.; Dunne, A. P.; Cantwell, N.; Crerand, P. T.; Foulkes, W. A.; Setters, M. E.; Moir, I.; Chisnall, J. P.; Sadler, D.; Law, D.; Charlton, R.; Stiles, N. P.; Best, G.; Herd, D. G.; Quixall, A.; Moore, G.; Gaskell, J. D.; Brennan, S. A.; Anderson, W. J.; Tranter, W.

OPPOSITE PAGE

Top: MANCHESTER UNITED 4 TOTTENHAM HOTSPUR 1   *9 November 1963.*
Denis Law is congratulated by Graham Moore after scoring the first goal of his hat-trick.
Moore was making his United debut. Bobby Charlton and David Herd are on the left. (BNPC)

Bottom Left: MANCHESTER UNITED YOUTH TEAM GROUP 1963/4   *Back Row:*
Fitzpatrick, McBride, Farrar, Rimmer, Duff, Noble (Captain). Front Row: Anderson, Best,
Sadler, Kinsey, J. Aston. (JG)

Bottom Right: Club physio Ted Dalton discusses an injury problem with Harry Gregg in
October 1963. (BNPC)

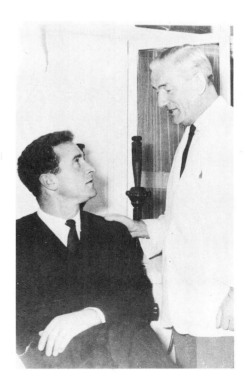

F.A. Semi-Finalists & European Fairs Cup Semi-Finalists   *Football League Champions*

MANCHESTER UNITED

Match No.	Date		Venue	Opponents	Result		Goalscorers	Attendance
1	Aug	22	H	West Bromwich Albion	D	2-2	Law, Charlton	52,007
2		24	H	West Ham United	L	1-3	Law	37,070
3		29	A	Leicester City	D	2-2	Sadler, Law	32,373
4	Sept	2	A	West Ham United	W	3-1	Connelly, Law, Best	45,123
5		5	A	Fulham	L	1-2	Connelly	36,291
6		8	H	Everton	D	3-3	Law, Connelly, Herd	63,024
7		12	H	Nottingham Forest	W	3-0	Herd 2, Connelly	45,012
8		16	A	Everton	W	2-1	Best, Law	49,968
9		19	A	Stoke City	W	2-1	Herd, Connelly	40,031
10		26	H	Tottenham Hotspur	W	4-1	Crerand 2, Law 2	53,058
11		30	A	Chelsea	W	2-0	Best, Law	60,769
12	Oct	6	A	Burnley	D	0-0		30,761
13		10	H	Sunderland	W	1-0	Herd	48,577
14		17	A	Wolverhampton Wanderers	W	4-2	Law 2, Herd, 1 o.g.	26,763
15		24	H	Aston Villa	W	7-0	Herd 2, Law 4, Connelly	36,807
16		31	A	Liverpool	W	2-0	Herd, Crerand	52,402
17	Nov	7	h	Sheffield Wednesday	W	1-0	Herd	50,178
18		14	A	Blackpool	W	2-1	Herd, Connelly	31,129
19		21	H	Blackburn Rovers	W	3-0	Best, Connelly, Herd	49,633
20		28	A	Arsenal	W	3-2	Law, Connelly	59,637
21	Dec	5	H	Leeds United	L	0-1		53,374
22		12	A	West Bromwich Albion	D	1-1	Law	28,504
23		16	A	Birmingham City	D	1-1	Charlton (pen)	25,721
24		26	H	Sheffield United	W	1-0	Best	37,295
25		28	A	Sheffield United	D	1-1	Herd	42,000
26	Jan	16	A	Nottingham Forest	D	2-2	Law 2	43,009
27		23	H	Stoke city	D	1-1	Law	50,392
28	Feb	6	a	Tottenham Hotspur	W	1-0	Law	58,639
29		13	H	Burnley	W	3-2	Best, Herd, Charlton	38,865
30		24	H	Sunderland	L	0-1		51,336
31		27	H	Wolverhampton Wanderers	W	3-0	Connelly Charlton 2	37,018
32	Mar	13	H	Chelsea	W	4-1	Best, Herd 2, Law	56,261
33		15	H	Fulham	W	4-1	Herd 2, Connelly 2	45,402
34		20	A	Sheffield Wednesday	L	0-1		33,549
35		22	A	Blackpool	W	2-0	Law 2	42,318
36	Apr	3	a	Blackburn Rovers	W	5-0	Charlton 3, Connelly, Herd	29,363
37		12	H	Leicester City	W	1-0	Herd	34,114
38		17	H	Leeds United	W	1-0	Connelly	52,368
39		19	A	Birmingham City	W	4-2	Best 2, Charlton, Cantwell	28,907
40		24	A	Liverpool	W	3-0	Law 2, Connelly	55,772
41		26	H	Arsenal	W	3-1	Best, Law 2	51,628
42		28	a	Aston Villa	L	1-2	Charlton	36,081

League Appearances

League Scorers

F.A. CUP

	Date		Venue	Opponents	Result		Goalscorers	Attendance
Rd 3	Jan	9	H	Chester	W	2-1	Best, Kinsey	45,660
Rd 4		30	A	Stoke City	D	0-0		53,009
Replay	Feb	3	H	Stoke City	W	1-0	Herd	50,814
Rd 5		20	H	Burnley	W	2-1	Law, Crerand	54,000
Rd 6	Mar	10	A	Wolverhampton Wanderers	W	5-3	Law 2, Herd, Best, Crerand	53,581
S/F		27	N	Leeds United	D	0-0		65,000
Replay		31	N	Leeds United	L	0-1		46,300

(at Hillsborough, Sheffield)
(at City Ground, Nottingham)

Players:
Gaskell, J. D.; Brennan, S. A; Dunne, A. P.; Setters, M. E.; Foulkes, W. A.; Stiles, N. P.; Connelly, J. M.; Charlton, R.; Herd, D. G.; Law, D.; Best, G.; Crerand, P. T.; Sadler, D.; Dunne, P. A. G.; Moir, I.; Fitzpatrick, J.; Aston, J.; Cantwell, N.; Kinsey, A.

OPPOSITE PAGE

Top: LEAGUE CHAMPIONS AND CHARITY SHIELD HOLDERS 1964/5 Team Group.
Back Row: Mr. L. Olive (Secretary), N. Stiles, T. Dunne, D. Gaskell, P. Dunne, P. Crerand, J. Fitzpatrick, Mr. J. Murphy (Ass. Manager). Centre Row: Mr. J. Crompton (Trainer), Mr. D. D. Haroun (Director), Mr. W. A. Young (Director), S. Brennan, D. Sadler, B. Foulkes, J. Aston, N. Cantwell, Mr. L. C. Edwards (Director), Mr. J. A. Gibson (Director), Mr. M. Busby (Manager). Front Row: J. Connelly, B. Charlton, D. Herd, D. Law, G. Best. (JG)

Bottom: MANCHESTER UNITED 0 LEEDS UNITED 0 F.A. Cup Semi-Final at Hillsborough 27th March 1965. David Herd heads the ball back into the Leeds goalmouth, policed by Jack Charlton. United lost the replay 0-1 at Nottingham. (JG)

FOOTBALL LEAGUE CHAMPIONS 1964/5

MANCHESTER UNITED

Match No.	Date	Venue	Opponents	Result	Goalscorers	Attendance
1	Aug 21	H	Sheffield Wednesday	W 1-0	Herd	37,524
2	24	A	Nottingham Forest	L 2-4	Aston, Best	33,744
3	28	A	Northampton Town	D 1-1	Connelly	21,140
4	Sept 1	H	Nottingham Forest	D 0-0		38,777
5	4	H	Stoke City	D 1-1	Herd	37,603
6	8	A	Newcastle United	W 2-1	Herd, Law	57,380
7	11	A	Burnley	L 0-3		30,235
8	15	H	Blackburn Rovers	D 2-2	Charlton, Law	30,401
9	18	H	Chelsea	W 4-1	Stiles	34,581
10	25	A	Newcastle United	W 5-0	Charlton, Aston	37,917
11	Oct 2	H	Arsenal	L 2-4	Charlton, Aston	56,757
12	9	A	Liverpool	W 2-0	Best, Law	58,161
13	16	H	Tottenham Hotspur	L 1-5	Charlton	58,051
14	23	A	Fulham	W 4-1	Herd 3, Charlton	32,716
15	30	H	Blackpool	W 2-1	Herd 2	24,703
16	Nov 6	a	West Bromwich Albion	D 2-2	Charlton, Law	38,823
17	13	A	Leicester City	W 5-0	Herd 2, Connelly, Charlton, Best	34,581
18	20	H	Sunderland	W 3-1	Best 2, Law	37,917
19	27	A	Liverpool	W 3-2	Best, Herd	32,924
20	Dec 4	H	West Bromwich Albion	W 3-2	Best 2, Herd	37,417
21	11	A	Tottenham Hotspur	W 5-1	Best, Herd, Charlton	32,624
22	18	H	Everton	D 0-0	Charlton, Law 2, Herd, 1 o.g.	39,270
23	27	H	Sunderland	D 0-0		54,102
24	Jan 1	A	Liverpool	L 1-2	Law	53,970
25	8	A	Sunderland	W 3-2	Best	39,162
26	15	H	Leicester City	W 5-0	Herd, Connelly	49,672
27	29	H	Sheffield Wednesday	W 3-1	Charlton, Herd 3	39,381
28	Feb 5	H	Northampton Town	W 6-2	Charlton 3, Law 2, Connelly	34,986
29	19	A	Stoke City	D 2-2	Herd, Connelly	36,667
30	26	H	Burnley	D 2-2	Sadler	33,018
31	Mar 12	A	Chelsea	L 0-2		49,892
32	19	H	Arsenal	W 2-1	Law, Stiles	47,246
33	Apr 9	H	Aston Villa	D 1-1	Cantwell	28,211
34	9	H	Leicester City	L 1-2	Connelly	42,593
35	16	A	Sheffield United	L 1-3	Sadler	22,330
36	25	A	Everton	D 0-0		50,843
37	27	H	Blackpool	W 2-1	Law, Charlton	26,983
38	30	A	West Ham United	L 2-3	Cantwell, Aston	36,416
39	May 7	A	West Bromwich Albion	D 3-3	Herd, Aston, Dunne, A.	22,609
40	9	A	Blackburn Rovers	W 4-1	Herd 2, Charlton, Sadler	14,513
41	16	H	Aston Villa	W 6-1	Herd 2, Sadler 2, Charlton, Ryan	23,034
42	19	H	Leeds United	D 1-1	Herd	35,008

F.A. CUP

Match No.	Date	Venue	Opponents	Result	Goalscorers	Attendance
Rd 3	Jan 22	H	Derby County	W 5-2	Law (2) (1 pen), Best (2), Herd	33,827
Rd 4	Feb 12	A	Rotherham United	D 0-0		54,263
Replay	Feb 15	H	Rotherham United	W 1-0	Connelly (after extra time)	23,500
Rd 5	Mar 5	A	Wolverhampton Wanderers	W 4-2	Law 2, Best, Herd	53,500
Rd 6	Mar 26	A	Preston North End	D 1-1	Herd	37,876
Replay	Mar 30	H	Preston North End	W 3-1	Law 2, Connelly	60,433
S/F	Apr 23	N	Everton	L 0-1	(at Burnden Park, Bolton)	60,000

Player columns (appearances, substitutions and scorers recorded across the season):
Dunne, P. A. G.; Brennan, S. A.; Dunne, A. P.; Crerand, P. T.; Foulkes, W. A.; Stiles, N. P.; Anderson, W. J.; Charlton, R.; Herd, D. G.; Best, G.; Aston, J.; Connelly, J. M.; Gaskell, J. D.; Cantwell, N.; Law, D.; Fitzpatrick, J.; Gregg, H.; Sadler, D.; Noble, R.; Ryan, J.; McBride, P.

League Appearances · Substitute Appearances · League Scorers

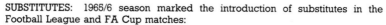

SUBSTITUTES: 1965/6 season marked the introduction of substitutes in the Football League and FA Cup matches:
Code: S* denotes substitute used
4* denotes player substituted
S denotes substitute not used
Note: Substitute appearances total includes used substitutes only.

Top: MANCHESTER UNITED 1 STOKE CITY 1   4 September 1965   John Connelly leaps over the Stoke 'keeper in this United attack, supported by Denis Law (No. 10). Maurice Setters, recently transferred to City, is on the right. (JG)

Bottom: FA CHARITY SHIELD 1965   MANCHESTER UNITED 2 LIVERPOOL 2   Old Trafford. Cantwell and Crerand watch agonisingly as the ball hits the back of the United net. (MMUSC)

MANCHESTER UNITED

Match No.	Date	Venue	Opponents	Result	Goalscorers	Attendance
1	Aug 20	H	West Bromwich Albion	W 5-3	Best, Stiles, Law 2, Herd	41,343
2	23	A	Everton	W 2-1	Law 2	60,657
3	27	A	Leeds United	L 1-3	Best	45,092
4	31	H	Everton	W 3-0	Foulkes, Connelly, Law	61,114
5	Sept 3	H	Newcastle United	W 3-2	Herd, Connelly, Law	44,448
6	7	A	Stoke City	L 0-3		44,337
7	10	A	Tottenham Hotspur	L 1-2	Law	56,295
8	17	H	Manchester City	W 1-0	Law	62,500
9	24	H	Burnley	W 4-1	Law, Herd, Crerand, Sadler	52,697
10	Oct 1	A	Nottingham Forest	L 1-4	Charlton	41,864
11	8	H	Blackpool	W 2-1	Law 2 (1 pen)	33,555
12	15	H	Chelsea	D 1-1	Law	56,789
13	29	A	Arsenal	W 1-0	Sadler	45,387
14	Nov 5	H	Chelsea	W 3-1	Aston 2, Best	55,988
15	12	A	Sheffield Wednesday	W 2-0	Charlton, Herd	46,942
16	19	A	Southampton	W 2-1	Charlton 2	29,498
17	26	H	Sunderland	W 5-0	Herd 4, Law	44,687
18	30	A	Leeds United	D 0-0		53,486
19	Dec 3	H	Aston Villa	W 2-1	Law, Best	39,014
20	10	A	Liverpool	D 2-2	Best 2 (1 pen)	39,937
21	17	H	West Bromwich Albion	W 4-3	Herd 3, Law	62,500
22	26	A	Sheffield United	L 1-2	Herd	42,752
23	27	H	Sheffield United	W 2-0	Crerand, Herd	59,392
24	31	A	Tottenham Hotspur	D 0-0		53,486
25	Jan 14	H	Tottenham Hotspur	W 1-0	Herd	57,366
26	21	A	Manchester City	D 1-1	Foulkes	63,000
27	Feb 4	H	Burnley	D 1-1	Sadler	40,165
28	11	H	Nottingham Forest	W 1-0	Law	62,727
29	25	A	Blackpool	W 4-0	Charlton 2, Law, 1 o.g.	47,158
30	Mar 3	H	Arsenal	D 1-1	Aston	63,363
31	11	A	Newcastle United	D 0-0		37,430
32	18	H	Leicester City	W 5-2	Herd, Charlton, Law, Sadler	50,281
33	25	A	Liverpool	D 0-0		53,813
34	27	H	Fulham	W 2-2	Best, Stiles	47,290
35	Apr 1	A	Fulham	W 2-1	Foulkes, Stiles	51,673
36	10	H	West Ham United	W 3-0	Charlton, Best, Law	61,308
37	18	A	Sheffield Wednesday	D 2-2	Charlton 2	51,101
38	22	A	Southampton	W 3-0	Charlton, Law, Sadler	54,921
39	29	H	Sunderland	D 0-0		43,570
40	May 6	H	Aston Villa	W 3-1	Aston, Law, Best	55,782
41	13	A	West Ham United	W 6-1	Charlton, Crerand, Foulkes, Best, Law 2 (1 pen)	38,424
42	13	H	Stoke City	D 0-0		61,071

F.A. CUP

	Date	Venue	Opponents	Result	Goalscorers	Attendance
Rd 3	Jan 28	H	Stoke City	W 2-0	Law, Herd	63,500
Rd 4	Feb 18	H	Norwich City	L 1-2	Law	63,405

Players (appearance columns): Gaskell, J. D.; Brennan, S. A.; Dunne, A. P.; Fitzpatrick, J.; Foulkes, W. A.; Stiles, N. P.; Best, G.; Law, D.; Charlton, R.; Herd, D. G.; Connelly, J. M.; Crerand, P. T.; Gregg, H.; Sadler, D.; Aston, J.; Stepney, A. C.; Noble, R.; Cantwell, N.; Ryan, J.; Anderson, W. J.; McGuinness, W.; Kidd, B.

League Appearances, Substitute Appearances and League Scorers totals are recorded at the foot of each column.

DID YOU KNOW! United won the Football League Championship for the seventh time in 1966/7, with 60 points, four ahead of Runners-up Nottingham Forest. Bill Foulkes played in 61 consecutive FA Cup-ties for United between 9 January 1954 and 28 January 1967, until injury kept him out of the 4th round tie with Norwich City on 18 January 1967. He also played in 45 European Cup-ties and held the United League appearance record of 563 games until this was surpassed by Bobby Charlton.

OPPOSITE PAGE

Top: FULHAM 2 MANCHESTER UNITED 2   27 March 1967   Pat Crerand challenges Johnny Haynes at Craven Cottage. (JG)

Middle: TRAINING SESSION Easter 1967. Taken the day before Bobby Noble's motor accident on his way home from the Sunderland match. (Left to right): Tony Dunne, Alex Stepney, Bobby Noble, Jack Crompton, Joe Glanville, Bill Foulkes, George Best and David Sadler. (JG)

Bottom: LEAGUE CHAMPIONS & CHARITY SHIELD HOLDERS 1966/7.
Back Row: Mr. L. Olive (Secretary), N. Cantwell, D. Sadler, D. Herd, B. Foulkes, J. Ryan, J. Crompton (Trainer), Mr. J. Murphy (Ass. Manager). Middle Row: Mr. W. A. Young (Director), Mr. L. C. Edwards (Chairman), D. Gaskell, S. Brennan, B. Charlton, J. Aston, P. Crerand, A. Stepney, Mr. J. A. Gibson (Vice Chairman), Mr. D. D. Haroun (Director). Front Row: J. Fitzpatrick, N. Stiles, A. Dunne, Mr. M. Busby, C.B.E. (Manager), D. Law, G. Best, R. Noble. (JG)

FOOTBALL LEAGUE
CHAMPIONS

MANCHESTER UNITED

Match No.	Date	Venue	Opponents	Result		Goalscorers	Attendance
1	Aug 19	A	Everton	L	1-3	Charlton	61,400
2	23	H	Leeds United	W	1-0	Charlton	53,016
3	26	A	Leeds United	W	1-0	Charlton	51,286
4	Sept 2	A	West Ham United	W	3-1	Kidd, Sadler, Ryan	36,562
5	6	A	Sunderland	W	1-1	Kidd	51,527
6	9	H	Burnley	D	2-2	Burns, Crerand	55,809
7	16	A	Sheffield Wednesday	D	1-1	Best	47,274
8	23	H	Tottenham Hotspur	W	3-1	Best 2, Law	58,779
9	30	A	Manchester City	W	2-1	Charlton 2	63,000
10	Oct 7	H	Arsenal	W	1-0	Aston	60,197
11	14	A	Sheffield United	W	3-0	Kidd, Aston, Law (pen)	29,170
12	21	H	Coventry City	W	4-0	Aston, Kidd, Charlton	54,283
13	28	A	Nottingham Forest	L	1-3	Best	49,946
14	Nov 4	H	Stoke City	W	1-0	Charlton	51,041
15	8	A	Leeds United	L	0-1		43,999
16	11	H	Liverpool	W	2-1	Best 2	54,515
17	18	A	Southampton	W	3-2	Aston, Kidd, Charlton	48,732
18	25	H	Chelsea	D	1-1	Kidd	54,712
19	Dec 2	A	West Bromwich Albion	W	2-1	Best 2	52,568
20	9	H	Newcastle United	D	2-2	Kidd, Dunne	48,400
21	16	A	Everton	W	3-1	Sadler, Aston, Law	60,736
22	23	H	Leicester City	D	2-2	Charlton, Law	40,104
23	26	H	Wolverhampton Wanderers	W	4-0	Best 2, Kidd, Charlton	63,450
24	30	A	Wolverhampton Wanderers	W	3-2	Charlton, Aston, Kidd	53,940
25	Jan 6	H	West Ham United	W	3-1	Best 2, Charlton, Aston	54,498
26	20	H	Sheffield Wednesday	W	4-2	Best 2, Charlton, Kidd	55,284
27	Feb 3	A	Tottenham Hotspur	W	2-1	Best, Charlton	57,790
28	17	H	Burnley	L	1-2	Best	31,965
29	24	A	Arsenal	W	2-0	Best, l.o.g.	46,417
30	Mar 2	H	Chelsea	L	1-3	Kidd	62,471
31	16	A	Coventry City	L	0-2		47,110
32	23	H	Nottingham Forest	W	3-0	Charlton, Best	61,978
33	27	H	Manchester City	L	1-3	Herd, Brennan, Burns	63,004
34	30	A	Stoke City	W	4-2	Best, Gowling, Aston, Ryan	30,141
35	Apr 6	H	Liverpool	L	1-2	Best	62,637
36	12	A	Fulham	W	4-0	Best	40,182
37	13	A	Southampton	D	2-2	Charlton, Best, Aston	30,079
38	15	H	Fulham	W	3-0	Charlton, Best, Aston	60,465
39	20	H	Sheffield United	W	1-0	Law	55,033
40	29	A	West Bromwich Albion	L	3-6	Law, Kidd 2	43,412
41	May 4	H	Newcastle United	W	6-0	Kidd 2, Best 3 (2 pen), Sadler	59,976
42	11	A	Sunderland	L	1-2	Best	62,963

F.A. CUP

Rd 3	Jan 27	H	Tottenham Hotspur	D	2-2	Best, Charlton	63,500
Replay	31	A	Tottenham Hotspur	L	0-1		57,200

League Appearances
League Scorers
Substitute Appearances

Player columns: Stepndey, A. C.; Brennan, S. A.; Dunne, A. P.; Crerand, P. T.; Foulkes, W. A.; Stiles, N. P.; Best, G.; Law, D.; Charlton, R.; Kidd, B.; Aston, J.; Sadler, D.; Ryan, J.; Burns, F.; Fitzpatrick, J.; Kopel, F.; Herd, D. G.; Gowling; Rimmer, J. J.; Sartori, C.

DID YOU KNOW! Following United's European Cup victory over Benfica, manager Matt Busby received a knighthood from the Queen in recognition of his services to football. Brian Kidd celebrated his 19th birthday by scoring one of the extra-time goals at Wembley in the European Cup Final.

OPPOSITE PAGE

Top: EUROPEAN CUP FINAL   Manchester United 4 Benfica 1   24 May 1968 at Wembley. (Left): Charlton heads the first goal. (Right): Best restores the lead in extra time. (JG)

Middle Left: Bobby Charlton receives the trophy. (JG)

Middle Right: Matt Busby and Louis Edwards return with the victorious players and the Cup on a tour of Manchester. (JG)

Bottom: EUROPEAN CUP SEMI-FINAL   Real Madrid 3 Manchester United 2   15 May 1968   United go through on away goals rule. (Left): Sadler heads the second goal from Crerands free-kick and (Right): Goalmouth action with Kidd and Foulkes. (JG)

EUROPEAN CHAMPIONS

1968

MANCHESTER UNITED

Match No.	Date	Venue	Opponents	Result	Goalscorers	Attendance	Stepney, A. C.	Brennan, S. A.	Dunne, A. P.	Crerand, P. T.	Foulkes, W. A.	Stiles, N. P.	Best, G.	Kidd, B.	Charlton, R.	Law, D.	Aston, J.	Sadler, D.	Kopel, F.	Fitzpatrick, J.	Gowling, A.	Burns, F.	Ryan, J.	Morgan, W.	Sartori, C.	James, S. R.	Rimmer, J. J.	Murphy, N.	Match No.
1	Aug 10	H	Everton	W	2-1	Best, Charlton	63,000	1	2	3	4	5	6	7	8	9	10	11	S											1
2	14	A	West Bromwich Albion	L	1-3	Charlton	38,299	1	2	3	4	5*		6	7	8	9	10	11	S*										2
3	17	A	Manchester City	D	0-0		63,000	1		3			6	7	8	9			11*	5	2	4	10	S*						3
4	21	H	Coventry City	W	1-0	Ryan	51,201	1		3	S		6	11	8	9			5	2	4		10	7						4
5	24	H	Chelsea	L	0-4		54,870	1	S	3	4		6	11	8	9			5	2			10	7						5
6	28	H	Tottenham Hotspur	W	3-1	Fitzpatrick 2, 1 o.g.	62,649	1	2	3			6	11	8	9	10		5		4			7						6
7	31	A	Sheffield Wednesday	L	4-5	Best, Law 2, Charlton	51,931	1	2	3*			6	11	8	9	10		5		4		S*	7						7
8	Sept 7	H	West Ham United	D	1-1	Law	63,274	1	S	2		5	6	11		9	10		8		4		3	7						8
9	14	A	Burnley	L	0-1		33,220	1	2		4		6	11	S	9	10		8		4		3	7						9
10	21	H	Newcastle United	W	3-1	Best 2, Law	47,262	1		2	4*		6	11	S*	9	10		5		8		3	7						10
11	Oct 5	H	Arsenal	D	0-0		61,843	1		2	4	5	6	11		9	10				8	S	3	7						11
12	9	A	Tottenham Hotspur	D	2-2	Crerand, Law	56,205	1		2	4	5	6	11		9	8				10		3*	7	S*					12
13	12	A	Liverpool	L	0-2		53,391	1	2		4		6			9			3	8	10		7		11	5		S		13
14	19	H	Southampton	L	1-2	Best	46,026	1		2	4	5*	6	11		9			8	3	S*			7	10					14
15	26	A	Queens Park Rangers	W	3-2	Best, Law, 1 o.g.	31,138	1		2	4		6	11	8	9	10		5		S			7						15
16	Nov 2	H	Leeds United	D	0-0		54,000	1	2	3	4		6	11	8	9	10		5		S			7						16
17	9	A	Sunderland	D	1-1	1 o.g.	33,151	1	2	3	4		6	11	8	9			5	S				7	10					17
18	16	H	Ipswich Town	D	0-0		45,796	1	2	3	4		6	11	8*	9	10		S*					7						18
19	23	A	Stoke City	D	0-0		30,639	1		3	4		6	8		9			2	10			S	7	11	5				19
20	30	H	Wolverhampton Wanderers	W	2-0	Best, Law	49,764	1		3	4		6*	11		9	10		5	2	S*			7	8					20
21	Dec 7	A	Leicester City	L	1-2	Law (pen)	36,303	1		2	4		6	11		9	10		5	S			3	7	8					21
22	14	H	Liverpool	W	1-0	Law	59,000	1		2	4		6	7		9	10			3	S			11	5					22
23	21	A	Southampton	L	0-2		26,194	1		2	4		6	7		9	10		8	S				11	5					23
24	26	A	Arsenal	L	0-3		62,218	1		2	4*		6	7	11	9	10			3				S*	5					24
25	Jan 11	A	Leeds United	L	1-2	Charlton	48,145	1		2	4		6	7		9	10		S	8			3	11	5					25
26	18	H	Sunderland	W	4-1	Law 3, Best	45,670		2				6	8		9	10			4			3	7	11	5	1	S		26
27	Feb 1	A	Ipswich Town	L	0-1		30,837	1		3	4		6	11	8	9			S		2			7	5					27
28	15	A	Wolverhampton Wanderers	D	2-2	Charlton, Best	44,023	1		3	4	S*		11	8	9			6		2			7	10*	5				28
29	Mar 8	H	Manchester City	L	0-1		63,388	1	2		4	5	6	11	8	9			S	10	3			7						29
30	10	A	Everton	D	0-0		57,746	1	2*	3	4	S*	6	7	8				11	10	9				5					30
31	15	A	Chelsea	L	2-3	James, Law (pen)	60,436	1		3	4		6	11	8	9				10	2			7	5					31
32	19	H	Queens Park Rangers	W	8-1	Morgan 3, Best 2, Stiles, Kidd, Aston	37,053	1		3	4		6	11	8			10	9		2			S	7	5				32
33	22	H	Sheffield Wednesday	W	1-0	Best	45,527	1		3	4		6	11	8			10	9	S	2				7	5				33
34	24	H	Stoke City	D	1-1	Aston	39,931	1		3	4		6	11	8			10	9	S*	2			7*		5				34
35	29	A	West Ham United	D	0-0		41,546	1		3*	4		6	11	8			10	9	S*	2			7		5				35
36	31	A	Nottingham Forest	W	1-0	Best (pen)	41,828	1		4	S	3		11	8			10	9	6	2			7		5				36
37	Apr 2	H	West Bromwich Albion	W	2-1	Best 2	38,846	1		4	S*	3		11	8				9	6	2			10*	7	5				37
38	5	H	Nottingham Forest	W	3-1	Morgan 2, Best	51,952	1		4	S	3		11	8			10	9	6	2				7	5				38
39	8	A	Coventry City	L	1-2	Fitzpatrick	45,398	1		4	S	3	9	8	10			11	6		2				7	5				39
40	12	A	Newcastle United	L	0-2		45,370		4			3	11	8	9			10	S	6	2				7	5	1			40
41	19	H	Burnley	W	2-0	Best, 1 o.g.	52,616	2		4	5		6	11	8			10	9		3				7	5	1			41
42	May 17	H	Leicester City	W	3-2	Best, Morgan, Law	45,900	1		4	5		6	11	8			10	9		S			3	7		1			42
			League Appearances					38	13	33	35	10	41	41	28	32	30	13	26	7	28	2	14	6	29	11	21	4	0	
			Substitute Appearances															1				2	1	2		2			0	
			League Scorers								1			1	18	1	5	14	2			3		1	6			4 o.g.	

F.A. CUP

	Date	Venue	Opponents	Result	Goalscorers	Attendance	Stepney	Brennan	Dunne	Crerand	Foulkes	Stiles	Best	Kidd	Charlton	Law	Aston	Sadler	Kopel	Fitzpatrick	Gowling	Burns	Ryan	Morgan	Sartori	James	Rimmer	Murphy	
Rd 3	Jan 4	A	Exeter City	W	3-1	Fitzpatrick, Kidd, 1 o.g.	18,500	1		2			6	7*	8	9	10		S*		4		3		11	5				
Rd 4	25	H	Watford	D	1-1	Law	63,498			3	S		6	8		9	10			2	4			7	11	5	1			
Replay	Feb 3	A	Watford	W	2-0	Law 2	34,099	1		3	4		6	11	8	9	10		S		2				7	5				
Rd 5	11	A	Birmingham City	D	2-2	Law, Best	52,500	1		3	4		6	11	8	9	10		S		2				7	5				
Replay	24	H	Birmingham City	W	6-2	Law 3 (1 pen), Crerand, Kidd, Morgan	61,932	1		3	4	S	6	11	8	9	10		S		2				7	5				
Rd 6	Mar 1	A	Everton	L	0-1		63,464	1		3	4		6	11	8	9	10		S		2				7	5				

WORLD CLUB CHAMPIONSHIP

	Date	Venue	Opponents	Result	Goalscorers	Attendance	Stepney	Brennan	Dunne	Crerand	Foulkes	Stiles	Best	Kidd	Charlton	Law	Aston	Sadler	Kopel	Fitzpatrick	Gowling	Burns	Ryan	Morgan	Sartori	James	Rimmer	Murphy	
1st leg	Sep 25	A	Estudiantes de Plata	L	0-1		70,000	1		2	4	5	6	11		9	10		8				3		7					
2nd leg	Oct 16	H	Estudiantes de Plata	D	1-1	Morgan	63,428	1	2		3	4	5	6	11	8	9	10*							7	S*				

OPPOSITE PAGE

Top: WORLD CLUB CHAMPIONSHIP: Manchester United 1 Estudiantes De Plata (Argentina) 1 Willie Morgan scores United's goal at Old Trafford but the 'Reds' lost 1-2 on aggregate. (JG)

Middle: EUROPEAN CUP SEMI-FINAL Manchester United 1 A.C. Milan 0 15 May 1968. Kidd and Best watch this shot go just wide United lost the tie 1-2 on aggregate. (JG)

Bottom: MANCHESTER UNITED 3 NOTTINGHAM FOREST 1 5 April 1969. Wille Morgan again, scoring the first goal. Alan Hill and John Winfield are the Foresters. (JG)

F.A. Cup Semi-Finalists & Third Place in Competition — *Position: 8th*

F.L. Cup Semi-Finalists *Wilf McGuinness appointed team manager*

MANCHESTER UNITED

Match No.	Date	Venue	Opponents	Result	Goalscorers	Attendance
1	Aug 9	A	Crystal Palace	D 2-2	Charlton, Morgan	48,080
2	13	H	Everton	L 0-2		60,161
3	16	H	Southampton	L 1-4	Morgan	47,436
4	19	A	Everton	L 0-3		53,185
5	23	A	Wolverhampton Wanderers	D 0-0		50,783
6	27	H	Newcastle United	D 0-0		53,267
7	30	H	Sunderland	W 3-1	Best, Kidd, Givens	50,590
8	Sept 13	A	Leeds United	D 2-2	Best 2	44,271
9	17	H	Liverpool	W 1-0	Morgan	59,387
10	20	A	Sheffield Wednesday	W 3-1	Kidd, Best 2	39,938
11	27	H	Arsenal	D 2-2	Best, Sadler	59,484
12	Oct	H	West Ham United	W 5-2	Burns, Best 2, Charlton, Kidd	58,579
13	Oct 4	A	Derby County	L 0-2		40,724
14	8	H	Coventry City	W 2-1	Aston, Law	31,044
15		H	Southampton	W 2-1	Best, Burns, Kidd	52,261
16		A	Nottingham Forest	L 1-2	Best	52,732
17	25	A	West Bromwich Albion	L 0-2		36,504
18	Nov 1	H	Stoke City	D 0-0	Kidd	42,006
19	8	A	Crystal Palace	W 2-1	Sartori, Morgan	41,643
20		H	Tottenham Hotspur	L 1-2	Kidd	60,514
21	22	A	Manchester City	L 0-4		63,013
22	29	H	Burnley	D 1-1	Charlton, Kidd 2	53,083
23	Dec 6	A	Chelsea	L 2-3?		49,244
24	13	H	Liverpool	W 4-1	Ure, Morgan, Charlton, 1 o.g.	47,682
25		A	Wolverhampton Wanderers	D 0-0		52,732
26		H	Sunderland	D 1-1	Best, Sadler	36,504
27	Jan 10	H	Arsenal	W 2-1	Sartori, Morgan	41,335
28	17	A	West Ham United	D 0-0		41,643
29		A	Leeds United	D 2-2	Sadler, Morgan (pen)	38,740
30	31	H	Derby County	D 2-2	Sadler, Kidd	59,584
31	Feb 7	H	Ipswich Town	W 1-0	Kidd	30,076
32	10	A	Ipswich Town	W 1-0	Charlton	55,262
33	14	A	Stoke City	D 2-2	Sartori, Morgan (pen)	38,740
34	28	H	Burnley	D 3-3	Crerand, Law, Best	39,826
35	Mar 21	H	Chelsea	L 1-2	Morgan	61,479
36	28	A	Manchester City	L 1-2	Kidd	60,286
37	30	H	Coventry City	D 1-1	Kidd	41,335
38	31	A	Nottingham Forest	W 2-1	Gowling, Charlton	39,223
39	Apr 4	A	Newcastle United	L 1-5	Charlton	42,550
40	8	H	West Bromwich Albion	W 7-0	Fitzpatrick 2, Charlton 2, Gowling 2, Best	29,396
41	13	A	Tottenham Hotspur	L 1-2	Fitzpatrick	41,808
42	15	H	Sheffield Wednesday	D 2-2	Best, Charlton	39,273

League Appearances

Substitute Appearances

League Scorers

F.A. CUP

	Date	Venue	Opponents	Result	Goalscorers	Attendance
Rd 3	Jan 3	A	Ipswich Town	W 1-0	1 o.g.	29,552
Rd 4	Jan 24	A	Manchester City	W 3-0	Morgan (pen), Kidd 2	63,417
Rd 5	Feb 7	A	Northampton Town	W 8-2	Best 6, Kidd 2	21,771
Rd 6	Feb 21	H	Middlesbrough	D 1-1	Sartori	63,418
Replay	Feb 25	H	Middlesbrough	W 2-1	Charlton, Morgan (pen)	55,000
SF	Mar 14	N	Leeds United	D 0-0	(at Hillsborough, Sheffield)	55,000
Replay	Mar 23	N	Leeds United	D 0-0	(after extra time) (at Villa Park, Birmingham)	62,000
2nd Replay	26	N	Leeds United	L 0-1	(at Highbury)	56,000
*	Apr 10	N	Watford	W 2-0	Kidd 2	15,105

* 3/4 Place Play-off (at Highbury)

Player column headings (right-hand side):

Rimmer, J. J. — Dunne, A. P. — Burns, F. — Crerand, P. T. — Foulkes, W. A. — Sadler, D. — Morgan, W. — Kidd, B. — Charlton, R. — Law, D. — Best, G. — Givens, D. J. — Brennan, S. A. — Stepney, A. C. — Fitzpatrick, J. — Edwards, P. — Aston, J. — Ure, I. J. F. — Gowling, A. — Sartori, C. — Stiles, N. P. — Ryan, J. — James, S. R.

OPPOSITE PAGE

Top: MANCHESTER UNITED 1969-70   Back Row: D. Givens, K. Goodeve, D. Sadler, A. Stepney, J. Connaughton, J. Rimmer, J. McInally, N. Murphy, J. Hall, A. Gowling. Centre Row: Sir. M. Busby C.B.E. (General Manager), Mr. J. Aston (Coach), W. Watson, P. Woods, J. Ryan, B. Foulkes, S. Brennan, B. Daniels, B. Kidd, P. Edwards, N. Kelly, Mr. W. McGuinness (Chief Coach), Mr. J. Murphy (Ass. Manager). Front Row: Mr. J. Crompton (Trainer), N. Stiles, W. Morgan, D. Law, R. Charlton, P. Crerand, A. Dunne, J. Aston Jnr., F. Burns. Kneeling: C. Sartori, J. Fitzpatrick, P. O'Sullivan, G. Best. (JG)

Middle: FA CUP SEMI-FINAL: Manchester United 0 Leeds United 0   14 March 1970   Sprake saves from Morgan, with Charlton and Best closing in, at Hillsborough. (BNPC)

Bottom: New Manager Wilf McGuinness talking to the United players before a training session. (JG)

MANCHESTER UNITED

Match No.	Date	Venue	Opponents	Result	Goalscorers	Attendance
1	Aug 15	H	Leeds United	L 0-1		59,523
2	19	H	Chelsea	D 0-0		51,079
3	22	A	Arsenal	L 0-4		54,137
4	26	A	Burnley	W 2-0	Law 2	28,442
5	29	H	West Ham United	D 1-1	Fitzpatrick	50,959
6	Sept 2	H	Everton	W 2-0	Best, Charlton	51,220
7	5	A	Liverpool	D 1-1	Kidd	52,542
8	12	H	Coventry City	W 2-0	Best, Charlton	48,912
9	19	A	Ipswich Town	L 0-4		27,776
10	26	H	Blackpool	W 2-0	Best, Charlton	46,647
11	Oct 3	A	Wolverhampton Wanderers	L 2-3	Gowling, Kidd	38,629
12	10	H	Crystal Palace	L 0-1		42,969
13	17	A	Leeds United	D 2-2	Fitzpatrick, Charlton	50,169
14	24	H	West Bromwich Albion	W 2-1	Kidd, Law	43,278
15	31	A	Newcastle United	L 0-1		45,195
16	Nov 7	H	Stoke City	D 2-2	Sadler, Law	47,553
17	14	A	Nottingham Forest	W 2-1	Gowling, Sartori	36,384
18	21	A	Southampton	L 0-1		30,202
19	28	H	Huddersfield Town	D 1-1	Best	45,306
20	Dec 5	A	Tottenham Hotspur	D 2-2	Best, Law	55,693
21	12	H	Manchester City	L 1-4	Kidd	52,686
22	19	A	Arsenal	L 1-3	Sartori	33,182
23	26	A	Derby County	D 4-4	Kidd, Best, Law 2	34,068
24	Jan 9	H	Chelsea	W 2-1	Morgan (pen), Gowling	53,482
25	16	H	Burnley	D 1-1	Aston	40,135
26	30	A	Huddersfield Town	W 2-1	Law, Aston	41,464
27	Feb 6	H	Tottenham Hotspur	W 2-1	Morgan (pen), Best	48,965
28	20	A	Southampton	W 5-1	Gowling 4, Morgan	36,060
29	23	A	Everton	L 0-1		52,544
30	27	H	Newcastle United	W 1-0	Kidd	41,902
31	Mar 6	A	West Bromwich Albion	L 3-4	Kidd, Best, Aston	41,112
32	13	H	Nottingham Forest	W 2-0	Best, Law	40,473
33	20	A	Stoke City	W 2-1	Best 2	40,005
34	Apr 3	A	West Ham United	L 1-2	Best	38,507
35	10	H	Derby County	L 1-2	Law	45,691
36	12	A	Coventry City	W 1-0	Gowling	41,766
37	13	A	Wolverhampton Wanderers	W 1-0	Best	33,849
38	17	A	Crystal Palace	W 5-3	Law 3, Best 2	39,146
39	19	H	Liverpool	L 0-2		44,004
40	24	A	Ipswich Town	W 3-2	Best (pen), Charlton, Kidd	31,662
41	May 1	H	Blackpool	D 1-1	Law	34,000
42	5	A	Manchester City	W 4-3	Best 2, Charlton, Law	43,626

FA CUP

	Date	Venue	Opponents	Result	Goalscorers	Attendance
Rd 3	Jan 2	H	Middlesbrough	D 0-0		47,924
Replay	5	A	Middlesbrough	L 1-2	Best	41,000

Players (appearance columns): Stepney, A. C.; Edwards, P.; Dunne, A. P.; Crerand, P. T.; Ure, I. J. F.; Sadler, D.; Fitzpatrick, J.; Stiles, N. P.; Charlton, R.; Kidd, B.; Best, G.; Morgan, W.; Law, D.; Rimmer, J. J.; Gowling, A.; Watson, W.; Burns, F.; James, S. R.; Aston, J.; Sartori, C.; O'Neil, T. P.; Young, A. T.; Donald, I.

League Appearances — Substitute Appearances — League Scorers

DID YOU KNOW? On 5 August 1970, United made history by taking part in the first ever penalty tie-breaker in English Senior Football. They beat Hull City 4-3 on penalties after a 1-1 draw at 90 minutes in the semi-final of the Watney Cup. In December 1970, with United dangerously close to the relegation zone, Wilf McGuinness was relieved of the manager's post, to resume duties as coach to the reserve team. Sir Matt Busby took over as caretaker-manager.

OPPOSITE PAGE

Top: THE OLD RIVALS. *Sir Matt Busby and Manchester City manager Joe Mercer, friends and rivals since the 1930's, are presented with momento's prior to the local 'derby' match in 1970. The occasion provided Eamonn Andrews with the opportunity to surprise Sir Matt with a second 'This is Your Life' appearance on Thames Television. (TT/JM)*

TRAINING SESSION PRIOR TO FA CUP SEMI-FINAL REPLAY v Leeds March 1970. (Left to Right): Kidd, Best, Crompton, McGuinness, Burns, Dunne, Edwards. (BNPC)

THE OLD RIVALS

MANCHESTER UNITED

Match No.	Date	Venue	Opponents	Result	Goalscorers	Attendance
1	Aug 14	A	Derby County	D 2-2	Law, Gowling	35,386
2	18	H	Chelsea	W 3-2	Kidd, Morgan (pen), Charlton	54,663
3	20	H	Arsenal **	W 3-1	Gowling, Charlton, Kidd (**at Anfield, Liverpool)	27,649
4	23	A	West Bromwich Albion ***	W 3-1	Best 2, Gowling (***at Victoria Ground, Stoke)	23,146
5	28	A	Wolverhampton Wanderers	D 1-1	Best	46,479
6	31	H	Everton	L 0-1		52,151
7	Sept 4	A	Ipswich Town	W 1-0	Best	45,656
8	11	H	Crystal Palace	W 3-1	Kidd, Law 2	43,720
9	18	A	West Ham United	W 4-2	Best 3, Charlton	53,339
10	25	H	Liverpool	D 2-2	Law, Charlton	55,642
11	Oct 2	H	Sheffield United	W 2-0	Best, Gowling	51,735
12	9	A	Huddersfield Town	W 3-0	Best, Law, Charlton	33,458
13	16	H	Derby County	W 1-0	Best	53,247
14	23	A	Newcastle United	W 1-0	Best	55,603
15	30	H	Leeds United	L 0-1		53,884
16	Nov 6	A	Manchester City	D 3-3	McIlroy, Kidd, Gowling	63,326
17	13	H	Tottenham Hotspur	W 3-1	McIlroy, Law 2	54,088
18	20	A	Leicester City	W 3-2	Kidd, Law 2	48,764
19	27	H	Southampton	W 5-2	Best 3, McIlroy, Kidd	30,323
20	Dec 4	A	Nottingham Forest	W 3-2	Law, Kidd 2	45,411
21	11	H	Stoke City	D 1-1	Law	33,875
22	18	A	Ipswich Town	D 0-0		29,213
23	27	H	Coventry City	D 2-2	Law, James	52,035
24	Jan 1	A	West Ham United	L 0-3		41,990
25	8	H	Wolverhampton Wanderers	L 1-3	McIlroy	47,626
26	22	H	Chelsea	L 0-1		55,927
27	29	A	West Bromwich Albion	L 1-2	Kidd	46,992
28	Feb 12	H	Newcastle United	L 0-2		44,983
29	19	A	Liverpool	L 0-3		54,000
30	Mar 4	A	Tottenham Hotspur	L 0-2	Burns	54,814
31	8	H	Everton	D 0-0		38,415
32	11	A	Huddersfield Town	W 2-0	Best, Storey-Moore	53,581
33	25	H	Crystal Palace	W 4-0	Gowling, Charlton, Storey-Moore, Law	41,550
34	Apr 1	A	Coventry City	W 3-2	Best, Storey-Moore, Charlton	37,870
35	3	H	Liverpool	L 0-3		54,000
36	4	A	Sheffield United	D 1-1	Sadler	45,045
37	8	H	Leicester City	L 0-2		38,649
38	12	A	Manchester City	L 1-3	Buchan	56,362
39	15	H	Southampton	W 3-2	Best (pen), Storey-Moore, Kidd	38,437
40	22	A	Nottingham Forest	W 3-2	Best, Storey-Moore, Kidd	35,063
41	25	A	Arsenal	L 0-3		49,125
42	29	H	Stoke City	W 3-0	Charlton, Storey-Moore, Best (pen)	34,959

F.A. CUP

Round	Date	Venue	Opponents	Result	Goalscorers	Attendance
Rd 3	Jan 15	A	Southampton	D 1-1	Charlton	30,190
Replay	19	H	Southampton	W 4-2	Sadler, Aston, Best 2	50,956
Rd 4	Feb 5	A	Preston North End	W 2-0	Gowling 2	27,025
Rd 5	26	H	Middlesbrough	D 0-0		53,850
Replay	29	A	Middlesbrough	W 3-0	Morgan (P), Best, Charlton	39,683
Rd 6	Mar 18	H	Stoke City	D 1-1	Best	54,226
Replay	22	A	Stoke City	L 1-2	Best (after extra time)	49,192

Players (column headings across appearance grid): Stepney, A. C.; O'Neil, T. P.; Dunne, A. P.; Gowling, A.; James, S. R.; Sadler, D.; Morgan, W.; Kidd, B.; Charlton, R.; Law, D.; Best, G.; Fitzpatrick, J.; Aston, J.; Burns, F.; Sartori, C.; McIlroy, S. B.; Edwards, P.; Buchan, M. M.; Storey-Moore, I.; Young, A. T.; Cnnaughton, J. P.

League Appearances
Substitute Appearances
League Scorers

OPPOSITE PAGE

Top: FRANK O'FARRELL *started his period as manager at the start of 1971/2 with these players: Back Row: M. Musgrove (Coach), J. Fitzpatrick, A. Gowling, P. Edwards, S. James, J. Rimmer, A. Stepney, D. Sadler, I. Ure, T. Dunne, B. Charlton, F. O'Farrell (Manager). Front Row: F. Burns, B. Kidd, D. Law, G. Best, W. Morgan, C. Sartori, J. Aston. P. Crerand. (JG)*

Bottom Right: DENMARK XI 2 MANCHESTER UNITED 3 *2 August 1972 In this friendly at Poleoto, Allan Simonsen scores the second Danish goal after outmanouvering Rimmer and Dunne in Copenhagen. (BNPC)*

Bottom Left: (above) THE GREAT MOORE MUDDLE. *Ian Moore finally signed for United after a transfer wrangle with Derby and his former club Forest.*
(Below): Ian scores on his United debut with this powerful header against Huddersfield at Old Trafford. (MMUSC)

The great Moore muddle

IAN MOORE at Derby: The fans he left behind.

Step-by-step, how the biggest squabble in Soccer unfolded

by
ROBERT FINDLAY Sports Editor

LAST night the biggest Power Game struggle in Soccer came to an end when 27-year-old Ian Moore finally signed for Manchester United in a £200,000 transfer deal.

The fortunes and futures of three big clubs had been at stake in the battle for Nottingham Forest's international forward.

Yesterday, as Forest disputed the deal and waited for him to _____ for duty, Ian Moore _____'s _____

around £200,000 after Everton and Wolves dropped out of the bidding.

But Nottingham Forest were against a transfer to Derby for two reasons. One, they believed Derby—unlike wealthy Manchester United—would not be able to pay cash down. Two, they feared fans would leave them to watch Moore play at nearby Derby.

Forest's cool thinking gave Frank O'Farrell a head start against his rival Brian Clough, whose style and temperament could hardly be more different.

The _____

Brian Clough decided to telephone Forest's manager, Matt Gillies, at nearby Nottingham and push for action — for his own bid for Moore. Gillies promised to ring back. In half an hour, but the time passed without a call.

"And the silence rang warning bells at the Derby club's HQ. Finally, Derby's chairman, Sam Longson, put through a call to Gillies, who admitted: 'Manchester United are meeting Moore at the moment.'

"Where?" asked Longson.

Gillies refused to say.

"I've got Ian Moore with me," he said. "He won _____

"staggered" and "distressed" Nottingham Forest were, said, deploring the game of _____ dignity it deserves.

However, he insisted: 'Ian Moore is our player.' And once it, he produced Moore charming football crowds Derby as 'our new signing.'

But after a few hours' puzzlement during which believed Clough had to behaved Clough into half 'We still expect to sign Moore he said.

On Friday Moore believes he belonged to Derby. I night, he was bound to the boss of Manchester United. But body believes that the team of the past 72 hours will affect _____ so determined to _____

Tommy Docherty appointed team manager

MANCHESTER UNITED

Match No.	Date	Venue	Opponents	Result	Goalscorers	Attendance
1	Aug 12	H	Ipswich Town	L 1-2	Law	51,489
2	15	A	Liverpool	L 0-2		54,779
3	19	A	Everton	L 0-2		52,348
4	23	H	Leicester City	D 1-1	Best (pen)	40,067
5	26	H	Arsenal	D 0-0		48,108
6	30	A	Chelsea	D 0-0		44,482
7	Sept 2	A	West Ham United	D 2-2	Best, Storey-Moore	32,372
8	9	H	Coventry City	L 0-1		37,073
9	16	A	Wolverhampton Wanderers	L 0-2		34,049
10	23	H	Derby County	W 3-0	Morgan, Storey-Moore, Davies	48,255
11	30	H	Sheffield United	L 0-1		37,347
12	Oct 7	A	West Bromwich Albion	D 2-2	Best (pen), Storey-Moore	39,209
13	14	H	Birmingham City	W 1-0	MacDougall	52,104
14	21	A	Newcastle United	L 1-2	Charlton	38,170
15	28	H	Tottenham Hotspur	L 1-4	Charlton	52,497
16	Nov 4	A	Leicester City	D 2-2	Best, Davies	32,575
17	11	H	Liverpool	W 2-0	Davies, MacDougall	53,944
18	18	A	Manchester City	L 0-3		52,050
19	25	H	Southampton	W 2-1	Davies, MacDougall	36,073
20	Dec 2	A	Norwich City	W 2-0	Storey-Moore, MacDougall	35,770
21	9	H	Stoke City	L 0-2		41,347
22	16	A	Crystal Palace	L 0-5		39,897
23	23	H	Leeds United	D 1-1	MacDougall	46,382
24	26	A	Derby County	L 1-3	Kidd	35,093
25	Jan 6	H	Arsenal	L 1-3	Kidd	56,194
26	20	A	West Ham United	D 2-2	Charlton (pen), Macari	50,878
27	24	H	Everton	D 0-0		58,970
28	27	A	Coventry City	D 1-1	Holton	42,911
29	Feb 10	H	Wolverhampton Wanderers	W 2-1	Charlton 2 (1 pen)	52,089
30	17	A	Ipswich Town	L 1-4	Macari	31,918
31	Mar 3	H	West Bromwich Albion	W 2-1	Kidd, Macari	46,735
32	10	A	Birmingham City	L 1-3	Macari	51,278
33	17	H	Newcastle United	W 2-1	Holton, Martin	48,426
34	24	A	Tottenham Hotspur	D 1-1	Graham	49,751
35	31	A	Southampton	W 2-0	Charlton, Holton	23,161
36	Apr 7	H	Norwich City	W 1-0	Martin	48,593
37	14	A	Crystal Palace	W 2-0	Kidd, Morgan	46,895
38	18	H	Stoke City	D 2-2	Macari, 1 o.g.	37,051
39	21	A	Leeds United	W 1-0	Anderson	45,450
40	23	H	Manchester City	D 0-0		61,500
41	28	H	Sheffield United	L 1-2	Kidd	57,280
42	28	A	Chelsea	L 0-1		44,184

F.A. CUP

Rd 3	Jan 13	A	Wolverhampton Wanderers	L 0-1		40,005

Players: Stepney, A. C.; O'Neil, T. P.; Dunne, A. P.; Morgan, W.; James, S. R.; Buchan, M. M.; Best, G.; Kidd, B.; Charlton, R.; Law, D.; Storey-Moore, I; McIlroy, S. B.; Young, A. T.; Sadler, D.; Fitzpatrick, J.; Donald, I.; Davies, W. R.; MacDougall, E. J.; Watson, W.; Edwards, P.; Forsyth, A.; Graham, G.; Holton, J. A.; Macari, L.; Martin, M. P.; Rimmer, J. J.; Anderson, W.; Fletcher, P.; Sidebottom, A.; Young, E. R.

League Appearances · Substitute Appearances · League Scorers

DID YOU KNOW? 1972/3 marked the end of a unique era for United with the departure from Old Trafford of Bobby Charlton, Denis Law and George Best. Charlton holds the club record of 606 league appearances, played between 6 October 1956 and 28 April 1973. In his International career he scored 49 goals in 106 games for England. Denis Law holds the goalscoring record for Scotland with 30 goals in 55 games.

CALL THE DOC!

Top: MANCHESTER UNITED MARCH 1973. This is the squad new manager Tommy Docherty took over, but it was soon to be dismantled. Back Row: T. Cavanagh (Trainer), T. Docherty (Manager), D. Sadler, D. Law, J. Holton, A. Stepney, M. Martin, G. Graham, W. Davies, A. Forsyth, M. Buchan, P. Crerand (Ass. Manager). Front Row: W. Morgan, T. MacDougall, T. Young, B. Charlton, L. Macari, B. Kidd, Ian Storey-Moore. (JG)

Middle Right: TOMMY DOCHERTY. He was appointed manager in early 1973. (MMUSC)

Middle Left: VATICAN CITY 23 March 1973. Officials and players of United had an audience with Pope Paul VI on their arrival in Rome for the English-Italian Tournament match against Lazio. (BNPC)

Bottom: MANAGERLESS!! In the tea-room at 'The Cliff' training ground 21 December 1972, following the dismissal of Frank O'Farrell and prior to Docherty's appointment. The players are (Left to Right): Buchan, Law, MacDougall, Dunne and Sadler. Directors (at rear) are Mr. A. Gibson, Mr. W. Young, Mr. Louis Edwards, Mr. Martin Edwards and Sir Matt Busby. (BNPC)

MANCHESTER UNITED

Match No.	Date	Venue	Opponents	Result	Goalscorers	Attendance
1	Aug 25	A	Arsenal	L 0-3		51,501
2	29	A	Stoke City	L 0-1	James	43,614
3	Sept 1	H	Queens Park Rangers	W 2-1	Holton, McIlroy	44,156
4	5	A	Leicester City	L 0-1		29,152
5	8	A	Ipswich Town	L 1-2	Anderson	22,023
6	12	H	Leicester City	L 1-2	Stepney (pen)	40,793
7	15	H	West Ham United	W 3-1	Kidd 2, Storey-Moore	44,757
8	22	A	Leeds United	D 0-0		47,058
9	29	H	Liverpool	D 0-0		53,882
10	Oct 6	A	Wolverhampton Wanderers	L 1-2	McIlroy	32,962
11	13	H	Derby County	W 1-0	Stepney (pen)	43,724
12	20	A	Birmingham City	D 0-0		48,957
13	27	A	Burnley	D 0-0		31,796
14	Nov 3	H	Chelsea	D 2-2	Young, Greenhoff	48,036
15	10	A	Tottenham Hotspur	L 1-2	Best	42,756
16	17	A	Newcastle United	L 2-3	Graham, Macari	40,252
17	24	H	Norwich City	D 0-0	McIlroy, Macari	36,338
18	Dec 8	H	Southampton	D 0-0		31,648
19	15	A	Coventry City	L 2-3	Best, Morgan	28,589
20	22	A	Liverpool	L 0-2		40,420
21	26	H	Sheffield United	L 1-2	Macari	38,653
22	29	H	Ipswich Town	W 2-0	McIlroy, Macari	36,365
23	Jan 1	A	Queens Park Rangers	L 0-3		32,339
24	12	A	West Ham United	L 1-2	Macari	34,147
25	19	H	Arsenal	L 1-3	James	38,589
26	Feb 2	H	Coventry City	L 0-1	McIlroy	25,313
27	9	H	Leeds United	D 2-2	Greenhoff, Houston	60,025
28	16	A	Derby County	L 2-2		29,987
29	23	H	Wolverhampton Wanderers	D 0-0	Macari	39,260
30	Mar 2	H	Sheffield United	W 1-0	Macari	29,203
31	13	A	Manchester City	D 0-0		51,331
32	16	H	Birmingham City	D 0-0		37,768
33	23	A	Tottenham Hotspur	L 0-1		36,278
34	30	H	Chelsea	W 3-1	Morgan, Daly, McIlroy	28,602
35	Apr 3	A	Burnley	D 3-3	McIlroy, Forsyth, Holton	33,336
36	6	A	Norwich City	W 2-0	Macari, Greenhoff	28,223
37	13	H	Newcastle United	W 1-0	McCalliog	44,751
38	15	H	Everton	W 3-0	McCalliog 2, Houston	48,424
39	20	A	Southampton	D 1-1	McCalliog (pen)	30,789
40	23	A	Everton	L 0-1		46,093
41	27	H	Manchester City	L 0-1		56,996
42	29	A	Stoke City	L 0-1		27,392

F.A. CUP

	Date	Venue	Opponents	Result	Goalscorers	Attendance
Rd 3	Jan 5	H	Plymouth Argyle	W 1-0	Macari	31,810
Rd 4	26	A	Ipswich Town	L 0-1		37,177

Players (appearance columns, listed right of table):

Stepney, A. C.; Young, A. T.; Buchan, M. M.; Daly, G. A.; Holton, J. A.; James, S. R.; Morgan, W.; Anderson, W.; Macari, L.; Graham, G.; Martin, M. P.; McIlroy, S. B.; Fletcher, P.; Sidebottom, A.; Sadler, D.; Kidd, B.; Greenhoff, B.; Storey-Moore, I.; Buchan, G.; Forsyth, A.; Best, G.; Griffiths, C. L.; Houston, S. M.; Bielby, P. A.; McCalliog, J.

Summary rows: League Appearances · Substitute Appearances · League Scorers

DID YOU KNOW? United's relegation fate was sealed on the last Saturday of the 1973/4 season that had seen the forwards score the fewest number of goals in a campaign since 1893/4. They found the net only 30 times in 42 matches. In the final game, against Manchester City at Old Trafford, Denis Law scored the City winner only minutes from time. After a crowd invasion of the pitch the match was abandoned, but the 0-1 result allowed to stand. United were relegated after 36 years in the First Division.

OPPOSITE PAGE

Top: BEATEN BY THE PUP! This dog brought some amusement ot Old Trafford on 14 December 1974 when it interrupted play against Orient. Lou Macari, with help from the referee, manages to chase it from the pitch in this marvellous photograph taken by Daily Mirror photographer P. Sheppard. (BPNC)

Bottom: SOUTHAMPTON 1 MANCHESTER UNITED 1   20th April 1974   United made a brave, vain attempt to avoid relegation, going six matches without defeat in March and April. Jim McCalliog is mobbed after scoring from the spot against fellow strugglers at the Dell. (BNPC)

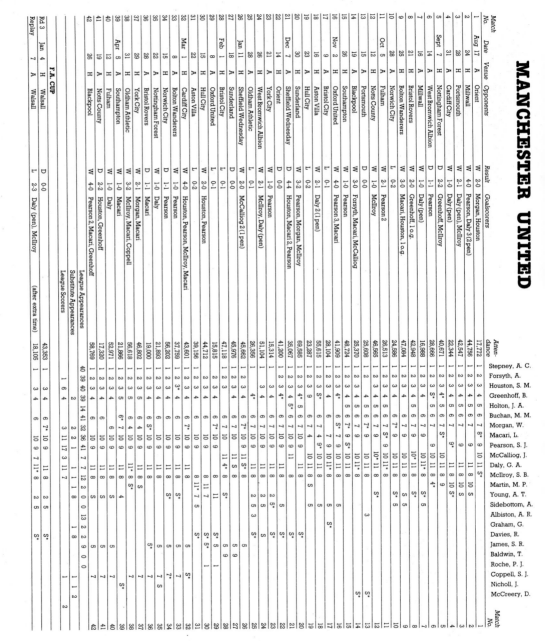

MANCHESTER UNITED

Match No.	Date	Venue	Opponents	Result	Goalscorers	Attendance
1	Aug 17	A	Orient	W 2-0	Morgan, Houston	17,772
2	24	H	Millwall	W 4-0	Pearson, Daly 3(2 pen)	44,756
3	28	A	Portsmouth	W 2-1	Daly(pen), McIlroy	42,547
4	31	A	Cardiff City	W 1-0	Daly(pen)	22,344
5	Sept 7	H	Nottingham Forest	D 2-2	Greenhoff, McIlroy	40,671
6	14	A	West Bromwich Albion	D 1-1	Pearson	28,666
7	16	A	Millwall	W 1-0	Daly(pen)	16,988
8	21	H	Bristol Rovers	W 2-0	Greenhoff, 1 o.g.	42,948
9	25	H	Bolton Wanderers	W 3-0	Macari, Houston, 1 o.g.	47,084
10	28	A	Norwich City	L 0-2		24,586
11	Oct 5	H	Fulham	W 2-1	Pearson 2	26,513
12	12	H	Notts County	W 1-0	McIlroy	46,565
13	15	A	Portsmouth	D 0-0		25,608
14	19	A	Blackpool	W 3-0	Forsyth, Macari, McCalliog	28,370
15	26	H	Southampton	W 1-0	Pearson	48,724
16	Nov 2	A	Oxford United	W 4-0	Pearson 3, Macari	41,909
17	9	H	Bristol City	L 0-1		28,104
18	16	H	Aston Villa	W 2-1	Daly 2 (1 pen)	55,615
19	23	A	Hull City	L 0-2		23,287
20	30	A	Sunderland	W 3-2	Pearson, Morgan, McIlroy	69,586
21	Dec 7	H	Sheffield Wednesday	W 4-4	Houston, Macari 2, Pearson	36,067
22	14	H	Orient	D 0-0		41,200
23	21	A	York City	W 1-0	Pearson	15,314
24	26	A	West Bromwich Albion	W 2-1	McIlroy, Daly(pen)	51,104
25	28	H	Oldham Athletic	L 0-1		26,356
26	Jan 11	H	Sheffield Wednesday	W 2-0	McCalliog 2 (1 pen)	45,662
27	18	A	Sunderland	D 0-0		45,976
28	Feb 1	H	Bristol Rovers	L 0-1		47,118
29	8	A	Oxford United	L 0-1		15,815
30	15	H	Hull City	W 2-0	Houston, Pearson	44,712
31	22	A	Aston Villa	L 0-2		39,156
32	Mar 1	H	Cardiff City	W 4-0	Houston, Pearson, McIlroy, Macari	43,601
33	8	A	Bolton Wanderers	W 1-0	Pearson	37,789
34	15	H	Norwich City	D 1-1	Pearson	56,202
35	22	A	Nottingham Forest	W 1-0	Daly	21,893
36	28	H	Bristol City	D 1-1	Macari	19,000
37	29	H	York City	W 2-1	Morgan, Macari	46,802
38	31	A	Oldham Athletic	W 3-2	McIlroy, Macari, Coppell	56,618
39	Apr 5	A	Southampton	W 1-0	Macari	21,866
40	12	H	Fulham	W 1-0	Daly	52,971
41	19	A	Notts County	D 2-2	Houston, Greenhoff	17,320
42	26	H	Blackpool	W 4-0	Pearson 2, Macari, Greenhoff	58,769

F.A. CUP

Rd 3	Jan 4	H	Walsall	D 0-0		43,353
Replay	7	A	Walsall	L 2-3	Daly (pen), McIlroy	18,105 (after extra time)

Players: Stepney, A. C.; Forsyth, A.; Houston, S. M.; Greenhoff, B.; Holton, J. A.; Buchan, M. M.; Morgan, W.; Macari, L.; Pearson, S. J.; McCalliog, J.; Daly, G. A.; McIlroy, S. B.; Martin, M. P.; Young, A. T.; Sidebottom, A.; Albiston, A. R.; Graham, G.; Davies, R.; James, S. R.; Baldwin, T.; Roche, P. J.; Coppell, S. J.; Nicholl, J.; McCreery, D.

League Appearances — Substitute Appearances — League Scorers

DID YOU KNOW? In winning the Division Two Championship in 1974/5, United attracted an average home attendance of 48,388, second only to Newcastle United's record of 56,473 for the second division, set in 1947/8.

OPPOSITE PAGE

Top: SECOND DIVISION CHAMPIONS 1974-5. (Left to Right): Tommy Docherty (Manager), S. Coppell, B. Greenhoff, L. Macari, G. Daly, M. Buchan, A. Forsyth, S. Pearson, S. McIlroy. (JG)

Bottom Right: UNITED CAPTAIN Martin Buchan receives the Division Two Championship trophy from the Football League President Dick Wragg. (BNPC)

Bottom Left: Supporters show their gratitude to the players for achieving promotion back to Division One at the first attempt. (MMUSC)

SECOND DIVISION CHAMPIONS 1974/5

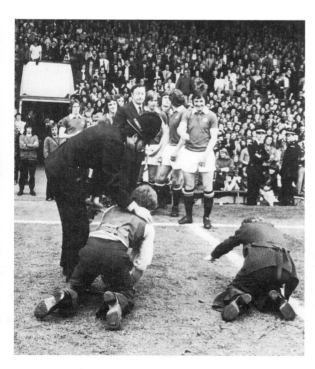

MANCHESTER UNITED

Match No.	Date	Venue	Opponents	Result		Goalscorers	Attendance
1	Aug 67	A	Wolverhampton Wanderers	W	2-0	Macari 2	32,348
2	19	H	Birmingham City	W	2-0	McIlroy 2	33,177
3	23	A	Sheffield United	W	5-1	Pearson 2, Daly, McIlroy, 1 o.g.	55,949
4	27	H	Coventry City	D	1-1	Pearson	52,169
5	30	A	Stoke City	W	1-0	1 o.g.	33,092
6	Sept 6	H	Tottenham Hotspur	W	3-2	Daly 2(1 pen), 1 o.g.	51,641
7	13	A	Queens Park Rangers	L	0-1		29,237
8	20	H	Ipswich Town	W	1-0	Houston	50,513
9	24	A	Derby County	L	1-2	Daly	33,187
10	27	A	Manchester City	D	2-2	McCreery, Macari	46,931
11	Oct 4	H	Leicester City	D	0-0		47,878
12	11	A	Leeds United	W	2-1	McIlroy 2	40,264
13	18	H	Arsenal	W	3-1	Coppell 2, Pearson	53,885
14	25	A	West Ham United	L	1-2	Macari	38,601
15	Nov 1	H	Norwich City	W	1-0	Pearson	50,587
16	8	A	Liverpool	L	1-3	Coppell	49,137
17	15	H	Aston Villa	W	2-0	Coppell, McIlroy	51,682
18	22	A	Arsenal	L	1-3	Pearson	40,102
19	29	H	Newcastle United	W	1-0	Daly	52,624
20	Dec 6	A	Middlesbrough	D	0-0		32,454
21	13	H	Sheffield United	W	4-1	Pearson 2, Hill, Macari	31,741
22	20	A	Wolverhampton Wanderers	W	1-0	Hill	44,269
23	23	H	Everton	D	1-1	Macari	41,732
24	27	A	Burnley	W	2-1	McIlroy, Macari	59,726
25	Jan 10	H	Queens Park Rangers	W	2-1	Hill, McIlroy	58,312
26	17	A	Tottenham Hotspur	D	1-1	Hill	49,189
27	31	H	Birmingham City	W	3-1	Forsyth, Macari, McIlroy	50,724
28	Feb 7	A	Coventry City	D	1-1	Macari	39,922
29	18	H	Liverpool	D	0-0		59,709
30	21	A	Aston Villa	L	1-2	Macari	50,094
31	25	H	Derby County	D	1-1	Pearson	59,632
32	28	A	West Ham United	W	4-0	Forsyth, Macari, McCreery, Pearson	57,220
33	Mar 13	H	Leeds United	W	3-2	Houston, Pearson, Daly	59,429
34	16	A	Norwich City	D	1-1	Hill	27,782
35	20	H	Newcastle United	W	4-3	Pearson 2, 2 o.g.s	41,427
36	27	A	Middlesbrough	W	3-0	Daly(pen), McCreery, Hill	58,527
37	Apr 10	A	Ipswich Town	L	0-3		34,889
38	17	H	Everton	D	1-1	McCreery, 1 o.g.	61,879
39	19	A	Burnley	W	1-0	Macari	27,418
40	21	A	Stoke City	L	0-1		53,879
41	24	H	Leicester City	L	1-2	Coyne	31,053
42	May 4	H	Manchester City	W	2-0	Hill, McIlroy	59,528

F.A. CUP

	Date	Venue	Opponents	Result		Goalscorers	Attendance
Rd 3	Jan 3	H	Oxford United	W	2-1	Daly (2 pens)	41,082
Rd 4	24	A	Peterborough United	W	3-1	Forsyth, McIlroy, Hill	56,352
Rd 5	Feb 14	A	Leicester City	W	2-1	Macari, Daly	34,000
Rd 6	Mar 6	H	Wolverhampton Wanderers	D	1-1	Pearson	59,433
Replay	9	A	Wolverhampton Wanderers	W	3-2	Pearson, Greenhoff, McIlroy (after extra time)	44,375
S/F	Apr 3	N	Derby County	W	2-0	Hill 2 (at Hillsborough, Sheffield)	55,000
FINAL	May 1	N	Southampton	L	0-1	(at Wembley)	100,000

Players (appearance columns): Stepney, A. C.; Forsyth, A.; Jackson, T.; Greenhoff, B.; Buchan, M. M.; Coppell, S. J.; McIlroy, S. B.; Pearson, S. J.; Macari, L.; Daly, G. A.; Nicholl, J. M.; McCreery, D.; Albiston, A. R.; Young, A. T.; Grimshaw, T.; Roche, P. J.; Hill, G. A.; Kelly, J. W.; Coyne, G.

League Appearances · Substitute Appearances · League Scorers (6 o.g.s)

OPPOSITE PAGE

Top: REPORTING FOR TRAINING 23 July 1976 Tommy Docherty and Tommy Cavanagh get the players together in this pre-season training session. (BNPC)

Bottom: MANCHESTER UNITED: F.A. Cup Winners & Charity Shield Holders 1976-7 Back Row: J. Nicholl, S. McIlroy, A. Stepney, B. Greenhoff, A. Albiston. Middle Row: Mr. Olive (Secretary), T. Cavanagh (Ass. Manager), Mr. M. Edwards (Director), Mr. Young (Director), Mr. Gibson (Director), Sir M. Busby (Director), Mr. Haroun (Director), D. McCreery, L. Brown (Physiotherapist). Front Row: S. Coppell, J. Greenhoff, M. Buchan, Mr. L. Edwards (Chairman), S. Pearson, L. Macari, G. Hill. (JG)

F.A. CUP WINNERS 1976/7

MANCHESTER UNITED

Match No.	Date	Venue	Opponents	Result	Goalscorers	Attendance
1	Aug 21	H	Birmingham City	D 2-2	Coppell, Pearson	58,898
2	24	A	Coventry City	W 2-0	Coppell, Pearson	26,775
3	28	A	Derby County	D 0-0		34,064
4	Sept 4	H	Tottenham Hotspur	L 2-3	Coppell, Pearson	60,723
5	11	A	Newcastle United	D 2-2	Pearson, B. Greenhoff	39,037
6	18	H	Middlesbrough	W 2-0	Pearson, 1 o.g.	56,712
7	25	A	Manchester City	W 3-1	Coppell, McCreery, Daly	48,861
8	Oct 2	A	Leeds United	W 2-0	Daly, Coppell	44,512
9	16	H	West Bromwich Albion	L 0-4		36,651
10	23	A	Norwich City	D 2-2	Daly (pen), Hill	34,356
11	30	H	Ipswich Town	L 0-1		57,416
12	Nov 6	A	Aston Villa	L 2-3	Pearson, Hill	46,324
13	20	H	Sunderland	D 3-3	Hill, Pearson, B. Greenhoff	42,685
14	27	A	Leicester City	D 1-1	Daly (pen)	26,421
15	Dec 18	H	West Ham United	W 2-0	Macari 2	55,366
16	27	A	Arsenal	L 1-3	McIlroy	39,572
17	Jan 1	H	Everton	W 4-0	Pearson, Houston, 1 o.g., Macari	56,786
18	22	A	Aston Villa	W 2-0	Pearson 2	55,446
19	Feb 5	A	Ipswich Town	L 1-2	Pearson	30,105
20	19	H	Coventry City	W 2-0	Macari 2	46,568
21	27	H	Bristol City	W 2-1	Pearson, B. Greenhoff	43,061
22	Mar 5	A	Birmingham City	W 3-2	Pearson, Houston, J. Greenhoff	35,316
23	12	A	West Bromwich Albion	L 1-2	Hill (pen), Coppell	54,044
24	16	H	Liverpool	W 1-0	Macari	46,946
25	19	A	Leeds United	W 1-0	Macari, McIlroy, Hill	57,487
26	23	H	Newcastle United	W 3-1	Pearson, Hill, Coppell	51,828
27	Apr 2	A	Norwich City	W 3-1	J. Greenhoff 3	58,595
28	9	H	Stoke City	W 3-0	Houston, Macari, Pearson	60,612
29	11	A	West Bromwich Albion	D 2-2	Pearson, Houston, J. Greenhoff	51,085
30	16	A	Sunderland	L 1-2	Hill 2	24,161
31	23	H	Everton	W 2-1	Hill 2	38,216
32	30	H	Leicester City	W 3-1	Houston, Macari, Pearson	53,102
33	May 3	A	Stoke City	L 1-2	J. Greenhoff	38,285
34	7	H	Queens Park Rangers	D 1-1	J. Greenhoff	49,161
35	11	A	Queens Park Rangers	D 0-0		38,785
36	14	H	Middlesbrough	L 0-3		21,744
37	16	A	Arsenal	W 1-0	Macari	50,788
38	16	A	Liverpool	L 0-1		50,123
39	7	A	Bristol City	D 1-1	Hill (pen)	32,166
40	11	A	Stoke City	D 3-3	Hill 2, McCreery	24,632
41	14	H	Arsenal	W 3-2	J. Greenhoff, Coppell, 1 o.g.	53,232
42	16	A	West Ham United	L 2-4	Hill, Pearson	29,311

F.A. CUP

Round	Date	Venue	Opponents	Result	Goalscorers	Attendance
Rd 3	Jan 8	H	Walsall	W 1-0	Hill	48,870
Rd 4	29	H	Queens Park Rangers	W 1-0	Macari	57,422
Rd 5	Feb 26	H	Southampton	D 2-2	Macari, Hill	58,103
Replay	Mar 8	A	Southampton	W 2-1	J. Greenhoff 2	29,137
Rd 6	19	H	Aston Villa	W 2-1	Houston, Macari	57,089
S/F	Apr 23	N	Leeds United	W 2-1	Coppell, J. Greenhoff (at Hillsborough, Sheffield)	55,000
FINAL	May 21	N	Liverpool	W 2-1	Pearson, J. Greenhoff (Wembley)	100,000

Summary rows: League Appearances 40 · Substitute Appearances · League Scorers · 4 o.g.s

Players:
Stepney, A. C.; Nicholl, J. M.; Houston, S. M.; Daly, G. A.; Greenhoff, B.; Buchan, M. M.; Coppell, S. J.; McIlroy, S. B.; Pearson, S. J.; Macari, L.; Hill, G. A.; Foggon, A.; McCreery, D.; Waldron, C.; McGrath, R. C.; Albiston, A. R.; Roche, P. J.; Paterson, S. W.; Clark, J.; Greenhoff, J.; Forsyth, A.; Jackson, T.

OPPOSITE PAGE

Top Left: 'KING TOM' A jubilant Tommy Docherty with the F.A. Cup following the victory over Liverpool. (MMUSC)

Top Right: F.A. CUP FINAL 1977   Manchester United 2 Liverpool 1 at Wembley. Lou Macari and Jimmy Greenhoff cannot conceal their delight as Macari's shot is deflected into the net by Greenhoff for the winning goal. (MMUSC)

Middle Left: The team returns to Manchester with the cup.

Bottom Left: MANCHESTER UNITED 2 ST. ETIENNE 0   5 October 1977.   Played at Plymouth, following crowd trouble at the 1st leg in France, United were ordered to play the 2nd leg away from Old Trafford. Jimmy Greenhoff is seen being foiled by the French 'keeper. (BNPC)

Bottom Right: ST. ETIENNE 1 MANCHESTER UNITED 1   European Cup Winners Cup. 4 September 1977. United defenders challenge the French centre forward Bartholemy. (BNPC)

F.A. CUP WINNERS 1976/7

Dave Sexton appointed team manager   *Position: 10th*

MANCHESTER UNITED

Match No.	Date	Venue	Opponents	Result	Goalscorers	Attendance
1	Aug 20	H	Birmingham City	W 4-1	Hill, Macari 3	28,086
2	24	H	Coventry City	W 2-1	Hill (pen), McCreery	55,726
3	27	A	Ipswich Town	D 0-0		59,547
4	Sept 3	A	Derby County	W 1-0	Macari	21,278
5	10	H	Manchester City	L 1-3	Nicholl	50,856
6	17	A	Chelsea	L 0-1		54,951
7	24	H	Leeds United	D 1-1	Hill	53,517
8	Oct 1	A	Liverpool	W 2-0	Macari, McIlroy	55,089
9	8	H	Middlesbrough	L 1-2	Coppell	27,052
10	15	A	Newcastle United	W 3-2	Coppell, Greenhoff J, Macari	55,096
11	22	H	West Bromwich Albion	L 0-4		26,822
12	29	A	Aston Villa	L 1-2	Nicholl	40,237
13	Nov 5	H	Norwich City	W 1-0	Pearson	44,729
14	12	A	Nottingham Forest	L 1-2	Hill	30,183
15	19	H	Arsenal	L 1-2	Pearson	53,055
16	26	A	Queens Park Rangers	D 2-2	Hill 2	24,367
17	Dec 3	H	Wolverhampton Wanderers	W 3-1	J. Greenhoff, McIlroy, Pearson	48,874
18	10	A	West Ham United	L 1-2	McGrath	54,374
19	17	H	Nottingham Forest	L 0-4		54,396
20	26	H	Everton	W 6-2	J. Greenhoff, Hill, Macari 2, McIlroy, l.o.g.	48,335
21	27	A	Leicester City	W 2-1	J. Greenhoff	24,706
22	31	A	Coventry City	L 0-3		53,501
23	Jan 14	A	Birmingham City	L 1-2	Coppell	23,321
24	21	H	Ipswich Town	W 2-1	McIlroy, Pearson	57,115
25	Feb 8	H	Derby County	W 4-0	Buchan, Hill 2 (1 pen), Pearson	43,457
26	11	A	Bristol City	D 1-1	Hill (pen)	32,849
27	25	H	Chelsea	D 2-2	Hill (pen), McIlroy	49,094
28	March 1	A	Liverpool	L 0-1		49,101
29	4	A	Leeds United	W 1-0	McIlroy	46,332
30	11	H	Middlesbrough	D 0-0		46,353
31	15	H	Newcastle United	L 0-1		25,825
32	18	A	Manchester City	D 2-2	Hill (2 pen)	58,398
33	25	H	West Bromwich Albion	D 1-1	McQueen	46,329
34	27	H	Leicester City	W 3-2	J. Greenhoff, Hill, Pearson	20,299
35	April 1	A	Everton	W 2-0	Coppell, Jordan	24,774
36	15	H	Aston Villa	L 1-3	Jordan	55,277
37	22	A	Arsenal	D 1-1	McIlroy	41,625
38	29	H	Queens Park Rangers	W 3-1	Grimes, Pearson 2 (1 pen)	40,809
39		A	Norwich City	W 3-0	Grimes, Jordan, McIlroy, Pearson	42,677
40		H	West Ham United	W 3-0	Grimes (pen), Jordan, McIlroy, Pearson	20,373
41		H	Bristol City	W 1-0	Pearson	54,089
42		A	Wolverhampton Wanderers	L 1-2	B. Greenhoff	25,868

F.A. CUP

	Date	Venue	Opponents	Result	Goalscorers	Attendance
Rd 3	Jan 7	H	Carlisle United	D 1-1	Macari	54,156
Replay	11	A	Carlisle United	W 4-2	Macari 2, Pearson 2	21,710
Rd 4	28	H	West Bromwich Albion	D 1-1	Coppell	57,086
Replay	Feb 1	A	West Bromwich Albion	L 2-3	Pearson, Hill	37,086 *(after extra time)*

League Appearances
Substitute Appearances
League Scorers

Players (appearance grid column headers):

- Stepney, A. C.
- Nicholl, J. M.
- Albiston, A. R.
- McIlroy, S. B.
- Greenhoff, B.
- Buchan, M. M.
- Coppell, S. J.
- McCreery, D.
- Pearson, S. J.
- Macari, L.
- Hill, G. A.
- Grimes, A. A.
- McGrath, R. C.
- Forsyth, A.
- Houston, S. M.
- Greenhoff, J.
- Rogers, M.
- Roche, P. J.
- Ritchie, A. T.
- Jordan, J.
- McQueen, G.

DID YOU KNOW? In the 1977/8 European Cup Winners Cup, crowd trouble at the away tie with St. Etienne of France led to United being expelled from the competition. However, UEFA relented and instead ordered the 2nd leg to be played away from Old Trafford. The match was played at Plymouth Argyle's ground. United won 2-0.

OPPOSITE PAGE

Top: MANCHESTER UNITED 1977-78. *Back Row: Tommy Cavanagh (Assistant Manager), A. Albiston, A. Forsyth, J. Nicholl, B. Greenhoff, P. Roche S. Houston, A. Stepney, G. McQueen, A. Grimes, T. Jackson, Dave Sexton (Manager). Front Row: S. Coppell, D. McCreery, C. McGrath, L. Macari, M. Buchan, J. Jordan, S. Pearson, J. Greenhoff, S. McIlroy. (RDSS)*

Middle Right: Sir Matt Busby leads out former United players prior to the Centenary match with Real Madrid. (BNPC)

Bottom: CENTENARY MATCH 1978. *Manchester United 4 Real Madrid 0. Sammy McIlroy leaves the Real defence in disarray to hammer goalwards. (BNPC)*

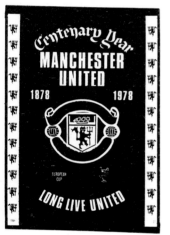

March No.	Date	Venue	Opponents	Result	Goalscorers	Attendance	Roche, P. J.	Greenhoff, B.	Albiston, A. R.	McIlroy, S. B.	McQueen, G.	Buchan, M. M.	Coppell, S. J.	Greenhoff, J.	Jordan, J.	Macari, L.	McCreery, D.	McGrath, R. C.	Nicholl, J. M.	Grimes, A. A.	Houston, S. M.	Sloan, T.	Thomas, M. R.	Ritchie, A. T.	Bailey, G. R.	Paterson, S. W.	Connell, T. E.	Moran, K. B.	Duxbury, M.	March No.
1	Aug 19	H	Birmingham City	W 1-0	Jordan	56,139	1	2	3	4	5	6	7	8	9	10	11													1
2	23	A	Leeds United	W 3-2	McQueen, McIlroy, Macari	36,845	1	2	3	4	5	6	7	8	9	10	11*	S												2
3	26	A	Ipswich Town	L 0-3		21,802	1	2	3	4	5	6	7	8	9	10	11*	S*												3
4	Sept 2	H	Everton	D 1-1	Buchan	53,982	1	2	3	4	5	6	7	8	9	10	11*	S*												4
5	9	A	Queens Park Rangers	D 1-1	J. Greenhoff	23,477	1	2	3	4	5	6	7	8	9	10		2*	S*											5
6	16	H	Nottingham Forest	D 1-1	J. Greenhoff	53,039	1	2	3	4	5	6	7	8	9	10	11*		S*											6
7	23	A	Arsenal	D 1-1	Coppell	45,393	1	2	3	4	5	6	7	8	9	10	11*			S*										7
8	30	H	Manchester City	D 1-1	Jordan	55,301	1	2	3	4	5	6	7	8*	9	10	4		S*											8
9	Oct 7	H	Middlesbrough	D 2-2	Macari, Jordan	45,402	1	2	3	4	5	6	7	8*	9	10	4			S	11									9
10	14	A	Aston Villa	D 2-2	McIlroy, Macari	36,667	1	2	3	4	5	6	7		9	10				S	11	8								10
11	21	H	Bristol City	L 1-3	J. Greenhoff	47,211	1	2	4*		5	6	7		9	10			3*	S	11	8								11
12	28	A	Wolverhampton Wanderers	W 4-2	J. Greenhoff 2, Jordan, B. Greenhoff	23,979	1	4		5	6	7		9	10			3*	2	S*	11	8								12
13	Nov 4	H	Southampton	D 1-1	J. Greenhoff	46,259	1	2	3	4	5	6	7		9	10	S*				11	8								13
14	11	A	Birmingham City	L 1-5	Jordan	23,877	1	5	3	4		6	7		9	10	2*		2	11	3									14
15	18	H	Ipswich Town	W 2-0	J. Greenhoff, Coppell	42,109	1	4	3		5	6	7		9	10	S*		2	11	3	8								15
16	21	H	Everton	L 0-3		42,126	1	4	3		5	6	7		9	10			2	S*	11	8								16
17	25	H	Chelsea	W 1-0	J. Greenhoff	38,162	1	4			5	6	7		9	10			2	3	11	8								17
18	Dec 9	A	Derby County	W 3-1	Ritchie, J. Greenhoff, McIlroy	23,180	1	4		5	6	7			10			2	3*	11	8	S*	9							18
19	16	H	Tottenham Hotspur	W 2-0	Ritchie, McIlroy	52,026	1	4		5	6	7			10			2	3	11	8		9							19
20	22	A	Bolton Wanderers	L 0-3		32,390	1	4		5	6	7			10	S*		2	3*	11	8		9							20
21	26	H	Liverpool	L 0-3		54,910	1	4		5	6	7			10			2	3	11	8	S	9							21
22	30	A	West Bromwich Albion	L 3-5	B. Greenhoff, McQueen, McIlroy	45,091	1	4		5	6	7			10	2*			3	11	8		9	S*						22
23	Feb 3	H	Arsenal	L 0-2		45460	1	4		5	6	7			10	2			3	11	8		9	S*						23
24	10	A	Manchester City	W 3-0	Coppell 2, Ritchie	46,151	1	4	3	5	6	7			10	2				9	11	8		S*						24
25	24	A	Aston Villa	D 1-1	J. Greenhoff (pen)	44,437	1	4	3	5	6	7			10	2				9*	11	8		S*						25
26	28	H	Queens Park Rangers	W 2-0	J. Greenhoff, Coppell	36,085	1	4	3	5	6	7			10*	2				9	11	8		S						26
27	March 3	A	Bristol City	W 2-1	Ritchie, McQueen	24,883	1	4	3	5	6	7			10	2				9	11	8		S*						27
28	20	A	Coventry City	L 3-4	Coppell 2, McIlroy	25,362	1	4	3	5	6	7			10	2				8*	11			9	S*					28
29	24	H	Leeds United	W 4-1	Ritchie 3, Thomas	51,191	1	4	3	5	6	7			10	2				8*	11	S*		9						29
30	27	A	Middlesbrough	W 2-2	McQueen, Coppell	20,138	1	4	3	5	6	7			10	2				S*	11	8		9						30
31	April 7	A	Norwich City	D 2-2	McQueen, Macari	19,382	1	4	3	5	6	7			10*	2				9	11	S						8		31
32	11	H	Bolton Wanderers	L 1-2	Buchan	49,617	1	4	3	5	6	7			10	2				9	11			8						32
33	16	A	Liverpool	L 0-2		46,608	1	4	3	5	6	7			10	2				9	11	S*		8*						33
34	16	H	Coventry City	D 0-0		43,035	1	4	3	5	6	7			10	2				9	11	S*		8*						34
35	18	A	Nottingham Forest	D 1-1	Jordan	33,074	1	4	3	5	6*	7			10	2				S*	11	8		9						35
36	21	H	Tottenham Hotspur	W 1-0	McQueen	36,665	1	4	3	5	6	7			10	2				S*	11	8		9						36
37	25	A	Norwich City	W 1-0	Macari	33,678	1	4	3	6*	7			10	2				S*	11	8		9					5		37
38	28	H	Derby County	D 0-0		42,546	1	4	3	6	7			10	2				S*	11	8		9					5		38
39	30	A	Southampton	D 1-1	Ritchie	21,616	1	4	3	6	7			10	2				6*	11*	8		9	3				5		39
40	May 5	A	West Bromwich Albion	L 0-1		27,960	1	4	3	6	7			10	2				S*	11	8		9					5		40
41	7	H	Wolverhampton Wanderers	W 3-2	Ritchie, Coppell 2	39,402	1	4	3	6	7			10	2				S*	11	8		9					5		41
42	16	H	Chelsea	D 1-1	Coppell	38,109	1	4	3	6	7			10*	2				S*	11	8		9					5		42

		F.A. CUP																											
Rd 3	Jan 15	H	Chelsea	W 3-0	Coppell, Grimes, J. Greenhoff	38,743	1	4	3	6	7			10	2				S*	11	8		9					5		Rd 3
Rd 4	31	A	Fulham	D 1-1	Grimes	26,229	1	4	3	6	7			10	2				S*	11	8		9					5		Rd 4
Replay	Feb 12	H	Fulham	W 1-0	J. Greenhoff	41,020	1	4	3	6	7			10	2				S*	11	8		9					5		Replay
Rd 5	20	A	Colchester United	W 1-0	J. Greenhoff	13,171	1	4	3	6	7			10	2				S*	11	8		9					5		Rd 5
Rd 5	Mar 10	A	Tottenham Hotspur	D 1-1	Thomas	51,800	1	4	3	6	7			10	2				9	11	8							5		Rd 5
Replay	14	H	Tottenham Hotspur	W 2-0	Jordan, McIlroy	55,584	1	4	3	6	7			10	2				9	11	8							5		Replay
SF	31	N	Liverpool	D 2-2	Jordan, B. Greenhoff (Maine Road, Manchester)	52,524	1	4	3	6	7			10	2				9	11	8							5		SF
Replay	Apr 4	N	Liverpool	W 1-0	J. Greenhoff (at Goodison Park, Liverpool)	53,069	1	4	3	6	7			10	2				9	11	8							5		Replay
FINAL	May 12	N	Arsenal	L 2-3	McQueen, McIlroy (at Wembley)	100,000	1	4	3	6	7			10	2				S*	11	8		9					5		FINAL

							League Appearances	14	32	32	40	36	37	42	33	30	31	14	0	19	25	21	3	25	18	28	1	2	1	0	
							Substitute Appearances		1		1				2			1	2		1	5	1	1	1	2		1			
							League Scorers	2	1		6	6	2	11	11	6	6				1				9						

OPPOSITE PAGE

Top: MANCHESTER UNITED — FA Cup Finalists 1979
T. Cavanagh (Ass. Manager), A. Albiston, A. Forsythe, J. Nicholl, B. Greenhoff, P. Roche, S. Houston, A. Stepney, G. McQueen, A. Grimes.
T. Jackson, D. Sexton (Manager).
Front Row: S. Coppell, D. McCreery, S. Paterson, L. Macari, M. Buchan, J. Jordan, S. Pearson, J. Greenhoff, S. McIlroy, L. Brown (Pyshio). (JG)

Bottom: FA CUP FINAL 1979 — Arsenal 3 Manchester United 2. 12 May 1979. In one of the most traumatic finals in Wembley's history, Arsenal snatched a last minute victory after United had recovered from a two-goal deficit. Three of the goals, two from the 'Red Devils', came in a sensational last five minutes of the matches. McQueen is seen scoring one of the United goals. (MMUSC)

Inset: FA Cup Runners-up Medal.

AT WEMBLEY AGAIN — 1979

MANCHESTER UNITED

Match No.	Date		Venue	Opponents	Result	Goalscorers	Attendance
1	Aug	18	A	Southampton	D 1-1	McQueen	21,768
2		22	A	West Bromwich Albion	W 2-0	McQueen, Coppell	53,377
3		25	H	Arsenal	D 0-0		44,380
4	Sept	1	H	Middlesbrough	W 2-1	Macari 2	51,015
5		8	A	Aston Villa	W 3-0	Coppell, Thomas (pen), Grimes	36,183
6		15	H	Derby County	W 1-0	I.o.g.	54,308
7		22	A	Wolverhampton Wanderers	L 1-3	Macari	35,503
8		29	H	Stoke City	W 4-0	Wilkins, McQueen 2, McIlroy	52,596
9	Oct	6	H	Brighton and Hove Albion	W 2-0	Coppell, Macari	52,641
10		10	A	West Bromwich Albion	L 0-2		27,713
11		13	H	Crystal Palace	D 1-1	Jordan	28,305
12		20	H	Bristol City	W 1-0	Macari	50,826
13		27	A	Ipswich Town	W 1-0	Grimes	50,215
14	Nov	3	A	Everton	D 0-0		50,067
15		10	H	Southampton	L 1-2	Macari	52,800
16		17	A	Manchester City	D 1-1	Macari	46,540
17		24	A	Crystal Palace	W 2-1	Macari, Coppell	37,708
18	Dec	1	H	Norwich City	W 5-0	Macari, Moran, Coppell, Jordan 2	51,389
19		8	A	Tottenham Hotspur	D 1-1	Thomas	57,471
20		15	H	Leeds United	W 1-0	Thomas	25,541
21		22	H	Nottingham Forest	W 2-1	McQueen, Macari	54,607
22		26	A	Coventry City	W 3-0	Jordan 2, McQueen	51,073
23		29	A	Liverpool	L 0-2		54,296
24	Jan	12	H	Arsenal	W 3-0	McQueen, Jordan, McIlroy (pen)	30,587
25	Feb	2	A	Middlesbrough	W 3-1	Thomas, McIlroy, I.o.g.	27,783
26		9	H	Wolverhampton Wanderers	L 0-1		51,568
27		16	H	Stoke City	D 1-1	Coppell	28,389
28		23	A	Bristol City	W 4-0	Jordan 2, McIlroy, I.o.g.	43,329
29		27	H	Bolton Wanderers	W 2-0	McQueen, Coppell	47,546
30	March	1	A	Ipswich Town	L 0-6		30,229
31		12	H	Everton	W 2-0	Jordan 2	45,515
32		15	H	Brighton and Hove Albion	D 0-0		30,243
33		22	H	Manchester City	W 1-0	Thomas	56,387
34		29	H	Crystal Palace	W 2-0	Jordan, Thomas	33,056
35	April	2	A	Nottingham Forest	D 0-0		31,417
36		5	H	Liverpool	W 2-1	Thomas, Greenhoff	57,342
37		7	A	Bolton Wanderers	W 3-1	McQueen, Thomas, Coppell	31,902
38		12	H	Tottenham Hotspur	W 4-1	Ritchie 3, Wilkins	53,151
39		19	A	Norwich City	W 2-0	Jordan 2	23,274
40		23	H	Aston Villa	W 2-1	Jordan 2	45,201
41		26	H	Coventry City	W 2-1	McIlroy 2 (1 pen)	52,154
42	May	3	A	Leeds United	L 0-2		39,625

F.A. CUP

	Date		Venue	Opponents	Result	Goalscorers	Attendance
Rd 3	Jan	5	A	Tottenham Hotspur	D 1-1	McIlroy (pen)	45,207
Replay		9	H	Tottenham Hotspur	L 0-1		53,762 (after extra time)

League Appearances
Substitute Appearances
League Scorers

Players:
Bailey, G. R.
Nicholl, J. M.
Albiston, A. R.
McIlroy, S. B.
McQueen, G.
Buchan, M. M.
Coppell, S. J.
Wilkins, R. C.
Jordan, J.
Macari, L.
Thomas, M. R.
Ritchie, A. T.
Paterson, S. W.
Grimes, A. A.
Sloan, T.
Houston, S. M.
Moran, K. B.
McGrath, R. C.
Jovanovic, N.
Greenhoff, J.

DID YOU KNOW? *Martin Edwards succeeded his father, the late Louis Edwards as Chairman of Manchester United on 22 March 1980. On the same day Sir Matt Busby became the Club President and United beat Manchester City 1-0 in the 'Centenary Derby' league match at Old Trafford.*

OPPOSITE PAGE

Top: Manchester United 2 Everton 1. 25 October 1980. McDonagh and Lyons combine to foil new £1.28 million signing, Garry Birtles on his Old Trafford debut, with Steve Coppell in attendance. (MMUSC)

Bottom: MANCHESTER UNITED — 1980/81
Back Row: K. Moran, N. Jovanovic, J. Nicholl, A. Ritchie, J. Jordan, A. Grimes.
Middle Row: T. Cavanagh (Ass. Manager), D. Sexton (Manager), S. Houston, J. Greenhoff, P. Roche, G. Bailey, G. McQueen, L. Brown (Physio).
Front Row: A. Albiston, S. Coppell, R. Wilkins, L. Macari, M. Buchan, M. Thomas, S. McIlroy. (JG)

MANCHESTER UNITED

Match No.	Date	Venue	Opponents	Result	Goalscorers	Attendance
1	Aug 16	H	Middlesbrough	W 3-0	Macari, Thomas, Grimes	54,394
2	19	A	Wolverhampton Wanderers	L 0-1		31,965
3	23	A	Birmingham City	D 0-0		28,661
4	30	H	Sunderland	D 1-1	Jovanovic	51,498
5	Sept 6	A	Tottenham Hotspur	D 0-0		40,995
6	13	H	Leicester City	W 5-0	Coppell, Grimes, Jovanovic 2, Macari	43,229
7	20	A	Leeds United	D 0-0		32,539
8	27	H	Manchester City	D 2-2	Coppell, Albiston	55,918
9	Oct 4	A	Nottingham Forest	W 2-1	Macari, Coppell	29,801
10	8	H	Aston Villa	D 3-3	McIlroy 2 (1 pen), Coppell	49,036
11	11	H	Arsenal	D 0-0		38,831
12	18	A	Ipswich Town	D 1-1	McIlroy (pen)	28,572
13	25	H	Stoke City	W 2-1	Jordan, Macari	24,534
14	Nov 1	H	Everton	W 2-1	Jordan, Coppell	54,260
15	8	A	Crystal Palace	L 0-1		31,449
16	12	H	Coventry City	D 0-0		42,794
17	22	H	Wolverhampton Wanderers	D 0-0		37,959
18	29	H	Liverpool	L 1-3	Jovanovic	20,606
19	Dec 6	A	Brighton and Hove Albion	W 4-1	Jordan 2, McIlroy, Duxbury	23,401
20	13	H	Southampton	D 1-1	Jordan	46,840
21	20	A	Norwich City	D 2-2	Coppell, 1 o.g.	18,780
22	26	A	Stoke City	D 2-2	Macari, Jordan	26,514
23	27	A	Arsenal	L 1-2	Macari	39,568
24	Jan 10	A	Middlesbrough	D 0-0		33,730
25	17	A	West Bromwich Albion	L 1-3	Jovanovic	57,049
26	31	H	Brighton and Hove Albion	W 2-1	McQueen, Macari	30,326
27	Feb 7	A	Sunderland	L 0-2		42,208
28	21	H	Birmingham City	W 2-0	Jordan, Macari	31,910
29	28	A	Leicester City	L 0-1		26,514
30		H	Tottenham Hotspur	D 0-0		40,642
31	March 7	A	Manchester City	L 0-1		50,114
32	14	H	Leeds United	L 0-1		45,733
33	18	A	Southampton	D 3-3	Jordan 2, McIlroy (pen)	22,698
34	21	A	Aston Villa	D 1-1	1 o.g.	42,916
35	28	H	Nottingham Forest	D 1-1		38,205
36	April 4	H	Ipswich Town	W 2-1	Thomas, Nicholl	46,685
37	11	A	Everton	W 1-0	Jordan	28,856
38	14	H	Crystal Palace	W 1-0	Duxbury	37,954
39	18	A	Coventry City	W 2-0	Jordan, 2	20,201
40	20	A	Liverpool	W 1-0	McQueen	31,276
41	25	H	West Bromwich Albion	W 2-1	Jordan, Macari	44,442
42	25	H	Norwich City	W 1-0	Jordan	40,165

Player columns (appearance grid):

Bailey, G. R. · Nicholl, J. M. · Albiston, A. R. · McIlroy, S. B. · Moran, K. B. · Buchan, M. M. · Coppell, S. J. · Greenhoff, J. · Jordan, J. · Macari, L. · Thomas, M. R. · Grimes, A. A. · Roche, P. J. · Ritchie, A. T. · McGrath, R. C. · Duxbury, M. · Jovanovic, N. · McGarvey, S. · McQueen, G. · Sloan, T. · Birtles, G. · Whelan, A. G. · Wilkins, R. C.

League Appearances
Substitute Appearances
League Scorers

F.A. CUP

	Date	Venue	Opponents	Result	Goalscorers	Attendance
Rd 3	Jan 3	H	Brighton and Hove Albion	D 2-2	Duxbury, Thomas	42,199
Replay	7	A	Brighton and Hove Albion	W 2-0	Nicholl, Birtles	26,915
Rd 4	24	A	Nottingham Forest	L 0-1		34,110

DID YOU KNOW? Uniteds 18 drawn games in 1980-1 is a record for the club. Garry Birtles signed from Nottingham Forest for £1,250,000, achieving his boyhood ambition to play for United. At the end of the season Manager Dave Sexton was succeeded by Ron Atkinson.

OPPOSITE PAGE

Top Left: £3 MILLION PEN. Bryan Robson signs for United at a British Record fee of £1.8 million, watched by new Manager Ron Atkinson. The same pen was used by Andy Gray to sign registration forms for Wolves in his £1.2 million transfer from Aston Villa. (MMUSC)

Top Right: UEFA Cup. Valencia 2 Manchester United 1. 29 Sept. 1983. Gary Bailey saves as Spanish striker Tendillo challenges in this exciting goalmouth incident at the Gran Mestrellas Stadium. (BPNC)

Bottom: FRANK STAPLETON DEBUT. Coventry 2 Manchester United 1. 29 August 1981. Ron Atkinson's first signings were Stapleton and John Gidman. Both made their debuts in the opening match of 1981/2 at Coventry, here Frank goes up to meet this cross but is beaten to it by the City 'keeper. (MMUSC)

MANCHESTER UNITED

Match No.	Date	Venue	Opponents	Result	Goalscorers	Attendance
1	Aug 29	A	Coventry City	L 1-2	Macari	19,329
2	31	H	Nottingham Forest	L 0-1		51,496
3	Sept. 5	A	Ipswich Town	L 1-2	Stapleton	45,596
4	12	H	Aston Villa	D 1-1	Stapleton	37,661
5	19	A	Swansea City	W 1-0	Birtles	47,309
6	22	H	Middlesbrough	W 2-0	Birtles, Stapleton	19,895
7	26	A	Arsenal	D 0-0		39,795
8	30	H	Leeds United	W 1-0	Stapleton	47,019
9	Oct 3	A	Wolverhampton Wanderers	W 5-0	Stapleton, McIlroy 3, Birtles	46,837
10	10	H	Manchester City	W 2-0	Birtles, Stapleton	52,037
11	17	H	Birmingham City	D 1-1	Coppell	48,800
12	21	A	Middlesbrough	W 2-1	Moses, Albiston	38,342
13	24	H	Liverpool	W 2-1	Moran, Albiston	41,438
14	31	A	Notts County	W 2-1	Birtles, Moses	45,928
15	Nov 7	H	Sunderland	W 5-1	Moran, Robson, Stapleton 2, Birtles	27,070
16	21	A	Tottenham Hotspur	L 1-3	Birtles	35,534
17	28	H	Brighton and Hove Albion	W 2-0	Birtles, Stapleton	41,911
18	Dec 5	A	Southampton	L 2-3	Stapleton, Robson	24,404
19	Jan 6	H	Everton	D 1-1	Stapleton	40,461
20	23	A	Stoke City	W 3-0	Coppell, Stapleton (pen), Birtles	19,793
21	27	H	West Ham United	L 0-2		41,291
22	30	H	Notts County	L 0-1		24,115
23	Feb 6	A	Aston Villa	W 4-1	Moran 2, Robson, Coppell	43,184
24	13	H	Wolverhampton Wanderers	W 1-0	Birtles	22,481
25	20	H	Arsenal	D 0-0		43,833
26	27	A	Manchester City	D 1-1	Moran	57,830
27	March 6	A	Coventry City	L 0-1		19,657
28	17	H	Birmingham City	W 1-0	Birtles	34,499
29	20	A	Notts County	W 3-1	Coppell 2, Stapleton	17,048
30	27	H	Sunderland	D 0-0		40,726
31	April 3	A	Leeds United	D 0-0		30,963
32	7	H	Liverpool	L 0-1		48,371
33	10	A	Everton	D 3-3	Coppell 2, Grimes	29,317
34	12	H	West Bromwich Albion	W 1-0	Moran	38,717
35	17	A	Tottenham Hotspur	W 2-0	Coppell (pen), McGarvey	50,724
36	20	A	Ipswich Town	L 1-2	Gidman	25,763
37	24	H	Brighton and Hove Albion	W 1-0	Wilkins	20,785
38	May 1	A	Southampton	W 1-0	McGarvey	40,038
39	5	A	Nottingham Forest	W 1-0	Stapleton	18,449
40	8	A	West Ham United	D 1-1	Moran	26,337
41	12	H	West Bromwich Albion	W 3-0	Moran, Birtles, Coppell	19,707
42	15	H	Stoke City	W 2-0	Robson, Whiteside	43,072

F.A. CUP

Rd 3	Jan 2	A	Watford	L 0-1		26,104

League Appearances
Substitute Appearances
League Scorers

Players: Bailey, G. R.; Gidman, J.; Albiston, A. R.; Wilkins, R. C.; McQueen, G.; Buchan, M. M.; Coppell, S. J.; Birtles, G.; Stapleton, F. A.; Macari, L.; McIlroy, S. B.; Duxbury, M.; Moses, R. M.; Moran, K. B.; Robson, B.; Roche, P. J.; Nicholl, J. M.; McGarvey, S.; Grimes, A. A.; Whiteside, N.; Davies, A.

DID YOU KNOW? A new system of 3 points for a win was introduced by the Football League in 1981-2, in an effort to encourage more attacking football. At the end of the season Garry Bailey was the first winner of the 'Golden Gloves' trophy, conceding only 22 goals in 39 matches. In the 1982 World Cup Finals, United's Bryan Robson scored the fastest goal in the competition, for England against France, in only 27 seconds. Bryan Robson signed for a British Record Fee of £1,800,000.

OPPOSITE PAGE

Top & Bottom Right: FA CHARITY SHIELD 24 August 1983 Robson scores United's second goal against Liverpool at Wembley. (BNPC)

Garry Bailey and Bryan Robson celebrate United's victory with the Shield. (BNPC)

Bottom Left: MANCHESTER UNITED 2 MANCHESTER CITY 2 23 October 1982 McQueen and Stapleton cause trouble for the City defence at Old Trafford. (BNPC)

F.A. Cup Winners & Milk Cup Finalists   *Position: 3rd*

MANCHESTER UNITED

Match No.	Date	Venue	Opponents	Result	Goalscorers	Attendance
1	Aug 28	H	Birmingham City	W 3-0	Moran, Stapleton, Coppell	48,673
2	Sep 1	A	Nottingham Forest	W 3-0	Wilkins, Whiteside, Robson	23,996
3	Sep 4	A	West Bromwich Albion	L 1-3	Robson	24,928
4	Sep 8	H	Everton	W 2-1	Whiteside, Robson	43,186
5	Sep 11	H	Ipswich Town	W 3-1	Whiteside 2, Coppell	43,140
6	Sep 18	A	Southampton	W 1-0	Macari	21,700
7	Sep 25	A	Arsenal	D 0-0		43,198
8	Oct 2	H	Luton Town	D 1-1	Grimes	17,009
9	Oct 9	H	Stoke City	W 1-0	Robson	43,132
10	Oct 16	A	Liverpool	D 0-0		40,853
11	Oct 23	H	Manchester City	D 2-2	Stapleton 2	57,334
12	Oct 30	A	West Ham United	L 1-3	Moran	32,478
13	Nov 6	H	Brighton and Hove Albion	L 0-1		18,379
14	Nov 13	H	Tottenham Hotspur	W 1-0	Muhren	47,869
15	Nov 20	A	Aston Villa	L 1-2	Stapleton	35,487
16	Nov 27	H	Norwich City	W 3-0	Muhren, Robson 2	34,579
17	Dec 4	A	Watford	W 1-0	Whiteside	25,669
18	Dec 11	H	Notts County	W 4-0	Whiteside, Stapleton, Robson, Duxbury	33,618
19	Dec 18	A	Swansea City	D 0-0		15,748
20	Dec 27	H	Sunderland	D 0-0		48,283
21	Dec 28	A	Coventry City	L 0-3		18,945
22	Jan 1	H	Aston Villa	W 3-1	Stapleton 2, Coppell	41,545
23	Jan 3	A	West Bromwich Albion	D 0-0		39,123
24	Jan 15	H	Birmingham City	W 2-1	Whiteside, Robson	19,333
25	Jan 22	A	Nottingham Forest	W 2-0	Coppell (pen), Muhren	38,615
26	Feb 5	H	Ipswich Town	W 3-0	Stapleton, Macari, 1 o.g.	23,804
27	Feb 26	H	Liverpool	D 1-1	Muhren	57,397
28	Mar 2	H	Stoke City	W 1-0	Robson	21,266
29	Mar 5	A	Manchester City	W 2-1	Stapleton 2	45,400
30	Mar 19	H	Brighton and Hove Albion	D 1-1	Albiston	36,264
31	Mar 22	A	West Ham United	W 2-1	Stapleton, McGarvey	30,227
32	Apr 2	H	Coventry City	W 3-0	Stapleton, Macari, 1 o.g.	36,814
33	Apr 4	A	Sunderland	D 0-0		31,486
34	Apr 9	H	Southampton	D 1-1	Robson	37,120
35	Apr 19	A	Everton	L 0-2		21,715
36	Apr 23	H	Watford	W 2-0	Cunningham, Grimes (pen)	43,048
37	Apr 30	A	Norwich City	D 1-1	Whiteside	22,986
38	May 2	A	Arsenal	L 0-3		23,602
39	May 7	H	Swansea City	W 2-1	Robson, Stapleton	35,784
40	May 9	H	Luton Town	W 3-0	McGrath 2, Stapleton	34,213
41	May 11	A	Tottenham Hotspur	L 0-2		32,803
42	May 14	A	Notts County	L 2-3	McGrath, Muhren	14,395

F.A. CUP

	Date	Venue	Opponents	Result	Goalscorers	Attendance
Rd 3	Jan 8	H	West Ham United	W 2-0	Coppell, Stapleton	44,143
Rd 4	Jan 29	A	Luton Town	W 2-0	Moses, Moran	20,516
Rd 5	Feb 19	A	Derby County	W 1-0	Whiteside	33,022
Rd 6	Mar 12	H	Everton	W 1-0	Stapleton	58,198
S/F	Apr 16	N	Arsenal	W 2-1	Robson, Whiteside (at Villa Park, Birmingham)	46,535
FINAL	May 12	N	Brighton and Hove Albion	D 2-2	Stapleton, Wilkins (after extra time) (at Wembley)	100,000
Replay	May 26	N	Brighton and Hove Albion	W 4-0	Robson (2), Whiteside, Muhren (pen) (Wembley)	92,000

Player columns: Bailey, G. R.; Duxbury, M.; Albiston, A. R.; Wilkins, R. C.; Moran, K. B.; McQueen, G.; Robson, B.; Muhren, A. J. H.; Stapleton, F. A.; Whiteside, N.; Coppell, S. J.; Buchan, M. M.; Grimes, A. A.; Macari, L.; Moses, R. M.; McGrath, P.; McGarvey, S.; Gidman, J.; Wealands, J.; Cunningham, L. P.; Davies, A.; Beardsley, P.

Substitute Appearances
League Appearances
League Scorers

OPPOSITE PAGE

Top: FA CUP WINNERS 1983: Back Row: Gordon MacQueen, Scott McGarvey, Mike Duxbury, Gary Bailey, Jeff Wealands, Paul McGrath, Ashley Grimes, Norman Whiteside. Middle Row: Jim McGregor (physio), John Gidman, Kevin Moran, Lou Macari, Steve Coppell, Alan Davies, Frank Stapleton, Mick Brown (coach). Front Row: Remi Moses, Arnold Muhren, Bryan Robson, Ron Atkinson (Manager), Ray Wilkins, Arthur Graham, and Arthur Albiston. (JG)

Bottom: EUROPEAN CUP-WINNERS CUP Quarter Final 2nd leg MANCHESTER UNITED 3 BARCELONA 0 21 March 1984 Barcelona's Maradona is grounded by Moran and Duxbury as United pull a 2-goal deficit round to enter the Semi-Final where they were eliminated by Juventus. (MMUSC)

F.A. CUP WINNERS 1983

1983-4

Division One

European Cup Winners Cup Semi-Finalists

Position: 4th

MANCHESTER UNITED

Match No.	Date	Venue	Opponents	Result	Goalscorers	Attendance
1	Aug 27	H	Queens Park Rangers	W 3-1	Muhren 2 (1 pen), Stapleton	48,742
2	29	A	Nottingham Forest	L 1-2	Moran	43,005
3	Sep 3	A	Stoke City	W 1-0	Muhren	23,704
4	6	H	Arsenal	W 3-2	Moran, Stapleton, Robson	42,703
5	10	H	Luton Town	W 2-0	Muhren (pen), Albiston	41,013
6	17	A	Southampton	L 0-3		20,674
7	24	H	Liverpool	W 1-0	Stapleton	56,121
8	Oct 1	A	Norwich City	D 3-3	Whiteside 2, Stapleton	19,680
9	15	H	West Bromwich Albion	W 3-0	Graham, Whiteside, Albiston	42,221
10	22	A	Sunderland	W 1-0	Wilkins (pen)	26,826
11	29	H	Wolverhampton Wanderers	W 3-0	Stapleton 2, Robson	41,880
12	Nov 5	A	Aston Villa	L 1-2	Robson	45,077
13	12	H	Leicester City	D 1-1	Robson	24,409
14	19	A	Watford	W 4-1	Stapleton 3, Robson	43,111
15	27	A	West Ham United	W 1-0	Graham	23,355
16	Dec 3	H	Everton	L 0-1		43,664
17	10	A	Ipswich Town	W 2-0	Graham, Crooks	19,779
18	16	H	Tottenham Hotspur	W 4-2	Graham 2, Moran 2	33,616
19	26	A	Coventry City	D 1-1	Muhren (pen)	21,453
20	27	H	Notts County	D 3-3	Crooks, McQueen, Moran	41,544
21	31	H	Stoke City	D 2-2	Whiteside, Hogg	40,164
22	Jan 2	A	Liverpool	D 1-1	Whiteside	45,122
23	13	A	Queens Park Rangers	D 1-1	Whiteside	16,309
24	21	H	Southampton	W 3-2	Robson, Stapleton, Muhren	40,371
25	Feb 4	H	Norwich City	D 0-0		36,891
26	7	A	Birmingham City	D 2-2	Whiteside, Hogg	19,967
27	12	A	Luton Town	W 5-0	Robson 2, Whiteside 2, Stapleton	11,265
28	18	H	Wolverhampton Wanderers	W 1-0	Whiteside	20,676
29	25	H	Sunderland	W 2-1	Moran 2	40,615
30	Mar 3	H	Aston Villa	W 3-0	Moses, Whiteside, Robson	32,874
31	10	H	Leicester City	W 2-0	Moses, Hughes	39,473
32	17	H	Arsenal	W 4-0	Muhren 2, Stapleton, Robson	48,942
33	31	A	West Bromwich Albion	L 0-2		27,964
34	Apr 7	H	Birmingham City	W 1-0	Robson	39,891
35	14	A	Notts County	L 0-1		13,911
36	17	H	Watford	W 4-1	Hughes 2, McGrath, Wilkins	20,764
37	21	H	Coventry City	D 0-0		38,524
38	28	H	West Ham United	W 1-0	Stapleton	44,124
39	May 5	A	Everton	D 1-1	Hughes	28,817
40	7	H	Ipswich Town	L 1-2	Hughes	44,257
41	12	A	Tottenham Hotspur	D 1-1	Whiteside	39,790
42	16	A	Nottingham Forest	L 0-2		23,651

Players: Bailey, G. R.; Duxbury, M.; Albiston, A. R.; Wilkins, R. C.; Moran, K. B.; McQueen, G.; Robson, B.; Muhren, A. J. H.; Stapleton, F. A.; Whiteside, N.; Graham, A.; Macari, L.; Gidman, J.; Moses, R. M.; McGrath, P.; Crookes, G. A.; Wealands, J.; Hogg, G.; Hughes, M.; Davies, A.; Blackmore, C.

F.A. CUP

Round	Date	Venue	Opponents	Result	Attendance
Rd 3	Jan 7	A	A.F.C Bournemouth	L 0-2	14,782

DID YOU KNOW? Manchester United's operating profit of £1,731,200 for 1983/4 is a record for a British club. Arnold Muhren scored the goal that gave United their 1-0 win over Stoke City on 3 September 1983 to register the club's 1,000th victory in the First Division, achieved against 51 different opponents.

OPPOSITE PAGE

Top Left: 25 YEARS AFTER MUNICH: 6 February 1983. Supporters gather to pay homage under the Munich Memorial at Old Trafford. (BNPC)

Top Right: UNITED IN BELFAST: Manchester United 4 Liverpool 3 3 August 1983 at Windsor Park. Stapleton (left) and Robson salute the winning goal from Lou Macari in this testimonial match for Irish F.A. Secretary Billy Drennan. (BNPC)

Bottom: GORDON STRACHAN. Following protracted transfer negotiations, complicated by a prior claim to his signature from F.C. Cologne of West Germany, Gordon joined United in the summer of 1984. He soon began to repay the £600,000 fee, and scored 17 league and F.A. Cup goals in 1984/5. Here he scores his second goal against Nottingham Forest on 8 December. (MMUSC)

MANCHESTER UNITED

Match No.	Date	Venue	Opponents	Result	Goalscorers	Attendance
1	Aug 25	H	Watford	D 1-1	Strachan (pen)	53,668
2	28	A	Southampton	D 0-0		22,183
3	Sep 1	A	Ipswich Town	D 1-1	Hughes	20,876
4	5	H	Chelsea	D 1-1	Olsen	48,398
5	8	H	Newcastle United	W 5-0	Olsen, Strachan 2 (1 pen), Hughes, Moses	54,915
6	15	A	Coventry City	W 3-0	Robson, Whiteside 2	18,312
7	22	A	Liverpool	D 1-1	Strachan	56,638
8	29	H	West Bromwich Albion	W 2-1	Robson, Strachan (pen)	26,401
9	Oct 6	A	Aston Villa	L 0-3		37,132
10	13	H	West Ham United	W 5-1	McQueen, Brazil, Strachan, Moses, Hughes	47,559
11	20	A	Tottenham Hotspur	W 1-0	Hughes	54,516
12	27	H	Everton	L 0-5		40,769
13	Nov 2	A	Arsenal	W 4-2	Robson, Strachan 2, Hughes	32,279
14	10	H	Leicester City	W 3-2	Brazil, Hughes, Strachan (pen)	23,840
15	17	A	Luton Town	W 2-0	Whiteside 2	21,630
16	24	H	Sunderland	L 2-3	Robson, Hughes	25,405
17	Dec 1	A	Norwich City	W 2-0	Robson, Hughes	36,635
18	8	H	Nottingham Forest	L 2-3	Strachan 2 (1 pen)	25,902
19	15	A	Queens Park Rangers	W 3-0	Gidman, Duxbury, Brazil	36,134
20	22	H	Ipswich Town	W 3-0	Strachan (pen), Robson, Gidman	35,168
21	26	A	Stoke City	W 1-2	Stapleton	20,985
22	29	A	Chelsea	W 3-1	Hughes, Moses, Stapleton	42,197
23	Jan 1	H	Sheffield Wednesday	L 1-2	Hughes	47,625
24	12	A	Coventry City	L 0-1		35,992
25	Feb 2	H	West Bromwich Albion	W 2-0	Strachan 2	36,681
26	9	A	Newcastle United	D 1-1	Moran	31,798
27	23	H	Arsenal	W 1-0	Whiteside	48,612
28	Mar 2	A	Everton	L 0-1		51,150
29	12	H	Tottenham Hotspur	W 2-1	Hughes, Whiteside	42,918
30	15	A	West Ham United	D 2-2	Stapleton, Robson	16,674
31	23	H	Aston Villa	W 4-0	Hughes 3, Whiteside	40,541
32	31	A	Liverpool	W 1-0	Stapleton	34,880
33	Apr 3	H	Leicester City	W 2-1	Robson, Stapleton	35,590
34	6	H	Stoke City	W 5-0	Hughes 2, Olsen 2, Whiteside	42,940
35	9	A	Sheffield Wednesday	L 0-1		39,380
36	21	A	Luton Town	L 1-2	Whiteside	10,320
37	24	H	Southampton	D 0-0		31,291
38	27	H	Sunderland	D 2-2	Robson, Moran	38,979
39	May 4	A	Norwich City	W 1-0	Moran	16,006
40	6	H	Nottingham Forest	W 2-0	Gidman, Stapleton	43,334
41	11	A	Queens Park Rangers	W 3-1	Brazil 2, Strachan	20,483
42	13	A	Watford	L 1-5	Moran	20,047

F.A. CUP

	Date	Venue	Opponents	Result	Goalscorers	Attendance
Rd 3	Jan 5	H	A F C Bournemouth	W 3-0	Strachan, McQueen, Stapleton	32,080
Rd 4	26	H	Coventry City	W 2-1	Hughes, McGrath	38,039
Rd 5	Feb 15	H	Blackburn Rovers	W 2-0	Strachan, McGrath	22,692
Rd 6	Mar 9	A	West Ham United	W 4-2	Whiteside (3) (1 pen), Hughes	46,769
SF	Apr 13	N	Liverpool	D 2-2	Hughes, Stapleton (a.e.t.) (at Goodison Park)	51,690
Replay	17	N	Liverpool	W 2-1	Robson, Hughes (at Maine Road)	45,775
FINAL	May 18	N	Everton	W 1-0	Whiteside (at Wembley)	100,000

Players:

Bailey, G. R.
Duxbury, M.
Albiston, A. R.
Moses, R. M.
Moran, K. B.
Hogg, K.
Robson, B.
Strachan, G. D.
Hughes, M.
Brazil, A. B.
Olsen, J.
Whiteside, N.
Muhren, A. J. H.
McQueen, G.
Gidman, J.
Stapleton, F. A.
Garton, W.
McGrath, P.
Blackmore, C.
Pears, S.
Davies, A.

OPPOSITE PAGE

Top: UEFA CUP QUARTER FINAL 1984/5. Videotron v Manchester United. 20 March 1985 in Hungary. After winning the 1st leg 1-0 at Old Trafford, United were 0-1 down in the away leg after extra time. With the aggregate at 1-1, Videotron won on penalties. (BNPC)

Middle Right: FA CUP WINNERS 1985. Bryan Robson holds the FA Cup aloft after United had beaten Everton 1-0, playing with only ten men after Kevin Moran had been sent-off. (MMUSC)

Centre Inset: FA CUP WINNERS MEDAL

Middle Left: NORMAN WHITESIDE. His sensational individual goal at Wembley won the FA Cup for United in dramatic fashion. (MMUSC)

Bottom: UEFA CUP 1984/5. Manchester United 2 Dundee United 2   28 November 1984   Dundee defender Malpas gives away the penalty which Gordon Strachan scored for United, who won the return leg 3-2 (BNPC)

F.A. CUP WINNERS 1985

MANCHESTER UNITED

Match No.	Date	Venue	Opponents	Result	Goalscorers	Attendance
1	Aug 17	A	Aston Villa	W 4-0	Whiteside, Hughes 2, Olsen	49,743
2	20	H	Ipswich Town	W 1-0	Robson	18,777
3	24	A	Arsenal	W 2-1	Hughes, McGrath	37,145
4	26	H	West Ham United	W 2-0	Hughes, Strachan	50,773
5	31	A	Nottingham Forest	W 3-1	Hughes, Barnes, Stapleton	26,274
6	Sept 4	H	Newcastle United	W 3-0	Stapleton 2, Hughes	51,102
7	7	A	Oxford United	W 3-0	Whiteside, Robson, Barnes	51,820
8	14	H	Manchester City	W 3-0	Robson (pen), Albiston, Duxbury	48,723
9	21	A	West Bromwich Albion	W 5-1	Brazil 2, Strachan, Blackmore, Stapleton	25,068
10	28	H	Southampton	W 1-0	Hughes	52,449
11	Oct 5	A	Luton Town	D 1-1	Hughes	17,454
12	12	H	Queens Park Rangers	W 2-0	Hughes, Olsen	48,845
13	19	A	Liverpool	D 1-1	McGrath	54,492
14	26	H	Chelsea	W 2-1	Olsen 2	42,485
15	Nov 2	A	Coventry City	W 2-0	Olsen, Hughes	46,748
16	9	H	Sheffield Wednesday	L 0-1		48,105
17	16	A	Tottenham Hotspur	D 0-0		54,575
18	23	H	Leicester City	L 0-3		22,008
19	30	A	Watford	D 1-1	Brazil	42,181
20	Dec 7	H	Ipswich Town	W 1-0	Stapleton	37,981
21	14	A	Aston Villa	W 3-1	Blackmore, Strachan, Hughes	27,626
22	21	H	Arsenal	L 0-1		44,386
23	26	A	Everton	L 1-3	Stapleton	42,551
24	Jan 1	H	Birmingham City	W 1-0	C. Gibson	43,095
25	11	A	Oxford United	W 3-1	Whiteside, Hughes, C. Gibson	13,280
26	18	H	Nottingham Forest	L 2-3	Olsen 2 (1 pen)	46,717
27	Feb 2	A	West Ham United	L 1-2	Robson	22,642
28	9	H	Liverpool	D 1-1	C. Gibson	38,044
29	22	H	West Bromwich Albion	W 3-0	Olsen 3 (2 pen)	45,193
30	Mar 1	A	Southampton	L 0-1		19,012
31	15	A	Queens Park Rangers	L 0-1		23,407
32	19	H	Luton Town	W 2-0	Hughes, McGrath	33,668
33	22	H	Manchester City	D 2-2	C. Gibson, Strachan (pen)	51,274
34	29	A	Birmingham City	D 1-1	Robson	22,551
35	31	H	Everton	D 0-0		51,189
36	Apr 5	A	Coventry City	W 3-1	C. Gibson, Robson, Strachan	17,160
37	9	H	Chelsea	L 1-2	Olsen (pen)	45,355
38	13	H	Sheffield Wednesday	L 0-2		32,331
39	16	A	Newcastle United	W 4-2	Robson (pen), Hughes 2, Whiteside	31,840
40	19	A	Tottenham Hotspur	D 0-0		32,357
41	26	H	Leicester City	W 4-0	Stapleton, Hughes, Blackmore, Davenport (pen)	38,840
42	May 3	A	Watford	D 1-1	Hughes	18,414

F.A. CUP

	Date	Venue	Opponents	Result	Goalscorers	Attendance
Rd 3	Jan 9	H	Rochdale	W 2-0	Stapleton, Hughes	38,500
Rd 4	25	A	Sunderland	D 0-0		35,484
Replay	29	H	Sunderland	W 3-0	Whiteside, Olsen (2)(1 pen)	43,402
Rd 5	Mar	A	West Ham United	D 1-1	Stapleton	26,441
Replay	9	H	West Ham United	L 0-2		30,441

Players: Bailey, G. R.; Gidman, J.; Albiston, A. R.; Whiteside, N.; McGrath, P.; Hogg, G.; Robson, R. M.; Moses, R. M.; Hughes, M.; Stapleton, F. A.; Olsen, J.; Duxbury, M.; Strachan, G. D.; Barnes, P.; Brazil, A. B.; Blackmore, C.; Moran, K. B.; Garton, W.; Gibson, C.; Dempsey, M.; Turner, C.; Wood, N.; Gibson, T.; Sivebaek, J.; Davenport, P.; Higgins, M.

(Rows below the fixtures list: League Appearances, Substitute Appearances, League Scorers)

DID YOU KNOW? United won all of their first 10 league matches in 1985/6. The record is 11 consecutive opening wins, by Spurs in 1960/1.

THE SIGNING THAT NEVER WAS.... but please read on

JOHNNY SIVEBAEK signs on the dotted line for Manchester United watched by Ron Atkinson and Martin Edwards. But that was "THE SIGNING THAT NEVER WAS" for the picture above was taken in December when he signed for the Reds the first time and then the transfer was called off for medical reasons. Come January, the doctors think it over once again, and Johnny finally signs for United for £200,000.

Welcome Johnny....

★★★★★

COMINGS AND GOINGS

Top left: JOHN SIVEBAEK belatedly signs for United as the feature from Echoes from Old Trafford *explains (MMUSC)*

Top right: COLIN GIBSON arrived from Aston Villa, and TERRY GIBSON from Coventry City. (MMUSC)

Below: MARK HUGHES joined Barcelona for £2 million, as reported here in The Times *of Malta. (TM)*

Bottom left: PETER DAVENPORT arrives from Forest, as covered in Daily Mirror. *(BNPC)*

Bottom right: JESPER OLSEN blasts a shot past the post in the 0—0 F.A. Cup round 4 tie at Roker Park. (MMUSC)

TARGET MAN: Forest striker Peter Davenport is top of United's list.

IT'S RED PETER

United swoop

MANCHESTER UNITED will splash out £600,000 within the next 48 hours on Nottingham Forest striker Peter Davenport.

HUGHES TRANSFER TO BARCELONA CONFIRMED

LONDON, March 21.

● Manchester United striker Mark Hughes has signed a contract to play for Barcelona next season, it was confirmed today.

The Welsh international will join the Spanish champions and European Cup semifinalists in a two million sterling deal, subject to a satisfactory medical examination.

Manchester United and Hughes, 22, issued a joint statement today, ending weeks of speculation about the transfer.

The fee was agreed a couple of months ago. The transfer has been confirmed despite reports that Barcelona's English manager Terry Venables has decided to resign and leave Spain at the end of the season.

EUROPEAN COMPETITIONS RECORD 1956 – 86

EUROPEAN CHAMPIONS CUP

1956 – 57
Prelim. Round, 1st leg: 12 Sept. A. v. ANDERLECHT RSC
2 – 0, scorers: Viollet, Taylor.
Atten: 35,000. Wood, Foulkes, Byrne, Colman, Jones,
Blanchflower, Berry, Whelan, Taylor, Viollet, Pegg.
Prelim. Round, 2nd leg: 26 Sept. H*. v. ANDERLECHT RSC
10 – 0, scorers: Whelan (2), Berry, Violett (4), Taylor (3).
Atten: 43,635. Wood, Foulkes, Byrne, Colman, Jones,
Edwards, Berry, Whelan, Taylor, Viollet, Pegg.
Round 1, 1st leg: 17 Oct. H*. v. BORUSSIA DORTMUND
3 – 2, scorers: Viollet (2), O.g. (Burgsmueller).
Atten: 75,598. Wood, Foulkes, Byrne, Colman, Jones,
Edwards, Berry, Whelan, Taylor, Viollet, Pegg.
Round 1, 2nd leg: 21 Nov. A. v. BORUSSIA DORTMUND
0 – 0. *Atten: 45,000.* Wood, Foulkes, Byrne, Colman, Jones,
McGuinness, Berry, Whelan, Taylor, Edwards, Pegg.
Quarter-final, 1st leg: 16 Jan. A. v. ATLETICO BILBAO
3 – 5, scorers: Taylor, Violett, Whelan.
Atten: 45,000. Wood, Foulkes, Byrne, Colman, Jones,
Edwards, Berry, Whelan, Taylor, Viollet, Pegg.
Quarter-final, 2nd leg: 6 Feb. H*. v. ATLETICO BILBAO
3 – 0, scorers: Viollet, Taylor, Berry.
Atten: 65,000. Wood, Foulkes, Byrne, Colman, Jones,
Edwards, Berry, Whelan, Taylor, Viollet, Pegg.
Semi-final, 1st leg: 11 April A. v. CF REAL MADRID
1 – 3, scorer: Taylor. *Atten: 134,000.*
Wood, Foulkes, Byrne, Colman, Blanchflower, Edwards,
Berry, Whelan, Taylor, Violett, Pegg.
Semi-final, 2nd leg: 25 April H. v. CF REAL MADRID
2 – 2, scorers: Taylor, Charlton.
Atten: 61,676. Wood, Foulkes, Byrne, Colman, Blanchflower,
Edwards, Berry, Whelan, Taylor, Charlton, Pegg.
(H. denotes game played at Maine Road.)*

1957 – 58
Prelim. Round, 1st leg: 25 Sept. A. v. SHAMROCK ROVERS
6 – 0, scorers: Whelan (2), Taylor (2), Berry, Pegg.
Atten: 45,000. Wood, Foulkes, Byrne, Goodwin,
Blanchflower, Edwards, Berry, Whelan, Taylor, Viollet, Pegg.
Prelim. Round, 2nd leg: 2 Oct. H. v. SHAMROCK ROVERS
3 – 2, scorers: Violett (2), Pegg.
Atten: 33,754. Wood, Foulkes, Byrne, Colman, Jones,
McGuinness, Berry, Webster, Taylor, Viollet, Pegg.
Round 1, 1st leg: 21 Nov. H. v. DUKLA PRAGUE
3 – 0, scorers: Webster, Taylor, Pegg.
Atten: 60,000. Wood, Foulkes, Byrne, Colman, Blanchflower,
Edwards, Berry, Whelan, Taylor, Webster, Pegg.
Round 1, 2nd leg: 4 Dec. A. v. DUKLA PRAGUE
0 – 1. *Atten: 35,000.* Wood, Foulkes, Byrne, Colman,
Jones, Edwards, Scanlon, Whelan, Taylor, Webster, Pegg.
Quarter-final, 1st leg: 14 Jan. H. v. RED STAR BELGRADE
2 – 1, scorers: Charlton, Colman.
Atten: 63,000. Gregg, Foulkes, Byrne, Colman, Jones,
Edwards, Morgans, Charlton, Taylor, Viollet, Scanlon.
Quarter-final, 2nd leg: 5 Feb. A. v. RED STAR BELGRADE
3 – 3, scorers: Violett, Charlton (2).
Atten: 52,000. Gregg, Foulkes, Byrne, Colman, Jones,
Edwards, Morgans, Charlton, Taylor, Viollet, Scanlon.
Semi-final, 1st leg: 8 May H. v. AC MILAN
2 – 1, scorers: Viollet, E. Taylor (pen.).
Atten: 44,882. Gregg, Foulkes, Greaves, Goodwin, Cope,
Crowther, Morgans, E. Taylor, Webster, Viollet, Pearson.
Semi-final, 2nd leg: 14 May A. v. AC MILAN 0 – 4.
Atten: 80,000. Gregg, Foulkes, Greaves, Goodwin, Cope,
Crowther, Morgans, E. Taylor, Webster, Viollet, Pearson.

1965 – 66
Prelim. Round, 1st leg: 22 Sept. A. v. HJK HELSINKI
3 – 2, scorers: Herd, Connelly, Law.
Atten: 15,000. Gaskell, Brennan, Dunne, Fitzpatrick, Foulkes,
Stiles, Connelly, Charlton, Herd, Law, Aston.
Prelim. Round, 2nd leg: 6 Oct. H. v. HJK HELSINKI
6 – 0, scorers: Connelly (3), Best (2), Charlton.
Atten: 30,388. P.A.G. Dunne, Brennan, Dunne, Crerand,
Foulkes, Stiles, Connelly, Best, Charlton, Law, Aston.
Round 1, 1st leg: 17 Nov. A. v. ASK VORWAERTS
2 – 0, scorers: Law, Connelly.
Atten: 40,000. Gregg, Dunne, Cantwell, Crerand, Foulkes,
Stiles, Best, Law, Charlton, Herd, Connelly.
Round 1, 2nd leg: 1 Dec. H. v. ASK VORWAERTS
3 – 1, scorers: Herd (3).
Atten: 30,082. P.A.G. Dunne, Dunne, Cantwell, Crerand,
Foulkes, Stiles, Best, Law, Charlton, Herd, Connelly.
Quarter-final, 1st leg: 2 Feb. H. v. SL BENFICA
3 – 2, scorers: Herd, Law, Foulkes.
Atten: 64,035. Gregg, Dunne, Cantwell, Crerand, Foulkes,
Stiles, Best, Law, Charlton, Herd, Connelly.
Quarter-final, 2nd leg: 9 Mar. A. v. SL BENFICA
5 – 1, scorers: Best (2), Connelly, Crerand, Charlton.
Atten: 75,000. Gregg, Brennan, Dunne, Crerand, Foulkes,
Stiles, Best, Law, Charlton, Herd, Connelly.
Semi-final, 1st leg: 13 April A. v. PARTIZAN BELGRADE
0 – 2. *Atten: 60,000.* Gregg, Brennan, Dunne, Crerand,
Foulkes, Stiles, Best, Law, Charlton, Herd, Connelly.
Semi-final, 2nd leg: 20 April H. v. PARTIZAN BELGRADE
1 – 0, scorer: O.g. (Soskic).
Atten: 62,500. Gregg, Brennan, Dunne, Crerand, Foulkes,
Stiles, Anderson, Law, Charlton, Herd, Connelly.

1967 – 68
Round 1, 1st leg: 20 Sept. H. v. HIBERNIANS (Malta)
4 – 0, scorers: Sadler (2), Law (2).
Atten: 43,912. Stepney, Dunne, Burns, Crerand, Foulkes,
Stiles, Best, Sadler, Charlton, Law, Kidd.
Round 1, 2nd leg: 27 Sept. A. v. HIBERNIANS (Malta) 0 – 0.
Atten: 23,217. Stepney, Dunne, Burns, Crerand, Foulkes,
Stiles, Best, Sadler, Charlton, Law, Kidd.
Round 1, 1st leg: 15 Nov. A. v. FK SARAJEVO 0 – 0.
Atten: 45,000. Stepney, Dunne, Burns, Crerand, Foulkes,
Sadler, Fitzpatrick, Kidd, Charlton, Best, Aston.
Round 2, 2nd leg: 29 Nov. H. v. FK SARAJEVO
2 – 1, scorers: Aston, Best.
Atten: 62,801. Stepney, Brennan, Dunne, Crerand,
Foulkes, Sadler, Burns, Kidd, Charlton, Best, Aston.
Quarter-final, 1st leg: 28 Feb. H. v. KS GORNIK ZABRZE
2 – 0, scorers: O.g. (Florenski), Kidd.
Atten: 63,500. Stepney, Dunne, Burns, Crerand, Sadler, Stiles,
Best, Kidd, Charlton, Ryan, Aston.
Quarter-final, 2nd leg: 13 Mar. A. v. KS GORNIK ZABRZE
0 – 1. *Atten: 105,000.* Stepney, Dunne, Burns, Crerand,
Sadler, Stiles, Fitzpatrick, Kidd, Charlton, Best, Herd.
Semi-final, 1st leg: 24 April H. v. CF REAL MADRID
1 – 0, scorer: Best.
Atten: 63,200. Stepney, Dunne, Burns, Crerand, Sadler, Stiles,
Best, Kidd, Charlton, Law, Aston.
Semi-final, 2nd leg: 15 May A. v. CF REAL MADRID
3 – 3, scorers: O.g. (Zocco), Sadler, Foulkes.
Atten: 120,000. Stepney, Brennan, Dunne, Crerand, Foulkes,
Stiles, Best, Kidd, Charlton, Sadler, Aston.
Final: 29 May Wembley v. SL BENFICA
4 – 1, scorers: Charlton (2), Best, Kidd.
Atten: 100,000. Stepney, Brennan, Dunne, Crerand, Foulkes,
Stiles, Best, Kidd, Charlton, Sadler, Aston.

1968 – 69
Round 1, 1st leg: 18 Sept. A. v. WATERFORD
3 – 1, scorer: Law (3).   Atten: 48,000. Stepney, Dunne, Burns, Crerand, Foulkes, Stiles, Best, Sadler, Charlton, Law, Kidd. (Sub: Rimmer 1).
Round 1, 2nd leg: 20 Oct. H. v. WATERFORD
7 – 1, scorers: Stiles, Law (4), Burns, Charlton.
Atten: 41,750. Stepney, Dunne, Burns, Crerand, Foulkes, Stiles, Best, Sadler, Charlton, Law, Kidd.
Round 2, 1st leg: 13 Nov. H. v. RSC ANDERLECHT
3 – 0, scorers: Kidd, Law (2).
Atten: 51,000. Stepney, Brennan, Dunne, Crerand, Sadler, Stiles, Ryan, Kidd, Charlton, Law, Sartori.
Round 2, 2nd leg: 27 Nov. A. v. RSC ANDERLECHT
1 – 3, scorer: Sartori.
Atten: 35,000. Stepney, Kopel, Dunne, Crerand, Foulkes, Sadler, Fitzpatrick, Stiles, Charlton, Law, Sartori.
Quarter-final, 1st leg: 26 Feb. H. v. SK RAPID VIENNA
3 – 0, scorers: Best (2), Morgan.
Atten: 63,118. Stepney, Fitzpatrick, Dunne, Crerand, James, Stiles, Morgan, Kidd, Charlton, Law, Best.
Quarter-final, 2nd leg: 5 Mar. A. v. SK RAPID VIENNA
0 – 0.   Atten: 52,000. Stepney, Fitzpatrick, Dunne, Crerand, James, Stiles, Morgan, Kidd, Charlton, Sadler, Best.
Semi-final, 1st leg: 23 April A. v. AC MILAN 0 – 2.
Atten: 88,000. Rimmer, Brennan, Fitzpatrick, Crerand, Foulkes, Stiles, Morgan, Kidd, Charlton, Law, Best. (Sub: Burns, 6).
Semi-final, 2nd leg: 15 May H. v. AC MILAN
1 – 0, scorer: Charlton.
Atten: 63,103. Rimmer, Brennan, Burns, Crerand, Foulkes, Stiles, Morgan, Kidd, Charlton, Law, Best.

EUROPEAN CUP WINNERS CUP
1963 – 64
Round 1, 1st leg: 25 Sept. A. v. WILLEM II
1 – 1, scorer: Herd.
Atten: 20,000. Gregg, Dunne, Cantwell, Crerand, Foulkes, Setters, Herd, Chisnall, Sadler, Law, Charlton.
Round 1, 2nd leg: 15 Oct. H. v. WILLEM II
6 – 1, scorers: Law (3), Charlton, Chisnall, Setters.
Atten: 42,672. Gregg, Dunne, Cantwell, Crerand, Foulkes, Setters, Herd, Chisnall, Sadler, Law, Charlton.
Round 2, 1st leg: 3 Dec. A. v. TOTTENHAM HOTSPUR
0 – 2.   Atten: 57,447. Gaskell, Dunne, Cantwell, Crerand, Foulkes, Setters, Quixall, Stiles, Herd, Law, Charlton.
Round 2, 2nd leg: 10 Dec. H. v. TOTTENHAM HOTSPUR
4 – 1, scorers: Herd (2), Charlton (2).
Atten: 48,639. Gaskell, Dunne, Cantwell, Crerand, Foulkes, Setters, Quixall, Chisnall, Sadler, Herd, Charlton.
Quarter-final, 1st leg: 26 Feb. H. v. SPORTING LISBON
4 – 1, scorers: Law (3) (2 pen.), Charlton.
Atten: 60,297. Gaskell, Brennan, Dunne, Crerand, Foulkes, Setters, Herd, Stiles, Charlton, Law, Best.
Quarter-final, 2nd leg: 18 Mar. A. v. SPORTING LISBON
0 – 5. Atten: 50,000. Gaskell, Brennan, Dunne, Crerand, Foulkes, Setters, Best, Chisnall, Herd, Law, Charlton.

1977 – 78
Round 1, 1st leg: 14 Sept. A. v. AS ST. ETIENNE
1 – 1, scorer: Hill.
Atten: 33,678. Stepney, Nicholl, Albiston, McIlroy, Greenhoff, Buchan, McGrath, McCreery, Pearson, Coppell, Hill. (Sub: Grimes 4, Houston 5).
Round 1, 2nd leg: 5 Oct. H. v. AS ST. ETIENNE
2 – 0, scorers: Pearson, Coppell.
Atten: 31,634. Stepney, Nicholl, Albiston, McIlroy, Greenhoff, Buchan, Coppell, J. Greenhoff, Pearson, Macari, Hill. (Sub: McGrath 9).
Round 2, 1st leg: 19 Oct. A. v. FC PORTO 0 – 4.
Atten: 60,000. Stepney, Nicholl, Albiston, McIlroy, Houston, Buchan, McGrath, McCreery, Coppell, Macari, Hill. (Sub: Forsyth 5, Grimes 7).
Round 2, 2nd leg: 2 Nov. H. v. FC PORTO
5 – 2, scorers: Coppell (2), O.g. (Murca) (2), Nicholl.
Atten: 51,831. Stepney, Nicholl, Albiston, McIlroy, Houston, Buchan, McGrath, Coppell, Pearson, McCreery, Hill.
1983 – 84
Round 1, 1st leg: 14 Sept. H. v. DULKA PRAGUE
1 – 1, scorer: Wilkins (pen.).
Atten: 39,745. Bailey, Duxbury, Albiston, Wilkins, Moran, McQueen, Robson, Muhren, Stapleton, Macari, Graham. (Sub: Moses 8, Gidman 7).
Round 1, 2nd leg: 27 Sept. A. v. DULKA PRAGUE
2 – 2, scorers: Robson, Stapleton.
Atten: 28,850. Bailey, Duxbury, Albiston, Wilkins, Moran, McQueen, Robson, Muhren, Stapleton, Whiteside, Graham.
Round 2, 1st leg: 19 Oct. A. v. JSK SPARTAK VARNA
2 – 1, scorers: Robson, Graham.
Atten: 40,000. Bailey, Duxbury, Albiston, Wilkins, Moran, McQueen, Robson, Muhren, Stapleton, Whiteside, Graham.
Round 2, 2nd leg: 2 Nov. H. v. JSK SPARTAK VARNA
2 – 0, scorer: Stapleton (2).
Atten: 39,079. Bailey, Duxbury, Albiston, Moses, Moran, McQueen, Robson, Muhren, Stapleton, Whiteside, Graham. (Sub: Dempsey 5, Hughes 10).
Quarter-final, 1st leg: 7 Mar. A. v. FC BARCELONA 0 – 2.
Atten: 70,000. Bailey, Duxbury, Albiston, Wilkins, Moran, Hogg, Robson, Muhren, Stapleton, Hughes, Moses. (Sub: Graham 10)
Quarter-final, 2nd leg: 21 Mar. H. v. FC BARCELONA
3 – 0, scorers: Robson (2), Stapleton.
Atten: 58,547. Bailey, Duxbury, Albiston, Wilkins, Moran, Hogg, Robson, Muhren, Stapleton, Whiteside, Moses. (Sub: Hughes 10).
Semi-final, 1st leg: 11 April H. v. JUVENTUS
1 – 1, scorer: Davies.
Atten: 58,171. Bailey, Duxbury, Albiston, McGrath, Moran, Hogg, Graham, Moses, Stapleton, Whiteside, Gidman. (Sub: Davies 11).
Semi-final, 2nd leg: 25 April A. v. JUVENTUS
1 – 2, scorer: Whiteside.
Atten: 64,655. Bailey, Duxbury, Albiston, Wilkins, Moran, Hogg, McGrath, Moses, Stapleton, Hughes, Graham, (Sub: Whiteside 9).

EUROPEAN ANALYSIS

	Pl.	W	D	L	F	A	Players used	Top scorers
European Cup	41	26	7	8	100	45	48	14 Law
European Cup- -Winners Cup	18	8	5	5	35	27	49	6 Law
Inter-Cities Fairs Cup	11	6	3	2	29	10	12	8 Law, Charlton
U.E.F.A. Cup	16	6	6	4	17*	14*	37	3 Muhren, Robson, Strachan
World Club Cup	2	0	1	1	1	2	14	1 Morgan
	88	46	22	20	186	103	* Penalties scored in the Videoton tie-breaker, not included.	

INTER-CITIES FAIRS CUP AND U.E.F.A. CUP RECORD

INTER-CITIES FAIRS CUP

1964 – 65
Round 1, 1st leg: 23 Sept. A. v. DJURGARDENS IF
1 – 1, scorer: Herd.
Atten: 6,537. P.A.G. Dunne, Brennan, Dunne, Crerand,
Foulkes, Setters, Connelly, Charlton, Herd, Stiles, Best.
Round 1, 2nd leg: 27 Sept. H. v. DJURGADENS IF
6 – 1, scorers: Law (3) (1 pen.), Charlton (2), Best.
Atten: 38,437. P.A.G. Dunne, Brennan, Dunne, Crerand,
Foulkes, Stiles, Connelly, Charlton, Herd, Law, Best.
Round 2, 1st leg: 11 Nov. A. v. BORUSSIA DORTMUND
6 – 1, scorers: Herd, Charlton (3), Best, Law.
Atten: 18,000. P.A.G. Dunne, Brennan, Dunne, Crerand,
Foulkes, Stiles, Connelly, Charlton, Herd, Law, Best.
Round 2, 2nd leg: 2 Dec. H. v. BORUSSIA DORTMUND
4 – 0, scorers: Charlton (2), Law, Connelly.
Atten: 31,896. P.A.G. Dunne, Brennan, Dunne, Crerand,
Foulkes, Stiles, Connelly, Charlton, Herd, Law, Best.
Round 3, 1st leg: 20 Jan. H. v. EVERTON 1 – 1,
scorer: Connelly. *Atten: 49,075.* P.A.G. Dunne,
Brennan, Dunne, Crerand, Foulkes, Stiles, Connelly,
Charlton, Herd, Law, Best.
Round 3, 2nd leg: 9 Feb. A. v. EVERTON 2 – 1,
scorers: Connelly, Herd. *Atten: 54,397.* P.A.G. Dunne,
Brennan, Dunne, Crerand, Foulkes, Stiles, Connelly,
Charlton, Herd, Law, Best.
Quarter-final, 1st leg: 12 May A. v. RACING CLUB
STRASBOURG 5 – 0, scorers: Connelly, Herd, Law
(2), Charlton. *Atten: 28,911.* P.A.G. Dunne,
Brennan, Dunne, Crerand, Foulkes, Stiles, Connelly, Charlton,
Herd, Law, Best.
Quarter-final, 2nd leg: 19 May H. v. RACING CLUB
STRASBOURG 0 – 0. *Atten: 34,188.* P.A.G. Dunne,
Brennan, Dunne, Crerand, Foulkes, Stiles, Connelly,
Charlton, Herd, Law, Best.
Semi-final, 1st leg: 31 May H. v. TC FERENEVAROS
3 – 2, scorers: Law (pen.), Herd (2). *Atten: 39.902.*
P.A.G. Dunne, Brennan, Dunne, Crerand, Foulkes, Stiles,
Connelly, Charlton, Herd, Law, Best.
Semi-final, 2nd leg: 6 June A. v. TC FERENCVAROS 0 – 1.
Atten: 60,000. P.A.G. Dunne, Brennan, Dunne, Crerand,
Foulkes, Stiles, Connelly, Charlton, Herd, Law, Best.
Play-off: 16 June A. v. TC FERENCVAROS 1 – 2,
scorer: Connelly. *Atten: 90,000.* P.A.G. Dunne,
Brennan, Dunne, Crerand, Foulkes, Stiles, Connelly, Charlton,
Herd, Law, Best.

U.E.F.A. CUP

1976 – 77
Round 1, 1st leg: 15 Sept. A. v. AJAX AMSTERDAM 0 – 1.
Atten: 30,000. Stepney, Nicholl, Houston, Daly, Greenhoff,
Buchan, Coppell, McIlroy, Pearson, Macari, Hill.
(Sub: McCreery 4).
Round 1, 2nd leg: 29 Sept. H. v. AJAX AMSTERDAM
2 – 0, scorers: Macari, McIlroy. *Atten: 58,938.* Stepney,
Nicholl, Houston, Daly, Greenhoff, Buchan, Coppell,
McIlroy, McCreery, Macari, Hill. (Sub: Albiston 4,
Paterson 11).
Round 2, 1st leg: 20 Oct. H. v. JUVENTUS 1 – 0,
scorer: Hill. *Atten: 59,021.* Stepney, Nicholl, Albiston,
Daly, Greenhoff, Houston, Coppell, McIlroy, Pearson,
Macari, Hill. (Sub: McCreery 4).

Round 2, 2nd leg: 3 Nov. A v JUVENTUS 0 – 3.
Atten: 66,632. Stepney, Nicholl, Albiston, Daly, Greenhoff,
Houston, Coppell, McIlroy, Pearson, Macari, Hill.
(Sub: McCreery 8, Paterson 10).
1980 – 81
Round 1, 1st leg: 17 Sept. H. v. RTS WIDZEW LODZ 1 – 1,
scorer: McIlroy. *Atten: 38,037.* Bailey, Nicholl, Albiston,
McIlroy, Jovanovic, Buchan, Grimes, J. Greenhoff, Coppell,
Macari, Thomas. (Sub: Duxbury 2).
Round 1, 2nd leg: 10 Oct. A. v. RTS WIDZEW LODZ 0 – 0.
Atten: 35,000. Bailey, Nicholl, Albiston, McIlroy, Jovanovic,
Buchan, Grimes, Coppell, Jordan, Duxbury, Thomas.
(Sub: Moran 6).
1982 – 83
Round 1, 1st leg: 15 Sept. H. v. CF VALENCIA 0 – 0.
Atten: 46,588. Bailey, Duxbury, Albiston, Wilkins, Buchan,
McQueen, Robson, Grimes, Stapleton, Whiteside, Coppell.
Round 1, 2nd leg: 29 Sept. A. v. CF VALENCIA 1 – 2,
scorer: Robson. *Atten: 35,000.* Bailey, Duxbury,
Albiston, Wilkins, Moran, Buchan, Robson, Grimes,
Stapleton, Whiteside, Moses. (Sub: Macari 6, Coppell 11).
1984 – 85
Round 1, 1st leg: 19 Sept. H. v. RABA VASAS ETO GYOR
3 – 0, scorers: Robson, Muhren, Hughes.
Atten: 33,119. Bailey, Duxbury, Albiston, Moses, Moran,
Hogg, Robson, Muhren, Hughes, Whiteside, Olsen.
Round 1, 2nd leg: 30 Oct. A. v. RABA VASAS ETO GYOR
2 – 2, scorers: Brazil, Muhren (pen.).
Atten: 26,000. Bailey, Duxbury, Albiston, Moses, Moran,
Hogg, Robson, Muhren, Hughes, Brazil, Olsen.
(Sub: Gidman 7).
Round 2, 1st leg: 24 Oct. A. v. PSV EINDHOVEN 0 – 0.
Atten: 27,500. Bailey, Gidman, Albiston, Moses, Moran,
Hogg, Robson, Strachan, Hughes, Brazil, Olsen.
Round 2, 2nd leg: 7 Nov. H. v. PSV EINDHOVEN 1 – 0,
scorer: Strachan (pen.) after extra time. 90 minutes: 0 – 0.
Atten: 39,281. Bailey, Gidman, Albiston, Moses, Moran,
Hogg, Robson, Strachan, Hughes, Stapleton, Olsen.
(Sub: Whiteside 10, Garton 5).
Round 3, 1st leg: 28 Nov. H. v. DUNDEE UNITED 2 – 2,
scorers: Strachan (pen.), Robson.
Atten: 48,278. Bailey, Gidman, Albiston, Moses, McQueen,
Duxbury, Robson, Strachan, Hughes, Whiteside, Olsen.
(Sub: Stapleton 10).
Round 3, 2nd leg: 12 Dec. A. v. DUNDEE UNITED 3 – 2,
scorers: Hughes, Muhren, O.g. (McGinnis).
Atten: 22,500. Bailey, Gidman, Albiston, Moses, McQueen,
Duxbury, Robson, Strachan, Stapleton, Hughes, Muhren.
Quarter-final, 1st leg: 6 Mar. H. v. VIDEOTON 1 – 0,
scorer: Stapleton. *Atten: 35,432.* Bailey, Gidman,
Albiston, Duxbury, McGrath, Hogg, Strachan, Whiteside,
Hughes, Stapleton, Olsen.
Quarter-final, 2nd leg: 20 Mar. A. v. VIDEOTON 0 – 1.
After 90 minutes and extra time: 0 – 1: Videoton won 4 – 6
on penalties). Scorers: Whiteside, Olsen, Strachan, Gidman
(all penalties). *Atten: 25,000.* Bailey, Gidman, Albiston, Duxbury, McGrath,
Hogg, Robson, Strachan, Hughes, Stapleton, Whiteside.
(Sub: Olsen 7).

WORLD CLUB CHAMPIONSHIP 1968 – 69

1st leg: 25 Sept. A. v. ESTUDIANTES DE PLATA 0 – 1.
Atten: 70,000. Stepney, Dunne, Burns, Crerand, Foulkes,
Stiles, Morgan, Sadler, Charlton, Law, Best.

2nd leg: 16 Oct. H. v. ESTUDIANTES DE PLATA 1 – 1,
scorer: Morgan. *Atten: 63,428.* Stepney, Brennan,
Dunne, Crerand, Foulkes, Sadler, Morgan, Kidd, Charlton,
Law, Best. (Sub: Sartori 10).

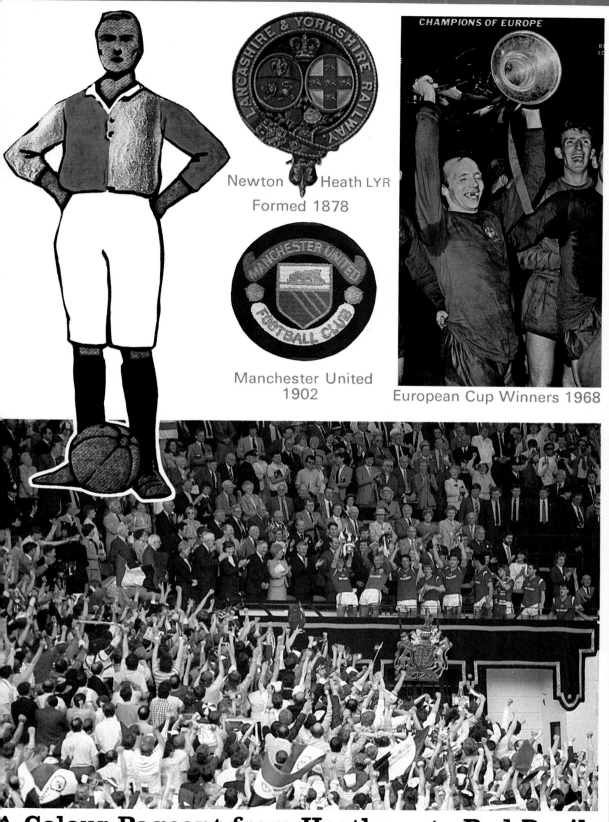

Newton Heath LYR
Formed 1878

Manchester United
1902

CHAMPIONS OF EUROPE

European Cup Winners 1968

A Colour Pageant from Heathens to Red Devils

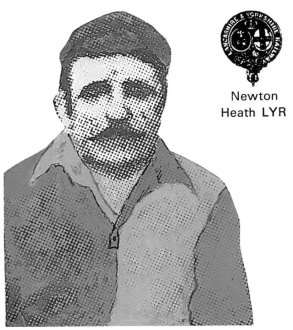

Newton
Heath LYR

MANCHESTER UNITED'S MASCOT WHEN THEY WON THE CUP IN 1909 WAS A SUPPORTER'S PET GOAT. IT WENT WITH THE TEAM TO THE FINAL AT CRYSTAL PALACE AND JOINED IN THE CELEBRATIONS FOLLOWING UNITED'S VICTORY OVER BRISTOL CITY.

UP THE UNITED

Above : R. DONALDSON,
Newton Heath 1891-1898 (KM)

Above : F.A. Cup Winners 1909 (MMUSC)

Below : F.A. Cup Winners 1948 (JG)

The Daily Dispatch
CUP FINAL SOUVENIR
MANCHESTER UNITED v. BLACKPOOL
WEMBLEY, APRIL 24, 1948

JOHNNY CAREY
Captain
Manchester United

HARRY JOHNSTON
Captain
Blackpool

1/-

Edited by ARCHIE LEDBROOKE

Duncan Edwards

Tommy Taylor

THE BUSBY BABES

MUNICH 1958

Back Row (left to right): Eddie Colman, Bill Foulkes, Ray Wood, Roger Byrne, Mark Jones, Duncan Edwards.
Front Row: Dennis Viollet, Johnny Berry, Tommy Taylor, Bill Whelan, David Pegg.

SHARP ELECTRONICS PROUD SPONSOR

MANCHESTER UNITED FOOTBALL CLUB

ESTADIO SANTIAGO BERNABE[U]

El miércoles 15 de mayo de 1968 — A LAS 8,30 DE LA NOC[HE]

XIII COPA DE EUROPA (Semifinal)

MANCHESTER UNITED-REAL MADRID C. de [F.]

(CAMPEON DE INGLATERRA) — (CAMPEON DE ESPAÑA)

VENTA DE LOCALIDADES

PRECIOS DE LAS LOCALIDADES (incluidos todos los impuestos)

LOCALIDADES DE ASIENTO SIN ENTRADA		DELANTERA Y FILAS
PREFERENCIA	Tribuna	300
	Grada	250
	1.ª Anfiteatro	200
	2.ª Anfiteatro	150
FONDOS NORTE Y SUR	Tribuna	200
	1.ª Anfiteatro	150
	2.ª Anfiteatro	125

LOCALIDADES DE PIE		
LATERAL	Cubierta	75
	Baja	75
	2.ª Anfiteatro Bajo y Alo...	50
	3.ª Anfiteatro	25
Paseo Fondo Norte y Sur, 2.ª Anfiteatro		75
Para niños, y militares sin graduación uniformados		10
Entradas Fondos Norte y Sur para socios Real Madrid		15
Entradas para localidades de asiento		100

ORDEN DE VENTA	DIAS Y HORAS	TAQUILLAS
Sres. abonados, abonados al tercer anfiteatro de pie y localidades de fondo norte y sur para socios del Real Madrid	2, 3, 4, 6 y 7, de 6 a 9 de la noche.	Taquillas interiores del Estadio, p...
Localidades de fondo norte y sur, exclusivamente para socios del Real Madrid	2, 3, 4, 6 y 7, de 6 a 9 de la noche.	Exteriores del Estadio, taquilla n... Avenida Monte Igueldo, 6, bar (V... Mesón de Paredes, 2 (Casa Marian... Menorca, 27 (Bar La Bolera). Almendrales, 35 (Bar Botafogo).
Para público, localidades sin numerar.		Bravo Murillo, 283 (Bar La Mezq... Joaquín García Morato, 147 (Casa ... Alcalá, 199 (Bar Los Charros). Plaza San Miguel, 9 (Bar San Mi... Luva 3, Cruz de los Caídos (Billares... Taquillas interiores del Estadio...

FOOTBALL LEAGUE CHAMPIONS 1966-7

J. P. MURPHY
(Assistant Manager)

J. CROMPTON
(Trainer)

FAMOUS FOOTBALLERS
Nº 1

R. CHARLTON
(Manchester Un. and England)

Robert (Bobby) Charlton, aged 28, has played for Manchester United since he was 17 and was capped for England 58 times up till the end of last season. In July he will be one of the strengths of England's attack in the World Cup series. Read about the making of Bobby Charlton and the impact of the World Cup on Britain in a 12-page feature starting on page 8.

A SERIES OF 48
ISSUED BY
THE SUNDAY TIMES
GRAYS INN ROAD. LONDON. ENGLAND.

nited lift Chris

Grantham Journal
CHRISTOPHER APPEAL

★ ★ ★ ★
THE REDS ARE COMING
★ ★ ★ ★

GRANTHAM
v.
MAN. UTD.

THURSDAY, 1st MAY 1986 — 7.00p.m. KICK-OFF

LONDON ROAD FOOTBALL GROUND, GRANTHAM

ts £2.00   Juniors £1.00 — available at ground or Candy Kitchen

Top Left : Matt Busby with three United winners of 'European Player of the Year' — Best, Charlton and Law (JG).

Centre Left : Bobby Charlton, from The Sunday Times Magazine feature on the 1966 World Cup (JG).

Bottom Left : Human Face of Soccer 1986. United sent a star-studded team to aid the appeal for Leukaemia victim Christopher Buckingham (KM).

1985 F.A. CUP WINNERS

Back Row (L. to R): RON ATKINSON (Manager), MICK BROWN (Asst. Manager), MARK HUGHES, GORDON McQUEEN, JESPER OLSEN, NORMAN WHITESIDE, STEVE PEARS (hidden), GARY BAILEY, FRANK STAPLETON, GRAEME HOGG, PAUL McGRATH.
Front Row (L. to R): GORDON STRACHAN, JOHN GIDMAN, ARTHUR ALBISTON, MIKE DUXBURY, BRYAN ROBSON, KEVIN MORAN.

MANCHESTER UNITED

MIKE DUXBURY   BRYAN ROBSON

1983 F.A. CUP WINNERS

✒ F.A. CHARITY SHIELD ᴥ

Manchester United were the first-ever winners of the F.A. Charity Shield when it was introduced in 1908, initially as a challenge match between the respective Champions of the Football League and the Southern League. Here are the results and United teams for each of the thirteen occasions the Club has competed for the Shield.
* denotes trophy shared — 6 months each.

1908 27 April v. QUEEN'S PARK RANGERS 1 − 1, scorer: Meredith. Attendance: 12,000 *(Park Royal)*. Moger, Stacey, Burgess, Duckworth, Roberts, Bell, Meredith, Bannister, J. Turnbull, A. Turnbull, Wall.
Replay 29 Aug. v. QUEEN'S PARK RANGERS 4 − 0, scorers: J. Turnbull (3), Wall. Attendance: 30,000 *(Stamford Bridge)*. Moger, Stacey, Burgess, Duckworth, Roberts, Bell, Meredith, Bannister, J. Turnbull, Picken, Wall.
1911 25 Sept. v. SWINDON TOWN 8 − 4, scorers: Halse (6), Turnbull, Wall. Attendance: 12,000 *(Stamford Bridge)*. Edmonds, Hofton, Stacey, Duckworth, Roberts, Bell, Meredith, Hamill, Halse, A. Turnbull, Wall.
1948 6 Oct. v. ARSENAL 3 − 4, scorers: Rowley, Burke, Mitten. Attendance: 31,000 *(Highbury)*. Crompton, Carey, Aston, Anderson, Chilton, Warner, Delaney, Morris, Burke, Rowley, Mitten.
1952 24 Sept. v. NEWCASTLE UNITED 4 − 2, scorers: Rowley (2), Byrne, Downie. Attendance: 11,381 *(Old Trafford)*. Wood, McNulty, Aston, Carey, Chilton, Gibson, Berry, Downie, Rowley, Pearson, Byrne.
1956 24 Oct. v. MANCHESTER CITY 1 − 0, scorer: Viollet. Attendance: 30,495 *(Maine Road)*. Wood, Foulkes, Byrne, Colman, Jones, Edwards, Berry, Whelan, Taylor, Violett, Pegg. (Sub: Gaskell).
1957 22 Oct. v. ASTON VILLA 4 − 0, scorers: Taylor (3), Berry (pen.). Attendance: 27,923 *(Old Trafford)*. Wood, Foulkes, Byrne, Goodwin, Blanchflower, Edwards, Berry, Whelan, Taylor, Violett, Pegg.
1963 17 Aug. v. EVERTON 0 − 4. Attendance: 54,840 *(Goodison Park)*. Gaskell, Dunne, Cantwell, Crerand, Foulkes, Setters, Giles, Quixall, Herd, Law, Charlton.
1965 14 Aug. v. LIVERPOOL 2 − 2*, scorers: Best, Herd. Attendance: 48,502 *(Old Trafford)*. Dunne, Brennan, A.P. Dunne, Crerand, Cantwell, Stiles, Best, Charlton, Herd, Law, Aston. (Sub: Anderson).
1967 12 Aug. v. TOTTENHAM HOTSPUR 3 − 3*, scorers: Charlton (2), Law. Attendance: 54,106 *(Old Trafford)*. Stepney, Brennan, A.P. Dunne, Crerand, Foulkes, Stiles, Best, Law, Charlton, Kidd, Aston.
1977 13 Aug. v. LIVERPOOL 0 − 0*. Attendance: 82,000 *(Wembley)*. Stepney, Nicholl, Albiston, McIlroy, B. Greenhoff, Buchan, Coppell, J. Greenhoff, Pearson, Macari, Hill. (Sub: McCreery).
1983 20 Aug. v. LIVERPOOL 2 − 0, scorer: Robson (2). Attendance: 92,000 *(Wembley)*. Bailey, Duxbury, Albiston, Wilkins, Moran, McQueen, Robson, Muhren, Stapleton, Whiteside, Graham. (Sub: Gidman).
1985 10 Aug. v. EVERTON 0 − 2. Attendance: 82,000 *(Wembley)*. Bailey, Gidman, Albiston, Whiteside, McGrath, Hogg, Robson, Duxbury, Hughes, Stapleton, Olsen. (Sub: Moses).

DID YOU KNOW? United's 1967 Charity Shield match with F.A. Cup holders Tottenham Hotspur featured one of the strangest goals ever scored at Old Trafford. Pat Jennings, the Spurs' goalkeeper drop-kicked a mighty clearance upfield, and to the surprise of everyone, the bounce of the ball deceived his opposite number, Alex Stepney, to enter the United net.

THE F.A. CHARITY SHIELD

A COLOUR PAGEANT FROM HEATHENS TO RED DEVILS

The publishers would like to express their appreciation to E.C.S. of Nottingham for producing the colour section on pages 245 to 252, and also to the following for their assistance and co-operation: Andrew Burslem, Sharp Electronics (UK) Ltd., Dave Smith, Manchester United Supporters Club, Graham Buttershaw, Football Monthly, Steve Brown, Sporting Pictures (UK) Ltd., Paul Cope, Phil Walsh, E.C.S., Roger Heaton (Artist), Keith Mellor (Designer), Joe Glanville (Consultant).

Opposite page: Top: Football Monthly 1985 F.A. Cup Winners poster. (FM/SP).
Bottom: F.A. Cup Winners 1983. Mike Duxbury (left), Bryan Robson (right). (JG).

FOOTBALL LEAGUE CUP

1960 – 61
Round 2: 19 Oct. A. v. EXETER CITY
1 – 1, scorer: Dawson.
Atten: 4,679. Gregg, Setters, Brennan, Stiles, Foulkes, Nicholson, Dawson, Lawton, Viollet, Pearson, Scanlon.
Replay: 26 Oct. H. v. EXETER CITY 4 – 1, scorers: Quixall (2/1 pen.), Giles, Scanlon.
Atten: 15,662. Gaskell, Dunne, Carolan, Stiles, Cope, Nicholson, Dawson, Giles, Quixall, Pearson, Scanlon.
Round 3: 2 Nov. A. v. BRADFORD CITY
1 – 2, scorer: Viollet.
Atten: 4,670. Gregg, Setters, Brennan, Brett, Foulkes, Nicholson, Dawson, Giles, Viollet, Pearson, Scanlon.

1966 – 67
Round 2: 14 Sept. A. v. BLACKPOOL
1 – 5, scorer: Herd.
Atten: 15,570. Dunne, Brennan, A.P. Dunne, Crerand, Foulkes, Stiles, Connelly, Best, Sadler, Herd, Aston.

1969 – 70
Round 2: 3 Sept. H. v.
MIDDLESBROUGH 1 – 0, scorer: Sadler.
Atten: 38,888. Stepney, Fitzpatrick, A.P. Dunne, Crerand, James, Sadler, Morgan, Kidd, Charlton, Givens, Best.
(Sub: Gowling).
Round 3: 24 Sept. H. v. WREXHAM 2 – 0, scorers: Kidd, Best.
Atten: 48,315. Stepney, Fitzpatrick, A.P. Dunne, Burns, Ure, Sadler, Morgan, Kidd, Charlton, Aston, Best.
Round 4: 15 Oct. A. v. BURNLEY 0 – 0.
Atten: 28,472. Stepney, Fitzpatrick, A.P. Dunne, Burns, Ure, Sadler, Morgan, Kidd, Charlton, Aston, Best.
Replay: 20 Oct. H. v. BURNLEY 1 – 0, scorer: Best (pen.).
Atten: 51,614. Stepney, Fitzpatrick, A.P. Dunne, Burns, Ure, Sadler, Morgan, Kidd, Charlton, Aston, Best. (Sub: Sartori 2)
Round 5: 12 Nov. A. v. DERBY COUNTY
0 – 0. *Atten: 38,893.* Stepney, Brennan, A.P. Dunne, Burns, Ure, Sadler, Sartori, Best, Charlton, Law, Aston.
Replay: 19 Nov. H. v. DERBY COUNTY
1 – 0, scorer: Kidd.
Atten: 57,122. Stepney, Fitzpatrick, A.P. Dunne, Burns, Ure, Sadler, Best, Kidd, Charlton, Law, Aston. (Sub: Sartori 10).
Semi-final, 1st leg: 3 Dec. A. v. MANCHESTER CITY 1 – 2, scorer: Charlton.
Atten: 55,799. Stepney, Edwards, A.P. Dunne, Burns, Ure, Sadler, Best, Kidd, Charlton, Stiles, Aston.
Semi-final, 2nd leg: 17 Dec. H. v. MANCHESTER CITY 2 – 2, scorers: Edwards, Law.
Atten: 63,418. Stepney, Edwards, Dunne, Stiles, Ure, Sadler, Morgan, Crerand, Charlton, Law, Best.

1970 – 71
Round 2: 9 Sept. A. v. ALDERSHOT
3 – 1, scorers: Best, Kidd, Law.
Atten: 18,509. Rimmer, Edwards, Dunne, Fitzpatrick, Ure, Sadler, Stiles, Law, Charlton, Kidd, Best. (Sub: James).
Round 3: 7 Oct. H. v. PORTSMOUTH
1 – 0, scorer: Charlton.
Atten: 32,068. Rimmer, Donald, Burns,

Fitzpatrick, Ure, Sadler, Morgan, Gowling, Charlton, Kidd, Best. (Sub: Aston 6).
Round 4: 28 Oct. H. v. CHELSEA
2 – 1, scorers: Charlton, Best.
Atten: 47,565. Rimmer, Edwards, Dunne, Fitzpatrick, James, Sadler, Law, Best, Charlton, Kidd, Aston. (Sub: Burns 7).
Round 5: 18 Nov. H. v. CRYSTAL PALACE 4 – 2, scorers: Fitzpatrick, Kidd (2), O.g. (McCormick).
Atten: 48,961. Rimmer, Watson, Dunne, Fitzpatrick, James, Sadler, Law, Best, Charlton, Kidd, Aston.
Semi-final, 1st leg: 16 Dec. H. v. ASTON VILLA 1 – 1, scorer: Kidd.
Atten: 48,889. Rimmer, Watson, Dunne, Fitzpatrick, James, Stiles, Sartori, Best, Charlton, Kidd, Aston.
Semi-final, 2nd leg: 23 Dec. A. v. ASTON VILLA 1 – 2, scorer: Kidd.
Atten: 63,000. Rimmer, Fitzpatrick, Dunne, Crerand, Ure, Sadler, Morgan, Best, Charlton, Kidd, Law.

1971 – 72
Round 2: 7 Sept. A. v. IPSWICH TOWN
3 – 1, scorers: Morgan (pen.), Best (2).
Atten: 28,143. Stepney, O'Neil, Dunne, Gowling, James, Sadler, Morgan, Kidd, Charlton, Best, Aston.
Round 3: 6 Oct. H. v. BURNLEY
1 – 1, scorer: Charlton.
Atten: 44,600. Stepney, O'Neil, Dunne, Gowling, James, Sadler, Morgan, Kidd, Charlton, Best, Aston.
Replay: 18 Oct. A. v. BURNLEY
1 – 0, scorer: Charlton.
Atten: 27,533. Stepney, O'Neil, Dunne, Gowling, James, Sadler, Morgan, Kidd, Charlton, Law, Best.
Round 4: 27 Oct. H. v. STOKE CITY 1 – 1, scorer: Gowling.
Atten: 47,062. Stepney, O'Neil, Burns, Gowling, James, Sadler, Morgan, Kidd, Charlton, Law, Best. (Sub: Aston 8).
Replay: 8 Nov. A. v. STOKE CITY 0 – 0.
Atten: 40,805. Stepney, O'Neil, Burns, Gowling, James, Sadler, Morgan, Kidd, Charlton, McIlroy, Best. (Sub: Aston 8).
Replay: 15 Nov. A. v. STOKE CITY
1 – 2, scorer: Best.
Atten: 42,249. Stepney, O'Neil, Burns, Gowling, James, Sadler, Morgan, McIlroy, Charlton, Sartori, Best.

1972 – 73
Round 2: 6 Sept. A. v. OXFORD UNITED 2 – 2, scorers: Law, Charlton.
Atten: 17,177. Stepney, O'Neil, Dunne, Buchan, James, Sadler, Morgan, Charlton, Law, Best, Storey-Moore. (Sub: McIlroy 3).
Replay: 12 Sept. H. v. OXFORD UNITED
3 – 1, scorers: Storey-Moore, Best (2).
Atten: 21,436. Stepney, Fitzpatrick, Buchan, Young, James, Sadler, Morgan, Law, Charlton, Best, Storey-Moore.
(Sub: McIlroy 8).
Round 3: 3 Oct. A. v. BRISTOL ROVERS 1 – 1, scorer: Morgan.
Atten: 33,597. Stepney, Donald, Dunne, Young, James, Buchan, Morgan, Kidd, Charlton, Best, Storey-Moore.
Replay: 11 Oct. H. v. BRISTOL ROVERS 1 – 2, scorer: McIlroy.
Atten: 29,348. Stepney, Watson, Dunne, Young, James, Buchan, Morgan, Kidd, Charlton, Best, Storey-Moore.

(Sub: McIlroy, 8).

1973 – 74
Round 1: 8 Oct. H. v.
MIDDLESBROUGH 0 – 1.
Atten: 23,906. Stepney, Buchan, Young, Greenhoff, Holton, James, Morgan, Daly, Macari, Kidd, Graham, (Sub: Buchan 9).

1974 – 75
Round 2: 11 Sept. H. v. CHARLTON ATHLETIC 5 – 1, scorers: Macari (2), McIlroy, Houston, O.g. (Warman).
Atten: 21,616. Stepney, Forsyth, Houston, Martin, Holton, Buchan, Morgan, McIlroy, Macari, McCalliog, Daly, (Sub: Young, 2).
Round 3: 9 Oct. H. v. MANCHESTER CITY 1 – 0, scorer: Daly (pen.).
Atten: 55,159. Stepney, Forsyth, Albiston, Greenhoff, Holton, Buchan, Morgan, McIlroy, Pearson, McCalliog, Daly. (Sub: Macari 9).
Round 4: 13 Nov. H. v. BURNLEY
3 – 2, scorers: Macari (2), Morgan.
Atten: 46,275. Stepney, Forsyth, Houston, Greenhoff, Sidebottom, Buchan, Macari, McIlroy, Pearson, McCalliog, Daly. (Sub: Morgan 4).
Round 5: 4 Dec. A. v MIDDLESBROUGH
0 – 0. *Atten: 36,005.* Stepney, Forsyth, Houston, Greenhoff, Holton, Buchan, Morgan, McIlroy, Pearson, Macari, Daly. (Sub: Young 7).
Replay: 18 Dec. H. v. MIDDLESBROUGH
3 – 0, scorers: Pearson, Macari, McIlroy.
Atten: 49,501. Stepney, Young, Houston, Greenhoff, Sidebottom, Buchan, Morgan, McIlroy, Pearson, Macari, Daly. (Sub: McCalliog 11).
Semi-final, 1st leg: 15 Jan. H. v. NORWICH CITY 2 – 2, scorer: Macari (2).
Atten: 58,010. Stepney, Forsyth, Houston, Greenhoff, James, Buchan, Morgan, McIlroy, Daly, Macari, McCalliog. (Sub: Young 9).
Semi-final, 2nd leg: 22 Jan. A. v. NORWICH CITY 0 – 1. *Atten: 31,621.* Stepney, Forsyth, Houston, Greenhoff, James, Buchan, Morgan, McIlroy, Daly, Macari, McCalliog. (Sub: Young, 5).

1975 – 76
Round 2: 10 Sept. H. v. BRENTFORD
2 – 1, scorers: Macari, McIlroy.
Atten: 25,286. Stepney, Nicholl, Houston, Jackson, Greenhoff, Buchan, Coppell, McIlroy, Pearson, Macari, Daly.
(Sub: Grimshaw, 4).
Round 3: 8 Oct. A. v. ASTON VILLA
2 – 1, scorers: Macari, Coppell.
Atten: 41,447. Stepney, Nicholl, Houston, Jackson, Greenhoff, Buchan, Coppell, McIlroy, Pearson, Macari, Daly.
Round 4: 12 Nov. A. v. MANCHESTER CITY 0 – 4. *Atten: 50,182.* Roche, Nicholl, Houston, Jackson, Greenhoff, Buchan, Coppell, McIlroy, Pearson, Macari, Daly. (Sub: McCreery 4).

1976 – 77
Round 2: 1 Sept. H. v. TRANMERE ROVERS 5 – 0, scorers: Daly (2), Macari, Pearson, Hill.
Atten: 37,586. Stepney, Nicholl, Houston, Daly, Greenhoff, Buchan, Coppell, McIlroy, Pearson, Macari, Hill.
(Sub: McCreery 8).

Round 3: 22 Sept. H. v. SUNDERLAND 2–2, scorers: Pearson, O.g. (Clarke). *Atten: 46,170.* Stepney, Nicholl, Daly, Greenhoff, Buchan, McCreery, McIlroy, Pearson, Macari, Hill.
Replay: 4 Oct. A. v. SUNDERLAND 2–2, scorers: Greenhoff, Daly (pen.). *Atten: 30,831.* Stepney, Nicholl, Houston, Daly, Waldron, Buchan, Coppell, McIlroy, McCreery, Greenhoff, Hill. (Sub: Albiston 10).
Replay: 6 Oct. H v. SUNDERLAND 1–0, scorer: Greenhoff. *Atten: 47,689.* Stepney, Nicholl, Houston, Daly, Greenhoff, Buchan, Coppell, McIlroy, McCreery, Macari, Hill. (Sub: Albiston 11).
Round 4: 27 Oct. H. v. NEWCASTLE UNITED 7–2, scorers: Houston, Hill (3), Pearson, Nicholl, Coppell. *Atten: 52,002.* Stepney, Nicholl, Albiston, Daly, Greenhoff, Houston, Coppell, McIlroy, Pearson, Macari, Hill. (Sub: McGrath 9).
Round 5: 1 Dec. H. v EVERTON 0–3. *Atten: 57,378.* Stepney, Forsyth, Albiston, Daly, Paterson, Greenhoff, Coppell, McIlroy, Pearson, Jackson, Hill. (Sub: McCreery 4).

1977 – 78
Round 2: 30 Aug. A. v. ARSENAL 2–3, scorers: McCreery, Pearson. *Atten: 36,171.* Stepney, Nicholl, Albiston, Grimes, Greenhoff, Buchan, McCreery, Pearson, Macari, Hill. (Sub: McGrath 5).

1978 – 79
Round 2: 30 Aug. H. v. STOCKPORT COUNTY, 3–2, scorers: Jordan, McIlroy, Greenhoff (pen.). *Atten: 41,761.* Roche, B. Greenhoff, Albiston, McIlroy, McQueen, Buchan, Coppell, J. Greenhoff, Jordan, Macari, Grimes.
Round 3: 4 Oct. H. v. WATFORD 1–2, scorer: Jordan. *Atten: 40,534.* Roche, Albiston, Houston, B. Greenhoff, McQueen, Buchan, Coppell, J. Greenhoff, Jordan, McIlroy, Grimes. (Sub: McCreery 4).

1979 – 80
Round 2, 1st leg: 29 Aug. A. v. TOTTENHAM HOTSPUR 1–2, scorer: Thomas. *Atten: 29,163.* Bailey, Nicholl, Albiston, Paterson, McQueen, Buchan, Ritchie, Wilkins, Jordan, Macari, Thomas.
Round 2, 2nd leg: 5 Sept. H. v. TOTTENHAM HOTSPUR 3–1, scorers: Thomas, Coppell, O.g. (Miller). *Atten: 48,292.* Bailey, Nicholl, Albiston, McIlroy, Houston, Buchan, Coppell, Wilkins, Jordan, Macari, Thomas. (Sub: Ritchie, 5).
Round 3: 26 Sept. A. v. NORWICH CITY 1–4, scorer: McIlroy. *Atten: 18,312.* Bailey, Nicholl, Albiston, McIlroy, McQueen, Buchan, Grimes, Wilkins, Coppell, Macari, Thomas. (Sub: Ritchie 4).

1980 – 81
Round 2, 1st leg: 27 Aug. H. v. COVENTRY CITY 0–1. *Atten: 31,656.* Bailey, Nicholl, Albiston, McIlroy, Jovanovic, Buchan, Coppell, J. Greenhoff, Ritchie, Macari, Thomas. (Sub: Sloan 8).
Round 2, 2nd leg: 2 Sept. A. v.

COVENTRY CITY 0–1. *Atten: 18,946.* Bailey, Nicholl, Albiston, McIlroy, Jovanovic, Buchan, Coppell, J. Greenhoff, Ritchie, Macari, Thomas.

MILK CUP
1981 – 82
Round 2: 1st leg: 7 Oct. A. v. TOTTENHAM HOTSPUR 0–1. *Atten: 39,333.* Bailey, Gidman, Albiston, Wilkins, Moran, Buchan, Coppell, Birtles, Stapleton, McIlroy, Robson. (Sub: Duxbury, 8).
Round 2, 2nd leg: 28 Oct. H. v. TOTTENHAM HOTSPUR 0–1. *Atten: 55,890.* Bailey, Gidman, Albiston, Wilkins, Moran, Buchan, Robson, Birtles, Stapleton, Moses, Coppell.

1982 – 83
Round 2, 1st leg: 6 Oct. H. v. BOURNEMOUTH 2–0, scorers: O.g. (Redknapp), Stapleton. *Atten: 22,091* Bailey, Duxbury, Albiston, Wilkins, Moran, McQueen, Robson, Grimes, Stapleton, Beardsley, Moses. (Sub: Whiteside 10).
Round 2, 2nd leg: 26 Oct. A. v. BOURNEMOUTH 2–2, scorers: Muhren, Coppell (pen.). *Atten: 13,226.* Bailey, Duxbury, Albiston, Wilkins, Grimes, Buchan, Robson, Muhren, Stapleton, Whiteside, Coppell. (Sub: Macari 4).
Round 3: 10 Nov. A. v. BRADFORD CITY 0–0. *Atten: 15,568.* Bailey, Duxbury, Albiston, Moses, McGrath, McQueen, Robson, Muhren, Stapleton, Whiteside, Coppell.
Replay: 24 Nov. H. v. BRADFORD CITY 4–1, scorers: Moses, Albiston, Moran, Coppell. *Atten: 24,981.* Bailey, Duxbury, Albiston, Moses, Moran, McQueen, Robson, Muhren, Stapleton, Macari, Coppell. (Sub: Whiteside i1).
Round 4: 1 Dec. H. v. SOUTHAMPTON 2–0, scorers: McQueen, Whiteside. *Atten: 28,378.* Bailey, Duxbury, Albiston, Moses, Moran, McQueen, Robson, Muhren, Stapleton, Whiteside, Coppell.
Round 5: 19 Jan. H. v. NOTTINGHAM FOREST 4–0, scorers: McQueen (2), Coppell, Robson. *Atten: 44,413.* Bailey, Duxbury, Albiston, Moses, Moran, McQueen, Robson, Muhren, Stapleton, Whiteside, Coppell.
Semi-final, 1st leg: 15 Feb. A. v. ARSENAL 4–2, scorers: Whiteside, Stapleton, Coppell (2). *Atten: 43,136.* Bailey, Duxbury, Albiston, Moses, Moran, McQueen, Robson, Muhren, Stapleton, Whiteside, Coppell.
Semi-final, 2nd leg: 23 Feb. H. v. ARSENAL 2–1, scorers: Coppell, Moran. *Atten: 56,635.* Bailey, Duxbury, Albiston, Moses, Moran, McQueen, Robson, Muhren, Stapleton, Whiteside, Coppell. (Sub: Wilkins 7).
Final: 26 Mar. Wembley v. LIVERPOOL 1–2, scorer: Whiteside. *Atten: 100,000.* Bailey, Duxbury, Albiston, Moses, Moran, McQueen, Wilkins, Muhren, Stapleton, Whiteside, Coppell.

(Sub: Macari 5).
1983 – 84
Round 2, 1st leg: 3 Oct. A. v. PORT VALE 1–0, scorer: Stapleton. *Atten: 19,885.* Bailey, Duxbury, Albiston, Wilkins, Moran, McGrath, Robson, Muhren, Stapleton, Whiteside, Graham. (Sub: Moses 2).
Round 2, 2nd leg: 26 Oct. H. v. PORT VALE 2–0, scorer: Whiteside, Wilkins (pen.). *Atten: 23,589.* Bailey, Gidman, Albiston, Wilkins, Duxbury, McQueen, Robson, Moses, Stapleton, Whiteside, Graham. (Sub: Hughes 10).
Round 3: 8 Nov. A. v. COLCHESTER UNITED 2–0, scorers: McQueen, Moses. *Atten: 13,031.* Bailey, Duxbury, Albiston, Wilkins, Moran, McQueen, Robson, Moses, Stapleton, Whiteside, Graham. (Sub: Macari 10).
Round 4: 30 Nov. A. v. OXFORD UNITED 1–1, scorer: Hughes. *Atten: 13,739.* Bailey, Duxbury, Albiston, Wilkins, Moran, McQueen, Robson, Moses, Stapleton, Whiteside, Hughes.
Replay: 7 Dec. H. v. OXFORD UNITED 1–1, scorer: Stapleton. *Atten: 27,459.* Bailey, Duxbury, Albiston, Wilkins, Moran, McQueen, Robson, Moses, Stapleton, Whiteside, Graham.
Replay: 19 Dec. A. v. OXFORD UNITED 1–2, scorer: Graham. *Atten: 13,912.* Wealands, Moses, Albiston, Wilkins, Moran, Duxbury, Robson, Muhren, Stapleton, Whiteside, Graham. (Sub: Macari 7).

1984 – 85
Round 2, 1st leg: 26 Sept. H. v. BURNLEY 4–0, scorers: Robson, Hughes (3). *Atten: 28,383.* Bailey, Duxbury, Albiston, Moses, Garton, Hogg, Robson, Muhren, Hughes, Whiteside, Graham. (Sub: Brazil 10).
Round 2, 2nd leg: 9 Oct. A. v. BURNLEY 3–0, scorers: Brazil (2), Olsen. *Atten: 12,690.* Bailey, Duxbury, Albiston, Moses, Moran, Hogg, Strachan, Blackmore, Stapleton, Brazil, Olsen.
Round 3: 30 Oct. H. v. EVERTON 1–2, scorer: Brazil. *Atten: 50,918.* Bailey, Gidman, Albiston, Moses, Moran, Hogg, Robson, Strachan, Hughes, Brazil, Olsen. (Sub: Stapleton 11).

1985 – 86
Round 2, 1st leg: 24 Sept. A. v. CRYSTAL PALACE 1–0, scorer: Barnes. *Atten: 21,506.* Bailey, Duxbury, Albiston, Whiteside, McGrath, Moran, Robson, Blackmore, Stapleton, Brazil, Barnes.
Round 2, 2nd leg: 9 Oct. H. v. CRYSTAL PALACE 1–0, scorer: Whiteside. *Atten: 26,118.* Bailey, Duxbury, Albiston, Whiteside, McGrath, Moran, Robson, Olsen, Hughes, Stapleton, Barnes. (Sub: Brazil 9).
Round 3: 29 Oct. H. v. WEST HAM UNITED 1–0, scorer: Whiteside. *Atten: 32,056.* Bailey, Duxbury, Albiston, Whiteside, Moran, Hogg, McGrath, Olsen, Hughes, Stapleton, Barnes. (Sub: Brazil 2).
Round 4: 26 Nov. A. v. LIVERPOOL 1–2, scorer: McGrath. *Atten: 41,291.* Bailey, Gidman, Blackmore, Whiteside, Moran, Hogg, McGrath, Strachan, Stapleton, Brazil, Olsen.

A CENTURY OF 'OWN GOALS'

Since gaining entry into the Football Alliance in 1889, and subsequently the Football League in 1893, the Newton Heath and Manchester United teams have obtained a most welcome Century. In senior league and cup competitions, they have been 'presented' with a total of 104 'own goals' by opposing players. This unique list of each of these scorers is specially compiled by Charles Zahra and Joseph Muscat.

FOOTBALL ALLIANCE

1889−90	H. Bootle	*Jardine*
	A. Crewe Alex.	*Osborne*
1890−91	H. Small Heath	*Bailey*
1891−92	A. Crewe Alex.	*Stafford*
	H. Lincoln C.	*Marnott*

FOOTBALL LEAGUE

1894−95	H. Newcastle U.	*McDermott*
1899−00	A. Grimsby T.	*Greenwood*
1902−03	A. Burnley	*Lockhart*
1904−05	H. Bradford C.	*Robinson*
1905−06	H. Burslem P V	*Hamilton*
	A. Barnsley	*Silto*
1906−07	H. Stoke	*Holford*
1907−08	H. Nottm. Forest	*Armstrong*
	H. Preston N.E.	*Rodway*
1910−11	H. Nottm. Forest	*Needham*
	H. Sunderland	*Milton*
1913−14	A. Sheffield Wed.	*Spoors*
	A. Blackburn R.	*Crompton*
1914−15	A. Blackburn R.	*Robinson*
1920−21	A. Oldham Ath.	*Hensley*
1922−23	H. Hull City	*Bell*
1923−24	A. Oldham Ath.	*Wynne*
	A. Coventry City	*Randle*
1927−28	A. West Ham U.	*Barrett*
1928−29	H. Leeds Utd.	*Turnbull*
1931−32	A. Oldham Ath.	*Vill*
1932−33	A. Southampton	*Campbell*
	H. Lincoln City	*Worthy*
1933−34	A. Fulham	*Keeping*
	H. Bradford City	*S. Barkas*
1934−35	A. Bolton Wndrs.	*Finney*
1935−36	H. Southampton	*Gurry*
1938−39	H. Bolton Wndrs.	*Hubbick*

World War Two Period

1939−40	A. Stockport	*Nelson*
1940−41	H. Everton	*Hall*

Other scorers in war period not known.

Post War Period

1946−47	A. Charlton Ath.	*Johnson*
	H. Blackburn R.	*Higgins*
1949−50	H. Bolton Wndrs.	*Gillies*
1951−52	A. Arsenal	*Daniels*
	H. Tottenham H.	*Ramsey*
	H. Chelsea	*McKnight*
1954−55	H. Newcastle Utd.	*Scoular*
	A. Arsenal	*Goring*
1956−57	A. Sunderland	*Morrison*
	A. Cardiff City	*McSeveney*
1957−58	H. Everton	*Jones*
	H. Aston Villa	*Dugdale*
1958−59	A. Chelsea	*Scott*
	H. Portsmouth	*Hayward*
1959−60	A. Leeds Utd.	*Gibson/Cush*
	H. Arsenal	*Dodgin*
	A. Wolverhampton	*Stuart*
1960−61	H. Blackpool	*Hauser*
1961−62	H. Manchester C.	*Ewing*
1962−63	H. Leyton Orient	*S. Charlton*
1964−65	A. Wolverhampton	*G. Harris*
1965−66	H. Tottenham H.	*Beal*
1966−67	H. Blackpool	*Hughes*
1967−68	A. Arsenal	*Storey*
1968−69	H. Tottenham H.	*Beal*
	A. Q.P.R.	*Hunt*
	A. Sunderland	*Hurley*
	H. Burnley	*Waldron*
1969−70	A. Liverpool	*Yeats*
1972−73	A. Stoke City	*Smith*
1974−75	H. Bristol Rvrs.	*Prince*
	H. Bolton Wndrs.	*McAllister*
1975−76	H. Sheff. Utd.	*Badger*
	A. Stoke City	*Dodd*
	H. Tottenham H.	*Pratt*
	A. Newcastle U	*Bird/Howard*
	H. Everton	*Kenyon*
1976−77	H. Middlesbrough	*McAndrew*

	H. Derby County	*Powell*
	H. Leeds Utd.	*Cherry*
	A. Norwich City	*Powell*
1977−78	A. Everton	*Ross*
1979−80	H. Derby County	*Hill*
	A. Derby County	*B. Powell*
	H. Bristol City	*Merrick*
1980−81	A. Norwich City	*Bond*
	H. Nottm. Forest	*Burns*
1982−83	H. Coventry City	*Gillespie*

F.A. CUP

1911−12	H. Blackburn Rvrs.	*Walmsley*
1945−46	H. Accrington St.	*Briggs*
1950−51	H. Oldham Ath.	*Whyte*
1953−54	A. Burnley	*Aird*
1959−60	H. Derby County	*Barrowcliffe*
1963−64	H. Sunderland	*Hurley*
1968−69	A. Exeter City	*Newman*
1969−70	A. Ipswich Town	*McNeil*

FOOTBALL LEAGUE CUP

1970−71	H. Crystal Pal.	*McCormick*
1974−75	H. Charlton Ath.	*Warman*
1976−77	H. Sunderland	*Clarke*
1979−80	H. Tottenham H.	*Miller*

MILK CUP

1982−83	H. Bournemouth	*Redknapp*

EUROPEAN CUP

1956−57	H. B. Dortmund	*Burgsmueller*
1965−66	H. P. Belgrade	*Soskic*
1967−68	H. Gornik Zabrze	*Florenski*
	A. Real Madrid	*Zocco*

EUROPEAN CUP WINNERS CUP

1977−78	H. Porto	*Murce*

U.E.F.A. CUP

1984−85	A. Dundee Utd.	*McG*

GENERAL INFORMATION — OWN GOALS

Goals scored in Football Alliance	5	by	4 different opposing teams
Goals scored in Football League	79	by	43 different opposing teams
Goals scored in F.A. Cup	8	by	8 different opposing teams
Goals scored in F.L./Milk Cup	5	by	5 different opposing teams
Goals scored in European matches	7	by	6 different opposing teams
Total in all competitions	**104 goals**		*(not including war period)*

A to Z
of
PLAYER
BIOGRAPHIES

ARTHUR ALBISTON is established amongst the most consistent full-backs in the Football League. He joined United as an apprentice in July 1973, turning professional the following year.

He made his first team debut in the Football League Cup against Manchester City at Old Trafford in October 1974, followed by his League debut six days later in a Second Division game at Portsmouth.

After representing Scotland at Schoolboy and Under 21 level, he eventually won his first full cap in 1984. His big breakthrough in the United side came in 1977, when he was brought into the team shortly before the F.A. Cup Final and went on to play an important part in United's victory over Liverpool. Since then he has achieved the distinction of being the only player in the clubs history to have won three F.A. Cup Winners medals.

REG ALLEN *was already regarded as one of the best goalkeepers in the country with Queens Park Rangers, before his £11,000 transfer to United during the summer of 1950.*

He quickly settled in Manchester, and it was not long before he was being watched by the England selectors. Before he had completed his first season with the club he had represented the Football League. His rise to International status was rather surprising because, during the war he spent some time in a prisoner-of-war camp, after being captured in North Africa.

During the League Championship winning season of 1951–52, he made a major contribution with 33 appearances. Sadly, he suffered a hand injury during the following season, which kept him out of the side, and shortly after his return to the team an illness which required prolonged treatment kept him out for the rest of the season.

This illness was to end his playing career, as he failed to fully recover and after a long and anxious consideration, the directors decided to terminate his contract, and he was forced to retire.

JOHNNY ANDERSON joined United as an amateur in 1937, after playing with Brindle Heath and representing Salford boys and the Lancashire schools side. He signed professional forms in November as a left back, but was soon converted to wing half.

With the "A" team he won a Championship medal, before joining the Navy. On his return he won a Central League Championship medal in the first post-war season.

On December 20th 1947 whilst travelling to Newcastle for a reserve team fixture he received a telegram telling him to return to Manchester as quickly as possible to play for the first team against Middlesbrough. He gave an impressive performance, and kept his place for the remainder of the season, winning an F.A. Cup winners medal against Blackpool, when he scored one of United's four goals.

The following season he managed only 13 appearances, and to ensure first-team football he gladly accepted a move to Nottingham Forest in 1949.

JOHN ASTON *Senior began his career with United during the summer of 1938, when he joined the club as a junior. Two years later on August 31st 1940, he made his United debut against Rochdale at Spotland, in the first match of the North section of the War-time League scoring one of United's goals. In his first season he scored 3 goals in his 10 games.*

During the next four years he was on military duty, and his next game was not until March 27th 1946, when he played at Blackpool. He played 3 more games towards the end of the season, all in the forward line, but the following season saw him switched to full-back where he finally established himself in the team.

During United's Cup winning season of 1947–48 he was the only player with a 100% appearance record in League and Cup games. Such consistency was noted by the England selectors and he won the first of his 16 caps on September 26th 1948 against Denmark.

He won a League Championship medal in 1952, but sadly there were to be no further honours as he made only a handful of appearances in 1953–54 before illness forced him to retire from the game. He was given a testimonial by the club in 1956, and later joined the United backroom staff.

As a schoolboy **JOHN ASTON** Junior played for both Manchester and Lancashire, before following his fathers footsteps and signing for United.

In 1964, he made a big impression in the Youth team, playing both wing half and outside left. After making steady progress he made his League debut against Leicester City on April 12th 1965.

He soon developed into a fast and tricky winger with an eye for goals and it was not long before he made the number 11 shirt his own, winning a championship medal in 1967 and a European Cup medal the following season. It was at Wembley in the European Cup Final that he had perhaps his best ever game for United, giving the Benfica defence a real runaround.

The following season, he unfortunately broke his leg against City at Maine Road, and although he made a complete recovery, he never managed to reach the heights of his Wembley performance again, though he did win England under-23 honours.

At the end of season 1971–72 he moved to Luton Town for a fee of around £30,000.

B

When goalkeeper **GARY BAILEY** *made his United debut on 18 November, 1979 he continued a family tradition, his father Roy had been Ipswich Town's custodian in their Championship team of 1962.*

The Bailey family moved to South Africa when Gary was only six years old, and before coming to Old Trafford on trial in the summer of 1978, he was playing for the Wittsrand University team in Johannesburg.

By coincidence his first game for United was against Ipswich, since then Gary has played more than 300 times for the club and represented England at Under-23, 'B' and full international levels.

FRANK BARSON began his playing career with Barnsley, at the age of 20, in 1911. Eight years later he was on his way to Aston Villa, where he won a Cup Winners medal and also an England cap. It is thought that he would have won more if he had not been so much of a physical player, being sent-off so many times.

In July 1922, United offered Villa £4,000 for his transfer, but Villa wanted £5,000. After much haggling United finally agreed to Villa's valuation, and so signed a hard tackling, but skilful centre-half, who had a keen attacking sense. He once entertained the Villa fans with a headed goal from all of 30 yards. He exerted a tremendous influence on the United team, and was soon made captain, taking them back to the First Division within three seasons.

His career with United lasted until May 1928, when he was given a free transfer, and he eventually signed for Watford.

Although **ALEC BELL** *was born in South Africa, his family moved to Scotland when he was a baby. He began his footballing life in Scottish junior sides and it was from that level of the game that he moved to United.*

He lined up alongside Charlie Roberts and Dick Duckworth, to form one of the best half back lines in the club's history. Such was the influence this combination had, the rest of the team played so well that United won both the Cup and the League during their time together.

Scotland also noticed Bell's play and in 1912 he represented his country. By now, United were looking to the future and in 1913 he moved across Lancashire to join Blackburn Rovers.

Born near Wrexham, **RAY BENNION** played as a professional for Crichton Athletic in the Cheshire County League. As a youngster, his ambitions were set much higher and he wrote to United for a trial.

He did enough to impress, and was signed in April 1920, going straight into the Central League team. After helping the reserves to their League title, he made his first team debut the following season against Everton at Goodison Park.

During that first season he shared the right half position with Cal Hilditch, but eventually made the position his own.

In 1923 he was selected to play for Wales, but turned down the chance so that he could play for United, who were going through a bad spell at that time. He was selected again, however, but not until two years later when he won the first of his 10 caps against Scotland, at Ninian Park.

His career with United lasted for another seven seasons, until November 1932, when he joined Burnley, much to the disappointment of United supporters.

Born at Irlams-o-the-Height, **GEOFF BENT** *captained Salford Boys to an English Schools Trophy win, before joining United in April 1949. He had to wait until December 11th 1954 before he got his first team chance, at Burnley.*

Had he preferred a transfer to reserve team football, he could have easily have got a place in the defence of any other First Division side, but he wanted to stay at

Old Trafford and wait for his chance of a regular place.

Sadly, it was never to come, as he died at Munich alongside his friends and team mates in 1958. Ironically he only made that fatal trip at the last minute as cover for Roger Byrne who had a slight injury. As he had only recently recovered from his second leg-break, he had not expected to go on the trip to Belgrade.

Outside right **JOHN BERRY** joined Birmingham City in December 1944 on his demob from the army, and scored just five goals in 103 appearances for the Midland side.

Ironically, one of those goals was against United at Old Trafford on trial in the summer of 1948–49, and Manager Matt Busby made up his mind that Berry was a player who could benefit his team. It took him 18 months to get his signature, but he finally signed for United in August 1951 for a fee of £25,000.

His United debut was at Bolton on September 1st, and he soon became one of the most consistent wingers in the game. His fine displays on United's right wing soon caught the eye of the England selectors, and he won the first of his caps on a tour of America in 1953. Unfortunately he was around at the same time as Matthews and Finney, therefore his International appearances were limited to only four games, plus an England "B" and a couple of Football League XI honours.

He won three League Championships medals, 1952, 1956 and 1957, but injuries he received at Munich forced him to retire from the game.

GARRY BIRTLES *began his career with Long Eaton United, before signing for Nottingham Forest, where he enjoyed almost instant success. In 87 League games he scored 32 goals and helped Forest to two European Cup victories and Football League Cup triumph, as well as winning three full and two under-21 caps. United boss Dave Sexton paid out £1,260,000 for his signature in October 1980, but he was unable to reproduce his Forest and England form, and after almost two years at Old Trafford, he was transferred back to the City Ground for £275,000.*

GEORGE BEST was arguably the greatest player that Britain has ever produced, but sadly he will be remembered by many for his activities off the field more than for his brilliance on it.

Best arrived in Manchester as a homesick 15-year-old in 1961, and after only a couple of days in Manchester he decided to return home to Belfast. He was persuaded to return and in May 1963 he signed professional forms. In September of the same year he made his debut as a 17-year-old against West Bromwich Albion at Old Trafford, six months later he won his first cap for Northern Ireland.

He won League and European Cup winners medals, English and European Footballer of the Year awards, 37 full International caps. He also had the dubious distinction of being sent off at League, European and International level. He became Britain's most exciting player and added thousands to the gate wherever he played. His individual brilliance won many matches for United. Between 1970 and 1972 his troubles off the field attracted constant national media interest and led to his contract being terminated by United.

Following an approach to Sir Matt Busby, he returned in November 1973 for a brief spell, playing his last game for the club against QPR in January 1974.

By this time, other leading clubs were wary of this wayward genius and his days at the highest level were prematurely over. Perhaps if he had not attempted so many comebacks at lower levels, the great memories of George Best would be much more satisfying.

SAM BLACK *was a founder member of the Newton Heath team and one of the club's legendary names.*

He was a consistent and popular player, captaining the side when it won its first trophy, the Manchester Senior Cup, in 1886.

He always played as an amateur, and on two occasions he captained the Manchester Association representative side against the Liverpool Association.

In his day he was reported as being "one of the finest backs that ever kicked a ball", and it was no surprise that in 1883, Blackburn Olympic, then the F.A. Cup holders tried to sign him.

When he did eventually leave the club he returned to his home town, and joined Burton Wanderers.

JACKIE BLANCHFLOWER, brother of the Spurs and Northern Ireland star Danny, came to United from Belfast junior football in 1950, as an inside forward. In his early days with the club the management worried about his lack of pace, but he moved back to wing half and soon began to show much more promise.

After impressive performances in the reserve side, he made his debut at Liverpool in December 1951. Before he could command a regular place in the United team, he was picked to play for his country. He shared the centre half spot with Mark Jones, but was capable of giving a first class performance in any position. Not only could he play outfield, but he was also a capable goalkeeper as he showed in the 1957 F.A. Cup Final against Aston Villa. Once, on a close season tour of Denmark, he actually played a whole game in goal.

Being such a versatile player, he was a great asset to the club, but sadly his full potential was never realised, as he had to retire from the game following the Munich disaster.

Shortly after the start of season 1936 – 37, **TOMMY BREEN** crossed the Irish Sea to join United from Belfast Celtic, and made his debut at Leeds United. Unfortunately his first touch of the ball was to pick it out of the net, after only ninety seconds play.

When he first began playing in Ireland he was a half-back or inside forward, only concentrating on goalkeeping after playing there in an emergency.

During his time with Belfast Celtic, he won international caps with Northern Ireland, and following his move to Old Trafford he was selected to play for both Northern and the Republic of Ireland. On the outbreak of war, he returned home to Ireland and rejoined Belfast Celtic. In 1946 – 47 when the United were in search of a goalkeeper they tried to obtain his services again, but he refused to return to England.

Born in Manchester with Irish parents, **SHAY BRENNAN** joined the club in December 1953, straight from school. He was an outstanding member of the Youth team, before graduating into the Central League side.

He suddenly found himself thrown into the first team immediately after Munich for the F.A. Cup tie against Sheffield Wednesday at Old Trafford, and celebrated by scoring twice, both from outside left.

Eventually, he was moved back to full back, with much success, winning his first International cap for Eire in May 1965, after F.A. honours with England. He did not gain a regular place in the side until the late sixties, when he formed a formidable partnership with Tony Dunne, helping United to both League and European honours.

At the end of season 1969 – 70, he was given a free transfer, due to the service he had given the club over the years. He moved to Ireland and joined Waterford, as player – manager.

MARTIN BUCHAN holds the unique distinction of captaining teams in F.A. Cup Finals in both England and Scotland.

His Scottish Cup success was with Aberdeen, who he joined from a local league side Banks O' Dee as an apprentice. Three years later, in August 1966, he

signed professional forms, and went on to make 131 league appearances for the Dons, leading them to their cup triumph in 1970. The following season he was voted Scottish Player of the Year.

In March 1972, United manager Frank O'Farrell paid £125,000 for the signature of the skilful, classy defender, who made his league debut for United a few days later at Tottenham.

Martin was already a Scottish International, having made his first appearance as a substitute against Portugal in October 1971, and went on to make 34 appearances for his country when many people felt he should have won many more.

He captained United to the Second Division title in 1975, and to three F.A. Cup Finals, in 1976 – 77 & 79, winning the second of his 'double' in 1977.

Sadly injuries began to keep him out of the United team, and in the summer of 1983 he was given a free transfer and joined Lancashire neighbours Oldham Athletic.

FRANCIS BURNS was captain of the Scottish schools side when he joined United upon leaving school in 1964. Shortly after that he won Scottish Youth and later, under-23 honours. His first team debut came in September 1967 against West Ham, after going on the clubs summer tour of Australia.

He was formerly a half-back, but switched successfully to full-back. Unfortunately injury forced him out of the side, and he had three cartilage operations in 18 months. However, he fought his way back, and was capped by Scotland during season 1969/70. A polished performer, his injury problems limited his opportunities at Old Trafford, and he moved to Southampton for a fee of £20,000 in 1972.

A transfer fee of £750 brought full back **HERBERT BURGESS** to the club, from Manchester City. He was in fact, one of the four City players who joined United following an enquiry by the Football Association in 1905.

His football began in local circles, but his mother was so against the game, that she would often burn his playing kit, before he signed for City from Glossop for £250 as a 21 year old.

In his days with City he won an F.A. Cup winners medal, and also played for England on four occasions.

Although he signed for United in 1905, it was in January 1907 before he could make his league debut, because of suspension.

Sadly his time with United was rather short, because after helping the club to the League Championship in 1907 – 08, he sustained a twisted knee while playing against Middlesbrough, an injury which not only kept him out of United's Cup winning team but also forced him into premature retirement.

ROGER BYRNE signed as an amateur from local junior team Ryder Boys Club, as an inside forward, in 1948.

His first team debut came during 1951 – 52, at Liverpool, on November 24th, and kept his place for the rest of the season. Although he had been signed as a forward, it was at left back that he made his debut.

Later in season 1951 – 52 he did however move back into the forward line to outside left and showed his attacking flair by scoring seven goals in six games, helping United to the Championship.

The following season he again played in both forward and defensive positions, but made the permanent move to left back.

Although he was short and slightly built, he was very fast on the recovery and showed a great deal of intelligence in his play. Before long he was representing England, winning his first cap in 1954 for the "B" team and later the full England side. It was also in 1954 that he was appointed club captain. He was soon an automatic choice for his country, but his life came to an end on the slush covered runway of Munich airport in 1958. If the accident had not

happened who knows what he may have led Manchester United, and England, to in later years.

NOEL CANTWELL, began his footballing career with Cork Athletic, and was transferred to West Ham United in September 1952, progressing from their third team to the first, in one season.

During his spell with the Hammers, whom he joined as a forward, he won a Second Division Championship medal in 1957 – 58 and also captained Eire on several occasions. During 1960 – 61 he was transferred to United on November 21st for a fee of around £30,000 which was at that time a record for a full-back. He made his debut for United against Bayern Munich in a friendly, that same day, and his league debut at Cardiff 5 days later.

In season 1962 – 63 he was appointed club captain, and led the club to their Cup Final victory.

Although he was a first class full-back, he also played well in the forward line, playing there for both United and Eire on numerous occasions.

He was elected Chairman of the Professional Footballers Association in 1966 and he also managed the Eire international side until September 1968.

JOHNNY CAREY was a brilliant captain and one of the greatest players ever to pull on the red shirt of Manchester United.

He arrived at Old Trafford as a 17-year-old in 1936, from St James Gate, Dublin for a £250 fee paid by Louis Rocca. His debut was on December 28th 1937 at Nottingham Forest, and he scored one of United's three goals, playing in those early days as an inside forward.

The following year, he was making his debut for the Republic of Ireland against Norway, and United turned down many offers for his services and fortunately were able to keep their finest asset.

At the restart of league football after the war, Matt Busby made him team captain, and it was under his guidance that United won the F.A. Cup, in 1948. That same season, he was named as "Footballer of the Year."

Season 1951 – 52 saw him lead United to the League title, but in 1953, he decided to retire, and became manager of Blackburn Rovers, and later Nottingham Forest.

During his great career, he played in nine different positions for the club and an equal number in International matches, in which he represented both Northern Ireland and the Republic. He also captained a Rest of Europe XI.

Now a Director of the club, nothing can be written about **BOBBY CHARLTON** which hasn't already appeared in print somewhere. His name will always be synonymous with Manchester United.

The fair-haired lad from Ashington, didn't take long to make an impression with the club after signing professional, in 1955, as a 17 year old.

Just a year later, he began his torment of First Division defences against Charlton Athletic, and scored twice, and since then his career went from strength to strength, winning almost every honour in the game.

His International debut came against Scotland at

259

Hampden Park, and again he scored. He soon became a regular in the England side and went on to break Billy Wright's record number of caps when he won his 106th in the 1970 World Cup in Mexico, four years after helping England to the trophy at Wembley.

Wembley was also the scene of his greatest personal triumph, captaining United when they defeated Benfica 4 – 1 in the European Cup Final. The following year he was awarded the O.B.E. for his services to football.

1970 – 71 saw him make his 564th league appearance for United, setting up a new club record, and in September 1972 he was awarded with a testimonial match against Celtic, and at the end of that season he decided to hang up his boots. His last match was in Italy against Verona, in the Anglo-Italian Cup, and he finished as he started, with a goal.

ALLENBY CHILTON signed as a junior, from Durham amateur side Seaham Colliery in 1938, and made his league debut a year later, on September 2nd 1939, at Charlton. But he then had to wait seven years to make his second appearance, due to the outbreak of the Second World War. During the war, when home on leave, he 'guested' for Charlton Athletic, and played for them in the War Cup Final of 1944, when they defeated Chelsea. The war also nearly ruined his career as he received leg wounds on the beaches at Normandy, but recovered in time to take up the number 5 shirt with United when league football resumed again.

He became an almost permanent fixture in the United line-up, and went on to help United to their F.A. Cup victory.

His consistent form was rewarded in 1951 when he was selected for the England team, and whether he should have won more than two caps was a controversial issue.

Up until February 1955, he had played a record of 175 successive league and cup games, and this run only came to an end as he felt that he was not playing to his normal form and that a rest might help.

But, a month later he was on the move from Old Trafford to Grimsby Town, whom he joined as player-manager, on a free transfer.

HENRY COCKBURN was signed as an amateur, on August 25th 1944, from local junior side Goslings.

As a youngster he was to have gone to Blackpool for trials, but a bout of influenza prevented it, and shortly afterwards United moved in and signed him.

He made his debut in the opening match of the season 1946 – 47 against Grimsby Town, and within a month he was chosen to play for England against Northern Ireland in Belfast.

Despite his lack of inches, he was a very clever player, with a hard tackle and the ability to distribute the ball with accuracy.

Although it was at half back he made his name, he was once an inside forward, and only changed positions during the war, when he "guested" for Accrington Stanley.

During his career with United he won many honours and admirers, and it was a sad day when he left to join Bury, in 1954.

EDDIE COLMAN played for Salford Boys and Lancashire Boys at both cricket and football, and was spotted playing for the Salford team at Old Trafford. He signed for the club upon leaving school, and was soon progressing through the junior sides, captaining the Youth team to their F.A. Youth Cup victory during 1954 – 55.

His breakthrough into the league side came at Bolton on November 12th 1955, and he remained in the side for the rest of the season.

Although he was small, he was a strong determined tackler, with tremendous skills which earned him the nickname of "swivel hips".

In November 1957, he celebrated his 21st birthday,

but three months later he died at Munich. At this point his career was just maturing and surely if it had not been prematurely ended he would have become one of the best half backs in British football.

JOHN CONNELLY began his playing career with St Helens Town, and was signed by Burnley in 1956. He was moved onto the wing, and was soon able to play on either flank.

He made his league debut during 1958 – 59 and the following season, he was a member of the side which won the league championship. 1960 also saw him win his first England cap.

His fine quick moving play and goalscoring ability was soon getting him the headlines on the sports pages, and on April 15th 1964, he signed for United at a fee of £60,000.

A friendly against City on May 7th 1964 marked his first appearance in a red shirt, and his league debut came at the start of the following season.

During 1964 – 65 he won back his England place with some fine performances for United, but in September 1966 he was transferred to Blackburn Rovers for a fee of £40,000.

STEVE COPPELL joined United as a part-time player in February 1975, for a fee of £30,000 from Tranmere Rovers. He had signed amateur forms with Tranmere while still studying at Liverpool University, in June 1973, making his initial appearance in league football in January of the following year.

His signing for United was intended to be an investment for the future but he soon forced himself into the United team, displacing Willie Morgan, who shortly afterwards left the club.

He soon proved to be a real bargain, and was a member of the England under-23 squad when still a part-timer, and after graduating from University in 1976 his career progressed even faster. England soon relied on his talents as much as United did, and when a knee injury forced him into an early retirement, it was a sad day for both club and country.

With United he played more than 400 games, and was rated by former boss Tommy Docherty as his best ever buy.

On his retirement he moved into management with Second Division side Crystal Palace.

Dundocher Hibs, a Scottish junior club, were the club from which Celtic signed **PAT CRERAND** in 1958. Soon he was developing into one of the finest wing-halves in Scotland. Season 1960 – 61 was perhaps his best with Celtic, winning Scottish under-23 and full caps and also a Cup runners-up medal. He soon became a Scotland regular, and his performances with Celtic were soon being widely noticed.

So much so that on February 6th 1963, Matt Busby paid Celtic around £56,000 for his signature. He made his first appearance against Bolton seven days later in a friendly in Ireland, and his league debut against Blackpool at Old Trafford, ten days after signing.

His skill and ball distribution soon made him a big favourite with the fans. It also helped United win the F.A. Cup in 1963, with Crerand playing a major part in the Final against Leicester.

1966, his International career came to an end after a clash with the Scottish selectors. This did not hinder his career with United, and he helped the club to the league championship and the European Cup.

Towards the end of his senior career, he spent more time coaching the youngsters. Later he took charge of the reserve team, and on the arrival of Tommy Docherty he became his assistant manager, until 1975/6 when he joined Northampton town.

Goalkeeper **JACK CROMPTON** was a product of the Manchester YMCA, Newton Heath Loco and Goslings, and he played his first game for United in

1944, against Stockport County, whilst still an amateur. In December of that year he signed professional forms.

His league debut came immediately after the war, and he went on to give United fine service over the years. He was a reliable and confident 'keeper, with a reputation for saving penalty kicks.

In the mid-fifties he actually captained the reserve team, which contained many of the famous "Busby Babes", to the Central League title.

During the season 1956 – 57 he left the club to become trainer-coach with Luton Town, and was the last of the 1948 cup winning team to leave the club. However, he returned after Munich to become trainer following Tom Curry's death.

This was a position he held until the early 1970's when he moved to Barrow as manager, before teaming up with Bobby Charlton at Preston.

He later returned to Old Trafford for a brief spell as a reserve team trainer.

Soon after taking over at Old Trafford, Tommy Docherty launched a scouting programme in Southern Ireland, and **GERRY DALY** was one of the players who were discovered, and he was signed in April 1973 for around £12,000, at the age of 19.

He had began his playing career with a junior side, Villa United, in 1972 before joining Bohemians, where he only stayed eight months before moving to United.

His first appearance for the club was in the Anglo Italian Cup against Bari on April 4th, at Old Trafford, and his league debut came on the opening day of season 1974 – 74 at Highbury against Arsenal .

He was by now a Republic of Ireland internationalist, having played his first match on May 6th 1973 in Poland, when he came on as substitute.

In season 1974 – 75 his form in mid-field helped to take United back into the First Division, and his all-out effort with non stop running also helped United to Wembley, and back amongst the top sides in the country, in season 1975 – 76.

The following season began well, but with the arrival of Jimmy Greenhoff in December, he found himself dropped from the team. He immediately asked for a transfer, which was refused, but when Derby County offered around £180,000 for him in March. United didn't stand in his way, and he moved to the Midlands.

Although born in Scotland, **ALEX DAWSON** was capped by England on schools, and in 1957 he signed for United on professional forms.

He developed quickly, in the junior and reserve teams, and made his first team debut on April 22nd at Old Trafford and scored in a 2 – 0 victory over Burnley.

He stayed in the side for the two remaining games of that season, and scored in both games. The following season, he made only one appearance before Munich, but following the disaster, he held a regular place.

Subsequently, he faded from the picture at Old Trafford, after showing so much promise as a strong, bulldozer-like centre forward, and in October 1961, he was transferred to Preston North End for a fee of

£20,000. During his spell with United he will be most remembered for his fine displays in the 1958 Cup semi-finals against Fulham when he scored three goals over the two games.

JIMMY DELANEY, *was Matt Busby's first signing for United when he became manager, in February 1946, for £4,000.*

As an 18-year-old, he was signed by Celtic from Lanarkshire junior football, and within two years he had won his first Scottish cap.

A broken arm kept him out of the game from 1939 until 1941, but he soon recovered his best form.

His signing for United surprised a few people as he was considered rather injury prone and also rather old to be starting a new career. But he soon proved everyone wrong and helped United to their F.A. Cup victory in 1948 and added an English winners medal to the Scottish one he had won with Celtic in 1937. He was also recalled to the Scottish International side after some fine games for United.

Shortly after the start of season 1950 – 51, he returned to Scotland and joined Aberdeen for a sum of £3,500, 4 years 9 months after joining United as a "short-term purchase."

It is interesting to note, that he was still playing in 1956, with Cork Athletic, and that he added a Northern Irish cup-winners medal to his collection in 1954, while with Derry City.

Scottish-born **NEIL DEWAR** regularly hit the headlines with his goal scoring achievements for Third Lanark, in the Scottish First Division. He first attracted attention south of the border during a representative match at Maine Road, when he scored a goal from 30 yards, for the Scottish League XI.
United's manager, Scott Duncan was at the match, and liked what he saw, and in the face of strong opposition signed him for a fee of £5,000 in 1933.
He had already won three Scottish caps before moving south, and he was soon charming the crowds in England with his fine individual style of play, following his debut in February 1933 against Preston North End, in which he scored. Shortly afterwards, he scored five goals in a friendly against Cowdenbeath, who were defeated 10 – 1.
Sadly his stay with the club wasn't a long one as he left at the end of the season and joined Sheffield Wednesday.

In the early days of Newton Heath, brothers **JACK DOUGHTY** *and* **ROGER DOUGHTY** *played significant parts in establishing the club as as footballing force. They both joined the club from the famous Welsh side, the Druids of Ruabon.*
Jack, played as a centre forward while Roger played inside left, and in one match for Wales against Northern Ireland, Jack scored four goals, and brother Roger two.
Wages in those early days were poor, with Jack Doughty receiving ten shillings a week for his services, whilst on turning professional he earned thirty shillings.
Both players enjoyed their football and of the two, perhaps Jack was the better player. He was a fast skilful player and difficult to shake off the ball. They were capable of playing in any of the forward positions, and would help each other get on the score sheet.
One brother would charge the defender out of the way, while the other would have a clear shot at goal.

JOHNNY DOWNIE was spotted by Bradford Park Avenue while playing for a Lanarkshire A.T.C. team, at centre forward, and was signed on amateur

forms. Before he became a professional at 19, he had made several appearances in the first team, mostly at inside left. He spent nearly 5 years with Bradford, and was their top scorer in season 1947 – 48.
In March 1949 he was signed by United for an £18,000 feee, and he made his debut at Charlton and scored in a 3 – 1 victory. He played in most of the remaining games that season, but during United's summer tour of Eire he injured his ankle, which troubled him for a spell and also affected his form. This meant a spell in the reserves, and in 1949 – 50 he only managed occasional appearances in the team. During 1950 – 51 he was strongly tipped for Scottish International honours, and also a transfer to Burnley, but neither materialised. The following season however he played a big part in United's title win scoring 11 goals in 31 league games.
He joined Luton Town in the summer of 1953 for £10,000.

Local born, **DICK DUCKWORTH**, *graduated through the junior side of Newton Heath, before making his debut in the first team during season 1903 – 04.*
He went on to become one of the best wing-halves ever to play for the club, forming a formidable half back line with Alec Bell and Charlie Roberts. This trio helped United to their F.A. Cup win, in 1909, with the strong commanding play of Dick Duckworth making a major contribution, and his remarkable understanding with outside right Billy Meredith.
Season 1909 – 10 saw him win his only England cap, something which surprised many people, but he did at least win four Football League caps.
He gave the club outstanding service up until the summer of 1919, when he was given a free transfer in recognition of his time spent with the club.

TONY DUNNE played for St. Finbars Youth Club, Dublin, before joining League of Ireland club Shelbourne.
On April 11th 1960, he was transferred to United for a fee of £5,000, plus an additional £500 when he had made ten league appearances and a further £500 when he won his first full cap.
He had already been capped at amateur level.
He made his Football League debut in October 1960 against Burnley, at Turf Moor, but had to wait until the following season before he got an extended run in the team.
He made the first of 24 international appearances during 1961 – 62, and had the honour of captaining the Republic against Hungary in June 1969.
From his very first appearance for United, when he came on as a substitute against Real Madrid, right up until his last, against Ipswich on February 17th 1973, he gave nothing but 100% effort. At the end of that season he joined Bolton Wanderers.

Accrington-born **MIKE DUXBURY**, *is one of the rare breed of players who can perform well in almost any position. He joined the club straight from school, progressing through the junior and reserve sides, before making his senior debut against Birmingham City at St. Andrews, as a substitute for Kevin Moran, on August 23rd 1980.*
One month later he was making his full league debut against local neighbours Manchester City at Old Trafford, almost four years after turning professional.
At the end of season 1980 – 81 he made such an impression on the supporters that they voted him their Young Player of the Year.
It was an injury to full back John Gidman that gave Mike an extended run in the team, and his form was so impressive that he was selected to play for England in 1984.

DUNCAN EDWARDS has often been called the most complete player ever to play in the Football League. As a schoolboy he was the target of every club in the country, after his displays in the England schoolboy team, of which he was captain.
The pressure to obtain his signature was so intense that United went to his home in the middle of the night to sign him, and the former Dudley schoolboy didn't take long to make an impression at Old Trafford.
He was soon playing for both England and United Youth sides, whilst also playing in the First Division. This lead to some of the F.A. Youth Cup opponents complaining about the unfair advantage United had in this competition. Perhaps they had a point, as Duncan helped his team mates to victory in 1953, 1954 and 1955.
His play progressed so quickly, that he was brought into the first team on April 4th 1953 against Cardiff City, at home, when he was aged 16 years 185 days old.
The England Under-23 team was his next stop, and at 18½, he was selected to play for the full England side, and so became the youngest player to play at this level. This was in April 1955, only two years after making his league debut, and four years after playing in the England schools side.
He was rated the outstanding prospect of British football, and he gained admirers wherever he played. He was a flawless, complete player. He tackled hard, and was an excellent passer of the ball. With legs like tree trunks and a huge chest, he had a devastating shot and was a formidable sight to his opponents in whatever position he filled.
Thousands of words have been written about Duncan, and had he survived Munich who knows what he may have achieved. Unlike his team mates he did not die on the runway at Munich airport, but 15 days later in the Rechts der Isar hospital. Had he survived, it was unlikely that he would have been able to play again, but with his courage and determination who knows?
Today, supporters travel to St. Francis's Church in Dudley, to see the stained glass windows to keep alive the memory of one of the truly all-time greats.

As a youngster, **ALEX FORSYTH** *spent some time with Arsenal as a junior player but failed to make much of an impression and returned home*

disappointed. Soon afterwards Partick Thistle offered him a chance of becoming a professional, and he made his debut for them during their Second Division title winning season of 1970 – 71.

The following season he soon obtained a regular place at left-back, and was chosen to go with the Scottish squad on tour in Brazil. He made his International debut at right-back against Yugoslavia in Belo Horizonte, in June 1972.

In December 1972, he was one of Tommy Docherty's early signings, when United paid Thistle £100,000 for him.

The Doc had been the Scottish manager when Alex made his International debut.

He took a few games to find his feet in the United side, but soon showed his paces as an attacking full-back and in 1974 – 75 helped the club to the Second Division title.

Shortly before the start of season 1978 – 79 he returned to Scotland and joined Rangers on loan, before signing on a permanent basis.

BILL FOULKES was working at the pit face, when United signed him as a part-time professional from Whiston Boys Club in St. Helens in 1946. Three years later he signed full professional forms.

He made his league debut on December 13th 1952 at Liverpool, and he went on to set up a club record in league appearances with a total of 563.

It was season 1953 – 54 before he obtained a regular first team place, and in October 1954 he won his only full England cap.

He was one of the survivors of the Munich crash, and he became captain of the side immediately afterwards. His qualities of leadership helped United through such a bleak period of time and back onto the road of success.

In season 1960 – 61, he switched from full-back to centre half where he played until the end of his career, the highlight of which must have been scoring United's equaliser against Real Madrid in the 1968 European Cup semi-final in Madrid, giving United their Final place.

Retirement came in 1970, when he was given the job of reserve team trainer. Because of his outstanding club loyalty he was given a testimonial in 1970, when United played City at Old Trafford. He later went to America as manager of Chicago Sting in the late 1970's.

G

DAVID GASKELL *was another of the many talented youngsters developed by United as a ground staff boy and through the junior sides. Although he didn't sign professional forms until 1957, he first appeared in the senior team on August 24th 1956 as a 16 year old, when he came on as a substitute for Ray Wood in the F.A. Charity Shield match at Maine Road, 2 months after joining the club.*

He had, however, to wait another 15 months for his league debut, which was against Tottenham at Old Trafford in November 1957.

During the 1961/62 season, injury cost him a place in the England under 23 side against Scotland.

In 1962 – 63, he made up for his disappointment by winning an F.A. Cup winners medal against Leicester City. He was at Old Trafford until 1968, when he left to join Bradford Park Avenue.

JOHN GIDMAN was born in Liverpool in 1954 and he signed for the Anfield club on leaving school, on amateur forms.

In 1970 he moved to Aston Villa, signing professional a year later.

Villa gave him his league debut during 1972 – 73, and he went on to make almost 200 appearances there, winning a League Cup winners award in 1977.

During his time with Villa, he almost lost his eye and then his life, in two separate accidents, before signing for Everton in October 1979, at a fee of £60,000.

He spent a couple of seasons at Goodison Park, where injuries still haunted him, before crossing the East Lancs. Road and joining United in a part exchange deal with Mickey Thomas, in July 1981.

The change of club saw his career improve, and his attacking full back style saw him again on the verge of the England team, but he failed to add to his solitary cap which he had won in 1977.

Injuries still plagued his career as both leg and back injuries kept him out of the team for long periods.

Dublin schoolboy **JOHNNY GILES** *played several times for Eire at schools level, before joining United after a short spell with Home Farm.*

He signed professional in 1958, and made his league debut in September 1959 against Tottenham at Old Trafford. Before the season had finished, he had won his first full International cap for Eire, at the age of 18.

In the United side he began as an inside forward, but was soon moved to the wing, with considerable success. Unfortunately he suffered a setback during 1960 – 61, when he broke his left leg at Birmingham in November.

Thankfully he soon recovered, and won back his first team place, and in 1963 he was in the Cup winning side at Wembley. However, although he was a regular member of the league side, he was allowed to leave United and join Leeds United for a fee of around £35,000, in August of the same year.

FREDDIE GOODWIN joined United as an amateur on leaving school, turning professional in October 1953. He played his first game in league football on November 20th 1954 against Arsenal at Old Trafford, as a 21 year old.

He was also a member of the Lancashire County Cricket club side but the presence of Eddie Colman restricted his senior United outings and Freddie at that time was referred to as the best reserve wing half in the country. But following Munich, he immediately stepped into the league side and kept his place, being noted for hard tackling and his ability to join in the attack.

Two years later, however, he lost his first team place, and was shortly after transferred to Leeds United in March 1960, for a fee of £10,000.

Oldham-born **IAN GREAVES** *joined United in 1952 from the Cheshire league club Buxton, and in October 1954 he made his debut away against Wolves.*

But like so many other players with United during that time he found his appearances limited, even although he could play in either full back position, link up well with the half backs and was a good distributor of a ball.

It was following the Munich disaster that he obtained a regular place, and kept it until injury put him on the side-lines and forced him to miss most of season 1959 – 60. During that season he underwent two operations, one for cartilage trouble and the other for the removal of scar tissue.

The following season, he just made two appearances in the Central League side, before joining Lincoln City. He left United with a Championship medal and F.A. Cup Runners-Up medal and many happy memories.

BRIAN GREENHOFF came to Old Trafford on

apprentice forms as a 15 year old in August 1968, signing professional in June 1970. He soon developed into one of the most versatile players at the club, capable of playing well in any position, including goalkeeper.

He made his league debut at Ipswich on September 8th 1973 at left half, and went on to play in most of the remaining games of that season, mainly at right back.

Having established himself in the team as a midfield man his future looked settled, but when Jim Holton broke his leg Brian moved into the centre of defence, to form a firm partnership with Martin Buchan.

Following his debut in 1973 – 74, he won England under 23 honours, and at the end of season 1975 – 76 he won his first full caps. In August 1979 he joined Leeds United for a fee of £350,000.

JIMMY GREENHOFF *joined Leeds United from school, and made his league debut for the Yorkshire club during 1962 – 63, in the second division.*

It took him almost three years to win a regular place, and he helped Leeds to the Football League cup and the Fairs Cup Final in 1968.

Although he looked settled with the Yorkshire club, he was sold to Birmingham City in the Summer of 1968, for £70,000. This transfer must have put him into the record books as the only player ever to be transferred during a League Cup Final, as he was sold between the first and second legs of the Fairs Cup Final.

His stay with Birmingham was brief, and less than a year later he was sold to Stoke City for £100,000.

With Stoke he won a second League Cup Winners medal in 1972.

In November 1976 a cash crisis at Stoke forced them sell some players, and United got themselves a bargain at £100,000.

During his spell with United he shouldered the main scoring responsibility and enjoyed the re-birth of his career, and he had the satisfaction of scoring the winning goal in the 1977 Cup Final.

Sadly, season 1979 – 80 saw him hit with injury, and he lost his first team place, and in December 1980, he re-joined his old manager Tony Waddington at Crewe, on a free transfer.

HARRY GREGG was a former Irish schools, youth and amateur International when he was introduced to league football by Doncaster Rovers in 1952 – 53, after they had signed him as a 19 year old from Coleraine.

The following season he won his first full cap, and his form was noted by United who paid out £23,000 for his services, a record for a goalkeeper at that time, in December 1957.

Two months after signing, he was one of the heroes at Munich, and by the end of the season, he had a F.A. Cup runners-up medal. During the summer he was voted the best goalkeeper in the 1958 World Cup Finals.

In the early sixties, he shared the No. 1 shirt with David Gaskell, missing the 1963 Cup Final through injury, and although he failed to make any appearances during 1964 – 65, he was back between the posts the following season.

But with the signing of Alex Stepney in 1966, he was given a free transfer, and in December of that year, he joined Stoke City.

JACK GRIMWOOD *began his career as an amateur with South Shields as a 16 year old, shortly before the start of the First World War. During the War South Shields had to suspend their league activities, and early in 1919 he was invited for a trial with United along with Joe Spence and Fred Hopkins, who were also playing in the North-East.*

In July of that year the club signed him as a professional, and after several reserve outings he made his League debut against Manchester City in October 1919.

For the next eight years he appeared regularly at

centre half, and when Frank Barson joined the club, he switched to wing half no less effectively. In 1927, he refused to accept new terms with the club and then changed his mind, but by that time United had decided to sell him, and he was transferred to Blackpool.

Leytonstone-born **HAROLD HALSE** was a star schoolboy player with Park Road School, Wanstead. On leaving school he was signed by non-league Barking Town, and later moved to Clapton Orient and Southend United where he began to make a name for himself.

While with Southend, he was introduced to Mr. J. J. Bentley the United secretary, and shortly afterwards joined the club for a fee of £350.

In his first game at Clayton, he scored within thirty seconds of the kick-off, and he soon set up a fine partnership with Billy Meredith as he helped United to two Championship wins and an F.A. Cup victory.

The F.A. Charity Shield match of 1911 saw him set up an individual goal scoring record, when he scored six, in United's 8 – 4 victory over Swindon Town at Stamford Bridge.

His performances didn't go unnoticed, as he was capped by England against Austria in 1909, and for the Football League, in 1908 and 1911.

However, shortly after his six Charity Shield goals he was transferred to Aston Villa, and went on to help them to F.A. Cup glory.

As a schoolboy, **JIMMY HANSON** won representative honours with both Manchester and England. On leaving school he played for various local non-league sides, and while still a Manchester North End player he played three games for United as an amateur, which saw him score three goals in one match. This led to his signing for the club as a professional in 1924.

He was soon showing his goalscoring ability in the Central League, and scored on his senior debut against Hull City, during the Second Division promotion winning season of 1924 – 25.

Unfortunately, his playing career came to an end on Christmas Day 1929, when he suffered a broken leg against Birmingham City at Old Trafford.

He tried to make a come-back in the United trial match at the start of the following season, but once again he had the misfortune to break his leg, and so his career came to a premature end.

A local youngster, **VINCE HAYES** progressed through the Newton Heath's club training scheme. After making his debut, he showed exceptional promise which helped him towards a regular place in the team.

Season 1905 – 06 saw him receive a benefit match against Barnsley on March 31st, and in 1909 he helped the club to their first F.A. Cup victory. During the following season, he was capped by the Football League and the Scottish League.

Season 1910 – 11 was his last with the club, and he went on to become manager of Preston North End, some time later.

DAVID HERD had the unusual experience of playing in the same team as his father, when he lined up for Stockport County, shortly after turning professional as a 17-year-old in 1951.

With County he soon became a noted goalscorer, and joined Arsenal for a fee of £8,000 in 1954. At Highbury he was the club's top scorer every season between 1958 and 1961.

In 1959 he won his first Scottish cap, and two years later he moved back to the Manchester area where he had spent his childhood, and joined United on July 26th 1961 for a fee of £40,000.

His first appearance in a United shirt was in Munich against F.C. Bayern in a pre-season friendly. His league debut came a few days later at West Ham.

Shortly after joining United he suffered a couple of injuries which kept him out of the side for a while, but he recovered and in season 1962 – 63 helped the club to the Cup Final, scoring twice in their three-one victory over Leicester.

His scoring touch never left him, and between seasons 1962 – 63 and 1964 – 65, he averaged 20 goals a season, and during 1966 – 67 he scored the 100th league goal of his career.

On March 18th 1967 he broke his leg while scoring against Leicester at Old Trafford, an injury which kept him out of the game until January 1968.

Due to his injury and his long spell out of the side, he could no longer be certain of a first team place, and during the close season of 1967 – 68, he moved to Stoke City.

A native of Northwich, **CAL HILDITCH** did not play football seriously until leaving school. Prior to the First World War, he played for Witton Albion, and during the hostilities he turned out for Altrincham where United's manager Jack Robson spotted him, and signed him as an amateur.

He became a professional in 1919, and in season 1919 – 20, he not only made his United debut but he also played for England against Wales.

During his distinguished career at half-back with the club, he was reputed never to have committed an intentional foul, and his fine play was respected by everyone in the game.

His career with the club spanned 17 years, and during 1926 – 27, he took over as player-manager after John Chapman was suspended by the F.A., but he stepped down again when Herbert Bamlett was appointed as manager. He left the club in 1932 to return home to Cheshire.

At one time it looked as if **GORDON HILL** had no chance of making the grade as a professional, as he was rejected by Queens Park Rangers, Southend United and even non-league Staines.

However, non-league Southall gave him a chance and with them he won three England amateur caps, before being spotted by Millwall.

He joined the London club in January 1973, and was soon a regular in their side. His fine wing play soon brought him the kind of attention usually given to players in the First Division, and soon the senior clubs were beginning to take notice.

Before any others could make a move, Tommy Docherty stepped in and paid Millwall £70,000 for him, in November 1975. He made his debut for United against Aston Villa at Old Trafford, and became an immediate crowd favourite.

His play continued to improve, and he was soon showing his goalscoring flair which helped him win England honours at under 23 and full level, as well as take United to the Cup Final in 1976.

1977, saw United at Wembley again and as in the previous seasons visit, he found himself being substituted. The following season he was leading scorer, but with the arrival of Dave Sexton he was expected to change his style and defend a bit more. This did not please him, and his old boss Tommy Docherty paid £250,000 for him in April 1978 and took him to Derby County.

GRAEME HOGG, has all the hallmarks of an old fashioned centre half, big, strong, hard-tackling and definite in his play. He joined the club from school in Aberdeen and progressed, like many before him, through the junior and youth sides before becoming a regular in the reserves.

His big chance came during 1983 – 84, when he made his debut in a F.A. Cup tie against Bournemouth, and he went on to establish himself in the team.

Season 1984 – 85 saw him command a regular place in the side and in the team march to Wembley he played in all but one of the previous rounds only to miss out on a Final place to Kevin Moran.

Locally developed full-back **RICHARD HOLDEN** made his league debut during 1904 – 05. He was a very strong and reliable full back who gave years of loyal service to the club, before a knee injury brought an end to his career in 1914.

Alongside Herbert Burgess he formed a formidable full-back partnership which helped the club to the F.A. Cup victory in 1909 and also the league title in 1908.

On October 15th 1910, he received a benefit from the club in the match against Newcastle United, and on his retirement from the game he joined the Royal Air Force.

"Six foot two — eyes of blue — big **JIM HOLTON** is after you," was the cry heard on grounds all over the country during the mid-seventies. The gentle giant began as an amateur with Celtic, and in 1967, he moved south to West Bromwich for trials, signing first as an amateur in December and as a professional four months later.

Although he made steady progress he failed to make their first team and after three years he was given a free transfer and joined Shrewsbury Town. On the opening day of 1971 – 72 he made his league debut and kept his place in the side.

His displays were noted by Scotland manager Tommy Docherty, when looking for under-23 players, and when the Doc became boss at Old Trafford he signed Jim for £80,000 in January 11th 1973.

Nine days later he made his United debut v. West Ham at home, and four months later he was playing for Scotland.

Just as he was on top form, he broke his leg at Sheffield Wednesday in December 1974, and during his come-back games prior to season 1975 – 76, he received a knee injury and while playing in the reserves broke his leg again. He joined Sunderland late in 1976 for around £75,000.

STEWART HOUSTON will probably be remembered by United fans as the unlucky player who missed the 1977 F.A. Cup Final due to a broken leg sustained at Bristol a couple of weeks before.

He joined Chelsea as a youngster and after only a handful of games he moved across London to Brentford for £17,000. He spent two successful years at Griffin Park, before signing for United in December 1973 for £55,000.

The change of divisions caused no problems, and he soon became the automatic choice at left back, helping United out of the Second Division in 1975, and to the Cup Final the following year. His performances for United in 1976 also earned him his only Scottish cap.

Sadly, after his broken leg, he was no longer an automatic choice, and at the end of 1979 – 80, he was given a free transfer and moved to Sheffield United.

Wrexham born **MARK HUGHES** burst into league football with a bang, and became one of the most feared strikers in the 1st division.

He joined United as a schoolboy and progressed through the juniors, and he was top scorer in the Youth side during 1981 and 1982.

After a couple of years in the reserves, he made his

senior debut at Oxford in the Milk Cup during 1983 – 84, and by the end of that season, he had represented Wales against England in his full International debut and scored.

He topped the United scoring chart in 1984 – 85, and his goal against Liverpool in the semi-final replay was only bettered by his effort against Spain at Wrexham. At the end of 1985 – 86 United accepted a bid of £2 million for Mark from Barcelona, and he left for Spain.

Born in Edinburgh, BILL JOHNSTON joined United on October 14th 1927, after playing for Hearts, Selby, Huddersfield and Stockport.

When United signed him they had to pay a fee of £3,000.

He was a brilliant schemer, and also a useful scorer of goals. But, after a couple of seasons with United he had a disagreement concerning terms and was put on the transfer list. He eventually joined Macclesfield in the Cheshire League.

However, United soon realised their mistake, and in May 1931 he was re-signed, but several injuries kept him out of the side, and in 1932 he left the club for a second time and joined Oldham Athletic.

A former England schoolboy player, **MARK JONES** was first noticed by Matt Busby while playing in a schools International at Old Trafford. His progress was noted and he joined the ground staff on leaving school.

He was patiently groomed to succeed Allenby Chilton and he made his league debut against Sheffield Wednesday in October 1950, but he had to wait another five years before he could make the No. 5 shirt his own.

A tall, well-built player, who adjusted to league football easily and made a big impact, but had always to be on top form to keep his place from Jackie Blanchflower. At the heart of the United defence, he added the necessary stability to the side, with his strong fearless play of an orthodox stopper. Sadly he failed to make the England team, but if he had not died at Munich he should have done so.

Signed by Dave Sexton in January 1978, JOE JORDAN, received a mixed reception from United fans upon his arrival, mainly due to his association with deadly rivals Leeds, to whom Sexton had to pay £350,000.

Morton was his first senior club, with whom he only played a handful of games before moving south to join Leeds United for a fee of £15,000 in October 1970. He wasn't long in making an impact south of the border and his aggressive style of play found him a marked man with opposing players, and referees.

More of a goal-maker than goalscorer, he helped Leeds to the league title in 1974 and two European Finals before moving to Manchester where he helped United to the 1979 cup final. During his spell with United he also added to his collection of Scottish caps helping his country to two World Cup Finals in the process.

BRIAN KIDD followed the same path as Nobby Stiles, from Collyhurst, via England schoolboys, to Old Trafford. Two years after signing professional he was a regular in the first team, and in 1967 he made his first team debut on the clubs Australian tour.

He made such an impression that he began the new season in the first team, making his debut officially in the F.A. Charity shield against Tottenham. 1967 – 68 was to be even more memorable for him as he scored for United in the European Cup Final against Benfica, on his 19th birthday.

But after such a bright start he found himself back in the reserves the following season for a time, but he soon regained his form and during 1969 – 70 and was selected to play for England.

In July 1974, he joined Arsenal for a fee of £110,000.

As a youngster, DENIS LAW looked anything but a future World class footballer, with his small frail build and his glasses to help a squint in one eye. But Andy Beattie at Huddersfield saw enough promise to sign him from school in 1955.

On Christmas Eve 1956, two months short of his 17th birthday, he made his league debut against Notts County at Meadow Lane, and in the return fixture on Boxing Day, he scored his first league goal.

He signed professional forms on February 25th 1957 and continued to make progress. So much so that on March 15th 1960, he signed for Manchester City at a cost of £56,000.

By this time he was an established Scottish International, having made his debut as an 18 year old against Wales at Cardiff. Perhaps his most notable feat during his period at City was in January 1961, when he scored six goals in an F.A. Cup tie, only for the match to be abandoned. Although he scored one in the replay, City were beaten, but he did have the satisfaction of being City's top scorer that season with 19 goals.

In 1961, he moved to Italy, to join Torino for £110,000. His career abroad began successfully, but clashes with the management forced him to refuse to play, and subsequently demand a transfer.

Matt Busby heard of his unrest, and on July 12th 1962 he returned to Britain and joined United for £115,000, and by the end of the season he had helped the club to F.A. Cup success. Championship medals

were to follow, but sadly he missed the European Cup triumph through injury.

Injuries were numerous as he went in search of goals, and defenders would try anything to stop him. This also saw him involved with referees, and he was ordered off on three occasions. For a decade he graced Old Trafford, one of the most popular players ever to don the red United jersey.

However, in the summer of 1973, he was given a free transfer, and was signed by neighbours City. He did return to Old Trafford once more as a player, on the last Saturday of league football 1973 – 74, when his goal put United into the second division. It was an ironic moment for the former "King" of Old Trafford.

One of the most popular players to play for United was **LOU MACARI**, perhaps due to his non-stop running and creative play.

He began his professional career with Celtic, and in his three seasons there, he won three Scottish league and two Cup medals along with Scottish caps at both full and under-23 level.

In January 1973, it looked as if he was going to sign for Liverpool, but Tommy Docherty persuaded him to Old Trafford, and a fee of £200,000 changed hands. He went straight into the United side and he made his debut against West Ham.

His collection of medals included F.A. Cup winners in 1977, and runners up in 1976 and 1979 plus a Milk Cup runners up and a Second Division Championship.

His loyalty to the club was rewarded at the end of season 1983 – 84 when he had a testimonial against his old club Celtic, in which he played for both sides.

In July 1984, he went into management with Swindon Town.

FRANK MANN was already a very experienced player, when the joined United in March 1923 from Huddersfield. His playing career began with his local amateur side Newark Town and other amateur clubs, before joining Leeds City and Lincoln City, as an amateur, and then Aston Villa, his first professional club.

He stayed at Villa for two years before moving to Huddersfield Town, where he played a part in the Yorkshire clubs F.A. Cup Finals of 1920 and 1922. With Huddersfield, he played mainly at inside forward, but was moved back to wing half after joining United, with whom he played regularly until season 1932 – 33.

DAVID McCREERY joined the club direct from school in 1973 after impressive performances with the Irish schools side.

He quickly made a name for himself, making his first team debut at Portsmouth on October 15th 1974 , when he came on as substitute.

Many of his appearances for the club were as substitute, but this did not prevent him from gaining full International honours for Ireland, his first cap coming against Scotland during 1975 – 76, again as substitute.

A fast, clever player, he was signed for QPR by his

former manager, Tommy Docherty for £200,000 in 1979.

PAUL McGRATH

PAUL McGRATH *is rated as one of the most skilful defenders in the first division. He was signed from St. Patricks Athletic in March 1982, and made his first appearances in friendly games prior to the start of season 1982 – 83.*

His first competitive appearance came in the Milk Cup, against Bradford City on November 10th, and his first league appearance came a few days later against Tottenham Hotspur at Old Trafford.

It wasn't until season 1984 – 85 that he made the team on a regular basis and he played a major part in United's march to Wembley, with performances that won him International honours with the Republic of Ireland.

Former England and Manchester Boys captain, **WILF McGUINNESS**, signed in 1953, and after good progress through the junior sides, he made his league debut, aged 17, against Wolves at Old Trafford on October 8th 1955.

A year later he was a member of the England Youth team and within the next three years he had represented the full under-23, and the Football League side.

After such a promising start to his career, it came as a great disappointment when he broke his leg against Stoke reserves on Dec. 12th 1959, and was forced to retire from the game.

The club found him a job as assistant youth team and reserve team boss, and during 1966 – 67, he surprised everyone by making a comeback in the reserves, and also being named as substitute for the first team.

During 1966, he helped England in their World Cup matches, and two years later, became manager of their Youth team, following a spell as trainer.

Following Sir Matt Busby's decision to retire in 1969, he was appointed chief coach, and at the start of season 1970 – 71 he took over the title of team manager.

Unfortunately things did not go well for him, and after a League Cup defeat by third Division Aston Villa, he relinquished his post to revert to managing the reserves. Shortly afterwards he left the club altogether, and eventually took up an appointment in Greece.

SAMMY McILROY, *has often been referred to as 'the last of the Busby Babes' since he was the last player signed by Matt Busby as a manager. He came to the club as an amateur in September 1969, turning professional two years later.*

His league debut came only three months later at Maine Road on November 6th, and he scored, and was soon being labelled the second George Best.

Thankfully his career took an entirely different path, and he went on to become a stylish mid-field player with both United and Northern Ireland, helping the club to the Second Division title in 1975 and the F.A. Cup in 1977, and winning over 70 caps for his country.

During 1973, his career almost came to an abrupt end, as he was badly hurt in a car crash, which kept him out of the game for some six months. He did however regain complete fitness and fought his way back into the United team, and totalling up some 320 league games and scoring 52 goals, before being transferred to Stoke City in February 1982.

HUGHIE McLENAHAN

HUGHIE McLENAHAN, was perhaps one of the best schoolboys to emerge from the Manchester area, and attracted a lot of attention while playing for both Manchester and England schools.

He was keen to join United, but surprisingly with a number of clubs after his signature, he signed for Stockport County on amateur forms. It was not long however, before he realised that he had made a mistake, and United again showed an interest.

Chief scout at the time, Louis Rocca, learned that County were to have a fund raising bazaar, and

decided to make a move. At this time, Rocca was one of Manchesters best makers of ice cream, and he offered to send three freezers of the stuff to the bazaar, free of charge. He then asked about the possibility of signing McLenahan, and was told that the matter would be considered. When the freezers arrived, County agreed to the transfer.

This was in 1927, and shortly afterwards he made his debut at right half against Tottenham at White Hart Lane. His play was progressing well but suffered a setback in August 1928, when he broke his leg in two places at Villa Park.

However, he made a comeback to the United side and captained the side on many occasions, before leaving in 1936, when he moved to Notts County.

Born in Barrow, **FRANK McPHERSON** *began his football career with Chesterfield, before returning to his native Barrow from whom he joined United in 1922.*

During his playing days he had perhaps the hardest shot of any forwards of this time, and perhaps the smallest feet as he only took size four boots.

He was also a very good sprinter which helped in his days as a winger, before moving to centre forward.

His stay with United lasted some six years, and he was unfortunate to be a member of a side which seemed to lack a little in team work, especially among the forwards.

In September 1928, Watford made an offer for him, and he eventually agreed to move south, but prior to his move he had been playing for Manchester Central, at Belle Vue, while on the transfer list at Old Trafford.

GORDON McQUEEN

GORDON McQUEEN followed his friend and former team-mate Joe Jordan to Old Trafford when he moved across the Pennines from Leeds for a fee of £500,000, in February 1978.

He had joined Leeds in March 1972 for £35,000 as a replacement for Jackie Charlton, and he went on to become not only a regular for the Elland Road side but also for Scotland. With Leeds he played more than 150 games before this move, and he went on to pass that total while at Old Trafford.

His height helped United in both defence and attack and his mere presence caused panic in penalty areas, at home and abroad.

Cup Final appearances in 1979 and 1983 and a Milk Cup Final appearance in 1983 were the only honours he won at Old Trafford before injuries began to keep him out of the side, and eventually lead to him getting a free transfer at the end of 1984 – 85.

In the summer of 1985, with several options to choose from, he decided that his future lay abroad, and he went to Hong Kong to join Sienko as player-coach.

WILLIAM McGLENN

WILLIAM McGLENN *joined United from Blythe Spartans in May 1946. He immediately established himself in the senior team in 1946/47, but a year later was sidelined by a cartilage operation. Happily he recovered well and went on to make 122 league and F.A. Cup appearances for the 'Reds' before joining Lincoln City at the end of season 1951/52.*

Perhaps the first super-star of British football **BILLY MEREDITH** is still remembered as one of the best outside rights ever to play in League and International football.

He was born in the village of Chirk in North Wales, and after only six games with Northwich Victoria, he joined Manchester City in 1894.

His career since then was rather remarkable, appearing 367 times for City and another 303 times for United. Between 1895 and 1920, he was selected for Wales 71 consecutive internationals, but was released to play in only 48 of those plus 3 'victory' internationals in 1919.

Two League Championship medals, two Second

Division Championship medals, and two F.A. Cup winners medals came his way following almost 1,100 senior games in which he scored over 300 goals. Whilst under suspension by the F.A. in 1906, he joined United from City, and was one of the players who helped to form the Players Union during his fifteen year spell with the club.

He returned to neighbours City in 1921, and was almost 50 years of age when he finally decided to give up the game, and leave the fans with the memories of his wizardly dribbles down the wing, with a toothpick sprouting from the corner of his mouth.

While in retirement, he kept a public house in Manchester, but sadly at the age of 81 he died at Withington, Manchester on 19th April 1958, and is one of the greatest players to play for United.

JACK MEW *was a native of County Durham, and began playing in goal at Henden school, Sunderland before joining Blaydon United, and later Marley Hill Colliery.*

Sunderland followed his progress closely, but they were too slow in making a move and United signed him in 1910 – 11 season.

He went straight into the Central League side and helped them to the championship during 1912 – 13 season, as well as making his first team debut against Middlesbrough. However, he had to wait until after the First World War before he got a regular place in the first team, and he went on to play 500 senior games, and 125 reserve games for the club.

In 1920, he won the first of his two England caps, and three years later he left United and moved to Barrow, after being presented with a gold watch by the club in recognition of his services.

Although highly rated in League Football, **CHARLIE MITTEN**, failed to win International recognition. He was spotted playing in Scottish junior football, and signed for the club on 10th August 1936.

After progressing through the junior sides, he made his senior debut on 11th November 1939, having served the club as an office boy when not playing with the juniors.

During the War, he served in the R.A.F., and was selected to play for an England XI against Scotland in the Bolton disaster match Maine Road which was to be the closest he would get to International football.

When football resumed after the hostilities he became a regular in the United side, helping them to victory in the 1948 F.A. Cup Final.

At the end of season 1949 – 50, United went to the U.S.A. on tour, and shortly before the end of it, he was tempted to go and try his luck in Bogota, where English players were being offered big money to show their skills.

Matt Busby tried to talk him out of it and told him if he ever came back to England, United would have nothing at all to do with him. But it was to no avail as he decided to try his luck in Colombia, and he walked out on his United contract.

He lasted only one season with the Santa Fe club, and upon his return to Britain, he was suspended by F.I.F.A., and put on the transfer list by United. Fulham made him an offer which he accepted and he moved south, where he began to enjoy his football again.

Goalkeeper **HARRY MOGER** *already had a fine reputation when he moved north to join United from Southampton, during 1902 – 03, and went on to give the club fine service.*

He played a big part in the success of the teams of that period, helping them to the Championship in 1908, and the F.A. Cup the following year, and his fine handling and consistent play gave the players in front of him confidence. He gave United sterling service until leaving the club at the end of the 1911/12 season.

Born at Cheslyn Hay, near Walsall, **CHARLIE MOORE**, was signed for United from Hednesford on May 19th 1919.

He didn't take long to settle at the club, and soon formed a full back partnership with Jack Silcock.

Two years after joining the club, he injured an ankle in a charity match at Northwich and unfortunately it looked as if he wasn't going to recover. The club placed him on the open to transfer list and also paid him compensation for his injury.

No club made a move for him, and it began to look as if his career was finished, but a few months later he reported for training and surprised everyone by making a come back.

He went on to prove he was as good as ever, remaining a member of the first team for another eight seasons.

KEVIN MORAN *was a former Gaelic footballer who played with Pegasus in Dublin before turning to professional soccer with United in February 1978, since when he has received his fair share of injuries during his eight years with the club.*

He made his league debut against Southampton away, on April 30th 1979, and since then has become a strong central defender in the United side, after becoming a regular during season 1981 – 82.

The Republic of Ireland soon called upon his services, and has since collected over 20 full caps, following in the footsteps of many other Irish players who have played for United. He will always have the sad reputation as the first player to be sent off in a Wembley Cup Final. The decision was criticised by many, but fortunately it had no effect on the outcome of the match.

On leaving school at 15, **WILLIE MORGAN** joined the ground staff at Burnley, in 1960. Three years later, in April 1963, he made his league debut at Hillsborough against Sheffield Wednesday, and soon made the outside right spot his own. During season 1967 – 68, he was selected to play for Scotland at full international level, after failing to make both the schoolboy and under 23 teams.

After some dazzling displays for Burnley, Matt Busby paid a fee of £90,000 on August 24th 1968, for his services. He made his United debut four days later against Tottenham at Old Trafford.

During Frank O'Farrell's time with the club, he was moved back to mid-field, where he enjoyed much success and also captained the club, which he also did during the time of Tommy Docherty.

During 1974 – 75, he was substituted against Southampton at Old Trafford, and showed his feelings by leaving the ground before the end of the game.

In June 1975, he refused to go on tour with the club, and not surprisingly he was transferred a few weeks later, back to his old club Burnley for a fee of around £35,000.

KEN MORGANS *was a former Welsh Schoolboy Internationalist, who joined United in 1955 after assistant manager Jimmy Murphy spotted him playing for Swansea Boys at Maine Road. In April 1956, he turned professional.*

His progress was swift, and he made his league debut on December 21st 1956 against Leicester City.

He was a speedy winger, who was capable of playing on either wing and he developed a reputation for his accurate centres.

At Munich, he was slightly injured, and the after-effects of the disaster seemed to affect his play, although he did win Welsh under-23 honours.

In March 1961 he got the chance to return to Wales and join Swansea Town.

JOHNNY MORRIS was another player who joined United as a junior. In 1938 he came from amateur side St. Johns in Radcliffe, where he was originally a centre half.

During the war, he played in Tommy Walkers touring side, and on his demob re-joined United. After only four reserve games he won his place in the first team and soon formed a good partnership with Jimmy Delaney.

In 1948 he was playing so well that he played trials for the Football League, and in March of that year he won his first honour, against the Scottish League. Surprisingly two League caps were all the international honours that he won, although his displays at club level thrilled fans up and down the country.

After playing a major part in the Cup victory of 1948, an ankle injury early in season 1948 – 49 affected his play, but he soon regained his old form a few weeks later. However, in March 1949, following some disagreement, he was transferred to Derby County for a then record fee of £25,000.

Although **REMI MOSES** *was born in Manchester, he began his professional career with West Bromwich Albion in 1977, joining them from Corpus Christi Boys Club.*

He signed professional forms on his 18th birthday, and enjoyed three seasons with the Midlands club, where he won England under 21 honours.

When former Albion manager Ron Atkinson moved to take over United he did not forget the little hard tackling midfield player, and signed him in a £2.4 million package deal along with Bryan Robson (with Remi valued at £650,000), in October 1981.

He made his first appearance for United as substitute against Swansea City on September 19th, with his full debut at Middlesbrough three days later. It wasn't long before he was being likened to Nobby Stiles, and he was soon to become just as big a favourite with the supporters.

A sending off at Highbury in 1983, robbed him of a place in the Cup Final team, and in 1985 when Wembley was reached again he was missing again, this time through injury.

ARNOLD MUHREN was considered one of the World's best midfield players when Ipswich Town brought him to England from Dutch club Twente Enschede in August 1978. With the Suffolk side, he helped them to a U.E.F.A Cup win and also the runners up spot in the League twice, during his four seasons there.

When his contract came to an end in 1982, he joined United in the summer of that year as a free agent.

Along with Robson and Moses he formed a formidable mid-field for United and his skills were appreciated by supporters, especially during the cup run of 1983.

At the end of season 1984 – 85, he was given a free transfer by United and returned to his native Holland and joined Ajax, leaving the United following with fond memories of his fine skill and delicate touches.

In 1933 – 34, **GEORGE MUTCH** *moved south from Scottish league club Arbroath to join United. He was a strong and powerful inside forward, who soon fitted into the side.*

It wasn't until the following season, however, that he made his league debut, and he went on to play in all but two games, and ended up as the clubs leading scorer.

After four successful seasons at Old Trafford, he left the club, moving to Preston North End, where he won an F.A. Cup winners medal, and a Scottish International cap during 1937 – 38.

JIMMY NICHOLL, was signed as an apprentice in 1972 from Belfast schools football, and turned professional in March 1974. Though Canadian-born, he captained the Northern Ireland Youth team and made steady progress through the United junior sides, before making his league debut at Southampton, almost one year after signing pro. forms, in April 1975.

He went on to form a fine, young, defensive partnership with Arthur Albiston and he was soon a regular selection for both club and country.

He went on to play in more than 240 games for United before he joined Sunderland on loan in 1982, and shortly afterwards he made the move a permanent one.

JIMMY NICHOLSON *joined the club as an amateur in May 1958, turning professional in February 1960. Before he was 16, he had won Irish under-23 honours, and on August 24th 1960 he made his league debut in the full Northern Ireland team, to add to the under 23, 'B' and schoolboy caps he had already won.*

He was skilful in his play, and got through a lot of work, whether playing wing half or inside forward, and was also quick to snap up a goal scoring chance. But, he became one of the many young players who found the fight for first team football at Old Trafford very difficult, due to the form of others, and had to compete against the likes of Setters, Stiles and Crerand for a first team place.

So, when Huddersfield Town made a move for him in December 1964, the club agreed to let him go for a fee of £8,000.

As a boy, **BOBBY NOBLE** played for Cheshire schools and was also an England trialist at wing half. He joined United from school, and was soon captain of the Youth team which won the F.A. Youth cup in 1964. He was also a member of the England Youth team which won the European Youth Cup in the same year.

Playing full-back, he turned in some fine displays in the reserves, and his chance finally came on April 9th 1966 against Leicester City.

The following season, he won a place in the side early on, and quickly settled in at left back, with sharp tackling and neat distribution.

Unfortunately towards the end of the season, he was badly injured in a car crash and at one time his life was in danger. After a spell in hospital he gradually recovered, but after trying to recover his fitness he found he was unable to do so, and he eventually had to retire from the game.

O

The deal that brought **JESPER OLSEN** to Old Trafford was arranged in January 1984, but it was not until the summer of that year that the player left Ajax for a £200,000 fee.

The Danish International was capable of playing either in midfield or on the wing, where his excellent close control and goal-scoring ability soon made him a firm favourite with supporters.

He made his United league debut in the opening match of season 1984/85, and played a significant part in the march to Wembley, missing only a handful of games all season.

LES OLIVE is not one of the star names in United's history, nor one of the players with countless appearances and honours behind them, but he more than deserves a mention in any history of the club.

He joined the clubs office staff in September 1942, on leaving school, and three years later he found himself in the R.A.F. with whom he served until July 1948.

At the end of the war he returned to Old Trafford where he worked in the ticket office, and also assisted the 'A' and 'B' teams in the early 1950's. In 1952 – 53, he was playing in the Central League, and by now had appeared in every position except outside left for the club.

In April 1953 he found himself selected for the first team because the other goalkeepers were injured, and made his first of two senior appearances on the 11th April at Newcastle United, and kept his place for the following week.

But his main job was between the filing cabinets rather than the goal posts, and he was appointed assistant-secretary in March 1955, taking over from the late Walter Crickmer after Munich, since when he has been the club secretary.

P

ALBERT PAPE was involved in perhaps one of the most surprising transfers ever.

He had began his career with Notts County before moving to Rotherham County and then Clapton Orient, with whom he travelled north in February 1925, to play against United.

Shortly before the kick off, officials of the two club's got together and the player was transferred to United. His registration was approved by the League, over the telephone, and he made his United debut against his former team mates. Even more ironically, he also scored.

A product of Derbyshire and England schoolboy sides, **MARK PEARSON** joined United straight from school. He played for United and England Youths during 1957 – 58, and in the same season made his senior debut in the F.A. Cup tie against Sheffield Wednesday, when he was drafted into the side for the first match after the disaster.

He came in for some criticism, due to his rugged style of play, but this was put down to his inexperience. But, he did show that he had the makings of a good player.

The following season he was kept out of the side due to the form of Quixall and Charlton, but he made the most of the appearances he had.

His league appearances were also hampered by injury, and in October 1963, he was transferred to Sheffield Wednesday for £20,000, where he managed to play regular first division football.

A former Salford schoolboy, **STAN PEARSON** joined United at the age of 15, on the 4th of May 1936.

It was on November 13th 1937, that he got his first league game a few months after signing professional. This was at Chesterfield, and he showed tremendous promise, which he showed even more a month later, when he scored four goals from the outside right position against Swansea.

In 1939, he was well in the running for an England cap, but the war delayed this honour until 1948 when he won the first of his eight caps.

Upon the departure of Johnny Carey, he was named club captain, a fitting honour for the quick forward with a deceptive body swerve and tricky footwork. At one point during 1948, he had made over 70 consecutive appearances.

He left the club in February 1954 when he joined Bury, at a time when he could no longer command a first team place. He could have stayed longer as a member of the reserve team helping along the young players, but he wanted to end his career still playing senior football. Certainly one of the all-time greats of United's history.

STUART PEARSON joined Hull City as an amateur, and moved up through their junior sides, before making his debut for them on the last day of season 1969 – 70. The following season he managed to add to his initial appearance, but it wasn't until 1971 – 72 that he obtained a regular place in the side. Teams soon began to take notice of his goalscoring ability, but Tommy Docherty moved quicker than the others and signed him for United on May 3rd 1974, for £200,000.

He soon settled in his new surroundings and scored 17 goals in his first season, helping United back into the First Division.

Unfortunately, being a forward he took his share of knocks, and he often missed games through injury, but this did not stop him making both the England under-23 and full international side during season 1975 – 76.

His goals helped to re-establish United in the first division, and also helped to take them to the 1976 and 1977 Cup Finals, where in the latter he scored the opening goal.

It wasn't long before he was England's first choice centre forward, but with the signing of Joe Jordan his United future looked rather bleak, but he held off the challenge of both Jordan and Greenhoff, until injury put him on the sidelines.

During the first half of 1978 – 79 he was injured after only one and a half games of a comeback attempt, but was still offered an improved contract at the end of the season. However, he felt he would be better off elsewhere, and a fee of £220,000 took him south to West Ham United.

JAMES PEDDIE was a very reliable player with a deadly shot, who favoured a deep lying forward role. Before moving to Clayton he had played for Scottish league side Third Lanark and then Newcastle United from whom he joined United during 1902 – 03.

He soon became an important member of the team, and a reliable goal-scorer. He also formed a good understanding with a speedy forward called Allen which resulted in many goals.

He was a member of the club when it changed its name from Newton Heath to Manchester United, but left in the latter half of season 1906 – 07.

J. PEDEN was an Irishman who came to Newton Heath at the start of season 1893 after spells with both Linfield and Distillery. He had played for the Irish international side since 1888.

As an outside left he was a real crowd pleaser, and the supporters of that time took to him right from the start. His debut for the club, was against Blackburn Rovers in the opening match of season 1893 – 94, and his performance was so brilliant that he was carried from the pitch shoulder high by the 'Heathens' followers

As a youngster, **DAVID PEGG** played inside left for Doncaster Boys, Yorkshire Boys, England under 14's and England Boys. He joined United from school in 1951, and worked his way up to the first team and made his league debut at Old Trafford on December 6th 1952, aged 17, against Middlesbrough.

His first team appearances were limited until 1955 – 56, when he claimed the number eleven shirt on his own, and shortly afterwards went on to play for England 'B'.

Unfortunately he was playing at the same time as Matthews and Finney, and therefore his chance of a full England cap were limited, but he did manage to win one during 1956 – 57 against Eire.

He was considered a speedy ball player, with a useful shot, and was another of the great side which was destroyed at Munich, who would have been more successful as the years passed on.

JACK POWELL was a well-built full-back, who was born in Frwd near Wrexham. He joined the Druids after watching them play, despite never having played before, in 1879.

After only three games for them, he was selected to play for Wales against England. He was transferred to Bolton Wanderers four years later, where he stayed for three seasons.

A fault was discovered in his contract, and he left Bolton, only for an offer of employment to come from Newton Heath almost immediately. This led to him playing for the club, and he signed professional forms in October 1887.

He went on to become club captain, and gave both his club and country great service.

Q

ALBERT QUIXALL began his career with Sheffield Wednesday and made his debut, aged 17, in 1951. Two years later he was making his full England

debut, in October 1953, and two years later helped Wednesday to the Second Division title.

His ball playing skills won him many admirers, and in September 1958, Matt Busby paid what was then a record fee of £45,000 for his signature.

In his debut against Tottenham he showed what a good player he was, but following his transfer he took a little time to settle. He then went on to play consistently up until 1961 – 62, when he only played in half of United's games, but the following season he returned to his best form and helped the club to its cup success.

Season 1963 – 64 saw him again make only a few first team appearances, and in the close season he was transferred to Oldham Athletic for a fee of £7,000.

R

It was mid-way through season 1928 – 29, when **TOMMY REID** joined United from Liverpool. He was a well-built player who was fast off the mark and very difficult to knock off the ball.

His United debut came in February 1929, and he soon began to show his skills and goalscoring ability. Up until his departure to Oldham Athletic during 1932 – 33, he had remained a consistent goalscorer.

Captain of the 1909 F.A. Cup winning side, **CHARLIE ROBERTS** was signed from Grimsby Town on April 22nd 1904. He was 20 years old and was considered by many as the best centre-half in the second division. At 6ft. tall and weighing around 12 stone he was certainly a formidable player to play against.

He cost United £400 and was worth every penny. Soon he was club captain, and became one of the founder members of the Players Union, gaining much respect from his fellow professionals for the work he did in this capacity.

During 1904 – 05 he won England International honours and the following season represented the Football League.

In 1912, he left the club and joined Oldham Athletic, after giving United great service in his years with the club.

Captain of both club and country, **BRYAN ROBSON** was signed by Ron Atkinson in October 1981 for a British record fee of over £1.5 m.

He had begun his career with West Bromwich Albion in September 1972, turning professional in August 1974. During his time at the Hawthorns he suffered three broken legs, but always fought back to full fitness, and recovered well enough to be capped at Youth, under 21 and 'B' levels before making the senior side in 1980.

More than 250 games were completed for Albion before he joined United along with team mate Remi Moses in a £2.4 m deal, and he has since become recognised as the most complete player in British football.

With United, he has captained them to two F.A. Cup final victories since his debut at Tottenham in the League Cup on October 7th 1981, but due to injuries has also missed many important games in which the club could have achieved more success had he been fit. He remains a most important member of both the United and England side.

JACK ROWLEY is still regarded as one of the most prolific goalscorers in the immediate post-war period. He came from a footballing family, with two brothers also professionals and his father also an ex-player.

Wolves signed him as a 15 year-old, and he progressed through the ranks to their league side. He then spent five months on loan to Bournemouth, before joining United on November 22nd 1937 for a £3,500 fee.

During the war, he guested for Wolves and Tottenham, and set individual goalscoring records when he scored eight for Wolves against Derby, and seven for Spurs against Luton Town.

His first representative honour came in 1944 when he played against Wales in a war-time international, and later in 1948 and 1949 he played for both the Football League and the full England side.

In season 1946 – 47 he broke Sandy Turnbull's long-standing record of 25 goals in one season, and in 1950 – 51 he improved on his own record with 30 goals.

He was able to play in any forward position, and he possessed a powerful shot in both feet.

During 1954 – 55 he moved to Plymouth Argyle as player-manager, on a free transfer, in recognition of his service to United.

S

DAVID SADLER was one of the most sought-after teenagers in British football when playing as an amateur with Maidstone. He was finally persuaded to join United in November 1962, still as an amateur, but he did sign as a professional three months later. After playing in the reserves and junior sides, he made his league debut in August 1963 against Sheffield Wednesday, as a centre forward.

His first-team appearances were limited due to the playing strength of the club, but he waited patiently for his chance to come.

When it did he proved to be a very versatile player, capable of playing in both attack or defence. He gained England under-23 caps, and in 1968, he won his first full cap at Wembley against Northern Ireland.

In November 1973, he accepted a move to Preston North End, and for a fee of £20,000 he took the short trip across Lancashire.

A former Manchester and Lancashire schoolboy player, **ALBERT SCANLON** joined the United ground staff in 1951, and after the usual grooming in the junior and reserve sides he made his league debut at Old Trafford in November 1954 against Arsenal.

He took over the outside left spot from Jack Rowley and proved to be a worthy successor, with his boundless enthusiasm and powerful shot in either foot.

At Munich, he suffered leg injuries but made a swift recovery and soon regained his place in the team. His fine performances and goalscoring ability soon won him England under-23 honours and he was also tipped at the time for full caps, but none followed.

In November 1960, he was transferred to Newcastle United for a fee of £15,000.

MAURICE SETTERS was a hard working, strong-tackling wing half who made his league debut with Exeter City in 1954. In January 1955 he moved to West Bromwich Albion for a fee of £3,000 and made his first division debut the following November, at inside forward. While with Albion, he represented the Army and also captained the England under-23 side.

In January 1960 he moved to Old Trafford for a fee of £30,000 and made his United debut at home to Birmingham City, ten days after signing, on January 16th.

Although he played mostly at wing half with Albion, he turned in some good performances at full back shortly after joining United. In October 1961 a knee injury kept him out of the side, but he was soon back playing his usual game, and in the following season he helped the club to Wembley where he added a cup winners medal to his England schoolboy, youth and under-23 caps.

Two seasons later in November 1964, he was transferred to Stoke City.

Manager Jack Robson signed **JACK SILCOCK** from Eccles Borough in 1916 after watching him play for that club. His first match for United was against Oldham Athletic as a 16-year-old in the Lancashire Section of the war-time league.

Two years after signing he turned professional, and in 1921, after playing in an international trial at Burnley, he was chosen to play for England against Scotland and Wales. Later, he also toured Sweden with England.

He must be rated as one of the greatest defenders the club has ever had, and he used to volley the ball from defence to the feet of his forwards. His career with United lasted 18 years, and in 1934 he moved to Oldham Athletic. While with United he was given two benefits of £650 each.

Centre forward **JOE SPENCE** joined United as an amateur, aged 20 in 1919 from Scotswood, a club with which he had been most successful.

Shortly after signing, he turned professional and made his debut the same week, scoring four goals against Burnley.

He played for United over 14 seasons, and during that time celebrated scoring his 100th league goal, v. Cardiff at Old Trafford in October 1927. During this time he was subject to an inquiry from Sheffield Wednesday for his transfer, but this was turned down.

However, in May 1933 he was placed on the transfer list and shortly afterwards moved to Bradford City. His departure was a blow to many United supporters, as he was one of the most popular pre-war players, whose goalscoring ability thrilled the crowds wherever he played.

HARRY STAFFORD was a fast and reliable full back who first made his name with Crewe Alexandra, before moving to Newton Heath in 1896.

He lived in Crewe after signing and travelled to Manchester by train, often not knowing if he would get his train fare back from the club.

Soon he became club captain, and was granted a benefit for his services.

Because he was a bit of a showman, he decided to play the match at night with the aid of Welles lights. Unfortunately the night was rather windy and one lamp after another was blown out. With only one lamp left alight the referee abandoned the match, only to find half of the players already in the dressing rooms.

At a time when the club was in a poor financial way, a chance meeting by Stafford and Mr. J. H. Davies changed all this, with Davies and friends putting money into the club.

He went on to become a director of the club when his playing career finished in 1902 – 03, in which position he remained until 1904 – 05.

Dublin born **FRANK STAPLETON** progressed through the Arsenal junior sides before making his league debut for the Gunners in 1975. He soon became a regular goalscorer, and played for them in the F.A. Cup Finals of 1978 – 79 & 80, scoring against United in the 1979 match.

Prior to the start of season 1981 – 82 he moved north to join United for a tribunal fixed fee of around £1m., and he made his United league debut in the opening match of that season, at Coventry. His goalscoring ability followed him to Old Trafford and he was always well up the scoring charts, as well as finding the net regularly for the Republic of Ireland. Although noted for his ability as a striker he has contributed much to United as a stop-gap in other positions, particularly in the Milk Cup Final of 1983, and more so in the F.A. Cup Final of 1985, when he won his third winners medal.

ALEX STEPNEY *continued the tradition of great goalkeepers at the club, when he signed for United for a record breaking £52,000 in September 1966, only four months after being signed by Chelsea from Millwall for a record £50,000.*

His career had began with non-league Tooting and Mitcham as a 15-year-old, joining Millwall four years later, but only playing in their reserves in mid-week and still playing for Tooting on a Saturday. He soon joined Millwall full time in May 1963, and went on to win under-23 honours two years later, and in May 1966, he crossed London to Chelsea.

One game was all he managed with Chelsea before coming to United, and he made his league debut for them against City at home on September 17th. He soon settled, and helped the club to the League Championship in his first season, and to the European Cup the following season.

Although his brilliance and consistency helped United, his England progress was restricted due to the form of Gordon Banks, but he did manage one appearance for his country in 1968.

His times with the club were not always happy, and in 1970 he asked for a transfer after being dropped, but this was refused. Early in 1973/74 he found himself leading goalscorer at the club after successfully converting two penalty kicks, but could not stop the slide into Divison two.

22 clean sheets in 40 games helped take the club back to the First Division and two cup finals were also reached, before he was given a testimonial in February 1977. Two years later he eventually left the club, moving to America and Dallas Tornado.

Goalkeeper **ALF STEWARD** was born in Manchester, and at the end of World War I he signed amateur forms for Stalybridge Celtic, but lasted only one season. He then wrote to United for a trial, and after a couple of matches, against his old club, he was signed. (He was the last by Jack Robson before resigning).

In his first season 1920 – 21, he helped the reserves to the Central League title, but had to wait until 1923 before taking over from Jack Mew. He soon formed a fine understanding with Frank Barson, and his 6ft. 12st. physique also helped in his performances.

During the summer months he kept trim by playing cricket for Kidderminster in the Birmingham League. His career with United lasted until 1932, when he joined local club Manchester North End.

NOBBY STILES *won five England schoolboy caps in 1957 before joining the Old Trafford ground staff. In his early days his tackles were often mis-timed, so Matt Busby sent him to an eye specialist where it was found that an accident with a trolley bus some years earlier had impaired his vision. He was fitted with contact lenses, and his game immediately improved.*

After captaining the youth team he turned professional in 1959, and after playing in the first team during friendly matches in 1959 – 60, he made his league debut at Bolton on October 1st 1960.

He made a big impact in the team, but in season

1962 – 63 he missed the F.A. Cup Final, after playing in 31 league games.

1965 saw him selected for England, and a year later helped them to victory in the World Cup, and his victory jig round Wembley will always be remembered. He was now making up for missing the 1963 Cup win, as he helped United to League and European triumphs.

In 1971 he moved to the North East and joined Middlesbrough for £20,000.

In the summer of 1984, the transfer of **GORDON STRACHAN** to United was a rather long drawn out affair due to the involvement of West German club Cologne, who had made earlier negotiations with the player. However after weeks of talks between the clubs, Aberdeen and the U.E.F.A. officials, he finally joined United from Aberdeen for a fee of £600,000.

He began his career in Scotland with Dundee, with his initial Senior appearance against Hearts in May 1975. Aberdeen then signed him in November 1977, and he became an important member of a successful team, which began to dominate the Scottish game. He won his first Scottish cap in 1980.

Since his transfer to United he has excited the crowds with his close control and ability to take on defenders.

A shoulder injury, while scoring at West Brom. early in 1985 – 86 kept him out of the side, but he soon returned to his best for both United and Scotland.

J.W. SUTCLIFFE *joined the club during the season 1902 – 03, but he had already made quite a name for himself in other fields before this. At one time he was an international at rugby football, but was expelled from the game as he was considered to be a professional.*

He then diverted his attention to the association game where he began with Bolton Wanderers as an inside forward and won five full caps with the Lancashire club.

Millwall were his next club, and by now he had moved to the position of goalkeeper, and it was in this position that he moved north to Clayton to join United, where he won Football League representative honours in season 1903 – 04.

IAN STOREY-MOORE holds the unique experience of being involved in the 'Transfer that never was'. More familiarly known in football as Ian Moore, on Saturday 4 March 1972, he was paraded by Derby County Manager Brian Clough at the Baseball Ground, as the club's new signing from Nottingham Forest. However, Forest refused to sanction the move and instead sold him to United for a £200,000 fee.

His career began in Scunthorpe youth soccer, signing professional for Forest in May 1962 and making his debut a year later. During 1966/67 he was capped at under-23 level, but a broken leg two years later halted his progress. He fought back to full fitness, only to fall victim to further injuries which limited him to one England cap. As a winger, he had an eye for goal and after finishing top scorer at Nottingham in 1968/69 and 1969/70 it was this talent that United hoped to capitalise on.

He scored on his debut against Huddersfield on 11 March 1972, but an injury in training soon after put him out for the rest of that season. He scored 11 goals in his 39 games for United and had made a big impact with supporters when yet another injury, received in 1973/74 forced him into retirement from League soccer.

The presence of **ERNIE TAYLOR** *in the immediate post-Munich side helped the club tremendously in that testing period.*

His playing career had started with Hylton Colliery Jnrs. before joining Newcastle in 1942, where he won an F.A. Cup winners medal in 1951.

Later that year he was transferred to Blackpool for £27,000, where he formed a formidable partnership with Stanley Matthews, winning another cup winners medal in 1953, and his only England cap a year later.

After the Munich disaster, Jimmy Murphy decided that Ernie Taylor could add the necessary experience to his young team, and he paid Blackpool £8,000 for his services.

With United he made Wembley again, but had to be content with a runners-up medal, but it was mostly thanks to his leadership on the field that they got that far.

He remained with the club until December 1958, when he left to return to his native north-east for another 'life-saving' mission at Sunderland, who were fighting relegation.

Barnsley-born **TOMMY TAYLOR** joined the ground staff of his local club in 1947, and two years later made his league debut.

After establishing himself in the first team, he was soon being noted as a promising player, and it was not long before various clubs were after his signature.

Matt Busby got there first, and in March 1953, he was signed for a fee of £29,999, so arranged that he would not become the first £30,000 player in the country. Arriving at Old Trafford with his boots wrapped in a paper parcel, made his league debut on March 7th against Preston and scored twice. A few weeks later, he was playing for England, and later for the Football League.

He had quickly established himself in the United side, and soon became a noted goalscorer, with a strong shot and excellent heading ability.

But Munich was also the end of the road for this talented player who undoubtedly would have gone onto greater things with United and England.

JIMMY TURNBULL *and* **'SANDY' TURNBULL** *were not related, but it is worthwhile to consider both their careers together. Both were Scotsmen, and they arrived at United round about the same time.*

Jimmy, a centre forward, joined the club from Leyton in 1907, while Sandy had arrived from neighbours City in January of the same year, along with Burgess, Meredith and Bannister following the troubles with the Hyde Road club, and he formed a fine partnership with Jimmy as his inside left.

Both players were always amongst the goals, with Sandy scoring the winner in the 1909 Cup Final against Bristol City, and they both helped the club to League Championship success.

Jimmy was first to leave the club, in 1910, when he moved to Bradford, while Sandy continued to convert Billy Meredith crosses into goals until he was sadly killed at Arras during the First World War.

DENIS VIOLLET was one of the many former schoolboy Internationals to join the club, signing professional forms in 1950. He graduated through the junior and reserve sides, being groomed to take over from Stan Pearson, by whom he was coached.

His first team debut came when he was 19, at Newcastle in April 1953, and to enable him to play he had to get weekend leave from the Army.

When he eventually took over from Pearson, he showed he had an eye for goals and often topped the goal charts. Representative honours soon came his way, and in 1956 – 57 he played for the Football League.

At Munich, he was injured, and took a little time to recover, but the following season he was soon back amongst the goals. In 1959, he was made club captain and in the same season he broke Jack Rowleys club scoring record of 30 league goals, when he scored 32.

A year later he won his first England cap, which was considered by most to be long overdue. He had shown his goalscoring ability with United over many seasons. He joined Stoke City in January 1962 for a fee of around £25,000.

Centre half **GEORGE VOSE** *signed professional for the club early on in season 1932 – 33, following some promising displays in the reserves. He had to wait until the following season however, before making his debut.*

Having got that out of the way, he went on to become a regular in the United line up, until the outbreak of war in 1939.

A fine hard-tackling defender, whose presence in the side helped steady the team during those struggling times in the 1930's when the club was going through a difficult period of their history.

It cost United a fee of £150 to sign outside left **GEORGE WALL** from Barnsley in 1906. He had marvellous ball control and packed a terrific shot in his left foot, and one of the best outside lefts ever to play for the club.

A year later after signing for the club he won the first of his seven England caps, against Wales, and he also represented the Football League on five occasions. His career with the club lasted until the outbreak of

the First World War in 1919 during which time he had helped win the F.A. Cup and the League Championship.

JOHN WARNER learned his football among the miners of South Wales, joining Swansea Town, where he won Welsh International honours.

He joined United on June 3rd 1938, but had to wait until November before making his debut at Aston Villa. His quick constructive style of play kept him in the team for the rest of the season, missing only one game.

During the War he helped with the United junior sides, and in the late 1940's he was captain of the reserve team. He was also United's 12th man at Wembley in 1948.

Although his first team appearances were few, he always gave everything, and was noted for his strong tackling and fine positional sense. At the end of the season 1950 – 51, he was given a free transfer and during the close season he joined Oldham Athletic as player-coach.

Another of the many Welshmen to play for United over the years, **COLIN WEBSTER** joined Cardiff City as a junior. He was then called up for National Service, and on completion of this he was given a free transfer. One of his team mates in the Army was Denis Viollet, who recommended him to United, and he was signed in 1952.

He made his first team debut in December 1953 at Portsmouth, but wasn't able to get an extended run in the side until the following season.

He was rather fortunate not to be involved in the Munich disaster, as he was unable to make the trip due to a bout of influenza which had confined him to bed.

In 1957, he won his first Welsh cap, and in 1958 he won an F.A. Cup runners up medal with United. The following October he returned to his native Wales, and joined Swansea Town.

ENOCH 'KNOCKER' WEST, was one of the finest goalscorers in the country during the years leading up to the First World War. He was signed from Nottingham Forest in the summer of 1910, after scoring almost a century of goals for the Midlands club, at a fee of £850.

He had spent five seasons with Forest, and was soon just as big a favourite with the United supporters as he had been with those at Forest.

During season 1911 – 12, he played for the Football League against the Scottish League, and it was unfortunate that his career was ended by the First World War, and his alleged involvement in the infamous 'Fixed' match against Liverpool in 1914.

BERT WHALLEY started his football career in the Manchester works league before moving to Staleybridge Celtic from whom he joined United in May 1934, with no fee involved.

He made his league debut against Doncaster on November 30th 1935, and most of his early appearances were at wing half, where his constructive play was used to good purpose.

In later seasons he prove a versatile player by playing at full back and centre half, and during his spells in the reserve side in the latter stages of his career he helped develop many of the young players.

Sadly an eye injury forced him to retire shortly after the start of season 1948 – 49, but he did not leave the club but stayed on to help with the coaching, and remained on the staff until he lost his life along with the players he helped, at Munich.

LIAM 'BILLY' WHELAN was one of the most skilful players in British football during the late 1950's. A former Republic of Ireland schoolboy, he came to United from Home Farm as an amateur at

the age of 18.

Within a week of his arrival he was a full time player and was soon a leading member of the youth team which won the F.A. Youth Cup in 1953.

His league debut came during season 1954 – 55, on March 26th at Preston, and it wasn't long before his deceiving body swerve was giving defences trouble. He created many chances for his team mates, and also managed to score numerous goals himself.

Not only did he establish himself in the United side, but also in the Republic of Ireland side, with whom he would have won more caps if he had not been another victim of the Munich disaster in 1958.

A former member of Stockport and England schools side, **JEFF WHITEFOOT**, had the chance to join numerous clubs, but signed for United in August 1949 as an amateur, and also began working in the club offices. He made rapid progress through the Juniors and the reserves, and he became the youngest player to play in the United league side, at the age of 16, when he turned out against Portsmouth at Old Trafford on 15 April 1950.

He continued his progress, and in 1954 he won England under-23 caps, and although not tall, he was well-built and could play equally well in either wing half positions or as an inside forward, where his ball playing ability created many openings for his team mates.

In 1957 he moved on to Grimsby Town for a short period before signing for Nottingham Forest.

NORMAN WHITESIDE was already being tipped for the top while still a schoolboy in Belfast.

Spotted by Bob Bishop, he joined United in May 1981, and less than a year later he was making his league debut at Brighton as a 16 year old.

He made his full league debut shortly afterwards in the last match of season 1981 – 82, and a matter of weeks later was the youngest player to appear in the World Cup Finals when he made his International debut, against Yugoslavia.

The following season he became the youngest player to score in a Wembley Final, when he scored in the Milk Cup Final against Liverpool.

A few months later he was back there scoring against Brighton in the F.A. Cup Final, and two years later his brilliant goal won the F.A. Cup for United against Everton.

RAY WILKINS began his playing career with Chelsea as a 15 year old in 1971, turning professional two years later. Over 200 senior games later he was signed by Dave Sexton (the man who had spotted him for Chelsea), for a fee of £825,000 in August 1979.

His play with United improved greatly, particularly when he teamed up in midfield with Bryan Robson. Ironically it was Robson who took over the captaincy of both United and England when Ray suffered a lengthy period of injury.

A talented player, it came as quite a surprise when Ron Atkinson accepted a fee of £1.5m from AC Milan for his transfer in the summer of 1984.

The career of **JACK WILSON** *is as interesting as any of the big name players the club has had. He came from Leadgate, County Durham and played for local junior sides before joining Newcastle United and playing for them in the Victory League towards the end of the First World War.*

In only his fourth game for the club, he met with a knee injury at West Brom., and following this failed to regain his past form. He was then put up for sale at £250, but no-one wanted to take the risk of signing him, and he eventually returned to Leadgate Park as player-manager.

Gradually his old form returned, after a spell with Durham County, he moved to Stockport Co. and began playing at wing half, instead of his usual forward position, and he enjoyed two seasons with them. A disagreement over terms saw him on the transfer list at £1,500, but he complained and this was reduced to £250.

In August 1926 United moved in and signed him for £500, after County appealed that it was too low. He then went on to become one of the best wing halves to play for club, and later became captain, until 1931/32, when he left Old Trafford.

RAY WOOD signed as an amateur with Newcastle during 1948 – 49, but was later released and joined Darlington, with whom he turned in some fine games before joining United on December 3rd 1949, making his debut a few hours later against Newcastle.

However, it was 1953 – 54 before the £5,000 signing gained regular first team football, and he then went on to win England under 23, 'B' and full caps as well

as representing the Football League.

He soon repaid his transfer fee and helped United to two League titles and also the 1957 Cup Final, when he was unfortunately injured. An accident which robbed United of the double that season.

The signing of Harry Gregg and an injury kept him out of the side, and in December 1958, he joined Huddersfield Town, after a fine career with United.

WILF WOODCOCK hailed from the Droylsden area of Manchester, and began his career with Stalybridge Celtic on an 'L' form, which meant that no other club could sign him before the end of the season.

As he was a very good inside forward, many clubs were after his signature as the end of season 1912 – 13 approached, but United were well prepared.

Louis Rocca stayed with him for most of the day, and as soon as the clock stopped striking midnight he

was signed at the home of manager Mangnall.

He went on to play for the club until season 1919 – 20, the season after he had won two full England caps.

BILLY WRIGGLESWORTH, began playing with Frickley Colliery in 1930, before moving to Chesterfield and then Wolves, where he gained the reputation of a fast and tricky winger.

He moved to Old Trafford in 1936, but only managed a handful of games before the outbreak of war halted his career. Most of his football with United was played during the war years, which was unfortunate for such a fine player.

Upon the resumption of league football after the hostilities he played in only four more games before moving across Lancashire in January 1947 to join Bolton Wanderers.

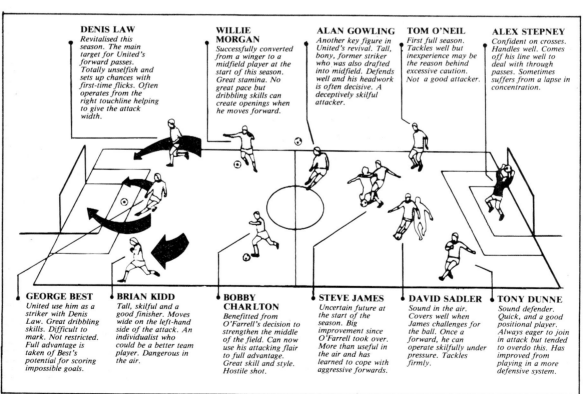

DENIS LAW
Revitalised this season. The main target for United's forward passes. Totally unselfish and sets up chances with first-time flicks. Often operates from the right touchline helping to give the attack width.

WILLIE MORGAN
Successfully converted from a winger to a midfield player at the start of this season. Great stamina. No great pace but dribbling skills can create openings when he moves forward.

ALAN GOWLING
Another key figure in United's revival. Tall, bony, former striker who was also drafted into midfield. Defends well and his headwork is often decisive. A deceptively skilful attacker.

TOM O'NEIL
First full season. Tackles well but inexperience may be the reason behind excessive caution. Not a good attacker.

ALEX STEPNEY
Confident on crosses. Handles well. Comes off his line well to deal with through passes. Sometimes suffers from a lapse in concentration.

GEORGE BEST
United use him as a striker with Denis Law. Great dribbling skills. Difficult to mark. Not restricted. Full advantage is taken of Best's potential for scoring impossible goals.

BRIAN KIDD
Tall, skilful and a good finisher. Moves wide on the left-hand side of the attack. An individualist who could be a better team player. Dangerous in the air.

BOBBY CHARLTON
Benefitted from O'Farrell's decision to strengthen the middle of the field. Can now use his attacking flair to full advantage. Great skill and style. Hostile shot.

STEVE JAMES
Uncertain future at the start of the season. Big improvement since O'Farrell took over. More than useful in the air and has learned to cope with aggressive forwards.

DAVID SADLER
Sound in the air. Covers well when James challenges for the ball. Once a forward, he can operate skilfully under pressure. Tackles firmly.

TONY DUNNE
Sound defender. Quick, and a good positional player. Always eager to join in attack but tended to overdo this. Has improved from playing in a more defensive system.

THE CLASS OF 1970 – 71 (BNPC)

Player	Seasons	League App	League Gls	FA Cup App	FA Cup Gls	L Cup App	L Cup Gls	Total App	Total Gls
Ainsworth A.	1933-34	2	0	0	0	0	0	2	0
Aitken J.	1895-96	1	0	2	0	0	0	3	0
Albiston A.R.	1974-86	303/6	6	34/2	0	36	0	410/6	6
Allan J.T.	1904-07	35	21	1	1	0	0	36	22
Allen R.A.	1950-53	75	5	5	2	0	0	80	7
Allman A.	1914-15	12	0	0	0	0	0	12	0
Ambler G.	1899-01	78	0	6	0	0	0	84	0
Anderson G.	1911-15	33	32	6	5	0	0	39	37
Anderson J.	1947-49	7/2	0	2	0	0	0	9/2	0
Anderson W.J.	1963-67	13/6	2	2	0	2	0	17/6	2
Anderson W.	1972-74	2	0	0	0	0	0	2	0
Arkesden T.A.	1902-06	72	25	9	8	0	0	81	33
Astley J.	1925-27	2	0	0	0	0	0	2	0
Aston J.	1964-72	139/16	25	12/3	1	5/2	1	156/21	27
Aston J.	1946-54	253	29	29	1	0	0	282	30
Bailey G.R.	1978-86	289	0	31	0	28	0	348	0
Bainbridge W.	1945-46	2	0	0	0	0	0	2	0
Bain D.	1922-24	22	0	0	0	0	0	22	0
Bain J.	1899-1900	2	0	0	0	0	0	2	0
Bain J.	1924-28	2	0	0	0	0	0	2	0
Baird H.	1936-38	49	15	4	3	0	0	53	18
Baldwin T.	1974-75	2	0	0	0	0	0	2	0
Ball J.	1929-35	47	15	3	0	0	0	50	18
Ball J.	1947-50	22	0	1	0	0	0	23	0
Ball W.H.	1902-03	4	0	0	0	0	0	4	0
Bamford T.	1934-38	98	52	12	4	0	0	110	56
Banks J.	1901-03	4	0	0	0	0	0	43	0
Bannister J.	1906-10	39	7	4	0	0	0	60	7
Barber J.	1922-24	56	3	0	0	0	0	2	0
Barlow C.	1919-22	3	0	4	0	0	0	7	0
Barlow J.	1922-24	29	7	2	0	0	0	31/1	7
Barnes P.	1985-6	12/1	3	3	0	1	0	15/1	3
Barrett F.	1896-00	118	0	10	0	0	0	128	0
Barson F.	1922-28	140	4	12	0	0	0	152	4
Beadsworth A.	1902-03	8	2	3	0	0	0	11	2
Beale R.H.	1912-15	106	0	7	0	0	0	113	0
Beardsley P.	1982-83	0	0	0	0	1	0	1/3	0
Beddowes J.H.	1904-07	33	0	2	0	0	0	35	0
Behan B.	1933-34	1	0	0	0	0	0	1	0
Bell A.	1902-13	279	12	29	1	0	0	308	12
Bennion S.R.	1921-32	286	2	15	0	0	0	301	2
Bent G.	1954-57	12	0	0	0	0	0	12	0
Berry J.J.	1951-58	247	37	15	4	0	0	262	41
Berry W.	1906-09	12	1	1	0	0	0	13	1
Best G.	1963-74	361	136	46	22	25	9	432	167
Bielby P.A.	1973-74	2/2	0	0	0	0	0	2/2	0
Birchenough H.	1902-03	25	0	5	0	0	0	30	0
Birch B.	1949-52	11	4	4	0	0	0	15	4
Birkett C.	1950-51	9	2	4	0	0	0	13	2
Birtles G.	1980-82	57/2	11	4	1	2	0	63/1	12
Bissett G.	1919-22	40	10	2	2	0	0	42	12
Blanchflower J.	1951-58	105	26	6	0	0	0	111	26
Black R.	1931-34	8	4	0	0	0	0	14	6
Blackmore C.	1983-86	14	3	2/2	0	2/2	0	19/2	3
Blackmore P.	1899-1900	1	0	0	0	0	0	1	0
Blackstock T.	1903-07	34	0	5	0	0	0	39	0

Player	Seasons	League App	League Gls	FA Cup App	FA Cup Gls	L Cup App	L Cup Gls	Total App	Total Gls
Blew H.	1905-06	1	0	0	0	0	0	1	0
Blott S.P.	1909-13	18	2	4	0	0	0	33	2
Bogan T.	1949-51	29	7	4	0	0	0	33	7
Bond J.E.	1951-53	20	4	0	0	0	0	21	4
Bonthron R.P.	1903-07	121	3	14	0	0	0	135	3
Booth W.	1900-01	2	0	0	0	0	0	2	0
Boyd H.	1896-99	52	32	6	2	0	0	58	32
Boyd W.	1934-35	6	4	0	0	0	0	6	4
Boyle T.	1928-30	16	6	1	0	0	0	17	6
Bradbury L.	1938-39	2	1	0	0	0	0	2	1
Bradley W.	1958-62	63	20	4	1	0	0	71	21
Brady W.	1892-93	20	0	1	0	0	0	21	0
Bratt J.H.	1960-61	1	0	0	0	0	0	1	0
Brazil A.B.	1984-86	18/13	8	0/1	0	4/3	3	22/17	11
Breedon J.	1935-39	33	0	0	0	0	0	33	0
Breen W.	1936-39	8	2	3	0	0	0	73	2
Brennan S.A.	1957-70	291/1	3	36	0	4	0	331	3
Brett F.B.	1921-22	10	0	0	0	0	0	10	0
Briggs W.R.	1960-62	9	0	2	0	0	0	11	0
Brisby	1986-87	3	0	0	0	0	0	3	0
Brooks W.H.	1898-99	3	0	0	0	0	0	3	0
Broome A.H.	1922-23	9	2	0	0	0	0	9	2
Broomfield H.C.	1907-08	2	0	0	0	0	0	2	0
Brown J.	1932-39	143	18	18	0	0	0	152	18
Brown R.B.	1947-49	4	2	0	0	0	0	7	2
Brown W.	1892-93	2	0	0	0	0	0	2	0
Brown W.	1896-97	7	2	2	0	0	0	9	2
Brown W.	1902-03	2	0	0	0	0	0	2	0
Bruce W.	1896-00	27	7	3	0	0	0	7	7
Bryant W.	1934-39	108	42	10	0	0	0	118	42
Buchan G.	1973-74	0/3	0	0	0	0/1	0	0/4	0
Buchan M.M.	1971-83	376	4	39	0	30	0	445	4
Buckle E.W.	1946-49	20	6	4	1	0	0	24	7
Buckley F.C.	1906-07	4	0	0	0	0	0	4	0
Bullock J.	1930-31	10	3	0	0	0	0	10	3
Burgess H.	1906-10	50	2	3	0	0	0	53	2
Burke R.S.	1946-49	28	16	6	6	0	0	34	22
Burns F.	1967-72	111/9	6	11/1	0	10/1	0	132/11	6
Byrne D.	1933-34	2	0	0	0	0	0	2	0
Byrne R.W.	1951-58	245	17	18	2	0	0	263	19
Cairns J.	1894-99	5	0	2	0	0	0	5	0
Campbell W.C.	1893-94	0	0	1	0	0	0	2	0
Cantwell N.	1960-67	123	6	14	2	0	0	137	8
Cape J.	1933-37	59	18	1	0	0	0	60	18
Capper A.	1911-12	1	0	0	0	0	0	1	0
Carey J.J.	1937-53	304	16	38	1	0	0	342	17
Carman H.R.	1897-98	3	0	0	0	0	0	3	0
Carolan J.	1958-61	66	0	4	0	1	0	71	0
Carson A.A.	1913-14	13	0	0	0	0	0	13	0
Cashmore A.A.	1913-14	3	1	0	0	0	0	3	1
Cartman H.R.	1922-23	3	0	0	0	0	0	3	0
Cartwright W.G.	1895-04	229	3	26	0	0	0	255	3
Cassidy J.	1892-93	4	0	0	0	0	0	4	0
Cassidy J.	1894-00	148	88	10	7	0	0	158	95
Cassidy L.	1947-52	4	0	0	0	0	0	4	0

PLAYER	SEASONS	LEAGUE App	LEAGUE Gls	FA CUP App	FA CUP Gls	L CUP App	L CUP Gls	TOTAL App	TOTAL Gls
Chalmers W.S.	1932-34	34	1	1	0	—	—	35	1
Chapman W.	1926-28	26	0	0	0	0	0	26	0
Charlton R.	1956-73	604/2	198	78	19	24	6	706/2	223
Chesters A.	1929-32	9	1	—	0	—	—	13	0
Chesters R.	1935-36	13	0	—	—	—	—	13	0
Chilton A.C.	1939-55	352	2	36	0	—	—	388	2
Chisnall J.P.	1961-64	35	8	8	1	—	—	43	9
Christie D.	1908-09	2	0	0	0	—	—	2	0
Chorlton T.	1902-03	—	—	—	—	—	—	—	—
Clarke J.	1913-14	4	0	0	0	—	—	4	0
Clarke J.	1899-00	1/1	0	0	0	—	—	1/1	0
Clarkin J.	1976-77	67	23	6	0	—	—	73	23
Clayton G.	1893-96	2	0	0	0	—	—	2	0
Cleaves H.	1956-57	—	—	—	—	—	—	—	—
Clements J.E.	1902-03	36	2	2	0	—	—	38	2
Clempson F.	1892-94	15	4	0	0	—	—	15	4
Cockburn H.	1949-53	243	4	32	0	—	—	275	4
Collinson C.	1945-55	7	0	0	0	—	—	7	0
Collinson J.	1946-47	—	—	—	—	—	—	—	—
Colman E.	1895-01	63	15	9	1	—	—	72	16
Colville J.	1955-58	85	0	9	0	—	—	94	0
Connachan J.	1892-93	9	0	—	—	—	—	—	—
Connaughton J.P.	1898-99	—	—	0	0	—	—	10	0
Connell T.E.	1971-72	10	4	0	0	0	0	4	0
Connelly J.M.	1978-79	4	0	—	—	0	0	—	—
Conner E.	1964-67	—	—	0	0	0	0	3	0
Cookson S.P.	1909-11	3	0	2	0	0	0	2	0
Cope R.	1914-15	2	0	13	0	13	0	93/1	24
Coppell S.J.	1956-61	79/1	22	0	0	0	0	14	2
Coupar J.	1974-83	320/2	53	36	4	25	9	381/2	66
Coupar J.	1892-93	21	4	0	0	—	—	21	4
Coyne G.	1901-02	10	0	0	0	—	—	10	0
Craig T.	1975-76	53	36	—	—	0	0	66	—
Craven C.	1889-90	0	0	—	—	—	—	1/1	0
Crerand P.T.	1938-39	11	2	2	0	0	0	11	2
Crompton J.	1962-71	304	10	43	4	4	0	351	14
Crooks G.A.	1945-56	191	0	20	0	0	0	211	0
Crowther S.	1983-84	6/1	2	0	0	—	—	6/1	—
Cunningham J.	1957-59	2	0	5	0	2	0	18	0
Cunningham L.P.	1898-99	15	3	0	0	5	0	17	3
Curry J.	1982-83	3/2	0	0	0	0	0	3/2	0
Dale J.	1908-11	13	0	2	0	—	—	14	0
Dale W.	1947-48	11	0	4	0	—	—	2	—
Dalton E.	1928-32	64	0	—	—	—	—	68	0
Daly G.A.	1907-08	2	0	0	0	—	—	2	0
Davidson J.	1973-77	107/4	23	9/1	1	17	1	133/5	32
Davidson W.R.	1893-94	28	1	3	0	—	—	31	1
Davies A.	1894-95	12	0	0	0	—	—	12	0
Davies J.	1981-84	7	2	0	0	0	0	8/1	2
Davies Jos	1892-93	0/8	0/2	—	—	0	0	0/10	—
Davies R.T.	1889-90	15/1	4	0	0	0	0	16/1	4
Davies W.R.	1974-75	11	0	0	0	0	0	11	0
Davenport P.	1972-73	80	44	10	3	0	0	93	53
Dawson A.D.	1985-86	2	0	0	0	0	0	2	0
Dawson P.	1956-62								
Dean H.	1931-32								

PLAYER	SEASONS	LEAGUE App	LEAGUE Gls	FA CUP App	FA CUP Gls	L CUP App	L CUP Gls	TOTAL App	TOTAL Gls
Delaney J.	1946-51	164	25	19	3	—	—	183	25
Dennis W.	1923-24	3	0	—	—	—	—	—	—
Dempsey M.	1985-86	1	0	0	0	—	—	1	0
Dewar N.	1932-34	36	14	0	0	—	—	36	14
Doherty J.	1952-58	25	7	1	0	—	—	26	7
Donaghy B.	1905-06	3	0	0	0	—	—	3	0
Donald I.	1970-73	4	0	0	0	2	0	6	0
Donaldson R.	1892-98	131	57	13	9	—	—	144	66
Donnelly A.	1908-13	34	0	3	0	—	—	37	0
Dougan	1938-39	0	0	—	—	—	—	—	—
Doughty J.	1889-90	0	0	2	2	—	—	2	2
Doughty R.	1889-90	2	2	2	0	—	—	4	2
Douglas W.	1893-96	55	0	1	0	—	—	56	0
Dow J.M.	1902-10	45	7	0	0	—	—	45	7
Downie A.L.B.	1902-10	170	12	18	2	—	—	188	14
Downie J.B.	1948-53	110	35	5	1	—	—	115	36
Draycott W.L.	1896-99	80	7	7	0	—	—	87	7
Duckworth R.	1903-14	225	11	27	0	—	—	252	11
Dunne A.P.	1960-73	414	2	54/1	0	21	0	489/1	2
Dunne P.A.G.	1964-67	45	0	2	0	6	0	53	0
Dunn W.	1897-98	11	2	0	0	—	—	12	—
Duxbury M.	1980-86	175/16	5	13/3	1	20/1	0	208/20	6
Dyer J.A.	1905-06	1	0	—	—	0	0	2	—
Edge A.	1891-92	0	0	—	—	—	—	—	—
Edmonds H.	1910-12	42	7	7	0	—	—	49	7
Edwards D.	1952-58	151	20	12	0	—	—	163	21
Edwards P.	1969-73	52/1	0	7	0	7	0	66/1	0
Ellis D.	1923-24	11	0	0	0	—	—	11	0
Errentz F.C.	1892-02	280	20	20	1	—	—	300	21
Errentz H.	1897-98	6	0	2	0	—	—	8	0
Evans H.	1923-24	2	0	0	0	—	—	—	—
Evans G.	1890-91	0	0	3	0	—	—	6	2
J.W. Fall	1893-94	23	3	3	0	—	—	26	0
Farman A.H.	1892-95	51	17	4	2	—	—	55	23
Feehan I.	1949-50	12	6	2	0	—	—	14	6
Ferguson D.	1927-28	8	4	0	0	—	—	4	0
Ferguson J.	1931-32	8	3	1	—	—	—	—	3
Ferrier R.	1935-38	18	0	0	0	12	0	19	—
Fitton G.A.	1931-33	12	3	0	0	—	—	12	3
Fielding W.J.	1946-47	6	0	1	0	—	—	7	0
Fitchett J.	1902-05	16	2	2	0	—	—	18	4
Fisher F.	1900-02	42	4	4	0	—	—	46	4
Fitzpatrick J.	1964-73	111/6	8	11	0	12	2	134/6	10
Fitzsimmons D.	1895-00	29	1	3	0	—	—	32	—
Fitzsimmons T.	1892-94	27	6	1	0	—	—	28	6
Fletcher P.	1972-74	2/5	0	0	0	0	0	2/5	0
Fogan A.	1976-77	0/3	0	0	0	0	0	0/3	0
Foley G.	1899-00	7	0	—	—	—	—	7	0
Ford J.B.	1908-10	35	2	2	0	—	—	37	—
Forster T.	1919-22	99/2	0	0	0	—	—	116/2	0
Forsyth A.	1952-78	563/4	10	61	0	—	—	627/4	7
Foulkes W.A.	1952-70	0	1	0	0	—	—	0	5
Fox	1914-15	51	0	1	—	—	—	52	7
Frame T.	1932-34	0	4	0	—	0	0	0	4

PLAYER	SEASONS	LEAGUE App	LEAGUE Gls	FA CUP App	FA CUP Gls	L CUP App	L CUP Gls	TOTAL App	TOTAL Gls
Gallimore S.	1930-34	72	19	4	1	0	0	76	20
Gardner R.	1935-37	16	1	2	0	0	0	18	1
Garton W.	1984-86	12	0	2	0	0	0	14	0
Garvey J.	1900-01	6	0	0	0	0	0	6	0
Gaskell J.D.	1956-67	97	0	16	0	1	0	114	0
Gaudie R.	1903-04	7	5	1	0	0	0	8	5
Gibson C.	1985-86	18	0	4	0	0	0	22	0
Gibson R.	1921-22	11	0	1	0	0	0	12	0
Gibson T.	1985-86	2/5	0	0	0	0	0	2/5	0
Gibson T.R.D	1950-55	108	0	6	0	0	0	114	0
Gidman J.	1981-86	94	4	9	0	5	0	108	4
Giles J.M.	1959-63	99	10	13	3	2	0	114	13
Gillespie M.	1896-00	73	18	8	4	0	0	81	22
Gipps T.	1912-15	22	0	0	0	0	0	22	0
Givens D.J.	1969-70	4/4	1	0	0	0	0	4/4	1
Gladwin G.	1936-39	26	4	1	0	0	0	27	4
Godsmark G.	1899-00	9	4	1	0	0	0	10	4
Goldthorpe E.H.	1922-25	27	15	3	1	0	0	30	16
Goodwin F.J.	1954-60	95	7	8	1	0	0	103	8
Goodwin W.	1920-22	7	0	0	0	0	0	7	0
Gourlay J.	1898-99	1	—	6/1	2	0	0	7/1	2
Gowling A.	1967-72	64/5	18	6	2	7/1	1	77/7	21
Graham A.	1983-85	33/4	5	1	0	6	1	40/4	6
Graham G.	1972-75	41/2	2	1	0	2	0	44/2	2
Graham J.	1893-94	4	0	0	0	0	0	4	0
Grassam W.	1903-05	29	11	8	5	0	0	37	16
Greaves I.D.	1954-60	67	0	6	0	0	0	73	0
Green E.	1933-34	9	4	0	0	0	0	9	4
Greenhoff B.	1973-79	218/3	13	24	2	19	2	261/3	17
Greenhoff J.	1976-81	94/3	26	18/1	9	4	1	116/4	36
Greenwood W.	1900-01	4	0	3	0	0	0	7	0
Gregg H.	1957-67	210	0	19	0	7	0	236	0
Griffiths C.L.	1973-74	7	0	0	0	0	0	7	0
Griffiths J.	1933-39	165	0	8	0	0	0	173	0
Griffiths W.	1896-05	159	27	17	3	0	0	176	30
Grimes A.A.	1977-83	62/28	10	5	0	6	0	73/28	10
Grimshaw T.	1975-76	0/1	0	0/1	0	0	0	0/2	0
Grimwood J.B.	1919-27	196	8	9	0	0	0	205	8
Grundy J.	1899-01	10	3	0	0	0	0	10	3
Hacking J.	1933-35	32	0	2	0	0	0	34	0
Hall J.	1925-26	3	0	0	0	0	0	3	0
Hall J.	1933-36	67	0	6	0	0	0	73	0
Hall P.	1903-04	4	0	0	0	0	0	4	0
Halse H.J.	1907-12	109	41	16	9	0	0	125	50
Halton R.	1936-37	8	2	0	0	0	0	8	2
Hamill M.	1911-14	57	0	2	0	0	0	59	0
Hanlon J.	1938-49	63	20	6	1	0	0	69	21
Hannaford C.	1924-30	11	0	1	0	0	0	12	0
Hanson J.	1924-30	138	48	9	5	0	0	147	53
Hardman H.P.	1908-09	4	2	0	0	0	0	4	2
Harris F.E.	1926-27	46	1	3	0	0	0	49	1
Harris T.	1919-22	4	0	0	0	0	0	4	2
Harrison C.	1889-90	0	0	3	0	0	0	4	5
Harrison	1903-04	0	—	0	0	0	0	1	0
Harrison W.E.	1920-22	44	5	2	0	0	0	46	5

PLAYER	SEASONS	LEAGUE App	LEAGUE Gls	FA CUP App	FA CUP Gls	L CUP App	L CUP Gls	TOTAL App	TOTAL Gls
Harrop R.	1957-59	10	0	0	0	1	0	11	0
Hartwell W.	1903-05	3	0	0	0	0	0	3	0
Haslam G.	1921-28	25	0	2	0	0	0	27	0
Hawksworth A.	1956-57	1	0	0	0	0	0	1	0
Haydock F.	1960-63	6	0	0	0	0	0	6	0
Hay J.T.	1889-90	1	0	0	0	0	0	1	0
Hayes J.V.	1900-11	115	2	14	0	0	0	129	2
Haywood J.F.	1913-15	8	0	2	0	0	0	10	0
Heathcote J.	1899-02	26	8	1	0	0	0	27	8
Henderson W.	1921-25	34	7	3	0	0	0	37	7
Hendry A.	1892-93	3	0	1	0	0	0	4	0
Hendry J.	1892-93	3	2	1	0	0	0	4	2
Herd D.G.	1961-68	201/1	114	15	10	21	6	237/1	130
Heron T.R.F.	1957-61	34	1	1	0	2	0	37	1
Heywood H.	1932-34	6	0	0	0	0	0	6	0
Higgins M.	1985-86	10	0	0	0	0	0	10	0
Higgins	1901-02	7	0	0	0	0	0	7	0
Higson J.	1901-02	7	4	1	0	0	0	8	4
Hilditch C.G.	1919-32	301	7	21	0	0	0	322	7
Hill G.A.	1975-78	100/1	39	17	7	7	3	124/1	49
Hillam C.E.	1933-34	8	0	0	0	0	0	8	0
Hine E.	1932-35	51	12	2	0	0	0	53	12
Hodge James	1910-20	81	0	6	0	0	0	87	0
Hodge John	1910-15	28	2	1	0	0	0	29	2
Hodges F.C.	1919-21	20	4	0	0	0	0	20	4
Hofton L.	1910-21	17	0	3	0	0	0	17	0
Hogg G.	1983-86	62	0	5	0	6	0	73	0
Holden R.H.	1904-13	104	12	12	0	0	0	116	12
Holton J.A.	1972-75	63	5	2	0	4	0	69	5
Holts J.	1899-00	7	1	0	0	0	0	7	1
Homer T.P.	1909-12	7	2	0	0	0	0	7	2
Hood W.	1892-93	32	3	3	2	0	0	35	7
Hooper A.	1909-14	25	1	0	0	0	0	25	1
Hopkin F.	1919-21	70	8	4	0	0	0	74	8
Hopkinson J.	1930-34	7	0	1	0	0	0	7	0
Hopkinson S.	1898-99	8	3	0	0	0	0	8	3
Houston S.M.	1973-80	204/1	13	22	2	16	1	242/1	16
Howarth J.T.	1921-22	2	0	0	0	0	0	2	0
Howarth R.	1926-27	2	0	0	0	0	0	2	0
Hudson E.	1913-15	11	0	0	0	0	0	11	0
Hughes M.	1983-86	85/4	37	10	5	5/1	4	100	46
Hulme A.	1907-09	4	0	0	0	0	0	4	0
Hunter G.C.	1913-15	22	0	0	0	0	0	22	0
Hunter R.	1958-59	3	2	0	0	0	0	3	2
Hunter W.	1912-13	1	0	0	0	0	0	1	0
Hurst D.J.	1902-03	20	4	5	0	0	0	25	4
Iddon R.	1925-27	2	0	0	0	0	0	2	0
Inglis W.W.	1925-29	14	0	0	0	0	0	14	0
Jackson T.	1975-77	18/1	0	0	0	4	0	22/1	0
Jackson W.	1899-01	60	12	2	0	0	0	62	14
James S.R.	1968-75	129	4	12	0	17/1	0	158/1	4
Jenkyns C.A.L.	1896-98	35	5	5	0	0	0	40	5
John W.R.	1936-39	15	0	0	0	0	0	15	0
Johnson S.	1900-01	1	0	0	0	0	0	1	0

PLAYER	SEASONS	LEAGUE App	LEAGUE Gls	FA CUP App	FA CUP Gls	L CUP App	L CUP Gls	TOTAL App	TOTAL Gls
Johnston W.G.	1927-32	71	24	6	3	0	0	77	27
Jones D.	1937-38	1	0	—	—	0	0	1	0
Jones E.P.	1957-58	1	0	0	0	0	0	1	0
Jones M.	1950-58	103	—	7	—	0	0	110	—
Jones O.J.	1898-99	1	—	0	—	0	0	1	—
Jones T.	1924-37	189	2	11	0	0	0	200	2
Jones T.J.	1934-35	20	4	2	0	0	0	22	4
Jordan J.	1977-81	109	37	11/1	2	4	2	124/1	41
Jovanovic N.	1979-81	20/1	4	1	—	2	—	23/1	4
Kelly J.W.	1975-76	0/1	—	0	—	0	0	0/1	—
Kennedy F.	1923-25	17	4	1	0	0	0	18	4
Kennedy P.A.	1954-55	1	—	0	—	0	0	1	—
Kennedy W.J.	1895-97	31	11	3	1	0	0	34	12
Kerr H.	1903-04	2	—	0	—	0	0	2	—
Kidd B.	1967-74	195/8	52	24/1	8	20	7	239/9	67
Kinloch J.	1892-93	1	0	0	0	0	0	1	0
Kinsey A.	1964-65	0	—	0	—	0	—	0	—
Knowles F.	1911-15	46	0	1	0	0	0	47	0
Kopel F.	1967-69	8/2	0	1	0	0	0	9/2	0
Lancaster J.G.	1949-50	4	0	0	0	0	0	4	0
Langford L.	1934-36	15	0	0	0	0	0	15	0
Lang T.	1935-37	12	0	1	0	0	0	13	0
Lappin H.H.	1900-03	25	3	0	0	0	0	25	3
Lawson R.R.	1900-01	3	0	0	0	0	0	3	0
Lawton N.	1959-63	36	6	1	0	7	0	44	6
Law D.	1962-73	305/4	171	44/2	33	11	3	360/6	207
Lee E.	1898-00	11	5	0	0	0	0	11	5
Leigh T.	1899-01	43	15	3	0	0	0	46	15
Leonard H.	1920-21	10	5	0	0	0	0	10	5
Lewis E.	1952-56	20	9	4	0	0	0	24	9
Lievesley L.	1922-23	2	0	0	0	0	0	2	0
Lievesley	1931-32	2	0	0	0	0	0	2	0
Linkson O.H.S.	1908-13	55	0	3	0	0	0	58	0
Livingstone G.T.	1908-14	43	0	3	0	0	0	46	0
Lochhead A.W.	1921-26	147	50	6	0	0	0	153	50
Longair W.	1894-95	50	—	0	—	0	0	50	—
Lowrie T.	1947-51	13	0	1	0	0	0	14	0
Lydon G.	1930-32	3	0	0	0	0	0	3	0
Lyner D.	1922-23	3	0	0	0	0	0	3	0
Lynn S.	1947-50	13	0	0	0	0	0	13	0
Lyons G.	1903-06	4	0	1	0	0	0	5	0
Macari L.	1972-84	311/18	78	31/2	8	22/5	10	364/25	96
MacDougal E.J.	1972-73	18	5	0	0	0	0	18	5
Mackie C.	1904-05	5	3	0	0	0	0	5	3
Manley T.	1931-39	188	40	7	1	0	0	195	41
Mann F.D.	1922-30	180	5	17	0	0	0	197	5
Mann H.	1931-32	13	0	0	0	0	0	13	0
Mann T.	1933-34	2	0	0	0	0	0	2	0
Marshall A.G.	1902-03	6	0	0	0	0	0	6	0
Martin M.P.	1972-75	33/6	0	2	0	1	0	36/6	0
Mathieson W.	1892-94	8	2	2	0	0	0	10	2
McBain N.	1921-23	42	2	1	0	0	0	43	2
McCalliog J.	1973-75	31	7	0/1	0	0	0	31/1	7
McCartney J.	1894-95	20	2	1	0	0	0	21	2
McCartney J.	1903-04	12	2	0	0	0	0	12	2
McCartney P.	1911-12	1	0	0	0	0	0	1	0
McClelland J.	1936-37	5	0	0	0	0	0	5	0
McCrae J.J.	1925-26	1	0	0	0	0	0	1	0
McCreery D.	1974-79	48/39	7	4/4	1	1/6	0	53/49	8
McDonald K.	1922-24	9	4	0	0	0	0	9	4
McDonald W.	1931-34	27	4	0	0	0	0	27	4
McFarlane N.W.	1953-54	—	0	0	0	0	0	—	0
McFarlane R.	1891-92	1	—	0	—	0	0	1	—
McFetridge D.	1894-95	—	0	0	0	0	0	—	0
McGarvey S.	1980-83	13/12	3	0	0	0	0	13/12	3
McGillivray C.	1933-34	3	0	0	0	0	0	3	0
McGillivray J.	1907-09	—	0	0	0	0	0	—	0
McGlen W.	1946-52	110	2	12	0	0	0	122	2
McGrath P.	1982-86	11/1	—	2	0	0	0	13/1	—
McGrath R.C.	1976-81	12/16	2	0/2	0	0	0	12/18	2
McGuinness W.	1955-60	81	2	2	0	0	0	83	2
McKay W.	1933-39	169	16	13	0	0	0	182	16
McLachlan G.	1929-33	110	4	6	0	0	0	116	4
McLenahan H.	1927-31	112	11	4	1	0	0	116	12
McIlroy S.B.	1971-82	320/22	58	25/3	6	35/2	6	380/27	70
McIlveney E.	1950-51	2	0	0	0	0	0	2	0
McMillan S.T.	1961-63	15	6	0	0	0	0	15	6
McMillan W.S.	1933-35	27	0	2	0	0	0	29	0
McNaught J.	1893-98	141	12	14	0	0	0	155	12
McNaughton J.	1893-94	—	—	—	—	0	0	—	—
McNulty T.	1949-54	57	0	2	0	0	0	59	0
McPherson F.	1923-28	159	46	16	0	0	0	175	46
McQueen G.	1977-85	184	20	16	2	21	4	221	26
McShane H.	1950-54	56	8	1	0	0	0	57	8
Meehan T.	1919-21	51	2	2	0	0	0	53	2
Mellor J.	1930-37	116	0	6	0	0	0	122	0
Menzies A.	1906-08	23	4	2	0	0	0	25	4
Meredith W.H.	1906-21	303	35	30	1	0	0	333	36
Mew J.W.	1912-26	186	0	13	0	0	0	199	0
Millar G.	1894-95	6	5	1	0	0	0	7	5
Millar J.	1923-24	4	—	0	—	0	0	4	—
Miller T.	1920-21	25	2	2	0	0	0	27	2
Mitchell A.	1892-94	54	4	4	0	0	0	58	4
Mitchell A.	1932-33	—	—	—	—	0	0	—	—
Mitten C.	1946-50	142	50	19	11	0	0	161	61
Moger H.H.	1903-12	245	0	23	0	0	0	268	0
Morgan H.	1900-01	20	5	3	0	0	0	23	5
Morgan W.	1896-03	142	7	8	1	0	0	150	8
Morgan W.	1968-75	236/2	24	24/1	3	26	4	286/3	31
Morgans K.G.	1957-61	17	8	2	0	0	0	19	8
Moir J.	1960-65	45	5	0	0	0	0	45	5
Montgomery A.	1905-06	3	0	0	0	0	0	3	0
Montgomery J.	1914-21	—	—	—	—	0	0	—	—
Moody J.	1931-32	50	0	1	0	0	0	51	0
Moore C.	1919-30	309	5	19	0	0	0	328	5
Moore G.	1963-64	18	4	1	0	0	0	19	4
Moran K.B.	1978-86	176/1	21	15	1	20	2	211/1	24
Moran T.	1902-04	28	4	4	0	0	0	32	4
Morris J.	1946-49	83	32	9	0	0	0	92	32
Morrison T.	1902-04	—	—	—	—	0	0	—	—
Morris B.	1935-36	—	—	—	—	0	0	—	—
Moses R.M.	1981-86	110/5	7	10	0	17/1	3	137/6	10

PLAYERS' CAREER

PLAYER	SEASONS	LEAGUE App	LEAGUE Gls	FA CUP App	FA CUP Gls	L CUP App	L CUP Gls	TOTAL App	TOTAL Gls
Muhren A.J.H.	1982-85	65/5	13	8	0	11	2	84/5	15
Murray R.D.	1937-38	4	0	0	0	0	0	4	0
Mutch G.	1934-38	112	46	8	3	0	0	120	49
Myerscough J.	1920-23	33	8	1	0	0	0	34	8
Nevin G.W.	1933-34	4	0	1	0	—	—	5	0
Newton P.	1933-34	2	0	0	0	—	—	2	0
Noble R.	1965-67	31	0	2	0	0	0	33	0
Nicol G.	1927-29	6	3	1	0	—	—	7	3
Nicholl J.M.	1974-82	188/9	3	22/4	0	14	0	234/13	3
Nicholson J.J.	1960-63	58	5	7	0	3	0	68	5
Norton J.	1913-15	37	5	0	0	—	—	37	5
Nuttall T.A.	1911-13	16	4	0	0	—	—	16	4
O'Brien W.	1901-02	1	0	—	—	—	—	1	0
O'Connell P.	1914-15	34	2	1	0	—	—	35	2
Olive R.L.	1952-53	2	0	0	0	—	—	2	0
Olsen J.	1984-86	61/2	16	9/2	2	5	1	75/4	19
O'Neil T.P.	1970-73	54	0	7	0	7	0	68	0
Owen G.	1889-90	—	—	5	0	—	—	5	0
Owen J.	1889-90	15	8	2	0	—	—	17	8
Owen W.	1898-90	0	0	2	0	—	—	2	0
Owen W.	1934-36	0	0	2	0	—	—	2	0
Paterson S.W.	1976-80	17	0	0	0	0	0	17	0
Partridge E.	1920-29	3/3	0	2	0	—	—	5/3	0
Parkinson R.	1899-00	148	50	9	9	—	—	160	59
Parker T.A.	1930-32	16	0	2	0	—	—	18	0
Parker A.	1893-94	17	0	1	0	—	—	17	0
Page A.	1924-26	11	0	4	0	—	—	15	0
Page L.A.	1931-33	18	5	1	0	—	—	12	6
Payne E.	1908-09	12	0	1	0	—	—	12	0
Pearson M.C.	1957-63	2	0	1	0	3	0	5/3	0
Pearson S.C.	1937-54	68	12	21	5	—	—	78	13
Pearson S.J.	1974-79	312	127	30	21	12	5	342	148
Pears S.	1984-85	138/1	55	22	5	5	5	172/1	65
Peddie J.H.	1902-07	4	0	—	—	—	—	5	0
Peden J.	1893-94	113	50	9	9	—	—	122	59
Pegg D.	1952-58	28	7	3	2	—	—	31	8
Pegg J.K.	1902-04	127	24	9	0	—	—	136	24
Pepper F.	1947-48	42	16	10	7	—	—	52	23
Perrins G.	1892-96	2	0	7	0	—	—	8	0
Peters J.	1894-96	7	0	1	0	—	—	8	0
Picken J.B.	1905-11	91	0	5	0	—	—	96	0
Pinner M.J.	1960-61	45	14	4	1	—	—	49	15
Porter W.	1934-38	112	40	8	7	—	—	120	47
Potts A.	1913-20	61	4	4	0	—	—	65	4
Powell J.	1889-90	27	6	1	0	—	—	28	6
Prentice J.H.	1919-20	0	0	—	—	—	—	2	0
Preston S.	1901-03	6	12	6	0	—	—	35	12
Prince D.	1893-94	0	0	—	—	—	—	2	0
Prince H.	1914-15	34	2	1	0	—	—	35	2
Pugh H.	1921-23	2	0	0	0	—	—	2	0
Quinn J.J.	1908-10	2	0	—	—	—	—	2	0
Quixall A.	1958-64	165	50	14	4	1	2	180	56
Radford C.	1920-24	91	0	5	0	—	—	96	0
Ramsden C.W.	1927-31	14	3	2	0	—	—	16	3
Ratcliffe G.	1898-99	1	0	0	0	—	—	1	0

PLAYER	SEASONS	LEAGUE App	LEAGUE Gls	FA CUP App	FA CUP Gls	L CUP App	L CUP Gls	TOTAL App	TOTAL Gls
Rawlings W.E.	1927-30	35	19	0	0	—	—	36	19
Read T.H.	1902-04	34	7	7	0	—	—	41	7
Redwood H.	1935-39	86	3	7	0	—	—	93	4
Redman W.	1950-54	36	0	2	0	—	—	38	0
Reid T.	1928-33	96	63	5	4	—	—	101	67
Rennox C.	1924-27	60	24	8	1	—	—	68	25
Richards C.H.	1902-03	8	0	2	0	—	—	11	2
Richards W.	1901-02	—	0	5	0	—	—	8	0
Richardson L.	1925-29	39	0	4	0	—	—	43	0
Ridding W.	1931-34	42	14	2	0	—	—	44	14
Ridgway J.A.	1895-98	13	3	3	0	—	—	16	3
Rimmer J.J.	1967-73	34	0	3	0	6	0	43	0
Ritchie A.T.	1977-81	26/7	12	3/1	0	3/2	0	32/10	12
Roach J.E.	1945-46	0	0	2	0	—	—	2	0
Robbie D.	1935-36	—	0	6	0	—	—	6	0
Roberts A.	1903-05	26	5	—	—	—	—	27	6
Robertson Alex	1904-06	9	0	0	0	—	—	9	0
Robertson S.	1903-04	25	6	7	0	—	—	32	7
Robertson T.	1903-36	4	0	—	—	—	—	4	0
Robertson W.S.	1933-36	47	6	3	1	—	—	50	7
Roberts	1898-00	10	2	—	—	—	—	10	2
Roberts C.	1903-13	270	24	30	0	—	—	300	25
Roberts R.H.A.	1913-14	10	2	—	—	—	—	10	2
Robinson M.	1931-32	10	3	—	—	—	—	10	3
Robinson J.W.	1919-22	21	0	—	—	—	—	21	0
Robson B.	1981-86	151/1	43	15	4	20	2	186/1	49
Robson J.W.	1919-10	—	0	4	0	—	—	3	0
Roche P.J.	1974-82	46	0	4	0	3	0	53	0
Rogers M.	1977-78	2	0	—	—	—	—	2	0
Rothwell C.	1893-95	—	0	1	0	—	—	1	0
Rothwell	1896-97	0	0	2	0	—	—	2	0
Rothwell H.	1902-03	21	0	6	0	—	—	27	0
Roughton W.G.	1936-39	86	0	6	0	—	—	92	0
Round E.	1913-14	—	0	1	0	—	—	1	0
Rowe J.	1909-10	173	4	—	—	—	—	180	56
Rowley H.B.	1928-37	56	15	7	4	—	—	56	15
Rowley J.F.	1937-55	380	182	42	27	—	—	422	209
Royals E.J.	1911-14	6	0	—	—	—	—	6	0
Ryan J.	1965-70	21/3	4	—	—	—	—	22/3	4
Sadler D.	1963-74	226/5	22	22/1	2	22	0	270/6	24
Sagar C.	1905-07	29	21	2	1	—	—	31	22
Sapsford G.D.	1919-22	52	16	—	—	—	—	53	17
Sartori C.	1968-72	26/12	4	9	0	3/2	0	38/14	5
Sarvis	1922-23	—	0	—	—	—	—	2	0
Saunders J.	1901-03	115	34	6	0	—	—	124	36
Savage R.	1937-38	4	0	—	—	—	—	4	0
Sawyer F.	1899-01	2	0	3	0	—	—	2	0
Sawyers T.	1900-01	—	0	—	—	—	—	5	0
Scanlon A.	1954-61	115	34	6	0	3	0	124	36
Scott J.	1921-22	3	0	—	—	—	—	3	0
Schofield G.W.	1920-22	2	30	—	—	—	—	2	30
Schofield J.A.	1900-07	158	30	22	3	—	—	180	33
Schofield J.A.	1903-04	3	0	—	—	—	—	3	0
Scott J.	1921-23	23	0	—	—	—	—	24	0
Setters M.E.	1959-65	159	12	25	1	—	—	186	13
Sharpe W.H.	1891-92	0	0	—	—	—	—	2	0
Sheldon J.	1910-12	26	3	—	—	—	—	26	3
Sidebottom A.	1972-75	16	0	—	—	2	0	20	0
Silcock J.	1919-34	423	2	27	0	—	—	450	2

PLAYER	SEASONS	LEAGUE App	LEAGUE Gls	FA CUP App	FA CUP Gls	L CUP App	L CUP Gls	TOTAL App	TOTAL Gls
Siveback J.	1985-86	2/1	0	0	0	0	0	2/1	0
Slater J.F.	1891-92	0	0	—	—			0	—
Sloan T.	1978-81	4/7	0	0	0	/1	0	4/8	0
Smith A.	1926-27	5	—	0	0			5	—
Smith J.	1937-39	36	14	5	1			41	15
Smith L.	1902-03	8	—	0	0			8	—
Smith R.	1894-00	87	33	6	3			93	36
Smith T.G.	1923-27	83	12	7	0			90	12
Smith W.	1900-02	19	2	1	0			20	2
Sneddon J.	1891-92	0	0	4	0			4	0
Spence J.W.	1919-33	481	157	28	11			509	168
Spencer C.W.	1928-30	46	0	2	0			48	0
Spratt W.	1914-20	14	8	0	0			14	8
Stacey G.	1907-15	240	8	27	0			267	8
Stafford H.	1895-03	185	13	13	1			198	14
Stapleton F.A.	1981-86	179/10	53	19	4	22/1	7	220/11	64
Stephenson R.	1895-96	2	2	—	—			2	2
Stepney A.C.	1966-78	433	2	44	0	35	0	512	2
Steward A.	1920-32	308	17	17	0			325	17
Steward W.	1892-95	76	5	6	0			82	5
Steward W.	1932-34	46	7	3	0			49	7
Stiles N.P.	1960-71	311	17	38	0	7	0	356	17
Stones H.	1893-95	6	0	6	0			12	0
Storey-Moore I.	1971-74	39	11	4	2	1	0	44	12
Strachan G.D.	1984-86	68/1	20	2	0	12	2	83/1	22
Street E.	1902-04	21	0	1	0			22	0
Sutcliffe J.W.	1903-04	21	0	7	0			28	0
Sweeney E.	1925-30	27	5	5	1			32	6
Tapken N.	1938-39	14	0	2	0			16	0
Taylor C.	1927-30	21	0	2	0			23	0
Taylor E.	1957-59	22	2	6	2			28	4
Taylor J.	1921-22	7	0	0	0			7	0
Taylor J.	1924-26	3	0	0	0			3	0
Taylor T.	1952-58	166	112	9	6			175	118
Thomas H.	1921-30	128	12	6	1			134	13
Thomas M.R.	1978-81	90	11	13	2	5	2	108	15
Thompson J.E.	1936-38	6	0	0	0			6	0
Thompson J.	1913-14	3	0	2	0			5	0
Thompson W.	1893-94	3	0	2	0			5	0
Thomson A.	1928-31	3	2	2	0			5	2
Thomson E.	1907-09	4	0	1	0			5	0
Toms W.	1919-21	13	3	1	0			14	3
Topping H.	1932-35	12	0	0	0			12	0
Tranter H.	1963-64	1	0	0	0			1	0
Travers G.E.	1913-15	21	4	0	0			21	4
Turnbull A.	1906-15	220	92	26	10			247	102
Turnbull J.	1907-10	69	36	10	5			79	41
Turner C.	1985-86	17	0	3	0	0	0	20	0
Turner J.	1898-99	3	0	0	0			3	0
Turner R.	1902-03	3	0	0	0			3	0
Turner R.	1923-24	2	0	0	0			2	0
Tyler S.	1969-71	0/1	0	0	0	0	0	0/1	0
Ure I.J.F.	1969-71	47	0	8	0	10	0	65	0
Valentine R.	1904-06	9	0	0	0			9	0
Vance J.	1895-97	11	0	0	0			11	0
Vincent E.	1931-34	64	1	1	0			65	1
Viollet D.S.	1952-62	259	159	18	5	2	1	279	165
Vose G.	1933-39	195	1	14	0			209	1
Waldron C.	1976-77	3	0	—	—	1	—	4	—
Walker D.	1962-63	1	0	0	0	1	0	2	0
Walker R.	1898-99	2	0	0	0			2	0
Wall G.	1905-15	288	88	30	9			318	97
Walton J.A.	1951-52	2	0	0	0			2	0
Walton J.W.	1945-48	21	2	2	0			23	2
Warburton A.	1929-34	35	10	4	0			39	10
Warner J.	1892-93	22	0	1	0			23	0
Warner J.	1935-39	11	0	2	0			13	0
Wassall J.	1935-50	102	6	13	0			115	6
Watson W.	1935-39	45	0	2	0			47	0
Wealands J.	1970-73	2	0	0	0			2	0
Webster C.	1953-59	65	26	9	4			74	30
Wedge F.E.	1897-98	7	6	1	2			8	8
West E.J.	1910-15	167	71	15	8			182	79
Wetherell J.	1896-97	3	0	2	0			5	0
Whalley A.	1909-20	98	8	9	0			107	8
Whalley H.	1935-47	32	2	6	0			38	2
Whelan A.G.	1954-58	79	43	6	4			85	47
Whitefoot J.	1949-56	93	0	2	0			95	0
Whitehouse J.	1900-03	58	10	5	0			63	10
Whitehurst W.	1955-56	1	1	—	—			1	1
Whiteside K.D.	1907-08	2	0	0	0			2	0
Whiteside N.	1981-86	130/12	32	19	6	18/2	8	167/14	46
Whitney J.	1895-01	3	0	3	0			3	0
Whittaker W.	1895-96	3	3	0	0			3	3
Whittle J.	1931-32	3	0	1	0			4	0
Wilcox T.W.J.	1908-09	2	0	0	0			2	0
Wilkins R.C.	1979-84	158/2	7	14/1	2	10	1	182/3	10
Wilkinson H.	1903-04	2	0	0	0			2	0
Williams D.R.	1927-29	31	0	5	0			36	0
Williams F.	1902-03	7	0	2	0			9	0
Williams F.	1930-31	3	0	1	0			4	0
Williams H.	1904-07	35	7	4	1			39	8
Williams H.	1922-23	3	0	2	0			5	0
Williams W.	1901-02	4	2	0	0			4	2
Williamson H.	1907-08	2	0	0	0			2	0
Williamson J.	1919-20	1	0	1	0			2	0
Wilson E.	1889-90	2	0	0	0			2	0
Wilson J.T.	1926-32	130	3	10	0			140	3
Wilson T.	1907-08	3	0	0	0			3	0
Winterbottom W.	1936-38	25	0	2	0			27	0
Wombwell R.	1904-07	47	3	4	0			51	3
Woodcock W.	1913-20	59	2	3	1			62	3
Wood J.	1922-23	15	4	1	0			16	4
Wood R.E.	1949-59	178	0	15	0			193	0
Woods M.J.	1985-86	0/1	0	0	0	0	0	0/1	0
Worrall H.	1893-94	6	0	0	0			6	0
Wrigglesworth W.	1936-47	27	6	7	3			34	9
Yates W.	1906-07	6	0	0	0			6	0
Young A.T.	1971-76	69/13	2	5/4	0			70/17	2
Young J.	1906-07	2	1	0	0			2	1

1939 – 40

16 Sept.	A.	Bolton Wndrs.	2 – 2
23 Sept.	H.	Oldham Ath.	3 – 1
30 Sept.	H.	Manchester C.	2 – 3
7 Oct.	A.	Stoke City	2 – 2
14 Oct.	A.	Blackpool	4 – 6
4 Nov.	A.	Sheffield Utd.	0 – 3
16 Dec.	H.	Sheffield Utd.	1 – 2
25 Dec.	A.	Manchester C.	1 – 1
26 Dec.	H.	Manchester C.	3 – 1
1 Jan.	H.	Blackpool	1 – 4
17 Feb.	H.	Birmingham	6 – 2
2 Mar.	A.	Preston N.E.	0 – 0
22 Mar.	A.	Bury	1 – 3
25 Mar.	H.	Preston N.E.	5 – 1

1942 – 43

22 Aug.	A.	Manchester C.	5 – 1

1943 – 44

21 Aug.	A.	Manchester C.	2 – 2

1944 – 45

19 Aug.	A.	Manchester C.	2 – 2

1945 – 46

20 Mar.		Services XI (BAOR)	1 – 2
		(in Hamburg, Germany)	

1947 – 48

16 May		Shelbourne Select	4 – 3
		(at Dalymount Park)	
19 May	A.	Linfield Select	3 – 2

1948 – 49

29 May	A.	Shamrock Rv.	2 – 2

1949 – 50

10 May	A.	Toronto Lge. XI	5 – 0
14 May		American Soccer XI	9 – 2
		(at New York)	
17 May		Fall River	2 – 0
		(at Massachusetts)	
21 May		American Soccer XI	2 – 2
		(at New Jersey)	
25 May		Joe Simpkins Club	5 – 0
		(at St. Louis)	
31 May		Los Angeles Select	7 – 1
		(at Los Angeles)	
4 June		Atlas Club	6 – 6
		(at Los Angeles)	
7 June	A.	Montreal XI	2 – 1
9 June		Jonkopping	4 – 0
		(at New York)	
11 June		Besiktas	2 – 1
		(at New Jersey)	
14 June		English Int. (FA XI)	2 – 4
		(at Toronto, Canada)	

1949 – 50

21 June		Jonkopping	1 – 3
		(at Chicago)	

1950 – 51

26 Sept.	A.	Aberdeen	5 – 3
22 May	A.	Copenhagen XI	2 – 2
25 May	A.	Copenhagen XI	2 – 1
27 May	A.	Odense	4 – 1
29 May	A.	F.All. Aalborg	0 – 1
31 May	A.	Jutland XI	3 – 0

1951 – 52

26 Sept.	H.	Hapoel F.C.	6 – 0
23 Feb.	H.	Manchester C.	4 – 2
29 Mar.	H.	Hibernian	1 – 1
9 May		Nwk/Port/Sc/Am Sel.	4 – 0
		(at Kearny)	
11 May		Phil/Am National Sel.	4 – 0
		(at Philadelphia)	
13 May		Montreal All Stars	10 – 0
		(at Montreal)	
18 May		New York Sel. XI	5 – 1
		(at New York)	
21 May		Fall River	11 – 1
		(at Massachusetts)	
25 May		Stuttgart Kickers	5 – 2
		(at New York)	

1951 – 52

27 May		Chicago All Stars	6 – 1
		(at Chicago)	
1 June		Atlas F.C.	2 – 0
		(at Los Angeles)	
8 June		Atlas F.C.	4 – 3
		(at Los Angeles)	
14 June		Tottenham Hotspur	0 – 5
		(at Toronto)	
15 June		Tottenham Hotspur	1 – 7
		(At New York)	

1952 – 53

11 Nov.	A.	Aust. Wien F.C.	1 – 0
2 May	A.	Millwall	4 – 4

1953 – 54

5 Oct.	A.	Millwall	1 – 2
28 Oct.	A.	Kilmarnock	3 – 0
9 Dec.		Western Command	4 – 1
		(at Wrexham)	
30 Jan.	A.	Bristol Rovers	1 – 0

1954 – 55

29 Sept.	A.	Clyde	1 – 4
15 Nov.	A.	Hibernian	3 – 1
12 Mar.	A.	Lincoln City	3 – 2
3 May	A.	Danish F.A. XI	1 – 0
6 May	A.	Copenhagen XI	1 – 0
8 May	A.	Copenhagen XI	3 – 1
10 May	A.	Gothenburg S. All.	4 – 2

1955 – 56

28 Sept.	A.	Hibernian	0 – 5
4 Oct.	A.	Bury	5 – 1
19 Oct.	A.	Clyde	1 – 2
28 Jan.	A.	Leeds United	4 – 1
9 April	A.	Dundee	1 – 5
23 April		Home Farm Select	4 – 0
		(at Dalymount Park)	
1 May	A.	Gothenburg	4 – 0
5 May	A.	Copenhagen Comb.	3 – 1
6 May	A.	Copenhagen Comb.	6 – 0
8 May	A.	Helsingborg	5 – 1

1956 – 57

21 May	A.	Copenhagen Comb.	3 – 2
23 May	A.	Copenhagen Comb.	4 – 3

1957 – 58

14 Aug.	A.	Berliner Stadtlf	3 – 0
17 Aug.	A.	Hannover 1896	4 – 2

1958 – 59

13 Aug.	A.	Munich Comb. XI	3 – 4
16 Aug.	A.	Hamburg Sports	0 – 2
24 Sept.	A.	BSC Young Boys	0 – 2
1 Oct.	H.	BSC Young Boys	3 – 0
24 Jan.	A.	Swansea Town	6 – 4
11 Feb.	H.	Wiener Sports	1 – 0
28 April	A.	S.C. Feyenoord	5 – 3

1959 – 60

8 Aug.	A.	Bayern Munich	2 – 1
12 Aug.	A.	Hamburg Sp. Ver	1 – 2
10 Oct.	H.	C.F. Real Madrid	1 – 6
11 Nov.	A.	C.F. Real Madrid	5 – 6
12 Mar.	A.	Manchester C.	3 – 1
21 Mar.	A.	Hibernian	4 – 0
5 April		Shamrock Rovers	2 – 3
		(at Dalymount Park)	
14 May		Heart of Midlothian	2 – 2
		(at Toronto)	
15 May		German American XI	2 – 1
		(at New York)	
18 May		TSV Munich 1860	2 – 4
		(at New York)	
25 May		Catholic Youth XI	4 – 0
		(at St. Louis)	
28 May		Heart of Midlothian	3 – 2
		(at Vancouver)	
1 June		Heart of Midlothian	0 – 4
		(at Los Angeles)	
5 June		Pacific Coast Stars	4 – 2
		(at San Francisco)	
8 June		New England Stars	7 – 0
		(at Massachusetts)	
12 June		Ukranian Nationals	10 – 1
		(at Philadelphia)	

1960 – 61

13 Oct.	H.	C.F. Real Madrid	2 – 3
21 Nov.	H.	Bayern Munich	3 – 1
1 Mar.	A.	Chester	6 – 0
2 May	A.	A.C. Torino	2 – 1
10 May	A.	Tevere Roma	2 – 3
14 May	A.	Malta Lge. XI	2 – 0

1961 – 62

9 Aug.	A.	Bayern Munich	2 – 0
11 Aug.	A.	First Vienna	1 – 1
13 Dec.	H.	C.F. Real Madrid	3 – 1
20 May	A.	Valencia	3 – 5
23 May		Amsterdam Stars XI	2 – 1
		(at Feyenoord Stadium)	

1962 – 63

25 Sept.	H.	S.L. Benfica	2 – 2
29 Oct.	H.	First Vienna	3 – 1
2 Feb.		Coventry City	2 – 2
		(in Dublin)	
13 Feb.		Bolton Wanderers	4 – 2
		(at Cork)	
19 Feb.		Comb. Irish XI	4 – 0
		(at Dalymount Stadium)	
29 May	A.	Juventus	1 – 0
1 June	A.	A.S. Roma	3 – 2
6 June	A.	Livorno	2 – 0

1963–64
13 Aug. A. Eint. Frankfurt 1–1

1964–65
12 Aug. A. Hamburg Sp. Ver 3–1
14 Aug. A. Shamrock Rvrs. 4–2

1965–66
8 Aug. A. S.V. Hannover 0–2
10 Aug. A. I.F.C. Nuremburg 0–2

1966–67
6 Aug. A. Glasgow Celtic 1–4
10 Aug. A. Bayern Munich 1–4
12 Aug. A. FK Austria Memph. 2–5
17 May S.L. Benfica 1–3
 (at Los Angeles)
23 May Dundee 2–4
 (at San Francisco)
28 May Auckland Assoc. 8–1
31 May New Zealand XI 11–0
4 June Queensland 7–0
7 June Sydney Rep XI 3–0
11 June Victorian XI 1–1
12 June North NS Wales XI 3–0
18 June New South Wales 3–1
21 June Victorian State XI 4–0
24 June South Australia 5–1
27 June Western Australia 7–0

1967–68
15 Aug. H. Italian Olympic XI 2–0

1968–69
31 July A. Hamburg Sports 2–0
5 May A. Shamrock Rvrs. 4–0
8 May A. Waterford 3–0

1969–70
31 July A. Staevnet Select 6–2
2 Aug. A. F.C. Zurich 9–1
26 April A. Bermuda Nat. XI 4–2
30 April A. Bermuda F.U. 6–1
5 May A.S. Bari 2–1
 (at New York)
13 May Eintracht Frankfurt 2–1
 (at San Francisco)
17 May Eintracht Frankfurt 2–3
 (at Los Angeles)

1970–71
21 Jan. A. Bohemians 2–0
12 Feb. A. Blackburn Rvrs. 2–0
25 May A. Aust. Klagenfurt 3–0
28 May A. Styria Select 3–0
1 June A. Grasshoppers 3–2

1971–72
4 Aug. A. Luton Town 2–0
7 Aug. A. Fulham 1–2
9 Aug. H. Coventry City 3–1
30 Nov. A. St. Ouen's 4–0
18 May A. R.D.C. Mallorca 1–1
24 May A. Panathanaikos 1–1
30 May A. Tel Aviv XI 2–1

1972–73
29 July A. Torquay Utd. 0–0
31 July A. AFC Bournemouth 1–3
2 Aug. A. Danish Olympic 3–2
5 Aug. A. West Berlin XI 2–2
23 Oct. A. Aberdeen 2–5
30 Dec. H. Hull City 2–1
1 Feb. A. Bohemians 3–1
4 Feb. A. F.C. Du Porto 0–0

1973–74
3 Aug. A. Hamburg Sports 0–0
11 Aug. A. Ross Co. F.C. 2–0
15 Oct. Shamrock Rovers 2–1
 (at Dalymount Park)
9 Mar. H. Glas. Rangers 2–3

1974–75
3 Aug. A. A.S. Oostende 2–1
6 Aug. A. Staevnet Sel. XI 1–0
8 Aug. A. Holstebro B K 4–0
10 Aug. A. Hull City 1–1
4 Sept. H. Rep. of Ireland 0–2
6 Nov. Shelbourne 1–1
 (at Dalymount Park)
8 May F.C. Basle 1–3
 (at Der Stadt Stadium)
10 May A. F.C. Lausanne 5–0
27 May A. Persepolis S.C. 1–1
1 June A. PSSI Tamtana 0–0
3 June Ajax Amsterdam 2–3
 (in Indonesia)
8 June A. Hong Kong 2–1
15 June Western Australia 2–1
18 June Australia XI 4–0
22 June Queensland 3–0
24 June Auckland F.C. 2–0

1975–76
3 Aug. A. Halskov I.F. 3–0
5 Aug. A. Hvidovre I.F. 3–1
7 Aug. A. Holstebro 3–2
12 Aug. H. Red Star Belgrade 4–4
24 May A. Vancouver 0–0
26 May A. Chicago Stings 2–2
29 May A. Dallas Tornados 2–2

1976–77
30 July A. I.F.C. Nuremburg 2–1
8 Aug. A. Red Star Belgrade 1–2
11 Aug. Home Farm Sel. XI 3–0
 (at Lansdowne Road)

1977–78
1 Aug. A. Werder Bremen 2–3
3 Aug. A. Rosenborg 8–0
8 Aug. A. Hamarkameratene 4–0
10 Aug. A. Stromsgodset I.F. 9–2
21 May Ajax Amsterdam 0–3
 (at Brann Stadium)
24 May A. Brann Bergen 3–1
28 May A. Tampa Bay 1–2
30 May A. Tulsa Roughnecks 2–1

1978–79
29 July A. F.C. Cologne 1–1
1 Aug. A. Schalke 04 1–1
10 Aug. A. Holstebro Ballklub 1–0

1979–80
28 July V.F.B. Stuttgart 0–0
 (at Brotzinger Valley Stadium)
1 Aug. A. V.F.L. Bochum 1–1
7 Aug. A. Staevnet Select 2–0
9 Aug. A. F.A. Aalborg 4–0
6 May A. Portland Timbers 1–0

1980–81
26 July A. I.F.C. Nuremburg 1–1
30 July A. F.K. Austria 2–2
6 Aug. A. I.F.K. Vasteras 1–0
8 Aug. A. Gefle IF/Brynas 2–1
1 Dec. Home Farm XI 3–0
 (at Tolka Park)
10 Feb. A. Linfield 1–0
7 May A. Israel Sel. XI 1–0
7 June A. Malaysia Sel. 0–0
10 June Sabah Selection 1–0
 (in Borneo)
14 June Selangor Selection 4–1
 (in Borneo)

1981–82
8 Aug. A. Bohemians 3–1
11 Aug. A. Port Vale 1–0
18 Aug. A. E.I.K. I.F. 1–0
20 Aug. A. V.N.D. Hanko 4–0
24 Aug. A. Blackpool 2–2
11 Nov. A. Poole Town 3–0
26 Dec. A. Hibernian 1–1
30 Dec. A. Portsmouth 3–0
16 Jan. A. Oldham Ath. 3–1
9 Mar. A. Linfield 5–1
29 Mar. A. Barnet 2–0

1982–83
4 Aug. A. Valur Reykjavik 5–1
5 Aug. A. K.A. 7–1
15 Mar. St. Patrick's Ath. 2–0
 (at Dalymount Park)

1983–84
25 Jan. A. Algerian Nat. XI 0–0
21 Feb. A. Libya XI 2–0

1984–85
5 Aug. A. Shamrock Rvrs. 2–0
14 Aug. H. Ajax Amsterdam 1–1
20 Jan. A. Oldham Ath. 2–1
24 May Southampton 0–1
 (at Port of Spain)
26 May Jamaica XI 3–1
 (at Kingston)

1985–86
3 Aug. A. Bristol City 1–0
25 Feb. A. Glasgow Celtic 3–0
12 Mar. A. Maccabi Haifa 1–1
1 May A. Grantham Tn. 3–0
11 May A. Singapore 2–0
15 May A. Rajpracha F.C. 2–0
17 May A. South China A.A. 2–2

FOOTBALL ALLIANCE AND FOOTBALL LEAGUE RECORD

Season	Pl.	W	D	L	F	A	Pts.	Posn.
ALLIANCE LEAGUE								
1889-90	22	9	2	11	40	45	20	8
1890-91	22	7	3	12	36	55	17	9
1891-92	22	12	7	3	69	33	31	2
FOOTBALL LEAGUE — DIVISION ONE								
1892-93	30	6	6	18	50	85	18	16
1893-94	30	6	2	22	36	72	14	16
FOOTBALL LEAGUE — DIVISION TWO								
1894-95	30	15	8	7	78	44	38	3
1895-96	30	15	3	12	66	57	33	6
1896-97	30	17	5	8	56	34	39	2
1897-98	30	16	6	8	64	35	38	4
1898-99	34	19	5	10	67	43	43	4
1899-1900	34	20	4	10	63	27	44	4
1900-01	34	14	4	16	42	38	32	10
1901-02	34	11	6	17	38	53	28	15
1902-03	34	15	8	11	53	38	28	5
1903-04	34	20	8	6	65	33	48	3
1904-05	34	24	5	5	81	30	53	3
1905-06	38	28	6	4	90	28	62	2
FOOTBALL LEAGUE — DIVISION 1								
1906-07	38	17	8	13	53	56	42	8
1907-08	38	23	6	9	81	48	52	1
1908-09	38	15	7	16	58	68	37	13
1909-10	38	19	7	12	69	61	45	5
1910-11	38	22	8	8	72	40	52	1
1911-12	38	13	11	14	45	60	37	13
1912-13	38	19	8	11	69	43	46	4
1913-14	38	15	6	17	52	62	36	14
1914-15	38	9	12	17	46	62	30	18
1919-20	42	13	14	15	54	50	40	12
1920-21	42	15	10	17	64	68	40	13
1921-22	42	8	12	22	41	73	28	22
FOOTBALL LEAGUE — DIVISION 2								
1922-23	42	17	14	11	51	36	48	4
1923-24	42	13	14	15	52	44	40	14
1924-25	42	23	11	8	57	23	57	2
FOOTBALL LEAGUE — DIVISION 1								
1925-26	42	19	6	17	66	73	44	9
1926-27	42	13	14	15	52	64	40	15
1927-28	42	16	7	19	72	80	39	18
1928-29	42	14	13	15	66	76	41	12
1929-30	42	15	8	19	67	88	38	17
1930-31	42	7	8	27	53	115	22	22
FOOTBALL LEAGUE — DIVISION 2								
1931-32	42	17	8	17	71	72	42	12
1932-33	42	15	13	14	71	68	43	6
1933-34	42	14	6	22	59	85	34	20
1934-35	42	23	4	15	76	55	50	5
1935-36	42	22	12	8	85	43	56	1
FOOTBALL LEAGUE — DIVISION 1								
1936-37	42	10	12	20	55	78	32	21
FOOTBALL LEAGUE — DIVISION 2								
1937-38	42	22	9	11	82	50	53	2
FOOTBALL LEAGUE — DIVISION 1								
1938-39	42	11	16	15	57	65	38	14
1946-47	42	22	12	8	95	54	56	2
1947-48	42	19	14	9	81	48	52	2
1948-49	42	21	11	10	77	44	53	2
1949-50	42	18	14	10	69	44	50	4
1950-51	42	24	8	10	74	40	56	2
1951-52	42	23	11	8	95	52	57	1
1952-53	42	18	10	14	69	72	46	2
1953-54	42	18	12	12	73	58	48	4
1954-55	42	20	7	15	84	74	47	5
1955-56	42	25	10	7	83	51	60	1
1956-57	42	28	8	6	103	54	64	1
1957-58	42	16	11	15	85	75	43	9
1958-59	42	24	7	11	103	66	55	2
1959-60	42	19	7	16	102	80	45	7
1960-61	42	18	9	15	88	76	45	7
1961-62	42	15	9	18	72	75	39	15
1962-63	42	12	10	20	67	81	34	19
1963-64	42	23	7	12	90	62	53	2
1964-65	42	26	9	7	89	39	61	1
1965-66	42	18	15	9	84	59	51	4
1966-67	42	24	12	6	84	45	60	1
1967-68	42	24	8	10	89	55	56	2
1968-69	42	15	12	15	57	53	42	11
1969-70	42	14	17	11	66	61	45	8
1970-71	42	16	11	15	65	66	43	8
1971-72	42	19	10	13	69	61	48	8
1972-73	42	12	13	17	44	60	37	18
1973-74	42	10	12	20	38	48	32	21
FOOTBALL LEAGUE — DIVISION 2								
1974-75	42	26	9	7	66	30	61	1
FOOTBALL LEAGUE — DIVISION 1								
1975-76	42	23	10	9	68	42	56	3
1976-77	42	18	11	13	71	62	47	6
1977-78	42	16	10	16	67	63	42	10
1978-79	42	15	15	12	60	63	45	9
1979-80	42	24	10	8	65	35	58	2
1980-81	42	15	18	9	51	36	48	8
1981-82	42	22	12	8	59	29	78	3
1982-83	42	19	13	10	56	38	70	3
CANON LEAGUE — DIVISION 1								
1983-84	42	20	14	8	71	41	74	4
1984-85	42	22	10	10	77	47	76	4
1985-86	42	20	11	11	64	53	71	5

Here is the record of both Newton Heath and Manchester United against all Football League opposition from entering the League in 1892 up until the end of the 1985/6 season.

	Pl.	W	D	L	F	A	Pts		Pl.	W	D	L	F	A	Pts
Arsenal	132	56	27	51	214	208	140	Leeds United	66	25	19	22	92	82	70
Aston Villa	108	47	22	39	202	177	122	Lincoln	28	13	4	11	46	40	30
Accrington	2	0	2	0	5	5	2	Loughborough	10	7	2	1	29	7	16
Birmingham City	80	33	23	24	113	96	94	Luton Town	26	18	5	3	60	19	46
Brighton & H. A.	8	5	2	1	12	4	14	Manchester City	108	39	38	31	152	149	118
Bolton Wanderers	90	33	20	37	128	137	86	Middlesbrough	72	34	15	23	132	119	85
Burnley	102	47	16	39	180	157	110	Millwall	8	5	2	1	18	5	12
Bristol City	34	14	10	10	47	39	38	Newcastle United	104	48	23	33	194	172	122
Blackburn Rovers	62	25	15	22	116	103	65	Norwich City	30	17	10	3	55	26	47
Bury	38	19	7	12	58	46	45	Nottingham Forest	74	34	17	23	135	108	90
Burton Wanderers	6	2	1	3	8	10	5	Notts County	44	18	12	14	66	55	52
Burton Swifts	14	7	4	3	36	21	18	New Brighton T.	6	4	0	2	11	6	8
Burton United	10	7	2	1	25	8	16	Nelson	2	1	0	1	2	1	2
Blackpool	80	43	17	20	149	94	103	Northampton T.	2	1	1	0	7	3	3
Barnsley	30	17	9	4	55	21	43	Orient	12	6	4	2	18	8	16
Bradford City	42	18	13	11	62	37	49	Oldham Athletic	30	12	9	9	56	37	33
Bradford Park A.	18	8	1	9	30	36	17	Oxford United	4	3	0	1	10	2	8
Brentford	10	4	2	4	19	19	10	Preston North End	64	26	20	18	107	79	72
Bristol Rovers	2	1	1	0	3	1	3	Port Vale	36	21	5	10	76	37	47
Chelsea	90	43	24	23	163	108	112	Portsmouth	42	16	12	14	55	49	44
Coventry City	44	18	10	16	65	51	52	Plymouth Argyle	12	6	2	4	20	20	14
Crewe Alexandra	4	4	0	0	15	1	8	Queens Park R.	18	11	3	4	36	21	29
Chesterfield	20	13	1	6	41	22	27	Rotherham United	6	4	1	1	14	7	9
Cardiff City	26	13	7	6	50	37	33	Sheffield Wed.	86	37	18	31	136	124	92
Crystal Palace	18	10	4	4	34	22	24	Stoke City	70	26	24	20	103	89	82
Charlton Athletic	32	18	7	7	65	46	43	Southampton	52	21	15	16	73	58	60
Derby County	68	25	21	22	116	112	71	Sunderland	94	36	23	35	153	162	98
Darwen	12	6	3	3	27	13	15	Swansea City	16	6	4	6	24	20	18
Doncaster Rovers	8	4	3	1	19	6	11	Sheffield United	78	32	15	31	125	118	79
Everton	114	41	29	44	168	190	112	Stockport County	18	9	2	7	29	18	20
Fulham	42	23	10	9	78	47	56	South Shields	6	4	1	1	10	3	9
Grimsby Town	36	16	6	14	64	63	38	Tottenham Hots.	98	42	27	29	154	137	116
Gainsboro' Town	20	13	5	2	36	14	31	Watford	8	3	4	1	11	9	13
Glossop North End	14	11	2	1	34	10	24	West Ham United	72	27	14	31	127	111	72
Hull City	14	8	3	3	28	15	19	West Bromwich A.	100	39	24	37	174	163	110
Huddersfield T.	42	18	15	9	78	60	51	Wolves	80	36	14	30	135	125	89
Ipswich Town	40	19	6	15	57	53	49	Walsall	12	7	4	1	31	8	18
Liverpool	106	37	31	38	150	146	108	York City	2	2	0	0	3	1	4
Leicester City	94	43	21	30	175	138	106								

NOTE: 1892/3 to 1980/1 — 2 points for a WIN and 1 point for a DRAW
1981/2 to 1985/6 — 3 points for a WIN and 1 point for a DRAW

TESTIMONIAL AND BENEFIT MATCH RESULTS 1986

Date	V	Opponents	Sc	For
12/5/48	A	Bohemians XI	1-2	J. Taylor
22/9/48	A	Hibernian	1-0	W. McCartney
1/6/48	A	Bohemians XI	3-1	C. Harris
25/4/51	A	Reading	4-4	J. Gulliver & F. Fisher
15/9/52	A	Hibernian	3-7	G. Smith
30/9/53	H	Hibernian	2-2	T. Curry
29/3/54	A	Q.P.R.	4-1	R. Allen
25/4/56	H	All-Stars XI	2-1	J. Aston
19/9/62	A	Real Madrid	2-0	—
4/8/68	A	Drumcondra XI at Dalymount Pk, Dublin	2-1	J. Whelan
10/11/70	H	Manchester City	0-3	W. Foulkes
3/5/72	A	Manchester City	3-1	A. Oakes
18/9/72	H	Glasgow Celtic	0-0	R. Charlton
13/11/72	A	West Ham United	2-5	R. Boyce
3/10/73	H	Ajax (Holland)	1-0	D. Law
24/10/73	H	Manchester City	1-2	A. Dunne
5/11/73	A	Partick Thistle	3-0	D. McKinnia
12/12/73	A	Stoke City	2-1	G. Banks
1/5/74	A	Chelsea	2-1	E. McCreadie
26/11/75	H	Man Utd XI 1968	7-2	P. Crerand
9/12/75	A	Plymouth Argyle	2-1	P. Middleton

Date	V	Opponents	Sc	For
17/5/76	A	Glasgow Celtic	0-4	J. Johnstone & R. Lennox
9/2/77	H	S. L. Benfica	2-1	A. Stepney
25/3/77	A	Manchester City	2-4	G. Pardoe
11/4/78	A	Preston North End	0-3	J. Sadler
5/5/78	A	Q.P.R.	2-4	D. Clements
17/9/79	A	Chelsea	3-5	P. Bonnetti
4/8/80	A	Glasgow Celtic United won 3-1 on pens.	0-0	D. McGrain
23/11/81	H	F.A. Cup XI 1977	4-4	S. McIlroy
7/12/81	A	Torquay United	2-4	T. Brown
10/8/82	A	Eire XI at Dalymount Pk, Dublin	4-2	D. Givens
12/8/82	A	Limerick	3-1	P. Nolan
3/8/83	N	Liverpool at Windsor Park, Belfast	4-3	W. Drennan
17/8/83	H	Aberdeen	2-2	M. Buchan
13/5/84	H	Glasgow Celtic	1-1	L. Macari
17/12/84	A	Scunthorpe United	5-5	I. Botham
20/7/85	A	Cambridge United	3-2	S. Fallon & S. Spriggs
1/8/85	A	Hereford United	1-0	C. Addison
23/10/85	A	Notts County	2-1	I. McCulloch

THE 'OLD RIVALS' — UNITED v CITY

The fierce local rivalry between the Manchester neighbours, United and City, dates back to 12 November 1881 when Newton Heath entertained West Gorton St. Marks at North Road and won 3-0. In 1888 West Gorton became Ardwick, until 1895 when the club changed finally to Manchester City. All the match results between the clubs are included in the various sections, and below is the full tabulated record of the local 'derby' games.

Competition	Pl	W	D	L	F	A	Pts
Football League	108	39	38	31	152	149	116
F.A. Cup	4	2	0	2	8	6	
Football League Cup	4	1	1	2	4	8	
F.A. Charity Shield	1	1	0	0	1	0	
Football Alliance	2	1	1	0	5	3	3
F.L. Jubilee Games	2	0	1	1	2	3	
Manchester/Salford Cup	1	1	0	0	5	2	
William Healey Cup	2	0	0	2	3	6	
Benefit Matches	2	1	0	1	5	5	
Testimonials	4	1	0	3	6	10	
Friendlies	36	19	7	10	69	48	
W.W.1 League & Cup	16	4	3	9	18	26	
W.W.2 League & Cup	25	9	4	12	42	47	
Manchester Cup	25	13	3	9	50	40	
Lancashire Cup	9	4	1	4	15	12	
TOTALS	241	96	59	86	385	365	

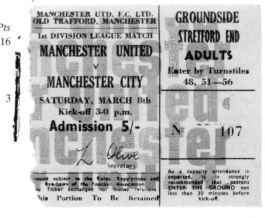

Above: LOCAL 'DERBY' DAY 1969.
Ticket for the Stretford End for the United v City League game on 8 March 1969. (RS)

TOURNAMENT & INVITATION MATCH RESULTS 1938-1986

Date		Opponents	Sc	Venue
FOOTBALL LEAGUE JUBILEE				
20/8/38	A	Manchester City	1-2	Maine Road
19/8/39	H	Manchester City	1-1	Old Trafford
CORONATION CUP				
13/5/53	QF	Glasgow Rangers	2-1	Hampden Pk.
16/5/53	SF	Glasgow Celtic	1-2	Hampden Pk.
MAJORCA TOURNAMENT				
15/5/62	SF	Mantova	3-0	Palma
16/5/62	F	Majorca	0-1	Palma
GLASGOW CHARITY CUP				
8/8/62	N	Glasgow All-Stars	4-2	Hampden Pk.
7/8/63	N	Glasgow All-Stars	1-2	Hampden Pk.
BRITISH WEEKS				
12/10/66	A	A.C. Florentina	2-1	Italy
24/10/77	A	Iran 'B'	2-0	Iran
ANNIVERSARY MATCHES				
28/5/64	A	Vizcaya XI	0-1	Spain
4/12/73	A	Portsmouth	1-1	Fratton Park
CENTENARY MATCHES				
7/8/78	H	Real Madrid	4-0	Old Trafford
14/8/82	A	Glentoran	2-0	Glentoran
8/12/82	A	Tranmere Rovers	0-2	Prenton Park
WATNEY CUP				
1/8/70	QF	Reading	3-2	Elm Park
5/8/70	SF	Hull City	1-1	Hull
		United won 5-4 on pens.		
8/8/70	F	Derby County	1-4	Derby
31/7/71	QF	Halifax Town	1-2	Shay
TORONTO CUP				
2/5/70	SF	A.S. Bari	1-0	Toronto
11/5/70	F	Glasgow Celtic	2-0	Toronto
ANGLO-ITALIAN CUP				
12/2/73	H	A.C. Florentina	1-1	Old Trafford
21/3/73	A	Lazio	0-0	Italy
4/4/73	H	A.S. Bari	3-1	Old Trafford
2/5/73	A	Hellas Verona	4-1	Italy
CITIES CUP TOURNAMENT — SPAIN				
17/8/73	SF	Penarol	6-5	Murcia
18/8/73	F	Real Murcia	0-1	Murcia
HITACHI CUP				
2/8/76	A	Sports Verein	3-1	Hamburg
4/8/76	A	A.Z. Alkmaar	0-0	Alkmaar
ADRIATIC CUP TOURNAMENT				
27/1/80	A	Hajduk Split	0-6	Yugoslavia
ABERDEEN TOURNAMENT				
1/8/81	SF	Southampton	1-3	Pittodrie
2/8/81	3/4 pl.	West Ham	0-1	Pittodrie
EUROPAC TOURNAMENT				
17/5/82	N	Vancouver W.C.	1-3	Empire St.
20/5/82	N	Seattle Sounders	0-3	Empire St.
22/5/82	N	Hajduk Split	2-1	Empire St.
CITY OF ZARAGOZA TROPHY-SPAIN				
19/8/82	SF	Honved S.E.	3-1	Zaragoza
20/8/82	F	Real Zaragoza	5-3	Zaragoza

Date		Opponents	Sc	Venue
Y.M.C.A. EXHIBITION MATCH				
2/5/51	H	Aberdeen	3-1	Old Trafford
FESTIVAL OF BRITAIN				
12/5/51	H	Red Star Belgrade	1-1	Old Trafford
MARGARET BAXTER MEMORIAL				
12/6/52	N	Toronto Ulster	4-2	Detroit
HENSHAWS BLIND INSTITUTION BENEFIT				
28/5/54	A	Manchester City	2-3	Maine Road
NORWICH & NORWICH CHARITY CUP				
5/5/54	A	Norwich City	1-2	Carrow Road
CHESHIRE HOMES BENEFIT				
16/4/56	A	Glasgow Celtic	2-2	Parkhead
BRITISH COMMONWEALTH CUP				
22/5/60	N	Hearts	3-0	New York
PRINCE OF WALES INVESTITURE				
26/7/69	A	Wales XI	2-0	Bangor
NEWPORT COUNTY BENEFIT				
8/12/76	N	South Wales XI	0-1	Cardiff
FRENCH CAMPAIGN AGAINST CANCER				
6/12/77	A	St. Ettienne	0-0	France
SOUTH ATLANTIC FUND				
2/8/82	A	Aldershot	3-1	Aldershot
JIM HEADRIGE MEMORIAL				
24/8/82	H	Bolton Wanderers	2-2	Old Trafford
SWAZISPA INTERNATIONAL CHALLENGE CUP				
4/6/83	N	Tottenham Hotspur	2-1	Somhlolo
11/6/83	N	Tottenham Hotspur	2-5	Somhlolo
TOWNSEND THORESEN CUP				
9/8/83	A	Brighton and H.A.	0-0	Brighton
AMSTERDAM INTERNATIONAL TOURNAMENT				
12/8/83	SF	S.C. Feyenoord	1-2	Olympic St.
14/8/83	3/4 pl	Ajax	0-1	Olympic St.
VITA CUP				
21/5/84	A	Bulova Sports	4-2	Hong Kong
WORLD SOCCER SERIES — AUSTRALIA				
26/5/84	N	Australia	0-0	Sydney
3/6/84	N	Nottingham Forest	1-0	Melbourne
6/6/84	N	Juventus	0-0	Sydney
		United lost 4-5 on pens.		
TERESA HERRERA TROPHY — SPAIN				
11/8/84	S/F	A.S. Roma	1-2	Riazor
13/8/84	3/4 p.	Athletico Bilbao	1-0	Riazor
ROTTERDAM A.D. TOURNAMENT				
17/8/84	SF	VFB Stuttgart	2-1	Feyenoord
19/8/84	F	S.C. Feyenoord	0-1	Feyenoord
SCREEN SPORT SUPER CUP				
18/9/85	H	Everton	2-4	Old Trafford
6/11/85	H	Norwich City	1-1	Old Trafford
4/12/85	A	Everton	0-1	Goodison Prk
11/12/85	A	Norwich City	1-1	Carrow Road
		Everton and Norwich qualified		
BRADFORD CITY DISASTER FUND				
6/8/85	N	Bradford City	1-3	Huddersfield
CHRISTOPHER BUCKINGHAM APPEAL				
1/5/85	A	Grantham Town	3-0	Grantham

NEWTON HEATH & MANCHESTER UNITED
INTERNATIONAL
PLAYERS

1887-1986

Newton Heath captain Jack Powell was the first club player to be capped at International level, when selected for Wales against England on 26 February 1887. He was quickly followed into Welsh colours by Jack Doughty three weeks later against Ireland, and Roger Doughty in March 1888, when all three appeared against Ireland at Wrexham. Wales won 11-0 and Jack scored four times and Roger twice. Charlie Roberts was the club's first England cap, in 1905, and since those early days up until the end of season 1985/6, in their colourful history Manchester United have provided 109 players to the national teams of England, Scotland, Wales, Northern Ireland and the Republic of Ireland. Eire in fact did not play independant International matches until 1924, previous Ireland teams were chosen from players both from the Republic and the Province. Many of the players listed won additional caps whilst with other clubs, but these appearances and totals refer solely to their period as Newton Heath and Manchester United players. For easy reference to the list, below are abbreviations for the opponents, and the year indicated refers to the season i.e. 1985 is the 1984/5 season, 1986 refers to World Cup Finals matches and friendlies prior to the tournament.

ABBREVIATIONS

A denotes Austria; Alb — Albania; Alg — Algeria; Arg — Argentina; Aus — Australia;
B — Bohemia; Bel — Belgium; Br — Brazil; Bul — Bulgaria; Ca — Canada; Ch — Chile;
Chn — China; Co — Colombia; Cy — Cyprus; Cz — Czechoslovakia; D — Denmark;
Ec — Ecuador; Ei — Eire; EG — East Germany; F — France; Fi — Finland; Gr — Greece;
G — Germany (pre-war); H — Hungary; Ho — Holland; Hon — Honduras; I — Italy;
Ic — Iceland; Ir — Iran; Is — Israel; K — Kuwait; L — Luxembourg; M — Mexico;
Mo — Morocco; Ma — Malta; N — Norway; Ni — Northern Ireland; Nz — New Zealand;
P — Portugal; Par — Paraguay; Pe — Peru; Pol — Poland; R — Rumania;
R of E — Rest of Europe; R of W — Rest of the World; S — Scotland; SA — South Africa;
Se — Sweden; Sp — Spain; Sw — Switzerland; T — Turkey; Tr — Trinidad & Tobago;
U — Uruguay; UK — Rest of United Kingdom; US — United States of America;
USSR — Russia; W — Wales; WG — West Germany; Y — Yugoslavia.

NOTES

RECORDS INCLUDE ALL 1986 WORLD CUP FINAL MATCHES

INDIVIDUAL PLAYERS APPEARANCE TOTALS ARE IN BRACKETS

INTERNATIONAL PLAYERS

ENGLAND

ASTON, John — 1949 v S, W, D, Sw, Se, N, F; 1950 v S, W, Ni, Ei, I, P, Bel, Ch, US; 1951 v Ni (17).

BAILEY, Gary — 1985 v Ei, M (2).

BERRY, Johnny — 1953 v Arg, Ch, U; 1956 v Se (4).

BRADLEY, Warren — 1959 v I, US, M (sub) (3).

BYRNE, Roger — 1954 v S, H, Y, Bel, Sw, U; 1955 v S, W, Ni, WG, F, Sp, P; 1956 v S, W, Ni, Br, Se, Fi, WG, D, Sp; 1957 v S, W, Ni, Y, D (2), Ei (2); 1958 v W, Ni, F (33).

CHARLTON, Robert — 1958 v S, P, Y; 1959 v S, W, Ni, USSR, I, Br, Pe, M. US; 1960 v W, S, Se, Y, Sp, H; 1961 v Ni, W, S, L, P, Sp, M, I, A; 1962 v W, Ni, S, A, Sw, Pe, L, P, H, Arg, Bul, Br; 1963 v S, F, Br, Cz, EG, Sw; 1964 v S, W, Ni, R of W, U, P, Ei, Br, Arg, Us (sub); 1965 v Ni, S, Ho; 1966 v W, Ni, S, A, Sp, WG (2), Y, Fi, N, Pol, U, M, F, Arg, P; 1967 v Ni, W, S, Cz; 1968 v W, Ni, S, USSR (2), Sp (2), Se, Y; 1969 v S, W, Ni, R (2), Bul, M, Br; 1970 v W, Ni, Ho (2), P, Co, Ec, Cz, R, Br, WG (106).

CHILTON, Allenby — 1951 v Ni; 1952 v F (2).

COCKBURN, Henry — 1947 v W, Ni, Ei; 1948 v S, I; 1949 v S, Ni, D, Sw, Se; 1951 v Arg, P; 1952 v F (13).

CONNELLY, John — 1965 v H, Y, Se; 1966 v W, Ni, S, A, N, D, U (10).

COPPELL, Steve — 1978 v I, WG, Br, W, Ni, S, H; 1979 v D, Ei, Cz, Ni (2), W (Sub), S. Bul, A; 1980 v D, Ni Ei (Sub), Sp, Arg, W, S, Bel, I; 1981 v R (sub), Sw, R, Br, W, S, Sw, H; 1982 v H, S, Fi, F, Cz, K, WG; 1983 v L, Gr (42).

DUXBURY, Mike — 1984 v L, F, W, S, USSR, Br, U, Ch; 1985 v EG, Fi (10).

DUCKWORTH, Dick — 1910 v SA (1).

EDWARDS, Duncan — 1955 v S, F, SP, P; 1956 v S, Br, Se, Fi, WG; 1957 v S, Ni, Ei (2), D (2); 1958 v W, Ni, F (18).

FOULKES, Bill — 1955 v Ni (1).

GREENHOFF, Brian — 1976 v W, Ni; 1977 v Ei, Fi, I, Ho, Ni, W, S, Br, Arg, U; 1978 v Br, W, Ni, S (sub), H (sub) (17).

HALSE, Harold — 1909 v A (1).

HILL, Gordon — 1976 v I; 1977 v Ei (sub), Fi (sub), L; 1978 v Sw (sub), L (6).

HILDITCH, C. G. — 1920 v SA (3).

KIDD, Brian — 1970 v Ni, Ec (sub) (2).

McGUINESS, Wilf — 1959 v Ni, M (2).

MEW, J. W. — 1921 v Ni (1).

PEARSON, Stuart — 1976 v W, Ni, S, Br, Fi; 1977 v Ei, Ho (sub), W, S, Br, Arg, U; 1978 v I (sub), WG, Ni (15).

PEARSON, Stanley — 1948 v S; 1949 v S, Ni; 1950 v Ni, I; 1951 v P; 1952 v S, I (8)

PEGG, David — 1957 v Ei (1).

ROBERTS, Charlie — 1905 v Ni, W, S (3).

ROBSON, Bryan — 1982 v H, Ni, W, Ho, S, Fi, F, Cz, WG, Sp; 1983 v D, Gr, L, S; 1984 v H, L, F, Ni, S, USSR, Br, U, Ch; 1985 v EG, Fi, T, Ei, R, Fi, S, M, I, WG, US; 1986 v M, P, Mo. (36).

ROWLEY, Jack — 1949 v Sw, Se, F; 1950 v Ni, I; 1952 v S (6).

SADLER, David — 1968 v Ni, USSR; 1970 v Ec (sub); 1971 v EG (4).

SILCOCK, Jack — 1921 v S, W; 1923 v Se (3).

SPENCE, Joe — 1926 v Bel; 1927 v Ni (2).

STEPNEY, Alex — 1968 v Se (1).

STILES, Nobby — 1965 v S, H, Y, Se; 1966 v W, Ni, S, A, Sp, Pol (2), WG (2), N, D, U, M, F, Arg, P; 1967 v Ni, W, S, Cz; 1968 v USSR; 1969 v R; 1970 v Ni, S (28).

TAYLOR, Tommy — 1953 v Arg, Ch, U; 1954 v Bel, Se; 1956 v S, Br, Se, Fi, WG; 1957 v Ni, Y (sub), D (2), Ei (2); 1958 v W, Ni, F (19).

VIOLLET, Denis — 1960 v H; 1962 v L (2).

WALL, George — 1907 v W; 1908 v Ni; 1909 v S; 1910 v W, S; 1912 v S; 1913 v Ni (7).

WILKINS, Ray — 1980 v D, Ni, Bul, Sp (2), Arg, W (sub), Ni, S, Bel, I; 1981 v Sp (sub), R, Br, W, S, Sw, H (sub); 1982 v Ni, W, Ho, S, Fi, F, Cz, K, WG, Sp; 1983 v D, WG; 1984 v D, Ni, W, S, USSR, Br, U, Ch (38).

WOOD, Ray — 1955 v Ni, W; 1956 v Fi (3).

INTERNATIONAL PLAYERS (continued)

NORTHERN IRELAND

ANDERSON, Trevor	1973 v Cy, E, S, W; 1974 v Bul, B (6).
BEST, George	1964 v W, U; 1965 v E, Ho (2), S, Sw (2), Alb; 1966 v S, E, Alb; 1967 v E; 1968 v S; 1969 v E, S, W, T; 1970 v S, E, W, USSR; 1971 v Cy (2), Sp, E, S, W; 1972 v USSR, Sp; 1973 v Bul; 1974 v P (32).
BLANCHFLOWER, Jackie	1954 v W; 1955 v E, S; 1956 vS, W; 1957 v S, E, P; 1958 v S, E, I (2) (12).
BREEN, Tommy	1937 v W, 1938 v E, S; 1939 v W, S (5).
BRIGGS, Ronnie	1962 v W (1).
CAREY, Johnny	1947 v E, S, W; 1948 v E; 1949 V E, S, W (7).
CROOKS, Billy	1922 v W (1).
GREGG, Harry	1958 v Cz, Arg, WG, F, W; 1959 v E, W; 1960 v S, E, W; 1961 v E, S; 1962 v S, Gr; 1964 v S, E (16).
HAMILL, Mickey	1912 v E; 1914 v E, S (3).
JACKSON, Tommy	1976 v Se, N, Y; 1977 v Ho, Bel, WG, E, S, W, Ic (10).
LYNER, D.	1923 v E (1).
McCREERY, David	1976 v S (sub), E, W; 1977 v Ho, Bel, WG, E, S, W, Ic; 1978 v Ic, Ho, Bel, S, E, W; 1979 v Ei, D, Bul (2), E, W, D (23).
McGRATH, Chris	1977 v Bel, WG, E, S, W, Ic (sub); 1978 v Ic, Ho, Bel, S, E, W; 1979 v Bul (sub), E (sub), E (sub) (15).
McILROY, Sammy	1972 v Sp, S (sub); 1974 v S, E; 1975 v N, Se, Y, E, S, W; 1976 v Se, N, Y, S, E, W; 1977 v Ho, Bel, E, S, W, Ic; 1978 v Ic, Ho, Bel, S, E, W; 1979 v Ei, D, Bul (2), E (2), S, W, D; 1980 v E, Ei, Is, S, E,W; 1981 v Se, P, S, P, S, Se; 1982 v S, Is (52).
McMILLAN, Sammy	1963 v E, S. (2).
McMILLEN, W. S.	1934 v E; 1935 v S; 1937 v S (3).
NICHOLL, Jimmy	1976 v Is, W (sub); 1977 v Ho, Bel, E, S, W, Ic; 1978 v Ic, Ho, Bel, S, E, W; 1979 v Ei, D, Bul, E, Bul, E, S, W, D; 1980 v E, Ei, Is, S, E, W, Aus (3); 1981 v Se, P, S, P, S, Se; 1982 v S, Is, E (41).
NICHOLSON, Jimmy	1961 v S, W; 1962 v E, W, Gr, Ho; 1963 v E, S, Pol (2) (10).
SLOAN, Tommy	1979 v S, W (sub), D (sub) (3)
WHITESIDE, Norman	1982 v Y, Hon, Sp, A, F; 1983 v WG, Alb, T; 1984 v A, T, WG, S, E, W, Fi; 1985 v R, Fi, Is, E, Sp, T; 1986 v Alg, Sp, Br (24).

SCOTLAND

ALBISTON, Arthur	1982 v Ni; 1984 v U, Bel, EG, W, E; 1985 v Y, Ic, Sp (2), W; 1986 v U (12).
BELL, Alec	1912 v Ni (1).
BUCHAN, Martin	1972 v W, Y, Cz, Br; 1973 v D (2), E; 1974 v WG, Ni, W, N, Br, Y; 1975 v EG, Sp, P; 1976 v D, R; 1977 v Fi, Cz, Ch, Arg, Br; 1978 v EG, W (sub), Ni, Pe, Ir, Ho; 1979 v A, N, P (32).
BURNS, Francis	1970 v A (1)
CRERAND, Paddy	1964 v Ni; 1965 v E, Pol, Fi; 1966 v Pol (5).
DELANEY, Jimmy	1947 v E; 1948 v E, W, Ni (13).
FORSYTH, Alex	1973 v E; 1975 v Sp, Ni (sub), R, EG; 1976 v D (6).
GRAHAM, George	1973 v E, W, Ni, Br (sub) (4).
HOLTON, Jim	1973 v W, Ni, E, Sw, Br; 1974 v Cz, WG, Ni, W, E, N, Z, Br, Y; 1975 v EG (15).
HOUSTON, Stewart	1976 v D (1)
JORDAN, Joe	1978 v Bul, Ni, E, Pe, Ir, Ho; 1979 v A, P, W (sub), Ni, E, N; 1980 v Bel, Ni (sub), W, E, Pol; 1981 v Is, W, E (20).
LAW, Denis	1963 v W, Ni, E, A, N, Ei, Sp; 1964 v W, E, N, WG; 1965 v W, Ni, E, Fi (2), Pol, Sp; 1966 v Ni, E, Pol; 1967 v W, E, USSR; 1968 v Ni; 1969 v Ni, A, WG; 1972 v Pe, Ni, W, E, Y, Cz, Br (35).

INTERNATIONAL PLAYERS (continued)

SCOTLAND (continued)

McBAIN, Neil	1922 v E (1).
McQUEEN, Gordon	1978 v Bul, Ni, W; 1979 v A, N, P, Ni, E, N; 1980 v Pe, A, Bel; 1981 v W (13).
MACARI, Lou	1973 v E (2), W (sub), Ni (sub); 1975 v Se, P (sub), W, E (sub), R; 1977 v Ni (sub), E (sub), Ch, Arg; 1978 v EG, W, Bul, Pe (sub), Ir (18).
MILLER, Tommy	1921 v E, Ni (2).
MORGAN, Willie	1972 v Pe, Y, Cz, Br; 1973 v D (2), E (2), W, Ni, Sw, Br; 1974 v Cz (2), WG (2), Ni, Bel (sub), Br, Y (20).
STRACHAN, Gordon	1985 v Sp (sub), E, Ic; 1986 v D, WG, U (6).

WALES

BENNION, Roy	1926 v S; 1927 v S; 1928 v S, E, Ni; 1929 v S, E, Ni; 1930 v S; 1932 v Ni (10).
BLACKMORE, Clayton	1985 v N (sub) (1).
DAVIES, Alan	1983 v Ni, Br; 1984 v E, Ni; 1985 v Ic (5).
DAVIES, Wyn	1973 v E, S (sub), Ni (3).
DOUGHTY, Jack	1887 v S, Ni; 1888 v E, S, Ni; 1889 v S; 1890 v E (7)
DOUGHTY, Roger	1888 v S, Ni; 1890 v E (32).
HUGHES, Mark	1984 v E, Ni; 1985 v Ic, Sp, Ic, N, S, Sp, N (9).
JENKYNS, Caesar	1897 v Ni (1).
JONES, Tommy	1926 v Ni; 1927 v E, Ni; 1930 v Ni (4).
MEREDITH, William	1907 v E, S, Ni; 1908 v E, Ni; 1909 v E, S, Ni; 1910 v E, S, Ni; 1911 v E, S, Ni; 1912 v E, S, Ni; 1913 v E, S, Ni; 1914 v E, S, Ni; 1920 v E, S, Ni (26).
MOORE, Graham	1964 v S, Ni (2).
OWEN, G.	1889 v S, Ni; 1892 v E; 1893 v Ni (4).
POWELL, Jack	1887 v E, S; 1888 v E, S, Ni (5).
THOMAS, H.	1927 v E (1).
WARNER, John	1939 v F (1)
WEBSTER, Colin	1957 v Cz; 1958 v H, M, Br (4).
WILLIAMS, D. R.	1929 v E, S (2)

REPUBLIC OF IRELAND

BREEN, Tommy	1937 v Sw, F.
BRENNAN, Seamus	1965 v Sp; 1966 v Sp, A, Bel; 1967 v Sp, T, Sp; 1969 v Cz, D, H; 1970 v S, Cz, D, H, Pol (sub), WG (16).
CANTWELL, Noel	1961 v S (2); 1962 v Cz (2), A; 1963 v Ic (2), S; 1964 v A, Sp, E; 1965 v Pol, Sp; 1966 v Sp (2), A, Bel; 1967 v Sp, T (19).
CAREY, Johnny	1938 v N, Cz, Pol; 1939 v Sw, Pol, H (2), G; 1946 v P, Sp; 1947 v E, Sp, P: 1948 v P, Sp; 1949 v Sw, Bel, P, Sp, Se; 1950 v Fi, E, Fi, Se; 1951 v N, Arg, N; 1953 v F, A (29).
CAROLAN, Joe	1960 v Se, Ch (2).
DALY, Gerry	1973 v Pol (sub), N; 1974 v Br (sub), U (sub); 1975 v Sw (sub); 1977 v E, T, F (8).
DUNNE, Anthony	1962 v A; 1963 v Ic, S; 1964 v A, Sp, Pol, N, E; 1965 v Pol, Sp; 1966 v Sp (2), A, Bel; 1967 v Sp, T, Sp; 1969 v Pol, D, H; 1970 v H; 1971 v Se, I, A (24).
DUNNE, Pat	1965 v Sp; 1966 v Sp (2), WG; 1967 v T (5).
GILES, Johnny	1960 v Se, Ch; 1961 v W, N, S (2); 1962 v Cz (2), A; 1963 v Ic, S (10).
GIVENS, Don	1969 v D, H; 1970 v S, Cz, D, H (6).
GRIMES, Ashley	1978 v T, Pol, N (sub); 1980 v Bul, US, Ni, E, Cy; 1981 v Cz, Pol; 1982 v Alg; 1983 v Sp (2) (13).
McGRATH, Paul	1985 v I (sub), Is, E, N (sub), Sw (sub) (5).
MARTIN, Mick	1973 v USSR, Pol. F, N; 1974 v Pol, Br, U, Ch; 1975 v USSR, T, Sw, USSR, SW (13).
MORAN, Kevin	1980 v Sw, Arg; 1981 v Bel, F, Cy, W (sub), Bel, Cz, Pol; 1982 v F, Alg; 1983 v Ic; 1984 v Ic, Ho, Ma, Is; 1985 v M (17).
ROCHE, Paddy	1975 v USSR, T, Sw, USSR, Sw; 1976 v T (6).
STAPLETON, Frank	1982 v Ho, F, Alg; 1983 v Ho, Sp, Ic, Ma, Sp; 1984 v Ic, Ho, Ma, Pol, Is, Chn; 1985 v N, D, I, Is, E, N, Sw (21).
WHELAN, Liam	1956 v Ho; 1957 v D, E (2) (4).

287

THE MALTA CONNECTION

The George Cross island of Malta has a unique association with Manchester United. Authors Charles Zahra and President Joseph Muscat are both prominent in the thriving Manchester United Supporters Club (Malta) based in Valletta, which boasts over 1,000 members on the island. United players and officials are regular guests of the club, and the dedicated worshippers from afar are sustained in their enthusiasm by treasured memories of two visits to their Mediterranean Isles, in 1961 and 1967. Here, former Malta club President John Scerri remembers the excitement of that initial occasion.

"Early in 1961 the founder of our branch of the Supporters Club, John Calleja, wrote to Matt Busby to enquire on the possibilities of bringing his team to Malta. To his surprise the response was encouraging, United were to play in Italy at the end of that season, and following some earnest negotiating and the consent of FIFA, the United board agreed to a match against the Malta League Select XI.

The Manchester party landed at Luqa Airport on 12 May 1961 to a resounding welcome from the expectant Island supporters anxious to see their favourites in the flesh. The volume of rapturous applause and cheering increased as Matt Busby emerged from the plane with his team, prompting one player to observe that "it was like a victorious team's homecoming after winning the cup.

Holidaying in Malta at that time was Tommy Docherty, then of Arsenal, and it was rumoured that he might 'guest' for United. Who could have foreseen then that he would be manager at Old Trafford one day. In the event, the thousands who thronged the Gzira Stadium saw these players take the field: Gaskell; Brennan, Cantwell; Stiles, Cope, Setters; Giles, Quixall, Dawson, Viollet and Moir. Following an eventful opening ten minutes during which Nobby Stiles cleared off the goal-line, the game developed into a one-sided affair and in the end the local amateurs had to bow to the supremacy of the professionals, who won 2-0. On 30 minutes, Albert Quixall's deftly flighted free-kick was converted by Noel Cantwell, then Maurice Setters added the second from Johnny Giles' corner. The 'Reds' visit had proved a marvellous success — and it sowed the seeds for further growth of the supporters movement in Malta."

MALTA 1961. The players of Manchester United and the Malta League XI before the big friendly fixture. (L to R), Back Row: Cilia, Taylor, Cantwell, Cini, Mackay, Zammit, D'Emmanuele, Theobald, Privitera, Cauchi and Borg. Front: Giles, Cope, Brennan, Quixall, Stiles, Dawson, Setters, Viollet, Moir and Gaskell. (MMUSC)

EUROPEAN CUP 1967/8

The second visit of Manchester United to Malta was in September 1967, for the return leg of the European Cup-tie encounter with Hibernians of Valletta, whose team coach Father Hilary Tagliaferro, recalls what proved to be his most momentous football experience.

"By far the most exciting period of my career as Coach to Hibernians Valletta F.C. was the three months of preparation during the hot summer months of 1967 for the two European Champions Cup matches against the illustrious Manchester United club.

The result in itself was not that important to us, that we were playing against the star-studded United side in a competitive game was sufficient honour in itself. Here was an opportunity for part-time, amateur players of Malta, to pit their skills against some of the world's greatest football artists like Bobby Charlton, George Best and Denis Law. It was a prospect to savour, and the Hibs players, encouraged by an enthusiastic crowd of 25,000, rose to the occasion. All the tactical, physical and psychological preparation was executed to perfection on that hot September afternoon. Hibs were never overawed, and in the end it was United who were thankful for the 0-0 draw, due to a stupendous save by Alex Stepney in the dying moments of the match. For Hibernians, the result was a just reward and tribute to the players who worked so hard at that game.

The shivering sensation down my spine as I had led the team out of the tunnel for the first leg at Old Trafford, to the tumultuous roar of the crowd that awaited us on that cold evening, is yet another unforgettable experience.

Once again the team displayed tactical knowledge and humbly presented a staunch resistance to a furious United onslaught, aided by a magnificent performance in goal by Freddie Mizzi. Our pride and prestige gained in glorious defeat was hightened further eight months later, in the knowledge that we had been vanquished by the ultimate Champions of Europe!

But what endurably remained from that European Cup experience was the human element. I made new friends: Sir Matt Busby, Bobby Charlton, Pat Crerand, Les Olive, Jack Crompton, the late Denzil Haroun, and most of all, Jimmy Murphy, with whom I have remained in contact ever since. I came to know all of these people so well, and found a high and profound reciprocal respect.

I learned that football is not just a game between two teams, but an encounter of high human values displayed on and outside the field of play."

MALTA 1967. The United team prior to the European Cup-tie against Hibernians. (L to R): Law, Stepney, Kidd, Best, Charlton, Foulkes, Sadler, Dunne, Stiles, Burns and Crerand. (JG)

WHO WROTE THIS LETTER? . . . .

Dear Sir
This is a picture
of my Grandad and a
friend of his Mr Stere
Bloomer.

YOU CAN FIND OUT IN . . .

HEATHENS & RED DEVILS
PICTORIAL MILESTONES OF MANCHESTER UNITED

A fascinating new collection of over 200 photographs and memorabilia from more than a century in the history of Newton Heath and Manchester United, superbly reproduced. It is a unique selection of rare and interesting pictorials from the club's formation in 1878 to the present time, including many illustrations never previously published. A must for all United supporters, and football enthusiasts everywhere. For details on this, and other forthcoming soccer books, please write to:

TEMPLE NOSTALGIA PRESS
Temple Printing (Nottm) Ltd., Wilford Crescent East, Nottingham.

Subscribers Limited Edition

Above: Subscribers orders from all over the world.

PICTORIAL HISTORY & CLUB RECORD OF MANCHESTER UNITED

★ ☆ ★ ☆ ★ ☆ ★

Presentation Copies
Manchester United

1 Manchester United Football Club   2 Sir Matt Busby C.B.E.

3 C. M. Edwards	4 R. Charlton C.B.E.	5 J. M. Edelson	6 J. A. Gibson
7 W. A. Young	8 E. M. Watkins	9 L. Olive	10 R. Atkinson
11 K. Merrett	12 K. Ramsden	13 C. Butler	14 S. Busby

Authors

15 Charles Zahra	16 Joseph Muscat	17 Iain McCartney	18 Keith Mellor

Contributors

19 David Meek Manchester Evening News	20 Alan Ormerod BNPC Library	21 Bryan Horsnell Football Monthly	22 Joe Glanville Consultant

Subscribers

23 Mick Hurst	37 Stephen Muscat	51 Geoff Greenstreet	65 Desmond Gould
24 John Gartside	38 Dr. Mario R. Sammut MD	52 Roy Morris	66 Alan Wyatt
25 John Camm	39 Micallef Ludovico	53 John Illingworth	67 Paul James Mellor
26 Geoffrey Wright	40 Michael Woodland	54 Jillian Borg-Cardona	68 Lee Gray
27 John Mason	41 Charles Cauchi	55 David Winterburn	69 Brian Smith
28 Bernard J. Grech	42 Joseph Catania	56 William Armstrong	70 Mr. Nicholas Galea
29 Mario Spiteri	43 Della-Ann Wilson	57	71-73 William B. Kilmurray
30 Eugene Warrington	44 Roy William Slape	58 T. A. Beavon	74 Nazzareno Schembri
31 David N. Robertson	45 W. J. J. Steadman	59 Mr. T. G. L. Humfryes	75 Edwin Farrugia
32 J. A. McCluskey	46 Gordon Atikinson	60 Mrs. M. S. Farrugia	76 Joe Mifsud
33 Keith Margerison	47 Paul Lawless	61 James J. Sharkey	77 Gareth M. Davies
34 Anthony Calleja	48 Simon Thomas	62 G. R. Williams	78 Yvonne Corlett
35 John White	49 Michael Penhaligon	63 Ian Jones	79 Alfred Aquilina
36 Mario Rapinett	50 Andrew John Rimmer	64 Ian Paul Dunn	80 Allan Sutcliffe

81 Craig Melvyn Scammell
82 Robert Brimicombe
83 A. Currall
84 John E. Scerri
85 Furtu Carvana
86 Nigel Baker
87 James A. Thomas
88 Dr. Carmel Galea
89 Martyn-John Parker
90 E. Stephen Edwards
91 Gina Bellhouse
92 Roderick J. Dean
93 David Barrie Johns
94 Mr. Sidney Proud
95 John Power
96 Alan Tyler
97 Michael McGurgan
98 Mark Lyon
99 Emanuel Caruana
100 Ian Standing
101 David Carney
102 Richard F. White
103 Wayne Dickinson
104 Gordon McKee
105 Brian David Cann
106 Bob Carlyon
107 Joseph Ciappara
108 Michael Stephen Gibson
109 P. R. Pinhey
110 J. A. Harris
111 Gordon Wallis
112 Steven Abbott
113 David and Leona Wilson
114 Frankie O'Rourke
115 Bernadette Kilkie
116 Ian Mellor
117 Tony Mellor
118 T. J. Surridge
119 Thomas Pentland
120 Kevin M. Comber
121 Richard Wells
122 Mr. Joseph Portelli
123 David Sullivan
124 A. and J. A. Waterman
125 Paul Stephen Marshall
126 George Ciappara
127 Mr. Silvio Frendo
128 Mr. Raymond Deidun
129 Howard Parry
130 Mr. Robert A. Stephenson
131 Joseph Bellia
132 Ralph Vella Gregory
133 Victor Radmilli
134 W. Needs
135 Norma Patricia Worton
136 David Geraint
   Mark Davies
137 D. Cave
138 Ron Hockings
139 Bernard Lewry
140 T. O'Brien
141 Roy Somerville
142 Dr. Jeremy Sides
143 Kevin McHugh,
   Alfred Donelan
144 David Sadler
145 Reidar Ånensen
146 Philip Soar
147 Mark Cleminson

148 Kevin Dorey
149 Christopher Buckingham
150 Gary Siddiqui
151 Gino Sciberras
152 Charlie Portelli
153 M. A. J. Bowden
154 William Smythe
155 Alun Williams
156 Mr. J. Burke
157 Johanna Tonge
158 S. R. Royle
159 J. E. P Kelly
160 Bill and Sandra King
161 Arthur McLeod
162 David Boswell
163 Ted Proudley
164 Damien M. McElvenny
165 Carl G. Riggall
166 Michael T. Moxon
167 K. A. Lawrenson
168 Colin Smythe
169 Steven Charles Andrew
170 Sid Woodhead
171 Paul Bowden
172 Carol Rothwell
173 Amos Smith
174 Nick Flint
175 William David Mercer
176 Darren Anthony Beswick
177 John Lord
178 Alan Mather
179 Mark William Fowler
180 John Thomason
181 Anthony Cooper
182 Roger Jones
183 Andrew Jackson
184 Mr. A. H. Brunt
185 Mr. H. N. Brunt
186 Mr. Alan Robertson
187 Brian Bowler
188 Bryan Michael Nield
189 Kevin Murphy
190 Michael Passmore
191 Andrew Goodrich
192 Mr. L. Burgess
193 Danny Finnegan
194 & 195 Nick Pearce
196 Ray Martin
197 Adam A. Bingham
198 A. T. Hill
199 Paul Topping
200 W. H. Greenhalgh
201 Raymond Abdilla
202 David J. Richardson
203 Lee Horsfield
204 Anthony T. Egan
205 Ian Bradbury
206 Neil David Pickup
207 Thomas Halliwell
208 Richard Werner
209 P. J. Harding
210 F. Kelly
211 Ron Pritchard
212 D. Swindell
213 Brendan Miskella
214 Wayne Miller
215 William Chetwynd
216 Mark Gerrard
217 Andrew David Shapley

218 Roger Hudson
219 Steven Baylis
220 John Rowlinson
221 William O'Neill
222 Philip Chaplin
223 Robert Tinker
224 Stewart Philip Griffin
225 Mr. Derek Fielding
226 J. C. Petrie
227 Martin Hardman
228 Graham Harrison
229 Trevor Thomas
230 M. E. Grunblat
231 David Marlor
232 J. Phillips
233 John Fitzgerald
234 Tony and Gloria
   Hayhurst
235 Craig Doherty
236 Gerald Hall
237 Julie Davies
238 Malcolm Rylance
239 Derek Cronshaw
240 Carl Holmes
241 Les Wraight
242 Andrew McMorine
243 Alan Jackson
244 Roy Florendine
245 Raymond Galea
246 Brian Holmes
247 Paul Nagel
248 Roy Carmichael
249 Ian Page
250 John Hemfrey
251 Roy M. Daniel
252 G. C. F. Openshaw
253 Michael Baker
254 Graham Bruton
255 John Gibbison
256 Edward Webb
257 Peter John Hudson
258 David Joseph Price
259 David John Cripwell
260 John Pond
261 Les Symes
262 Paul F. Entwistle
263 Derek Clarke
264 Arthur Beckett
265 David A. Howgate
266 Mr. Douglas F. Parker
267 Nigel G. Appleton
268 A. P. Wheatley
269 Roy Watts
270 Glen Watts
271 Stephen M. McEvoy
272-275 The Manchester
   Public Libraries
276 Mark McDonough
277 Grahame Stott
278 Paul Farmer
279 Norman Corry
280 Ian Horan
281 Stephen Hunter
282 Mr. J. W. Nussey
283 Mr. T. Entwistle
284 David Michael Woods
285 Kelvin Dickinson
286 Arthur H. Atkins
287 David Keith Gidley

288 Paul Anthony Godbeer
289 John Flint Penkethman
290 P. J. Thomas
291 Eddie Gibbons
292 Paul Steenson
293 Paul Jackson
294 John V. White
295 Stephen H. White
296 Steven J. Cross
297 Ian Mills
298 Nicholas Mills
299 Ernest T. Bullock
300 Peter Cheney
301 Clive Rayner
302 Gareth Pritchard
303 Mr. C. Massey
304 H. P. Kerr
305 Philip Roger Lugg
306 Colin Middleton
307 Peter Bolton
308 Bernard Law
309 J. Marsh, Irwin RGS FC
310 Mrs. A. C. Osborne
311 Terence J. Lomax
312 Mark Lingham
313 D. S. Humberston
314 Peter Ralph Foster
315 Mr. S. J. Cope
316 Norrie Tait
317 A. J. Scanlon
318 Mike Kibble
319 Debbie Thomas
320 Robin M. Morris
321 David Stephen Soper
322 Dave Plant
323 Frank Jones
324 John McCadden
325 Mr. N. F. R. Luxton
326 Fred Mayers
327 Duncan F. Murray
328 Clive Stone
329 Harry Isaacs
330 Harold Graham
331 Gary Newman
332 Morris Szeftel
333 John Good
334 Mr. Julian Douglas
   Manning
335 Michael Crick
336 Gino de Reland
337 Christopher Hackett
338 W. E. Mansell
339 N. Appleton
340 Gary Anthony Brown
341 G. K. Dutton
342 Michael J. Wells
343 Vincent Logan
344 Brian Potter
345 Frank Sydney Smith
346 Tom Birch
347 Ian Meadows
348 Mantzouranis Theodore
349 T. F. Rogerson
350 Jamie Newhall
351 James Martin Peters
352 Simon Kerr
353 Mark J. Warburton
354 & 355 D. H. Leggott
356 Ian Parkinson

357 Mr. John F. Tuckett
358 Dave Hunt
359 Richard Stocken
360 Alan Barnes
361 Thomas Haddock
362 John Crook
363 Don Marshall
364 Robert W. Mills
365 Matthew Roberts
366 Mr. S. Degiorgio
367 Christopher Roy Frost
368 Mr. Craig Jackson
369 Lars-Olof Wendler
370 William Davies
371 J. Brazzill
372 David John Stone
373 Peter Sanderson
374 David P. Hatton
375 Andrew Flack
376 Mr. Martin Spencer
377 Michael Holder
378 John Thorne
379 John Treffry
380 Andrew Yourglivch
381 Michael Wood
382 Malcolm Wood
383 Kenneth Beech
384 Mr. & Mrs. W. McGlen
385 Mr. Dave Kennedy
386 Douglas J. Nattan
387 Raymond White
388 Robin Woolman
389 Jonathan Michael Pinches
390 Alfred Roesberg
391 David Smyth
392 Dan Martinson
393 Charlie Grech
394 David Kirkby
395 Kevin Fox
396 J. A. Wilson
397 Nigel Robert Gallagher
398 Paul David Albert
399 Richard Charles Larcombe
400 M. Swart
401 Simon Bernstein
402 David Gregory
403 Brian Kidd
404 Joseph Wilson
405 David White
406-408 Stan Pearson
409 Tommy Heron
410 Alex MacLeod
411 Silvio Attard
412 Sammy McMillan
413 Phil Luff
414 Leslie Colin Badcock
415 A. L. Southwick
416 Darren Carter
417 Kyle Adam Blackshaw
418 Stuart R. Ross
419 Bill Robinson
420 Olav Ramstad
421 Neil A. Sternbach
422 Howard Roscoe
423 Alan Rhodes
424 Nicholas D. B. Harlow
425 Paul Evans
426 Michael Aitchison
427 Peter McDonald

428 Mr. Nigel Wilcock
429 Stephen Wilde
430 David Robert
     Charles Walton
431 Peter O'Connor
432 David Lee Jones
433 Jonathan Robin Lewin
434 Mrs. Sheila Jones
435 Mr. Philip Jones
436 Mr. Philip J. Bastard
437 Ronald Simm
438 Paul Adrian Tansey
439 Kay Sidebottom
440 Charles Herbet Shillito
441 James Kelly
442 Ian David Lovell
443 K. R. Beard
444 D. J. Haywood
445 Stephen Falp
446 Stuart Thomas Martin
447 Gerald Earnshaw
448 Trevor Buckley
449 Christer Svensson
450 Clifford Elson
451 Charles A. Long
452 Tracey Massey
453 Philip Bernard Loftus
454 Brian Anthony Carroll
455 Karen S. Lee
456 Adrian H. Hancock
457 Mark C. Paul
458 Stephen Copsey
459 Steven David Evans
460 Peter Edward Calvin
461 Richard James White
462 The Downie Family
463 Alan Sheen
464 Matthew Andrews
465 Adrian Mitchell
466 Paul Sutton
467 Mike Parnell
468 Alan Ibbotson
469 Roger Bampton
470 Ian Kevin Lindley
471 Mark Dunning
472 Michael L. Neale
473 Mr. M. Graham
474 Paul Needham
475 Adrian Mountford
476 Stuart Kenneth Falp
477 James Briggs
478 Greg Hunter
479 Steve Hunter
480 Andrew Gordon
481 Mr. Robert J. F. Titley
482 David Hewitt
483 Phillip Daniels
484 Roger Burke
485 Alan Moses
486 Philip A. Terry
487 James Andrew Mearns
488 Christopher Fenlon
489 Robert William Dale
490 Wendy Warren
491 Ian Mark Bosley
492 Stephen Williams
493 Kevin Robert Burston
494 Michael Bradbury
495 Paul Shelton
496 John Edwards

497 Andrew Bradley
498 Paul King
499 Chris Barron
500 Trevor Smith
501 Colin Illingworth
502 Brian Davies
503 Philip Lynch
504 Trevor W. Dent
505 Richard Stokes
506 Bryan Collins
507 Ian Chapman
508 Andrew Bowker
509 Patrick Harrington
510 Eric Burd
511 Patrick Burd
512 Kevin Burd
513 Leslie Smith
514 Peter John Howe Hall
515 Roger J. Groarke
516 John Ryan
517 Philip Ryan Rollinson
518 Martin Bartley
519 Paul Graham Hook
520 Mr. Barry Williams
521 John Roberts
522 David Smith
523 Elizabeth Warner
524 Stephen Colin Cheeseman
525 Chris Walton
526 G. Clee
527 Charles Haselden
528 Philip Brooks
529 Ray Dyer
530 Chris Berry
531 Andrew Pollard
532 Lynne Norcliffe
533 Andrew Gardner
534 Leslie Brown
535 Alan Jackson
536 Roy Richardson
537 Martin Bernard Gleaves
538 John D. Bennett
539 Nigel John Pallant
540 Maurice Pleace
541 Gary Latham
542 John Kane
543 Ernest Evans
544 Paul Christian Kelly
545 Sean S. MacGoey
546 David White
547 Terry Helps
548 Siobhan Welsh
549 Timothy Devall
550 Alan Gibson
551 Neil Boland
552 Neil Clark
553 Alec J. Watson
554 T. W. Woolhouse
555 David J. Hobbs
556 Richard D. Hill
557 Catherine A. Martin
558 Gregg Warren
559 James F. Gordon
560 Michael Sims
561 A. W. Fitzgerald
562 A. D. Walker
563 Wayne Gauden
564 Mr. Dennis Salt
565 Mr. Dave Salt

566 Huw Rhys Griffith
567 T. M. Clemow
568 David Britten
569 Barrie Bell
570 Geoffrey Green
571 John Davies
572 Donald Wilkinson
573 Paul Bowden
574 Gwenan Jones
575 Tony Denis Renton
576 R. W. G. Blewitt
577 Alison Debra Hocking
578 Andrew Michael Sutton
579 John Qvarnberg
580 Michael O'Brien-Kelly
581 William Thomas Jones
582 Robert Burse
583 Barry Raymond Dixon
584 Russell Unsworth
585 John David Chapman
586 William Wilkinson
587 David Bagshaw
588 Kevin Lockwood
589 Andrew Robinson
590 Michael John Dixon
591 Roger Coulston
592-597 The Manchester
       Public Libraries
598 Lionel Andrew Stanyon
599 Charles Zammit Moore
600 Ingemar Jönsson
601 Stephen Coyle
602 Phil Bradbury
603 M. J. Dobbin
604 Martin Muscat
605 Tony Lee Runeckles
606 John Connelly
607 David George Jackson
608 Andy Milne
609 Adrian Russell
610 Steven Alan Foster
611 Roger Everitt
612 Paul Brough
613 Mark Anthony Allen
614 Terence H. Radley
615 Gordon Stewart
616 Peter L. Keating
617 Nicholas H. W. Palin
618 John Howard
619 Francis Hopkins
620 Anthony Pickup
621 Martyn Carl Hoggarth
622 Colin Booth
623 Carl Tero
624 Mrs. Handford
625 Brian A. Pimblett
626 Colin Wilson
627 Adrian David Burch
628 Peter John Bardsley
629 Kenneth Leslie Baskerville
630 Robert Bithell
631 Philip A. Miles
632 Graham John Rose
633 Ian John Fowler
634 David Sutton
635 Jonathan M. Perkins
636 E. H. Megrath
637 Jack Rowley
638 David Ludwell

639 Rich Newman	710 Terence Atkinson	779 Brian Kinsley	849 Peter Huckerby
640 & 641 Mr. T. Beckett	711 Jonathan Mark Coomber	780 Denis Joseph Madigan	850 Elaine Huckerby
642 Brian Bracegirdle	712 Anthony James Exton	781 Noel E. Cantwell	851 Mr. Iain McFadyen
643 David Richard Ley	713 Stephen Irish	782 Gareth Roy Elliott	852 Paul John Sheehan
644 S. V. Ashton	714 Margaret McClelland	783 G. Bradley	853 Antony Shaw
645 J. A. Higham	715 Graham Lee	784 Carl Peter Wynne	854 Anthony Wright
646 Michael Lever	716 Martin F. Ingert	785 Andrew R. Le Tissier	855 Gerard Martin Wright
647 Diane Fussey	717 James E. Rushton	786 Stephen Edward	856 Hugh Michael Wright
648 Christine Osborne	718 Graham J. Mason	Humphrey	857 Michael Noel Wright
649 Hector Charles Fraser	719 Philip Campbell	787 Nick Hollowell	858-863 Trafford Borough
650 Christopher Stansfield	720 Robert Alan Darlington	788 Mr. Leslie Norman	Council
651 Graham Land	721 Colin Dunhill	789 Karen Morley	864 Andrew Mark Richmond
652 Michael William Smith	722 Mr. A. E. Lane	790 John Morley	865 Jonathan Webber
653 Howard Stones	723 Master R. Murphy	791 Michael Ford	866 Peter Graham
654 Paul Hession	724 Malcolm M. Key	792 Mark A. Booth	867 Giles Oakley
655 Phil Tozer	725 David Paul Elliott	793 Stephen Critchlow	868 Mark Lister
656 David Ings	726 James Ritchie	794 Steve Docksey	869 Bernard Jeffs
657 David Ian Crothers	727 Suleman Mahomed	795 R. A. J. Taylor	870 Jonathan S. Domnitz
658 Norman Crothers	728 Peter Richard Hallam	796 Ron Prestwood	871 Beverley Mills
659 Neil Day	729 David G. Weldon	797 Simon Eedle	872 Les Triggs
660 Mr. Philip Whitehead	730 Alex Mills	798 Antony Tune	873 Liam Flaherty
661 David John Feeley	731 Anthony Robert Austin	799 Miss Claire Snow	874 Jonathan Goodfellow
662 & 663 Martin E. James	732 Daniel Francis Bradley	800 Nigel F. Cavill	875 Alan Graham Bell
664 Andrew James	733 Dennis Moloney	801 Sammy Bacon	876 Jane Burchell
665 Simon Parkin	734 Diane Comyns	802 Alan Bartlett	877 Arnold Victor
666 Dennis Prescott	735 Edward Broadbent	803 R. J. McPake	878 Sean Charles Doyle
667 Mr. William R. Heaton	736 Richard Garstang	804 Philip Blears	879 J. S. Levy
668 Michael Wilkinson	737 Mr. Trevor Harris	805 Martin Taylor	880 C. H. Ashworth
669 Alan Wilkinson	738 Neil Greenwood	806 Graeme Eke	881 Nicholas Hodgson
670 Stephen Herron	739 Philip John Evans	807 Malcolm Smith	882 Andrew S. Ferguson
671 Alan J. Myers	740 Ian Tyers	808-810 Bill Green	883 Stuart Gent
672 Michael E. Harper	741 Alan Goate	811 John Graham Robinson	884 William Henry Wood
673 David John G. Clowes	742 Paul M. Overend	812 Gerard Carter	885 Paul Lindop
674 Stephen R. Tilley	743 Roy Cartlitch	813 Peter Challis	886 Alan Morris
675 Raymond Glenn Pearson	744 Mellony Ann Shepard	814 Raymond Saliba	887 Mr. Clive Anthony
676 F. Colin Fuller	745 Terence Martin	815 Gerald John Hutchinson	Thompson
677 Bryan Tinkler	746 Ian H. Sparrow	816 Joseph Bernard Smith	888 Ian Vacey
678 Keith Brown	747 Christopher Dare	817 Henry Eaton	889 Michael Swaffield
679 Michael A. Wheldon	748 Paul Phillip Gordon	818 David Chandler	890 David William Pearson
680 Mark Alan Bourne Phillips	749 Ian Pugh	819 Maurice Hadden	891 Donald Lee
681 David John Pearce	750 Stephen Richard White	820 Mr. Lyndon Williams	892 Anthony Roberts
682 Robert Clancy	751 Dennis Michael Fengl	821 Mr. Ian Manley	893 Thomas Walsh
683 Paul Hawkins	752 Kevin Michael Rabarts	822 Thomas Riley	894 Nigel R. S. King
684 Dave Stevenson	753 Brian John Gray	823 Arthur Booth	895 Paul Said
685 Alan F. Doyle	754 Christopher Burnell	824 Jeffrey Lewis	896 Ian Malcolm Jones
686 Alan Lee Bradshaw	755 Layne J. PAtterson	825 Alan James Wito	897 David Eeles
687 John Cobb	756 Steven Alexander Lamb	826 David J. Thompson	898 Keith Tickner
688 David John Gange	757 Gary Still	827 John Bage	899 David Mulligan
689 Tony Smith	758 Miss A. W. Wilde	828 Stephen Paul Renshall	900 John William Hudson
690 G. Saul	759 Mr. P. D. Wilde	829 Russell H. Moores	901 Barry M. Johnson
691 John Storey	760 Mr. J. H. Wilde	830 Winston Duncan	902 Dennis O'Sullivan
692 Laurence O'Donnell	761 George Christopher Ashton	831 Mark Meacock	903 Neil Waugh
693 Tan Chiea Poh	762 Ian John Wasley	832 Steven Thurgood	904 Paul Ellis
694 Jonathan Peter Carr	763 Julie Buckley	833 Martyn Smith	905 Alan Finch
695 Andrew Seamus Michael	764 Brian T. McDonnell	834 R. N. Black	906 Michael Edelson
Hynes	765 Mr. W. Shaw	835 Paul Rowland	907 Jack Abrahams
696 Eric Edward Morton	766 Paul Darren Mamigonian	836 Damian Hudson	908 Andrew Swetland
697 Gordon Johnson	767 Mr. A. Ratcliffe	837 Mr. Keith Johnson	909 R. Harris
698 Antony L. Harley	768 Allan Linton	838 Anthony Murphy	910 Graham Rose
699 Ian Houghton	769 Ron Berry	839 Jonathan Besant	911 Michael Joseph Day
700 Peter J. A. O'Hare	770 Stephen Hogben	840 Paul Stolworthy	912 John Lewis
701 Michael Francis Jane	771 Stephen Warner	841 Craig Raymond Musson	913 Jason Topping
702 Mr. R. D. England	772 Karen Jackson	842 Mr. P. Lunney	914 Colin Burridge
703 P. Young	773 Darren Robert Broadhurst	843 J. F. M. Tully	915 Harold Spence
704 Terry Siddall	774 Francis Burns	844 Kevin Grogan	916 Andy Prolze
705 Mr. R. Skiba	775 Brendan McCusker	845 Alan G. Ball	917 Roger Shipperley
706 Mario Bugeya	776 Alan H. Smith	846 Stuart Ball	918 Brian Norman Nugent
707 & 708 John Hill	777 Alkesh Patel	847 Brian Scorer	919 G. Farnell
709 Neil M. Glenn	778 Helge Conradsen	848 Geoff Allman	920 Brendan Powell

921 Derek Breddy
922 Kevin Henderson
923 Richard Evans
924 Kevin John May
925 Nigel Postill
926 Roger Brierley
927 A. D. Appleby
928 S. Watson
929 Louisa J. Wooller
930 Michael Russell
931 Alan B. Levy
932 Bill Browne
933 Cyril Hughes
934 Karlton Stratford
935 Patrick P. McAnea
936 Peter Doudney
937 Stuart George Grayshon
938 Jess Nunwa
939 Rosemary Cole
940 Albert Walker Allen
941 Barbara Neal
942 Michael James Finney
943 Simon R. Pilkington
944 John Tunnicliffe
945 Heinz Baller
946 Helmut Scheer
947 Dale Frederick Clarke
948 Göran Schönhult
949 Kieron O'Donovan
950 Martin Feeney
951 Ronald Gordon
952 Joe Davey
953 Michael Devins
954 Martin Gallagher
955 Bart McDonald
956 John Feeney
957 Maurice Langan
958 Donal Rosney
959 John Peacocke
960 Benny Murtagh
961 Michael Feeney
962 Robin McMaster
963 Mr. William Marshall
964 Muscat Joseph
965 Alfred Camilleri
966 Mario Peplow
967 John Occleston
968 Mark Douglas Patton
969 John Tweddell
970 & 971 David Godfrey
972 Peter Elder
973 Shaun McGowan-Griffin
974 Alan John Barnett
975 Patrick Allcorn
976 Jackie Lovell
977 Vic and Marcus Friday
978 Stephanie Butters
979 Zeev Bartur
980 Clive Scholes
981 G. A. Roden
982 John Stephen Eades
983 Dave Boult
984 P. W. Heppenstall
985 Leslie Kay
986 Colin Webster
987 Richard Price
988 Wendell Richards
989 Fred H. Johnson
990 Daniel Henkus

991 Andrew McCartney
992 Andrew J. Hey
993 Mark Oliver
994 J. T. Eksteen
995 S. Saengchote
996 John Hall
997 Val Wilson
998 Mr. M. B. Elliott
999 J. A. Kitson
1000 Temple Nostalgia Press
1001 Alan Leak
1002 Rune Dahlquist
1003 Grant Smethurst
1004 Melvyn Parker
1005 David Hargreaves
1006 Mr. George Calleja Gera
1007 Mr. Peter J. C. Lane
1008 David Dickens
1009 Julie Willey
1010 Elizabeth A. Roberts
1011 Graham Martin
1012 J. Clare
1013 Iain F. Smart
1014 Peter Moulds
1015 Mark Patrick Behan
1016 Michael Gregory
1017 Tony Douglas
1018 David Humphreys
1019 Lee Townley
1020 E. J. Nuttall
1021 Tomas Vesterberg
1022 Nicholas Wynn
1023 Tony Goss
1024 Alan Cann
1025 Michael John Hughes
1026 Paul N. Roughley
1027 Tim Bridle
1028 Mr. W. Gubb
1029 Roy Kennedy
1030 David Rourke
1031 Peter Rourke
1032 J. V. Croft
1033 Ian Griffiths
1034 David John Haworth
1035 Gavin Clarke
1036 David J. Rose
1037 Michael Kay
1038 Chris Kay
1039 Maurice Healey
1040 Mr. C. D. Simmonds
1041 John and Kathleen Bell
1042 & 1043 Mark Bailey
1044 Mark and Paul Taylor
1045 Raymond Gatt
1046 Steven Robert Mycock
1047 Frank S. Hammett
1048 Joe Farrugia
1049 Per Harald Larsen
1050 K. C. Ennion
1051 Stephen Magee
1052 Don Richards
1053 Andrew Moon
1054 Norman James Littler
1055 Gordon Neale
1056 Keith Heels
1057 Melvyn 'Cappy' Anderson
1058 Philip Andrew Holt
1059 Gerry Hadfield
1060 Graham Blant

1061 Ian Burley
1062 Ian Weafer
1063 Colin Williamson
1064 Steven J. Cooper
1065 Martin Day
1066 Simon Davies
1067 Scott James Hudson
1068 Leslie Scott
1069 Gary Spencer-Thompson
1070 Mark O'Callaghan
1071 Mr. Denis Cefai
1072 Mr. John W. Speight
1073 Paul Douglas
1074 Mark Douglas
1075 Rosemary Douglas
1076 Pete Langhorn
1077 Martyn James Harper
1078 John Muscat
1079 Kevin P. Stanton
1080 Mervyn Short
1081 Walter Peruzzi
1082 Simon Lawton
1083 T. Jagger
1084 Rory Sherman
1085 Michael John Doyle
1086 Raymond Vella
1087 Mr. G. R. Todd
1088 Wayne E. Ayto
1089 Susan J. Heath
1090 Mr. David Hollingsbee
1091 Stephen Newbatt
1092 Christopher Alder
1093 Paul O'Hare
1094 Rory Skinner
1095 Simon D. Rumsey
1096 John William Maddison
1097 Neil Mawer
1098 Alan Horswill
1099 Pete Hargreaves
1100 Harry Hargreaves
1101 Hugh Cattermole
1102 William Creddin
1103 Colin David Hadfield
1104 Roman Wychrij
1105 Robert Bolton
1106 Martin T. Bell
1107 Ian Soo
1108 Joseph Reilly
1109 Frank Bell
1110 Ian Briggs
1111 Mark Baggley
1112 John Menzies Library
   Services
1113 Basil W. Godley
1114 Kalevi Mikkonen
1115 Peter Smith
1116 David Owen
1117 Stuart Norman
1118 George Witham
1119 John Witham
1120 Ian Mills
1121 Lesley Elizabeth Willis
1122 Mike Bush —
   Nofotec Group
1123-1172 Sharp Electronics
   (UK) Ltd.
1173 Paul Clarkson
1174 Alan Bradshaw
1175 & 1176 Mr. P. McGuire

1177 Thomas D'Arcy
1178 Nicholas Blake
1179 Kieran Anthony
   O'Connor
1180 Declan Francis
   O'Connor
1181 Raymond Gregory
1182 David J. Handley
1183 James Robert Evans
1184 Stephen Lester
1185 Mark Ronaldson
1186 John Shard
1187 Martin Cyril Welbourn
1188 Bob Fidler
1189 Brian Wood
1190 Malcolm R. Edwards
1191 Irene Mary Mellor
1192 Ricardo Mendes
1193 Mr. David Dyson
1194 Stephen Pember
1195 Gary Smith
1196 Roy Smith
1197 Barrie Smith
1198 Patrick Eastham
1199 Ken Smales
1200 Joe Mercer
1201 Steve Brewer
1202 Keith Allen Schembi
1203 John Atkinson
1204 Manchester Public
   Libraries
1205 Paul David Ford
1206-1235 Sportspages
1236 Brian Cordes
1237 Tony Hall
1238 T. V. Thurley
1239 T. R. J. Hajder
1240 Martin & Josie Kilkie
1241 Tony Hughes
1242 Paul Bagguley
1243 Roger Heaton
1244 A. G. Anderson
1245 Association of Former
   Manchester United
   Players

Remaining subscribers unlisted

TEMPLE NOSTALGIA
Printed in England by
Temple Printing Ltd.
Trent Works
Wilford Crescent East
Nottingham

ACKNOWLEDGEMENTS

To compile a pictorial and statistical record of more than a century in the history of Manchester United requires the help, co-operation and generosity of a lot of people. The Publishers wish to express grateful thanks for assistance on the production of this publication by the following:

Firstly, our indebted thanks to Sir Matt Busby C.B.E. For the man who has done more than anyone in establishing the club's respect and status in World soccer to contribute the Foreword to this volume, we regard as indeed our great honour and privilege. Authors Charles Zahra, Joseph Muscat and Iain McCartney, for their untiring and momentous achievement in collating this work. Editor Keith Mellor, AOY Associates. Keith selected and compiled the illustrations, and designed the book and cover jacket. The project Consultant, Joe Glanville, his contribution is immeasurable and to whom the Editor is most grateful. Joe was a founder of the Malta branch of the Supporters Club and former President. Mike Bush, of Nofotec Group, assisted in research and provided his company facilities. Artist Roger Heaton, for graphics and artwork, and Armstrong Holmes Associates. Spectrum Graphics personnel Christopher Sharpe and Paul Slater, typesetting, and Alan Bartlett and Ian McLoughlin, layouts and artwork. Phil Walsh and Paul Cope, of E.C.S. Ltd for production of the colour section and cover jacket. David Meek of the *Manchester Evening News,* for his kind assistance. Andrew Burslem of Sharp Electronics (UK) Ltd., both for promotional sponsorship and colour photographs. Dave Smith, Manchester United Supporters Club, also for supplying colour photographs. Bryan Horsnell and Graham Buttenshaw of *Football Monthly,* and Steve Brown of Sporting Pictures (UK) Ltd. Sandy Busby at the Red Devils Souvenir Shop. John Scerri and Father Hilary Tagliaferro for the Malta feature. Ken Smales, Secretary of Nottingham Forest. Joe Mercer, former England team manager and captain. Alan Bradshaw, Manchester United Collectors Club. John Sumpter (JMS), Steve Phythian (CPS) and Ian Mellor for photographic services. Donald Wintersgill, of *The Guardian. The Times* of Malta, Ralph Gee and Colin Panter of the *Nottingham Evening Post* Picture Library. Georgette Hanson and Heather Ball for typing the copy material and correspondence. Barrie and Roy Smith, Louise and Bernadette Kilkie for subscriber mailing. The authors had other assistance from Ian Sparrow, the Jackson family of Southport, John Mason, Fiona Caplan, Edwin Farrugia, James Thomas, Keith Margerison, Les Triggs, Fred H. Johnson, Terry Frost, Ray Zahra, John Tucket, and all the kind contributors who are listed below in the caption credits. The Publishers particularly wish to acknowledge two most notable contributions. Firstly, the British Newspaper Printing Corporation, and its Chief Librarian Alan Ormerod for access to, and use of the Mirror Newspapers Picture Library, and for their most generous consent to reproduce the material. Finally at Manchester United, to Mr. Martin Edwards for his consent for the book, and to Mr. Les Olive and his friendly and helpful staff at Old Trafford.

CAPTION CREDITS

We gratefully acknowledge the generosity of the following people for their invaluable contributions, and their kind consent to reproduce the material. We have also been given some photographs where despite considerable effort, it has not been possible to discover whether or not they are subject to copyright. Should any such rights have been unintentionally infringed, an apology is made herewith.

BNPC	British Newspaper Printing Corporation (Courtesy of Alan Ormerod)	MMUSC	Malta Branch — Manchester United Supporters Club (Courtesy of Joe Muscat)
MUSC	Manchester United Supporters Club (Courtesy of Dave Smith)	FM	*Football Monthly*
		TT	Thames Television Ltd.
CPS	Contact Photographic Services	SE	Sharp Electronics (UK) Ltd.
G	*The Guardian*	BL	British Library
TM	*The Times* of Malta	JG	Joe Glanville
CZ	Charles Zahra	JM	Joe Mercer
IM	Iain McCartney	KM	Keith Mellor
ISM	Ian Mellor	BH	Bryan Horsnell
NW	Neville Westerman	PC	Paul Clarkson
RS	Roy Smith	KB	Kathleen Bell